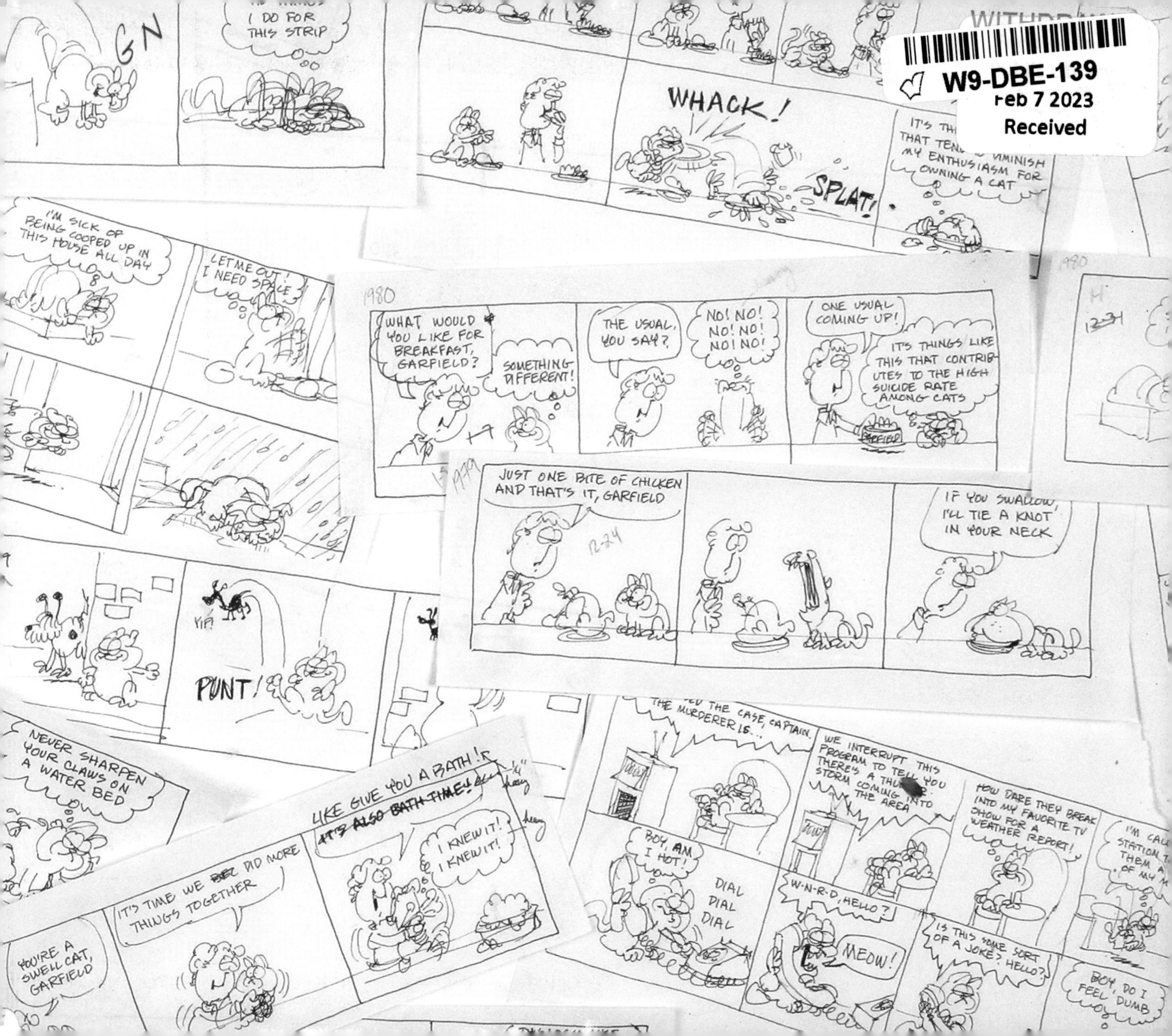

I DO FOR THIS STRIP
WHACK!
SPLAT!
IT'S TH... THAT TEN... ...IMINISH MY ENTHUSIASM FOR OWNING A CAT
I'M SICK OF BEING COOPED UP IN THIS HOUSE ALL DAY
LET ME OUT! I NEED SPACE
1980
WHAT WOULD YOU LIKE FOR BREAKFAST, GARFIELD?
SOMETHING DIFFERENT!
THE USUAL, YOU SAY?
NO! NO! NO! NO! NO! NO!
ONE USUAL COMING UP!
IT'S THINGS LIKE THIS THAT CONTRIBUTES TO THE HIGH SUICIDE RATE AMONG CATS
1980
JUST ONE BITE OF CHICKEN AND THAT'S IT, GARFIELD
IF YOU SWALLOW, I'LL TIE A KNOT IN YOUR NECK
YIP!
PUNT!
NEVER SHARPEN YOUR CLAWS ON A WATER BED
YOU'RE A SWELL CAT, GARFIELD
IT'S TIME WE DID MORE THINGS TOGETHER
LIKE GIVE YOU A BATH!
IT'S ALSO BATH TIME!
I KNEW IT! I KNEW IT!
THE MURDERER IS...
WE INTERRUPT THIS PROGRAM TO TELL YOU THERE'S A THU...R STORM COMING INTO THE AREA
HOW DARE THEY BREAK INTO MY FAVORITE TV SHOW FOR A WEATHER REPORT!
BOY, AM I HOT!
DIAL DIAL DIAL
W-N-R-D, HELLO?
MEOW!
IS THIS SOME SORT OF A JOKE? HELLO?
BOY, DO I FEEL DUMB

Garfield

30 YEARS OF LAUGHS
& LASAGNA

The life & times of a fat, furry legend!

Garfield

30 YEARS OF LAUGHS & LASAGNA

The life & times of a fat, furry legend!

SHUT UP AND FEED ME

BY JIM DAVIS

Ballantine Books • New York

Editors:	Scott Nickel, Mark Acey
Designer:	Thomas Howard
Art director:	Betsy Knotts
Art support:	Gary Barker, Lori Barker, Larry Fentz
Production:	Linda Duell

Published in the United States by Ballantine Books, an imprint
of Random House, a division of Penguin Random House LLC, New York.

BALLANTINE and colophon are registered trademarks of
Penguin Random House LLC.

NICKELODEON is a Trademark of Viacom International, Inc.

ISBN 978-0-345-50379-4

Printed in China on acid-free paper

randomhousebooks.com

9 8 7 6 5 4 3

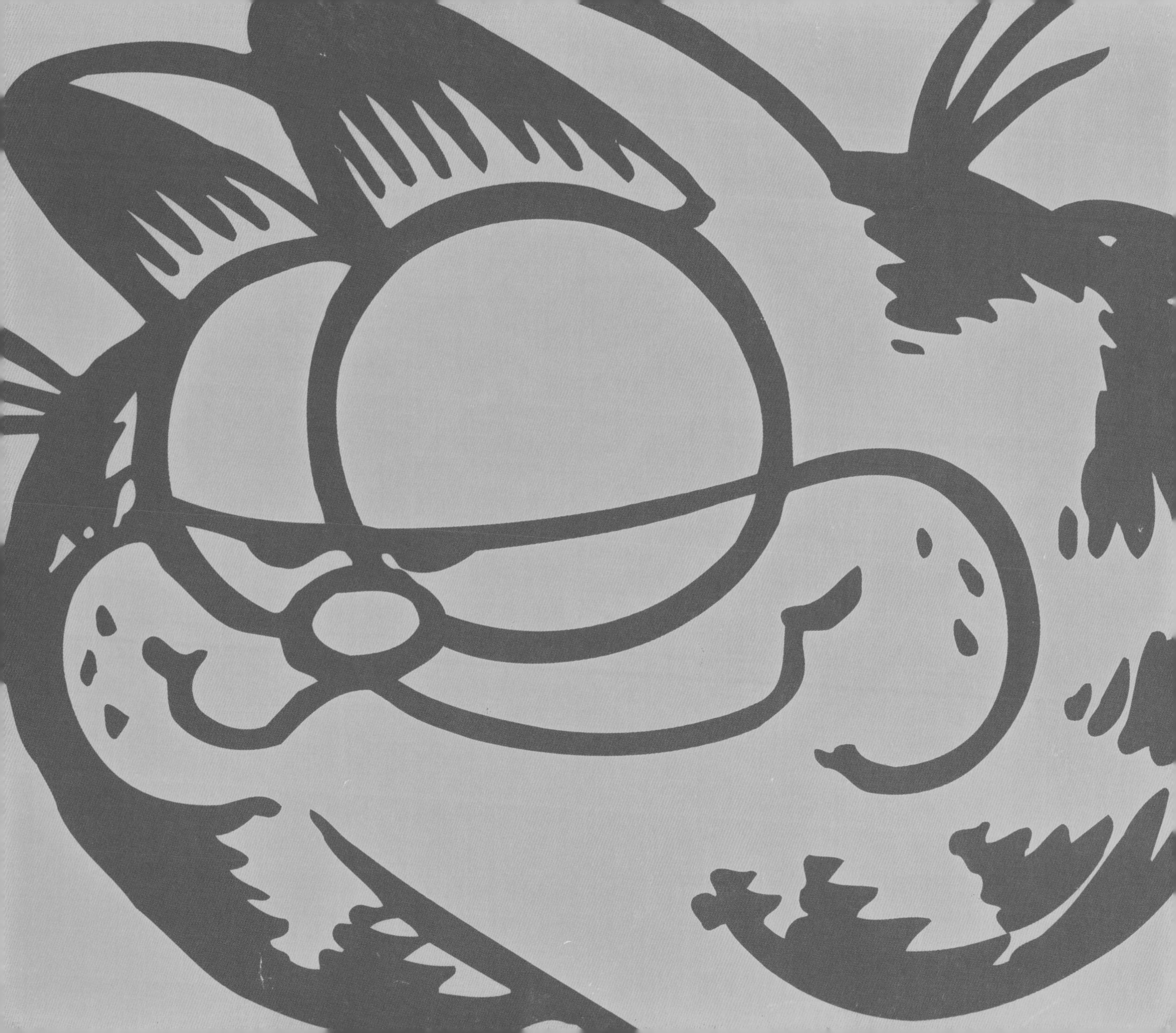

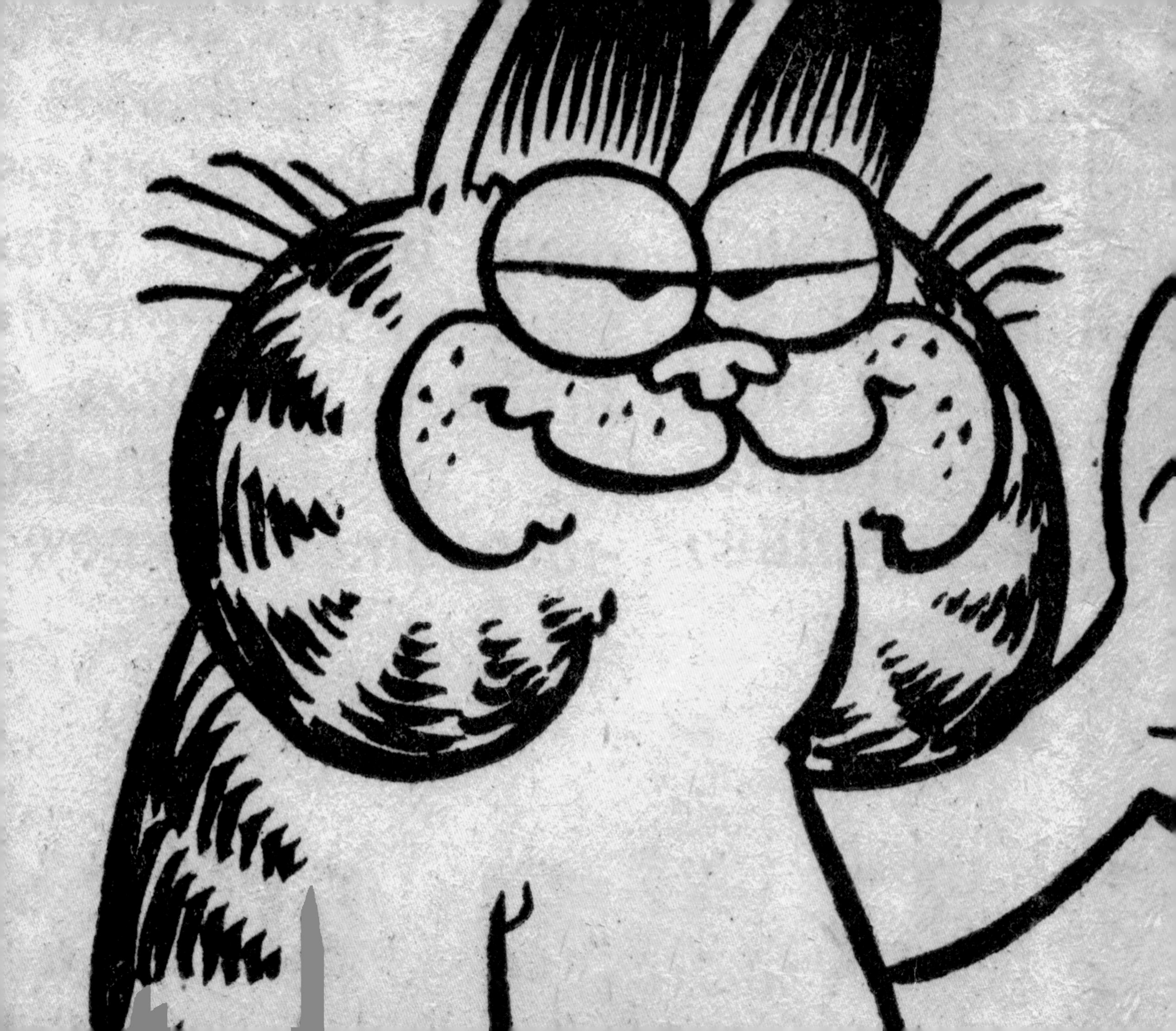

Contents

DEAN YOUNG
FOREWORD

PAGE
8

The First Decade
1978 – 1988

PAGE
10

The Second Decade
1988 – 1998

PAGE
92

The Third Decade
1998 – 2008

PAGE
174

JIM DAVIS
30 FAVES

PAGE
256

What goes around, comes around ... as now the Bumsteads happily prepare to return the favor by helping Garfield celebrate his big 3-0.

Jim and I have been best friends for almost thirty years. When he asked me to do this introduction, I instantly knew that it would border on blasphemy if I didn't dredge up at least one or two instances of minutia from our pithy past.

For instance, after a night of ribald frivolity before one of the many B.C. Open Golf Tournaments we played in, Jim decided that we should break into Tommy Smothers's room, ostensibly to clear it of interlopers, terrorists, or whatever. During the ensuing mayhem, Jim's glasses hit the floor only a nanosecond before I stepped on them.

I'll never forget the next morning at breakfast when he showed up wearing those broken glasses. He stuck his face right into mine (the right lens was so shattered that I couldn't even see his eyeball!) and said: "These are the only glasses I have to play golf in, Young!" I laughed so hard I cried ... and so did everyone else in the room. And I laughed all day ... especially when he'd look over at me with that shattered lens, pathetically mumbling about why he was having so much trouble connecting with the golf ball.

Then there was the time that I was going pretty fast in my boat with Jim and Marion and Mike Peters (*Mother Goose and Grimm*) all seated on the motor cushion behind me. They started hysterically screaming that Mike had fallen overboard. Just as cardiac arrest was about to kick in, Mike popped up from his hidden position behind my seat with a very subdued: "Gotcha, didn't we?"

FOREWORD

Anyway, I think you get the idea about the nature of our times together and the wonderful friendship we have shared over all these years, which brings me to the great honor of introducing Garfield's fabulous thirtieth-anniversary book.

My dad, Chic Young (*Blondie's* original creator), confided to me one time that doing a comic strip was like dragging around a big bag of bricks. Yeah, but it depends on your bricks. And I've always said Jim had some nice bricks!

It sure is fun to note that those bricks about that cynical cat have entertained millions of enthusiastic fans all around the world for three decades now. Every one of those little treasures is an exquisite menagerie of comedic timing, writing, and cartoon art. It's easy to see why his strip is continually voted one of the best on our planet by readers everywhere.

'Nuff said, it's time to get to the good part. Just turn the page and start enjoying thirty years of Jim's wonderful *Garfield* magic.

DEAN YOUNG

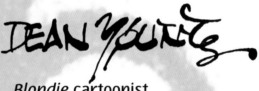

Blondie cartoonist

I WAS IN YOUR NEIGHBORHOOD, SO I THOUGHT I'D HAND DELIVER THIS
GEE THANKS, DAG
GARFIELD! WE GOT AN INVITATION TO BLONDIE AND DAGWOOD'S ANNIVERSARY PARTY!
FOOD!
"NO GIFTS. CASUAL DRESS. DIALOGUE AND LETTERING WILL BE PROVIDED"
YESSS! I WON'T EVEN HAVE TO THINK!
Distributed by Universal Press Syndicate
www.garfield.com
©2005 PAWS, INC. All Rights Reserved.

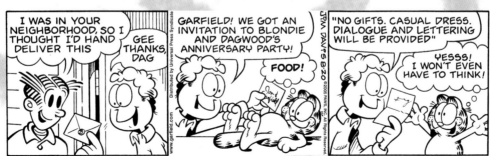

Blondie by Dean Young © 2008 King Features Syndicate, Inc.

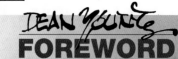

The First Decade
1978–1988

Finally! After nine years of assisting on the *Tumbleweeds* comic strip and submitting *Garfield* to newspaper syndicates, I got my chance.

I was hoping to earn enough money that I wouldn't have to take a second job to support my cartooning habit. I had grand plans for *Garfield*. I was going to get two—maybe three—hundred newspapers, and then someday maybe publish a book.

Well, after that book was published, *Garfield* caught on. Life became a blur as the strip garnered media attention. With all the hoopla came the opportunity to do animation and licensing.

With every new experience, I learned something new about my creation. Garfield morphed from a grumpy lump of wisecracking clay into the iconic "spokes-cat" for the '80s generation: the "Me Generation." What perfect timing!

With all this success, I felt confident that I'd be able to do the comic strip for, who knows, maybe twenty-five years.

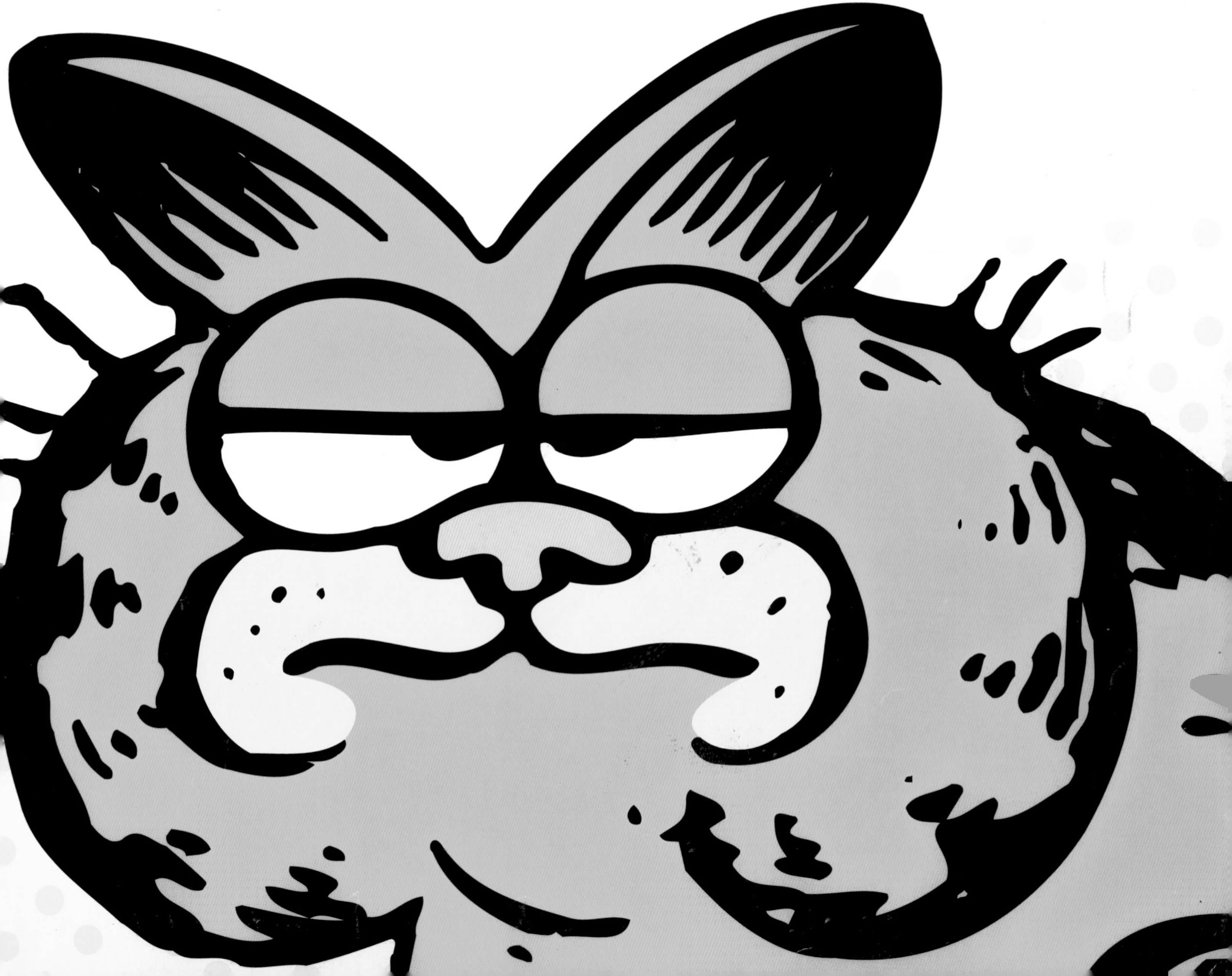

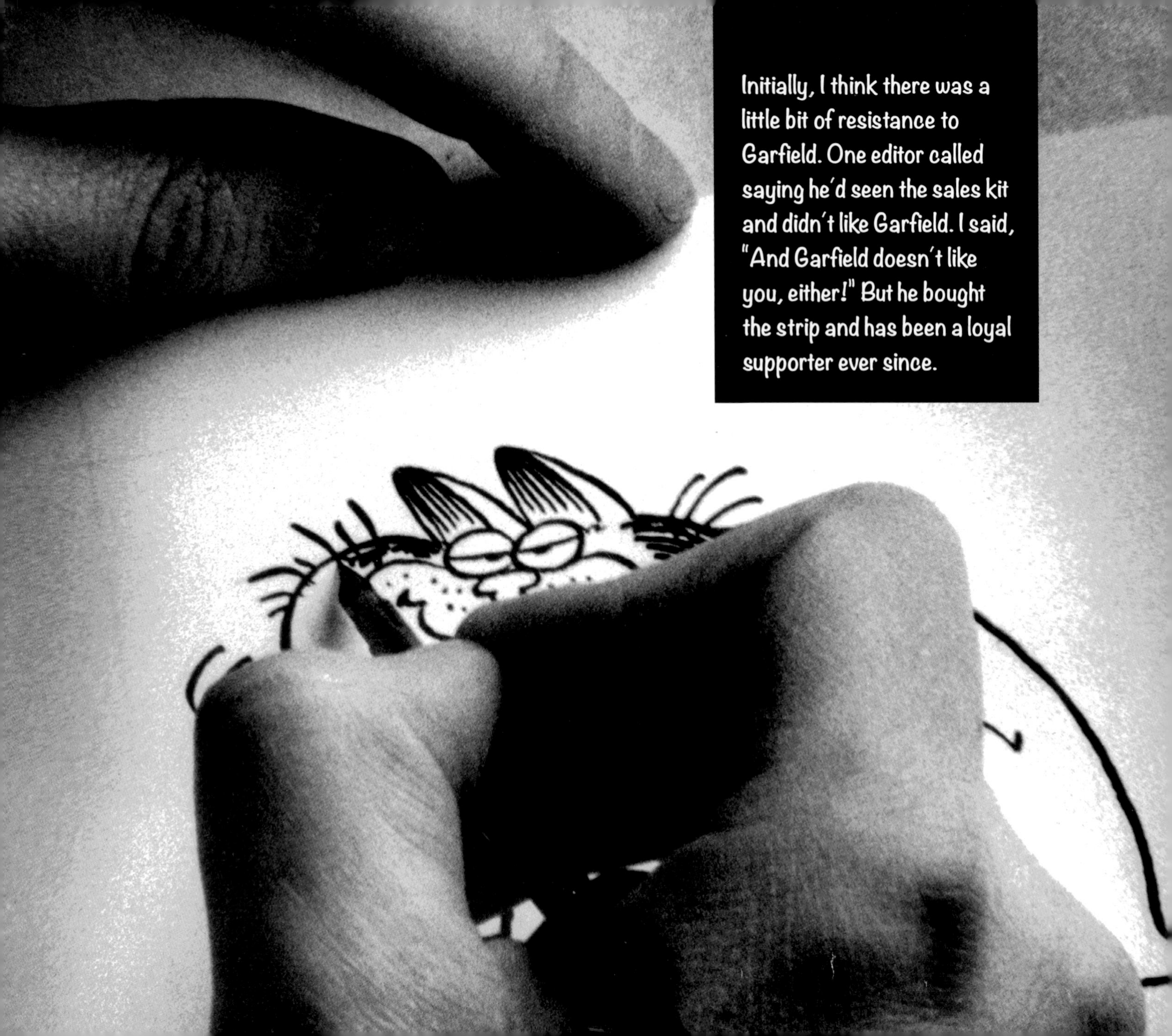

Initially, I think there was a little bit of resistance to Garfield. One editor called saying he'd seen the sales kit and didn't like Garfield. I said, "And Garfield doesn't like you, either!" But he bought the strip and has been a loyal supporter ever since.

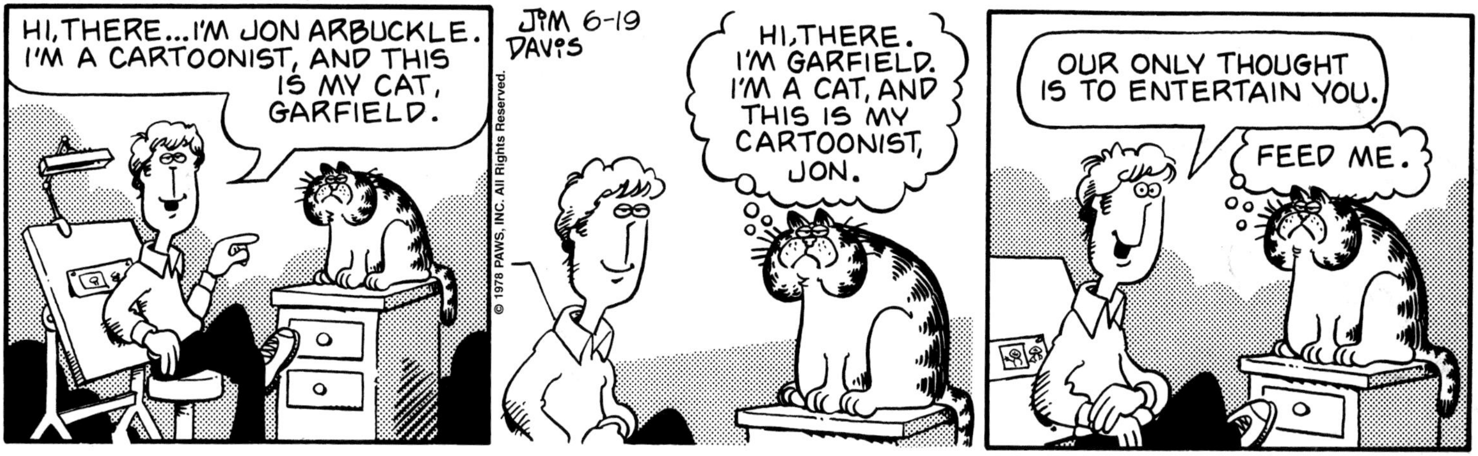
HI, THERE... I'M JON ARBUCKLE. I'M A CARTOONIST, AND THIS IS MY CAT, GARFIELD.
JIM DAVIS 6-19
© 1978 PAWS, INC. All Rights Reserved.
HI, THERE. I'M GARFIELD. I'M A CAT, AND THIS IS MY CARTOONIST, JON.
OUR ONLY THOUGHT IS TO ENTERTAIN YOU.
FEED ME.

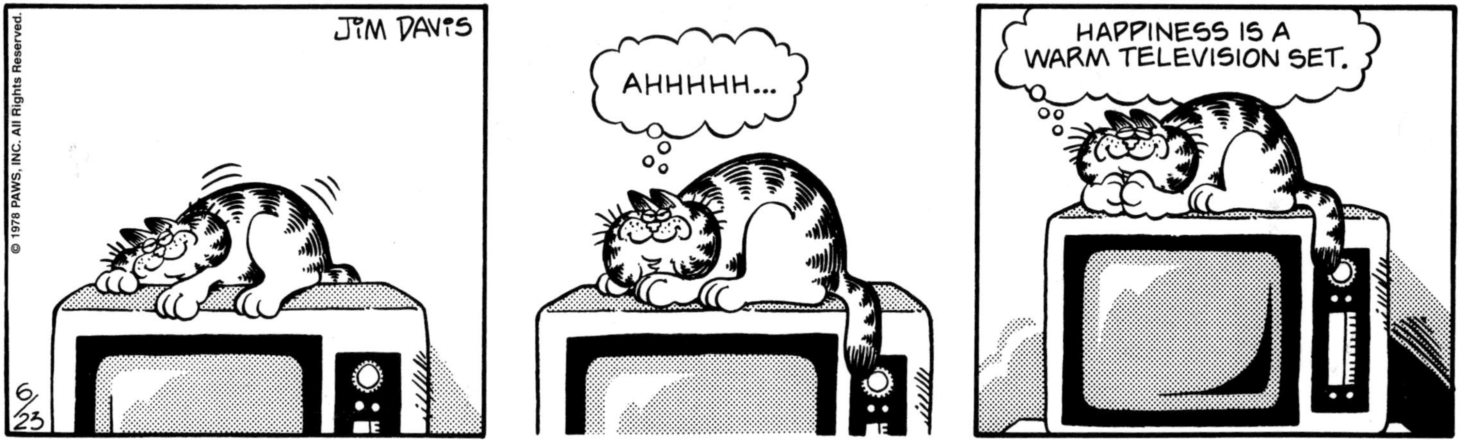
© 1978 PAWS, INC. All Rights Reserved.
JIM DAVIS
6/23
AHHHHH...
HAPPINESS IS A WARM TELEVISION SET.

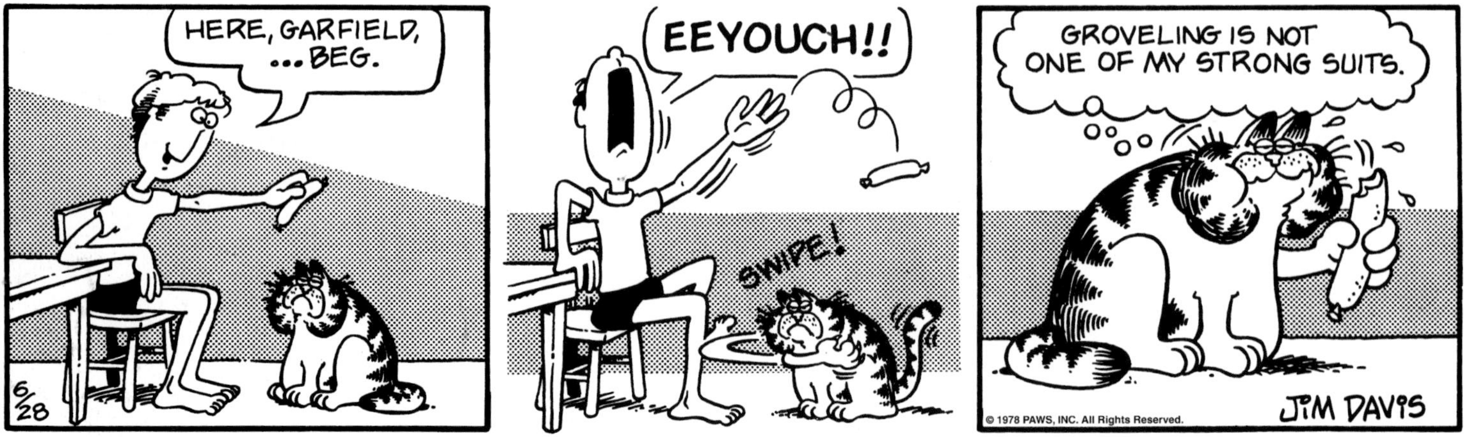
6/28
HERE, GARFIELD, ...BEG.
EEYOUCH!!
SWIPE!
GROVELING IS NOT ONE OF MY STRONG SUITS.
© 1978 PAWS, INC. All Rights Reserved.
JIM DAVIS

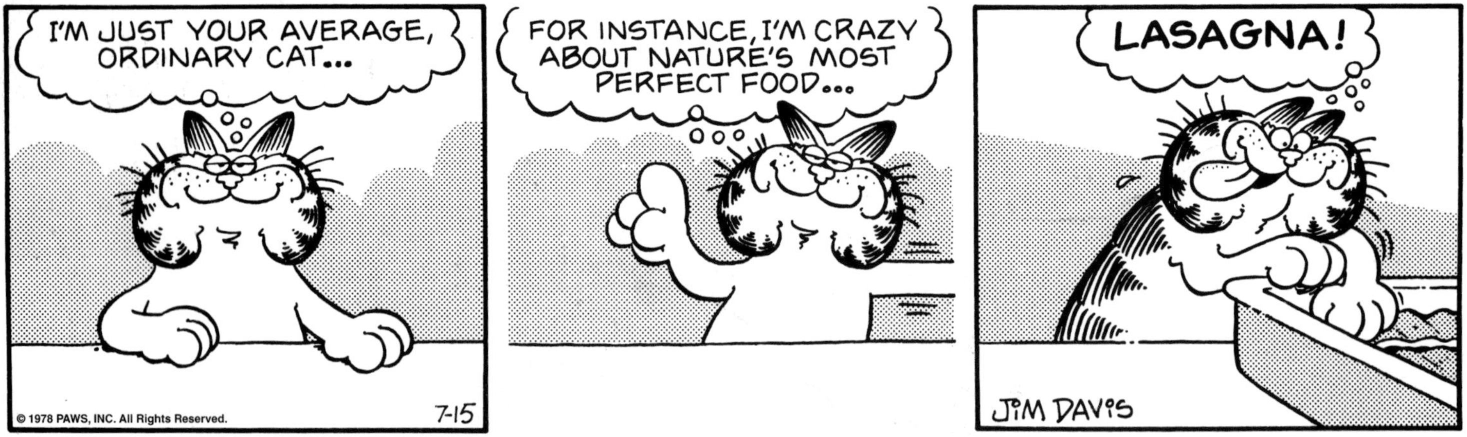
I'M JUST YOUR AVERAGE, ORDINARY CAT...
© 1978 PAWS, INC. All Rights Reserved.
7-15
FOR INSTANCE, I'M CRAZY ABOUT NATURE'S MOST PERFECT FOOD...
LASAGNA!
JIM DAVIS

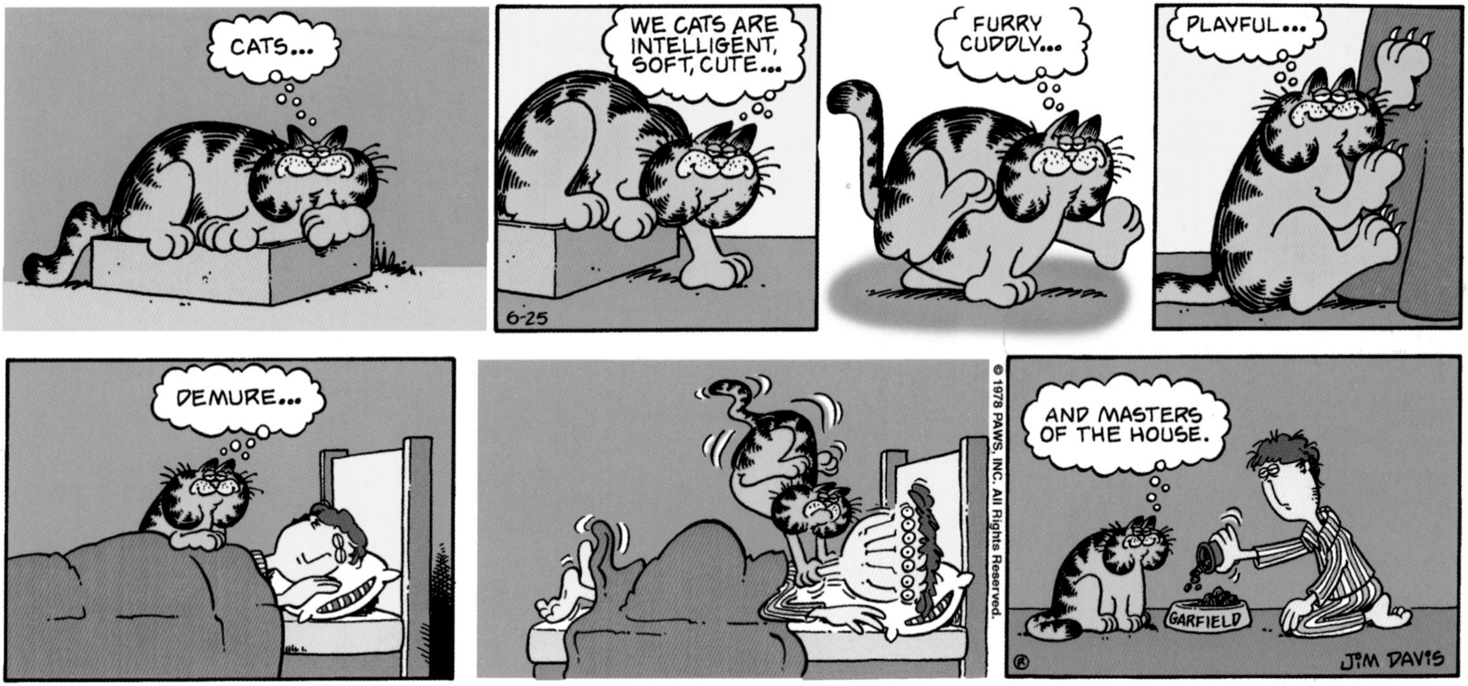
CATS...
WE CATS ARE INTELLIGENT, SOFT, CUTE...
6-25
FURRY CUDDLY...
PLAYFUL...
DEMURE...
© 1978 PAWS, INC. All Rights Reserved.
AND MASTERS OF THE HOUSE.
GARFIELD
®
JIM DAVIS

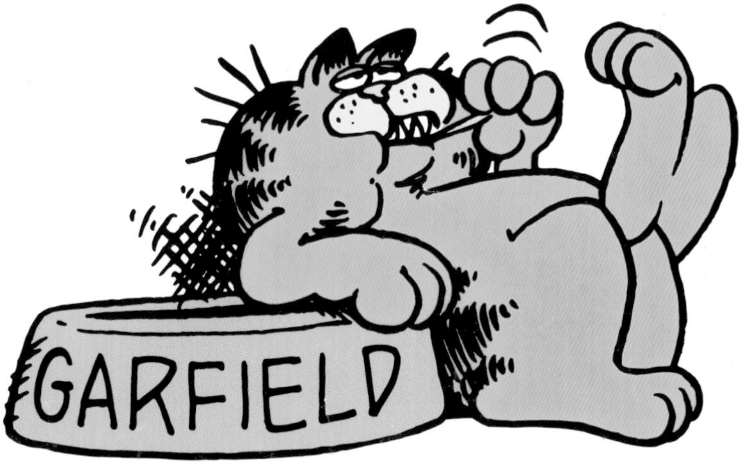
GARFIELD

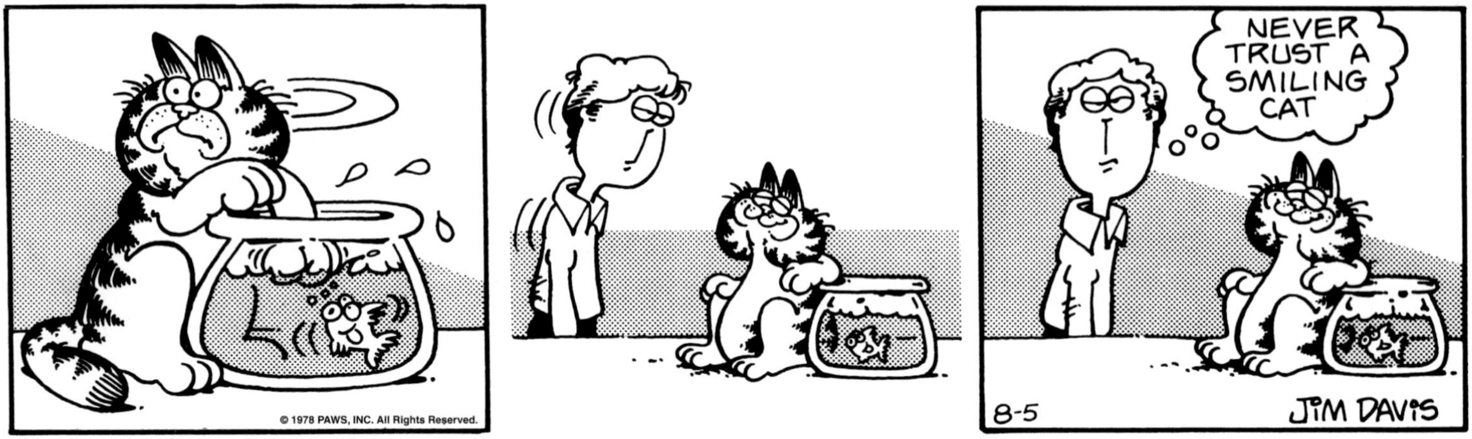
© 1978 PAWS, INC. All Rights Reserved.
NEVER TRUST A SMILING CAT
8-5
JIM DAVIS

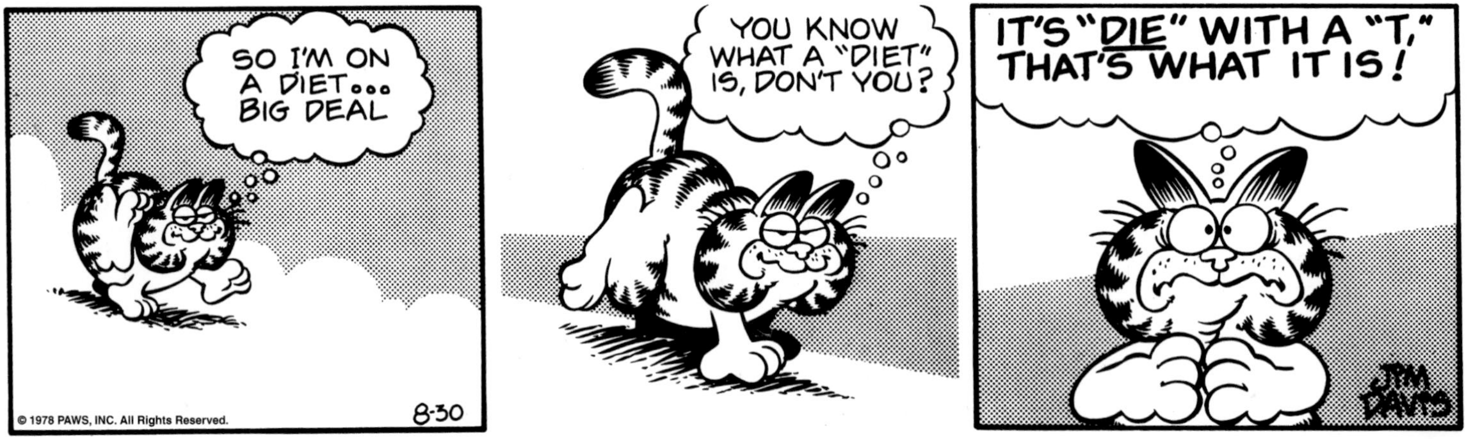
SO I'M ON A DIET... BIG DEAL
© 1978 PAWS, INC. All Rights Reserved.
8-30
YOU KNOW WHAT A "DIET" IS, DON'T YOU?
IT'S "DIE" WITH A "T," THAT'S WHAT IT IS!
JIM DAVIS

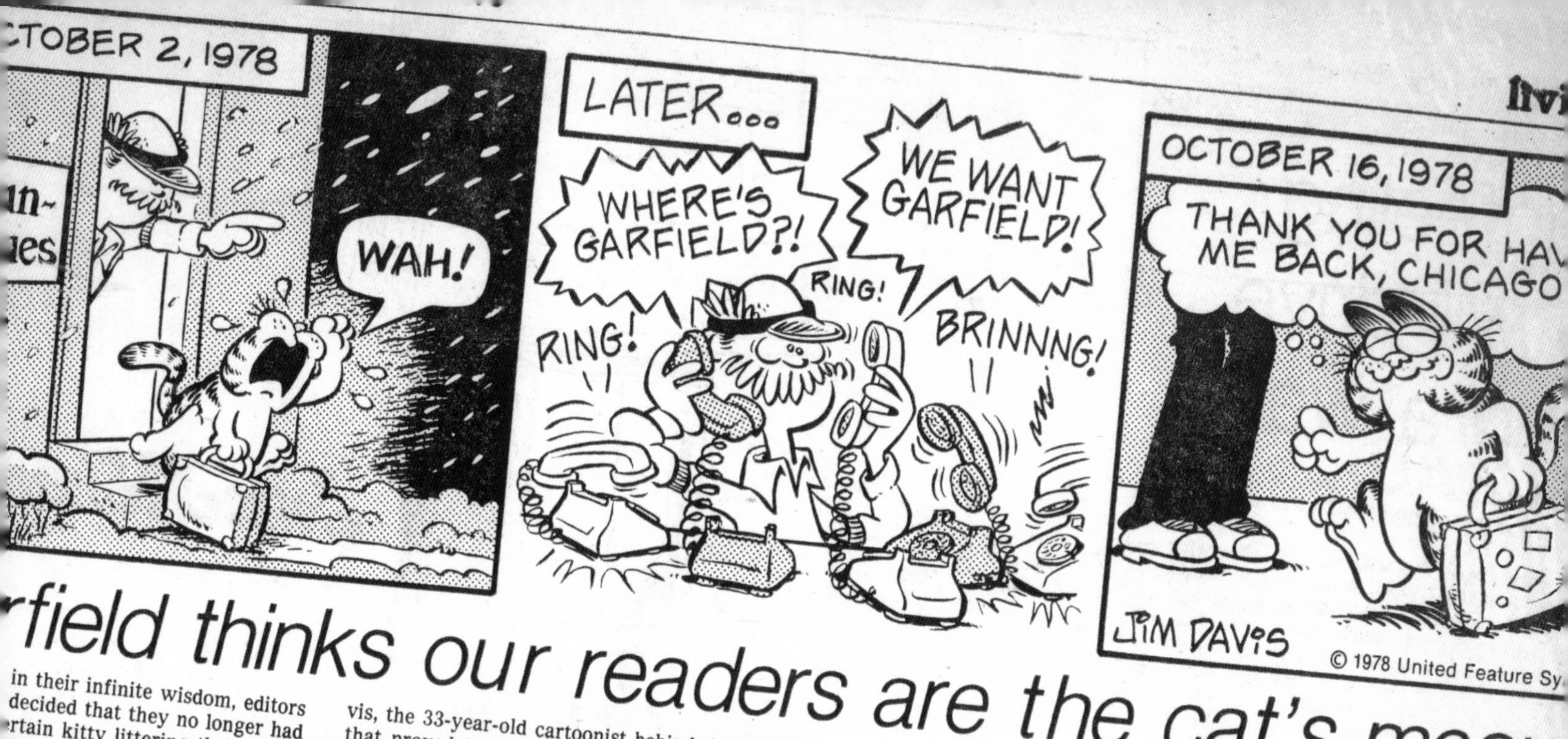
OCTOBER 2, 1978
WAH!
LATER...
WHERE'S GARFIELD?!
WE WANT GARFIELD!
RING!
RING!
BRINNNG!
OCTOBER 16, 1978
THANK YOU FOR HAV
ME BACK, CHICAGO
JIM DAVIS
© 1978 United Feature Sy
rfield thinks our readers are the cat's meow

Like anyone with a new feature, I watched and waited, hoping for a positive reaction to the strip. Several months went by and some new papers had signed on. I thought things were going pretty well. Then I learned that the *Chicago Sun-Times* had cancelled *Garfield*. I worried that it was the beginning of the end. But then the *Sun-Times* started receiving hundreds of letters and phone calls from a loyal and very vocal following of *Garfield* fans who had taken a liking to the cat. They demanded the strip be reinstated. It was, and since then, its circulation has continued to grow.

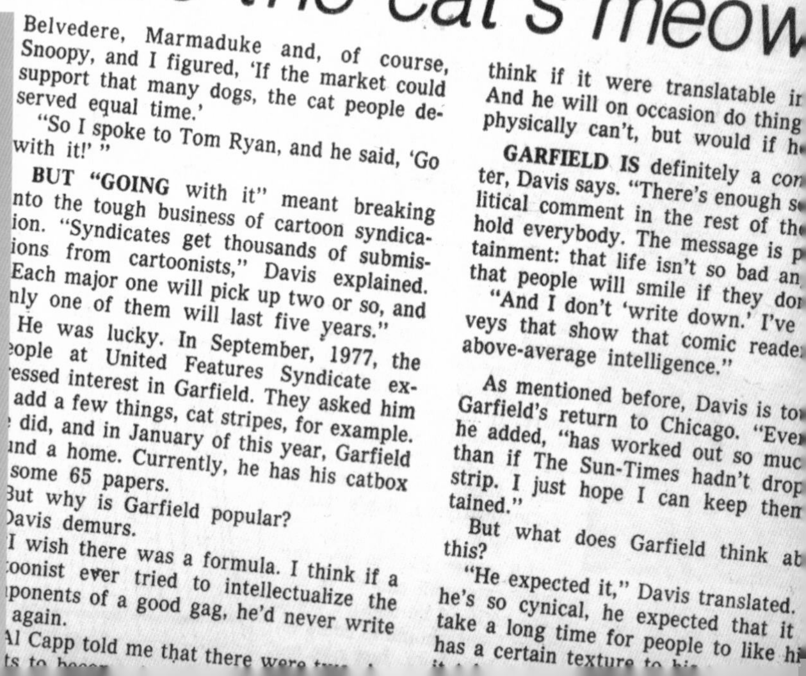

Belvedere, Marmaduke and, of course, Snoopy, and I figured, 'If the market could support that many dogs, the cat people deserved equal time.'

"So I spoke to Tom Ryan, and he said, 'Go with it!' "

BUT "GOING with it" meant breaking into the tough business of cartoon syndication. "Syndicates get thousands of submissions from cartoonists," Davis explained. "Each major one will pick up two or so, and only one of them will last five years."

He was lucky. In September, 1977, the people at United Features Syndicate expressed interest in Garfield. They asked him to add a few things, cat stripes, for example. He did, and in January of this year, Garfield found a home. Currently, he has his catbox in some 65 papers.

But why is Garfield popular?

Davis demurs.

"I wish there was a formula. I think if a cartoonist ever tried to intellectualize the components of a good gag, he'd never write again.

"Al Capp told me that there were ...

think if it were translatable ... And he will on occasion do thing... physically can't, but would if h...

GARFIELD IS definitely a con... ter, Davis says. "There's enough s... litical comment in the rest of the... hold everybody. The message is p... tainment: that life isn't so bad an... that people will smile if they do...

"And I don't 'write down.' I've ... veys that show that comic reade... above-average intelligence."

As mentioned before, Davis is to... Garfield's return to Chicago. "Eve... he added, "has worked out so muc... than if The Sun-Times hadn't drop... strip. I just hope I can keep them... tained."

But what does Garfield think ab... this?

"He expected it," Davis translated. ... he's so cynical, he expected that it ... take a long time for people to like hi... has a certain texture to his...

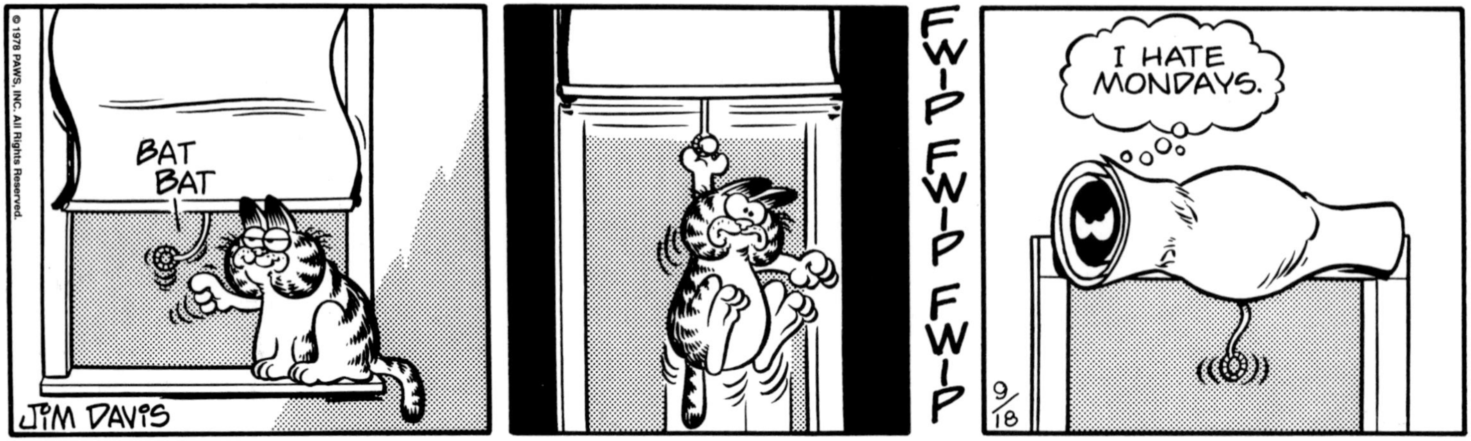
© 1978 PAWS, INC. All Rights Reserved.
BAT BAT
JIM DAVIS
FWIP FWIP FWIP FWIP
I HATE MONDAYS.
9/18

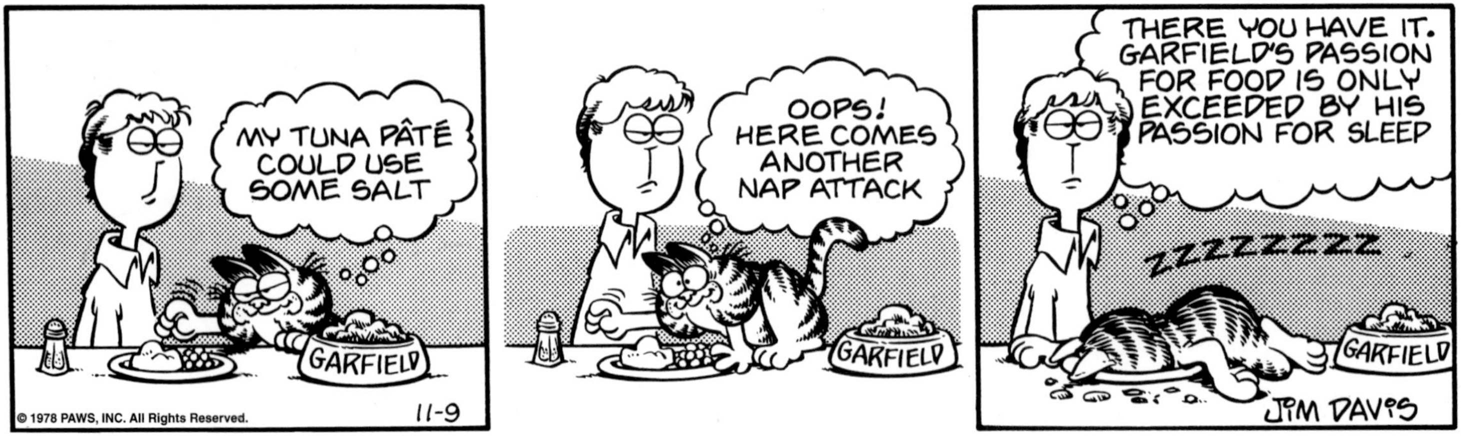
MY TUNA PÂTÉ COULD USE SOME SALT
GARFIELD
© 1978 PAWS, INC. All Rights Reserved.
11-9
OOPS! HERE COMES ANOTHER NAP ATTACK
GARFIELD
THERE YOU HAVE IT. GARFIELD'S PASSION FOR FOOD IS ONLY EXCEEDED BY HIS PASSION FOR SLEEP
ZZZZZZZZ
GARFIELD
JIM DAVIS

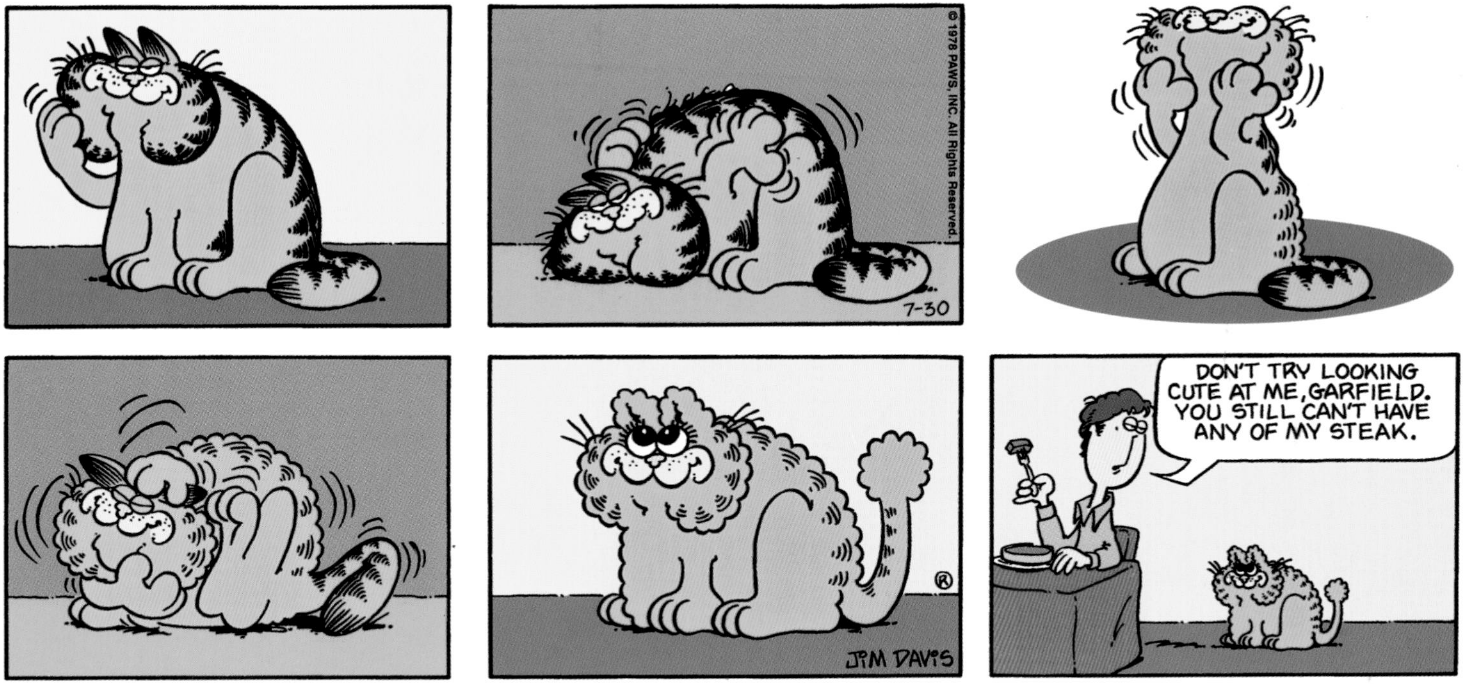
© 1978 PAWS, INC. All Rights Reserved.
7-30
DON'T TRY LOOKING CUTE AT ME, GARFIELD. YOU STILL CAN'T HAVE ANY OF MY STEAK.
JIM DAVIS

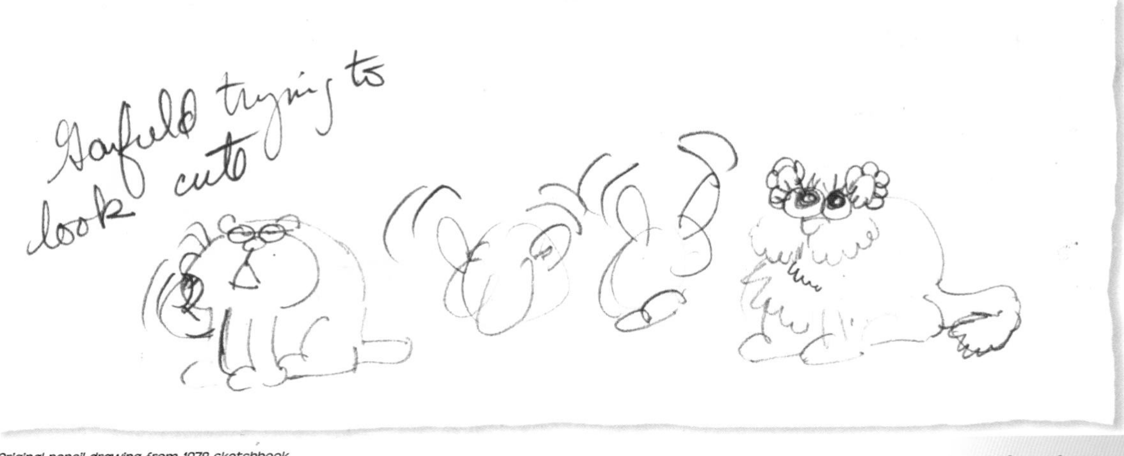
Garfield trying to look cute

Original pencil drawing from 1978 sketchbook.

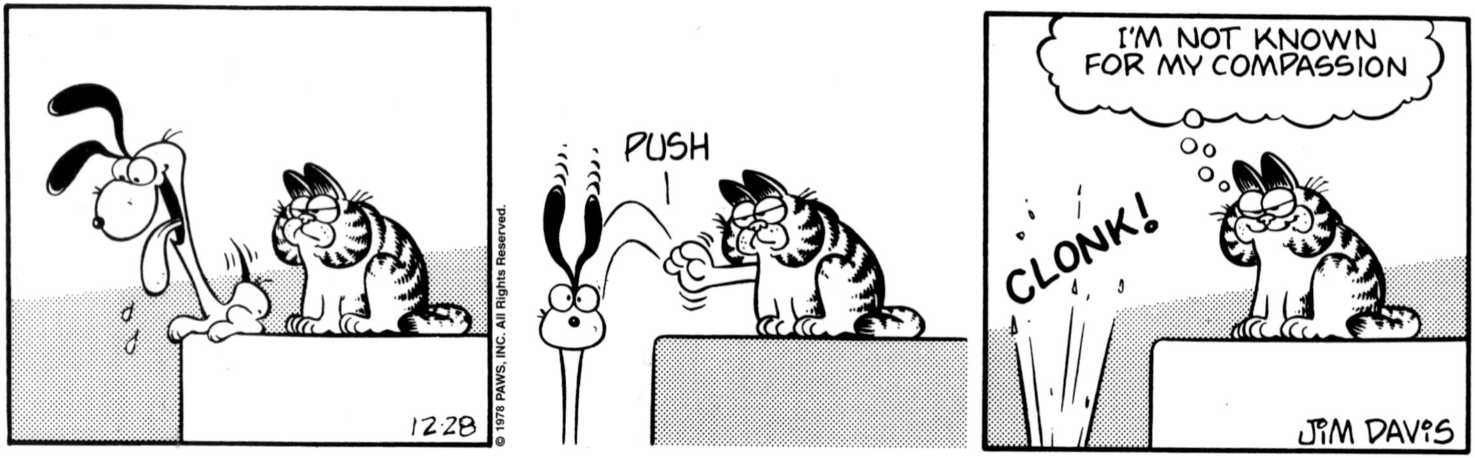
PUSH
CLONK!
I'M NOT KNOWN FOR MY COMPASSION
12·28
© 1978 PAWS, INC. All Rights Reserved.
JIM DAVIS

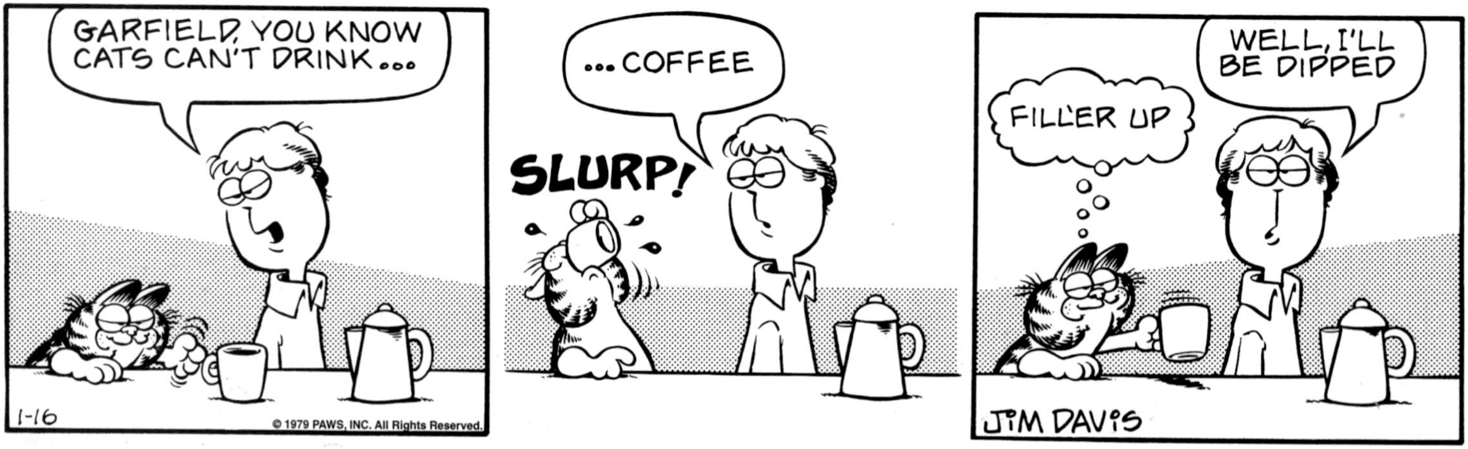
GARFIELD, YOU KNOW CATS CAN'T DRINK...
...COFFEE
SLURP!
FILL'ER UP
WELL, I'LL BE DIPPED
1-16
© 1979 PAWS, INC. All Rights Reserved.
JIM DAVIS

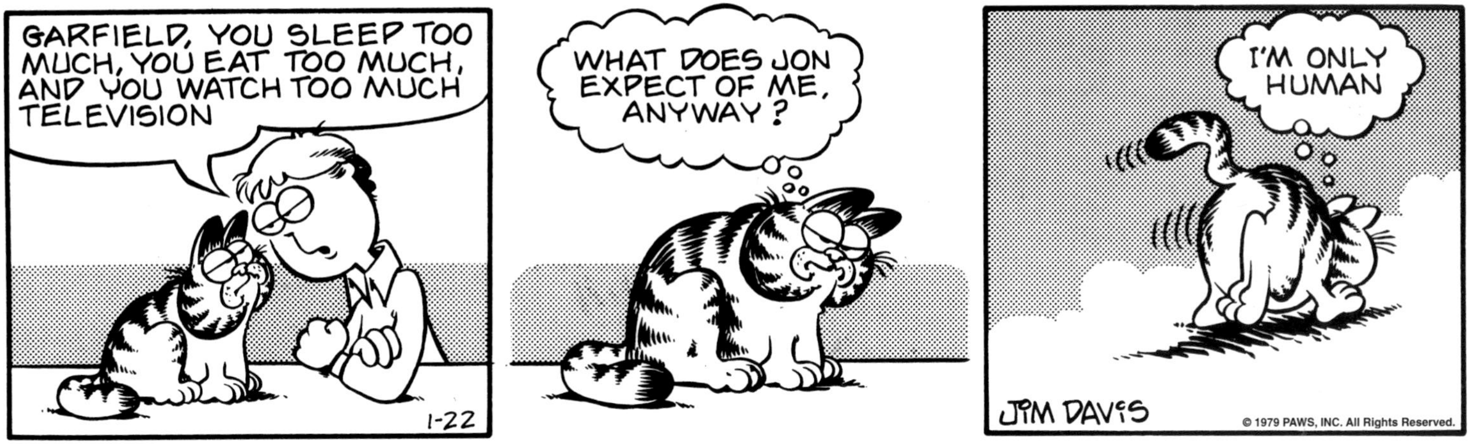
GARFIELD, YOU SLEEP TOO MUCH, YOU EAT TOO MUCH, AND YOU WATCH TOO MUCH TELEVISION
1-22
WHAT DOES JON EXPECT OF ME, ANYWAY?
I'M ONLY HUMAN
JIM DAVIS
© 1979 PAWS, INC. All Rights Reserved.

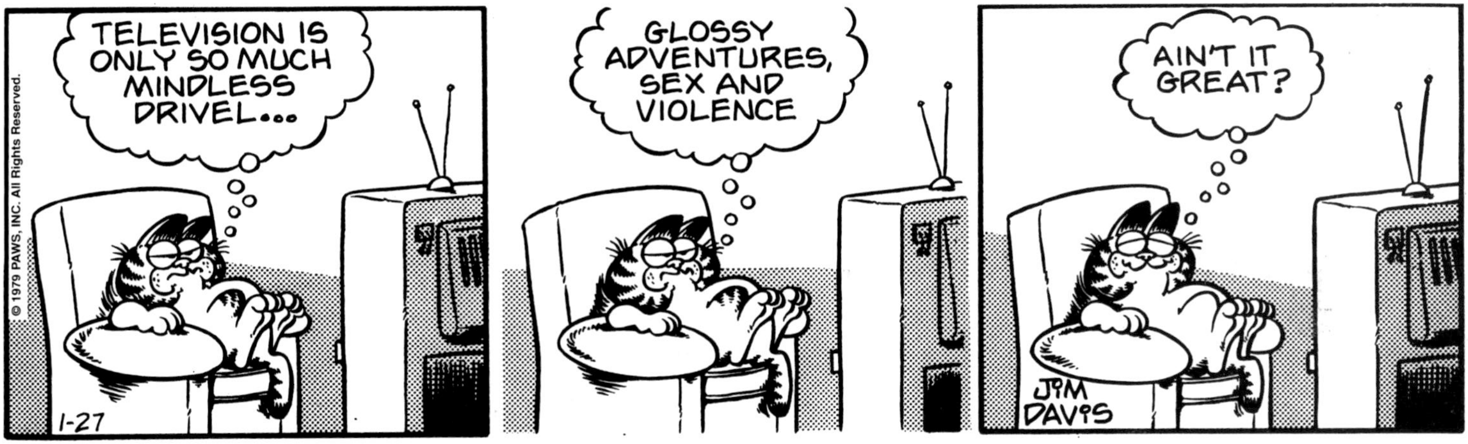
© 1979 PAWS, INC. All Rights Reserved.
TELEVISION IS ONLY SO MUCH MINDLESS DRIVEL...
1-27
GLOSSY ADVENTURES, SEX AND VIOLENCE
AIN'T IT GREAT?
JIM DAVIS

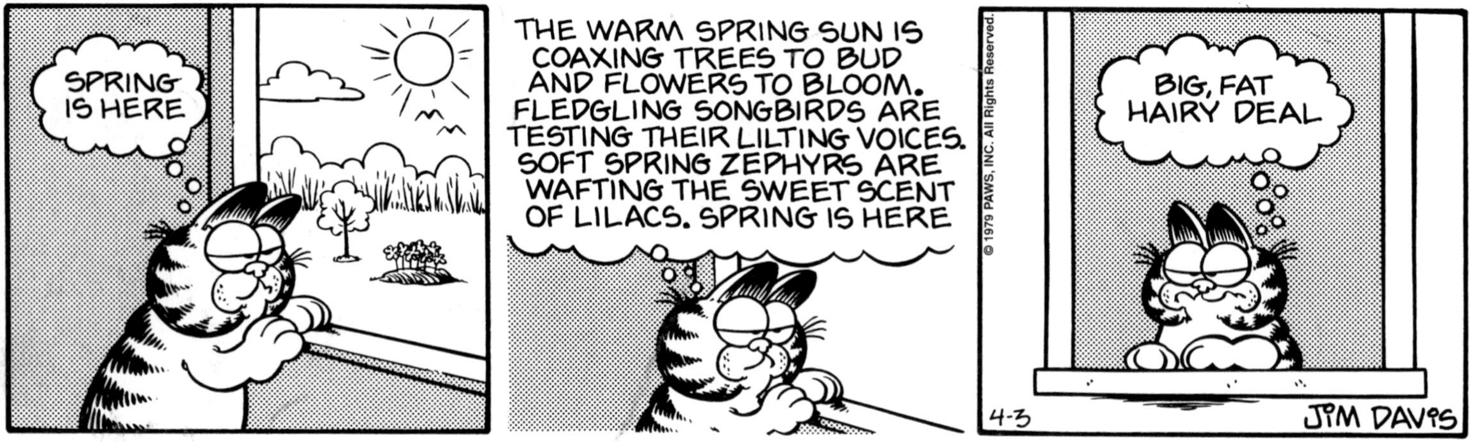
SPRING IS HERE
THE WARM SPRING SUN IS COAXING TREES TO BUD AND FLOWERS TO BLOOM. FLEDGLING SONGBIRDS ARE TESTING THEIR LILTING VOICES. SOFT SPRING ZEPHYRS ARE WAFTING THE SWEET SCENT OF LILACS. SPRING IS HERE
BIG, FAT HAIRY DEAL
© 1979 PAWS, INC. All Rights Reserved.
4-3
JIM DAVIS

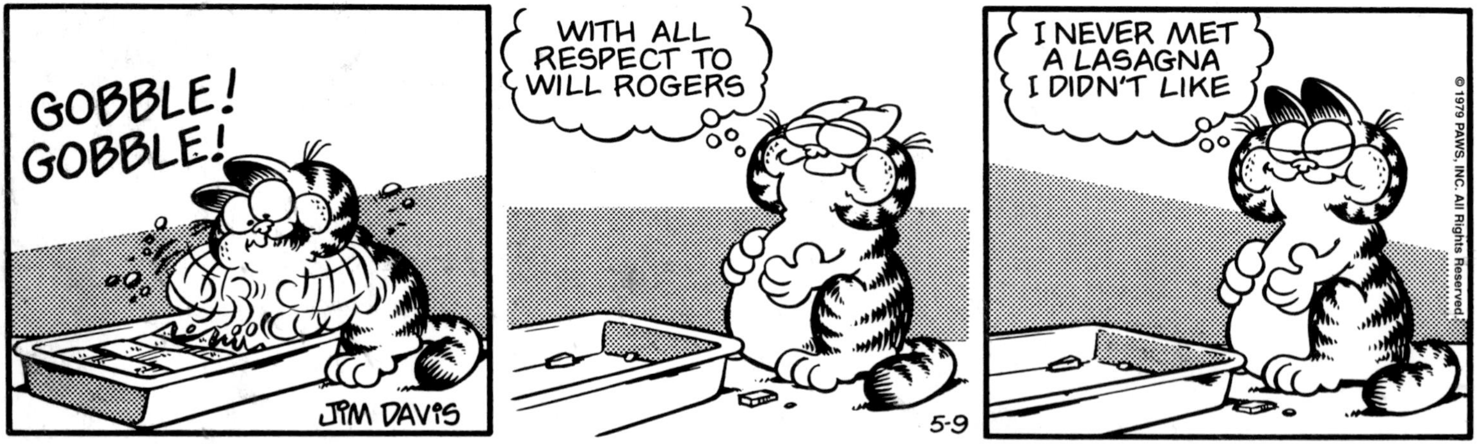
GOBBLE! GOBBLE!
JIM DAVIS
WITH ALL RESPECT TO WILL ROGERS
5-9
I NEVER MET A LASAGNA I DIDN'T LIKE
© 1979 PAWS, INC. All Rights Reserved.

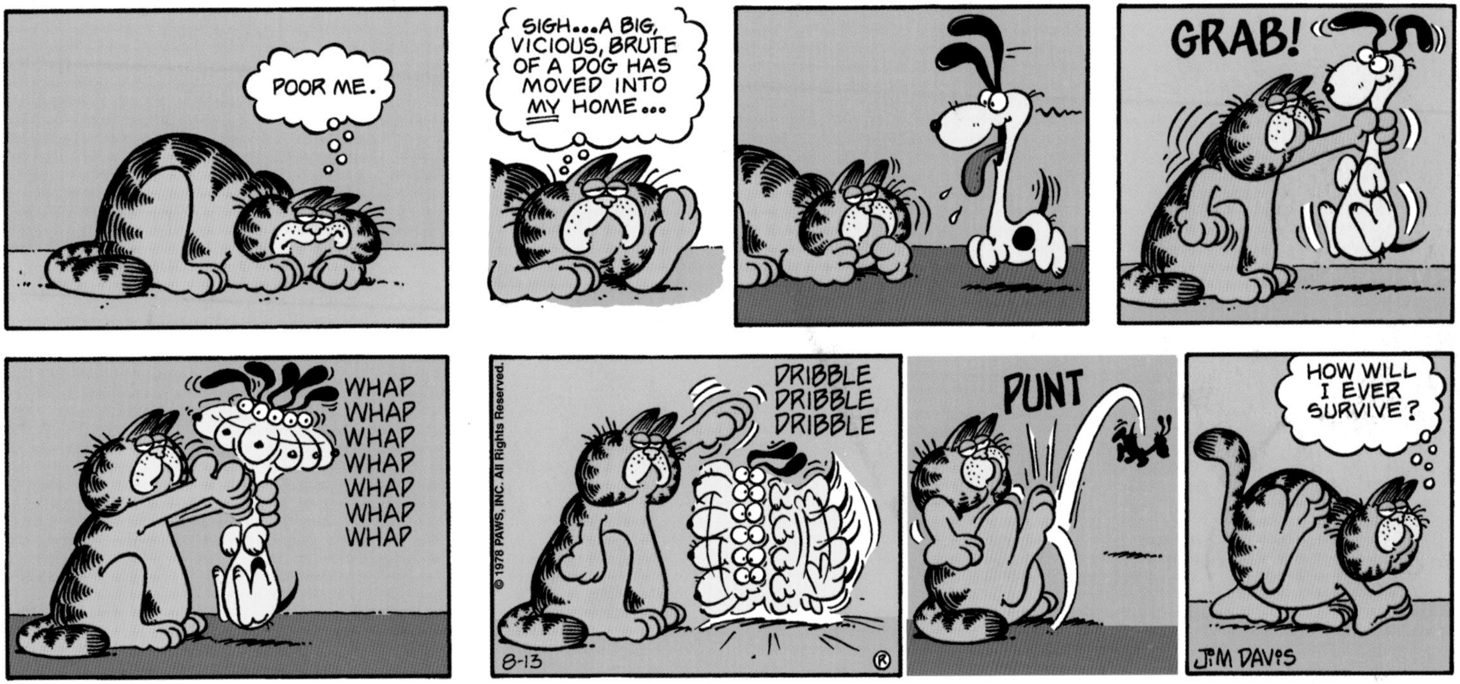
POOR ME.
SIGH...A BIG, VICIOUS, BRUTE OF A DOG HAS MOVED INTO MY HOME...
GRAB!
WHAP WHAP WHAP WHAP WHAP WHAP WHAP
© 1978 PAWS, INC. All Rights Reserved.
DRIBBLE DRIBBLE DRIBBLE
8-13
PUNT
HOW WILL I EVER SURVIVE?
JIM DAVIS

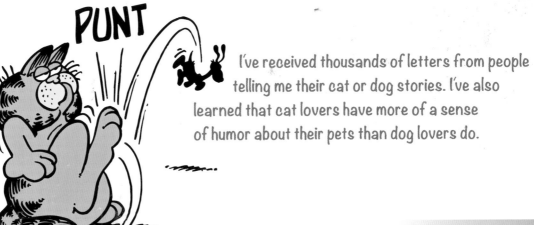

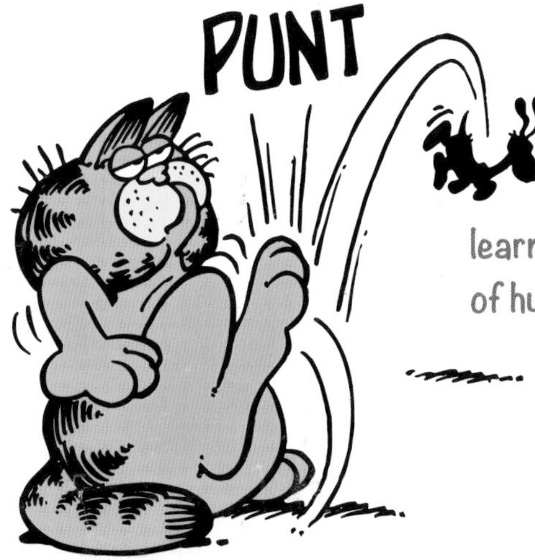
PUNT

I've received thousands of letters from people telling me their cat or dog stories. I've also learned that cat lovers have more of a sense of humor about their pets than dog lovers do.

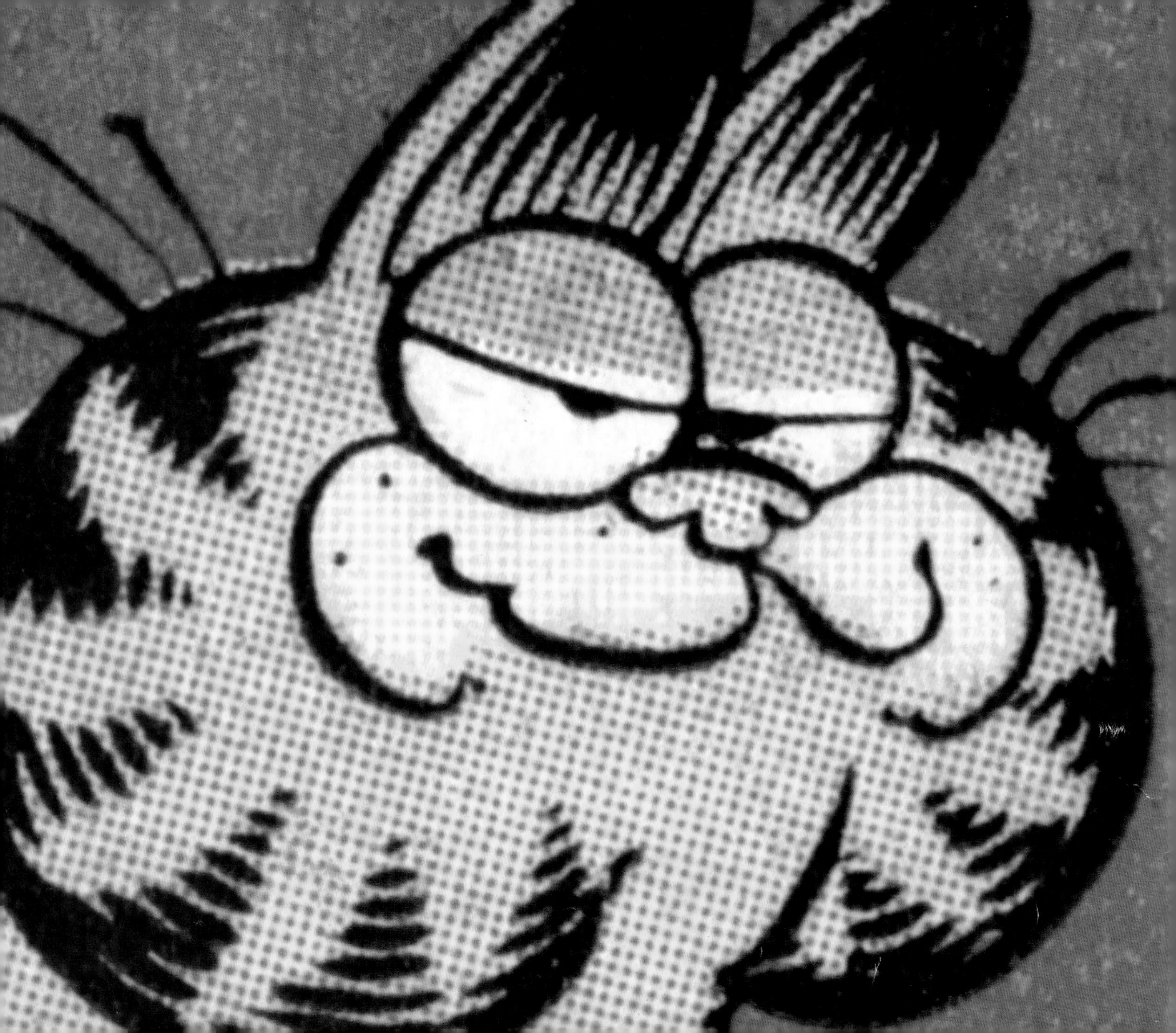

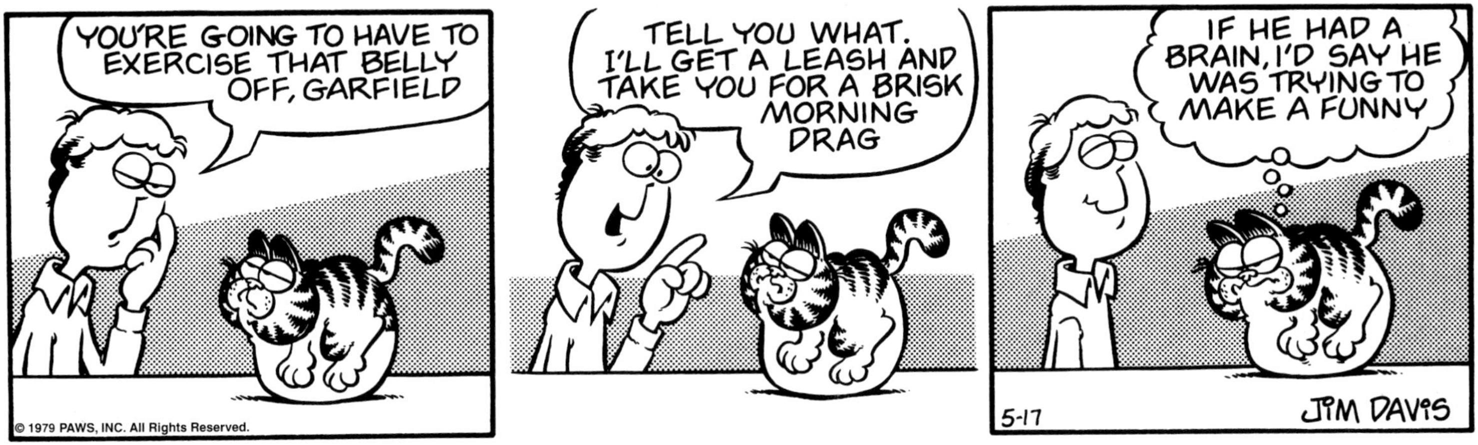
YOU'RE GOING TO HAVE TO EXERCISE THAT BELLY OFF, GARFIELD
TELL YOU WHAT. I'LL GET A LEASH AND TAKE YOU FOR A BRISK MORNING DRAG
IF HE HAD A BRAIN, I'D SAY HE WAS TRYING TO MAKE A FUNNY
© 1979 PAWS, INC. All Rights Reserved.
5-17
JIM DAVIS

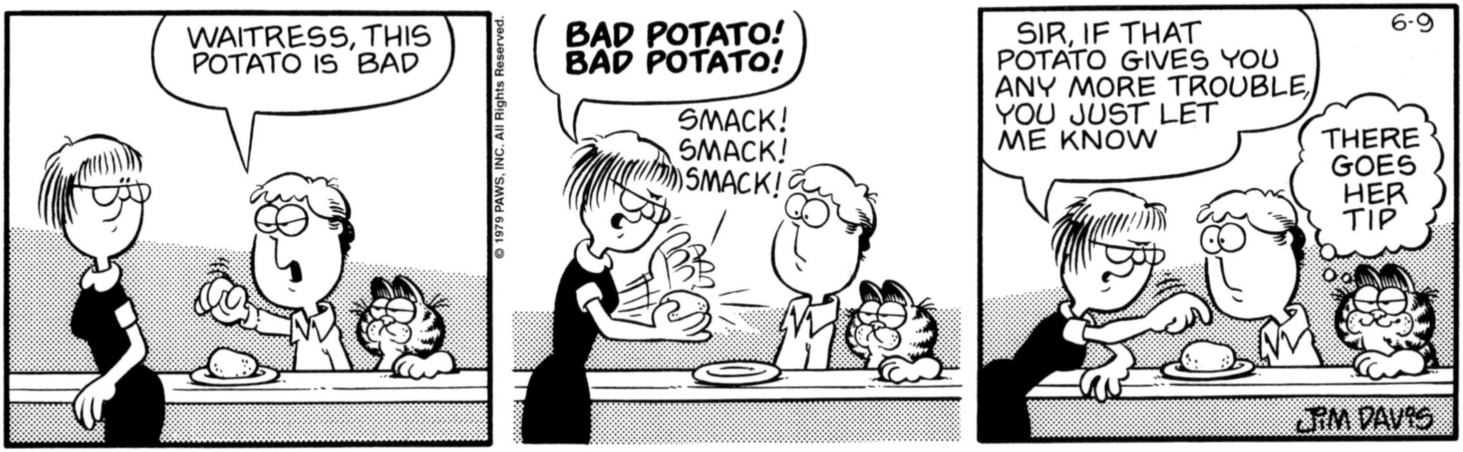
WAITRESS, THIS POTATO IS BAD
© 1979 PAWS, INC. All Rights Reserved.
BAD POTATO! BAD POTATO!
SMACK! SMACK! SMACK!
6-9
SIR, IF THAT POTATO GIVES YOU ANY MORE TROUBLE, YOU JUST LET ME KNOW
THERE GOES HER TIP
JIM DAVIS

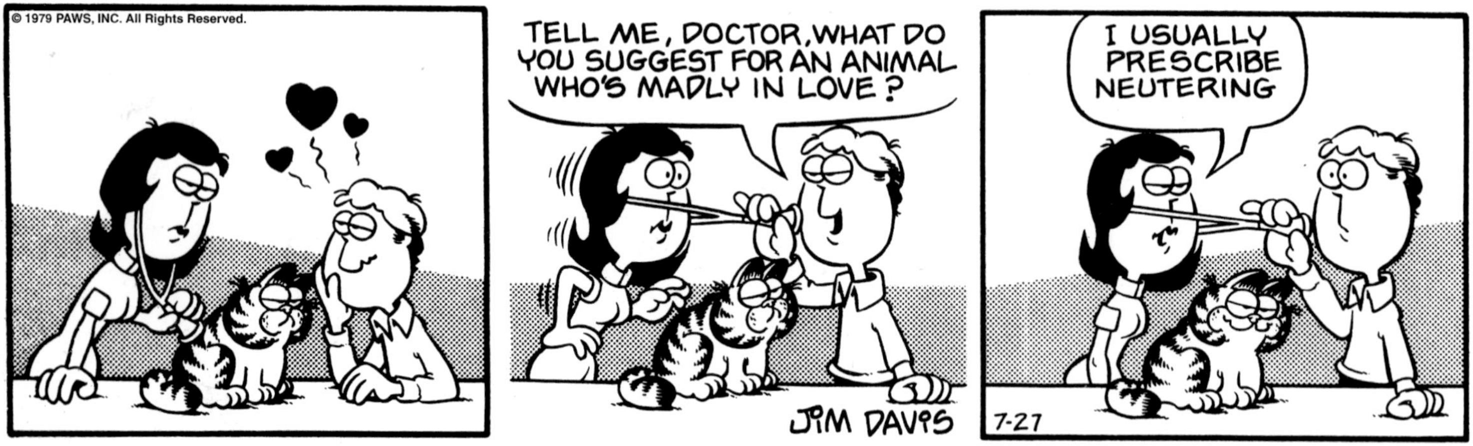
© 1979 PAWS, INC. All Rights Reserved.
TELL ME, DOCTOR, WHAT DO YOU SUGGEST FOR AN ANIMAL WHO'S MADLY IN LOVE ?
JIM DAVIS
I USUALLY PRESCRIBE NEUTERING
7-27

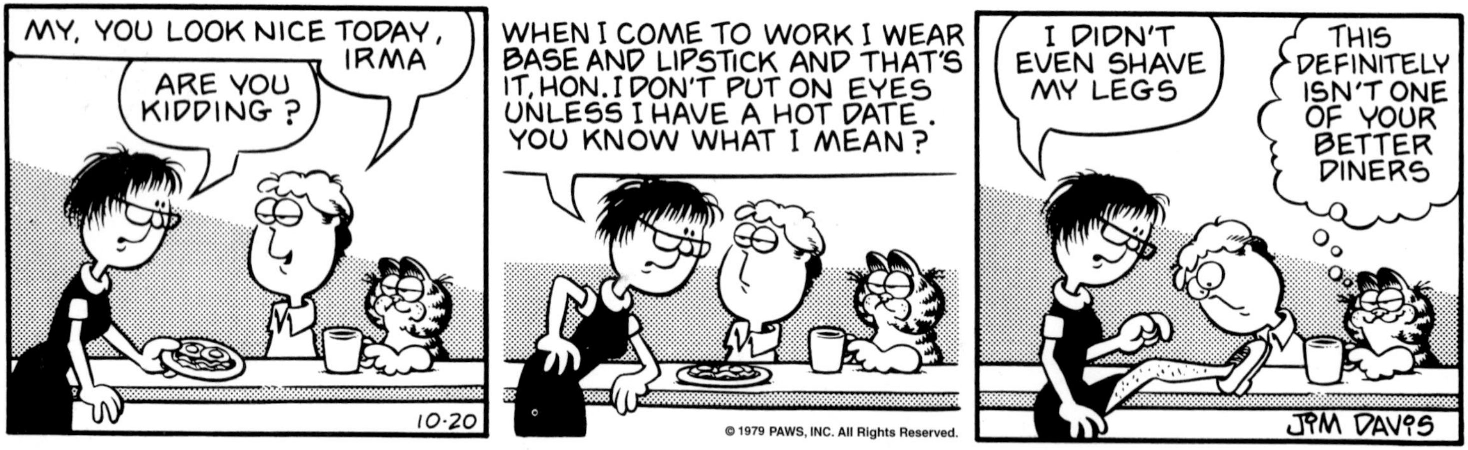
MY, YOU LOOK NICE TODAY, IRMA
ARE YOU KIDDING ?
10-20
WHEN I COME TO WORK I WEAR BASE AND LIPSTICK AND THAT'S IT, HON. I DON'T PUT ON EYES UNLESS I HAVE A HOT DATE. YOU KNOW WHAT I MEAN ?
© 1979 PAWS, INC. All Rights Reserved.
I DIDN'T EVEN SHAVE MY LEGS
THIS DEFINITELY ISN'T ONE OF YOUR BETTER DINERS
JIM DAVIS

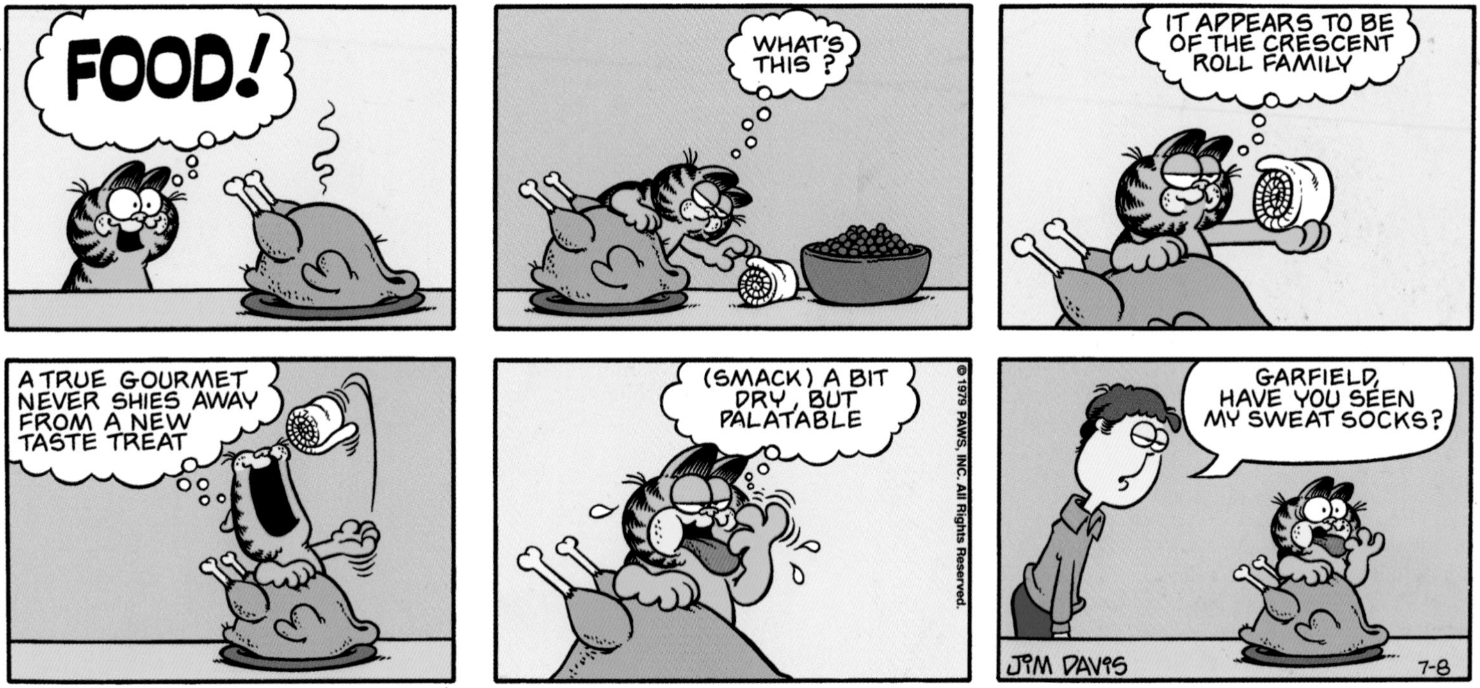
FOOD!
WHAT'S THIS ?
IT APPEARS TO BE OF THE CRESCENT ROLL FAMILY
A TRUE GOURMET NEVER SHIES AWAY FROM A NEW TASTE TREAT
(SMACK) A BIT DRY, BUT PALATABLE
© 1979 PAWS, INC. All Rights Reserved.
GARFIELD, HAVE YOU SEEN MY SWEAT SOCKS?
JIM DAVIS
7-8

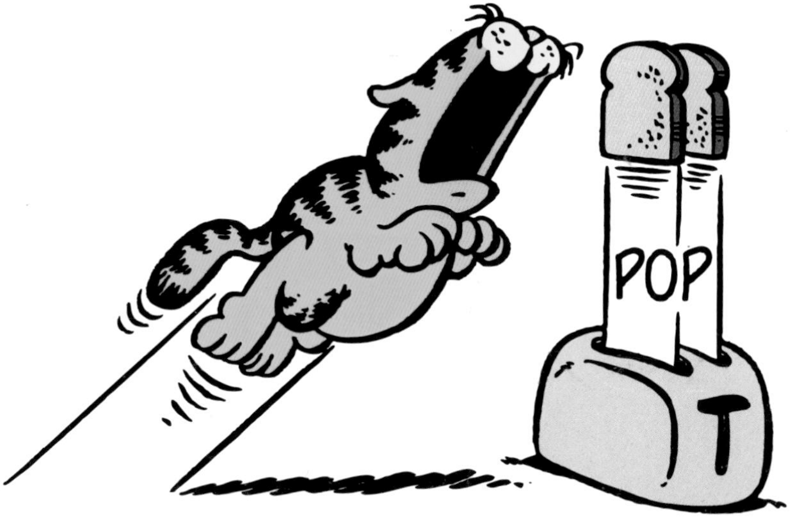
POP
T

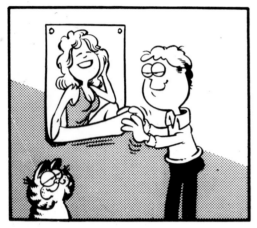

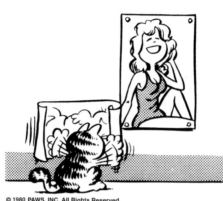

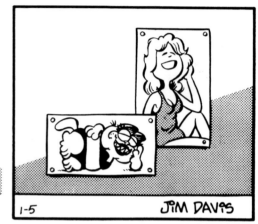

© 1980 PAWS, INC. All Rights Reserved.
1-5
JIM DAVIS

I decided to submit *Garfield* to one syndicate at a time. I figured that since I'd gone that long without being syndicated (I was thirty-two years old and had been trying for eight years), I'd only submit it to the larger syndicates one at a time. Maybe I was arrogant, but after eight years, I dreaded the thought of two syndicates taking the strip at the same time.

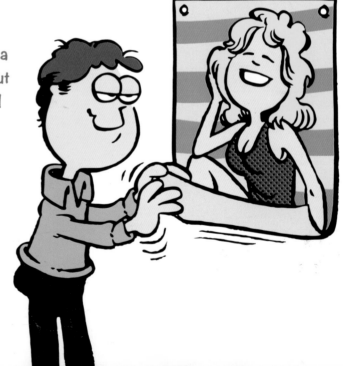

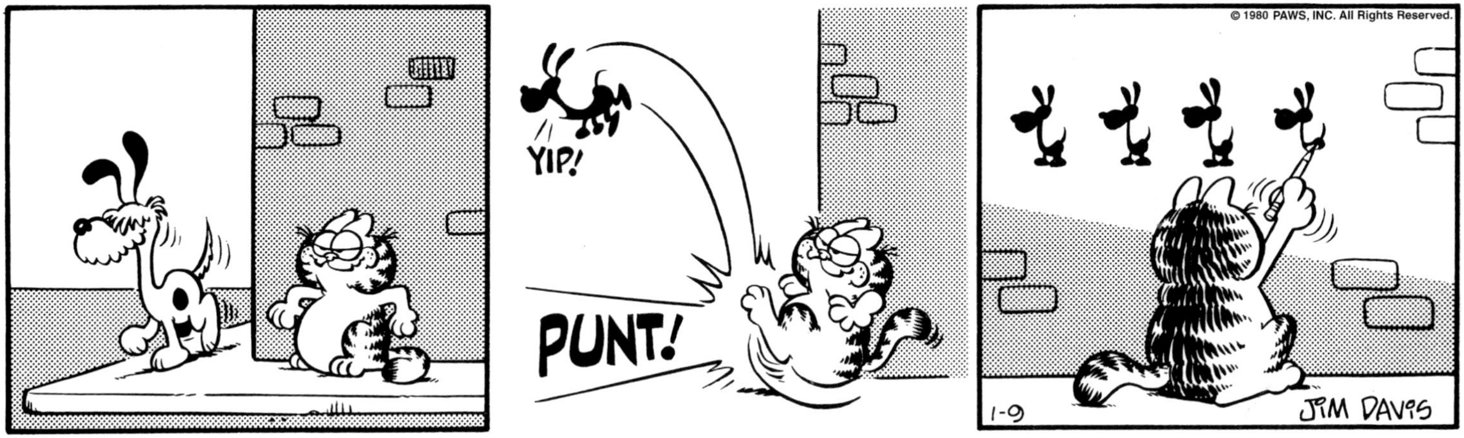
YIP!
PUNT!
© 1980 PAWS, INC. All Rights Reserved.
1-9
JIM DAVIS

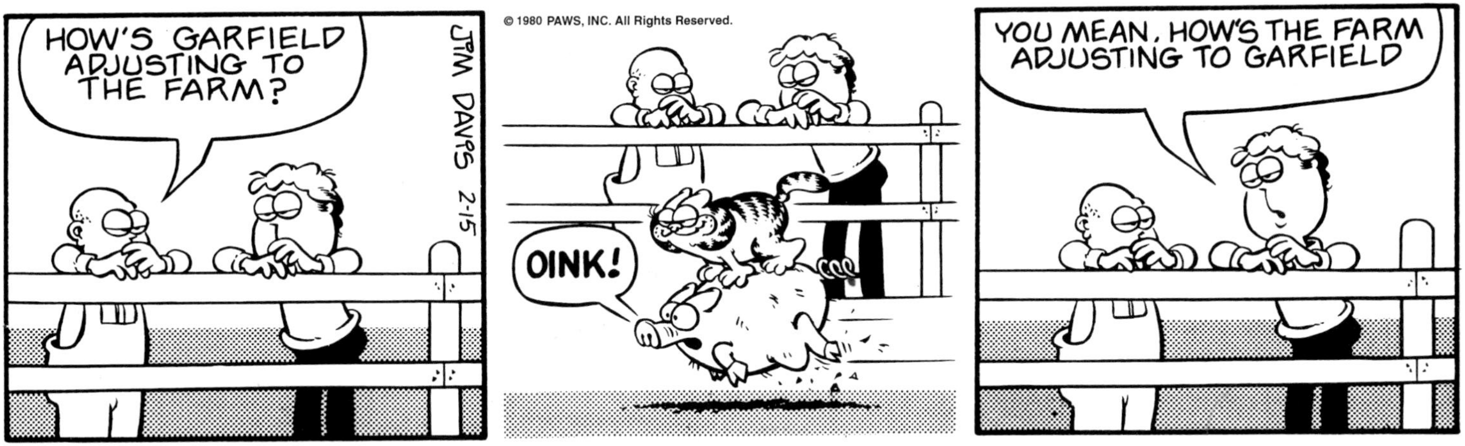
HOW'S GARFIELD ADJUSTING TO THE FARM?
JIM DAVIS 2-15
© 1980 PAWS, INC. All Rights Reserved.
OINK!
YOU MEAN, HOW'S THE FARM ADJUSTING TO GARFIELD

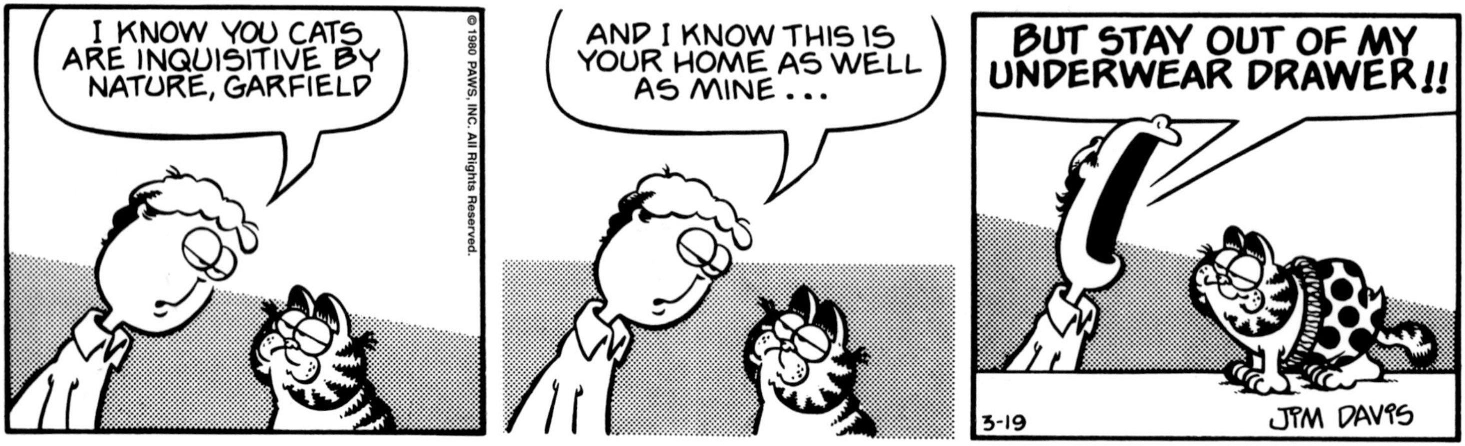
I KNOW YOU CATS ARE INQUISITIVE BY NATURE, GARFIELD
© 1980 PAWS, INC. All Rights Reserved.
AND I KNOW THIS IS YOUR HOME AS WELL AS MINE . . .
BUT STAY OUT OF MY UNDERWEAR DRAWER!!
3-19
JIM DAVIS

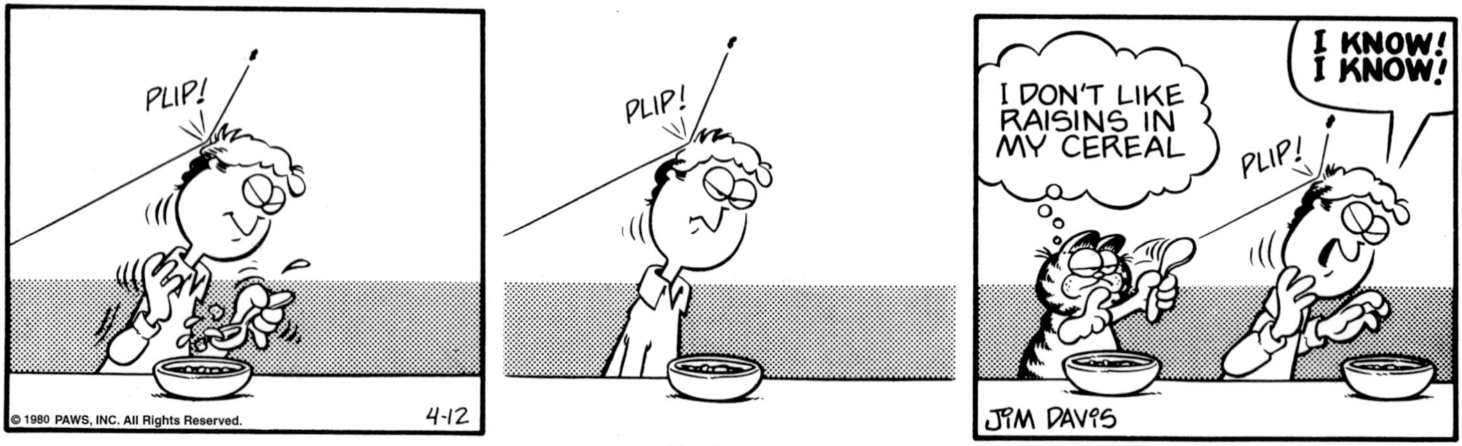
PLIP!
© 1980 PAWS, INC. All Rights Reserved.
4-12
PLIP!
I DON'T LIKE RAISINS IN MY CEREAL
PLIP!
I KNOW! I KNOW!
JIM DAVIS

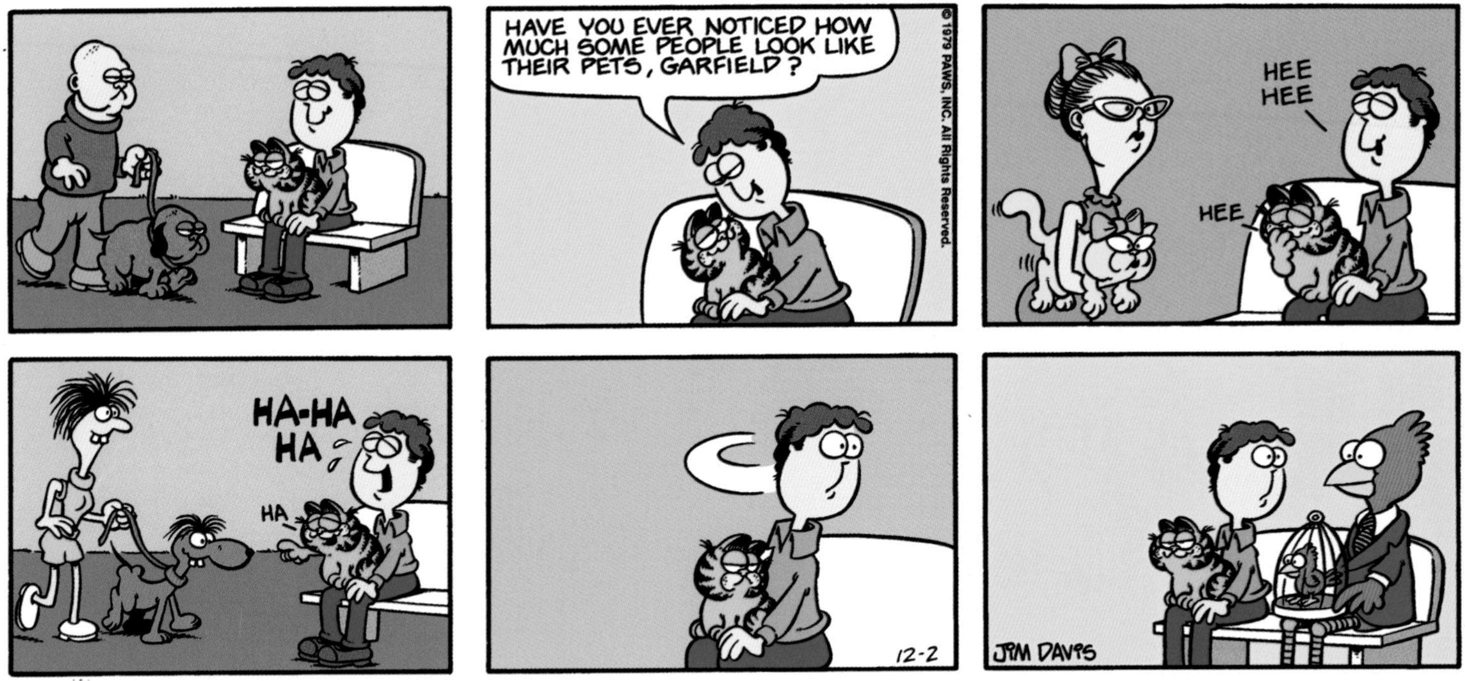
HAVE YOU EVER NOTICED HOW MUCH SOME PEOPLE LOOK LIKE THEIR PETS, GARFIELD?
© 1979 PAWS, INC. All Rights Reserved.
HEE HEE
HEE
HA-HA HA
HA
12-2
JIM DAVIS

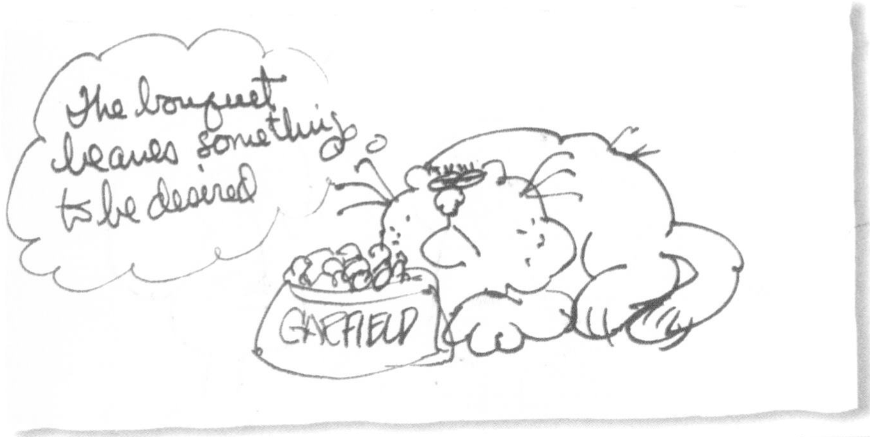
The bouquet leaves something to be desired
GARFIELD

Original pencil drawing from 1978 sketchbook.

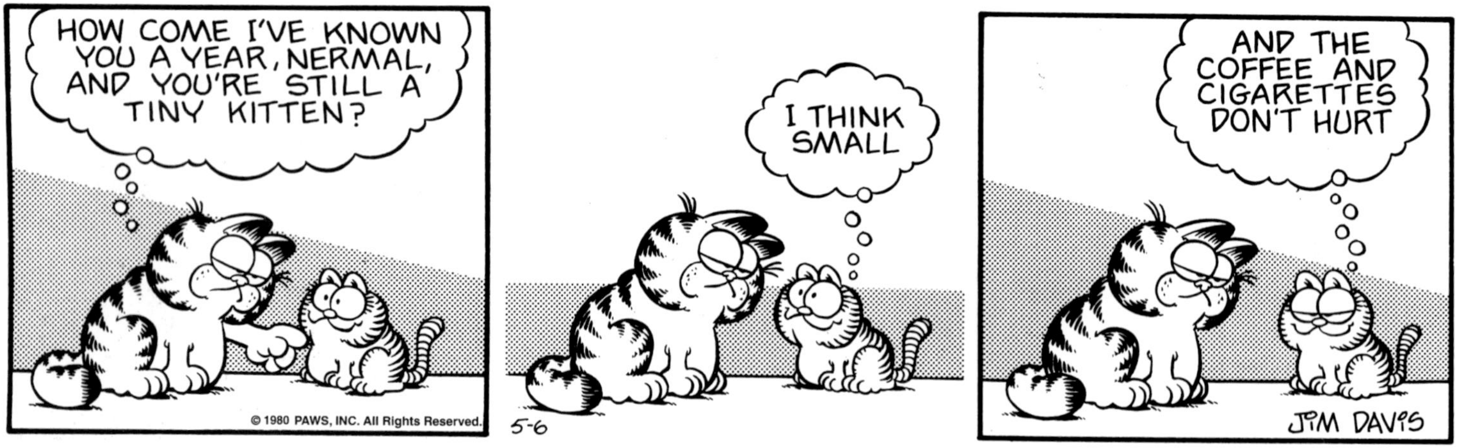
HOW COME I'VE KNOWN YOU A YEAR, NERMAL, AND YOU'RE STILL A TINY KITTEN?
© 1980 PAWS, INC. All Rights Reserved.
I THINK SMALL
5-6
AND THE COFFEE AND CIGARETTES DON'T HURT
JIM DAVIS

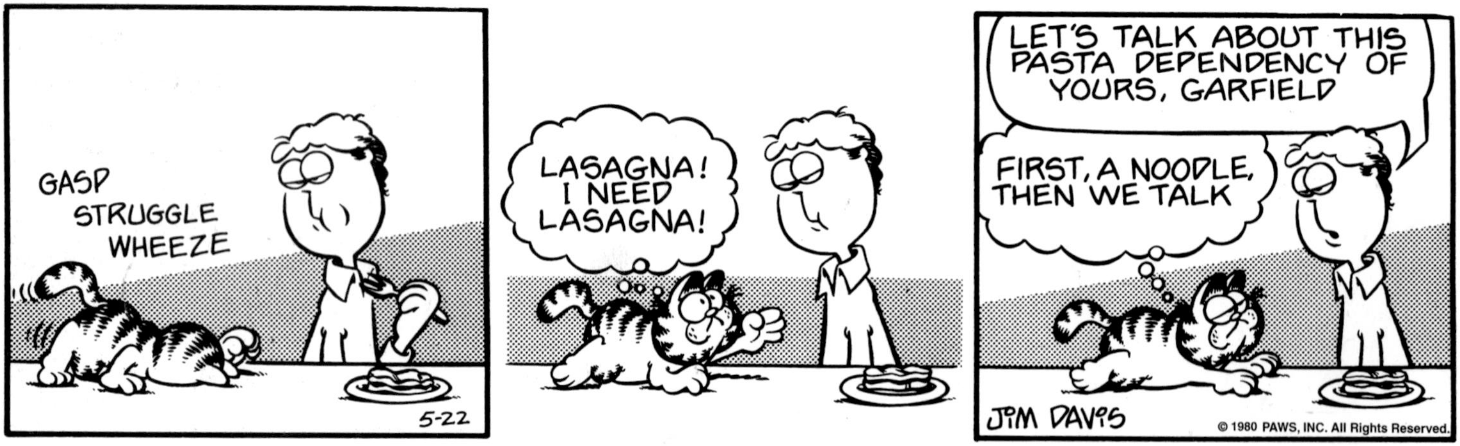
GASP
STRUGGLE
WHEEZE
5-22
LASAGNA! I NEED LASAGNA!
LET'S TALK ABOUT THIS PASTA DEPENDENCY OF YOURS, GARFIELD
FIRST, A NOODLE, THEN WE TALK
JIM DAVIS
© 1980 PAWS, INC. All Rights Reserved.

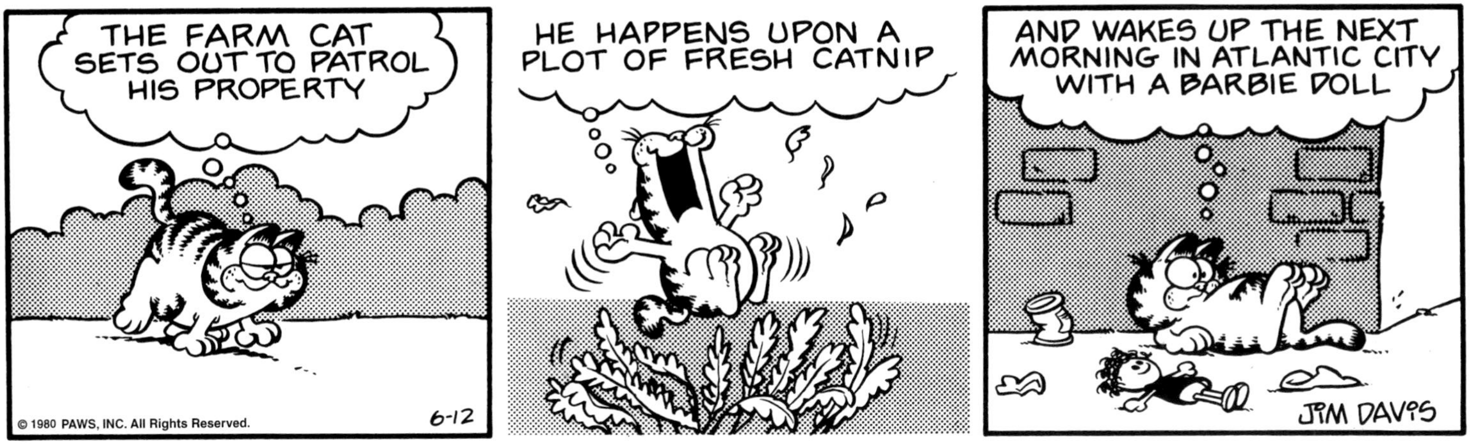
THE FARM CAT SETS OUT TO PATROL HIS PROPERTY
© 1980 PAWS, INC. All Rights Reserved.
6-12
HE HAPPENS UPON A PLOT OF FRESH CATNIP
AND WAKES UP THE NEXT MORNING IN ATLANTIC CITY WITH A BARBIE DOLL
JIM DAVIS

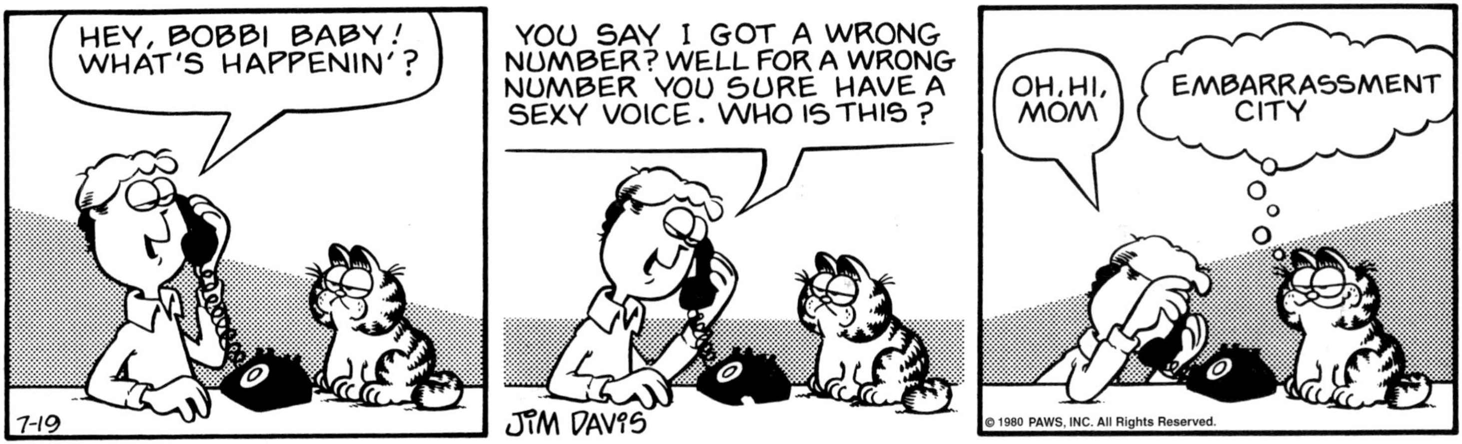
HEY, BOBBI BABY! WHAT'S HAPPENIN'?
7-19
YOU SAY I GOT A WRONG NUMBER? WELL FOR A WRONG NUMBER YOU SURE HAVE A SEXY VOICE. WHO IS THIS?
JIM DAVIS
OH, HI, MOM
EMBARRASSMENT CITY
© 1980 PAWS, INC. All Rights Reserved.

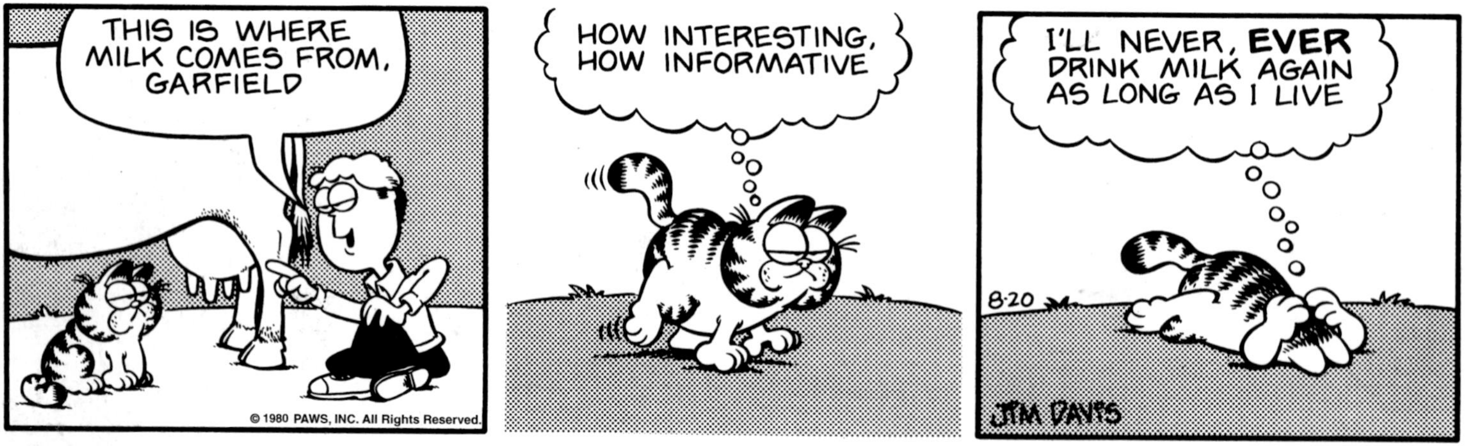
THIS IS WHERE MILK COMES FROM, GARFIELD
© 1980 PAWS, INC. All Rights Reserved.
HOW INTERESTING, HOW INFORMATIVE
I'LL NEVER, **EVER** DRINK MILK AGAIN AS LONG AS I LIVE
8-20
JIM DAVIS

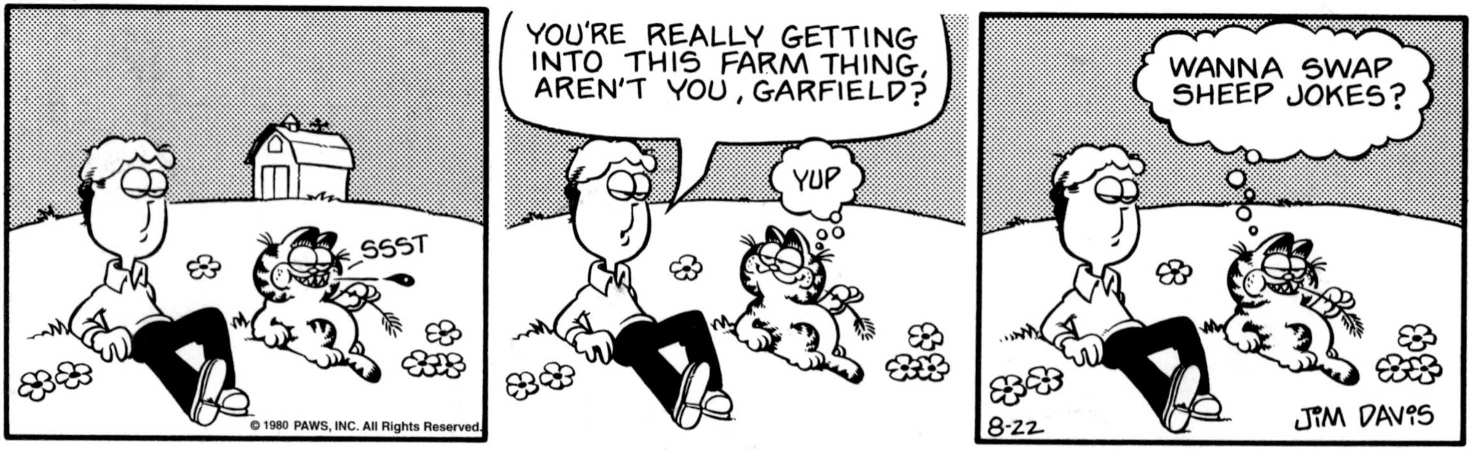
SSST
© 1980 PAWS, INC. All Rights Reserved.
YOU'RE REALLY GETTING INTO THIS FARM THING, AREN'T YOU, GARFIELD?
YUP
WANNA SWAP SHEEP JOKES?
8-22
JIM DAVIS

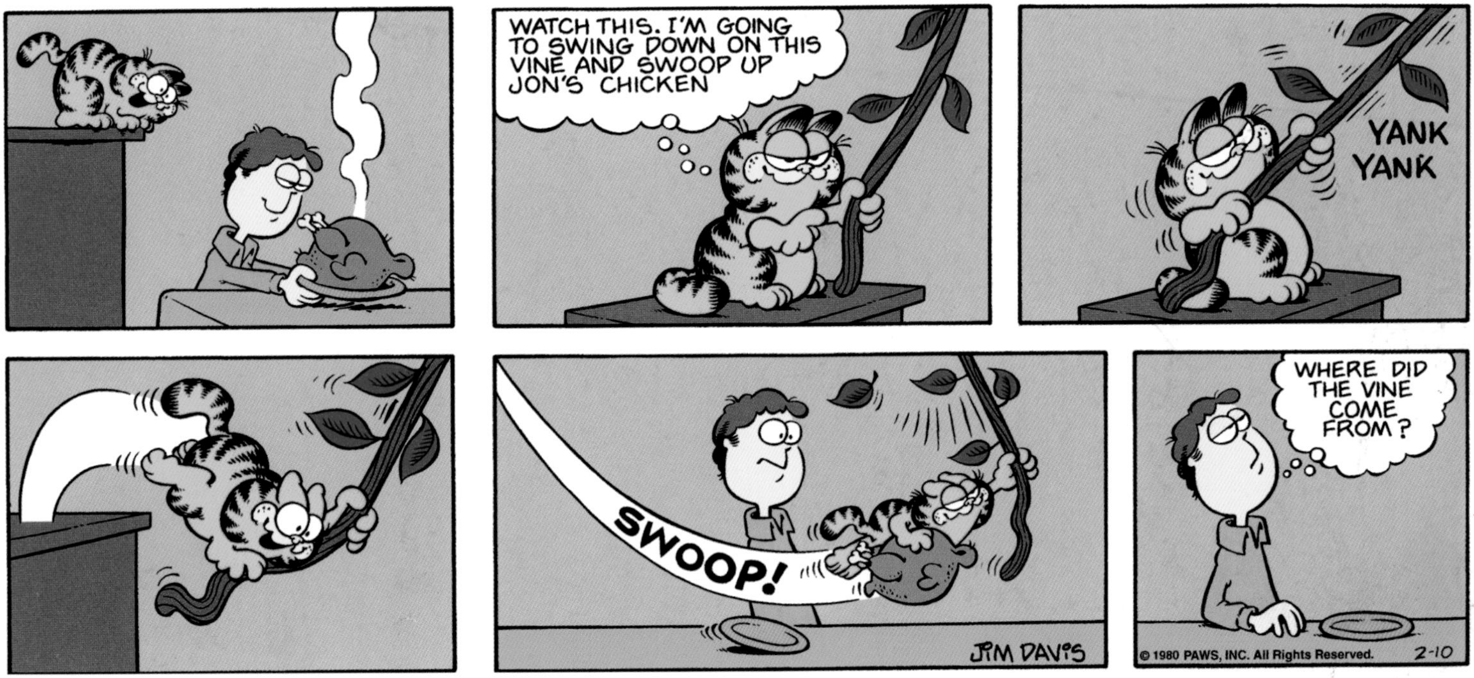
WATCH THIS. I'M GOING TO SWING DOWN ON THIS VINE AND SWOOP UP JON'S CHICKEN
YANK YANK
SWOOP!
JIM DAVIS
WHERE DID THE VINE COME FROM?
© 1980 PAWS, INC. All Rights Reserved.
2-10

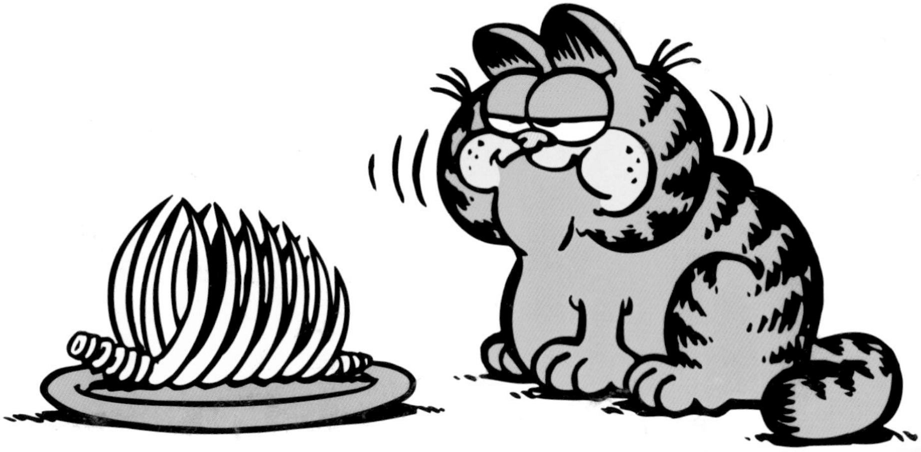

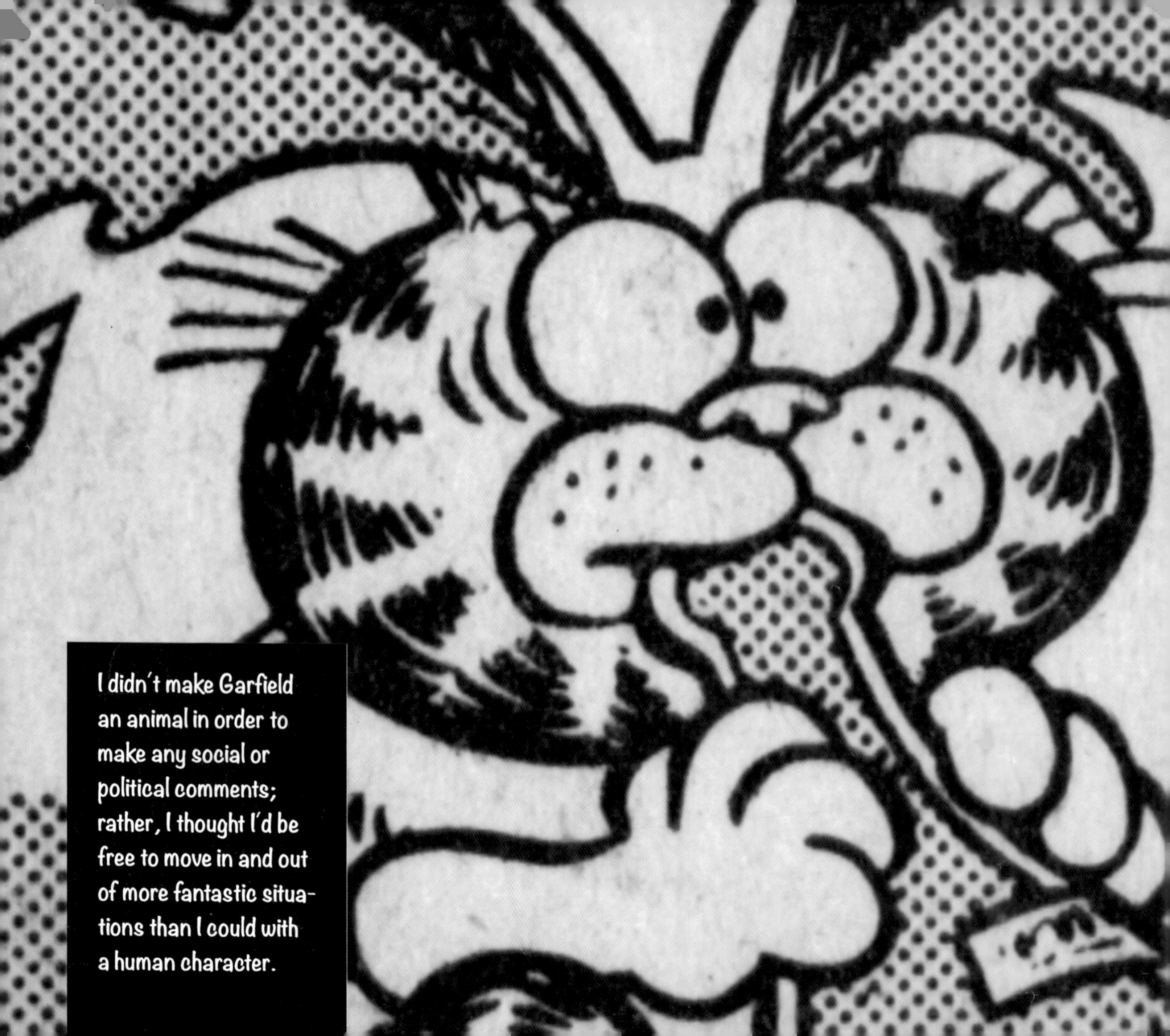

I didn't make Garfield an animal in order to make any social or political comments; rather, I thought I'd be free to move in and out of more fantastic situations than I could with a human character.

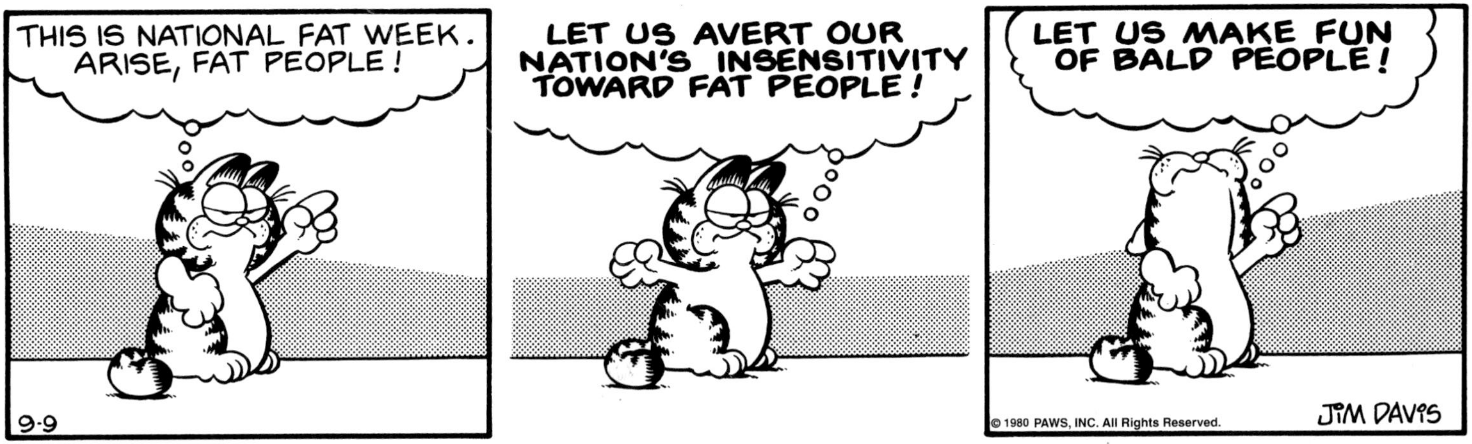
THIS IS NATIONAL FAT WEEK. ARISE, FAT PEOPLE!
9-9
LET US AVERT OUR NATION'S INSENSITIVITY TOWARD FAT PEOPLE!
LET US MAKE FUN OF BALD PEOPLE!
© 1980 PAWS, INC. All Rights Reserved.
JIM DAVIS

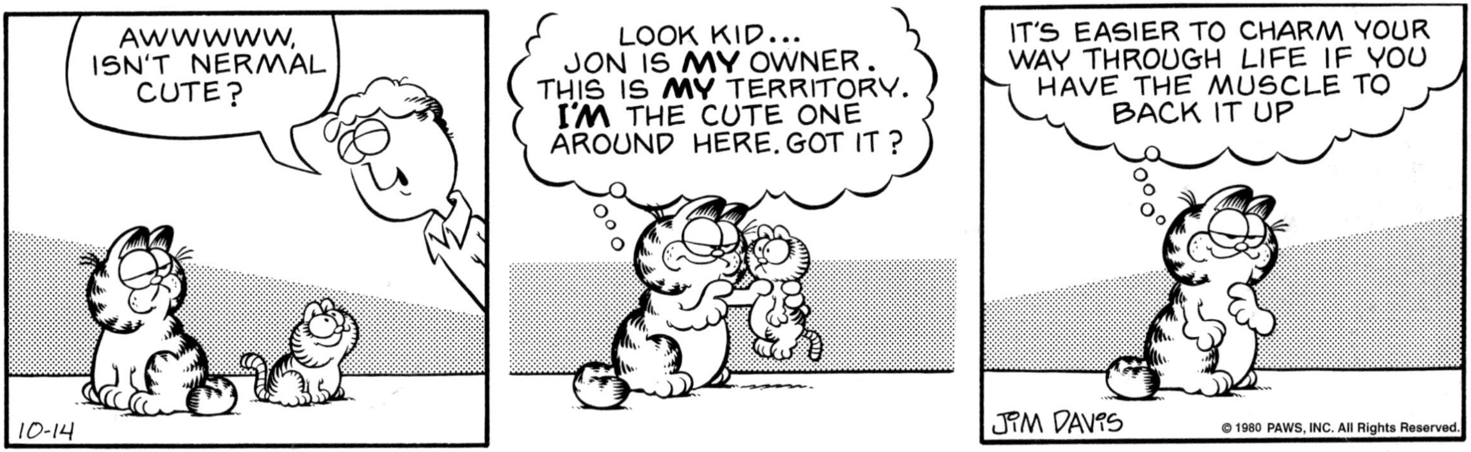
AWWWWW, ISN'T NERMAL CUTE?
10-14
LOOK KID... JON IS **MY** OWNER. THIS IS **MY** TERRITORY. **I'M** THE CUTE ONE AROUND HERE. GOT IT?
IT'S EASIER TO CHARM YOUR WAY THROUGH LIFE IF YOU HAVE THE MUSCLE TO BACK IT UP
JIM DAVIS
© 1980 PAWS, INC. All Rights Reserved.

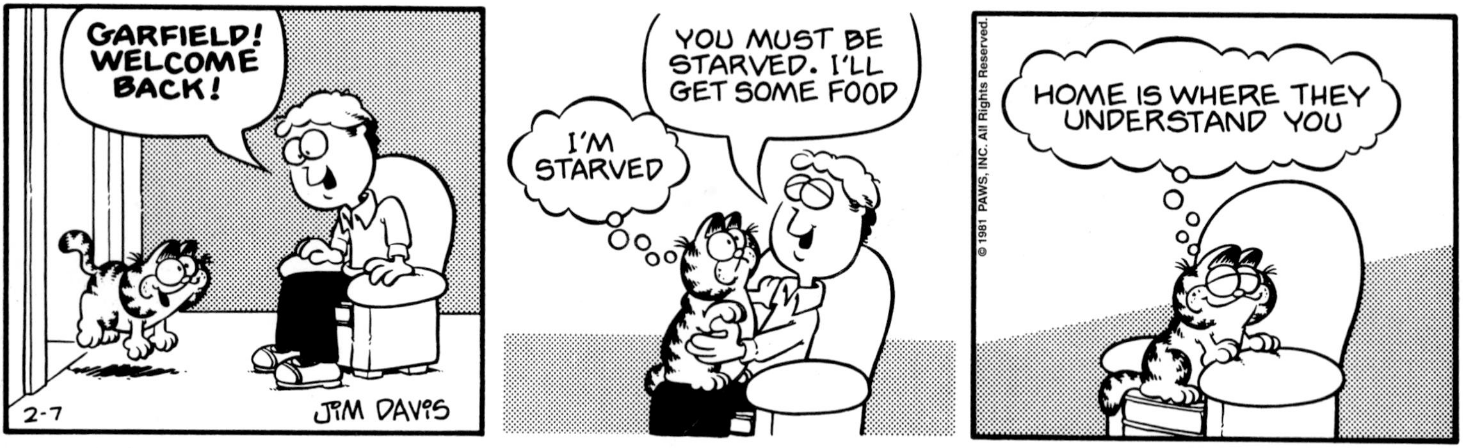
GARFIELD! WELCOME BACK!
2-7
JIM DAVIS
YOU MUST BE STARVED. I'LL GET SOME FOOD
I'M STARVED
© 1981 PAWS, INC. All Rights Reserved.
HOME IS WHERE THEY UNDERSTAND YOU

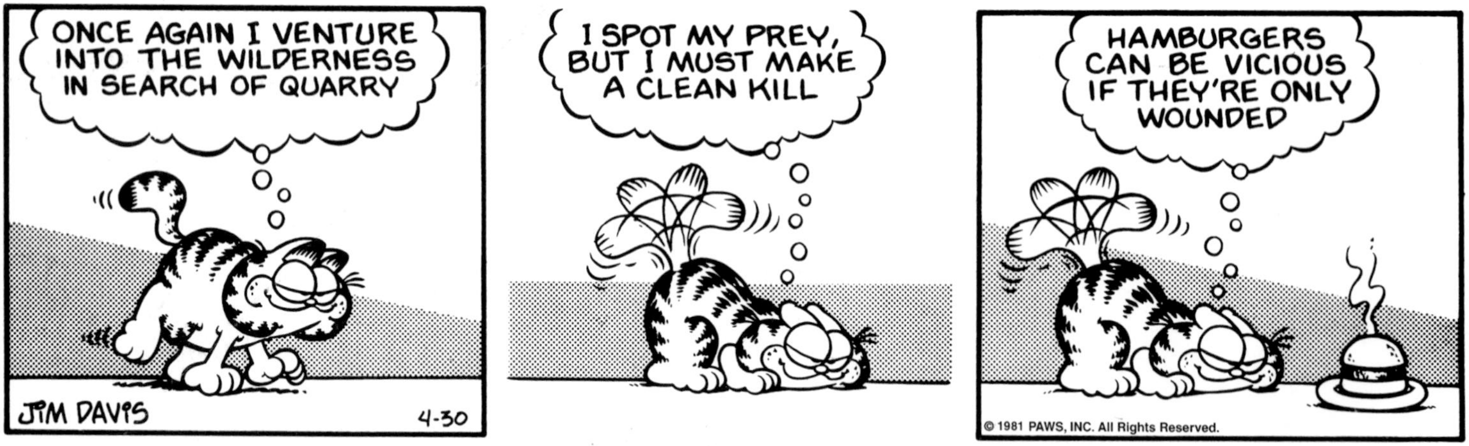
ONCE AGAIN I VENTURE INTO THE WILDERNESS IN SEARCH OF QUARRY
JIM DAVIS
4-30
I SPOT MY PREY, BUT I MUST MAKE A CLEAN KILL
HAMBURGERS CAN BE VICIOUS IF THEY'RE ONLY WOUNDED
© 1981 PAWS, INC. All Rights Reserved.

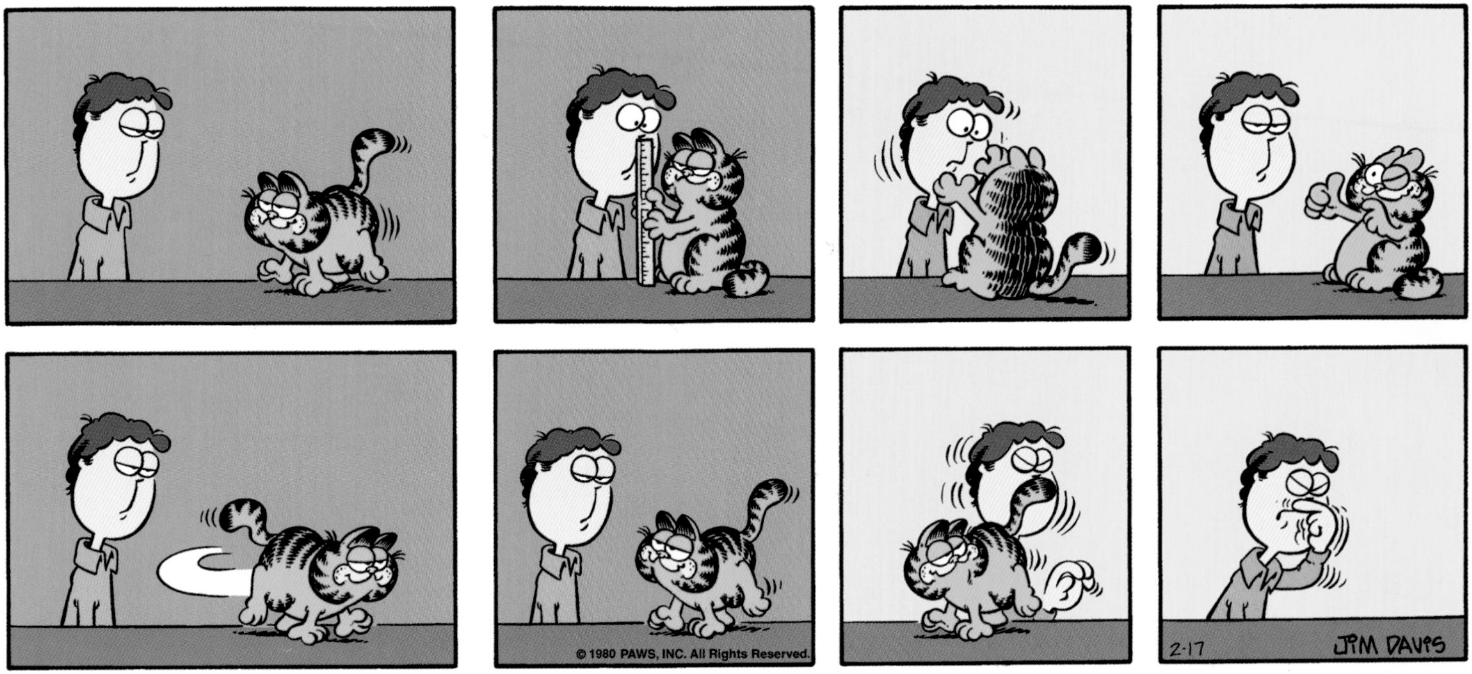
© 1980 PAWS, INC. All Rights Reserved.
2-17
JIM DAVIS

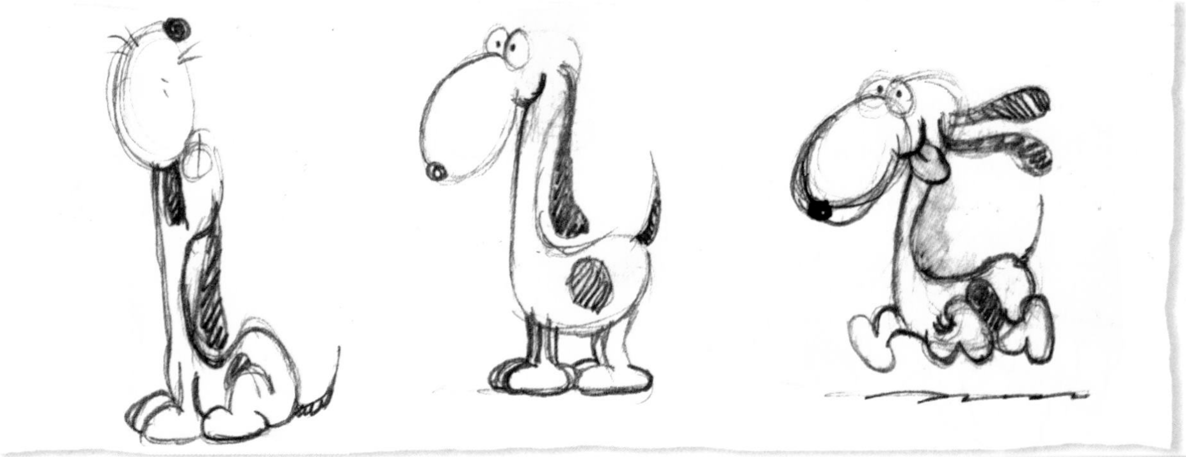

Early Odie concepts from 1978 sketchbook.

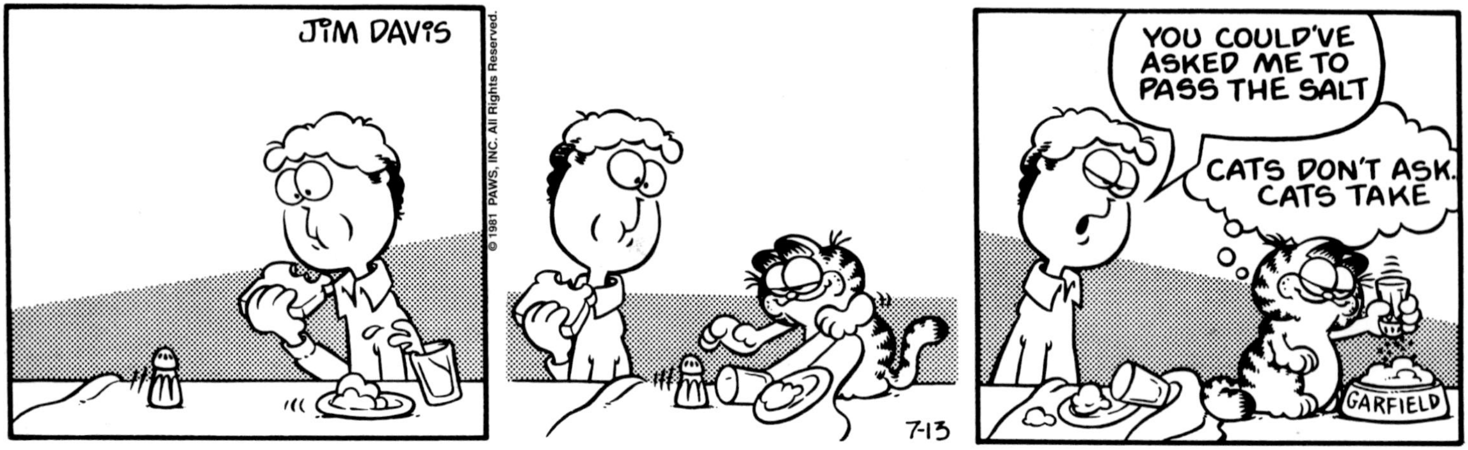
JIM DAVIS
© 1981 PAWS, INC. All Rights Reserved.
7-13
YOU COULD'VE ASKED ME TO PASS THE SALT
CATS DON'T ASK. CATS TAKE
GARFIELD

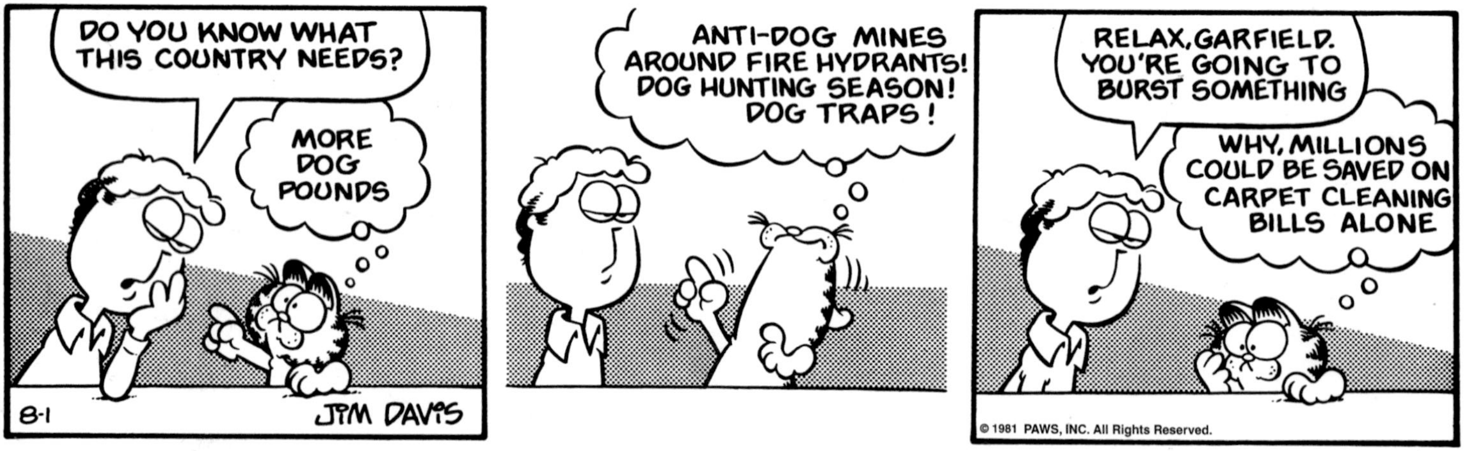
DO YOU KNOW WHAT THIS COUNTRY NEEDS?
MORE DOG POUNDS
8-1
JIM DAVIS
ANTI-DOG MINES AROUND FIRE HYDRANTS! DOG HUNTING SEASON! DOG TRAPS!
RELAX, GARFIELD. YOU'RE GOING TO BURST SOMETHING
WHY, MILLIONS COULD BE SAVED ON CARPET CLEANING BILLS ALONE
© 1981 PAWS, INC. All Rights Reserved.

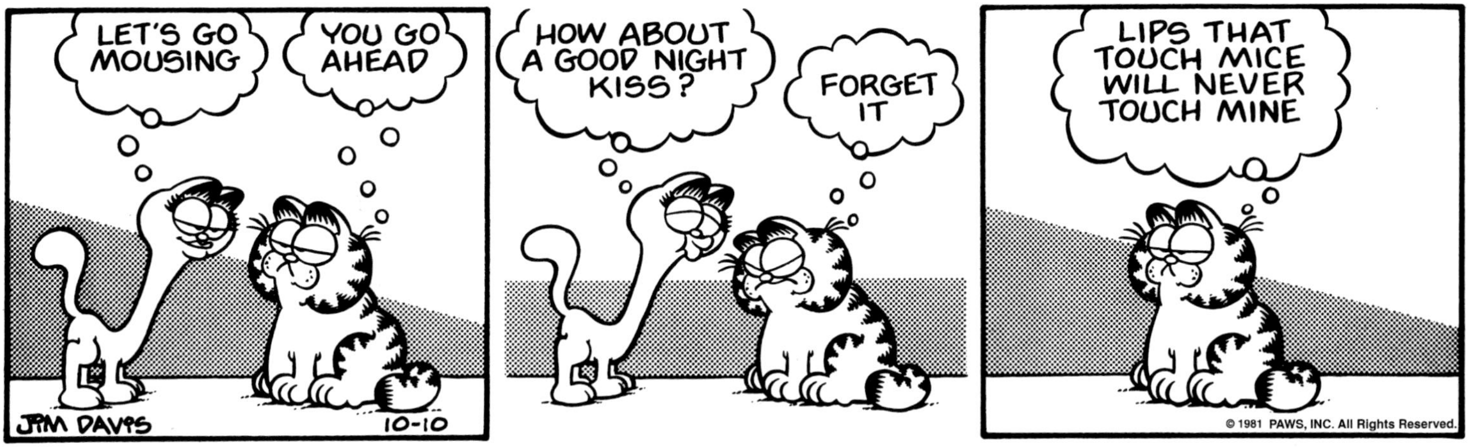
LET'S GO MOUSING
YOU GO AHEAD
JIM DAVIS
10-10
HOW ABOUT A GOOD NIGHT KISS?
FORGET IT
LIPS THAT TOUCH MICE WILL NEVER TOUCH MINE
© 1981 PAWS, INC. All Rights Reserved.

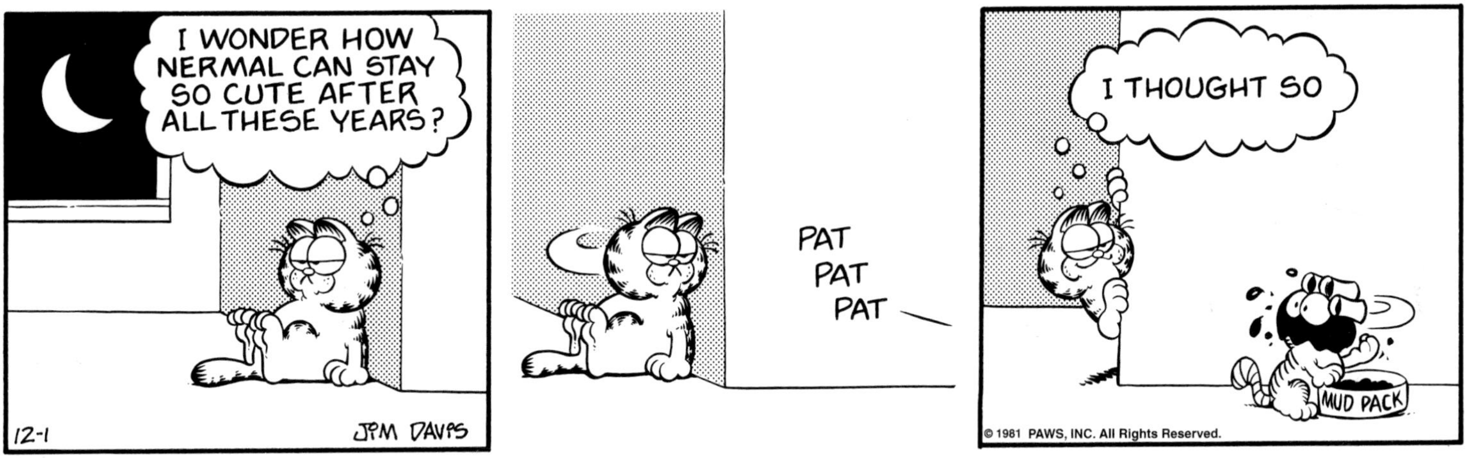
I WONDER HOW NERMAL CAN STAY SO CUTE AFTER ALL THESE YEARS?
12-1
JIM DAVIS
PAT
PAT
PAT
I THOUGHT SO
MUD PACK
© 1981 PAWS, INC. All Rights Reserved.

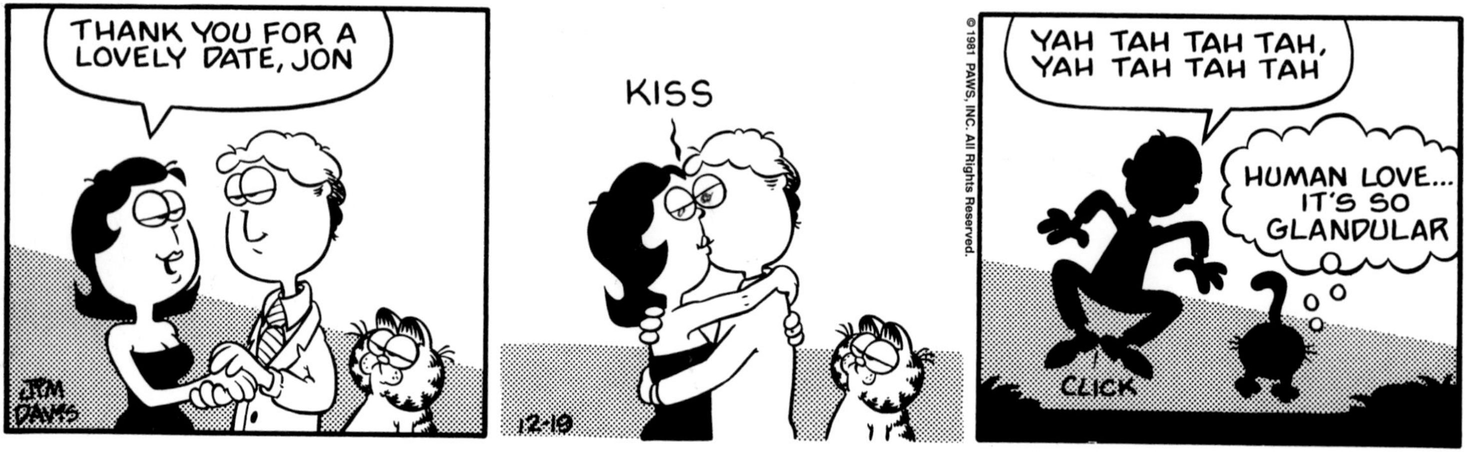
THANK YOU FOR A LOVELY DATE, JON
JIM DAVIS
12-19
KISS
© 1981 PAWS, INC. All Rights Reserved.
YAH TAH TAH TAH, YAH TAH TAH TAH
HUMAN LOVE... IT'S SO GLANDULAR
CLICK

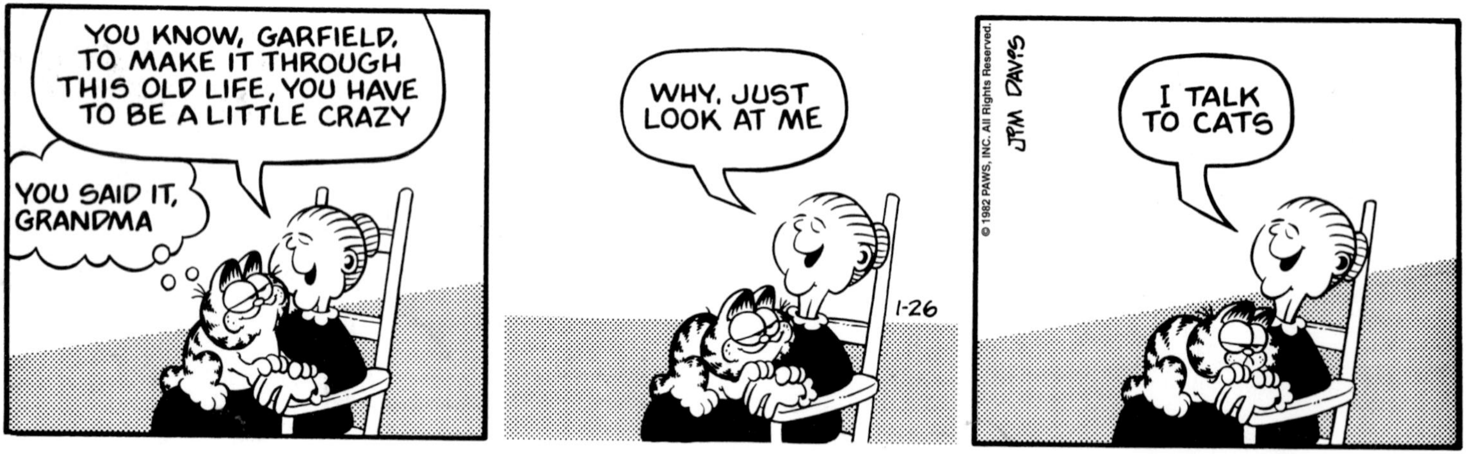
YOU KNOW, GARFIELD, TO MAKE IT THROUGH THIS OLD LIFE, YOU HAVE TO BE A LITTLE CRAZY
YOU SAID IT, GRANDMA
WHY, JUST LOOK AT ME
1-26
© 1982 PAWS, INC. All Rights Reserved.
JIM DAVIS
I TALK TO CATS

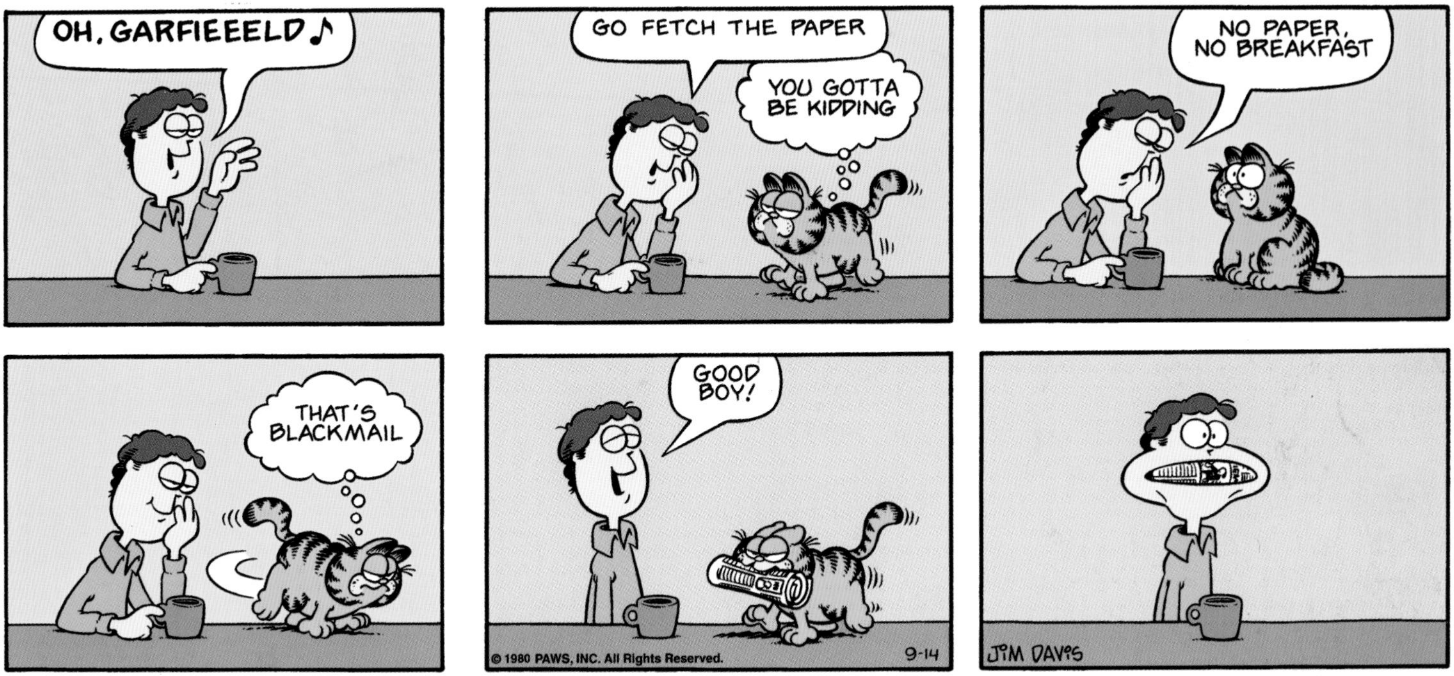
OH, GARFIEEELD♪
GO FETCH THE PAPER
YOU GOTTA BE KIDDING
NO PAPER, NO BREAKFAST
THAT'S BLACKMAIL
GOOD BOY!
© 1980 PAWS, INC. All Rights Reserved.
9-14
JIM DAVIS

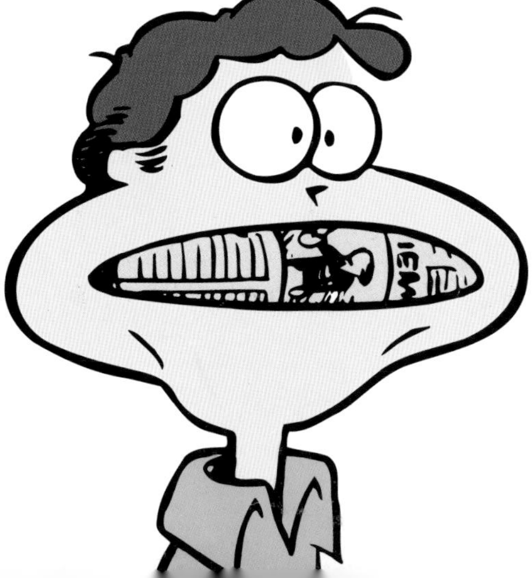

I feel a responsibility to balance the scales against what's really happening. The worse things are, the more humor is needed.

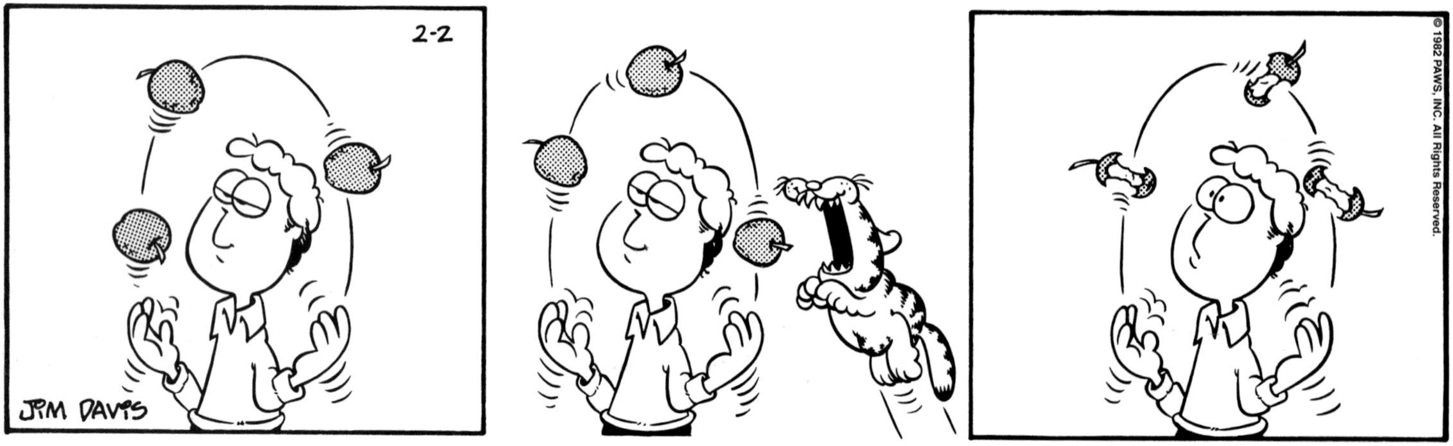
2-2
JIM DAVIS
© 1982 PAWS, INC. All Rights Reserved.

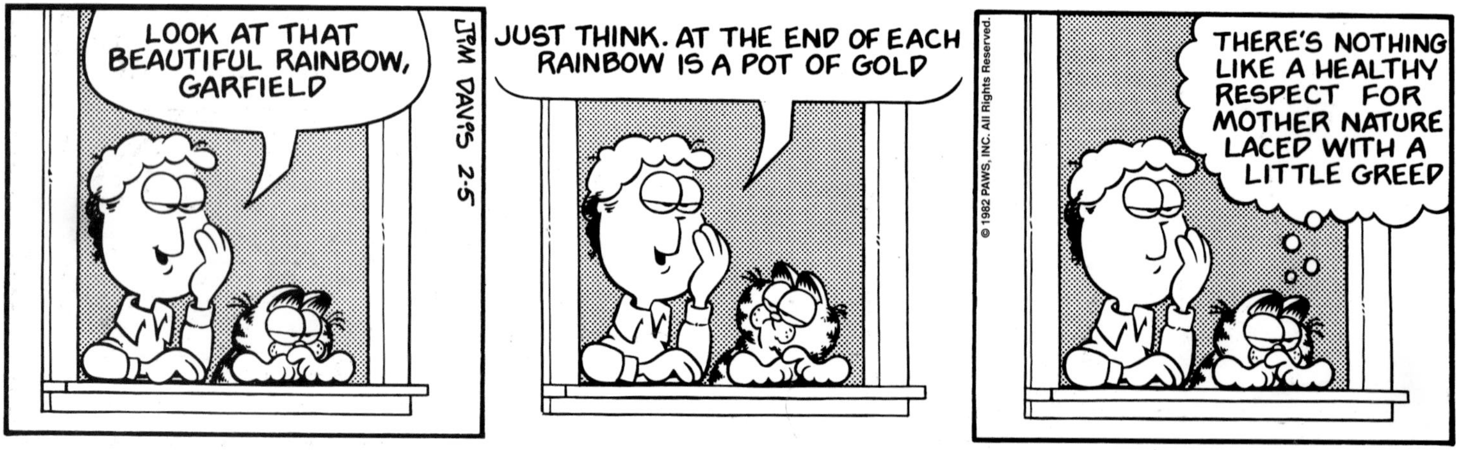
LOOK AT THAT BEAUTIFUL RAINBOW, GARFIELD
JIM DAVIS 2-5
JUST THINK. AT THE END OF EACH RAINBOW IS A POT OF GOLD
© 1982 PAWS, INC. All Rights Reserved.
THERE'S NOTHING LIKE A HEALTHY RESPECT FOR MOTHER NATURE LACED WITH A LITTLE GREED

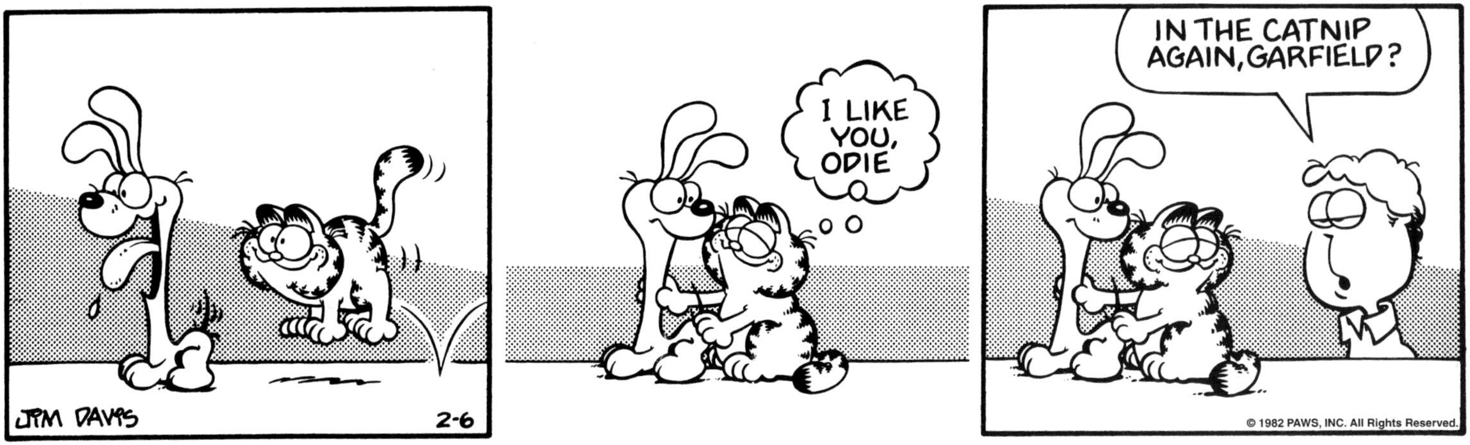
JIM DAVIS
2-6
I LIKE YOU, ODIE
IN THE CATNIP AGAIN, GARFIELD?
© 1982 PAWS, INC. All Rights Reserved.

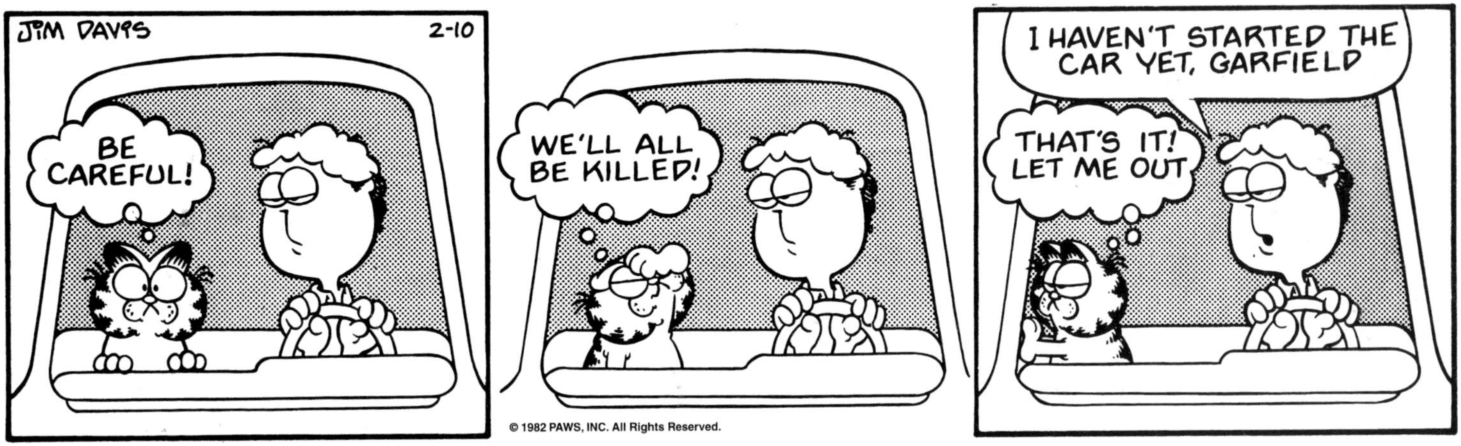
JIM DAVIS
2-10
BE CAREFUL!
WE'LL ALL BE KILLED!
I HAVEN'T STARTED THE CAR YET, GARFIELD
THAT'S IT! LET ME OUT

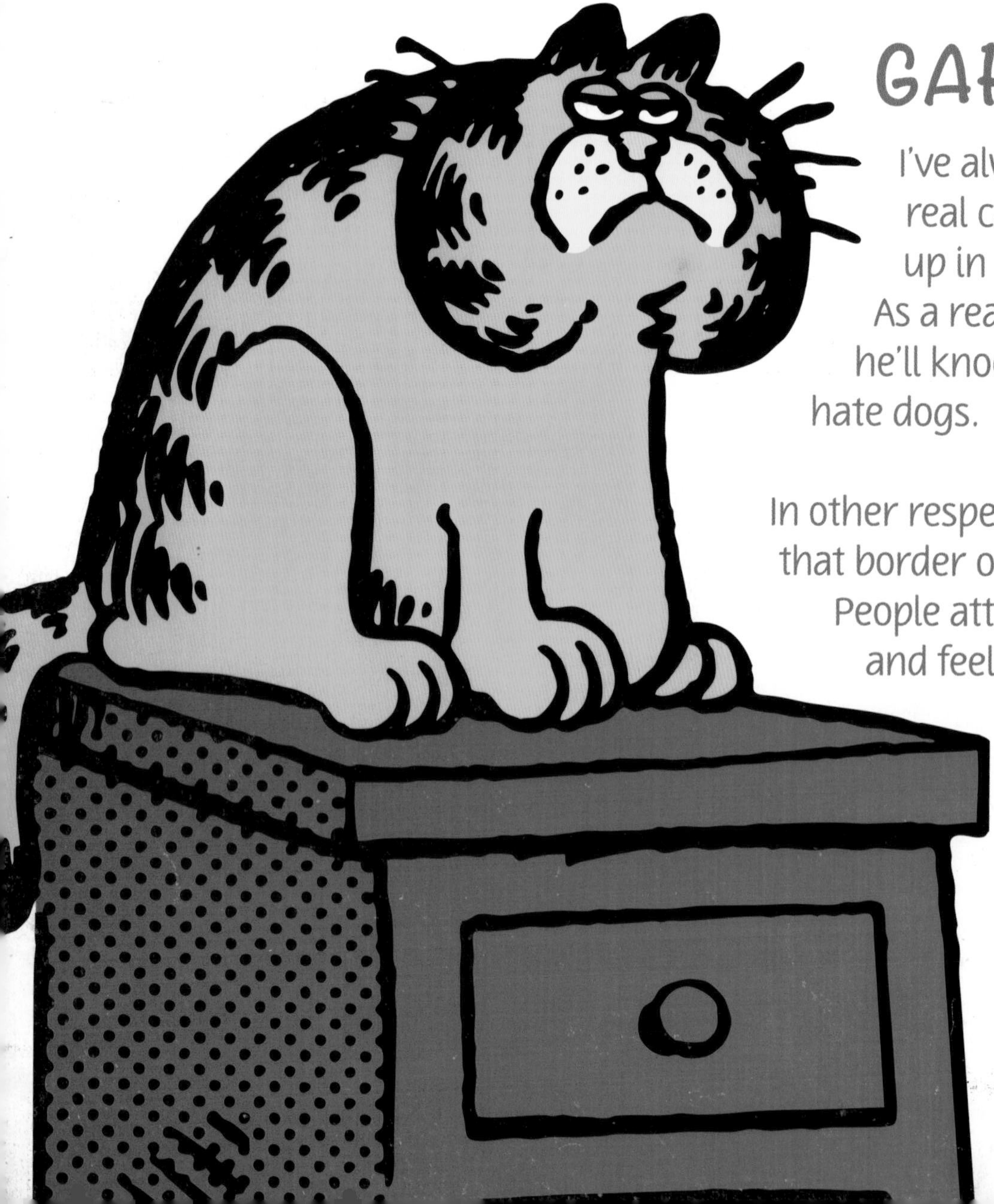

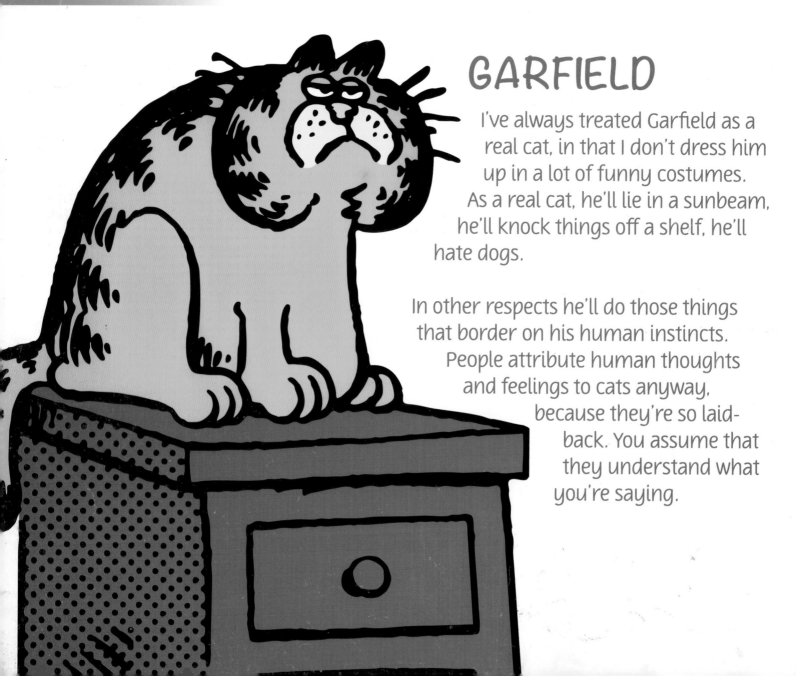

GARFIELD

I've always treated Garfield as a real cat, in that I don't dress him up in a lot of funny costumes. As a real cat, he'll lie in a sunbeam, he'll knock things off a shelf, he'll hate dogs.

In other respects he'll do those things that border on his human instincts. People attribute human thoughts and feelings to cats anyway, because they're so laid-back. You assume that they understand what you're saying.

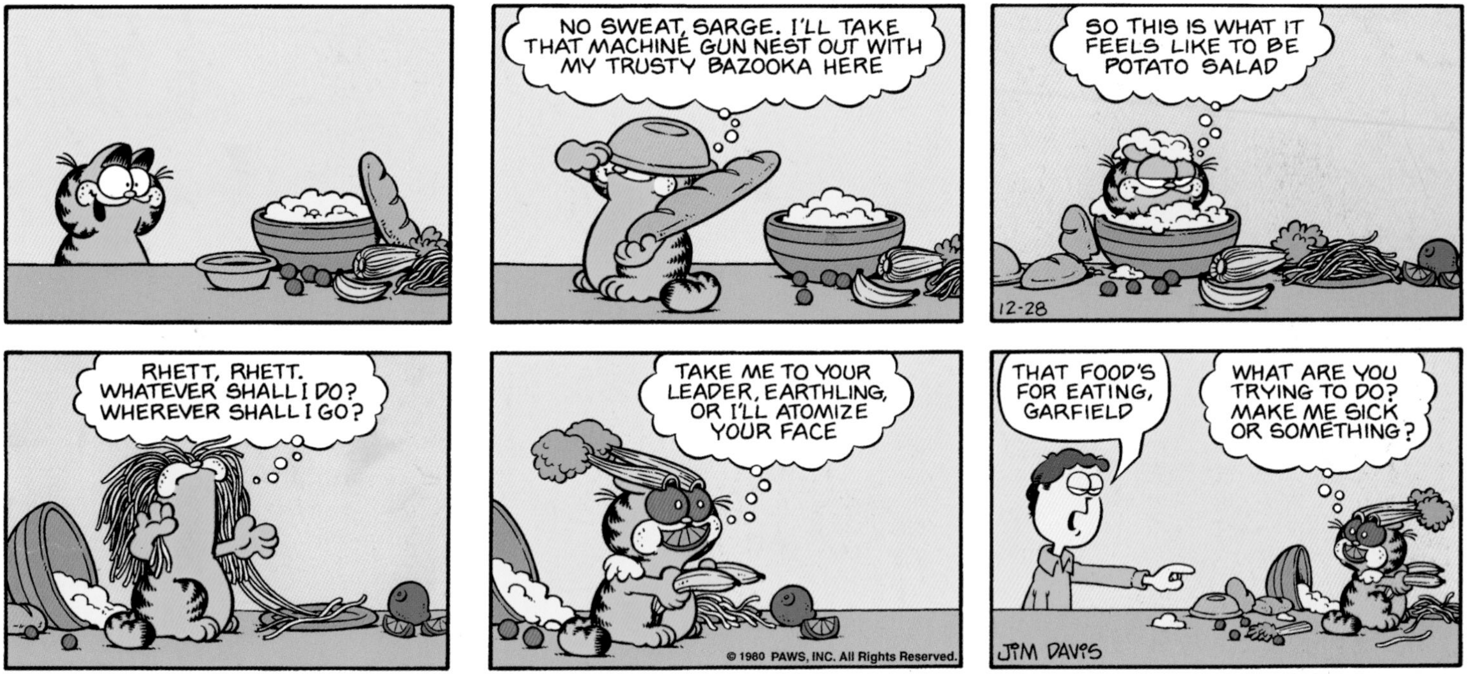
NO SWEAT, SARGE. I'LL TAKE THAT MACHINE GUN NEST OUT WITH MY TRUSTY BAZOOKA HERE
SO THIS IS WHAT IT FEELS LIKE TO BE POTATO SALAD
12-28
RHETT, RHETT. WHATEVER SHALL I DO? WHEREVER SHALL I GO?
TAKE ME TO YOUR LEADER, EARTHLING, OR I'LL ATOMIZE YOUR FACE
© 1980 PAWS, INC. All Rights Reserved.
THAT FOOD'S FOR EATING, GARFIELD
WHAT ARE YOU TRYING TO DO? MAKE ME SICK OR SOMETHING?
JIM DAVIS

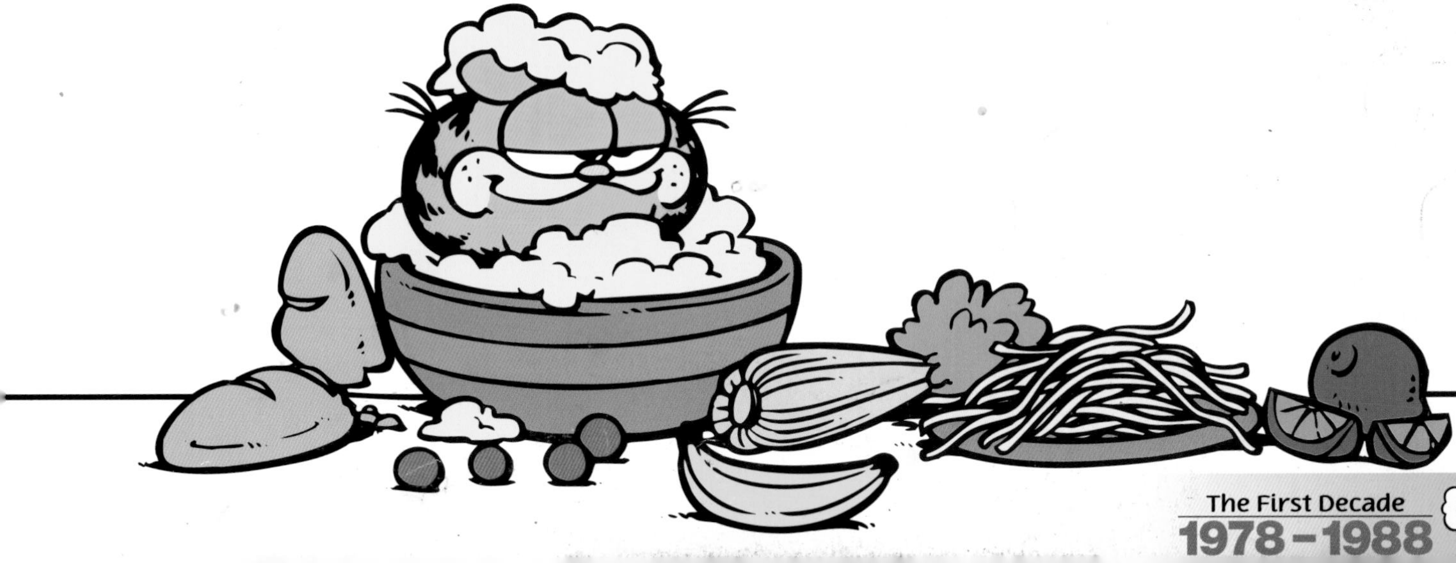

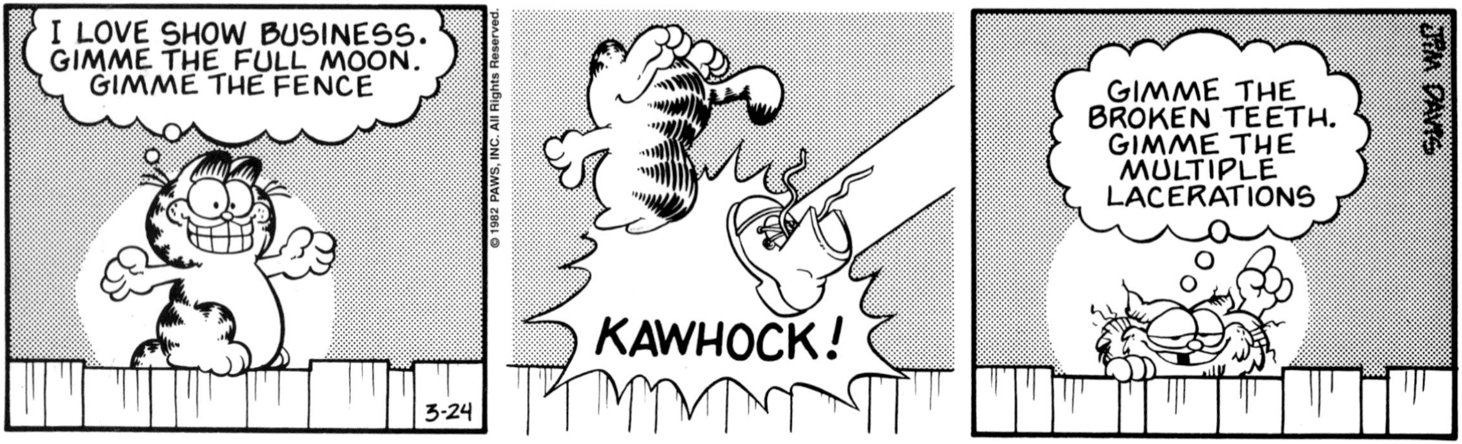
I LOVE SHOW BUSINESS. GIMME THE FULL MOON. GIMME THE FENCE
3-24
© 1982 PAWS, INC. All Rights Reserved.
KAWHOCK!
GIMME THE BROKEN TEETH. GIMME THE MULTIPLE LACERATIONS
JIM DAVIS

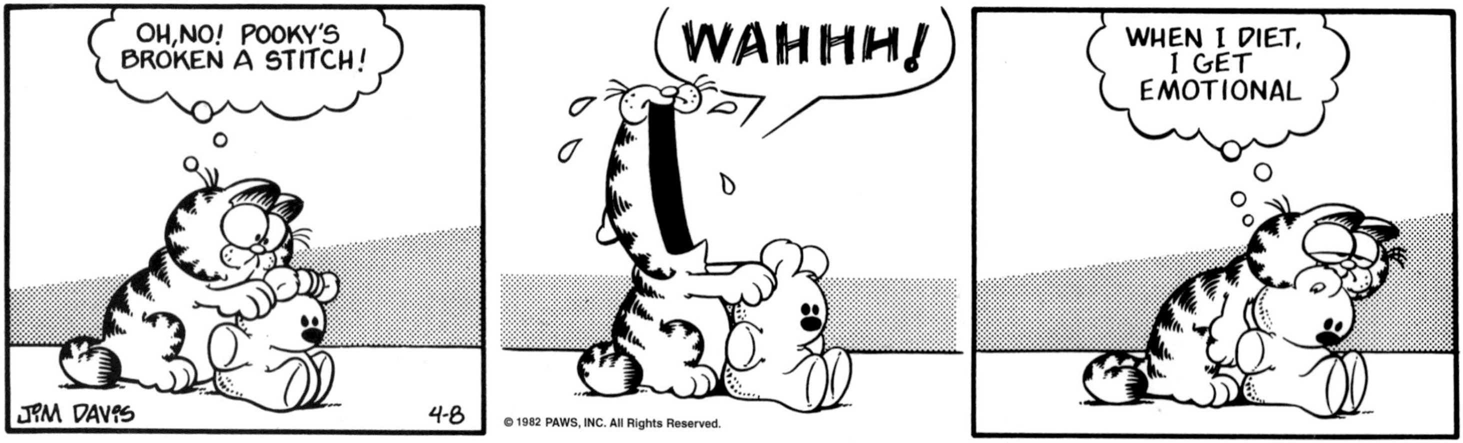
OH, NO! POOKY'S BROKEN A STITCH!
JIM DAVIS
4-8
WAHHH!
© 1982 PAWS, INC. All Rights Reserved.
WHEN I DIET, I GET EMOTIONAL

JIM DAVIS
4-20
I THINK ODIE'S GETTING AN IDEA
ODIE'S NOT TOO BRIGHT
© 1982 PAWS, INC. All Rights Reserved.

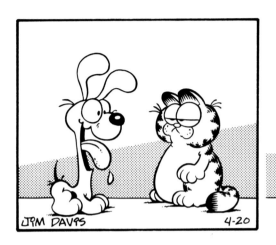

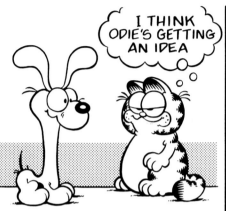

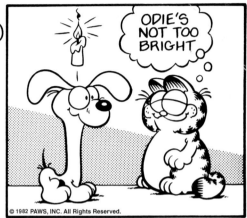

I took everything that Garfield wasn't and created Odie. Odie is trusting and a free spirit; he's always happy, even in a mindless sort of way. And, actually, over the years, he's become almost as popular as Garfield because of that, even though he's very hard to write for because he doesn't say anything.

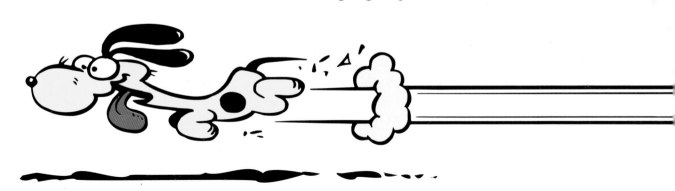

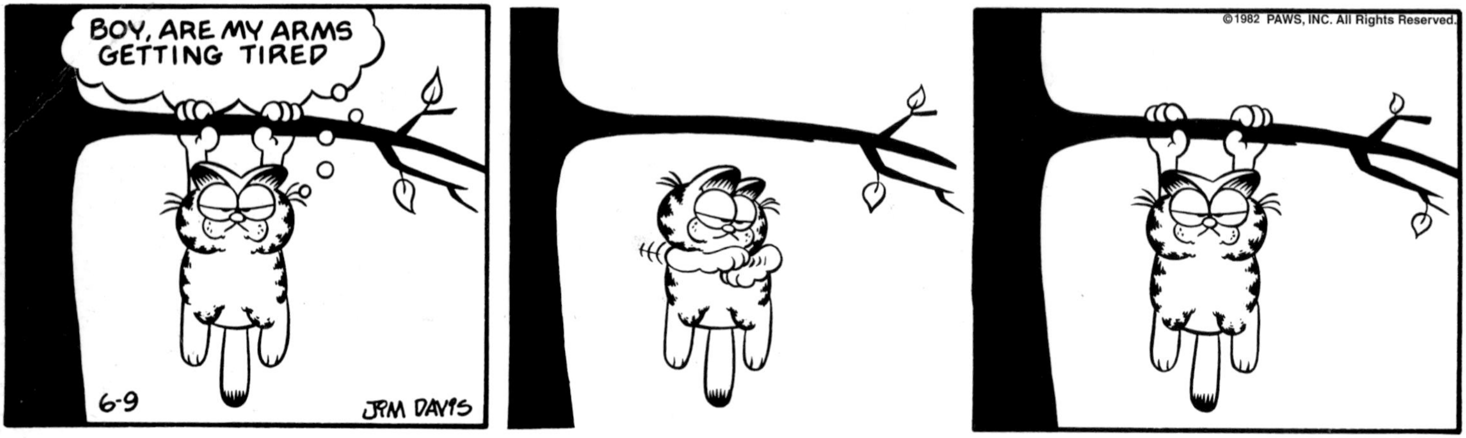
BOY, ARE MY ARMS GETTING TIRED
6-9
JIM DAVIS
©1982 PAWS, INC. All Rights Reserved.

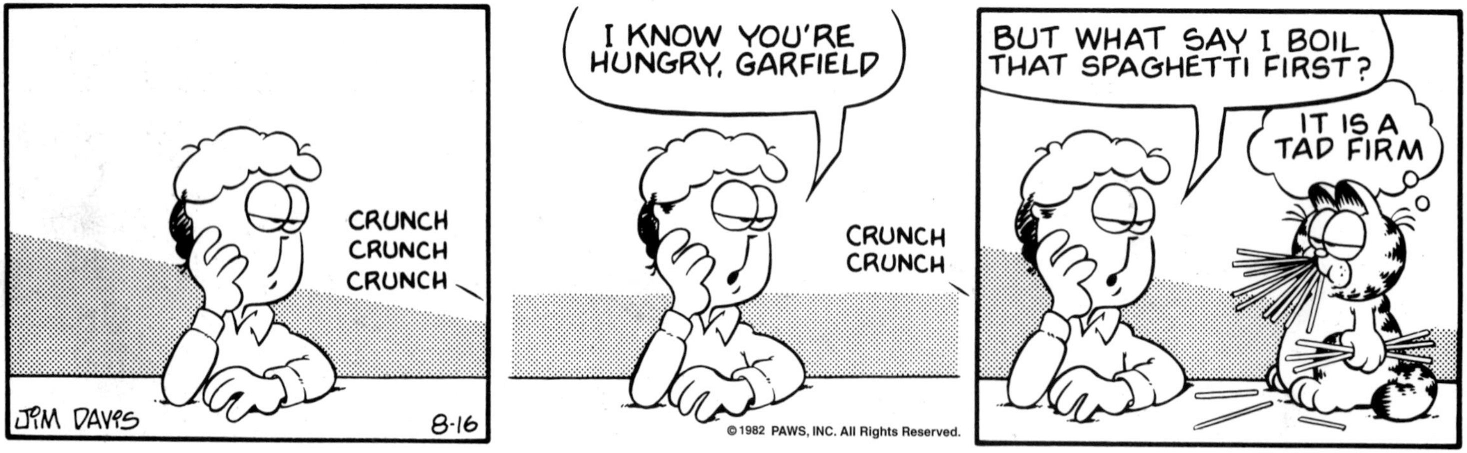
CRUNCH CRUNCH CRUNCH
JIM DAVIS
8-16
I KNOW YOU'RE HUNGRY, GARFIELD
CRUNCH CRUNCH
©1982 PAWS, INC. All Rights Reserved.
BUT WHAT SAY I BOIL THAT SPAGHETTI FIRST?
IT IS A TAD FIRM

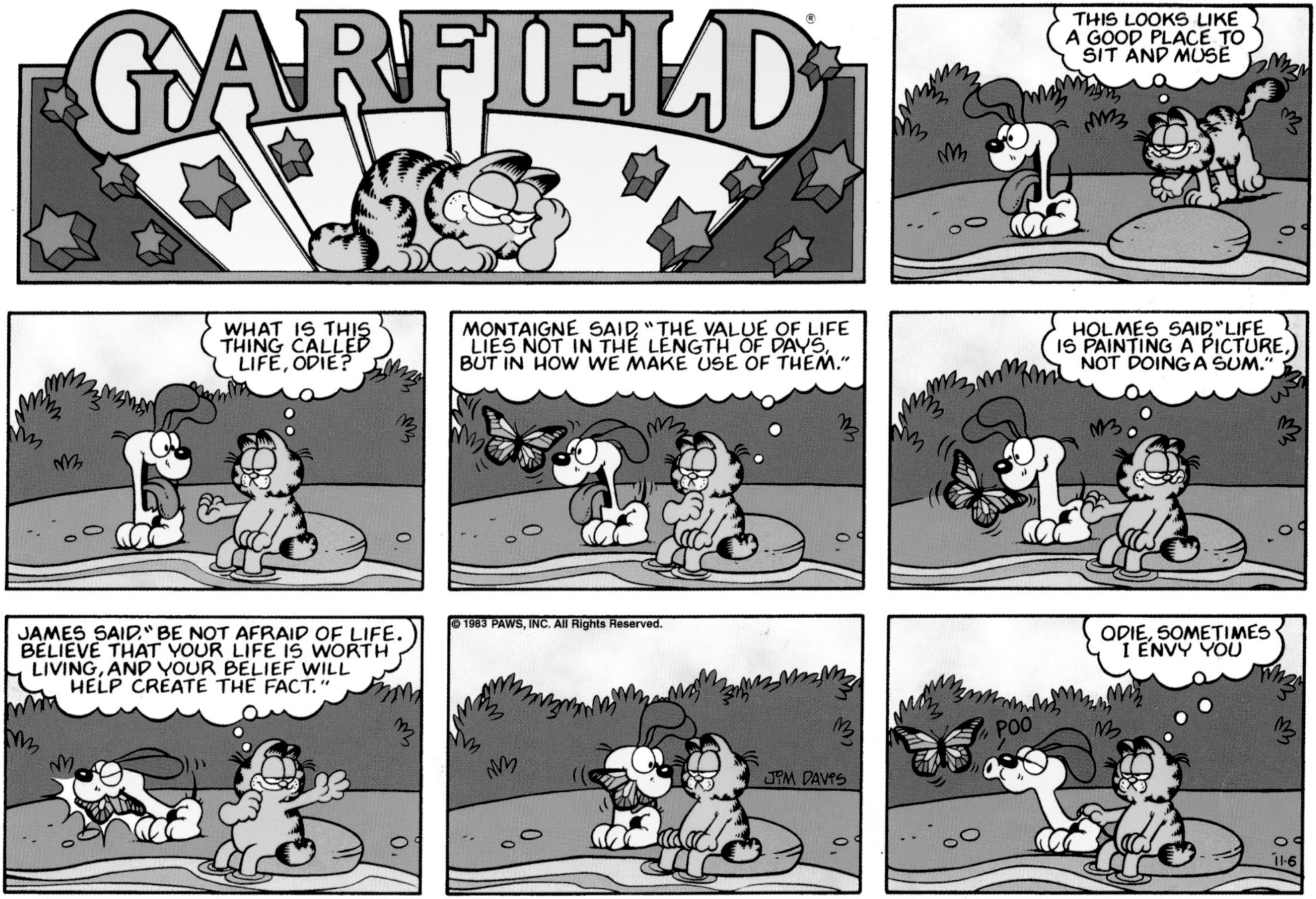
GARFIELD
THIS LOOKS LIKE A GOOD PLACE TO SIT AND MUSE
WHAT IS THIS THING CALLED LIFE, ODIE?
MONTAIGNE SAID, "THE VALUE OF LIFE LIES NOT IN THE LENGTH OF DAYS, BUT IN HOW WE MAKE USE OF THEM."
HOLMES SAID "LIFE IS PAINTING A PICTURE, NOT DOING A SUM."
JAMES SAID, "BE NOT AFRAID OF LIFE. BELIEVE THAT YOUR LIFE IS WORTH LIVING, AND YOUR BELIEF WILL HELP CREATE THE FACT."
© 1983 PAWS, INC. All Rights Reserved.
JIM DAVIS
POO
ODIE, SOMETIMES I ENVY YOU
11-6

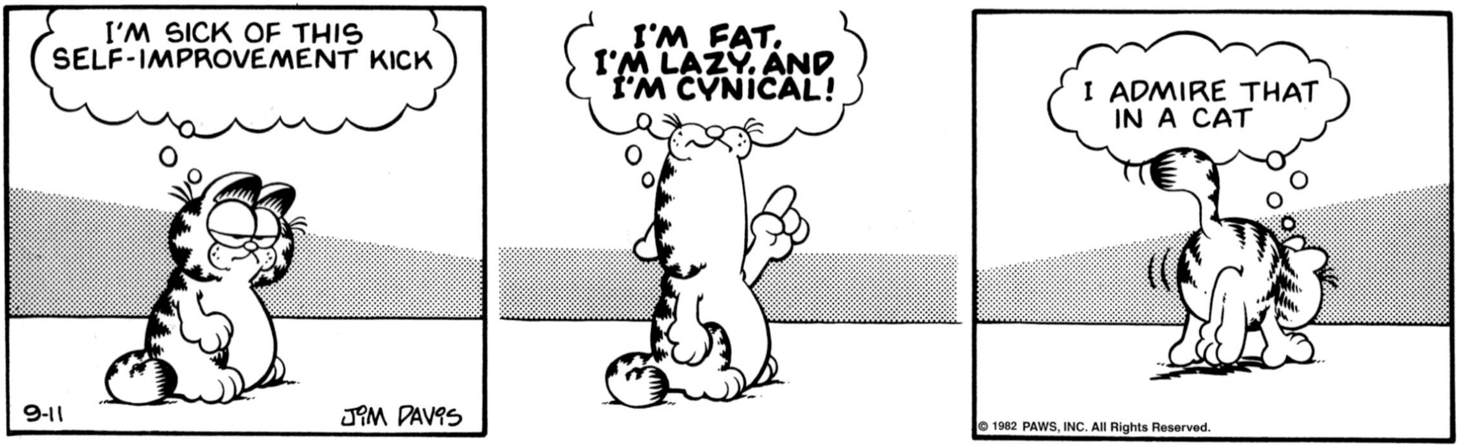
I'M SICK OF THIS SELF-IMPROVEMENT KICK
9-11
JIM DAVIS
I'M FAT. I'M LAZY. AND I'M CYNICAL!
I ADMIRE THAT IN A CAT
© 1982 PAWS, INC. All Rights Reserved.

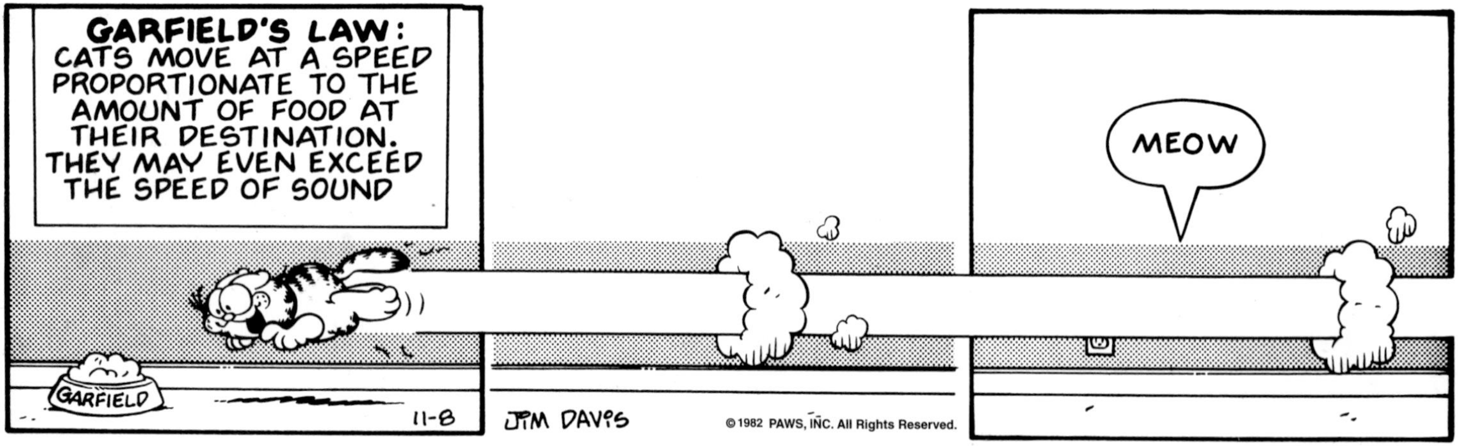
GARFIELD'S LAW: CATS MOVE AT A SPEED PROPORTIONATE TO THE AMOUNT OF FOOD AT THEIR DESTINATION. THEY MAY EVEN EXCEED THE SPEED OF SOUND
GARFIELD
11-8
JIM DAVIS
© 1982 PAWS, INC. All Rights Reserved.
MEOW

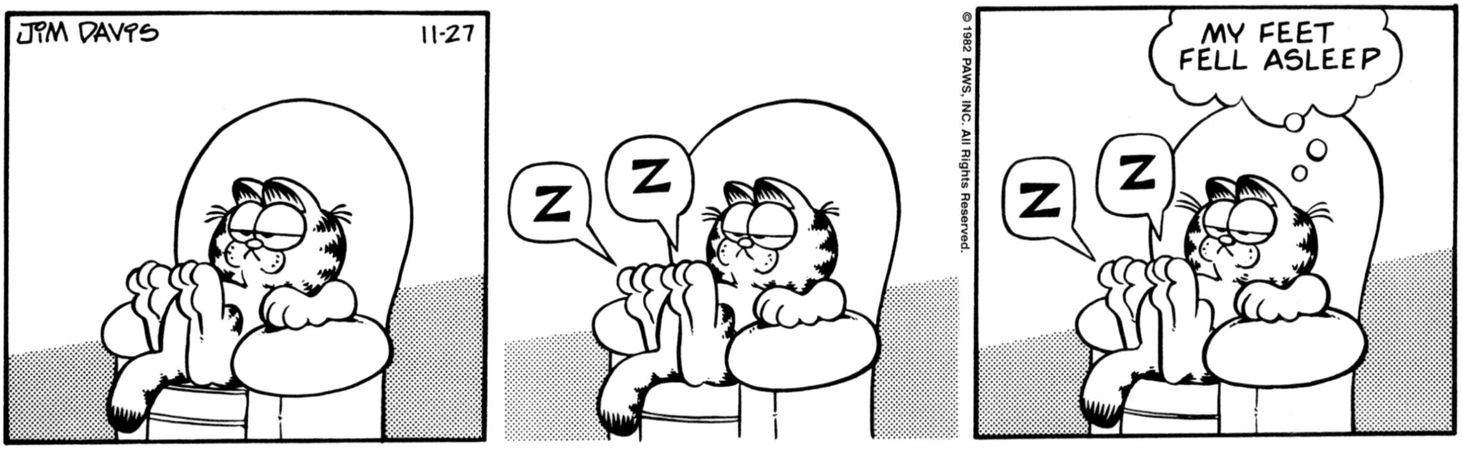
JIM DAVIS
11-27
Z
Z
© 1982 PAWS, INC. All Rights Reserved.
Z
Z
MY FEET FELL ASLEEP

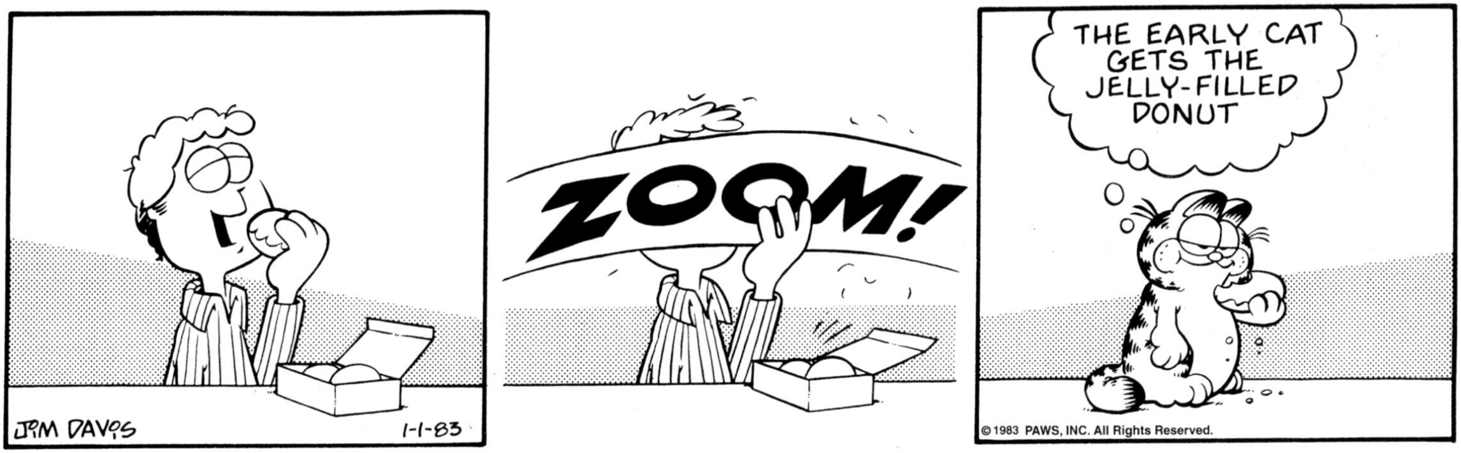
JIM DAVIS
1-1-83
ZOOM!
THE EARLY CAT GETS THE JELLY-FILLED DONUT
© 1983 PAWS, INC. All Rights Reserved.

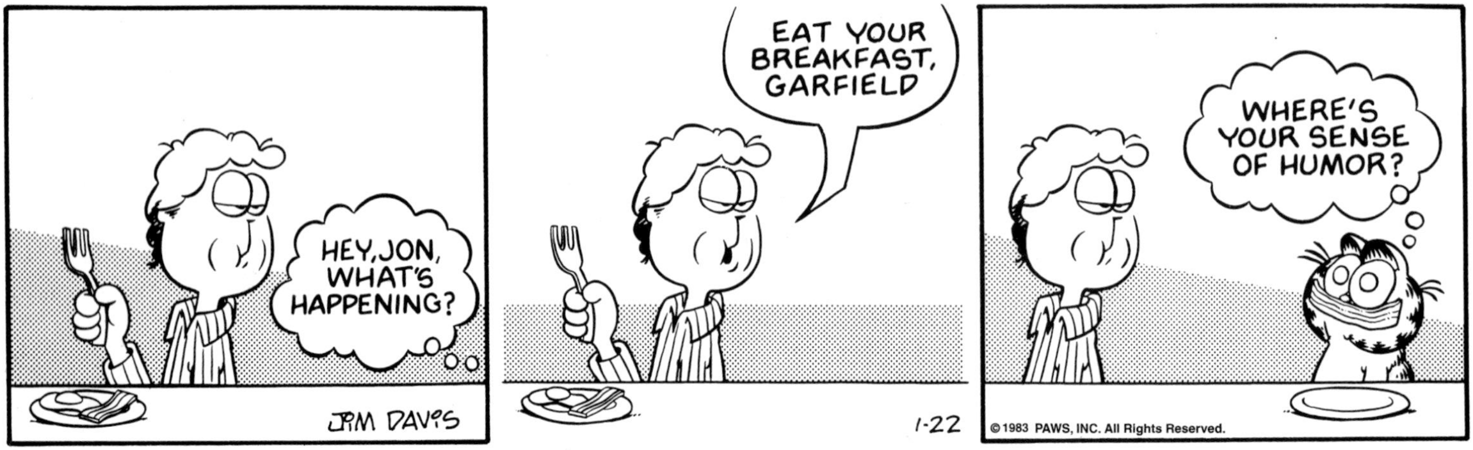
HEY, JON, WHAT'S HAPPENING?
JIM DAVIS
EAT YOUR BREAKFAST, GARFIELD
1-22
WHERE'S YOUR SENSE OF HUMOR?
© 1983 PAWS, INC. All Rights Reserved.

This whole line of work is to make people happy and smile. Getting paid for it is just a bonus. People should learn to laugh at themselves. That's the closest I come to making a statement.

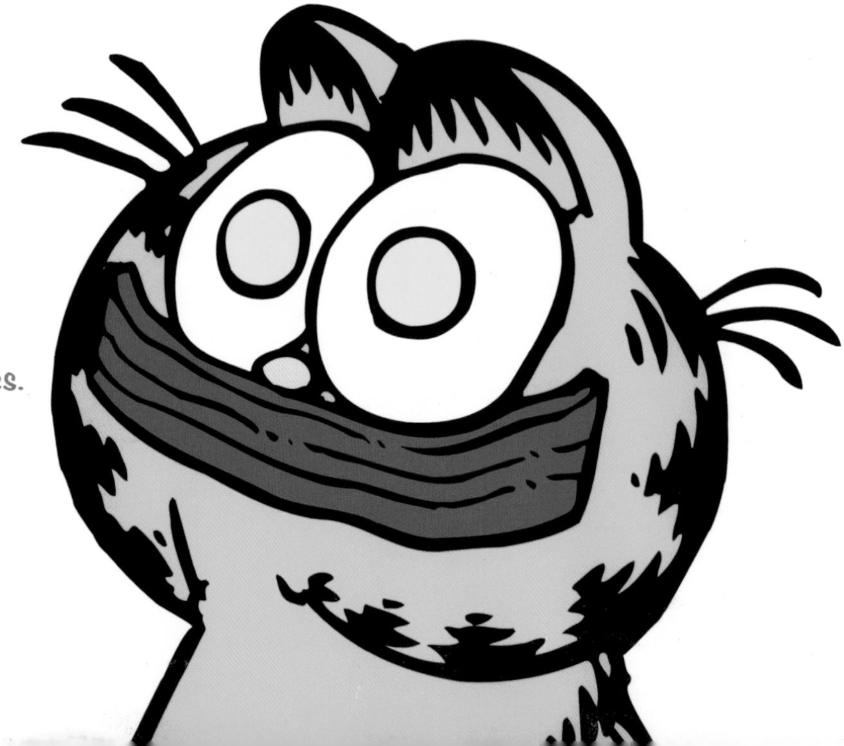

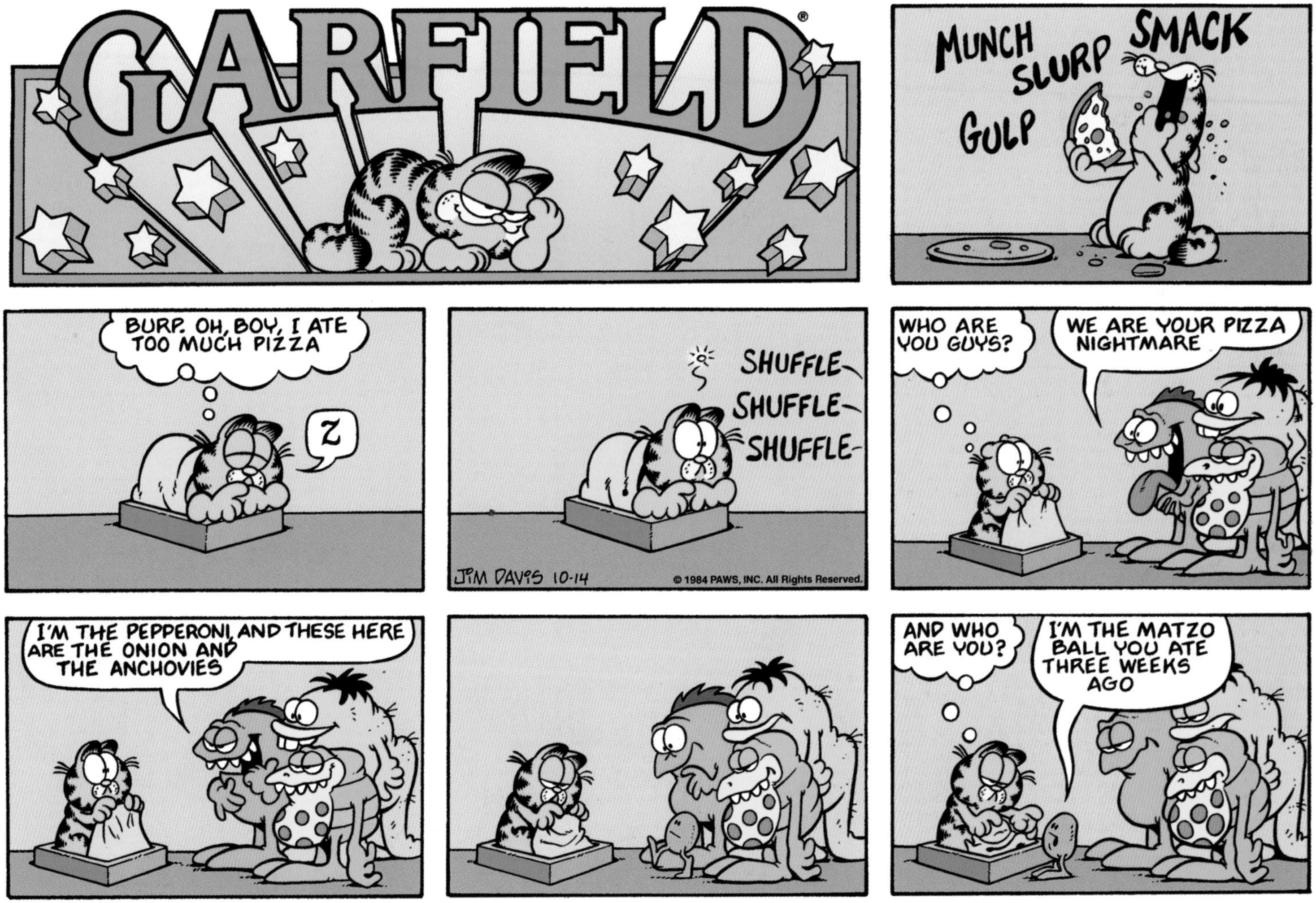
GARFIELD®
MUNCH
SLURP
SMACK
GULP
BURP. OH, BOY, I ATE TOO MUCH PIZZA
Z
SHUFFLE
SHUFFLE
SHUFFLE
JIM DAVIS 10-14
© 1984 PAWS, INC. All Rights Reserved.
WHO ARE YOU GUYS?
WE ARE YOUR PIZZA NIGHTMARE
I'M THE PEPPERONI, AND THESE HERE ARE THE ONION AND THE ANCHOVIES
AND WHO ARE YOU?
I'M THE MATZO BALL YOU ATE THREE WEEKS AGO

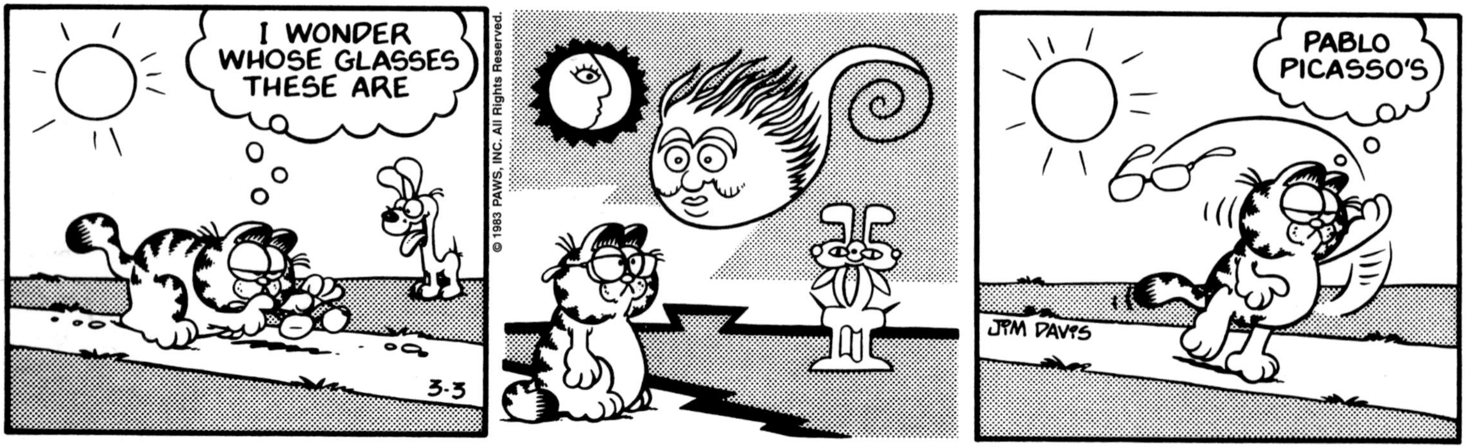
I WONDER WHOSE GLASSES THESE ARE
3-3
© 1983 PAWS, INC. All Rights Reserved.
PABLO PICASSO'S
JIM DAVIS

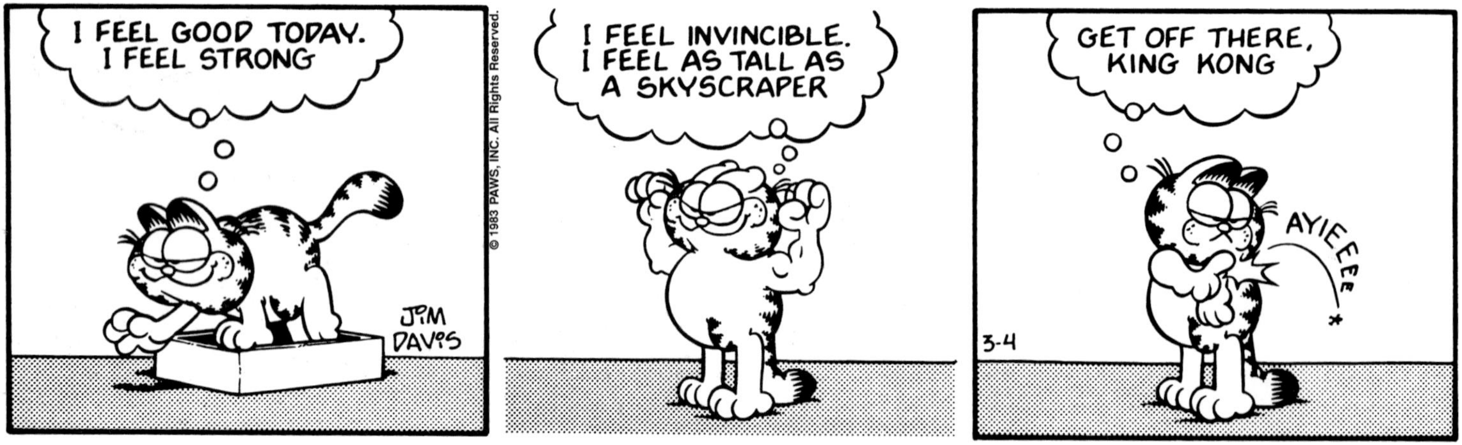
I FEEL GOOD TODAY. I FEEL STRONG
JIM DAVIS
© 1983 PAWS, INC. All Rights Reserved.
I FEEL INVINCIBLE. I FEEL AS TALL AS A SKYSCRAPER
GET OFF THERE, KING KONG
AYIEEEEE
3-4

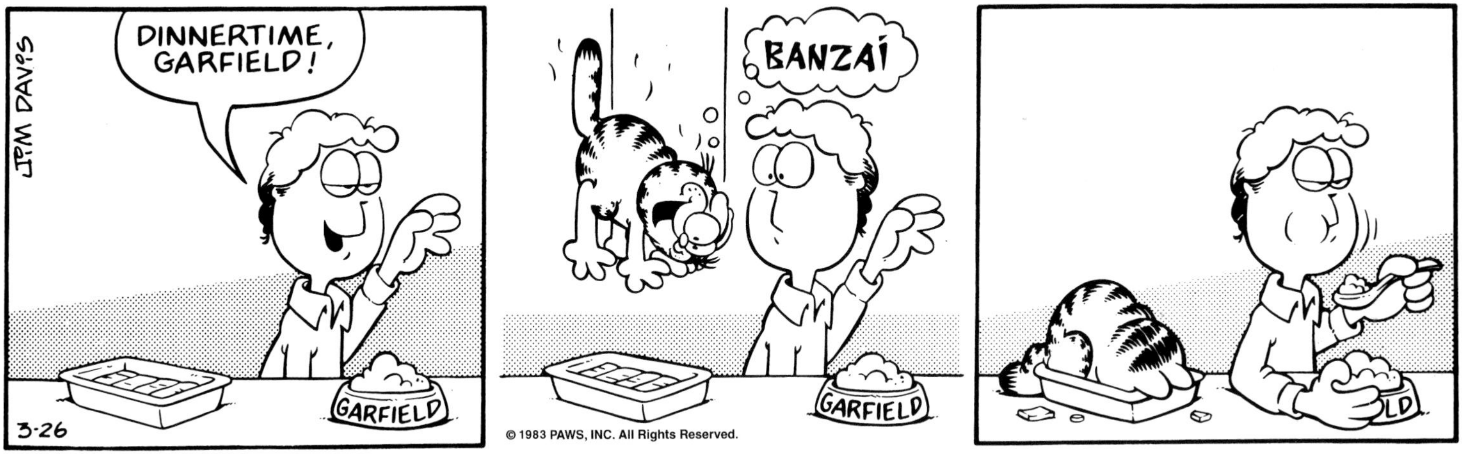
JIM DAVIS
DINNERTIME, GARFIELD!
GARFIELD
3-26
BANZAI
GARFIELD
© 1983 PAWS, INC. All Rights Reserved.
LD

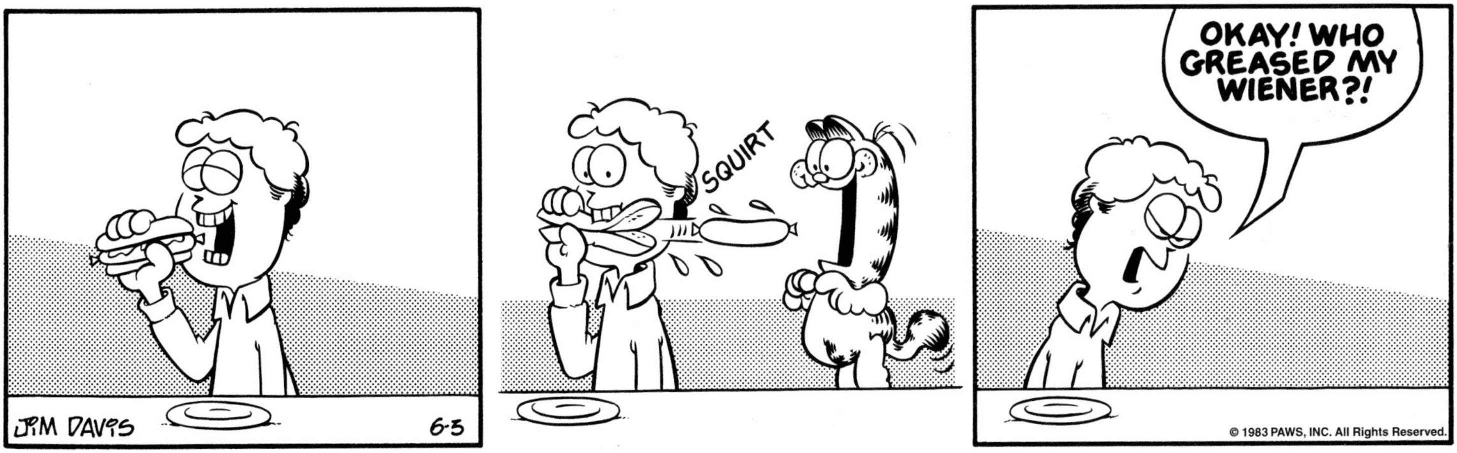
JIM DAVIS
6-3
SQUIRT
OKAY! WHO GREASED MY WIENER?!
© 1983 PAWS, INC. All Rights Reserved.

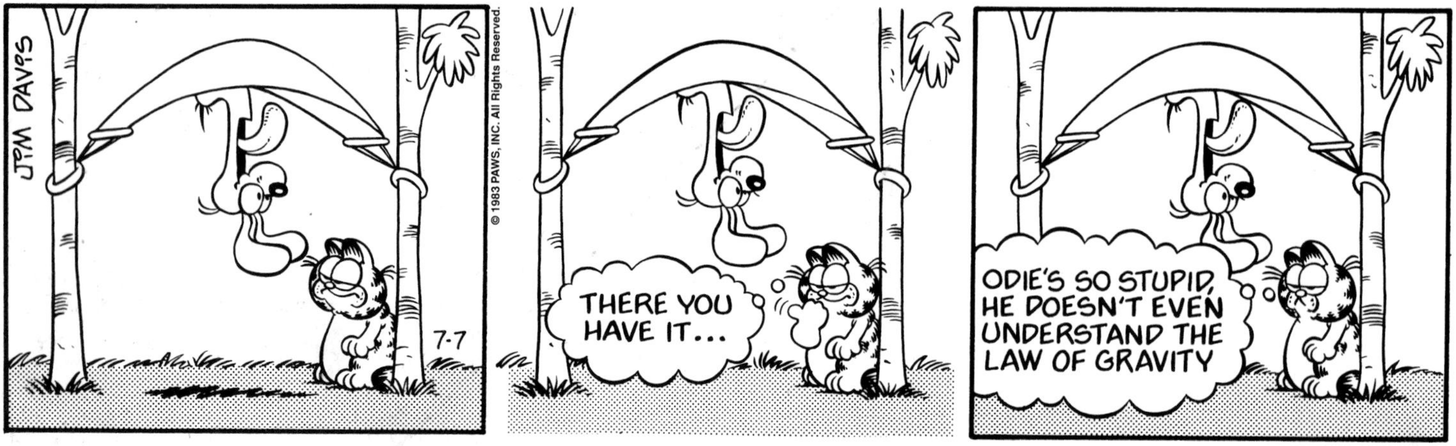
JIM DAVIS
© 1983 PAWS, INC. All Rights Reserved.
7-7
THERE YOU HAVE IT...
ODIE'S SO STUPID, HE DOESN'T EVEN UNDERSTAND THE LAW OF GRAVITY

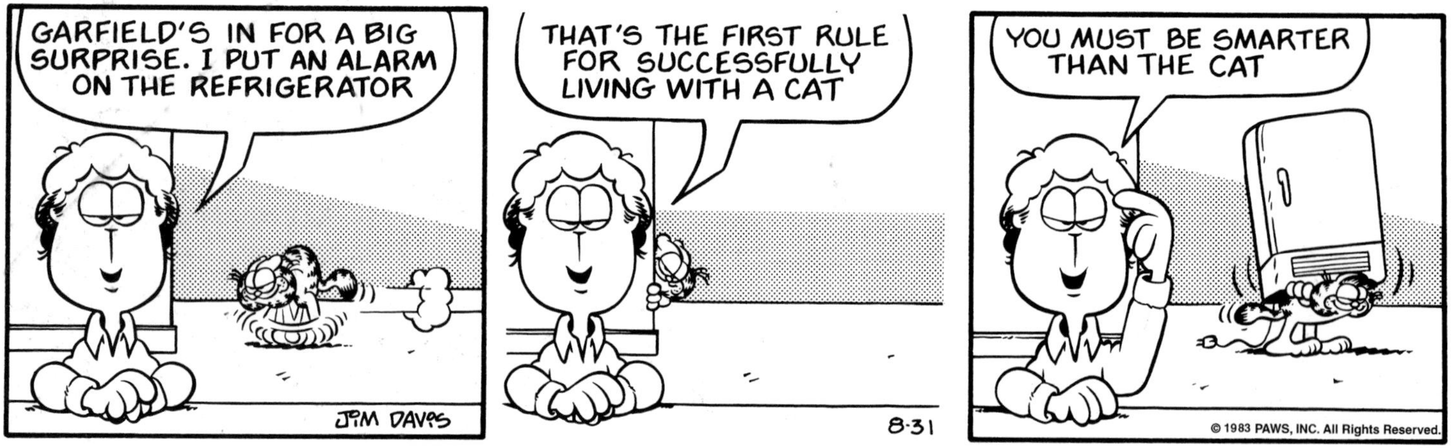
GARFIELD'S IN FOR A BIG SURPRISE. I PUT AN ALARM ON THE REFRIGERATOR
JIM DAVIS
THAT'S THE FIRST RULE FOR SUCCESSFULLY LIVING WITH A CAT
8-31
YOU MUST BE SMARTER THAN THE CAT
© 1983 PAWS, INC. All Rights Reserved.

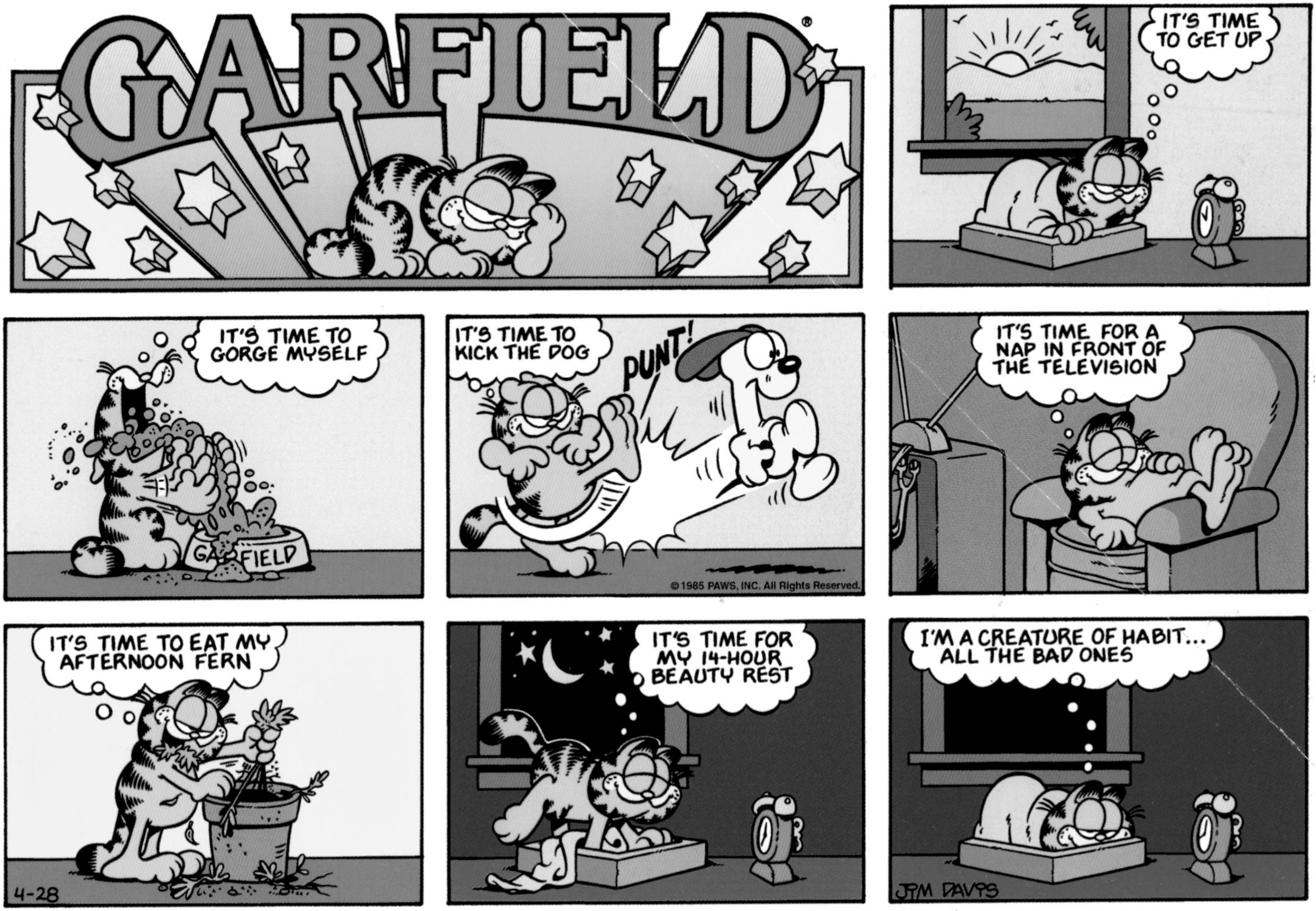
GARFIELD®
IT'S TIME TO GET UP
IT'S TIME TO GORGE MYSELF
GARFIELD
IT'S TIME TO KICK THE DOG
PUNT!
©1985 PAWS, INC. All Rights Reserved.
IT'S TIME FOR A NAP IN FRONT OF THE TELEVISION
IT'S TIME TO EAT MY AFTERNOON FERN
4-28
IT'S TIME FOR MY 14-HOUR BEAUTY REST
I'M A CREATURE OF HABIT... ALL THE BAD ONES
JIM DAVIS

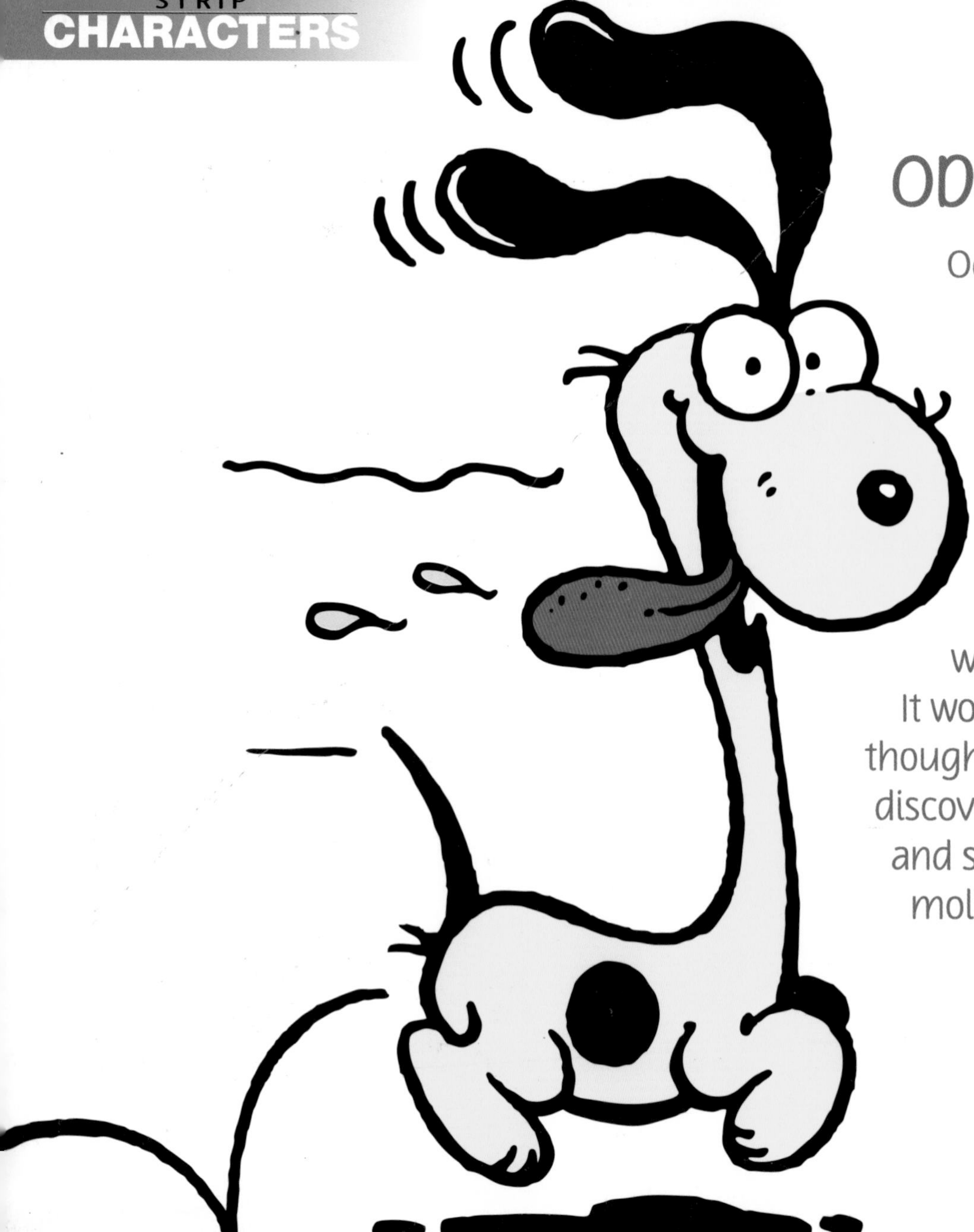

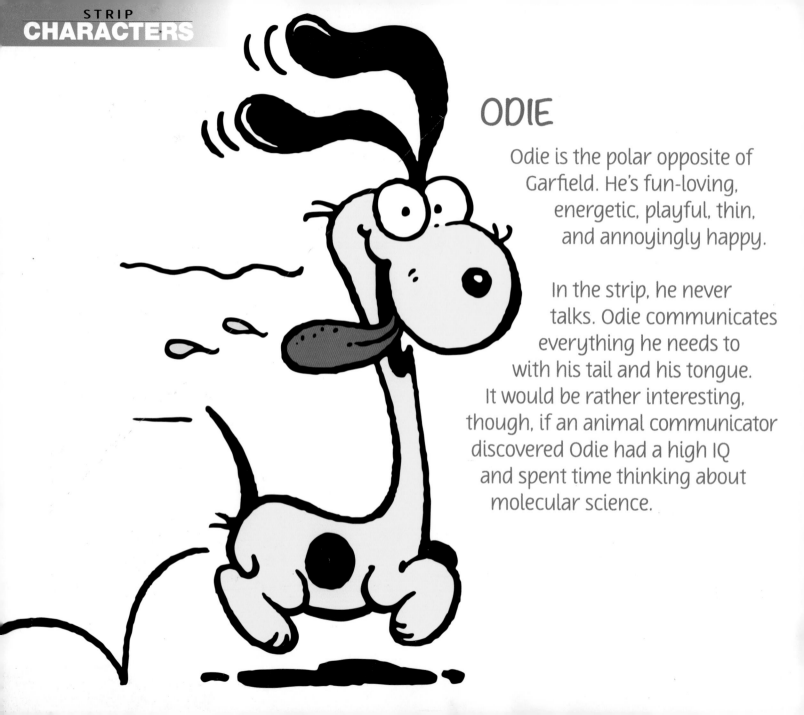

ODIE

Odie is the polar opposite of Garfield. He's fun-loving, energetic, playful, thin, and annoyingly happy.

In the strip, he never talks. Odie communicates everything he needs to with his tail and his tongue. It would be rather interesting, though, if an animal communicator discovered Odie had a high IQ and spent time thinking about molecular science.

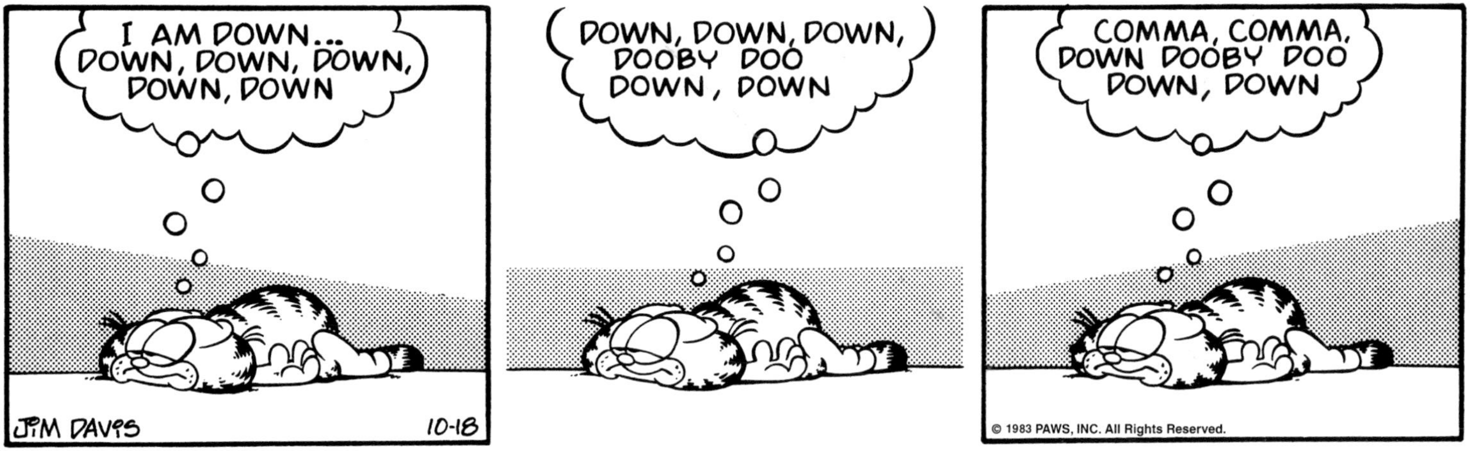
I AM DOWN... DOWN, DOWN, DOWN, DOWN, DOWN
JIM DAVIS
10-18
DOWN, DOWN, DOWN, DOOBY DOO DOWN, DOWN
COMMA, COMMA, DOWN DOOBY DOO DOWN, DOWN
© 1983 PAWS, INC. All Rights Reserved.

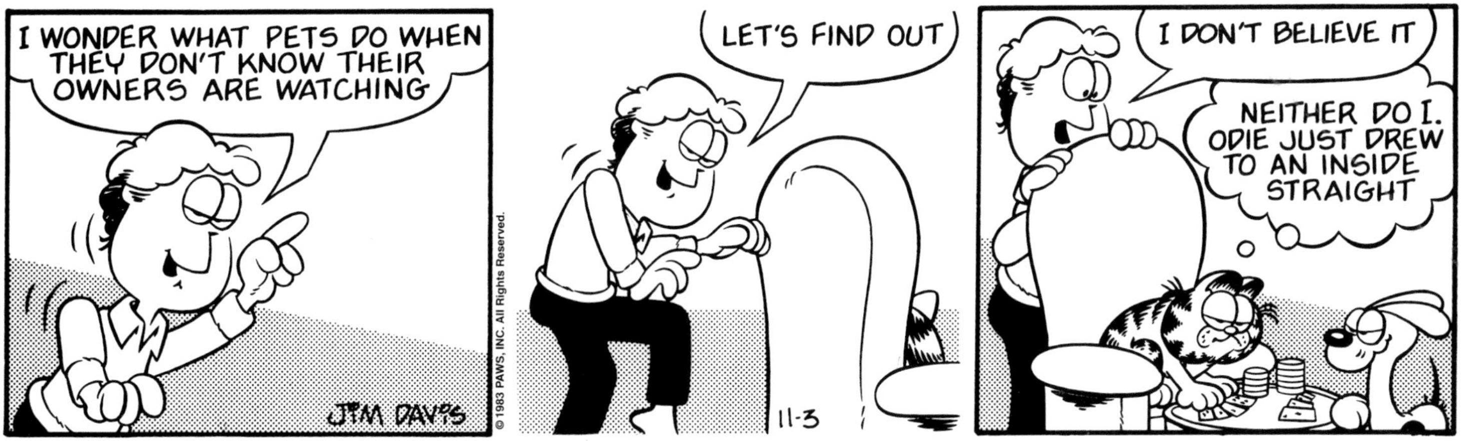
I WONDER WHAT PETS DO WHEN THEY DON'T KNOW THEIR OWNERS ARE WATCHING
JIM DAVIS
© 1983 PAWS, INC. All Rights Reserved.
LET'S FIND OUT
11-3
I DON'T BELIEVE IT
NEITHER DO I. ODIE JUST DREW TO AN INSIDE STRAIGHT

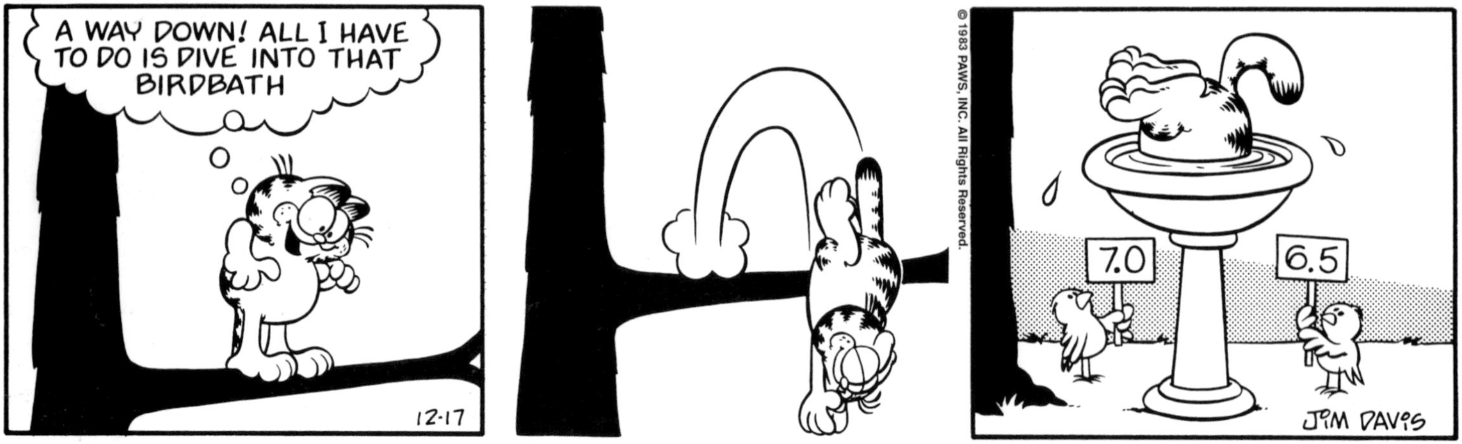
A WAY DOWN! ALL I HAVE TO DO IS DIVE INTO THAT BIRDBATH
12-17
© 1983 PAWS, INC. All Rights Reserved.
7.0
6.5
JIM DAVIS

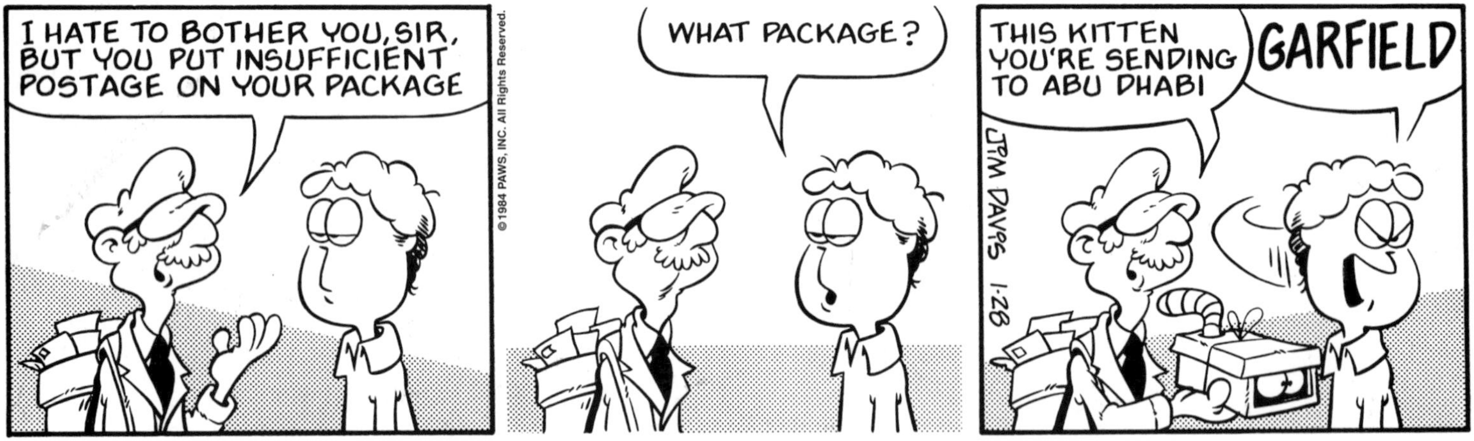
I HATE TO BOTHER YOU, SIR, BUT YOU PUT INSUFFICIENT POSTAGE ON YOUR PACKAGE
© 1984 PAWS, INC. All Rights Reserved.
WHAT PACKAGE?
THIS KITTEN YOU'RE SENDING TO ABU DHABI
GARFIELD
JIM DAVIS 1-28

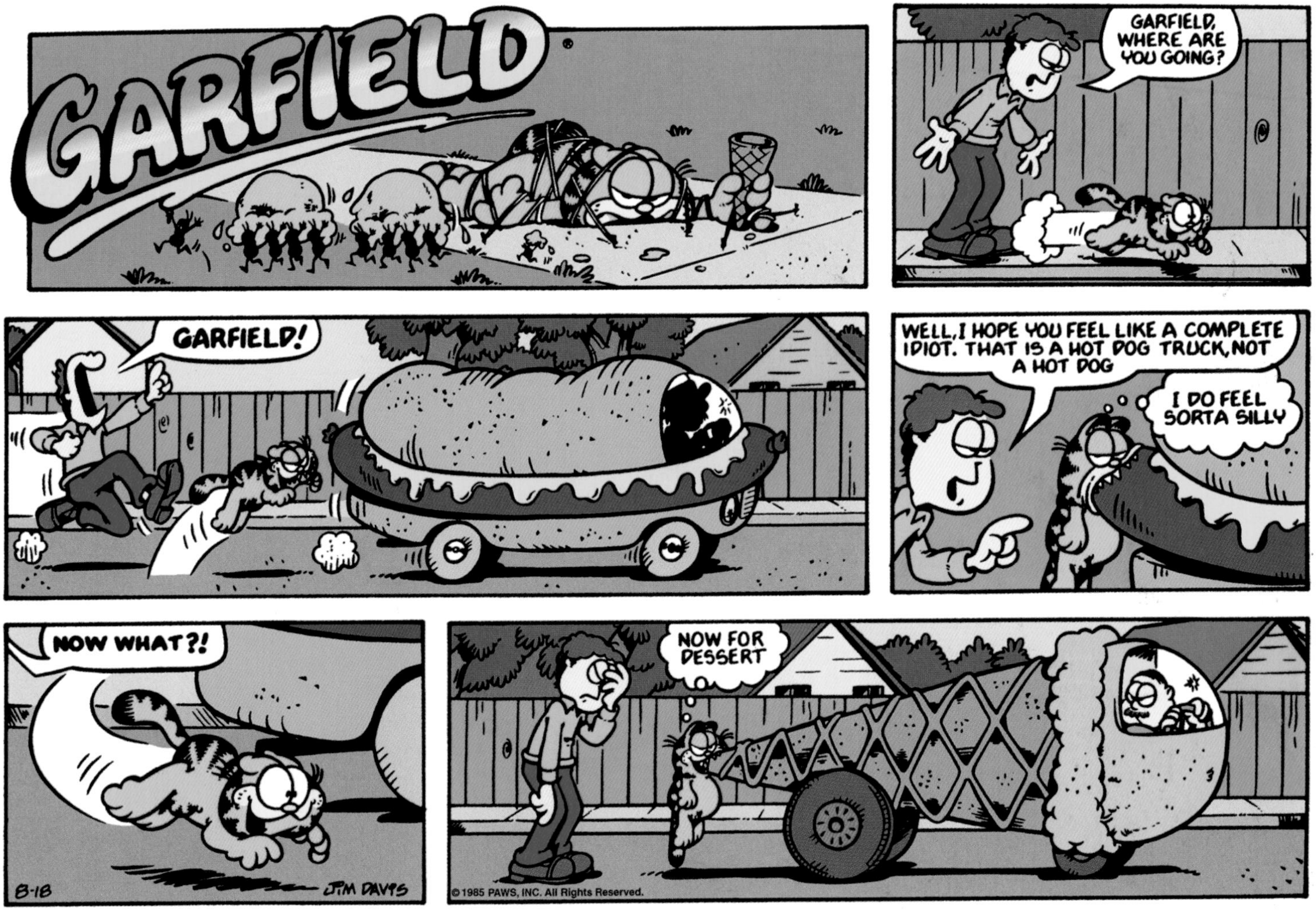
GARFIELD
GARFIELD, WHERE ARE YOU GOING?
GARFIELD!
WELL, I HOPE YOU FEEL LIKE A COMPLETE IDIOT. THAT IS A HOT DOG TRUCK, NOT A HOT DOG
I DO FEEL SORTA SILLY
NOW WHAT?!
NOW FOR DESSERT
8-18
JIM DAVIS
© 1985 PAWS, INC. All Rights Reserved.

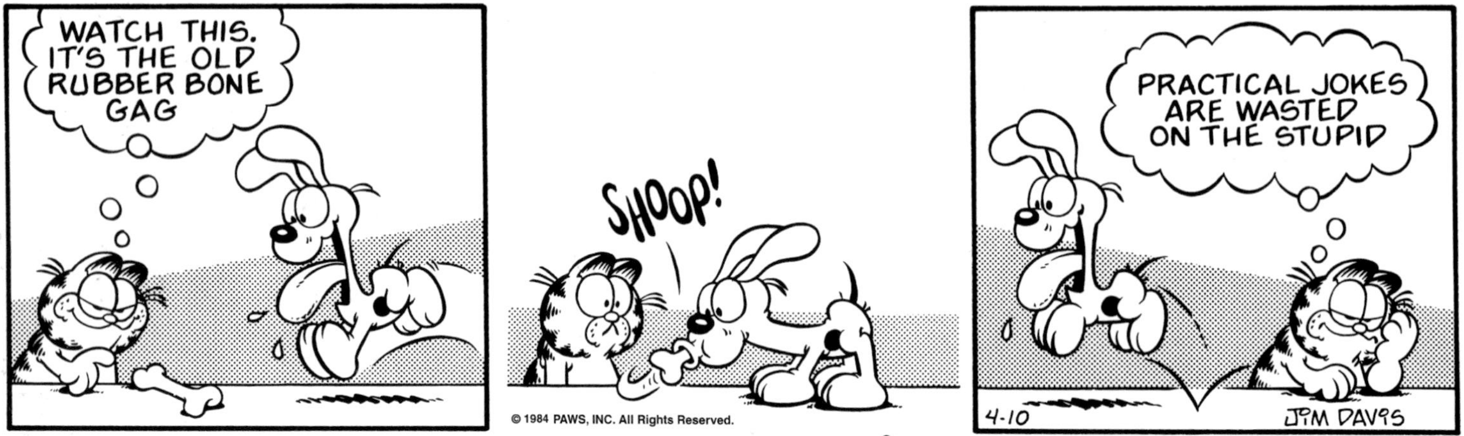
WATCH THIS. IT'S THE OLD RUBBER BONE GAG
SHOOP!
PRACTICAL JOKES ARE WASTED ON THE STUPID
4-10
JIM DAVIS

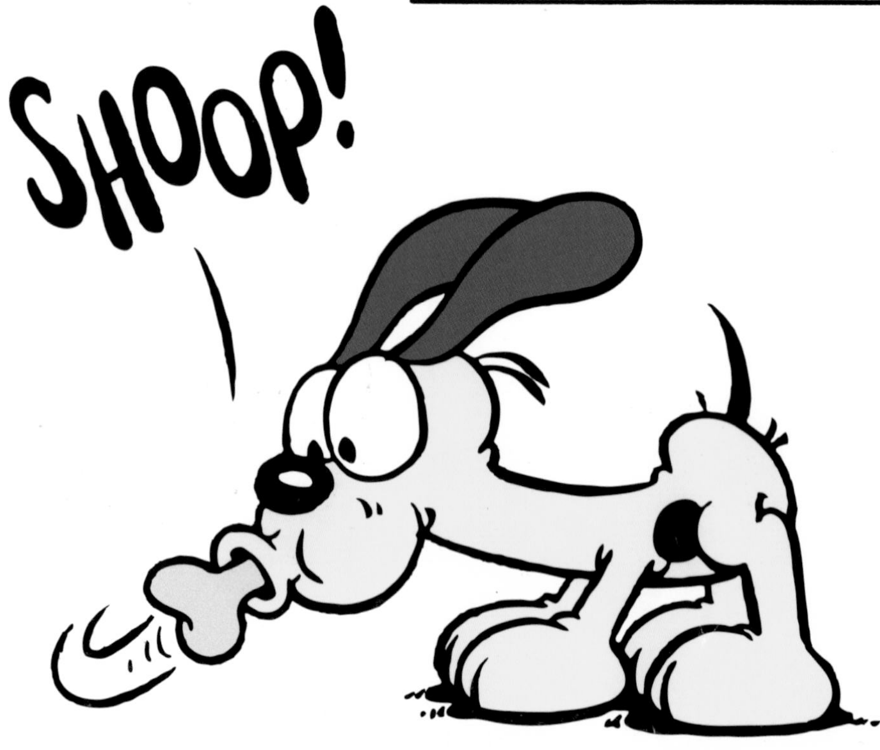
SHOOP!

To me, the eye has to flow through the gag. The timing of a strip gag is not the same as the timing of a spoken gag. A good gag in a comic strip cannot just be read—you have a fine balance between words and images.

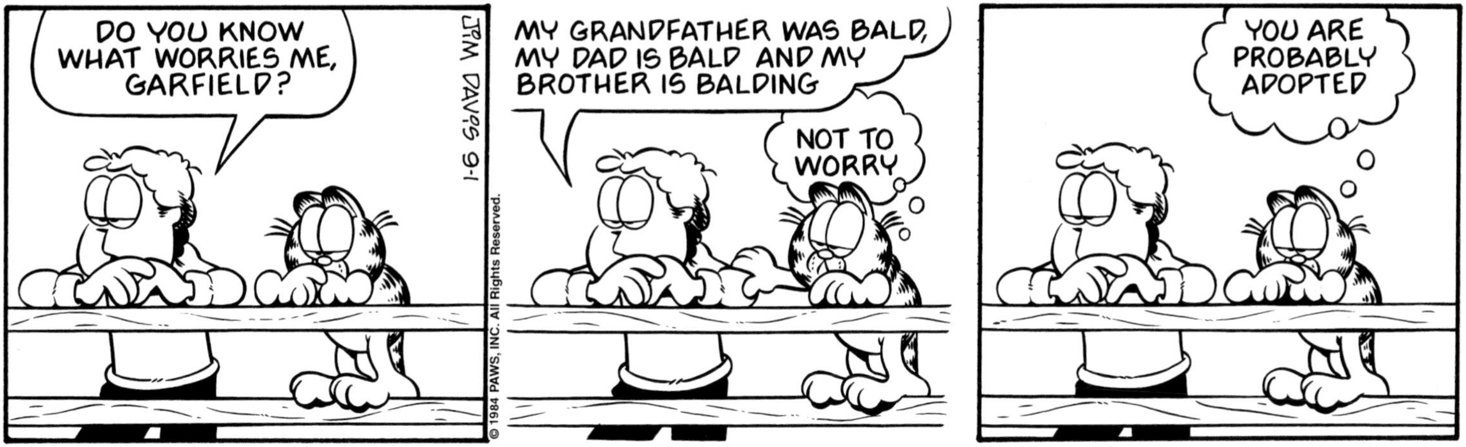
DO YOU KNOW WHAT WORRIES ME, GARFIELD?
JIM DAVIS 9-1
© 1984 PAWS, INC. All Rights Reserved.
MY GRANDFATHER WAS BALD, MY DAD IS BALD AND MY BROTHER IS BALDING
NOT TO WORRY
YOU ARE PROBABLY ADOPTED

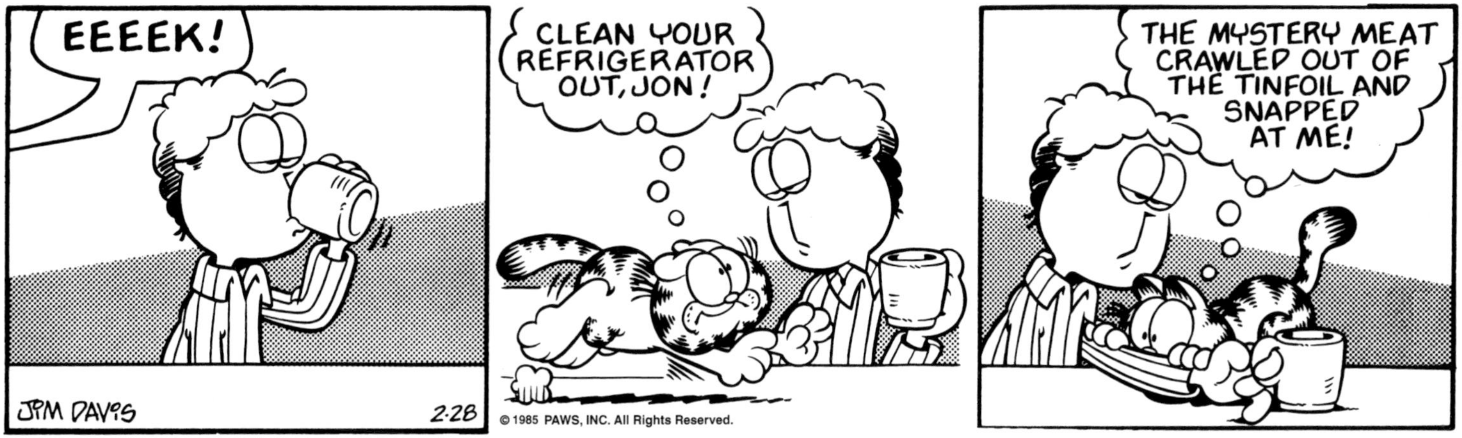
EEEEK!
JIM DAVIS
2-28
CLEAN YOUR REFRIGERATOR OUT, JON!
© 1985 PAWS, INC. All Rights Reserved.
THE MYSTERY MEAT CRAWLED OUT OF THE TINFOIL AND SNAPPED AT ME!

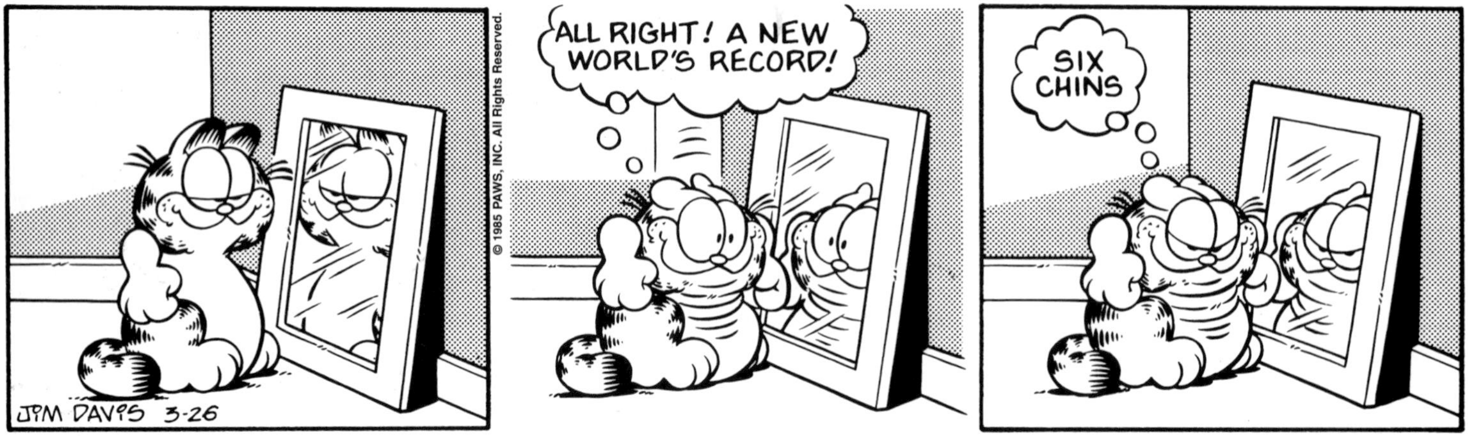
ALL RIGHT! A NEW WORLD'S RECORD!
SIX CHINS
JIM DAVIS 3-26
© 1985 PAWS, INC. All Rights Reserved.

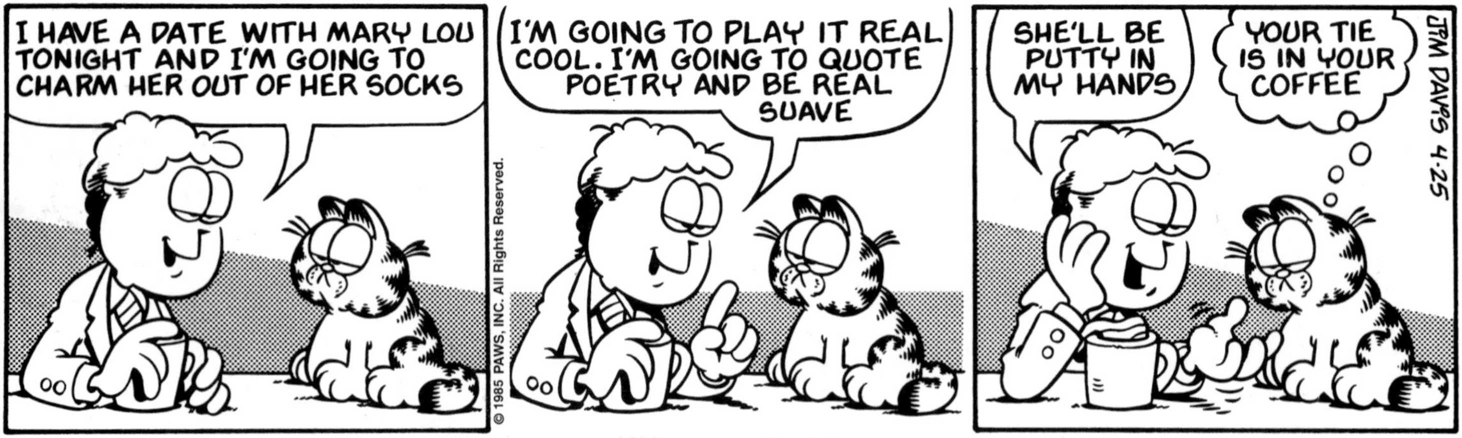
I HAVE A DATE WITH MARY LOU TONIGHT AND I'M GOING TO CHARM HER OUT OF HER SOCKS
I'M GOING TO PLAY IT REAL COOL. I'M GOING TO QUOTE POETRY AND BE REAL SUAVE
SHE'LL BE PUTTY IN MY HANDS
YOUR TIE IS IN YOUR COFFEE
JIM DAVIS 4-25
© 1985 PAWS, INC. All Rights Reserved.

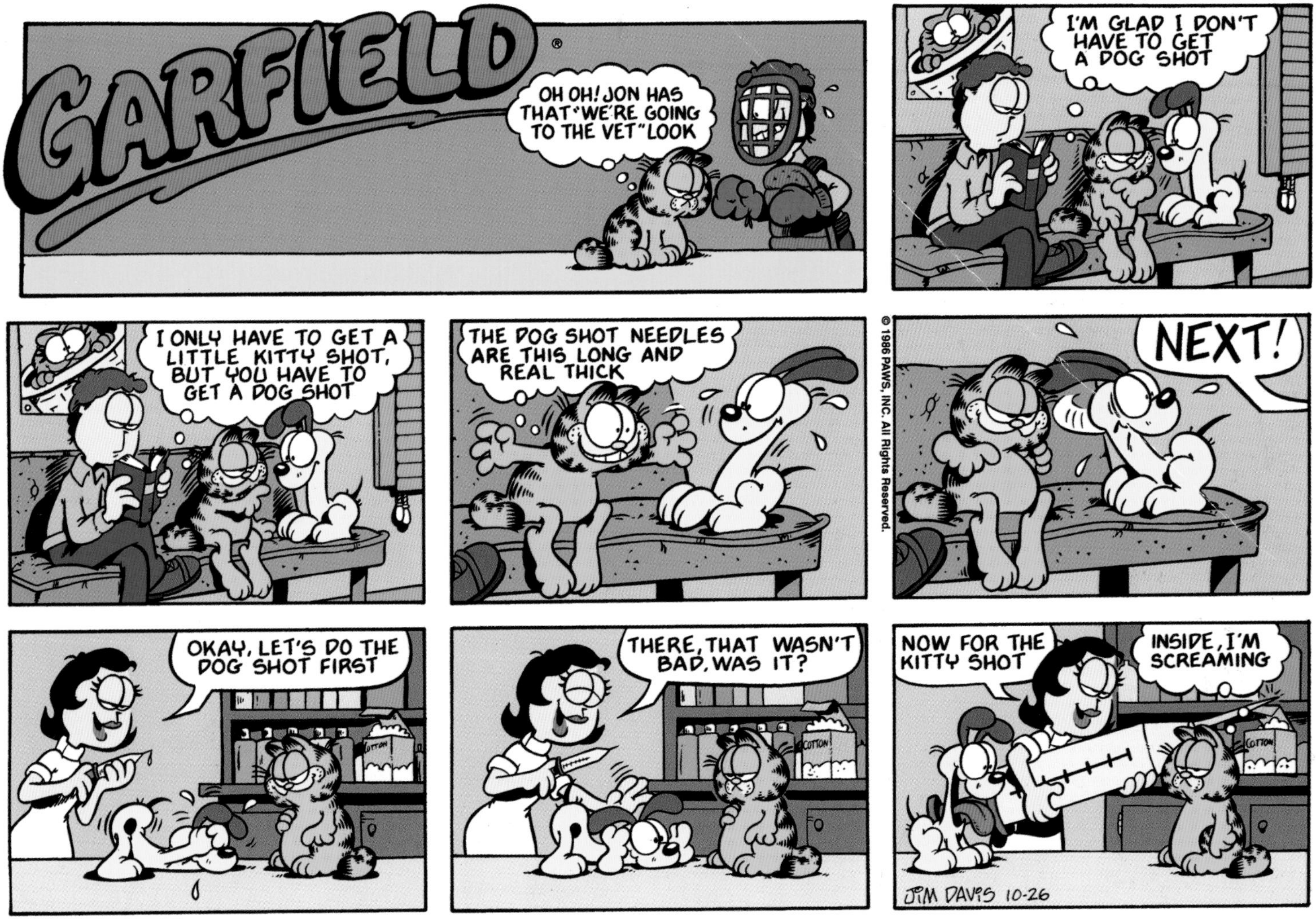
GARFIELD®
OH OH! JON HAS THAT "WE'RE GOING TO THE VET" LOOK
I'M GLAD I DON'T HAVE TO GET A DOG SHOT
I ONLY HAVE TO GET A LITTLE KITTY SHOT, BUT YOU HAVE TO GET A DOG SHOT
THE DOG SHOT NEEDLES ARE THIS LONG AND REAL THICK
© 1986 PAWS, INC. All Rights Reserved.
NEXT!
OKAY, LET'S DO THE DOG SHOT FIRST
THERE, THAT WASN'T BAD, WAS IT?
NOW FOR THE KITTY SHOT
INSIDE, I'M SCREAMING
COTTON
JIM DAVIS 10-26

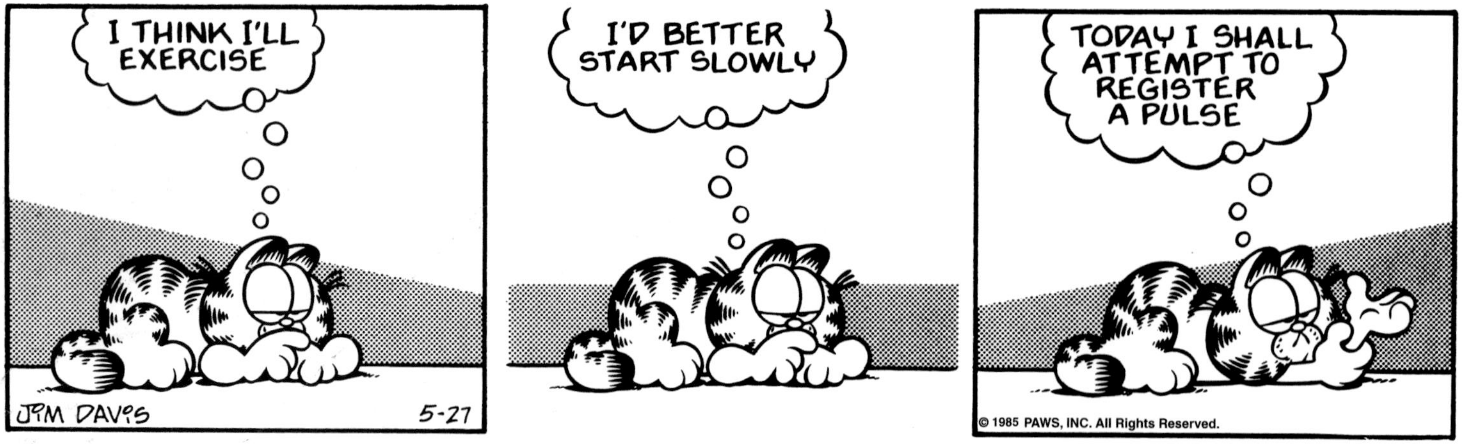
I THINK I'LL EXERCISE
I'D BETTER START SLOWLY
TODAY I SHALL ATTEMPT TO REGISTER A PULSE
JIM DAVIS
5-27
© 1985 PAWS, INC. All Rights Reserved.

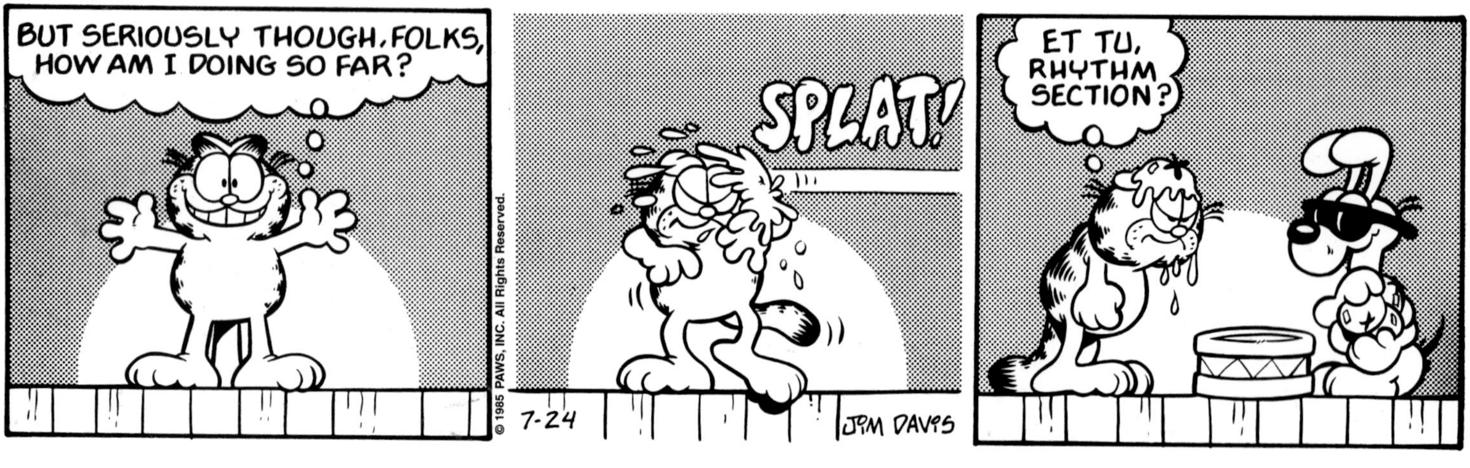
BUT SERIOUSLY THOUGH, FOLKS, HOW AM I DOING SO FAR?
SPLAT!
ET TU, RHYTHM SECTION?
© 1985 PAWS, INC. All Rights Reserved.
7-24
JIM DAVIS

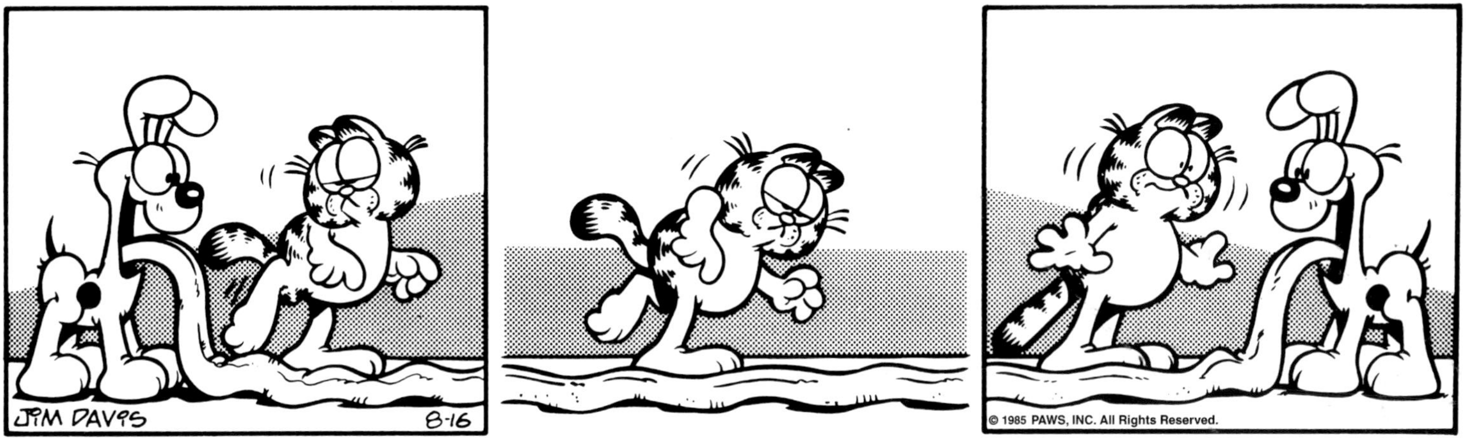
JIM DAVIS 8-16
© 1985 PAWS, INC. All Rights Reserved.

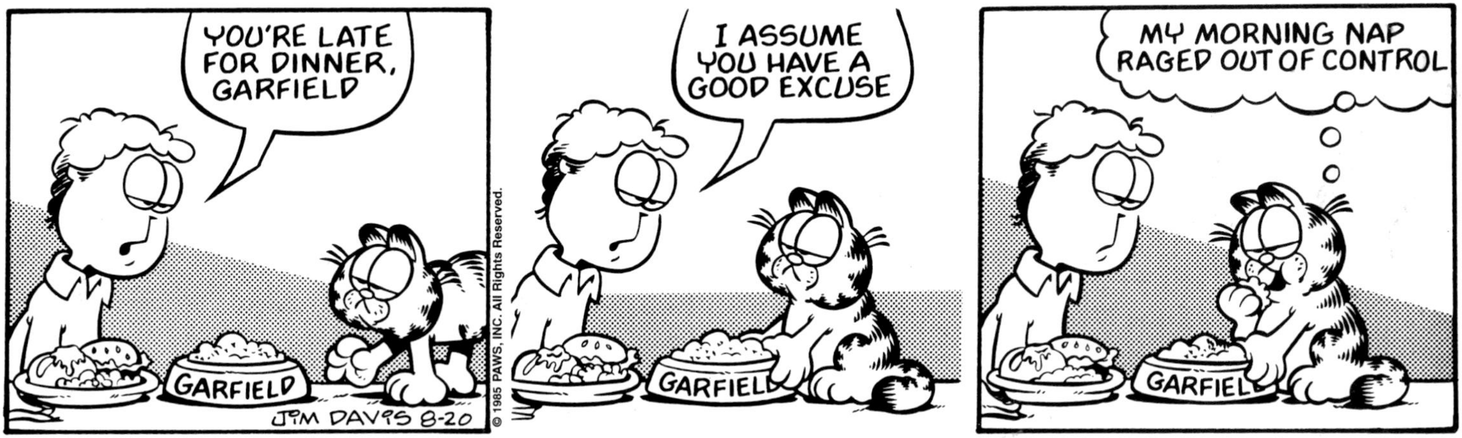
YOU'RE LATE FOR DINNER, GARFIELD
GARFIELD
JIM DAVIS 8-20
© 1985 PAWS, INC. All Rights Reserved.
I ASSUME YOU HAVE A GOOD EXCUSE
GARFIEL
MY MORNING NAP RAGED OUT OF CONTROL
GARFIEL

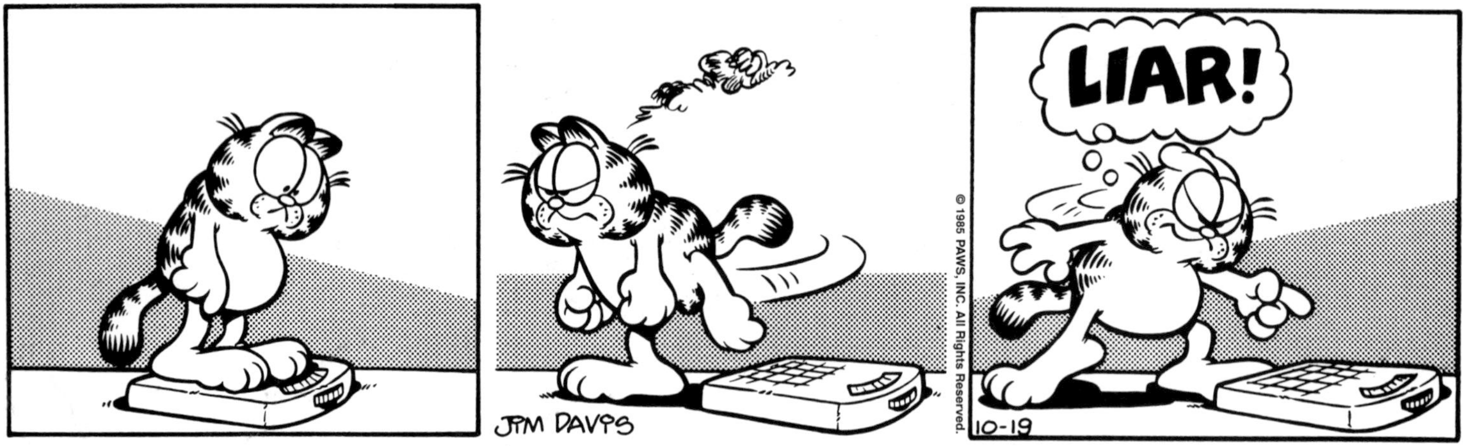
JIM DAVIS
© 1985 PAWS, INC. All Rights Reserved.
LIAR!
10-19

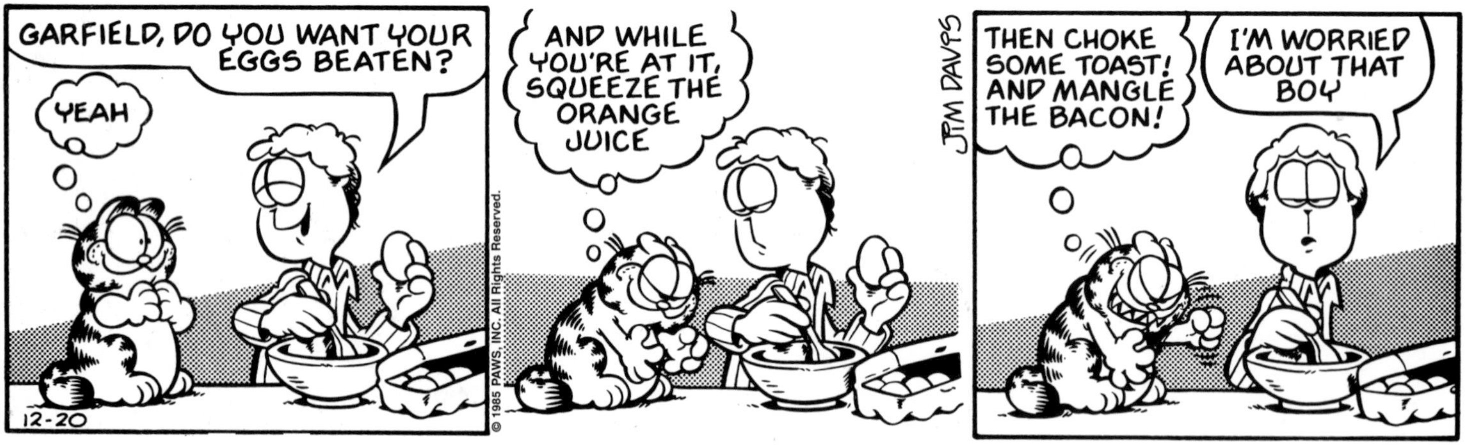
GARFIELD, DO YOU WANT YOUR EGGS BEATEN?
YEAH
12-20
© 1985 PAWS, INC. All Rights Reserved.
AND WHILE YOU'RE AT IT, SQUEEZE THE ORANGE JUICE
JIM DAVIS
THEN CHOKE SOME TOAST! AND MANGLE THE BACON!
I'M WORRIED ABOUT THAT BOY

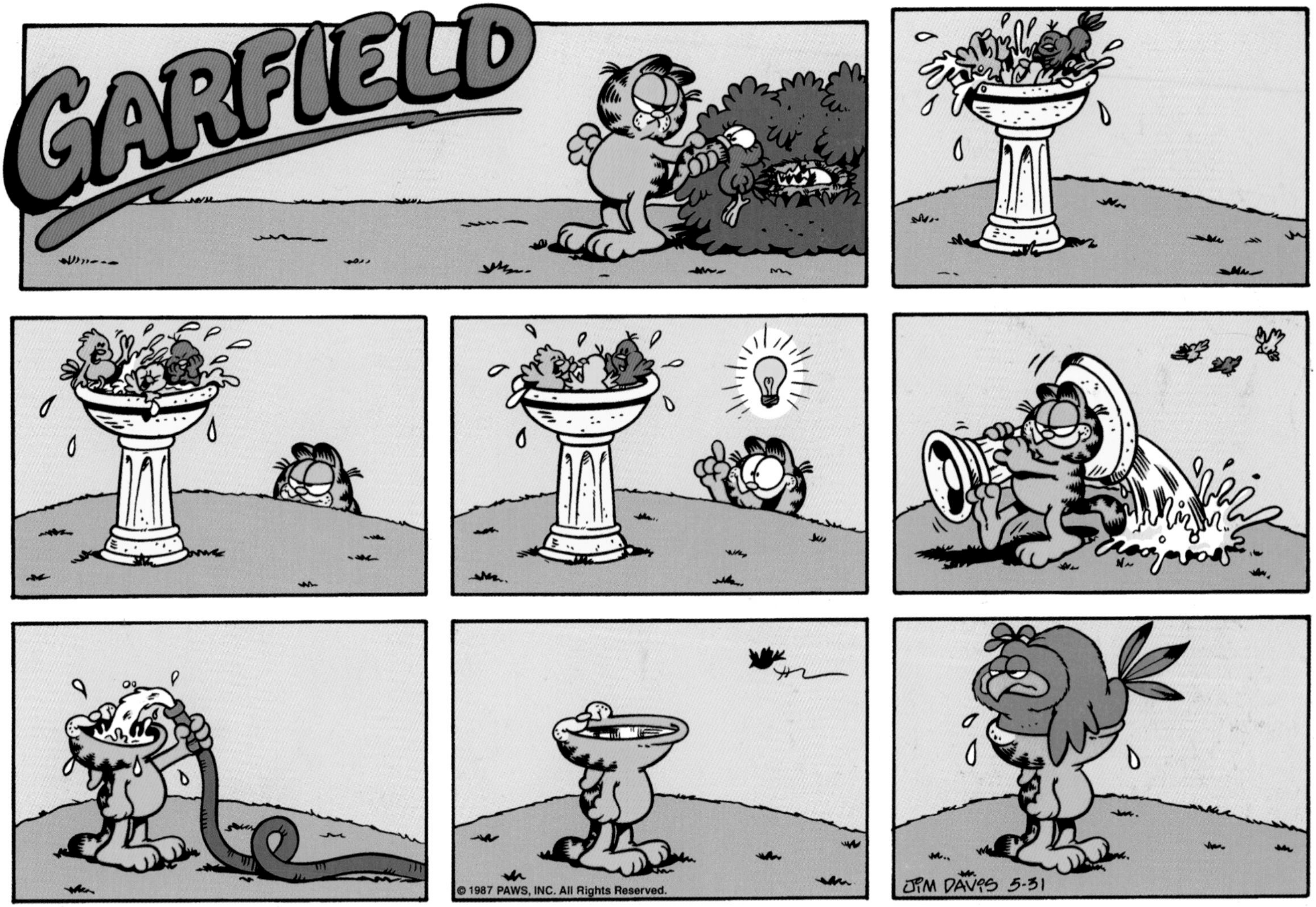
GARFIELD
© 1987 PAWS, INC. All Rights Reserved.
JIM DAVIS 5-31

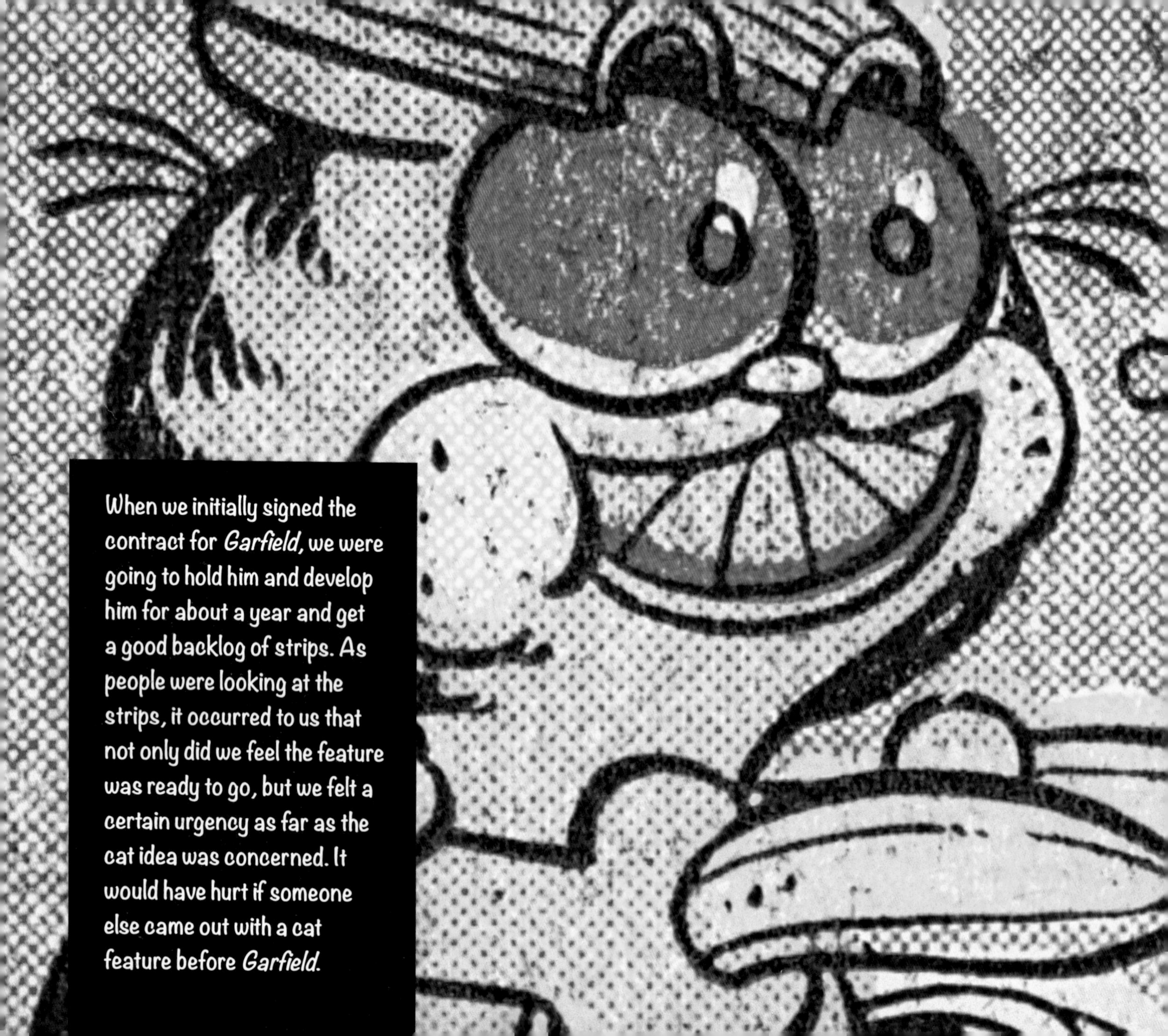

When we initially signed the contract for *Garfield,* we were going to hold him and develop him for about a year and get a good backlog of strips. As people were looking at the strips, it occurred to us that not only did we feel the feature was ready to go, but we felt a certain urgency as far as the cat idea was concerned. It would have hurt if someone else came out with a cat feature before *Garfield.*

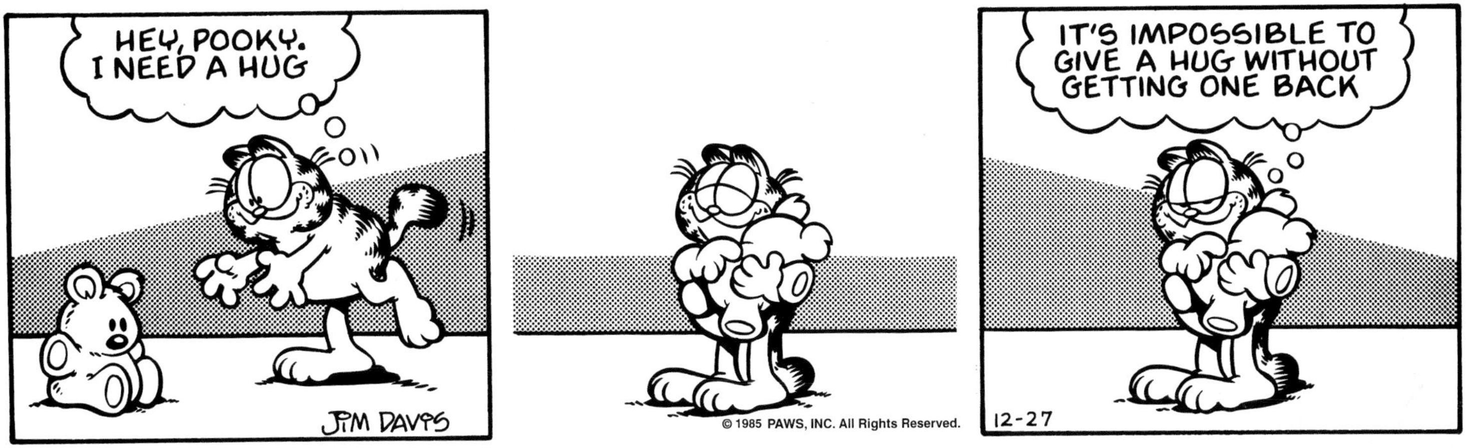
HEY, POOKY. I NEED A HUG
JIM DAVIS
© 1985 PAWS, INC. All Rights Reserved.
IT'S IMPOSSIBLE TO GIVE A HUG WITHOUT GETTING ONE BACK
12-27

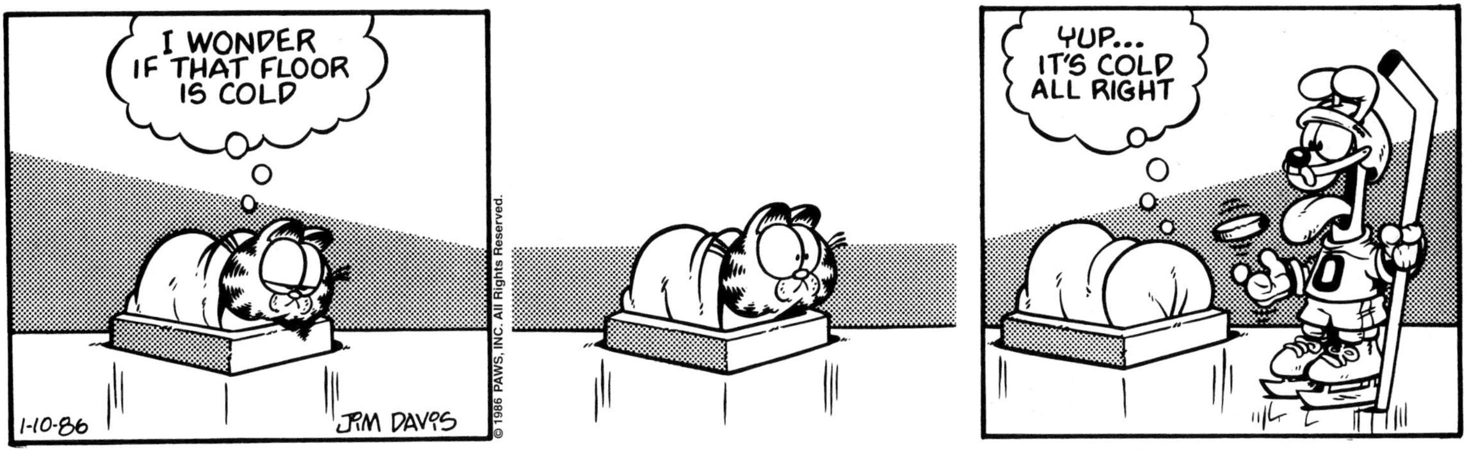
I WONDER IF THAT FLOOR IS COLD
1-10-86
JIM DAVIS
© 1986 PAWS, INC. All Rights Reserved.
YUP... IT'S COLD ALL RIGHT

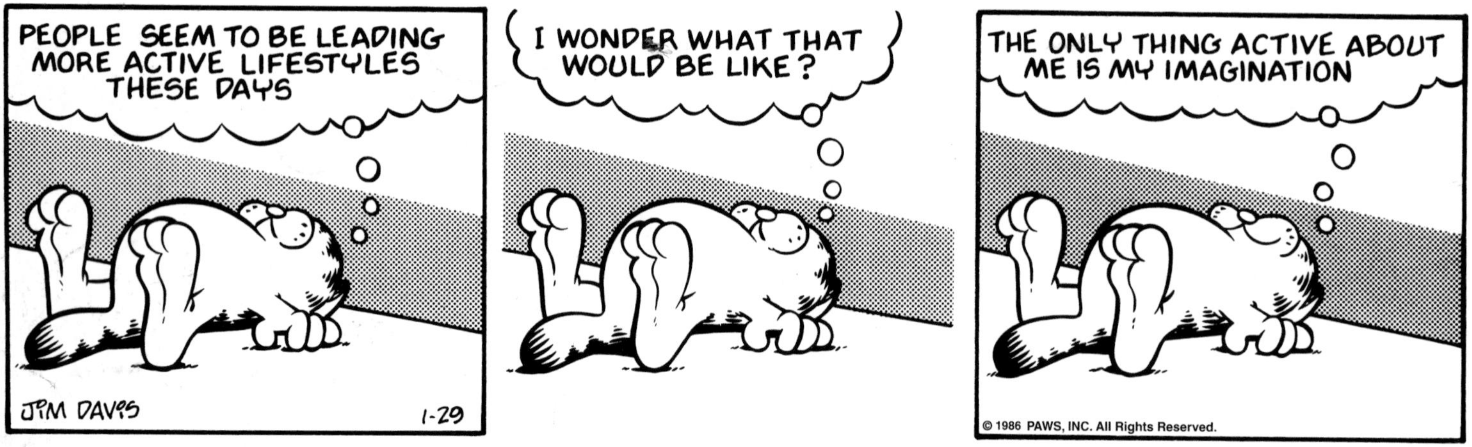
PEOPLE SEEM TO BE LEADING MORE ACTIVE LIFESTYLES THESE DAYS
JIM DAVIS
1-29
I WONDER WHAT THAT WOULD BE LIKE?
THE ONLY THING ACTIVE ABOUT ME IS MY IMAGINATION
© 1986 PAWS, INC. All Rights Reserved.

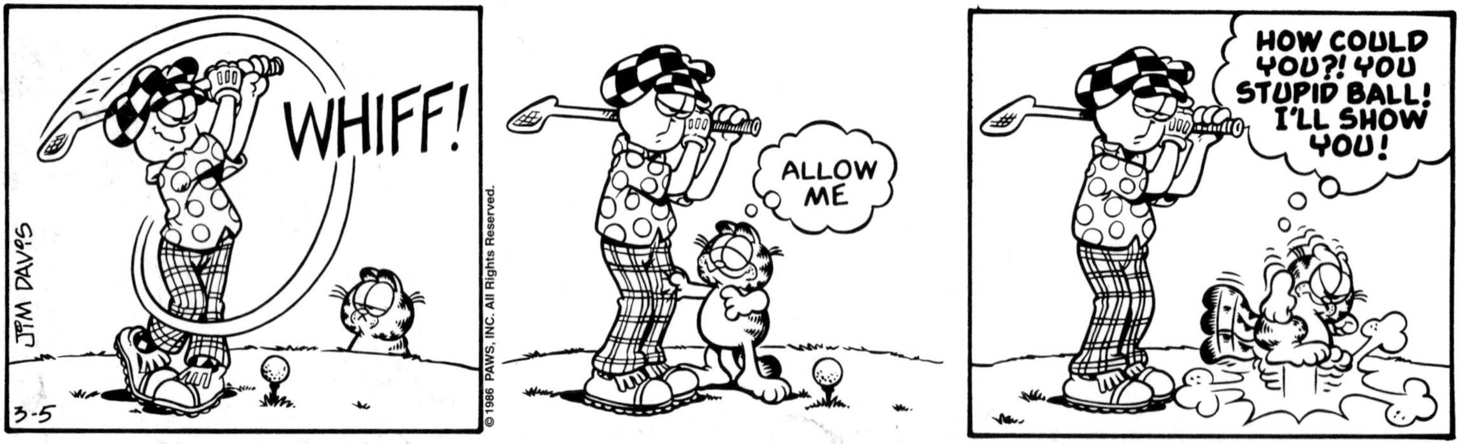
WHIFF!
JIM DAVIS
3-5
© 1986 PAWS, INC. All Rights Reserved.
ALLOW ME
HOW COULD YOU?! YOU STUPID BALL! I'LL SHOW YOU!

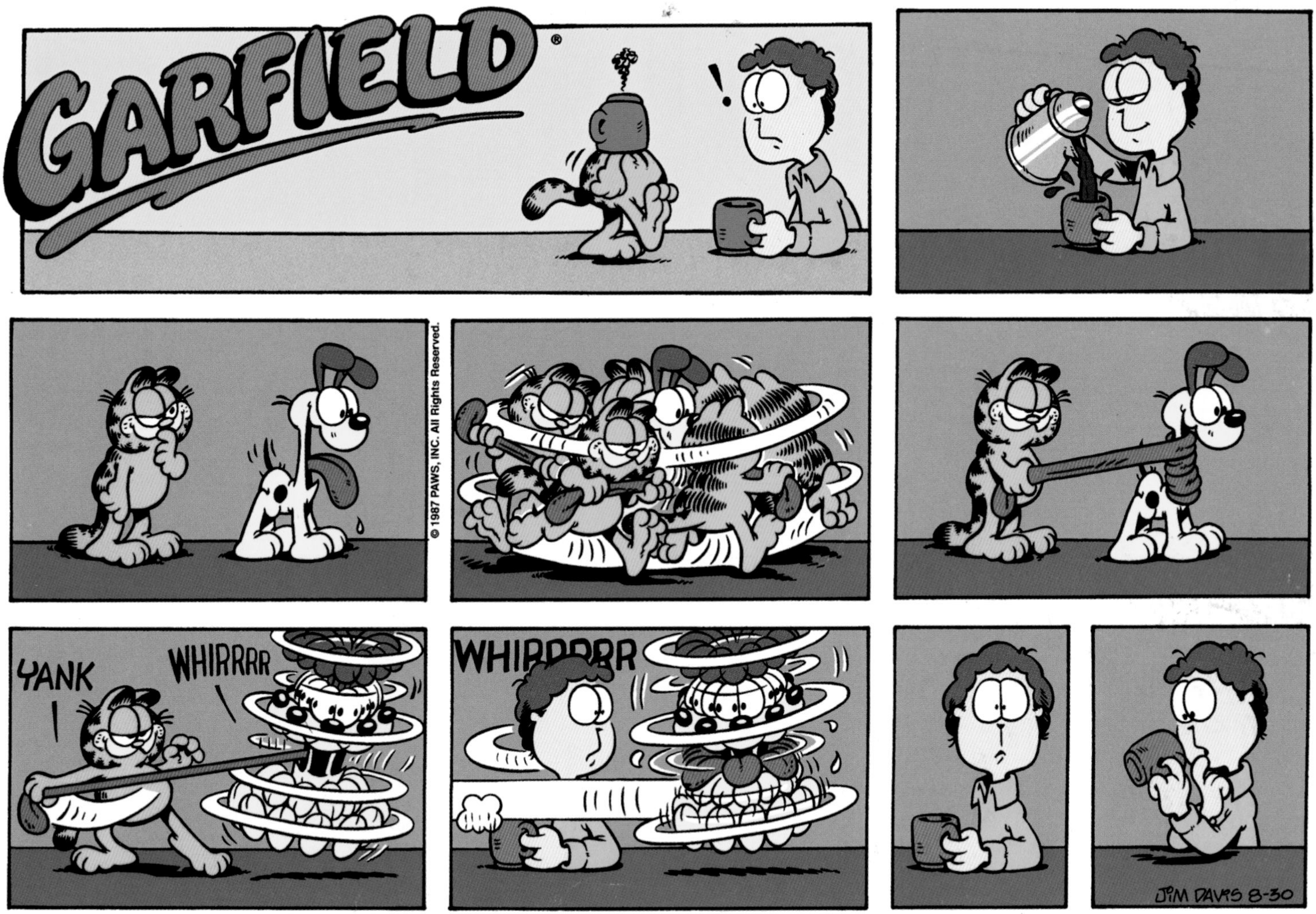
GARFIELD®
!
© 1987 PAWS, INC. All Rights Reserved.
YANK
WHIRRRR
WHIRRRRR
JIM DAVIS 8-30

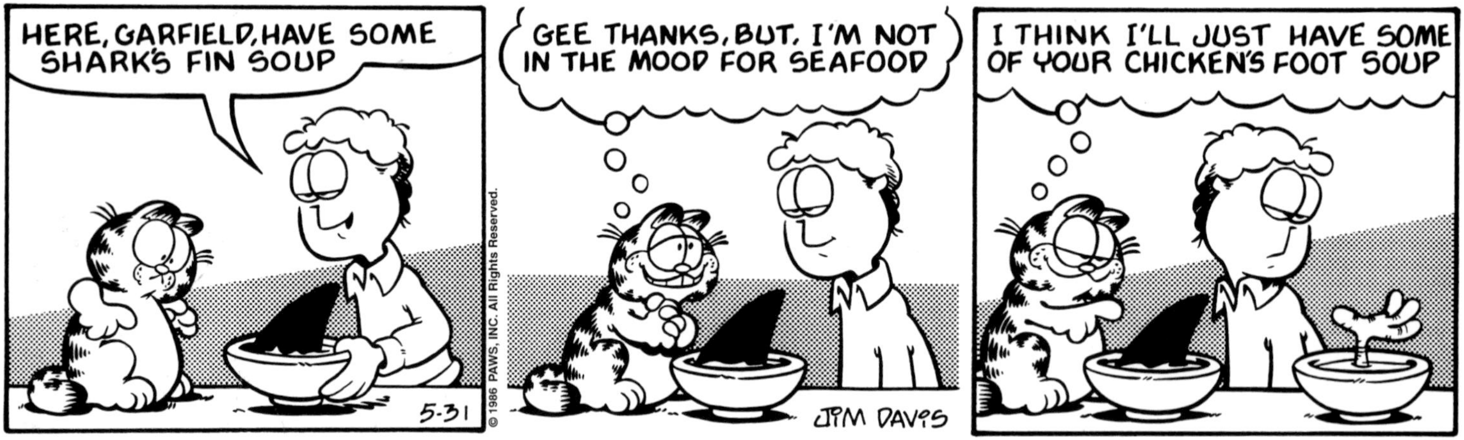
HERE, GARFIELD, HAVE SOME SHARK'S FIN SOUP
5-31
© 1986 PAWS, INC. All Rights Reserved.
GEE THANKS, BUT, I'M NOT IN THE MOOD FOR SEAFOOD
JIM DAVIS
I THINK I'LL JUST HAVE SOME OF YOUR CHICKEN'S FOOT SOUP

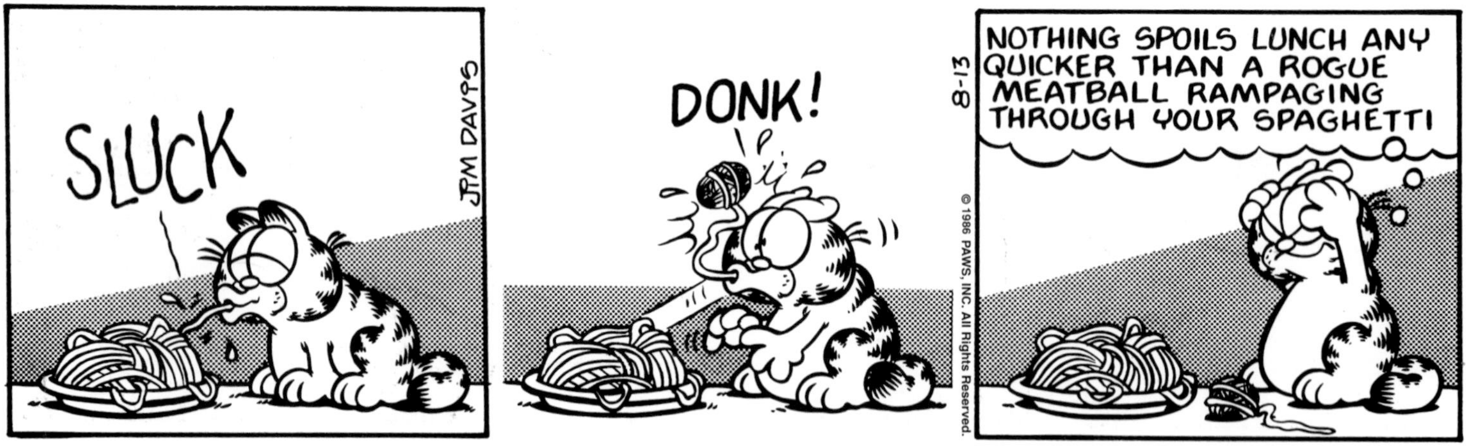
SLUCK
JIM DAVIS
DONK!
8-13
© 1986 PAWS, INC. All Rights Reserved.
NOTHING SPOILS LUNCH ANY QUICKER THAN A ROGUE MEATBALL RAMPAGING THROUGH YOUR SPAGHETTI

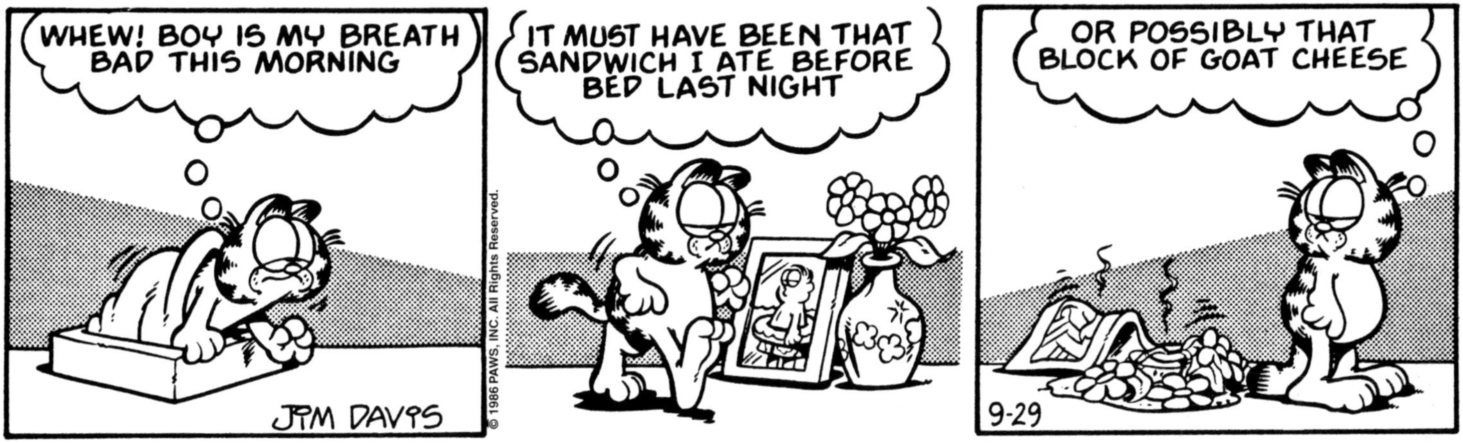
WHEW! BOY IS MY BREATH BAD THIS MORNING
JIM DAVIS
IT MUST HAVE BEEN THAT SANDWICH I ATE BEFORE BED LAST NIGHT
OR POSSIBLY THAT BLOCK OF GOAT CHEESE
9-29

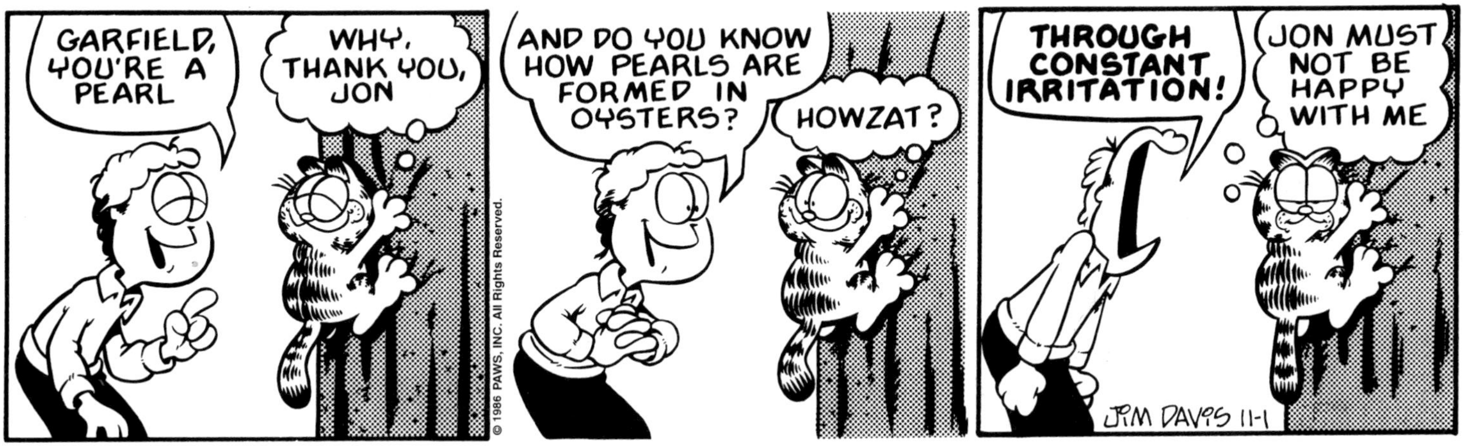
GARFIELD, YOU'RE A PEARL
WHY, THANK YOU, JON
AND DO YOU KNOW HOW PEARLS ARE FORMED IN OYSTERS?
HOWZAT?
THROUGH CONSTANT IRRITATION!
JON MUST NOT BE HAPPY WITH ME
JIM DAVIS 11-1

GARFIELD, DID YOU EAT MY JELLY FILLED DOUGHNUT?

IT WAS LIKE THIS, JON. IT HAPPENED TO BE A ROGUE DOUGHNUT WOUNDED IN A JUNGLE BAKERY

11-28

CRAZED WITH FEAR AND PAIN, IT CHARGED MY MOUTH AND I WAS FORCED TO EAT IT IN SELF-DEFENSE

IT'S TIMES LIKE THIS I WISH I UNDERSTOOD HIM

© 1986 PAWS, INC. All Rights Reserved.

JIM DAVIS

I think people honestly feel that cats think in English, that cats understand everything as they do; but obviously they don't talk, so I wanted to ride that line between here's what your cat is really thinking to give pet owners an insight without giving it away. To have Garfield really talk and Jon understand him would have made it more of a fantasy. I didn't want to do that. I wanted to create a very real world and then go out to the fantasy from there. And you'll notice that when Jon understands what Garfield is saying, it's something Garfield does with action, not a word that communicates it.

MEYOWR

WOOF

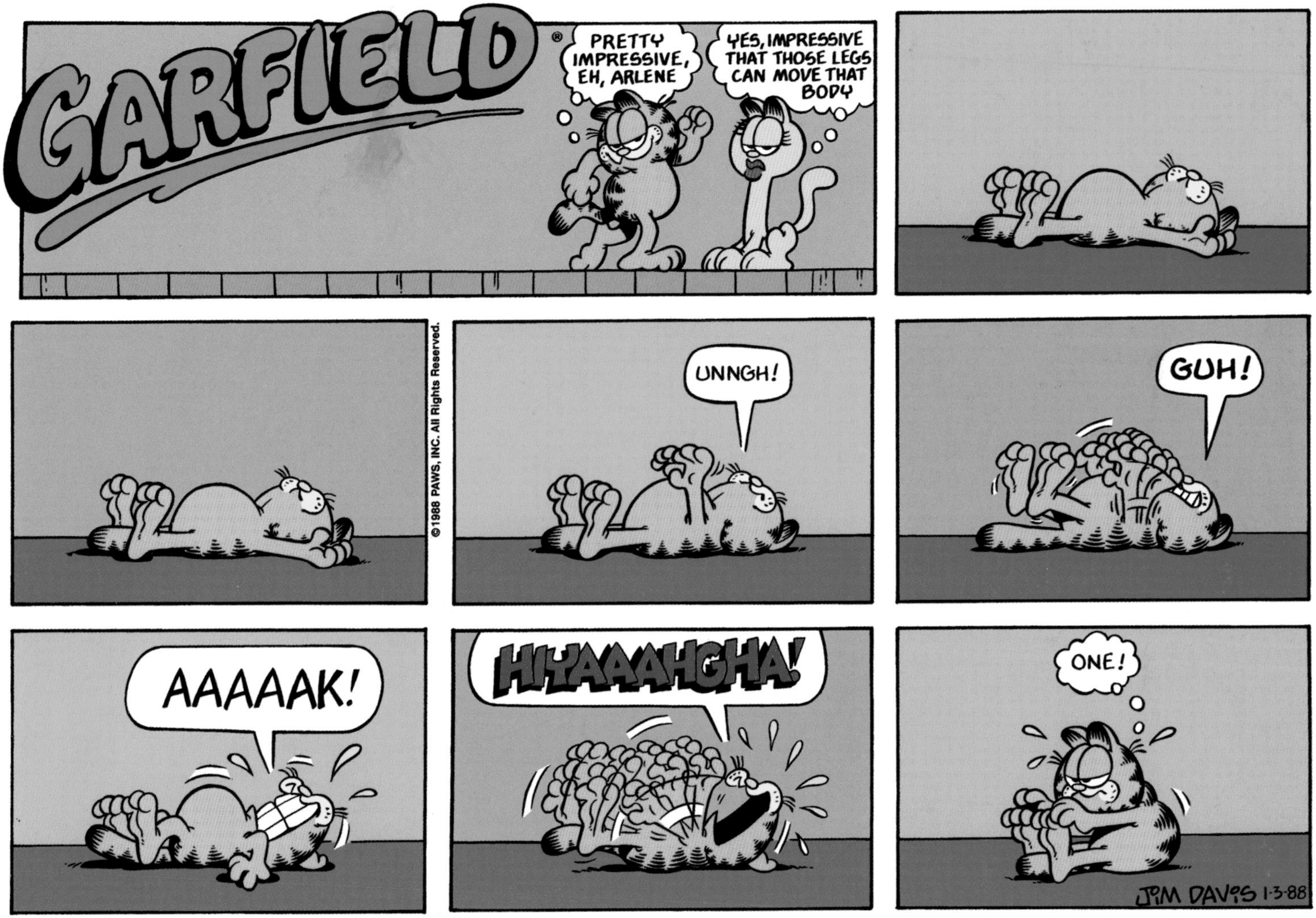
GARFIELD®
PRETTY IMPRESSIVE, EH, ARLENE
YES, IMPRESSIVE THAT THOSE LEGS CAN MOVE THAT BODY
UNNGH!
GUH!
AAAAAK!
HIYAAAHGHA!
ONE!
JIM DAVIS 1-3-88

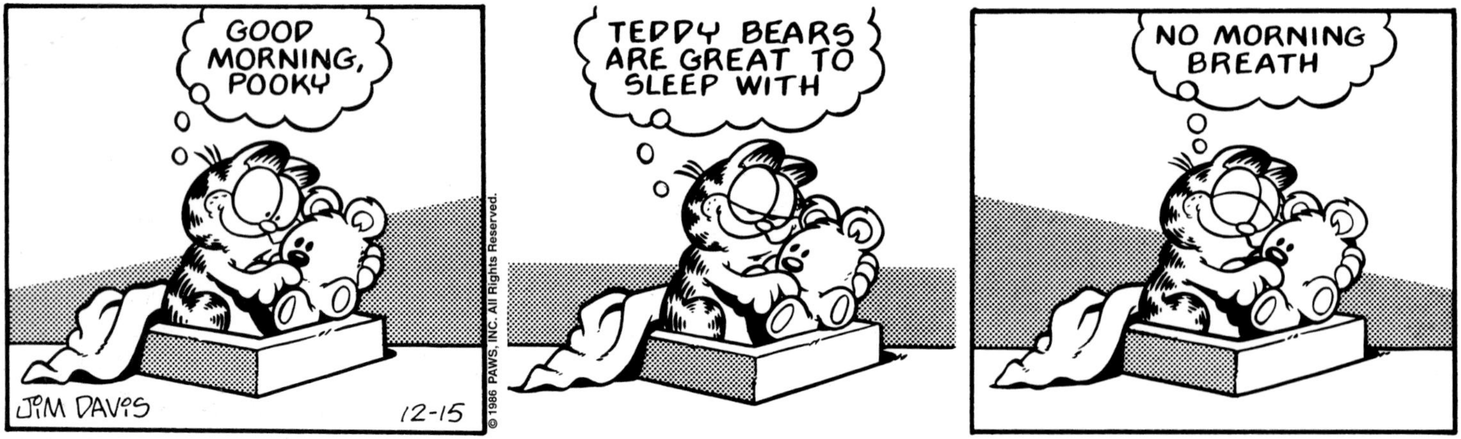
GOOD MORNING, POOKY
JIM DAVIS
12-15
© 1986 PAWS, INC. All Rights Reserved.
TEDDY BEARS ARE GREAT TO SLEEP WITH
NO MORNING BREATH

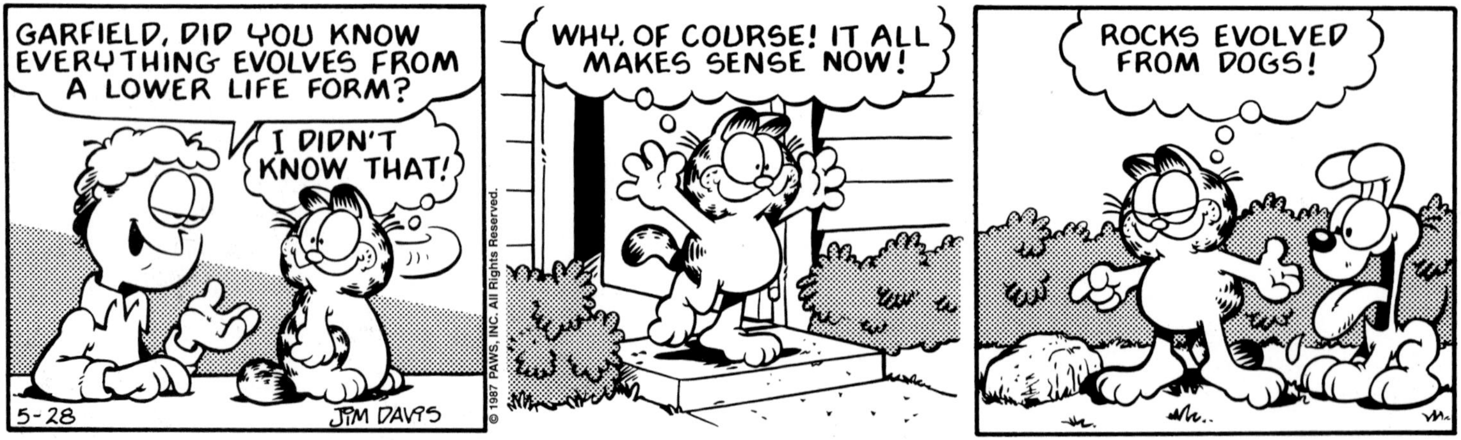
GARFIELD, DID YOU KNOW EVERYTHING EVOLVES FROM A LOWER LIFE FORM?
I DIDN'T KNOW THAT!
5-28
JIM DAVIS
© 1987 PAWS, INC. All Rights Reserved.
WHY, OF COURSE! IT ALL MAKES SENSE NOW!
ROCKS EVOLVED FROM DOGS!

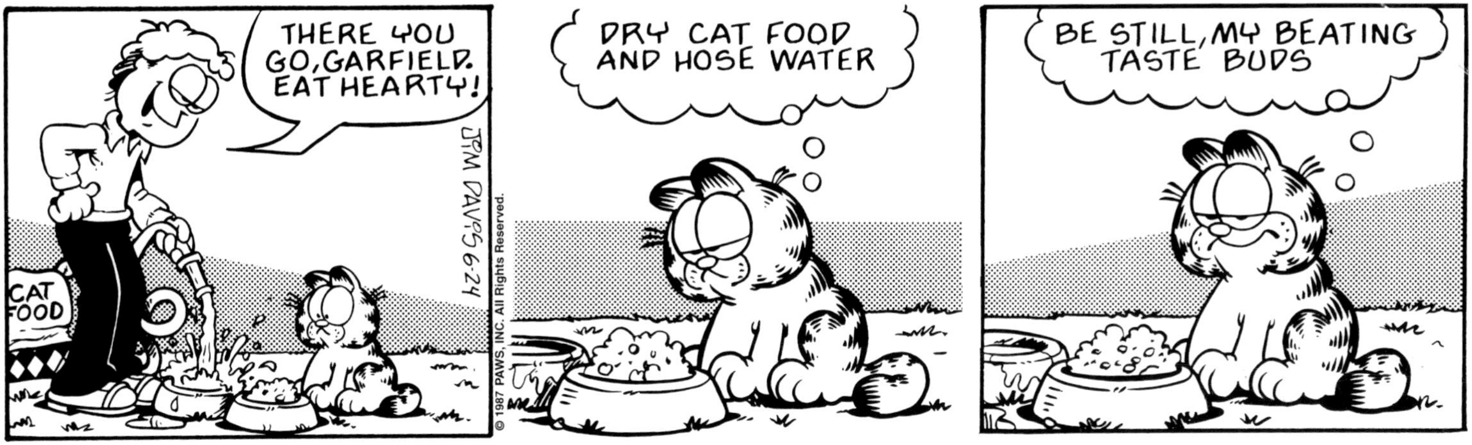
THERE YOU GO, GARFIELD. EAT HEARTY!
JIM DAVIS 6-24
© 1987 PAWS, INC. All Rights Reserved.
CAT FOOD
DRY CAT FOOD AND HOSE WATER
BE STILL, MY BEATING TASTE BUDS

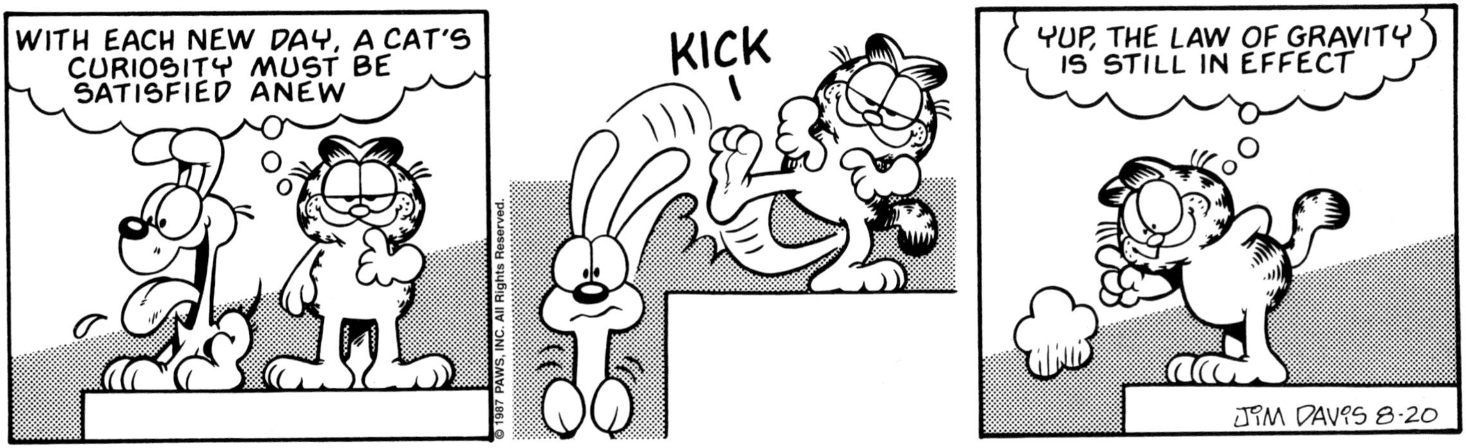
WITH EACH NEW DAY, A CAT'S CURIOSITY MUST BE SATISFIED ANEW
© 1987 PAWS, INC. All Rights Reserved.
KICK
YUP, THE LAW OF GRAVITY IS STILL IN EFFECT
JIM DAVIS 8-20

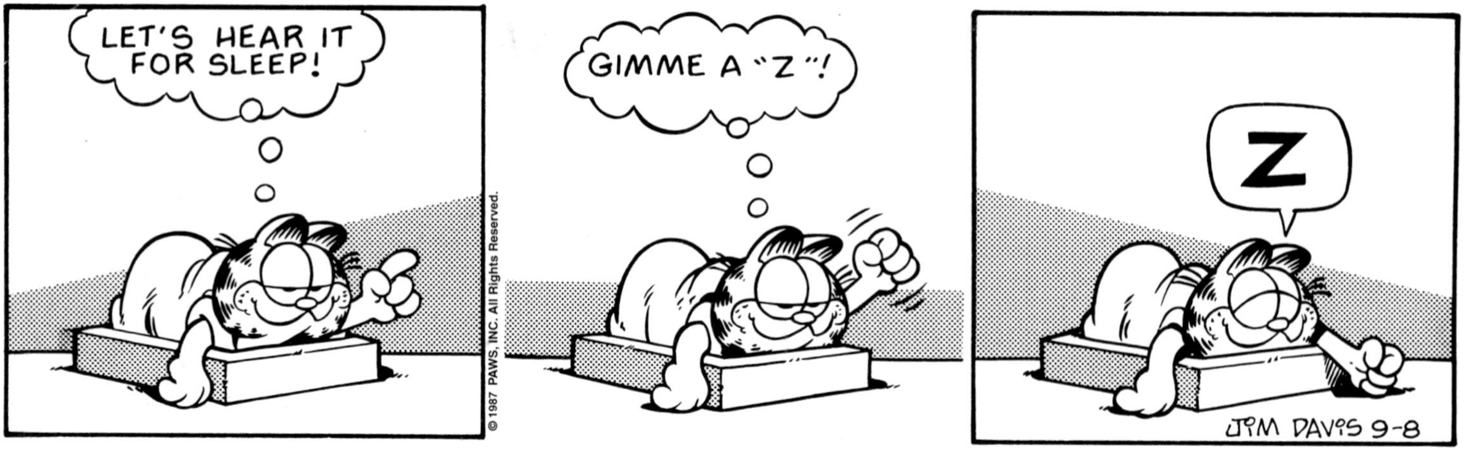
LET'S HEAR IT FOR SLEEP!
GIMME A "Z"!
Z
JIM DAVIS 9-8
© 1987 PAWS, INC. All Rights Reserved.

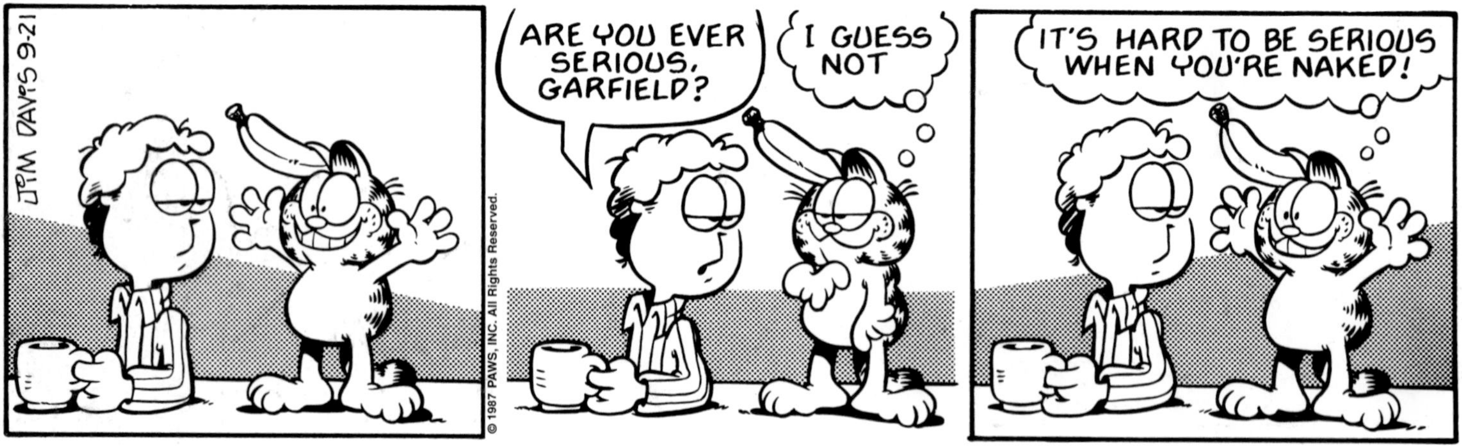
JIM DAVIS 9-21
ARE YOU EVER SERIOUS, GARFIELD?
I GUESS NOT
IT'S HARD TO BE SERIOUS WHEN YOU'RE NAKED!
© 1987 PAWS, INC. All Rights Reserved.

When I created Garfield, I suppose the logical thing would have been to sketch cats or use cat references to design the character. But I purposely didn't look at cats. I felt what I saw in my mind would be funnier and truer to Garfield's nature than any cat I could possibly have copied.

Early pencil drawing from 1978 sketchbook

WHAT'S THAT NUMBER ON YOUR BACK FOR, GARFIELD?

IT'S MANDATORY ATTIRE FOR MY NEW HOBBY

MARATHON SLEEPING

11-21   JIM DAVIS

JON

Jon Arbuckle is wishy-washy and a nerd...the perfect foil for Garfield's sarcastic humor.

Only those who read the first strip would know that Jon's a cartoonist. I made him a cartoonist because it always bugged me that nobody ever knew what Ozzie Nelson did for a living. (Incidentally, the strip was originally titled *Jon*, but Garfield kept hogging the spotlight, so I named it after him.)

In 2006, I decided to let Jon have a life, and he and Liz the vet finally got together and started dating. How long will the relationship last? Who knows? Jon's never had much luck with the ladies. Let's face it, Jon's not a stud; he's a dating dud.

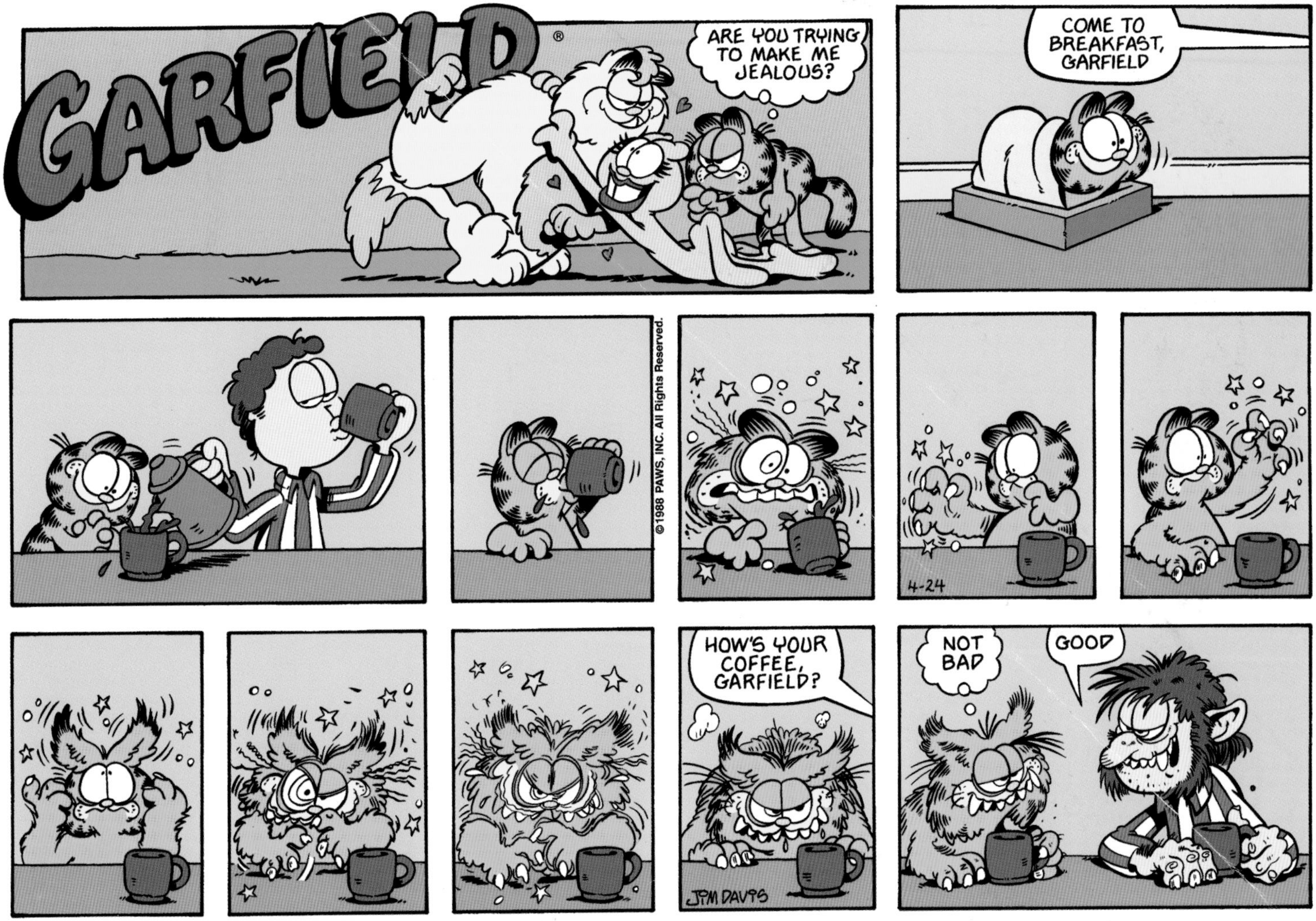
GARFIELD®
ARE YOU TRYING TO MAKE ME JEALOUS?
COME TO BREAKFAST, GARFIELD
© 1988 PAWS, INC. All Rights Reserved.
4-24
HOW'S YOUR COFFEE, GARFIELD?
JIM DAVIS
NOT BAD
GOOD

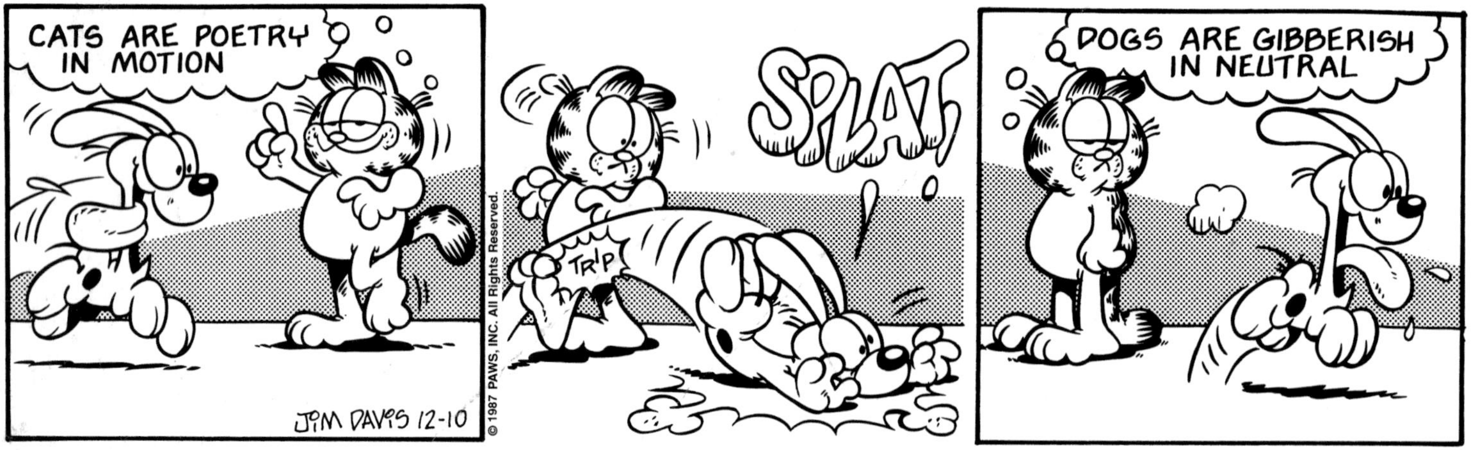
CATS ARE POETRY IN MOTION
JIM DAVIS 12-10
SPLAT
TRIP
© 1987 PAWS, INC. All Rights Reserved.
DOGS ARE GIBBERISH IN NEUTRAL

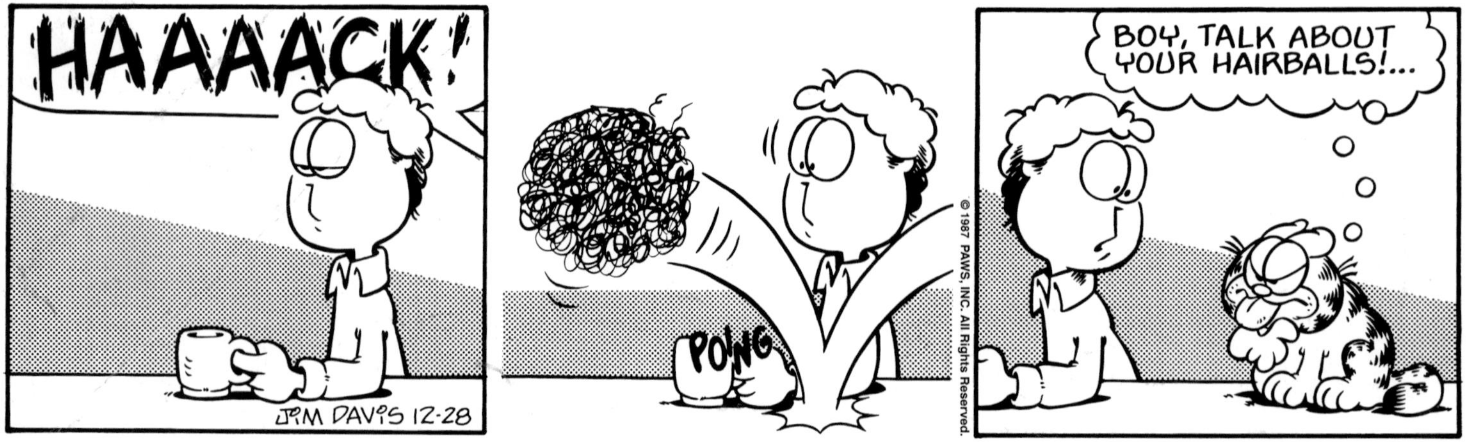
HAAAACK!
JIM DAVIS 12-28
POING
© 1987 PAWS, INC. All Rights Reserved.
BOY, TALK ABOUT YOUR HAIRBALLS!...

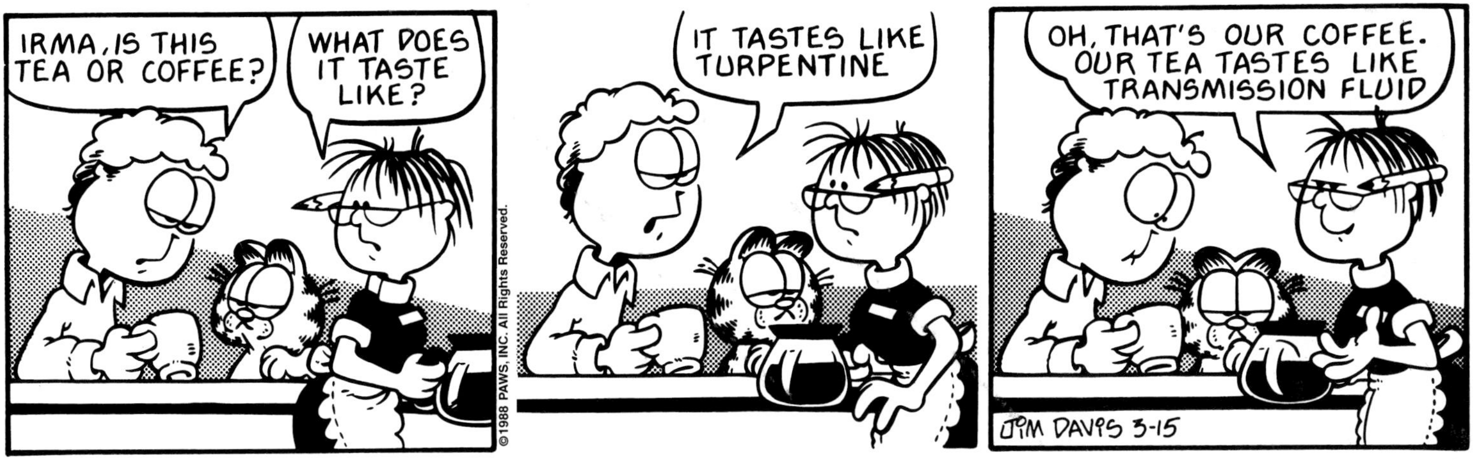
IRMA, IS THIS TEA OR COFFEE?
WHAT DOES IT TASTE LIKE?
© 1988 PAWS, INC. All Rights Reserved.
IT TASTES LIKE TURPENTINE
OH, THAT'S OUR COFFEE. OUR TEA TASTES LIKE TRANSMISSION FLUID
JIM DAVIS 3-15

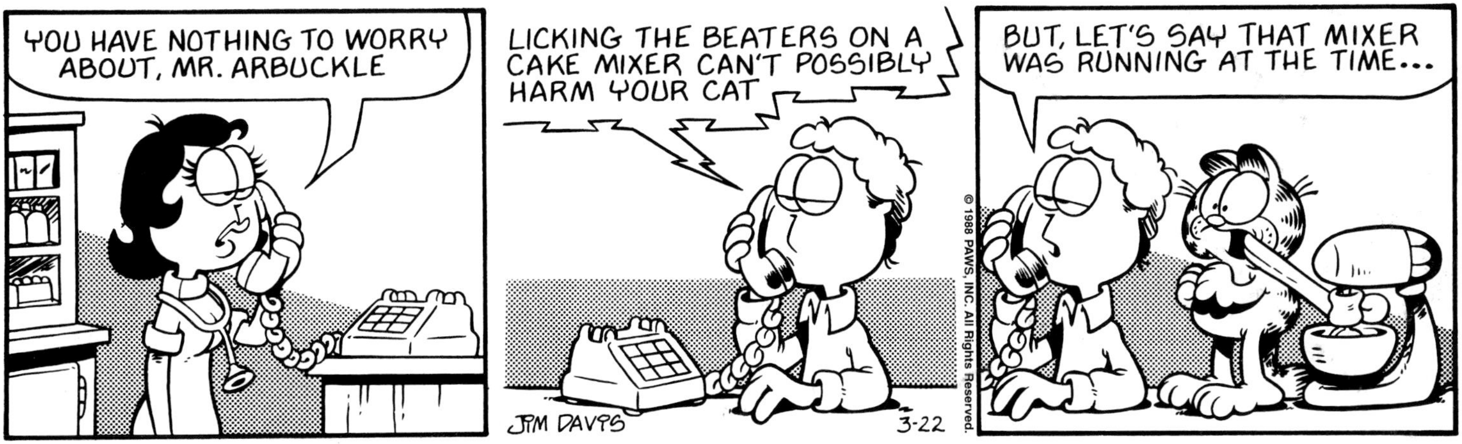
YOU HAVE NOTHING TO WORRY ABOUT, MR. ARBUCKLE
LICKING THE BEATERS ON A CAKE MIXER CAN'T POSSIBLY HARM YOUR CAT
JIM DAVIS
3-22
© 1988 PAWS, INC. All Rights Reserved.
BUT, LET'S SAY THAT MIXER WAS RUNNING AT THE TIME...

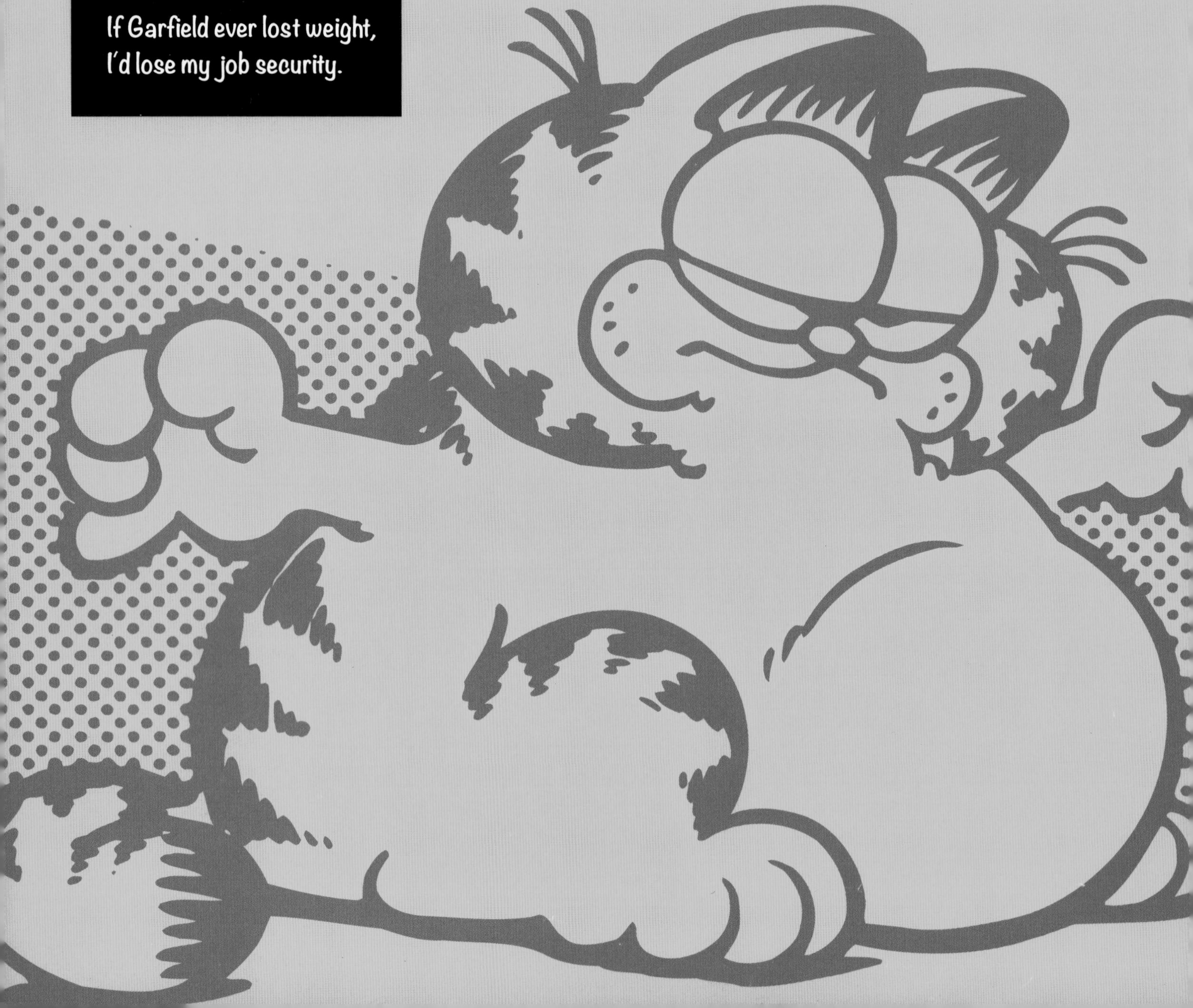

If Garfield ever lost weight,
I'd lose my job security.

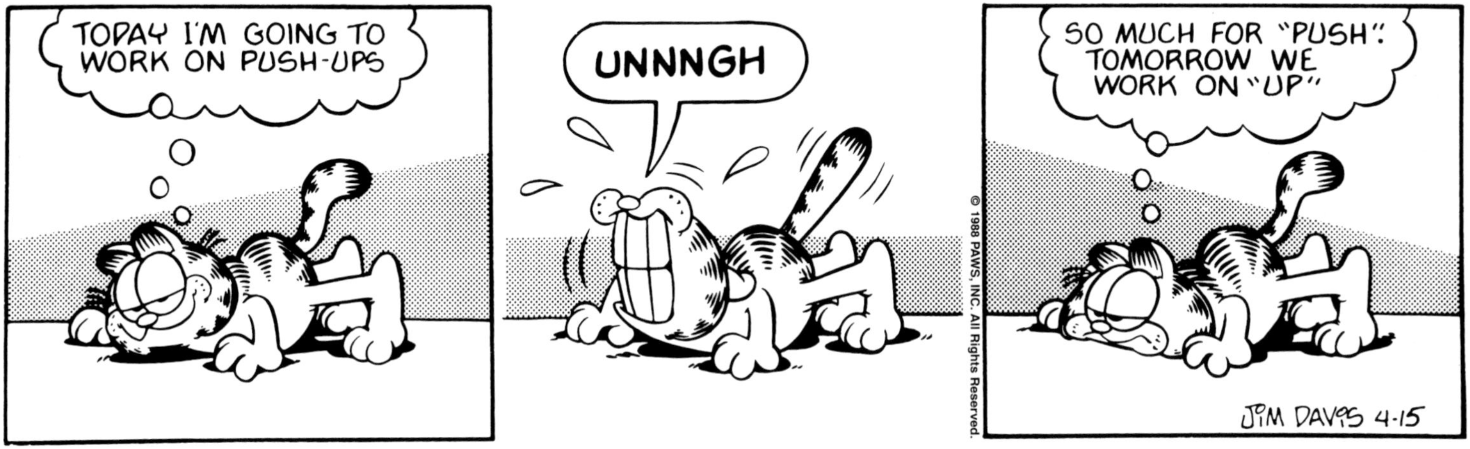
TODAY I'M GOING TO WORK ON PUSH-UPS
UNNNGH
SO MUCH FOR "PUSH". TOMORROW WE WORK ON "UP"
JIM DAVIS 4-15

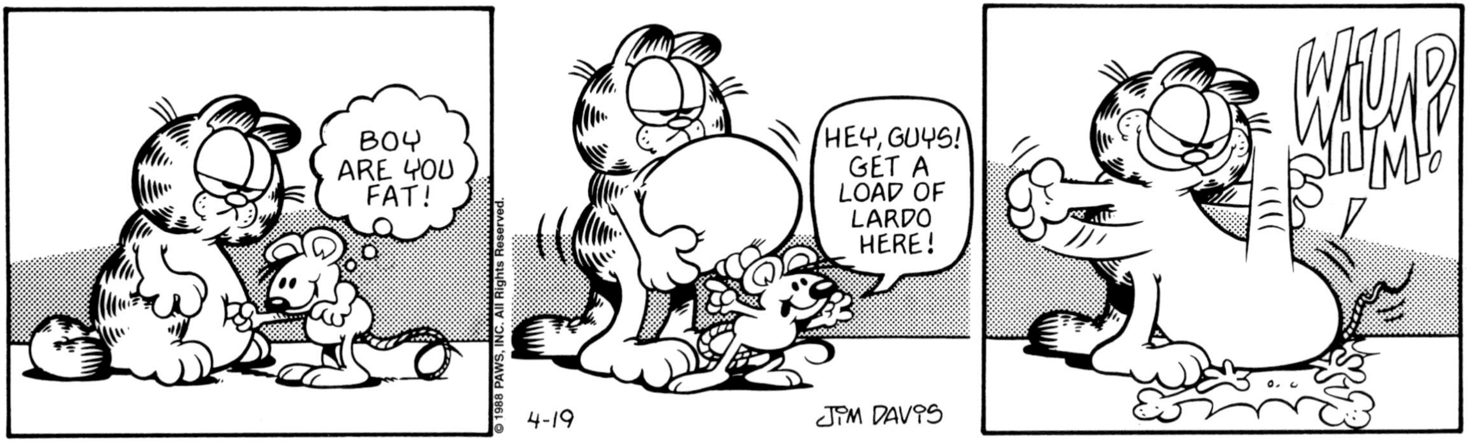
BOY ARE YOU FAT!
HEY, GUYS! GET A LOAD OF LARDO HERE!
WHUMP!
4-19
JIM DAVIS

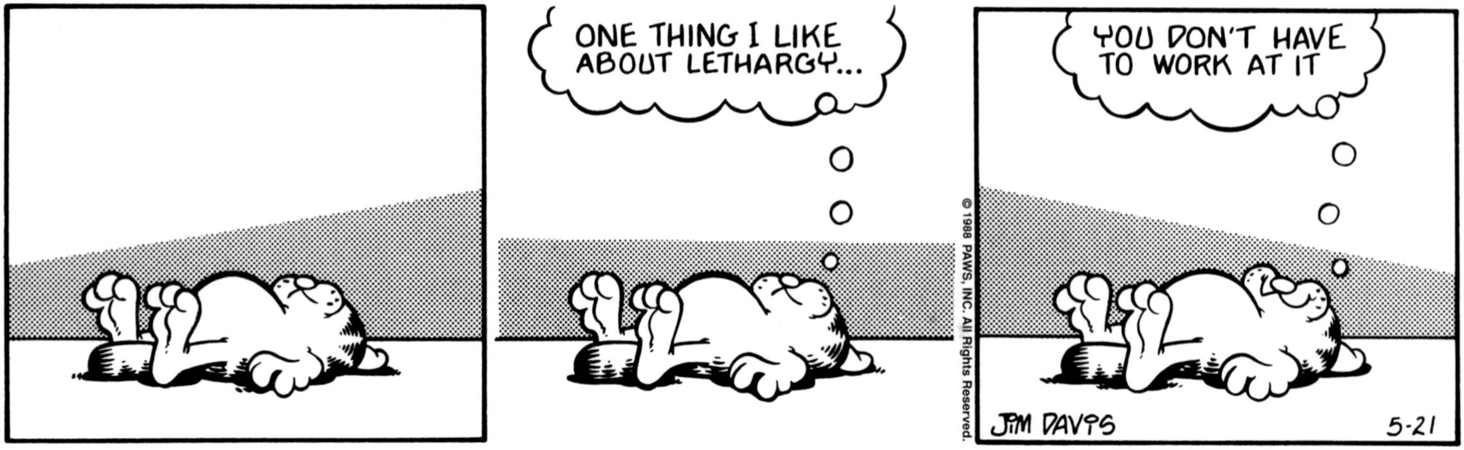
ONE THING I LIKE ABOUT LETHARGY...
YOU DON'T HAVE TO WORK AT IT
JIM DAVIS
5-21
© 1988 PAWS, INC. All Rights Reserved.

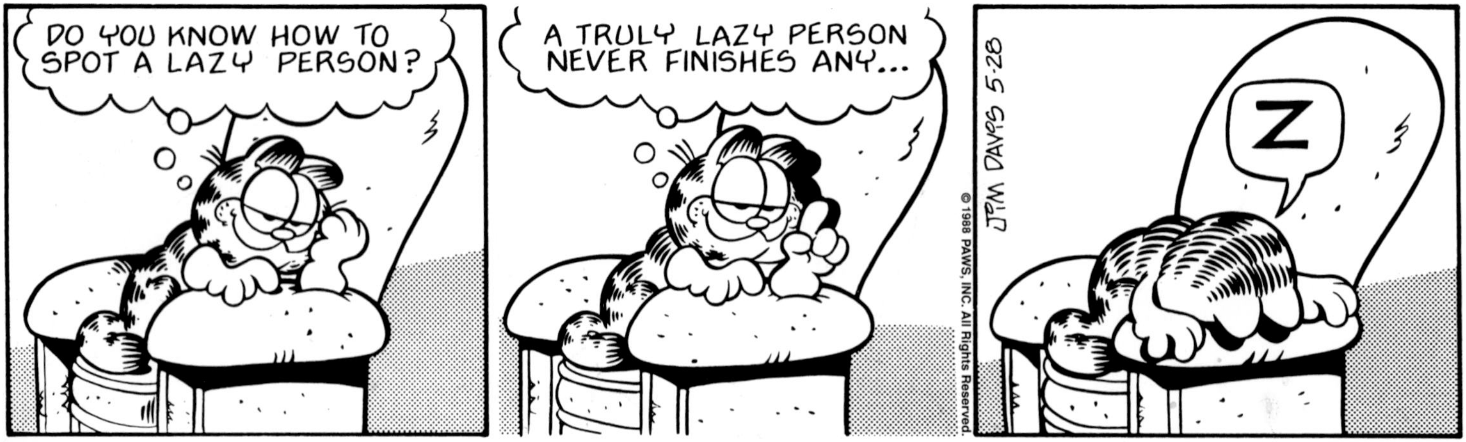
DO YOU KNOW HOW TO SPOT A LAZY PERSON?
A TRULY LAZY PERSON NEVER FINISHES ANY...
Z
JIM DAVIS 5-28
© 1988 PAWS, INC. All Rights Reserved.

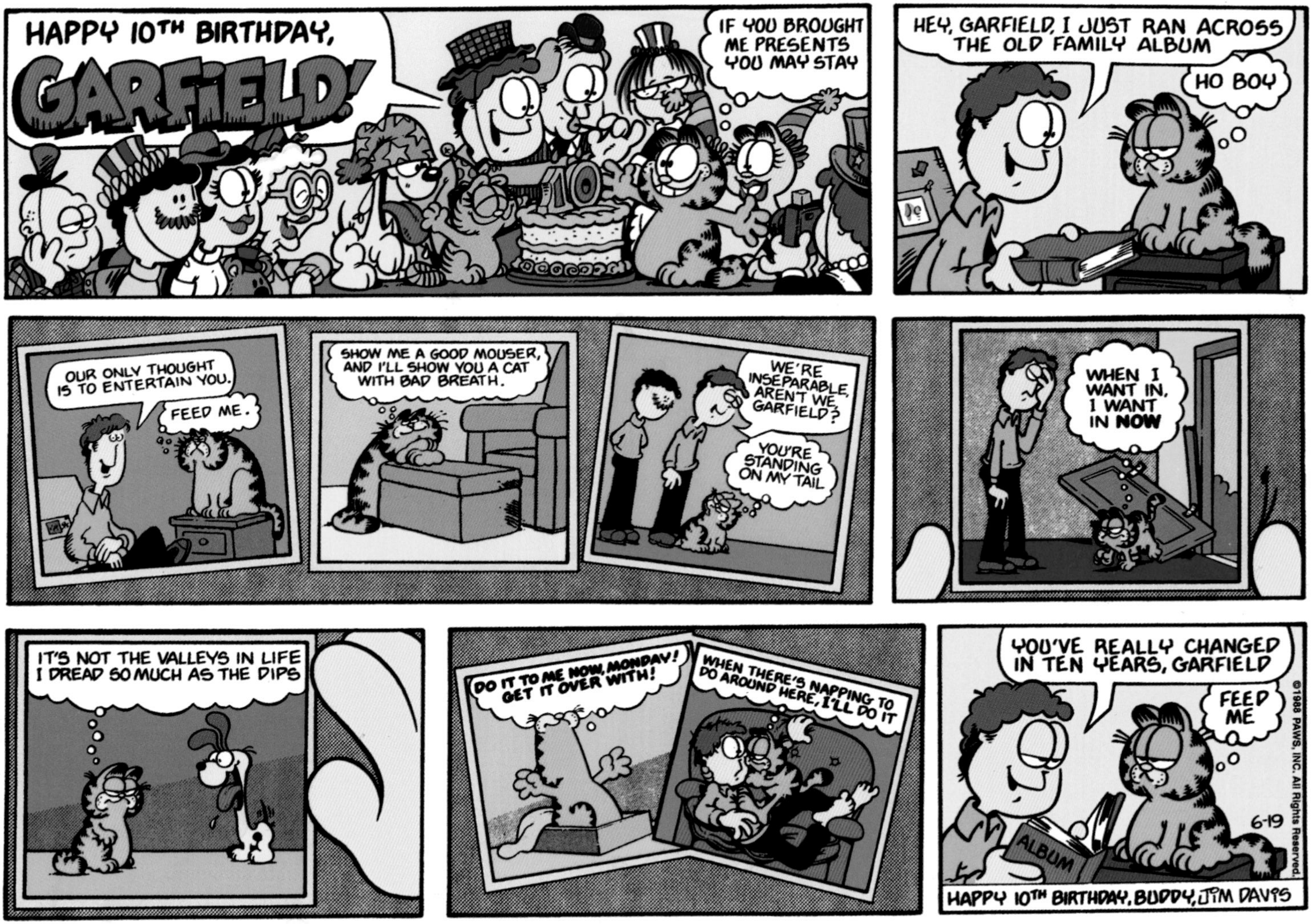
HAPPY 10TH BIRTHDAY, GARFIELD!
IF YOU BROUGHT ME PRESENTS YOU MAY STAY
HEY, GARFIELD, I JUST RAN ACROSS THE OLD FAMILY ALBUM
HO BOY
OUR ONLY THOUGHT IS TO ENTERTAIN YOU.
FEED ME.
SHOW ME A GOOD MOUSER, AND I'LL SHOW YOU A CAT WITH BAD BREATH.
WE'RE INSEPARABLE, AREN'T WE, GARFIELD?
YOU'RE STANDING ON MY TAIL
WHEN I WANT IN, I WANT IN **NOW**
IT'S NOT THE VALLEYS IN LIFE I DREAD SO MUCH AS THE DIPS
DO IT TO ME NOW, MONDAY! GET IT OVER WITH!
WHEN THERE'S NAPPING TO DO AROUND HERE, I'LL DO IT
YOU'VE REALLY CHANGED IN TEN YEARS, GARFIELD
FEED ME
ALBUM
6-19
©1988 PAWS, INC. All Rights Reserved.
HAPPY 10TH BIRTHDAY, BUDDY, JIM DAVIS

The Second Decade
1988–1998

Garfield matured in his second decade as he attracted readers from other countries. There are cat lovers all over the world who love to eat and sleep . . . go figure.

Garfield's support staff of creative and licensing people grew at Paws, Inc., the company I formed to take care of the fat cat's burgeoning brand. This allowed me to focus on the comic strip, my first love.

This decade was highlighted by the introduction of a new technological innovation called the Internet. With the electronic dissemination of information, would paper become a thing of the past? (Answer: You are reading this in a book, aren't you?)

However, after watching our children's no-fear approach to adapting to computers, we knew the Net was the way to introduce Garfield to the next generation of comics readers.

In 1996, Garfield.com was launched to little fanfare. Why? Because my low-tech cat still insisted on sleeping and eating . . . go figure.

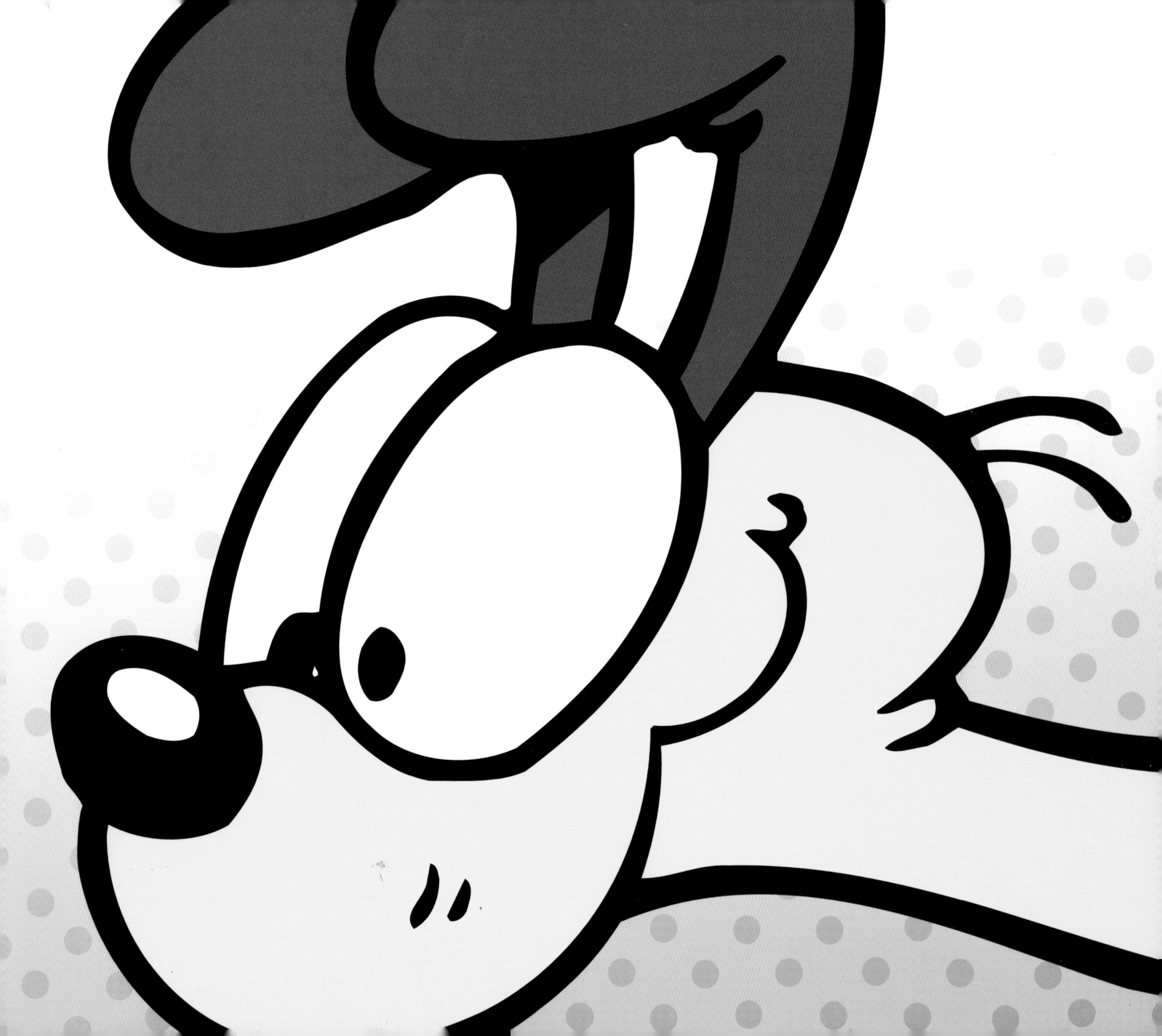

One of my philosophies of cartooning, especially when encouraging hopeful cartoonists, is that they should have fun doing the gags. If you have fun doing them, people will have fun reading them.

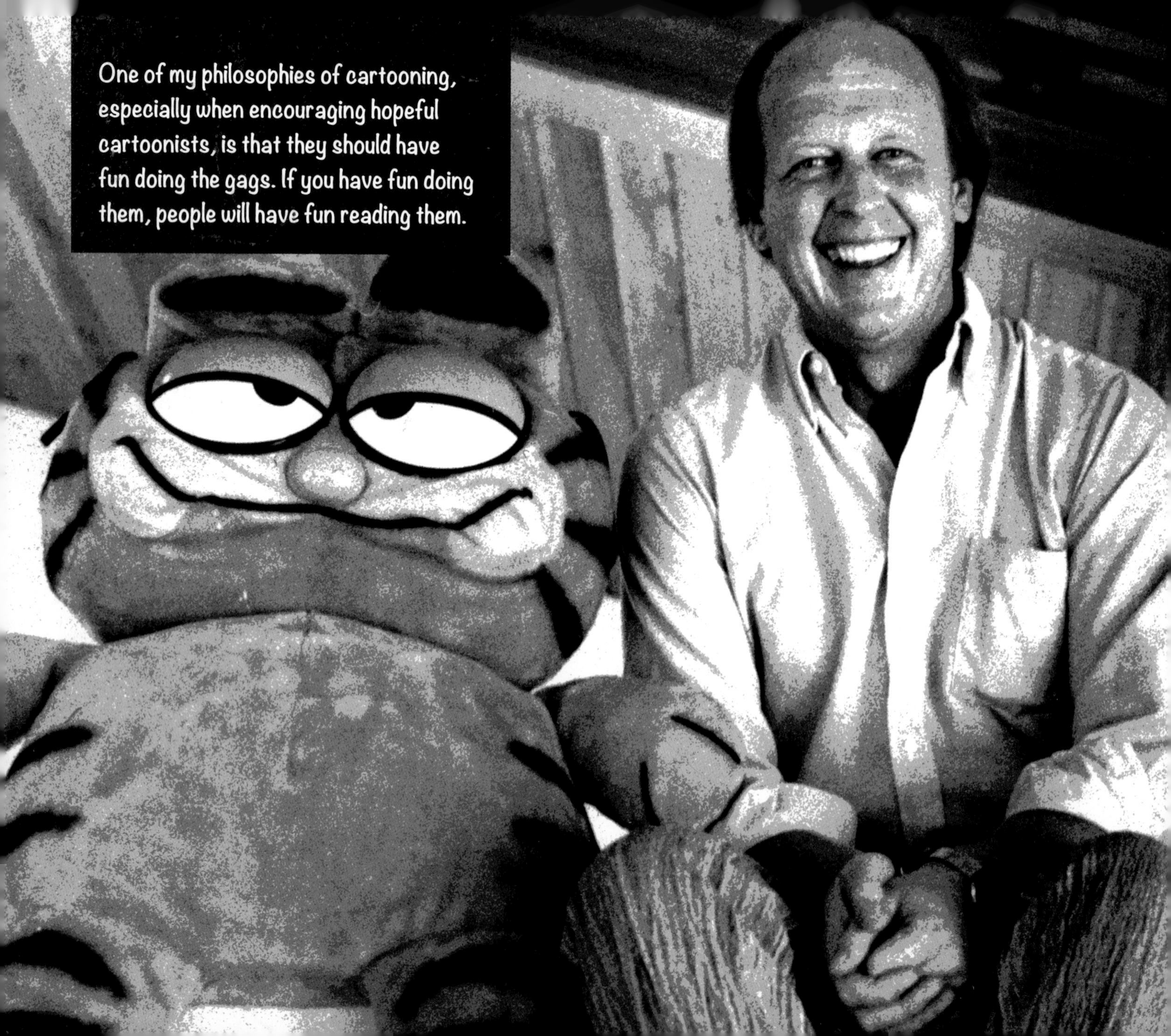

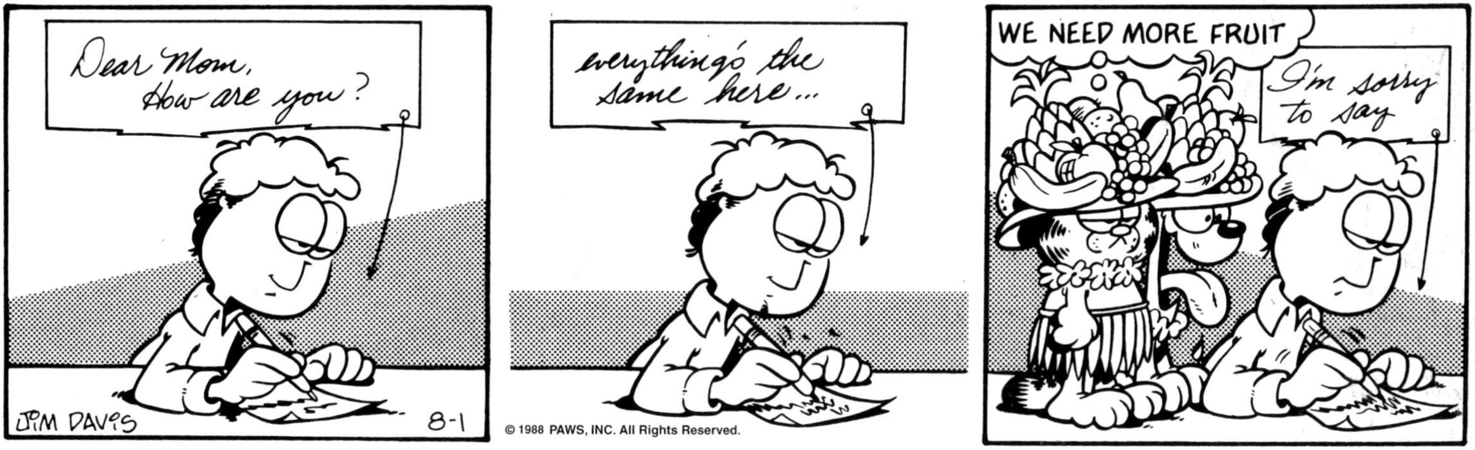
Dear Mom,
How are you?
JIM DAVIS
8-1
everything's the same here...
© 1988 PAWS, INC. All Rights Reserved.
WE NEED MORE FRUIT
I'm sorry to say

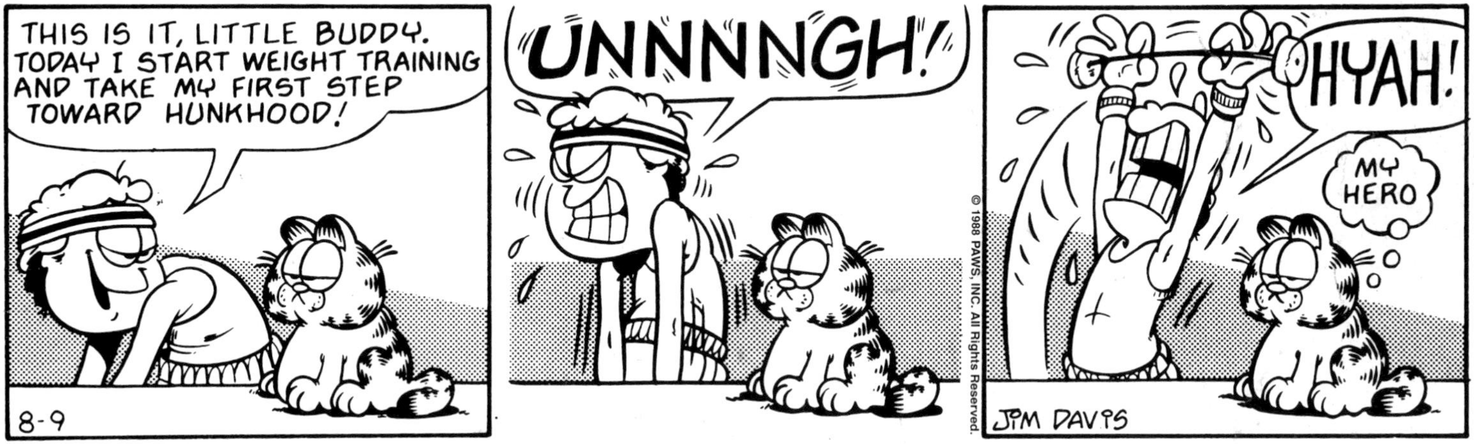
THIS IS IT, LITTLE BUDDY. TODAY I START WEIGHT TRAINING AND TAKE MY FIRST STEP TOWARD HUNKHOOD!
8-9
UNNNNGH!
© 1988 PAWS, INC. All Rights Reserved.
HYAH!
MY HERO
JIM DAVIS

I needed to put Garfield on his hind feet in order to let him dance in his first animated special. I liked it so well, I left him upright. It was actually Charles Schulz who did the first drawing of Garfield standing on his back feet.

IT'S GOING TO BE ONE OF THOSE MONDAYS

JIM DAVIS 11-14

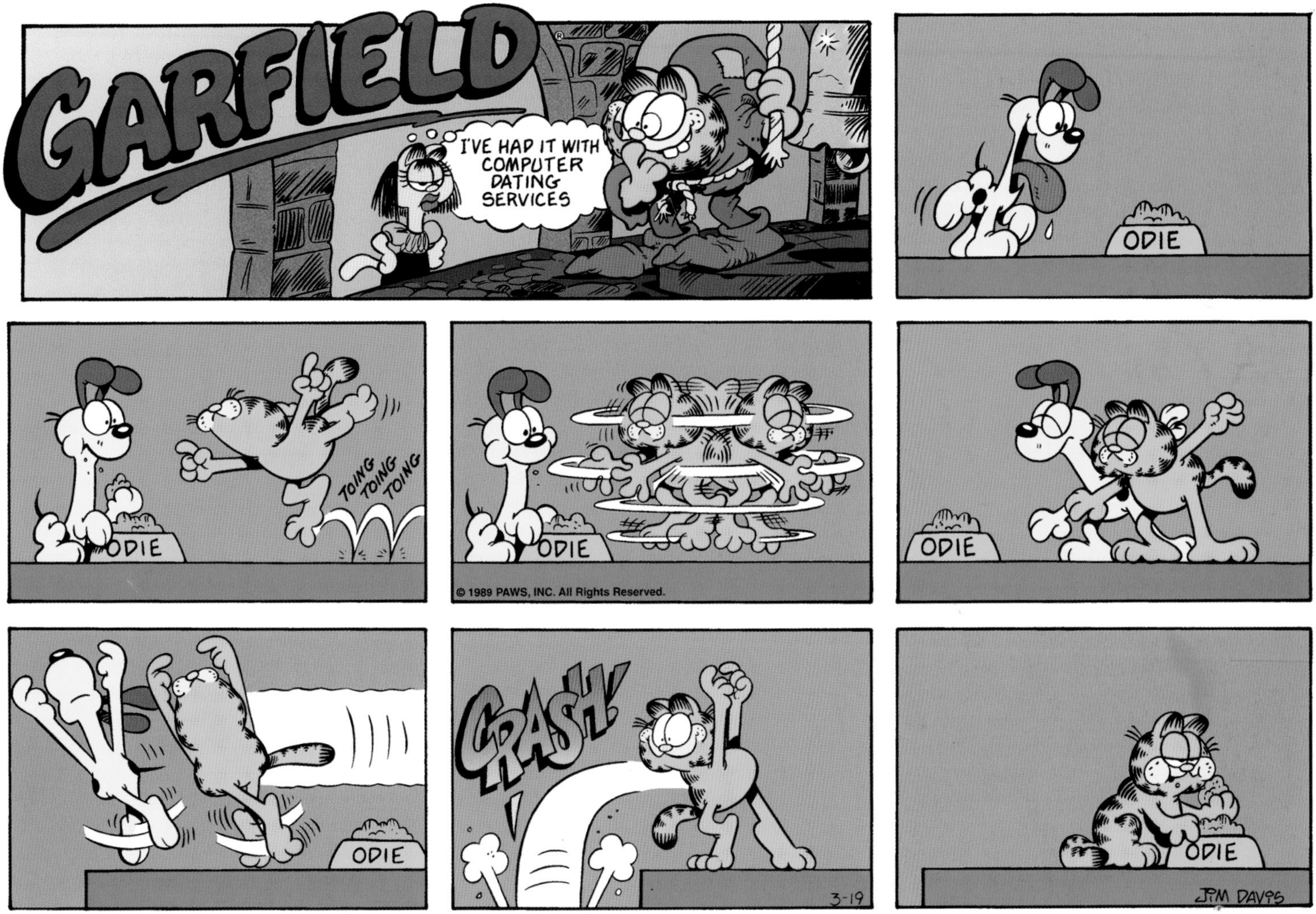
GARFIELD
I'VE HAD IT WITH COMPUTER DATING SERVICES
ODIE
ODIE
TOING TOING TOING
ODIE
© 1989 PAWS, INC. All Rights Reserved.
ODIE
ODIE
CRASH!
3-19
ODIE
JIM DAVIS

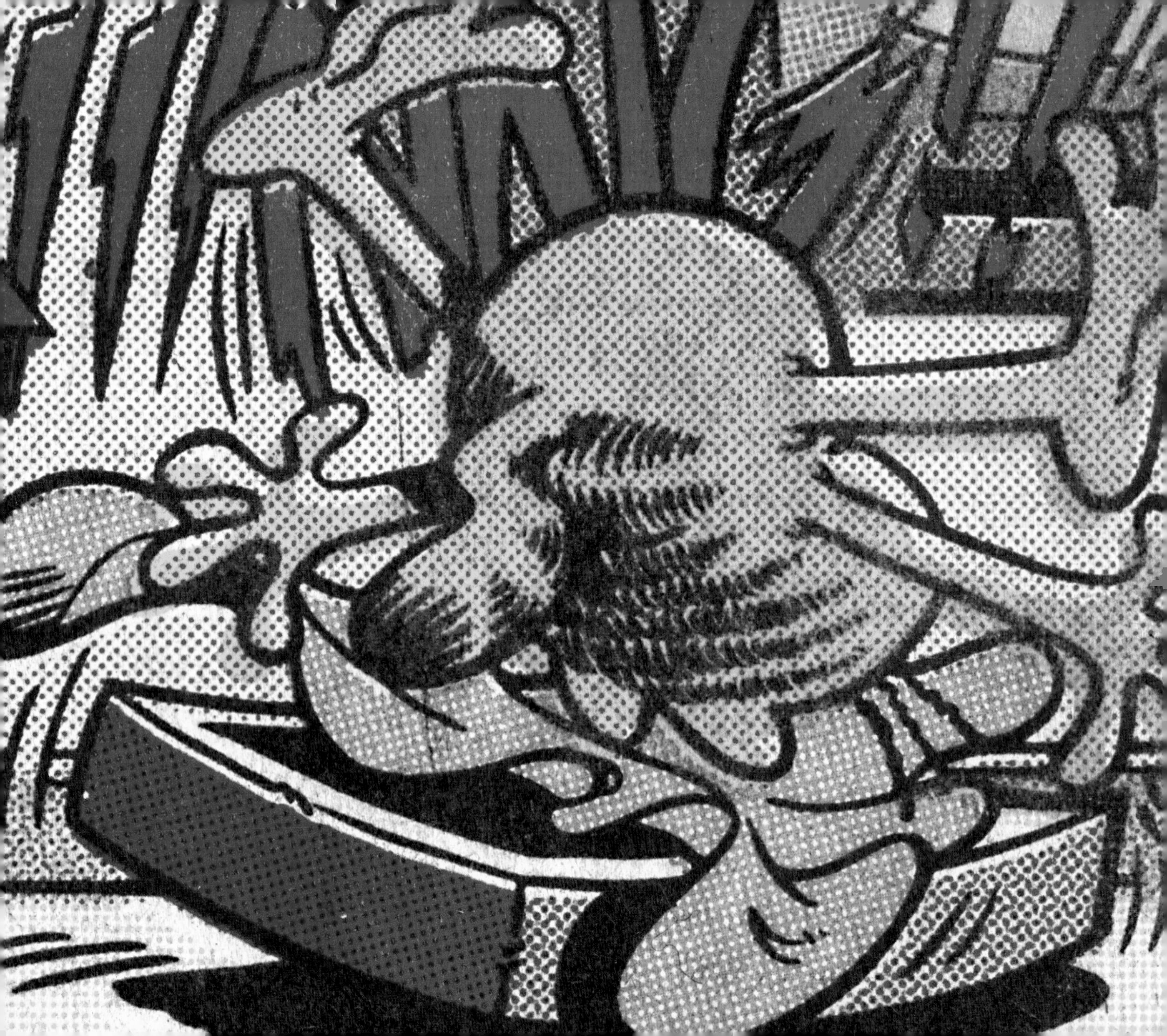

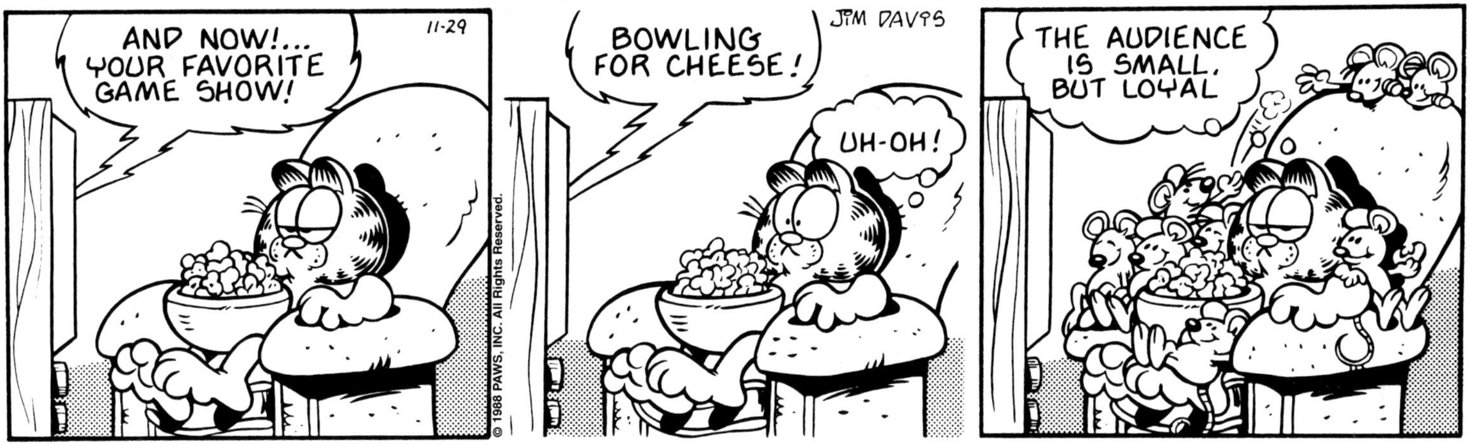
11-29
AND NOW!... YOUR FAVORITE GAME SHOW!
© 1988 PAWS, INC. All Rights Reserved.
JIM DAVIS
BOWLING FOR CHEESE!
UH-OH!
THE AUDIENCE IS SMALL, BUT LOYAL

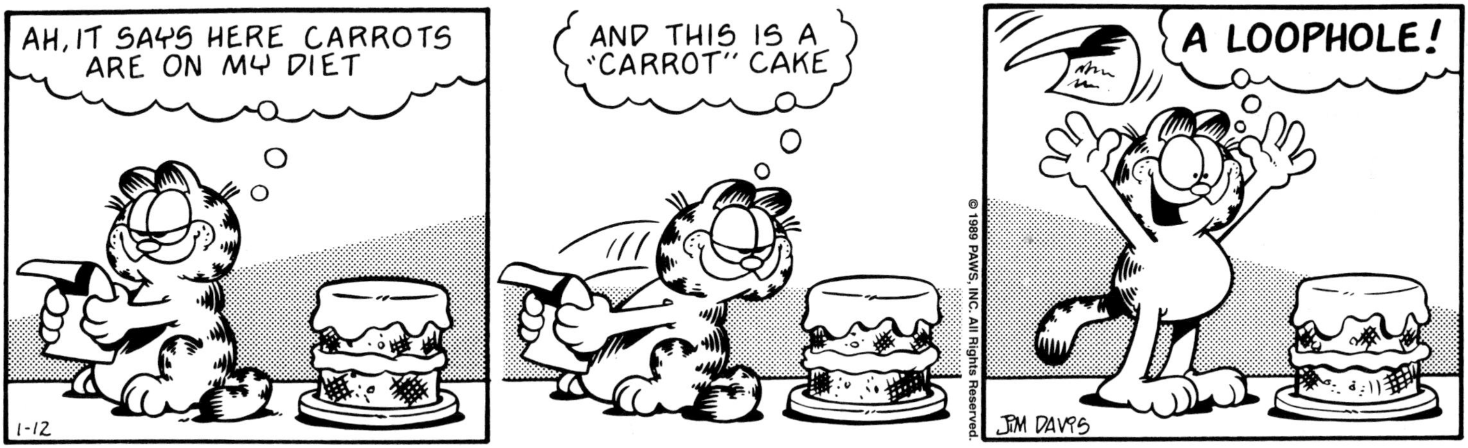
AH, IT SAYS HERE CARROTS ARE ON MY DIET
1-12
AND THIS IS A "CARROT" CAKE
© 1989 PAWS, INC. All Rights Reserved.
A LOOPHOLE!
JIM DAVIS

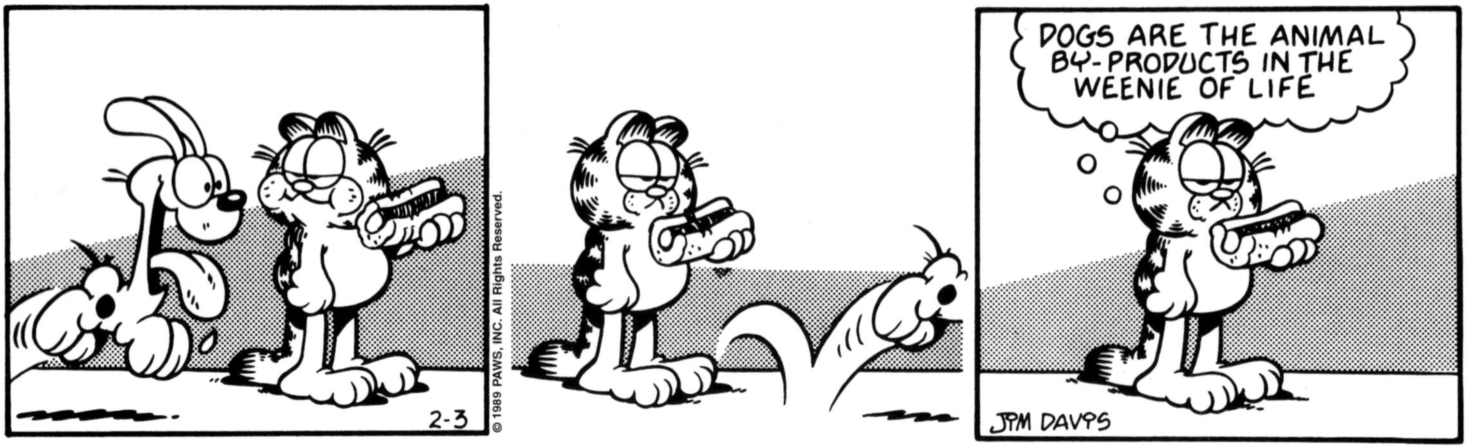
2-3
© 1989 PAWS, INC. All Rights Reserved.
DOGS ARE THE ANIMAL BY-PRODUCTS IN THE WEENIE OF LIFE
JIM DAVIS

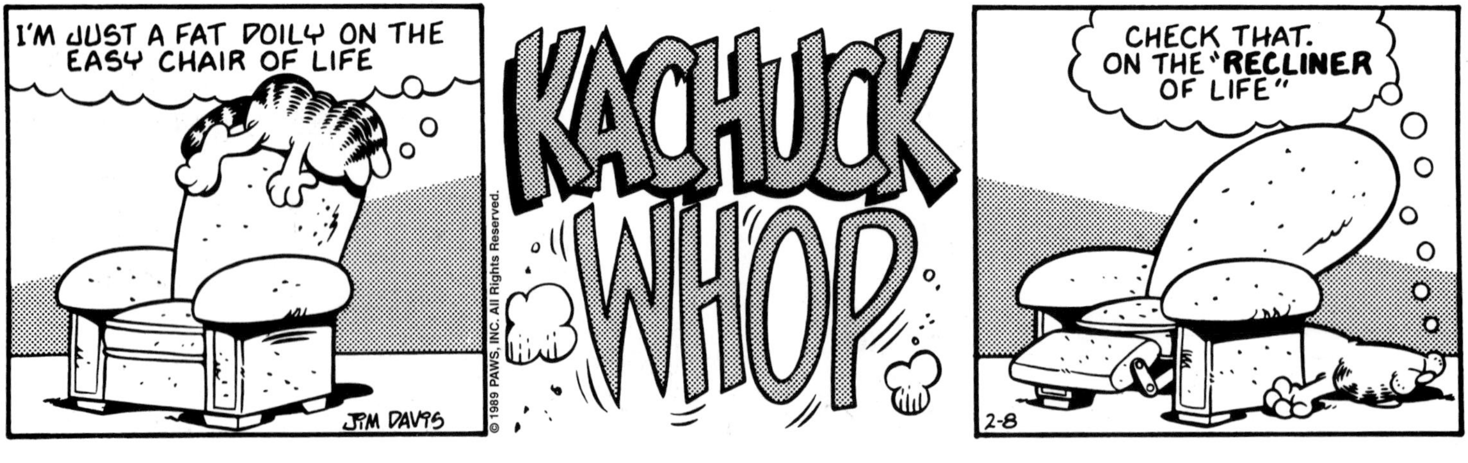
I'M JUST A FAT DOILY ON THE EASY CHAIR OF LIFE
JIM DAVIS
© 1989 PAWS, INC. All Rights Reserved.
KACHUCK
WHOP
CHECK THAT. ON THE "RECLINER OF LIFE"
2-8

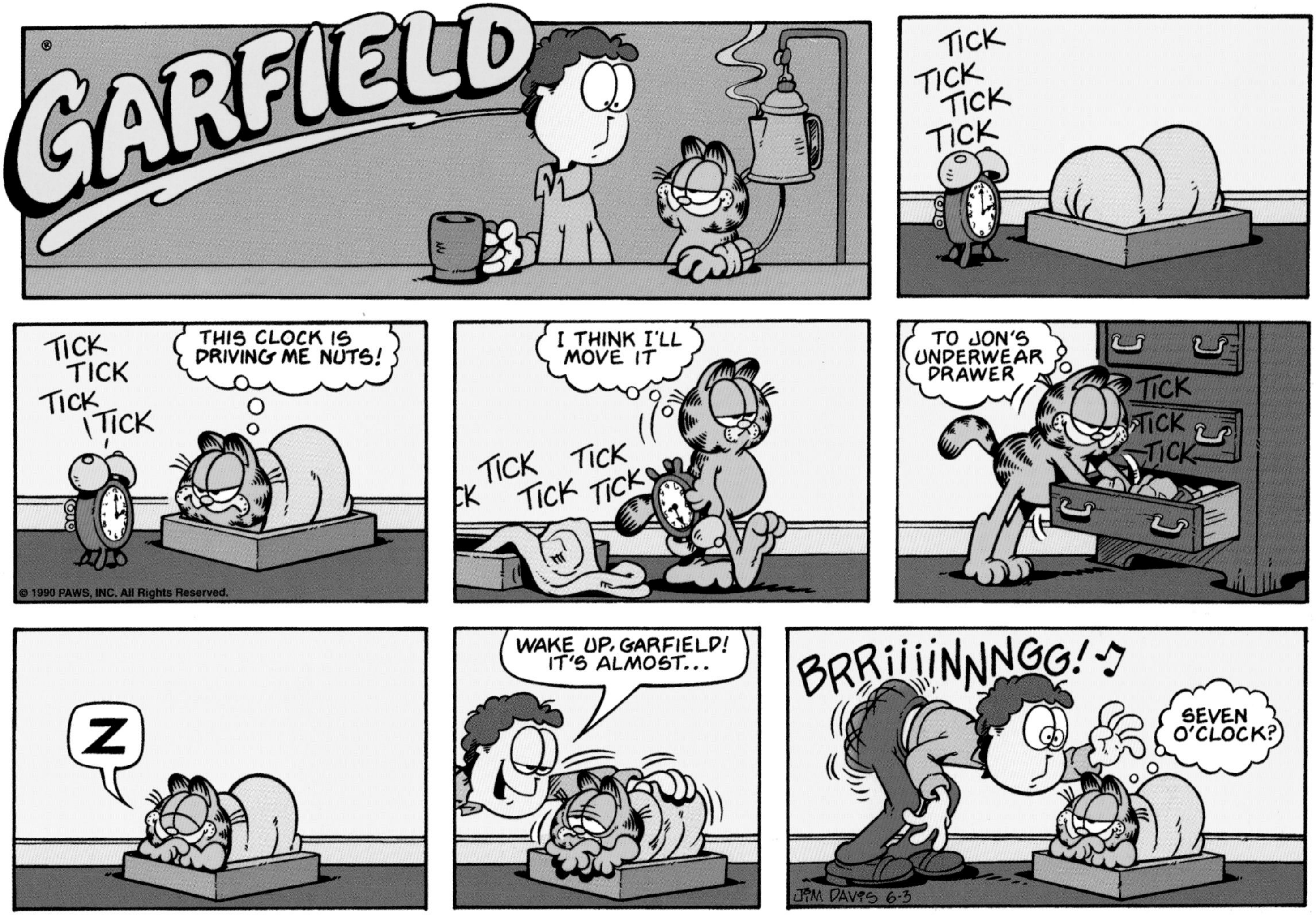
GARFIELD
TICK TICK TICK TICK
TICK TICK TICK TICK
THIS CLOCK IS DRIVING ME NUTS!
I THINK I'LL MOVE IT
TICK TICK TICK TICK
TO JON'S UNDERWEAR DRAWER
TICK TICK TICK
Z
WAKE UP, GARFIELD! IT'S ALMOST...
BRRiiiiNNNGG!
SEVEN O'CLOCK?
JIM DAVIS 6-3

Garfield's philosophy of life is to put yourself first. He is selfish, but unembarrassed by it. He pigs out and sleeps until noon and makes no apologies. Garfield is based on what I think all of us feel deep down inside—Garfield can get away with such bad behavior because he's a cat. If humans were to act this way, they would be despicable.

GARFIEL

HELLO? DEBBIE, MY SWEET?
YOU FAT GREEDY PIG! I OUGHTA SHAVE YOU BALD AND PUT YOU OUT IN THE COLD
CLICK
HELLO?
© 1989 PAWS, INC. All Rights Reserved.
5-30
JIM DAVIS

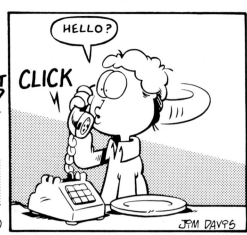

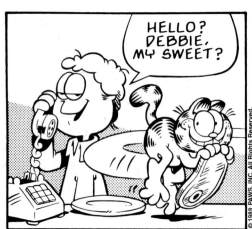

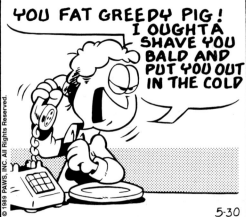

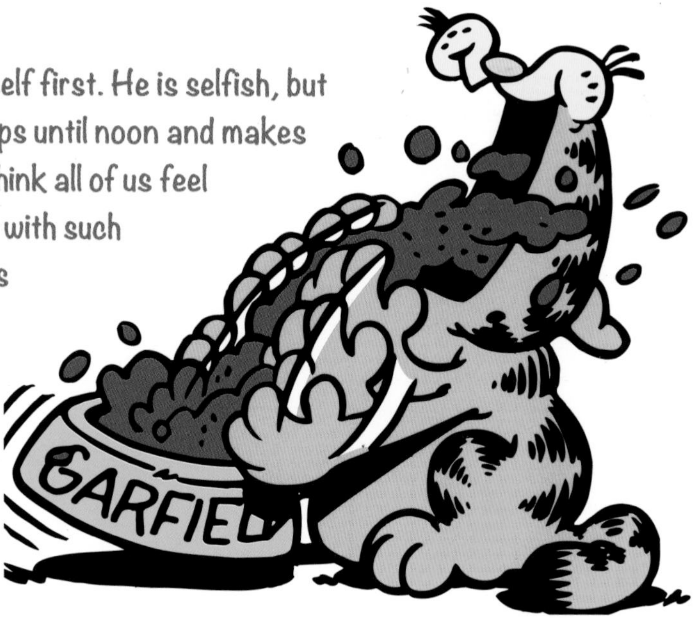

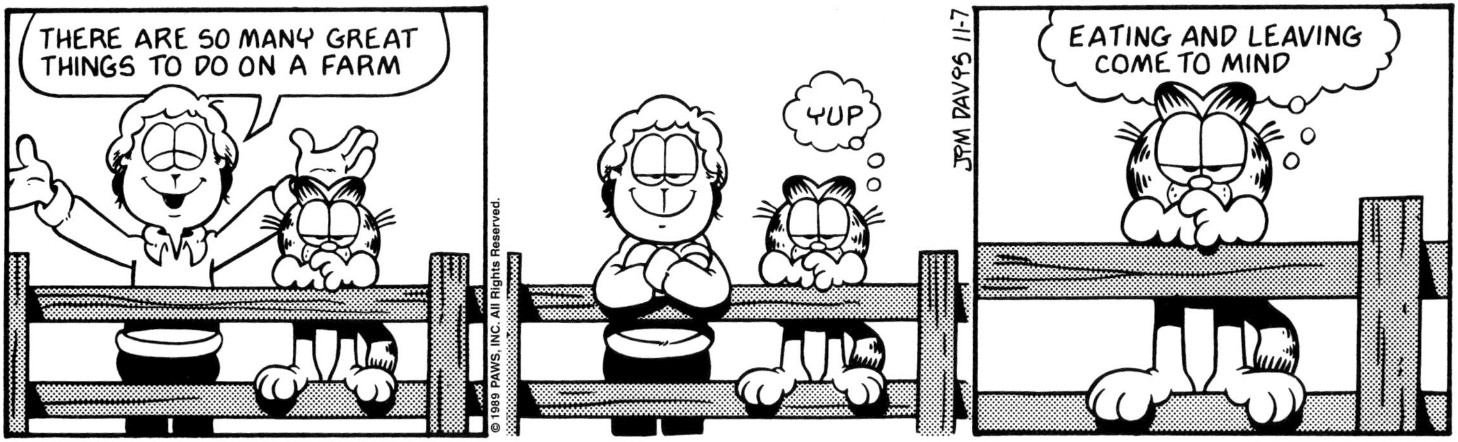
THERE ARE SO MANY GREAT THINGS TO DO ON A FARM
YUP
EATING AND LEAVING COME TO MIND
© 1989 PAWS, INC. All Rights Reserved.
JIM DAVIS 11-7

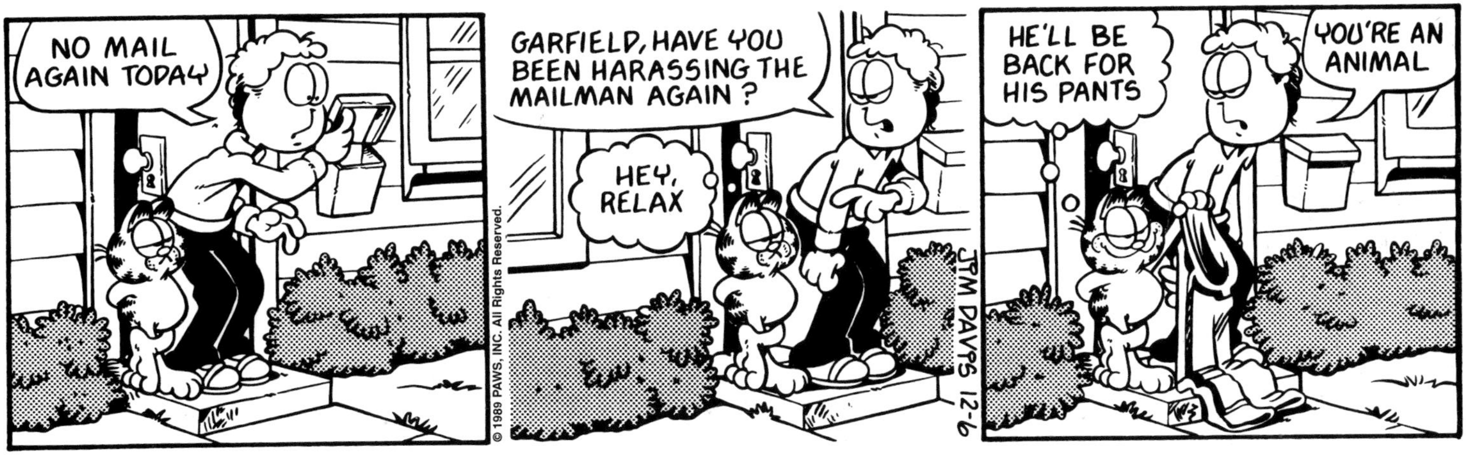
NO MAIL AGAIN TODAY
GARFIELD, HAVE YOU BEEN HARASSING THE MAILMAN AGAIN ?
HEY, RELAX
HE'LL BE BACK FOR HIS PANTS
YOU'RE AN ANIMAL
© 1989 PAWS, INC. All Rights Reserved.
JIM DAVIS 12-6

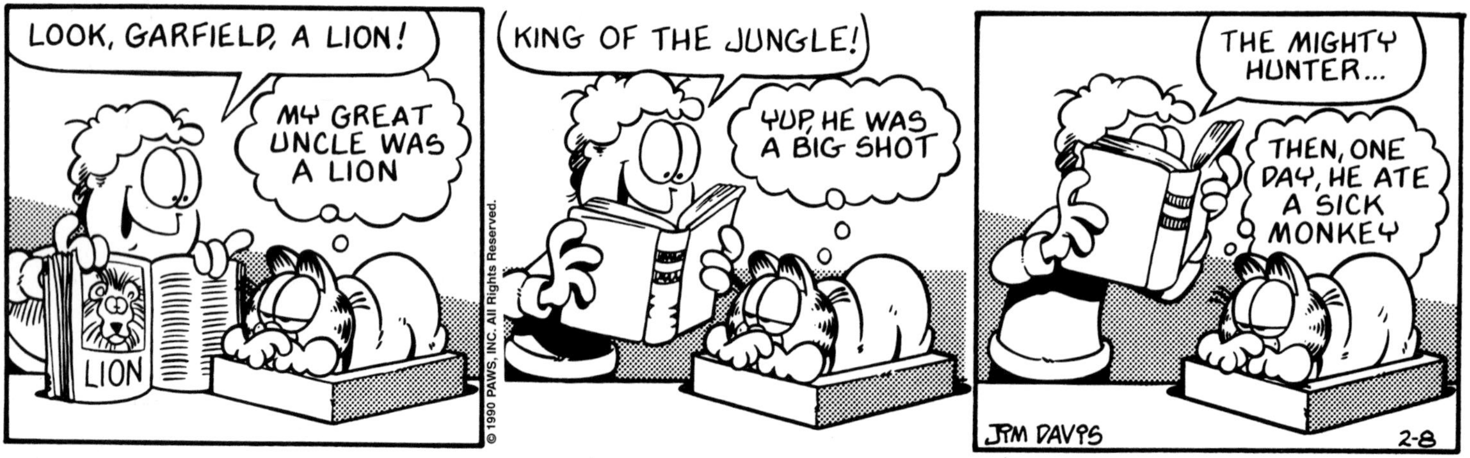
LOOK, GARFIELD, A LION!
MY GREAT UNCLE WAS A LION
LION
KING OF THE JUNGLE!
YUP, HE WAS A BIG SHOT
THE MIGHTY HUNTER...
THEN, ONE DAY, HE ATE A SICK MONKEY
JIM DAVIS
2-8
© 1990 PAWS, INC. All Rights Reserved.

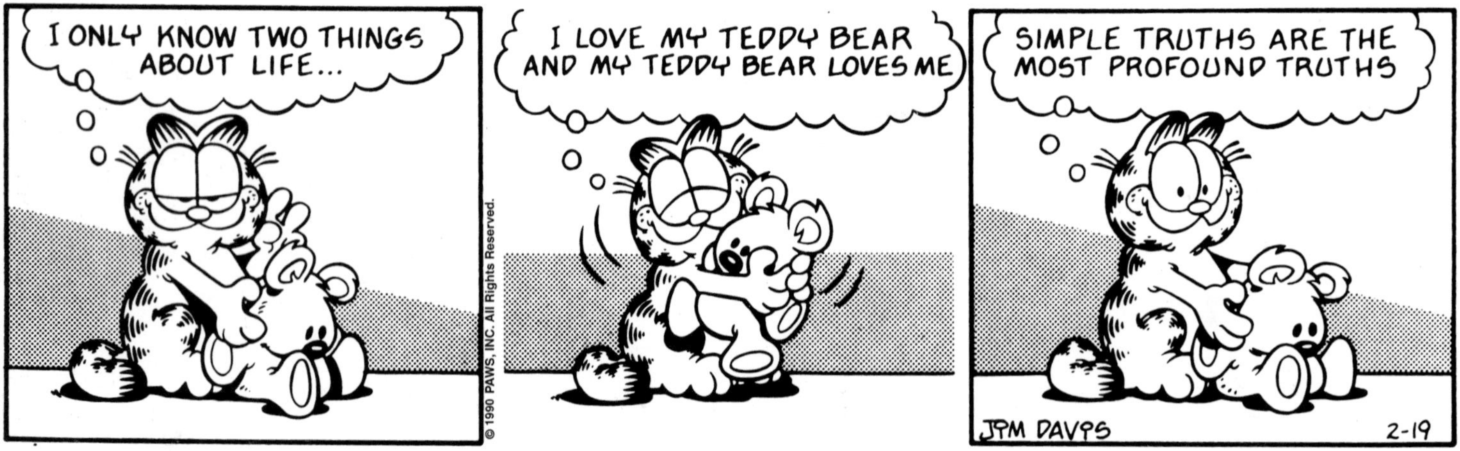
I ONLY KNOW TWO THINGS ABOUT LIFE...
I LOVE MY TEDDY BEAR AND MY TEDDY BEAR LOVES ME
SIMPLE TRUTHS ARE THE MOST PROFOUND TRUTHS
JIM DAVIS
2-19
© 1990 PAWS, INC. All Rights Reserved.

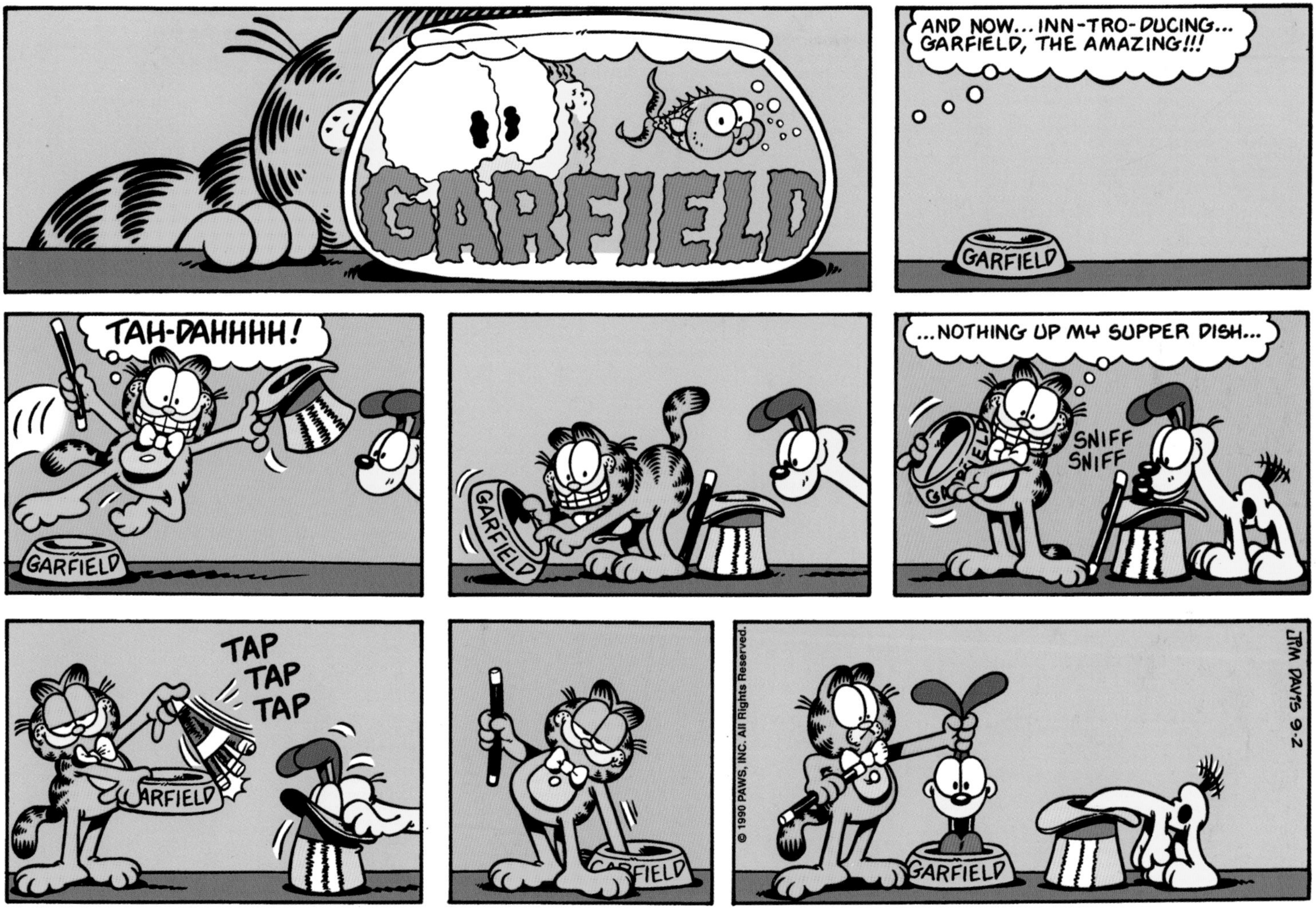
GARFIELD
AND NOW... INN-TRO-DUCING... GARFIELD, THE AMAZING!!!
GARFIELD
TAH-DAHHHH!
GARFIELD
GARFIELD
...NOTHING UP MY SUPPER DISH...
SNIFF SNIFF
TAP TAP TAP
© 1990 PAWS, INC. All Rights Reserved.
JIM DAVIS 9-2
GARFIELD

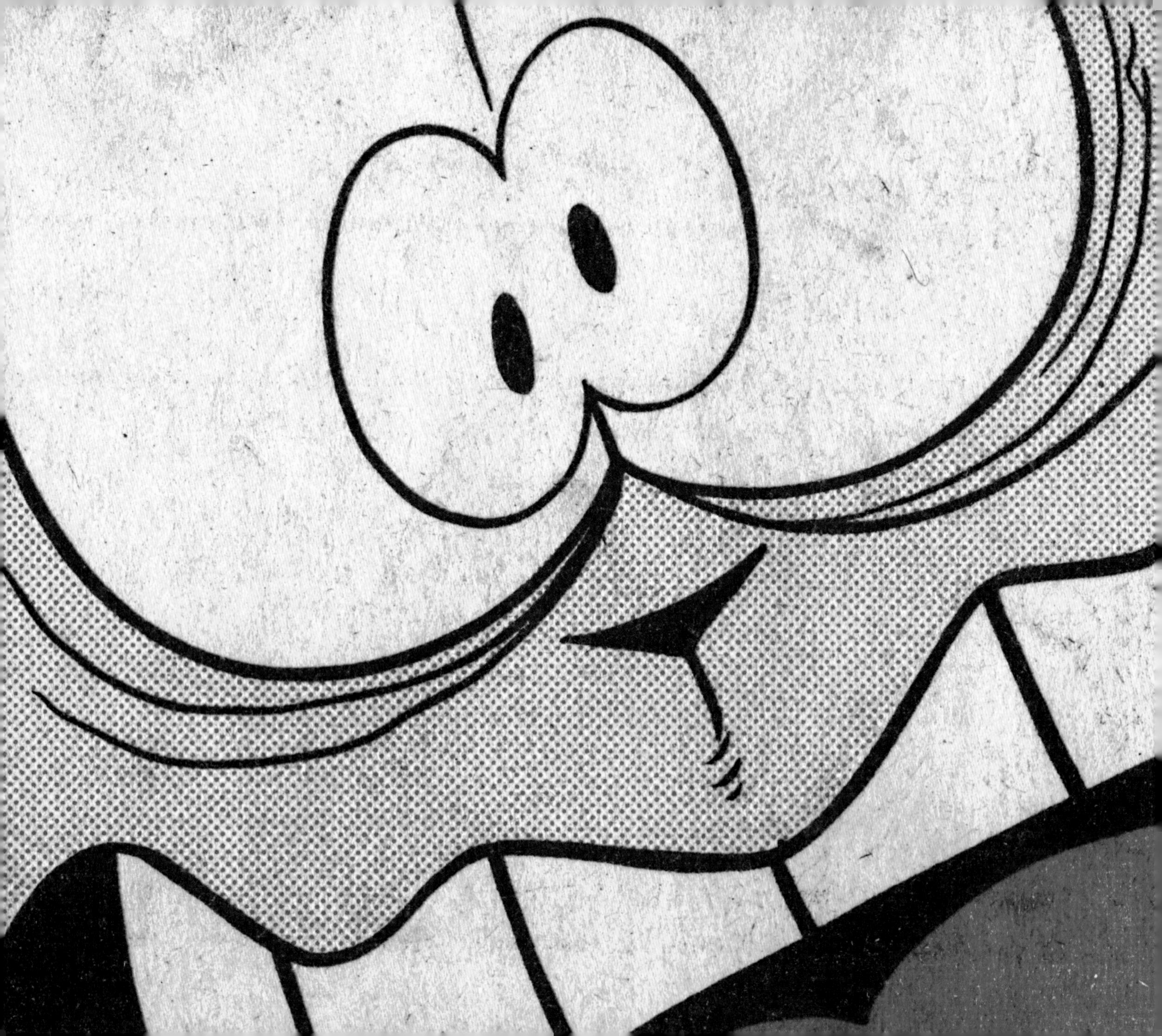

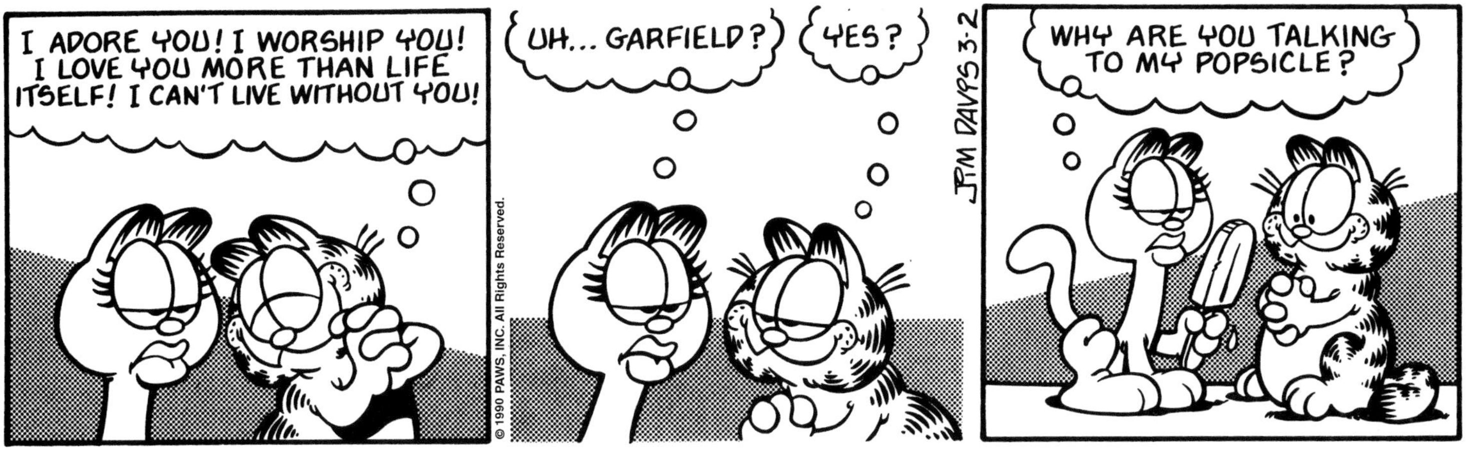
I ADORE YOU! I WORSHIP YOU! I LOVE YOU MORE THAN LIFE ITSELF! I CAN'T LIVE WITHOUT YOU!
UH... GARFIELD?
YES?
WHY ARE YOU TALKING TO MY POPSICLE?
© 1990 PAWS, INC. All Rights Reserved.

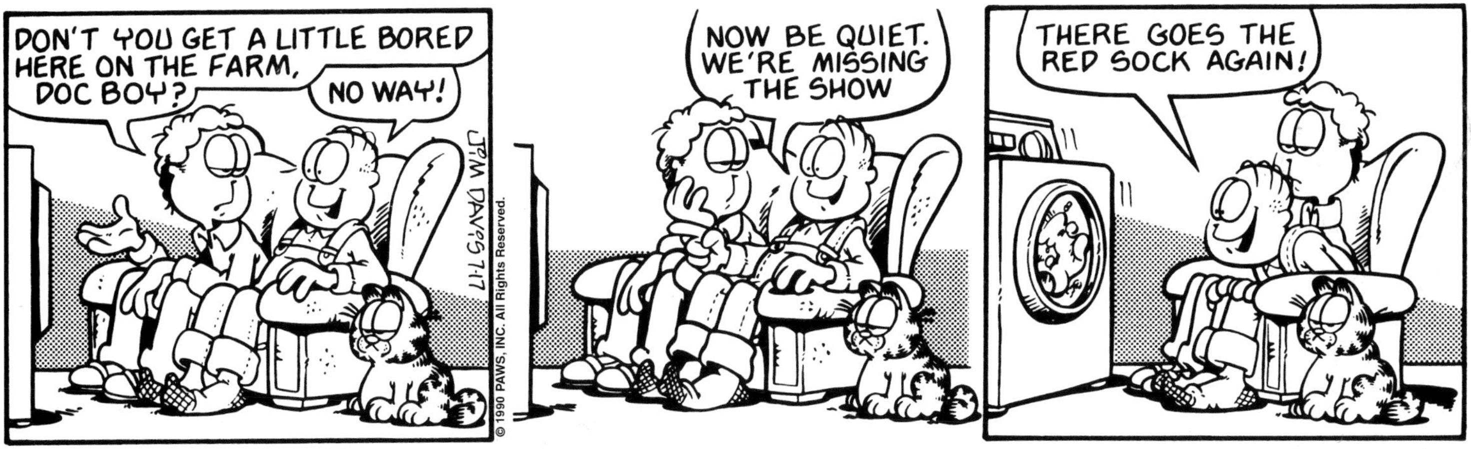
DON'T YOU GET A LITTLE BORED HERE ON THE FARM, DOC BOY?
NO WAY!
NOW BE QUIET. WE'RE MISSING THE SHOW
THERE GOES THE RED SOCK AGAIN!
© 1990 PAWS, INC. All Rights Reserved.

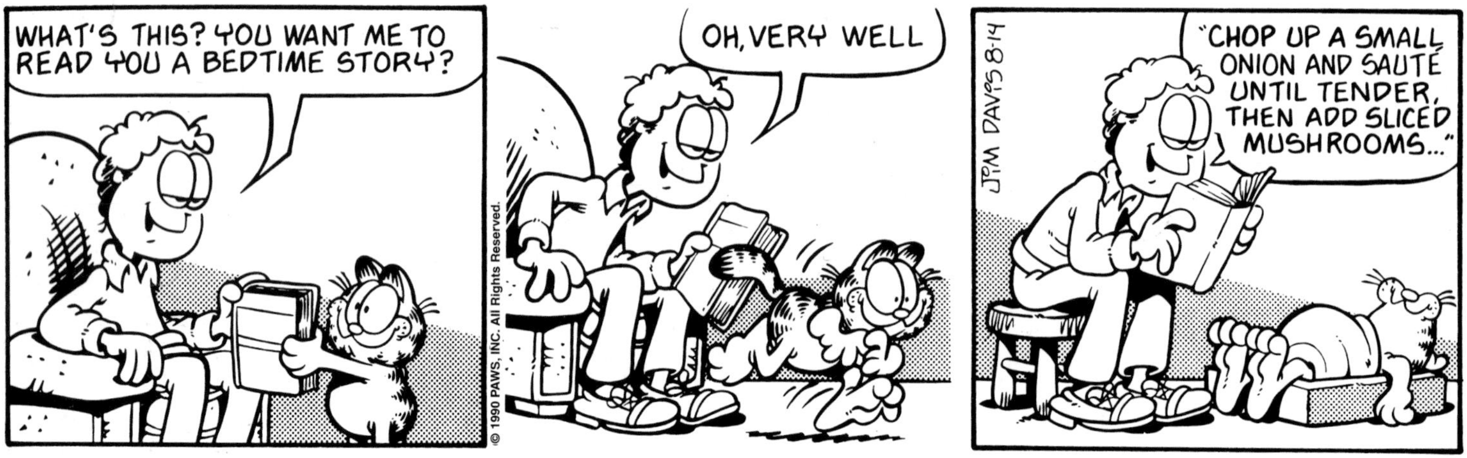
WHAT'S THIS? YOU WANT ME TO READ YOU A BEDTIME STORY?
OH, VERY WELL
© 1990 PAWS, INC. All Rights Reserved.
JIM DAVIS 8-14
"CHOP UP A SMALL ONION AND SAUTÉ UNTIL TENDER, THEN ADD SLICED MUSHROOMS..."

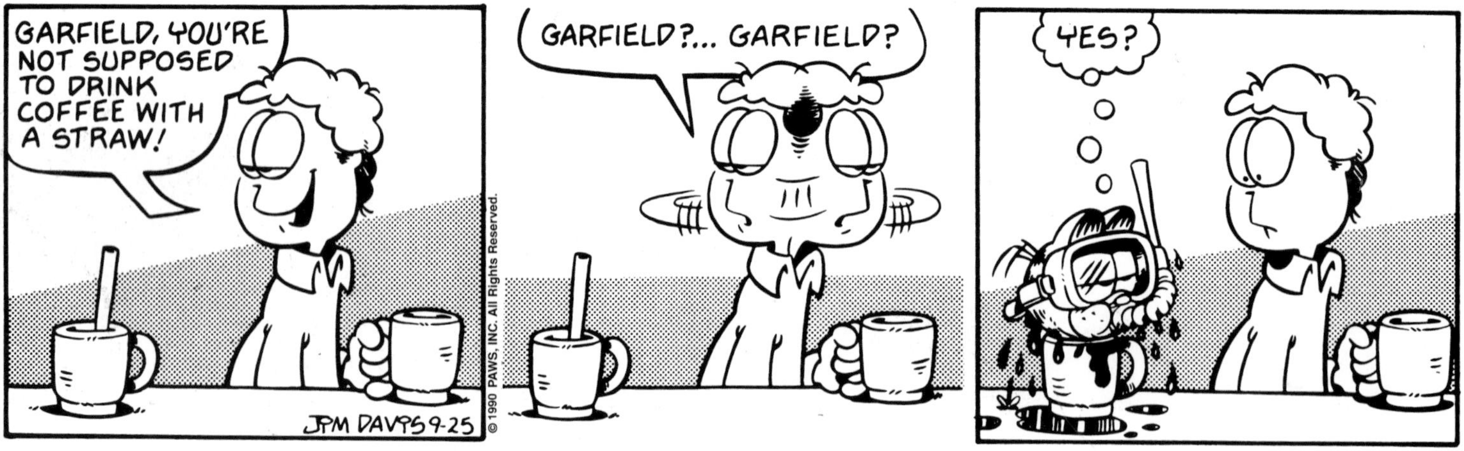
GARFIELD, YOU'RE NOT SUPPOSED TO DRINK COFFEE WITH A STRAW!
JIM DAVIS 9-25
© 1990 PAWS, INC. All Rights Reserved.
GARFIELD?... GARFIELD?
YES?

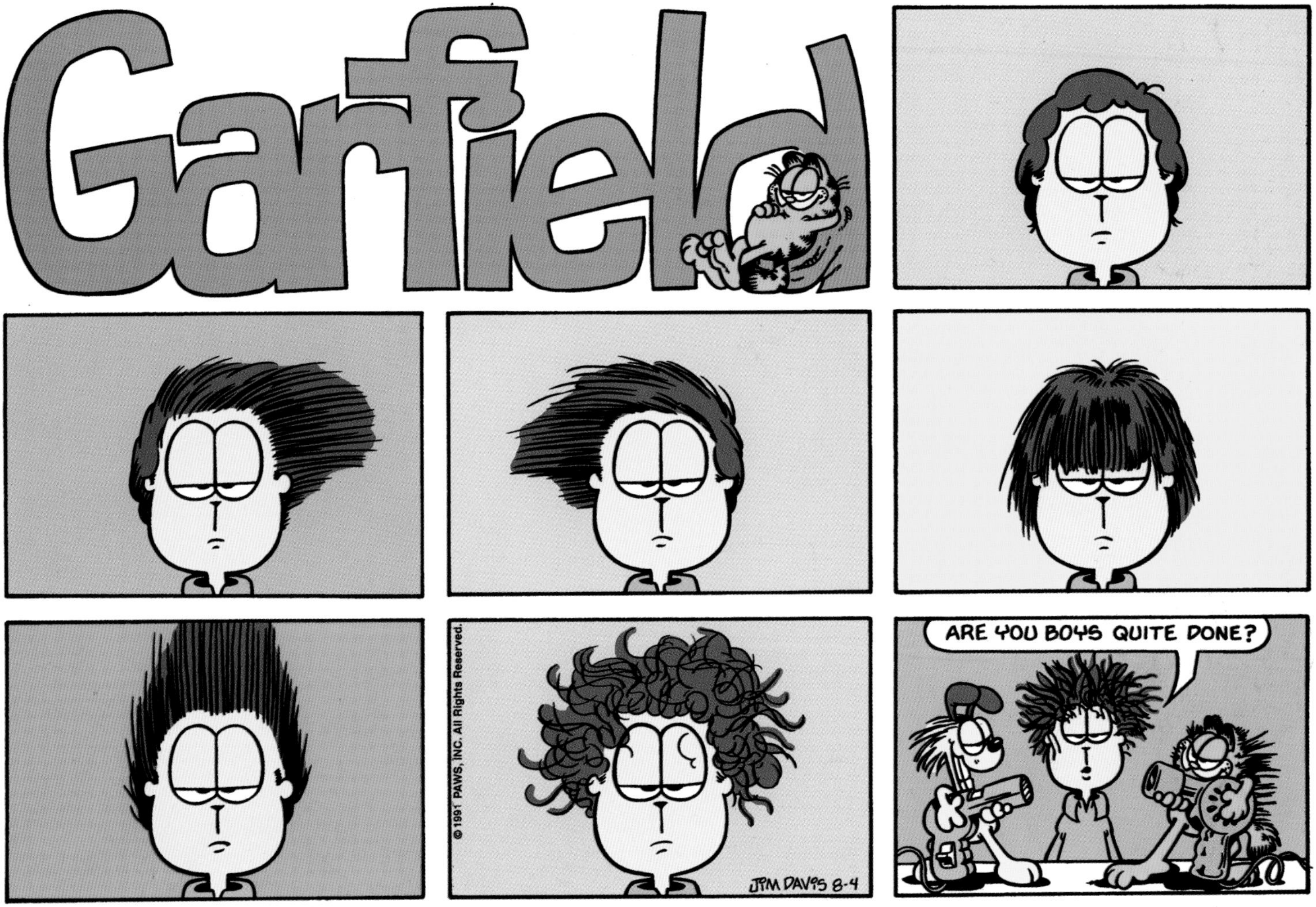
Garfield
© 1991 PAWS, INC. All Rights Reserved.
JIM DAVIS 8-4
ARE YOU BOYS QUITE DONE?

POOKY

My wife and I also named our Yorkshire terrier Pooky. Some days I call him "Poopy."

NERMAL

Nermal has one job: to annoy Garfield. Nermal is the little brother who won't leave you alone. Boy, does Garfield hate that.

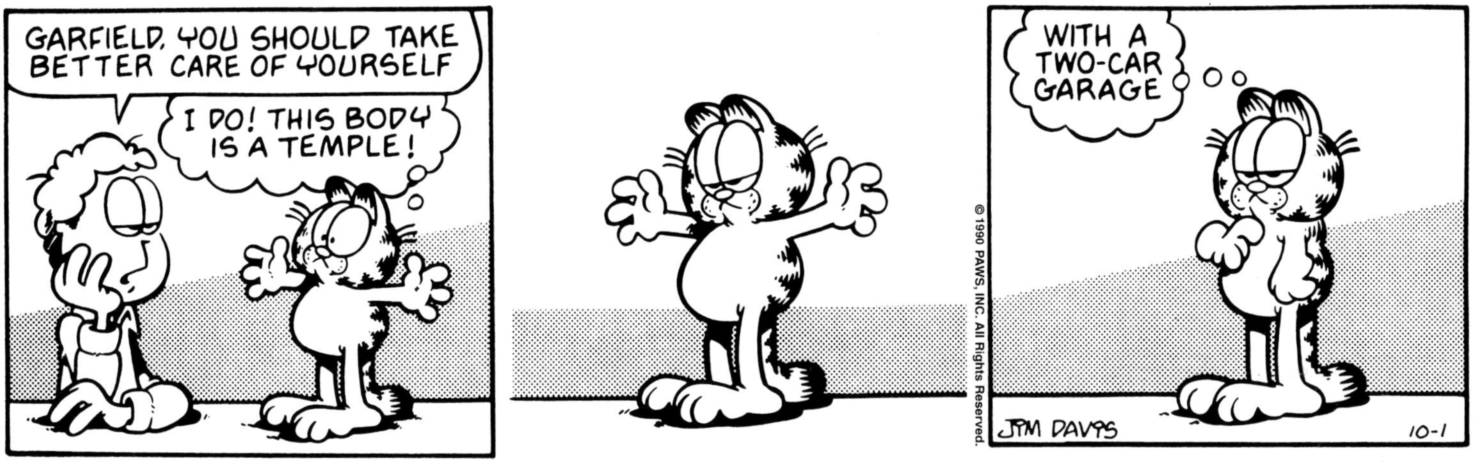
GARFIELD, YOU SHOULD TAKE BETTER CARE OF YOURSELF
I DO! THIS BODY IS A TEMPLE!
WITH A TWO-CAR GARAGE
© 1990 PAWS, INC. All Rights Reserved.
JIM DAVIS
10-1

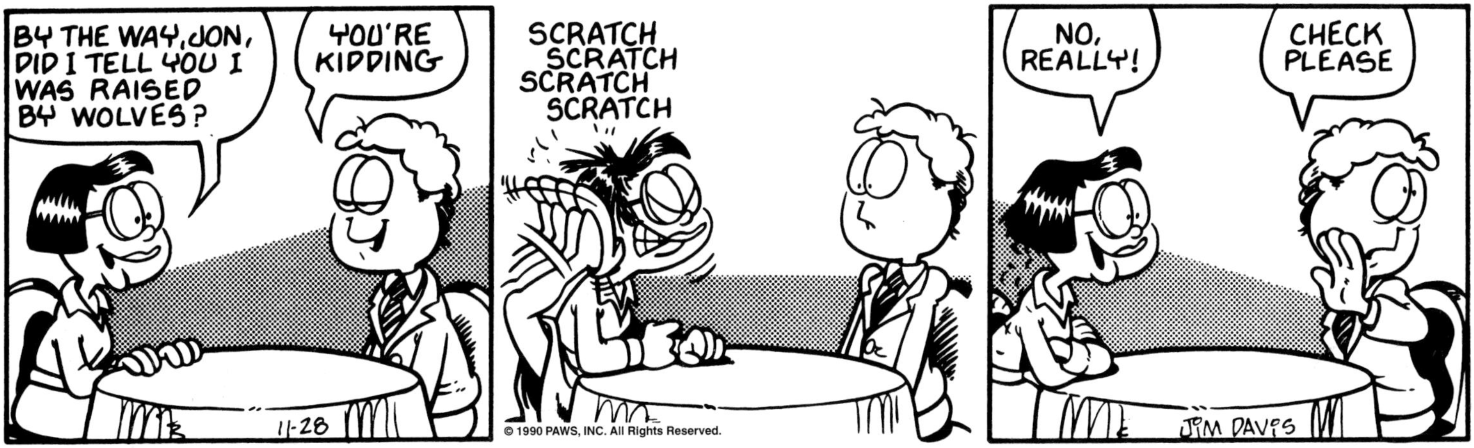
BY THE WAY, JON, DID I TELL YOU I WAS RAISED BY WOLVES?
YOU'RE KIDDING
11-28
SCRATCH SCRATCH SCRATCH SCRATCH
© 1990 PAWS, INC. All Rights Reserved.
NO, REALLY!
CHECK PLEASE
JIM DAVIS

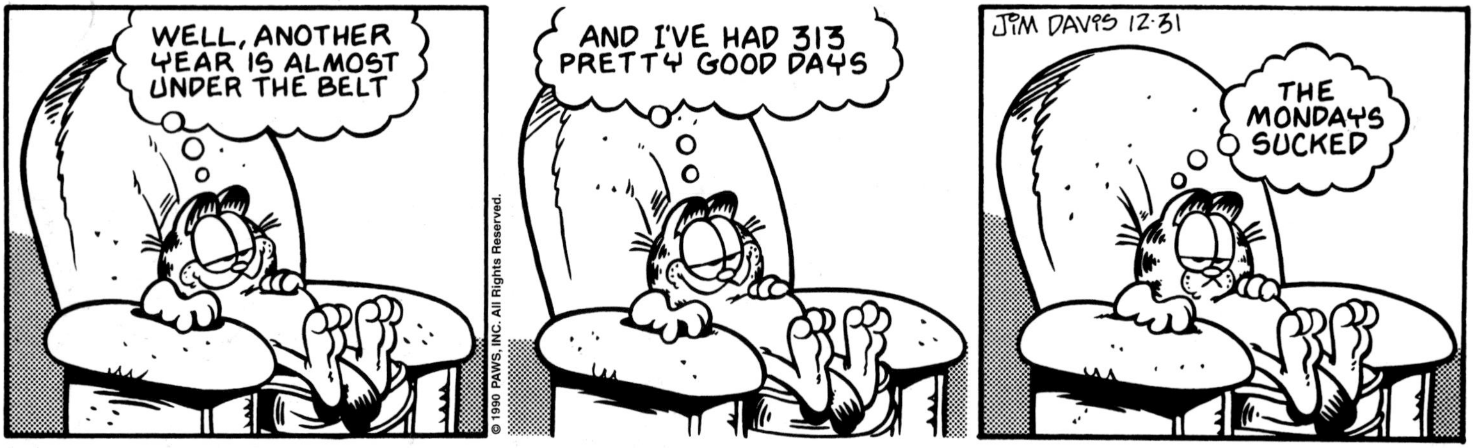
WELL, ANOTHER YEAR IS ALMOST UNDER THE BELT
AND I'VE HAD 313 PRETTY GOOD DAYS
JIM DAVIS 12-31
THE MONDAYS SUCKED

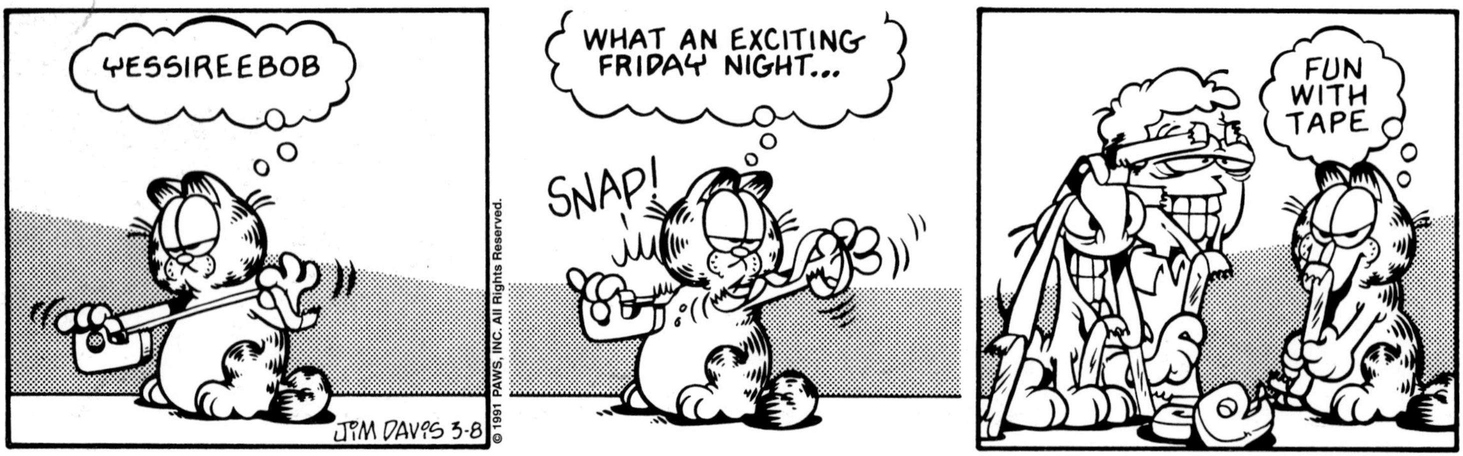
YESSIREEBOB
JIM DAVIS 3-8
WHAT AN EXCITING FRIDAY NIGHT...
SNAP!
FUN WITH TAPE

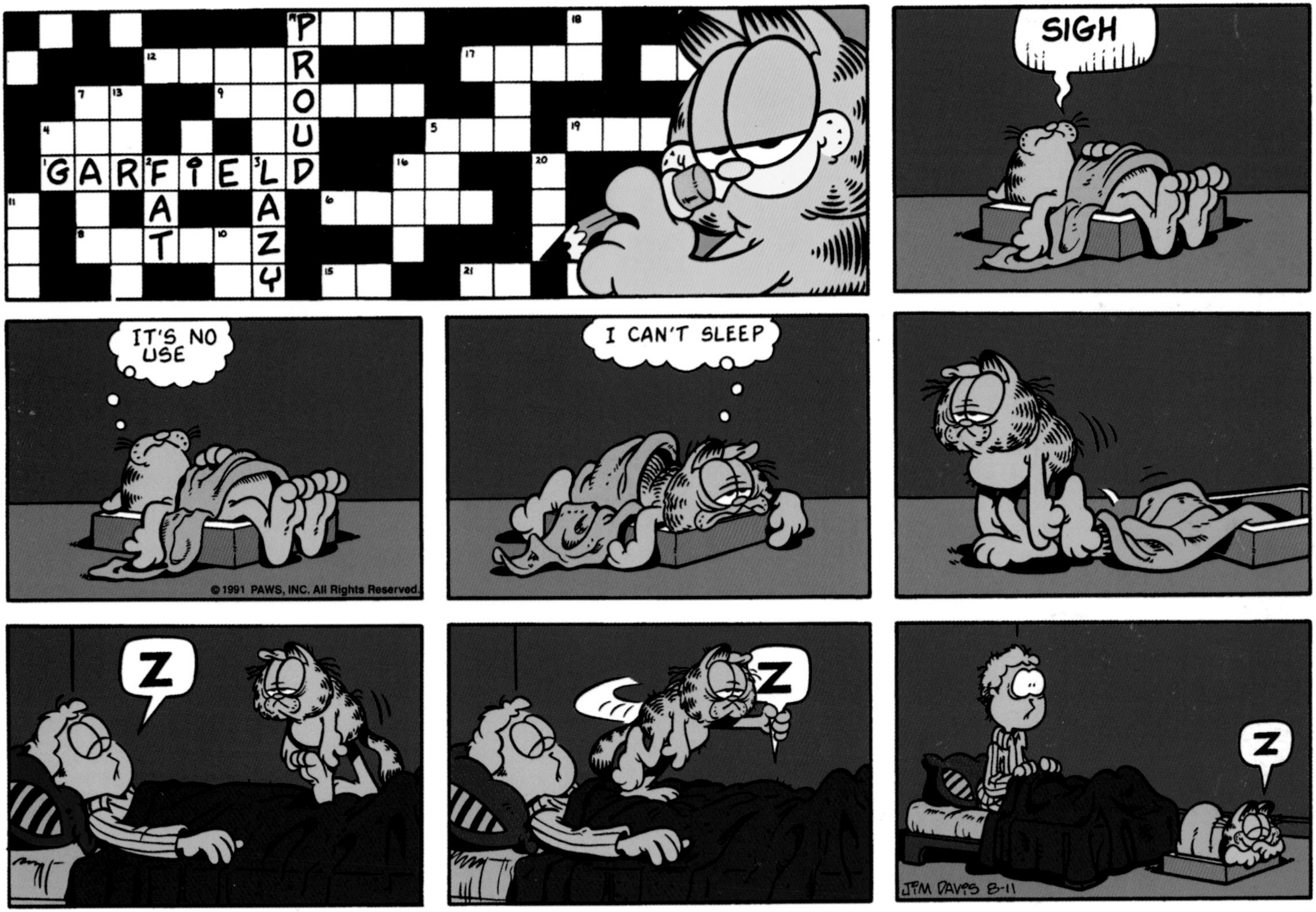

GARFIELD
PROUD
FAT
LAZY
SIGH
IT'S NO USE
I CAN'T SLEEP
© 1991 PAWS, INC. All Rights Reserved.
Z
Z
Z
JIM DAVIS 8-11

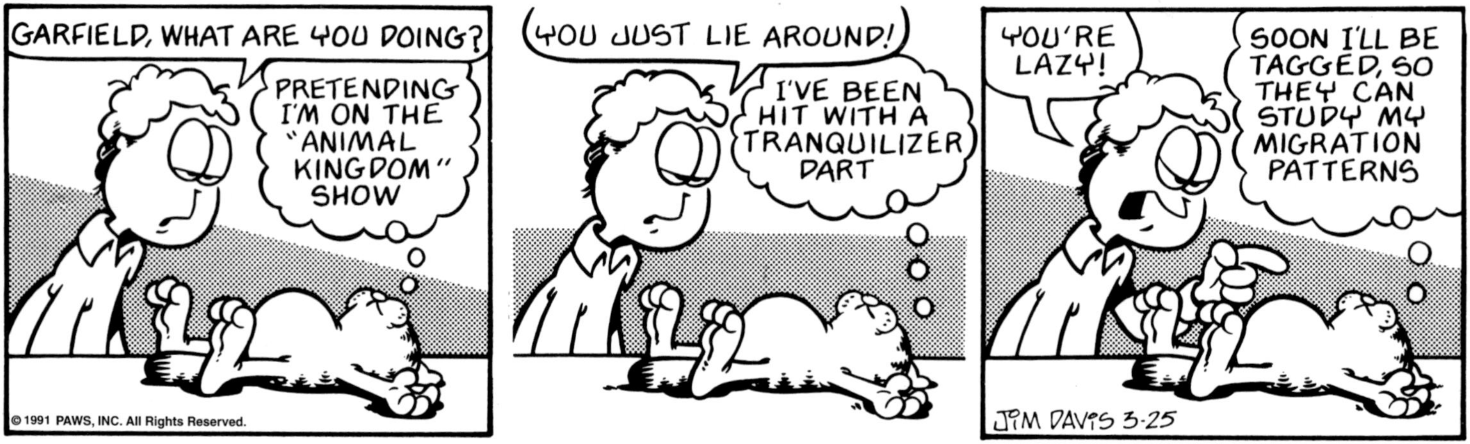
GARFIELD, WHAT ARE YOU DOING?
PRETENDING I'M ON THE "ANIMAL KINGDOM" SHOW
YOU JUST LIE AROUND!
I'VE BEEN HIT WITH A TRANQUILIZER DART
YOU'RE LAZY!
SOON I'LL BE TAGGED, SO THEY CAN STUDY MY MIGRATION PATTERNS
© 1991 PAWS, INC. All Rights Reserved.
JIM DAVIS 3-25

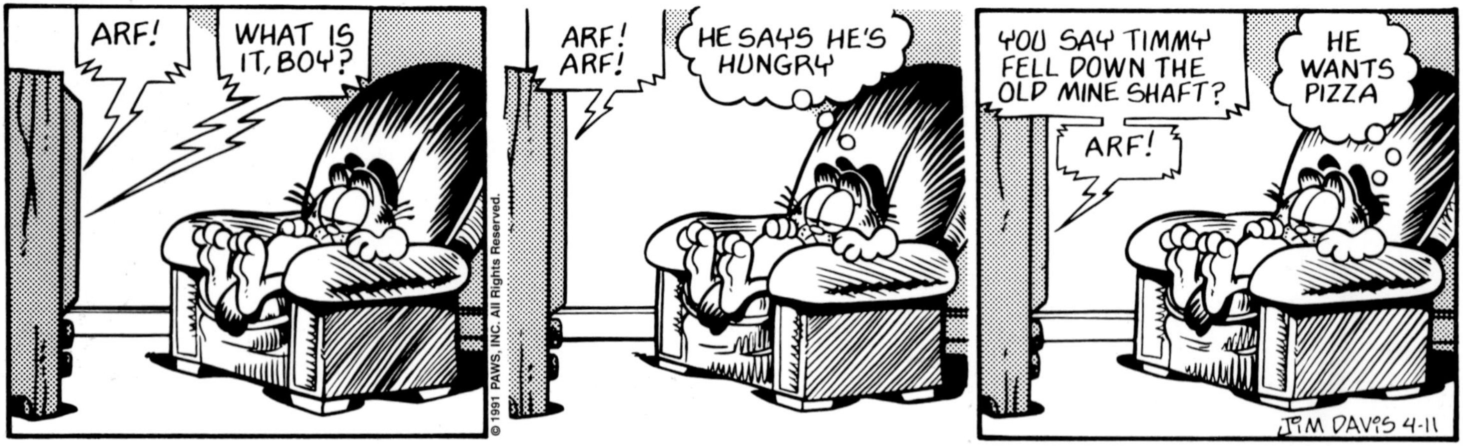
ARF!
WHAT IS IT, BOY?
ARF! ARF!
HE SAYS HE'S HUNGRY
YOU SAY TIMMY FELL DOWN THE OLD MINE SHAFT?
ARF!
HE WANTS PIZZA
© 1991 PAWS, INC. All Rights Reserved.
JIM DAVIS 4-11

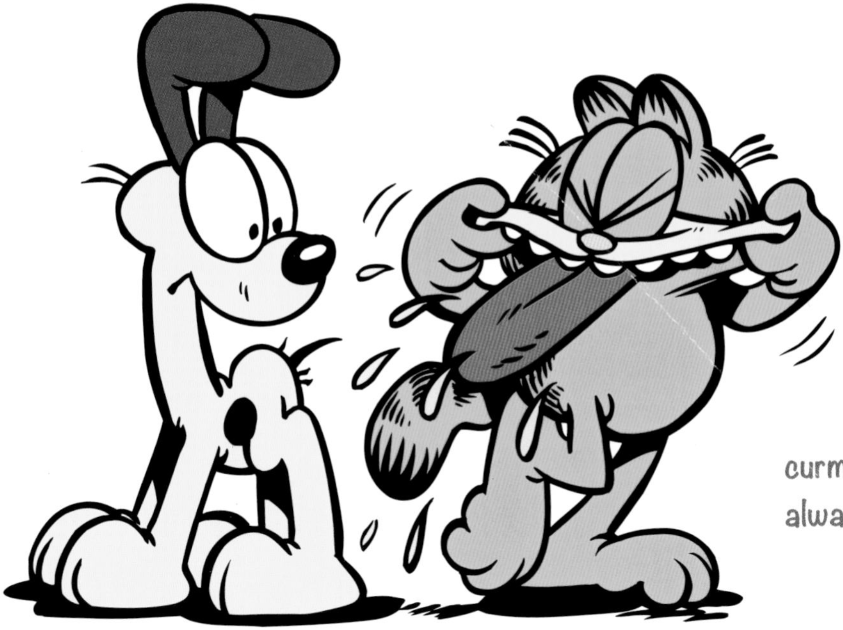

When I was developing Garfield in 1976, *All in the Family* was very popular, and Archie Bunker would say awful things and get laughs. Of course, that kind of character, the crusty old curmudgeon with a heart of gold, has always been popular.

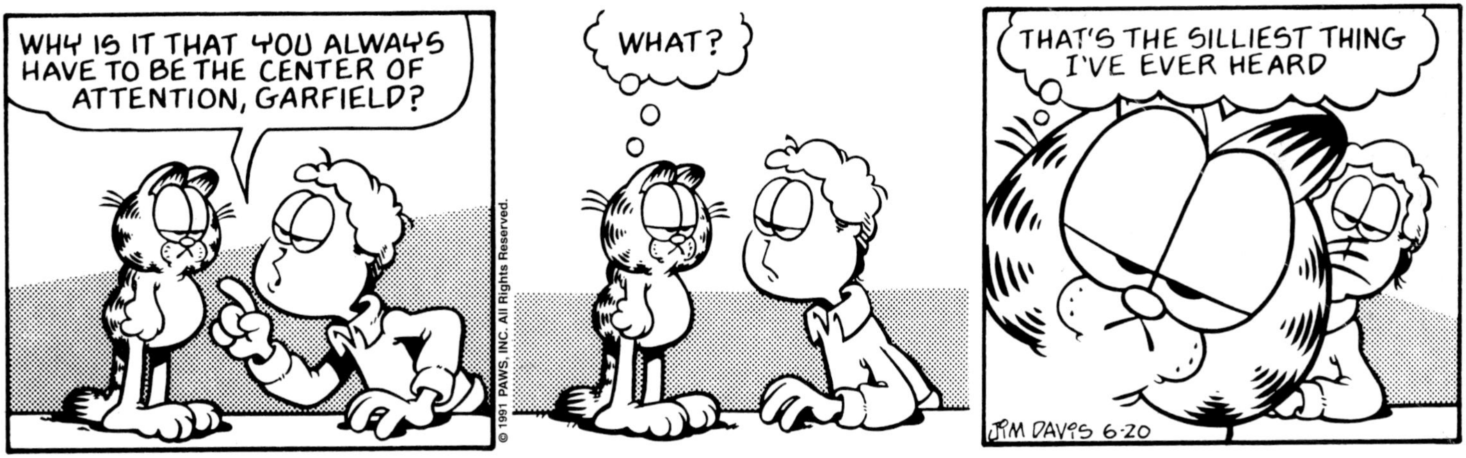
WHY IS IT THAT YOU ALWAYS HAVE TO BE THE CENTER OF ATTENTION, GARFIELD?
WHAT?
THAT'S THE SILLIEST THING I'VE EVER HEARD
JIM DAVIS 6-20

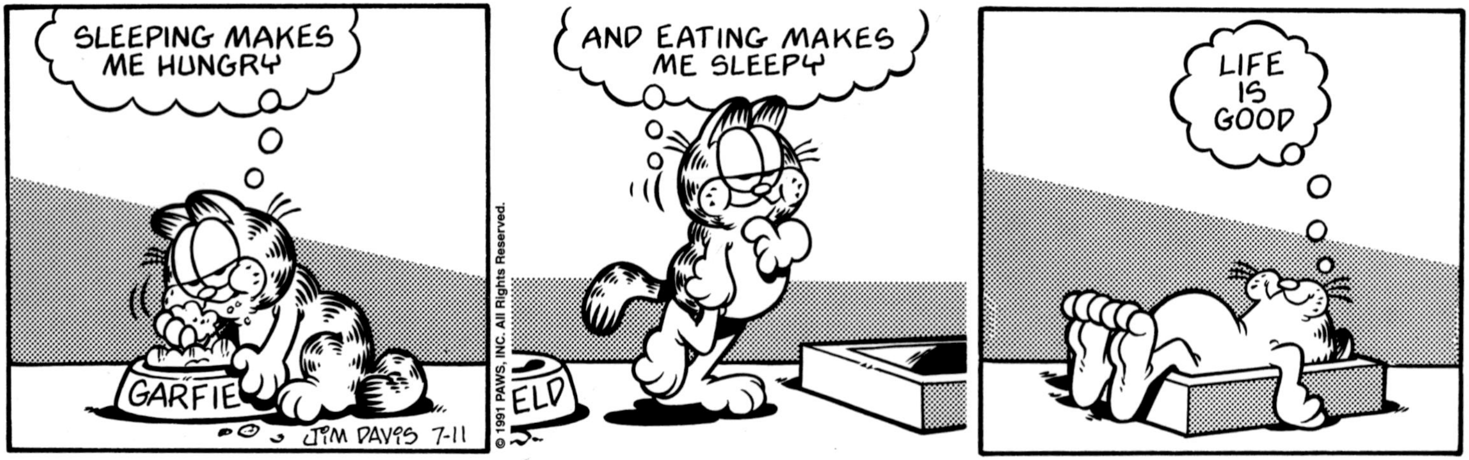
SLEEPING MAKES ME HUNGRY
GARFIELD
JIM DAVIS 7-11
© 1991 PAWS, INC. All Rights Reserved.
AND EATING MAKES ME SLEEPY
LIFE IS GOOD

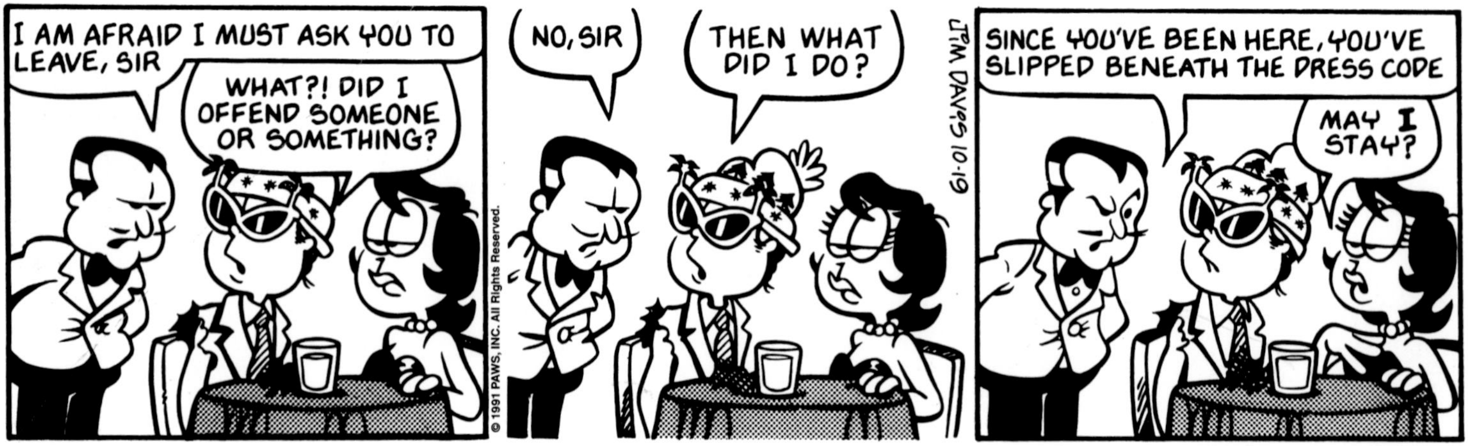
I AM AFRAID I MUST ASK YOU TO LEAVE, SIR
WHAT?! DID I OFFEND SOMEONE OR SOMETHING?
© 1991 PAWS, INC. All Rights Reserved.
NO, SIR
THEN WHAT DID I DO?
JIM DAVIS 10-19
SINCE YOU'VE BEEN HERE, YOU'VE SLIPPED BENEATH THE DRESS CODE
MAY I STAY?

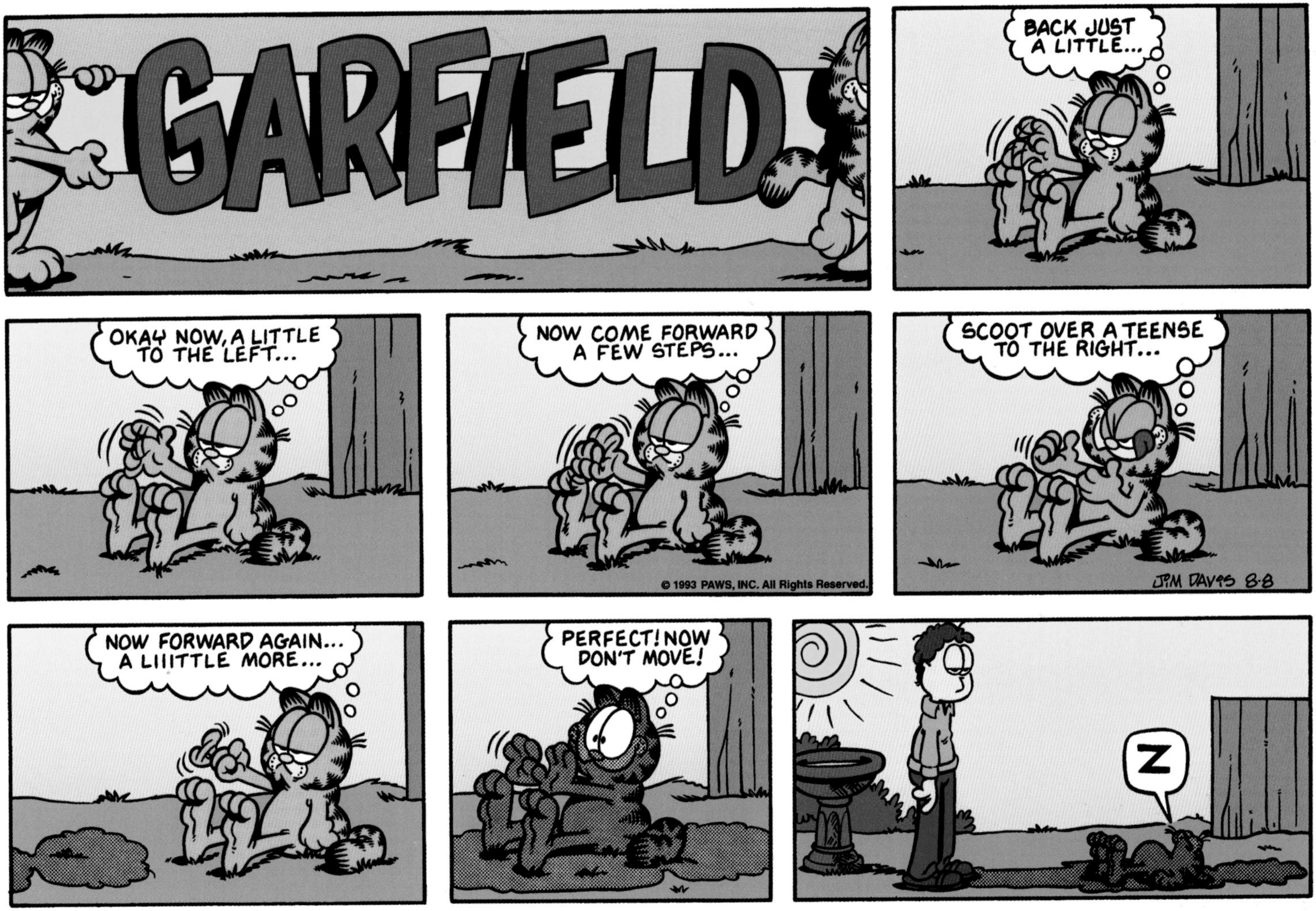
GARFIELD
BACK JUST A LITTLE...
OKAY NOW, A LITTLE TO THE LEFT...
NOW COME FORWARD A FEW STEPS...
SCOOT OVER A TEENSE TO THE RIGHT...
© 1993 PAWS, INC. All Rights Reserved.
JIM DAVIS 8-8
NOW FORWARD AGAIN... A LIIITTLE MORE...
PERFECT! NOW DON'T MOVE!
Z

Nothing funny ever occurs to me unless I'm concentrating on it very hard. I've never been able to observe a situation or have a gag pop into my mind during the night. I have to go in search of gag ideas. I once likened it to walking into a dark closet, taking gags off the shelf, and bringing them out. In the early days of *Garfield,* I never knew how big that closet was.

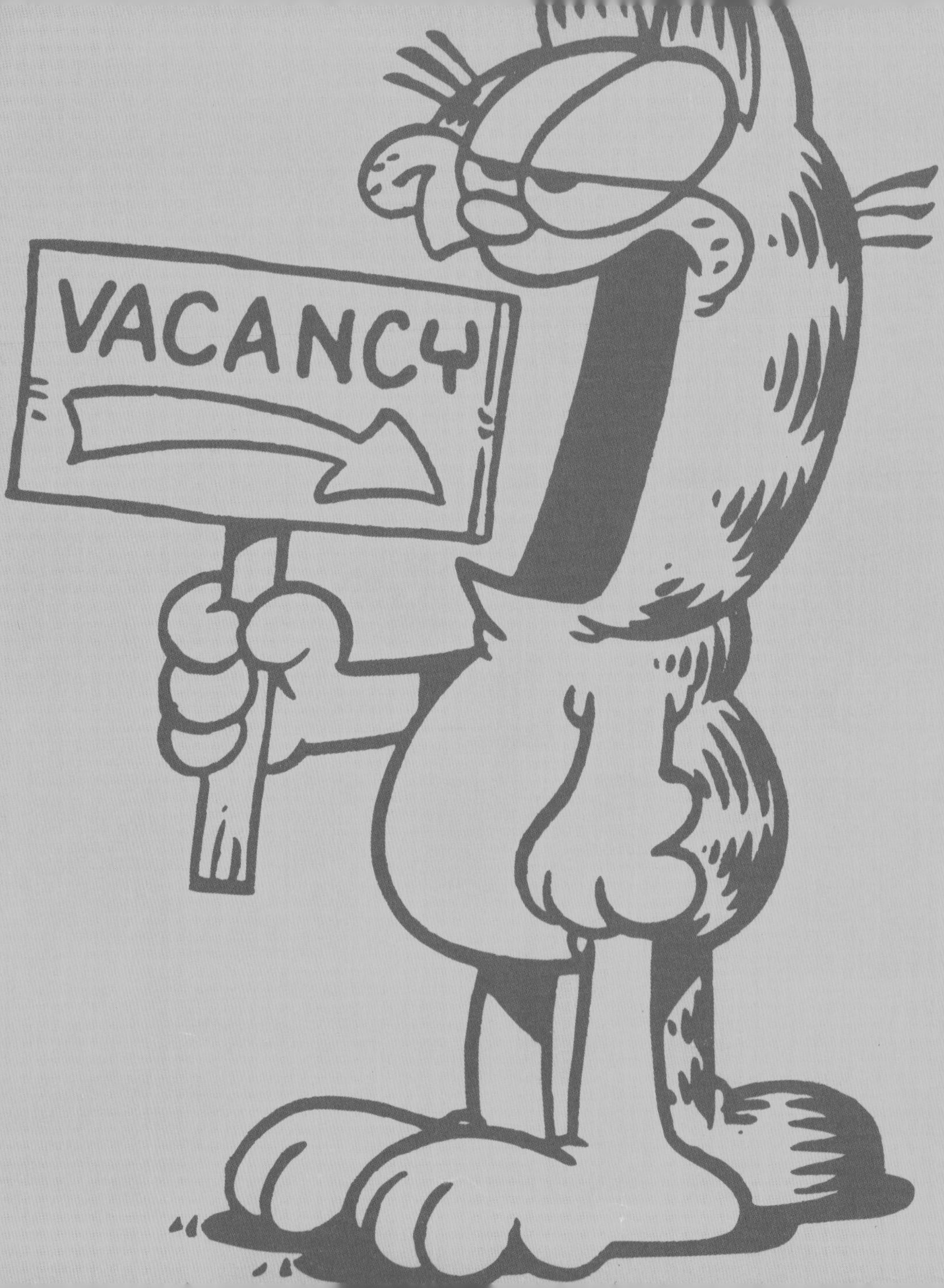
VACANCY

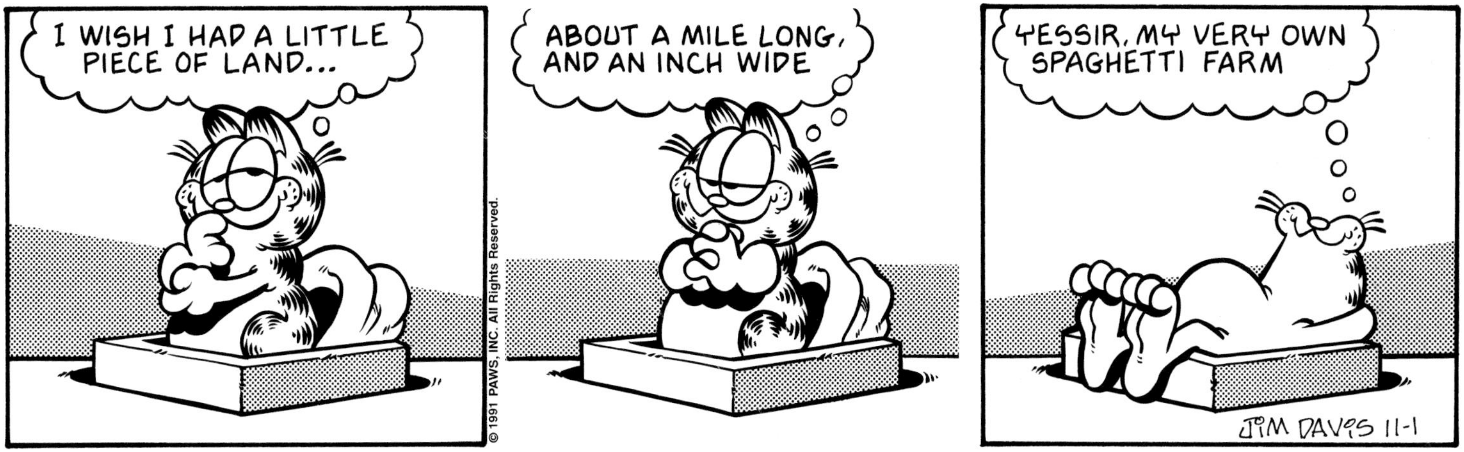
I WISH I HAD A LITTLE PIECE OF LAND...
ABOUT A MILE LONG, AND AN INCH WIDE
YESSIR, MY VERY OWN SPAGHETTI FARM
© 1991 PAWS, INC. All Rights Reserved.
JIM DAVIS 11-1

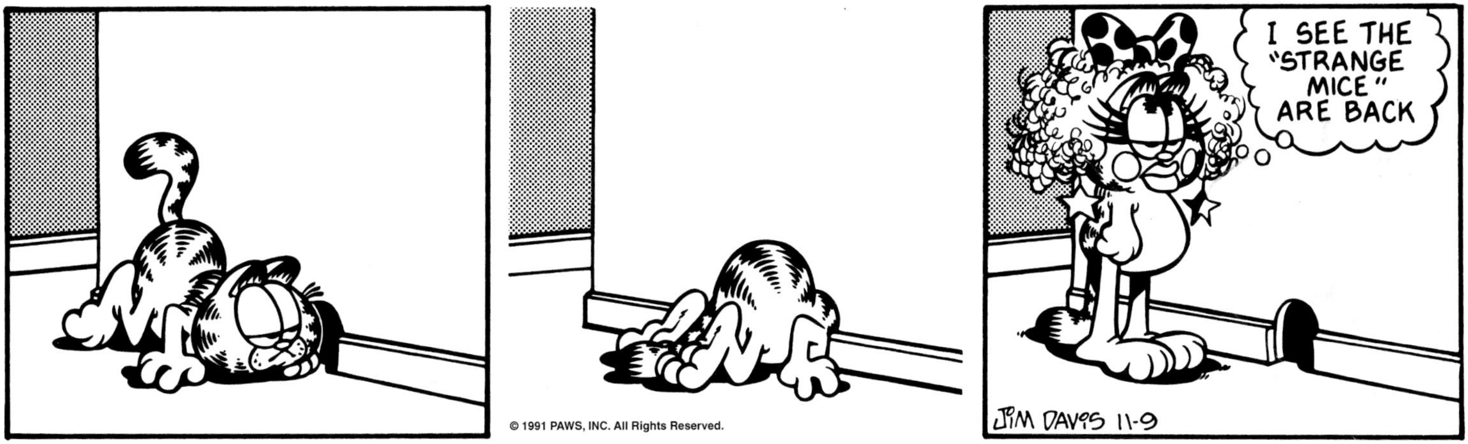
I SEE THE "STRANGE MICE" ARE BACK
© 1991 PAWS, INC. All Rights Reserved.
JIM DAVIS 11-9

I'm a sucker for physical comedy. I love pratfalls and slapstick humor. I also have a great deal of admiration for a well-timed punch line, a clever twist, or something that just really surprises you.

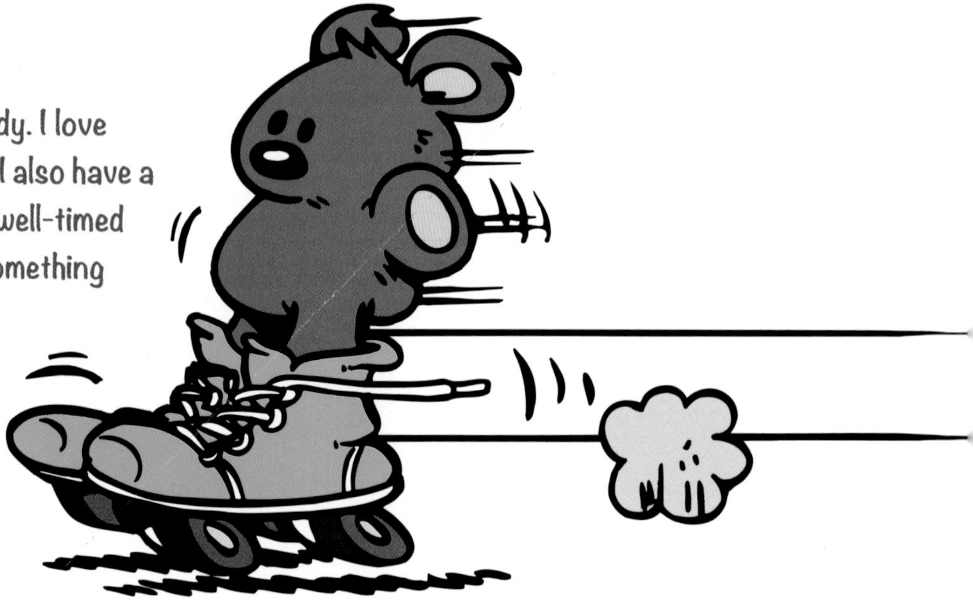

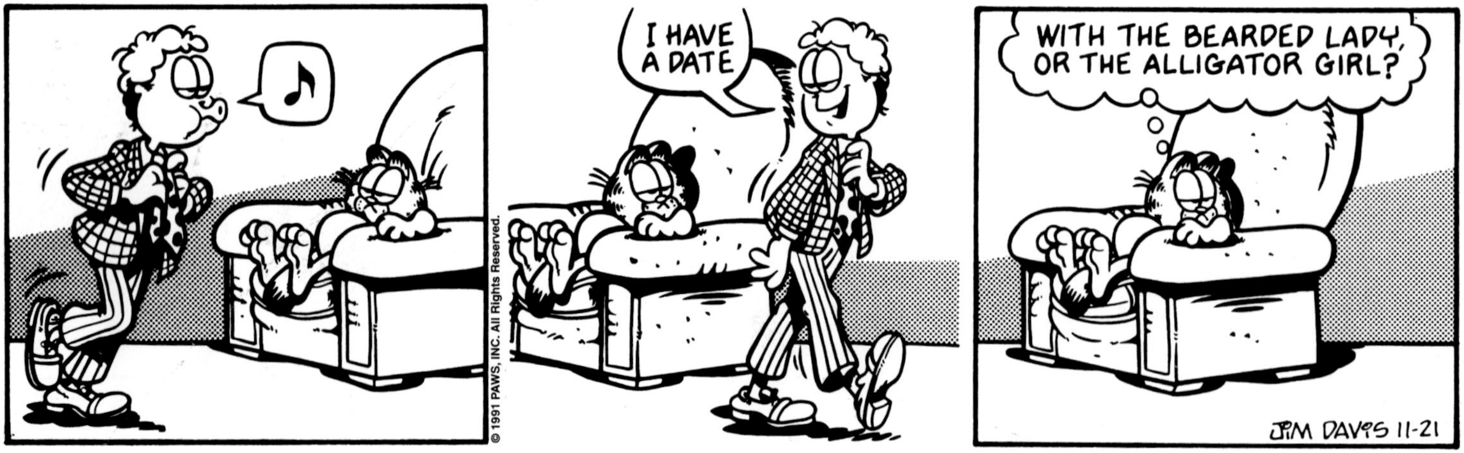
♪
I HAVE A DATE
WITH THE BEARDED LADY, OR THE ALLIGATOR GIRL?
JIM DAVIS 11-21

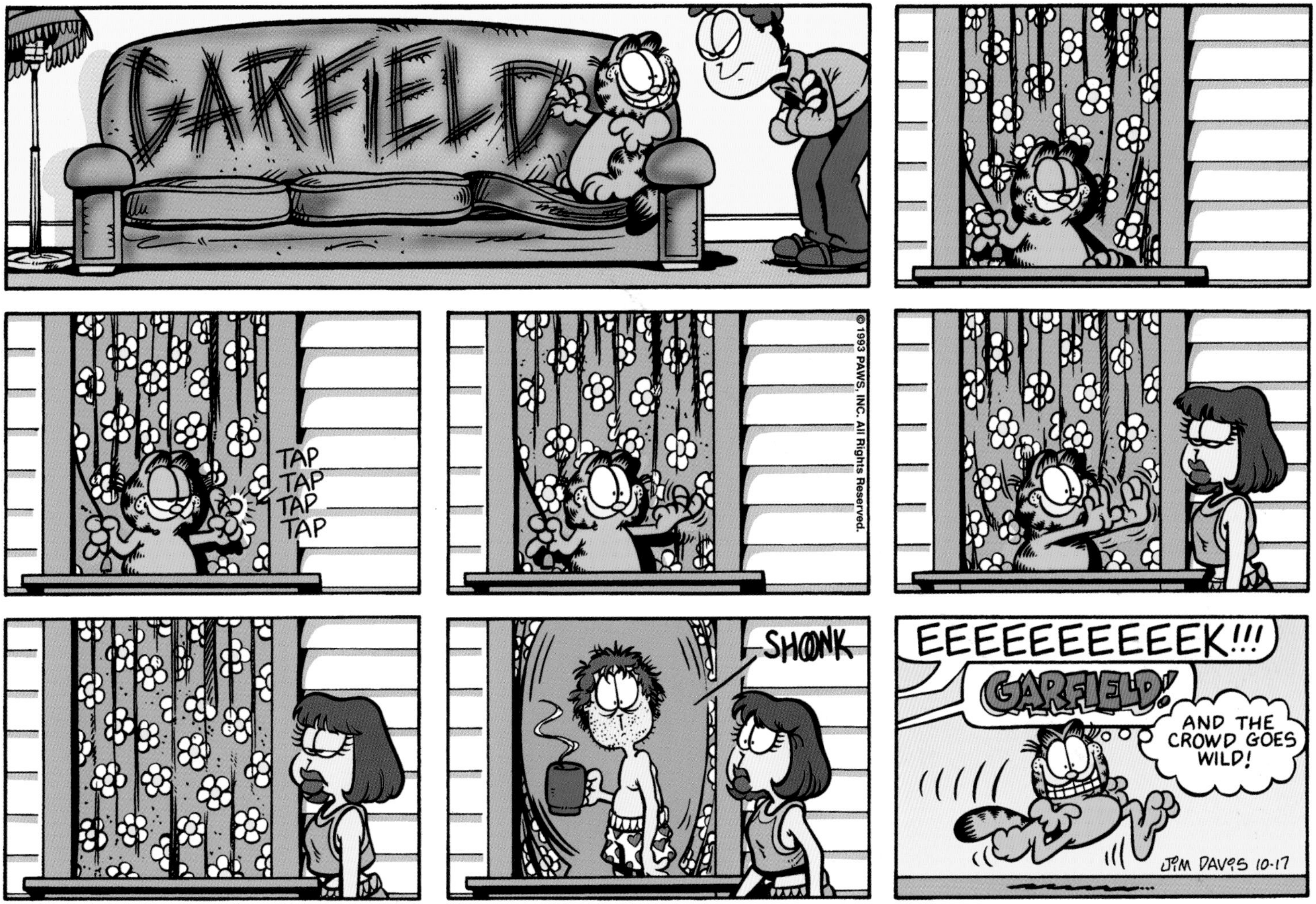
GARFIELD
TAP TAP TAP TAP
SHOONK
EEEEEEEEEEEK!!!
GARFIELD!
AND THE CROWD GOES WILD!
JIM DAVIS 10-17

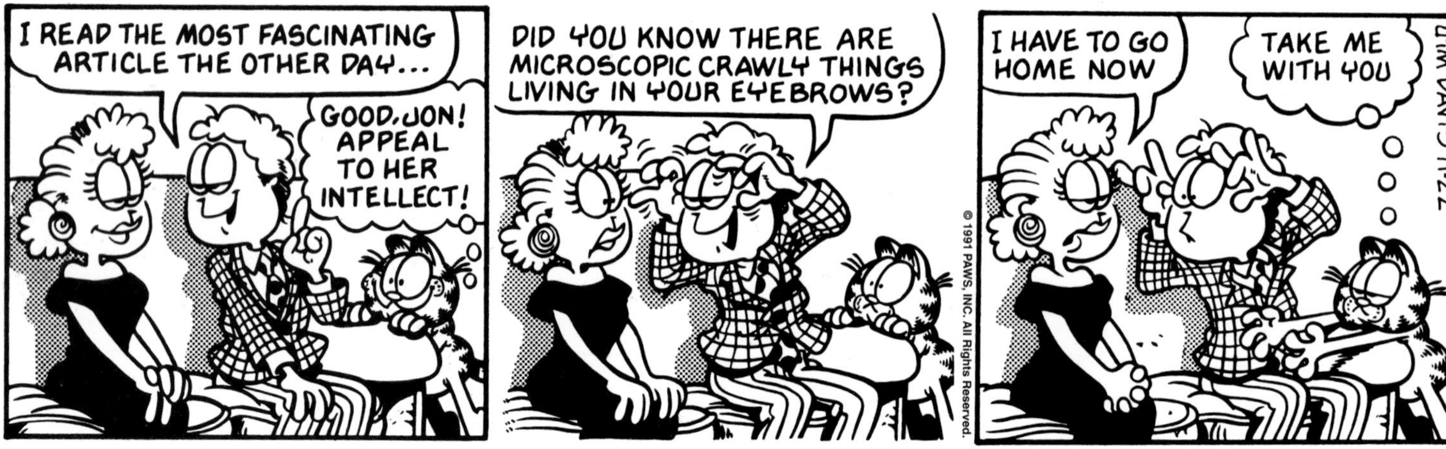
I READ THE MOST FASCINATING ARTICLE THE OTHER DAY...
GOOD, JON! APPEAL TO HER INTELLECT!
DID YOU KNOW THERE ARE MICROSCOPIC CRAWLY THINGS LIVING IN YOUR EYEBROWS?
© 1991 PAWS, INC. All Rights Reserved.
I HAVE TO GO HOME NOW
TAKE ME WITH YOU
JIM DAVIS 11-22

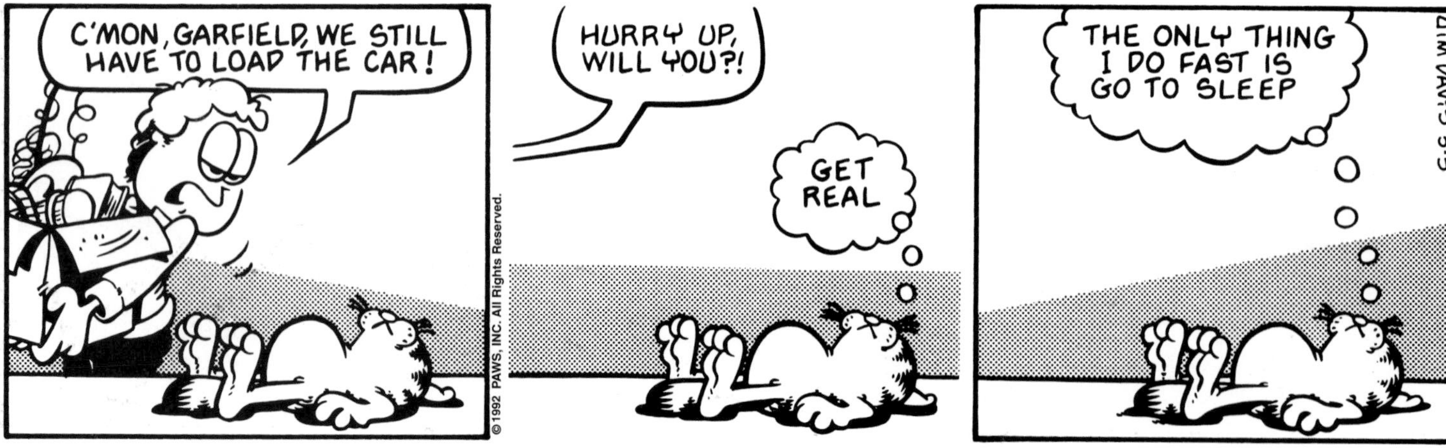
C'MON, GARFIELD, WE STILL HAVE TO LOAD THE CAR!
© 1992 PAWS, INC. All Rights Reserved.
HURRY UP, WILL YOU?!
GET REAL
THE ONLY THING I DO FAST IS GO TO SLEEP
JIM DAVIS 3-3

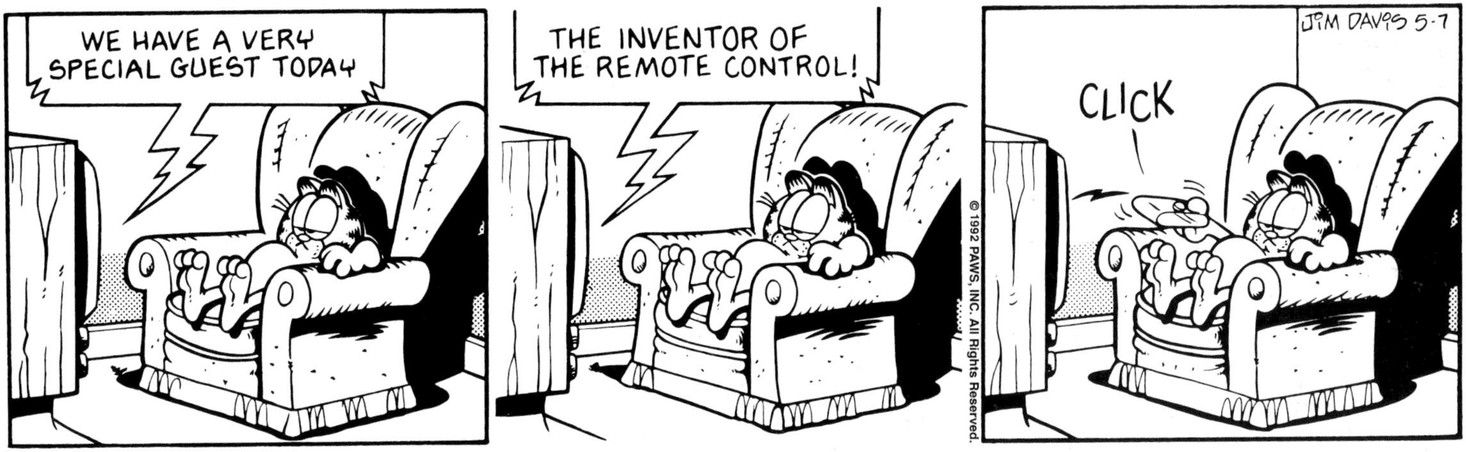
WE HAVE A VERY SPECIAL GUEST TODAY
THE INVENTOR OF THE REMOTE CONTROL!
JIM DAVIS 5-7
CLICK
© 1992 PAWS, INC. All Rights Reserved.

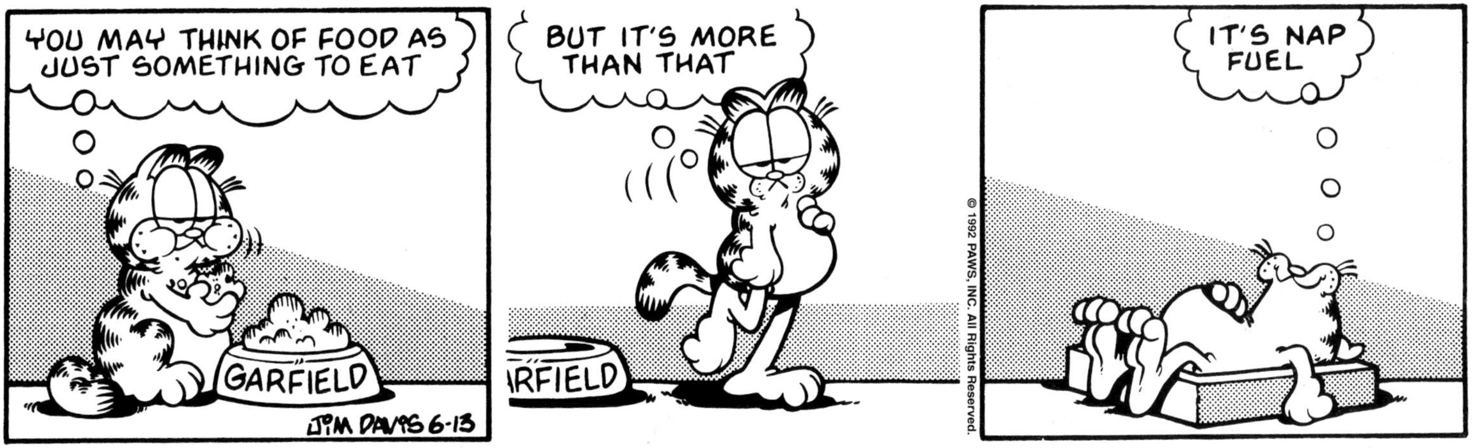
YOU MAY THINK OF FOOD AS JUST SOMETHING TO EAT
GARFIELD
JIM DAVIS 6-13
BUT IT'S MORE THAN THAT
ARFIELD
IT'S NAP FUEL
© 1992 PAWS, INC. All Rights Reserved.

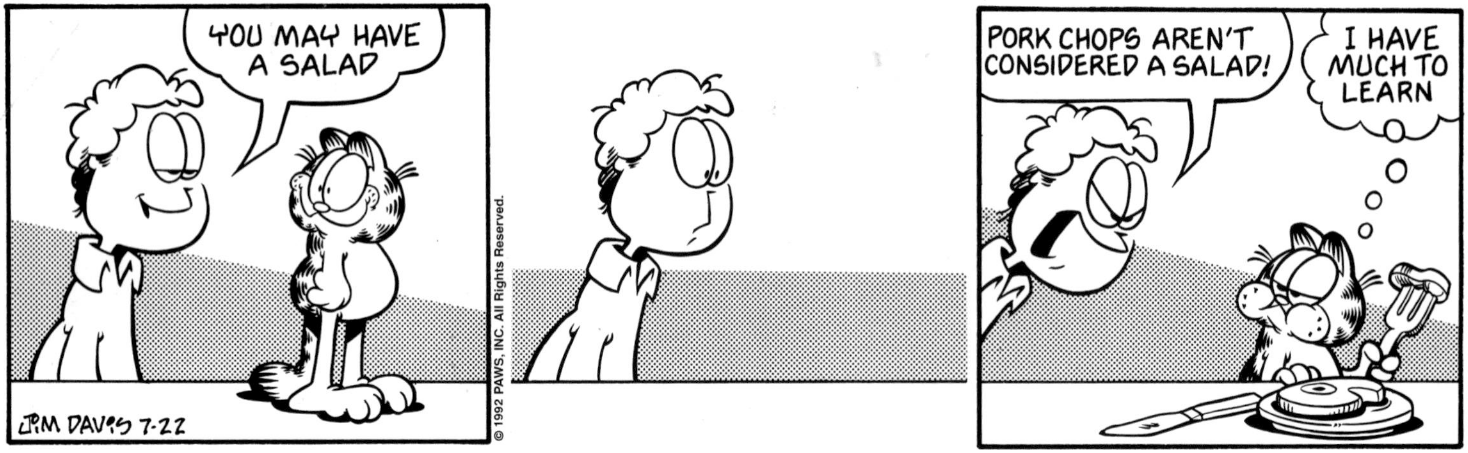

YOU MAY HAVE A SALAD
JIM DAVIS 7-22
© 1992 PAWS, INC. All Rights Reserved.
PORK CHOPS AREN'T CONSIDERED A SALAD!
I HAVE MUCH TO LEARN

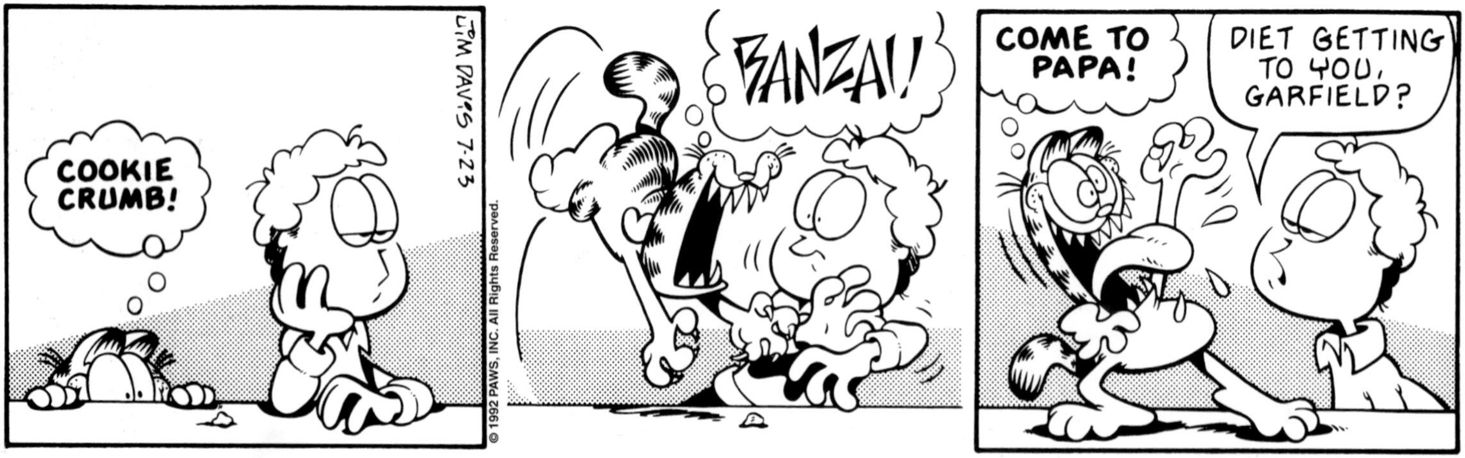

COOKIE CRUMB!
JIM DAVIS 7-23
© 1992 PAWS, INC. All Rights Reserved.
BANZAI!
COME TO PAPA!
DIET GETTING TO YOU, GARFIELD?

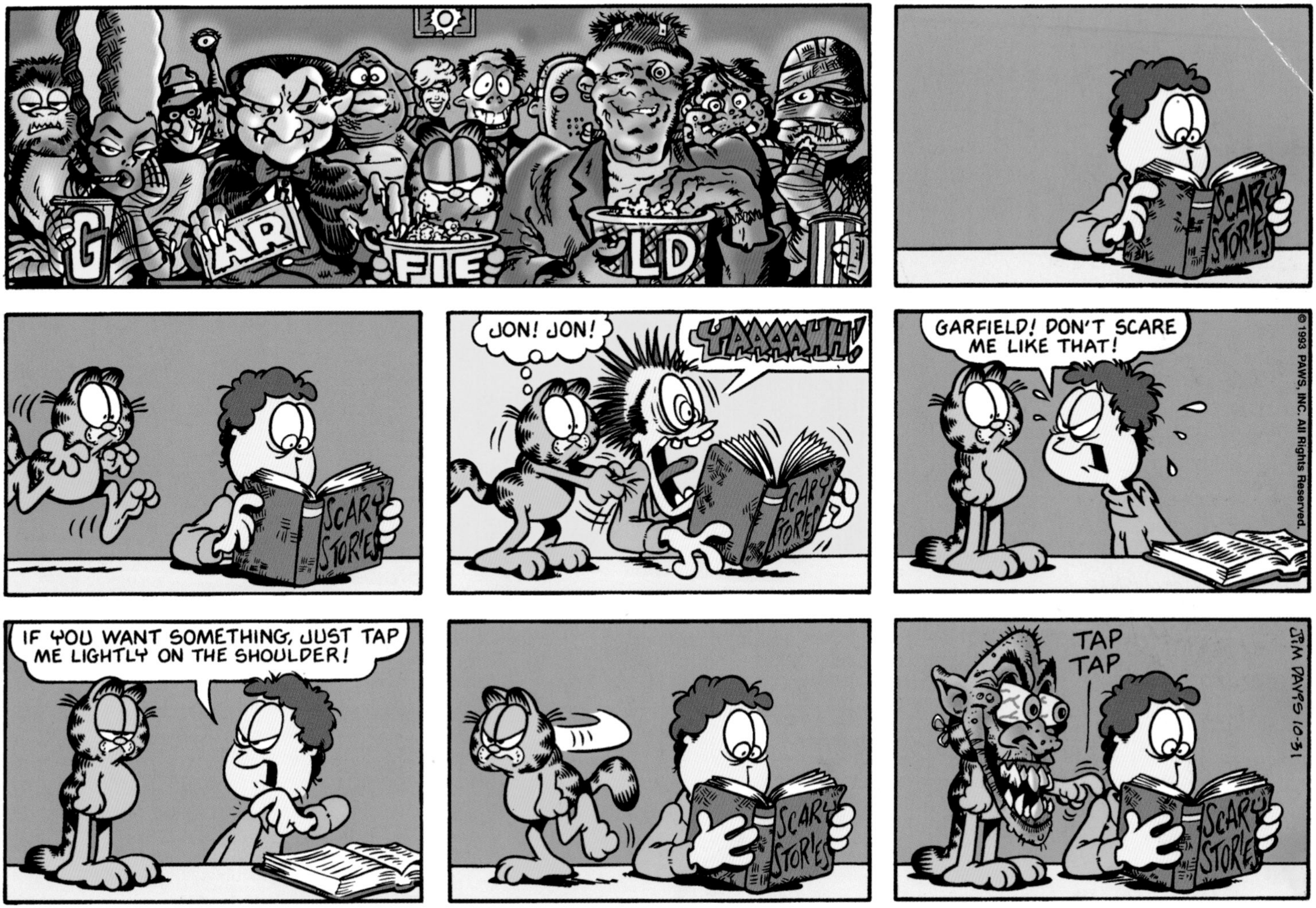

G
AR
FIE
LD
SCARY STORIES
JON! JON!
YAAAAAHH!
GARFIELD! DON'T SCARE ME LIKE THAT!
IF YOU WANT SOMETHING, JUST TAP ME LIGHTLY ON THE SHOULDER!
TAP TAP
JIM DAVIS 10-31

Chuck Jones, the great animator, said that every artist has a hundred thousand bad drawings in him, and the sooner you get those out of the way, every drawing is going to be good. It's absolutely true. I've always maintained there's no such thing as artistic talent, but there is such a thing as skill. The skill is born from a love of drawing. The more you enjoy it, the more you draw. The more you draw, the better you get. It's that simple.

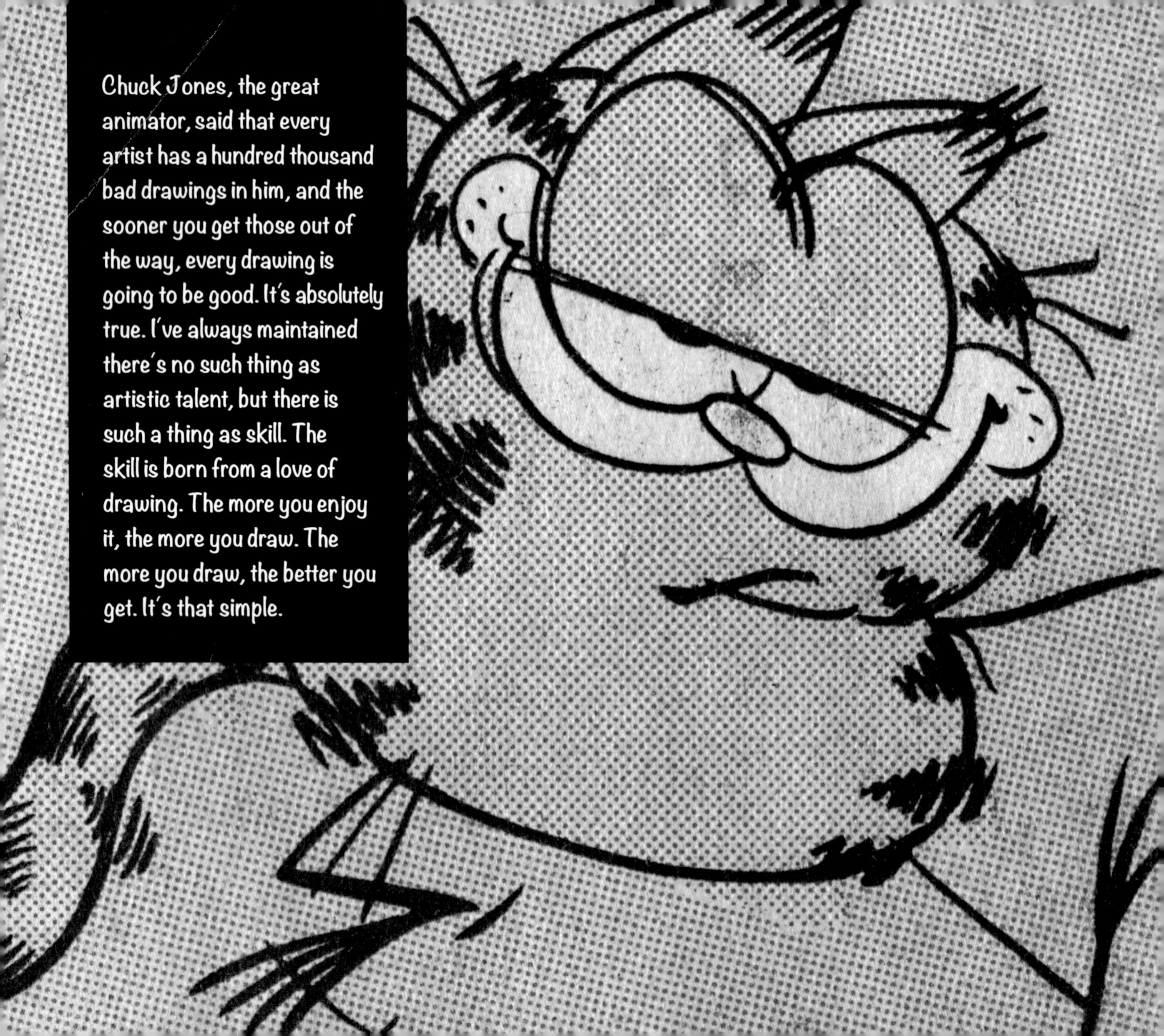

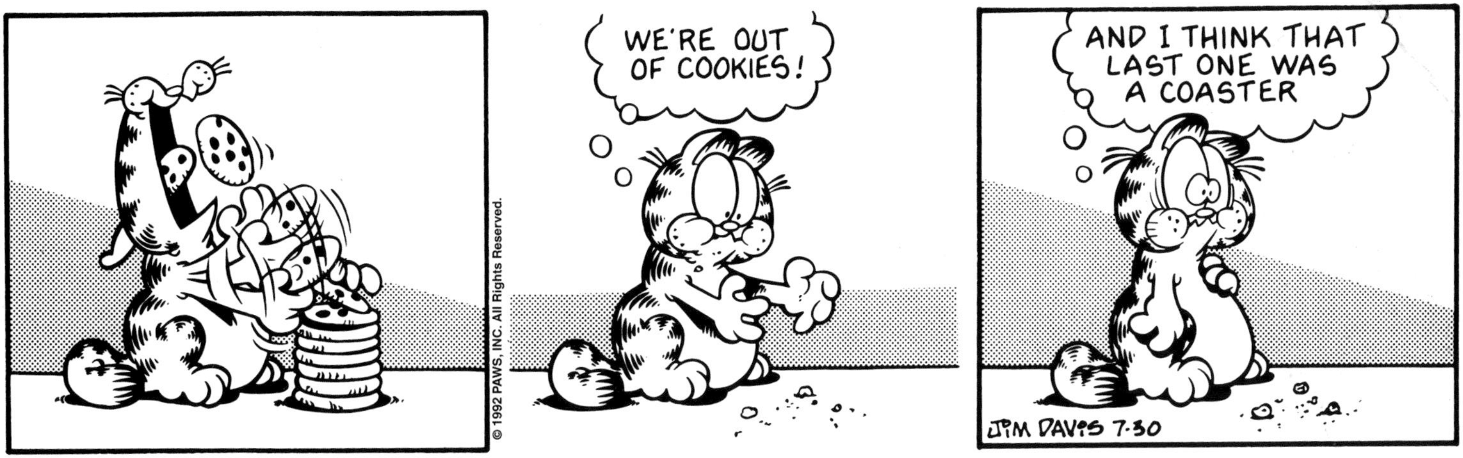
© 1992 PAWS, INC. All Rights Reserved.
WE'RE OUT OF COOKIES!
AND I THINK THAT LAST ONE WAS A COASTER
JIM DAVIS 7-30

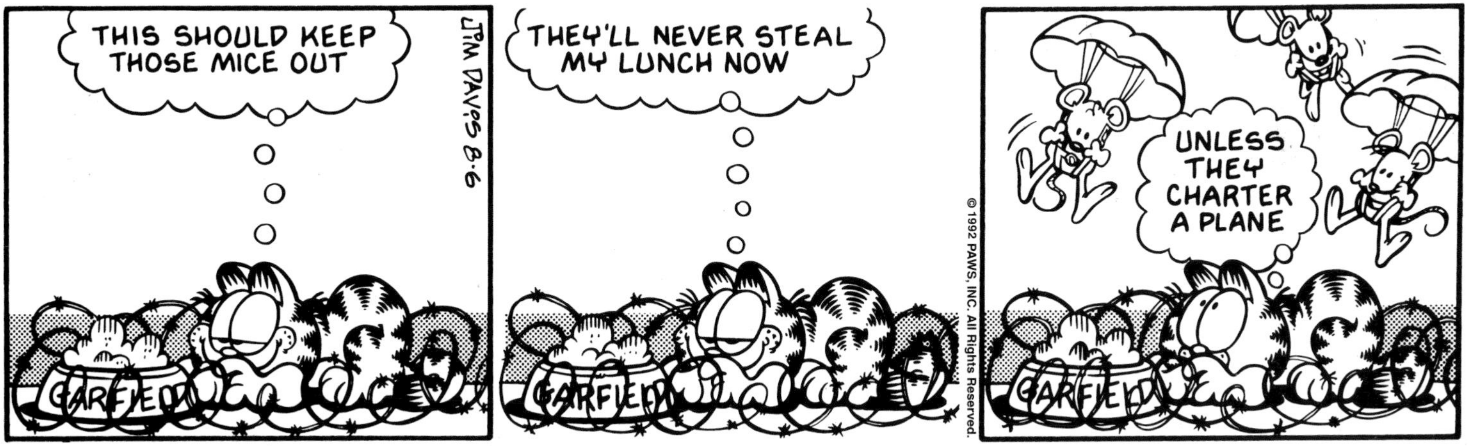
THIS SHOULD KEEP THOSE MICE OUT
JIM DAVIS 8-6
GARFIELD
THEY'LL NEVER STEAL MY LUNCH NOW
GARFIELD
© 1992 PAWS, INC. All Rights Reserved.
UNLESS THEY CHARTER A PLANE
GARFIELD

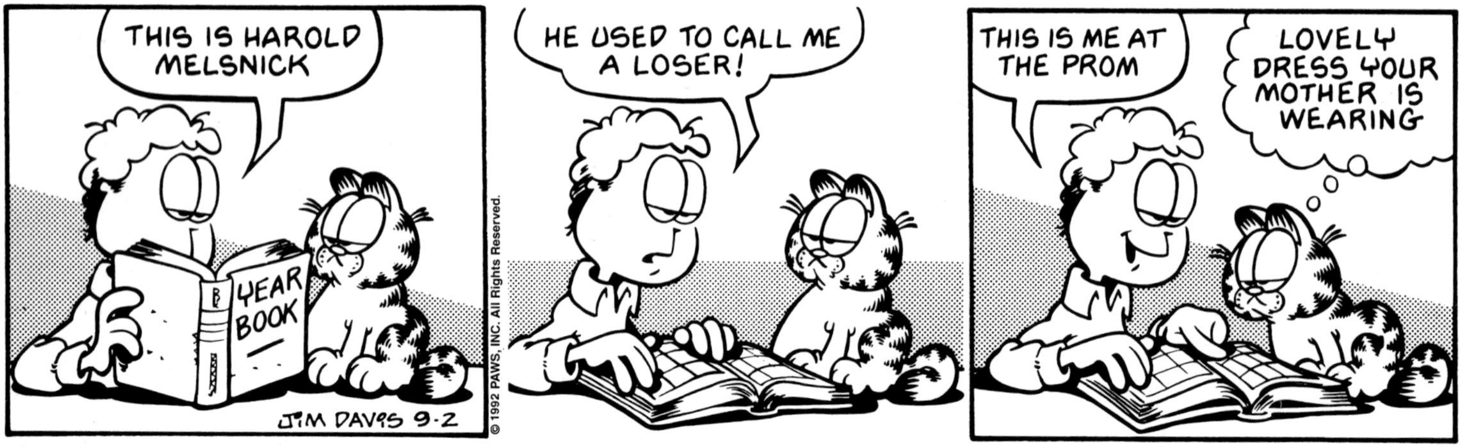
THIS IS HAROLD MELSNICK
YEAR BOOK
JIM DAVIS 9-2
© 1992 PAWS, INC. All Rights Reserved.
HE USED TO CALL ME A LOSER!
THIS IS ME AT THE PROM
LOVELY DRESS YOUR MOTHER IS WEARING

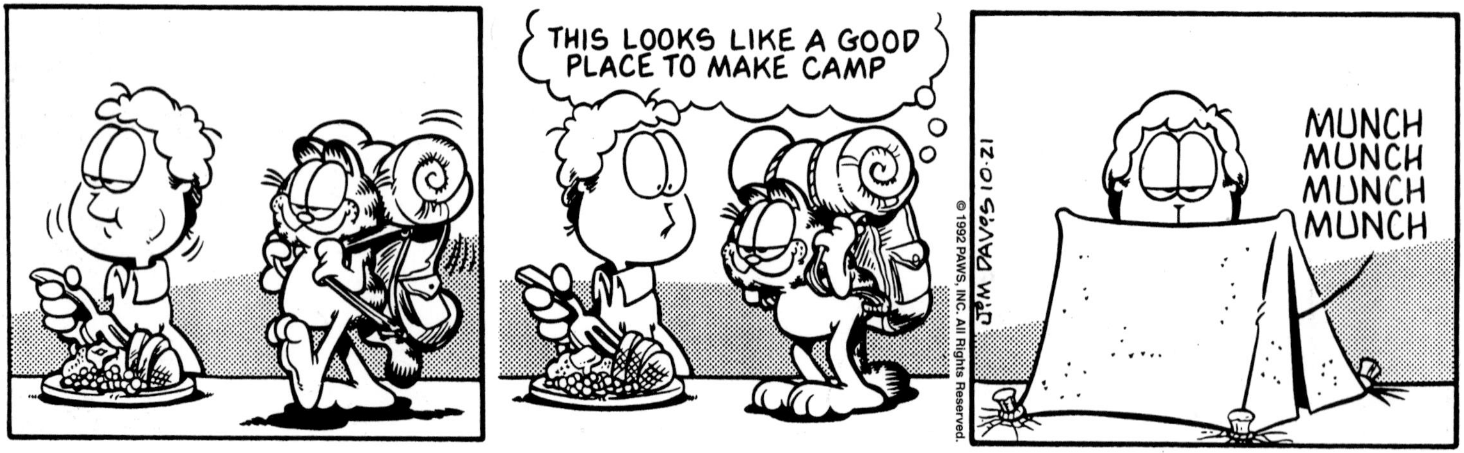
THIS LOOKS LIKE A GOOD PLACE TO MAKE CAMP
JIM DAVIS 10-21
© 1992 PAWS, INC. All Rights Reserved.
MUNCH
MUNCH
MUNCH
MUNCH

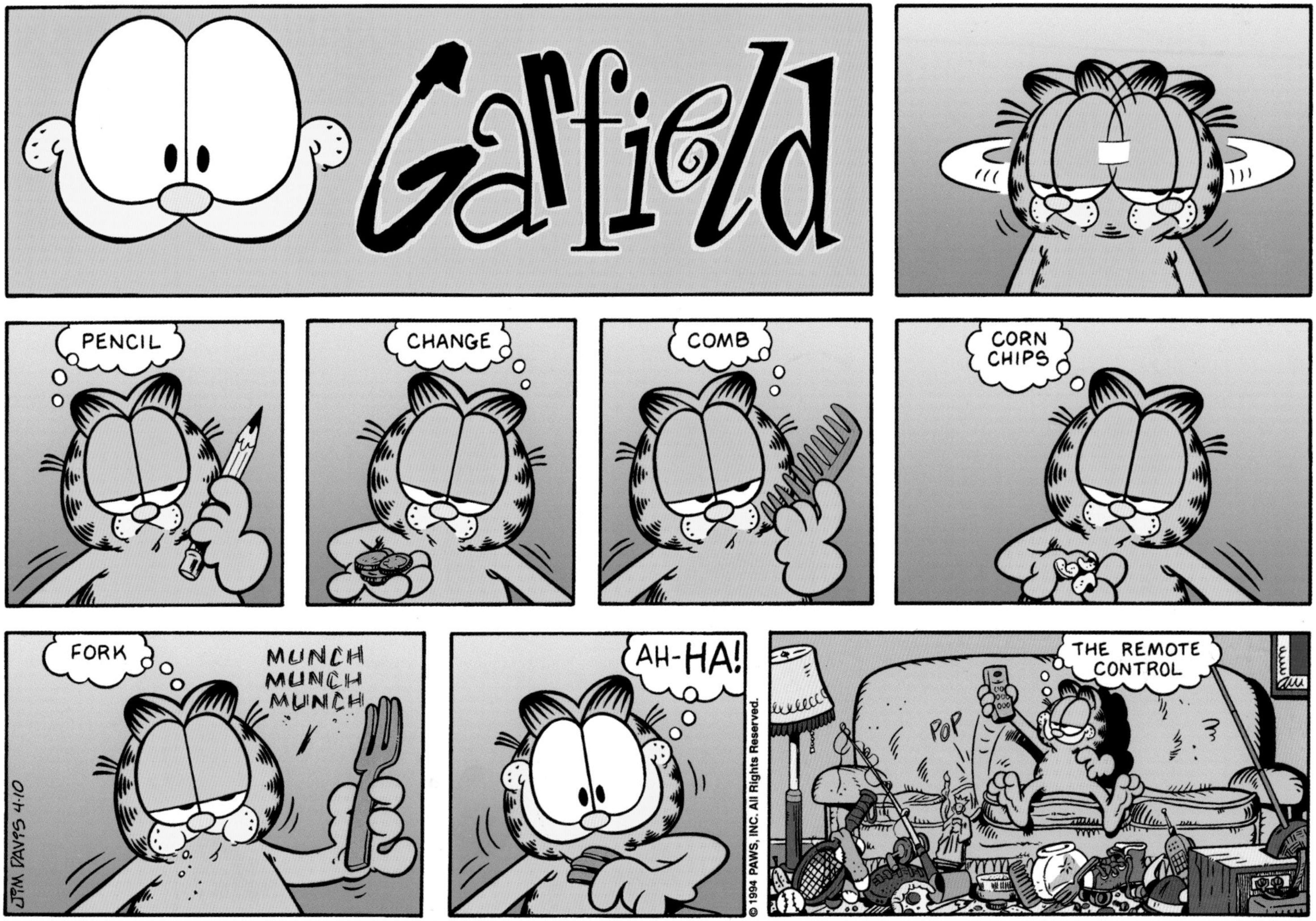
Garfield
PENCIL
CHANGE
COMB
CORN CHIPS
FORK
MUNCH MUNCH MUNCH
AH-HA!
JPM DAVPS 4-10
© 1994 PAWS, INC. All Rights Reserved.
THE REMOTE CONTROL
POP

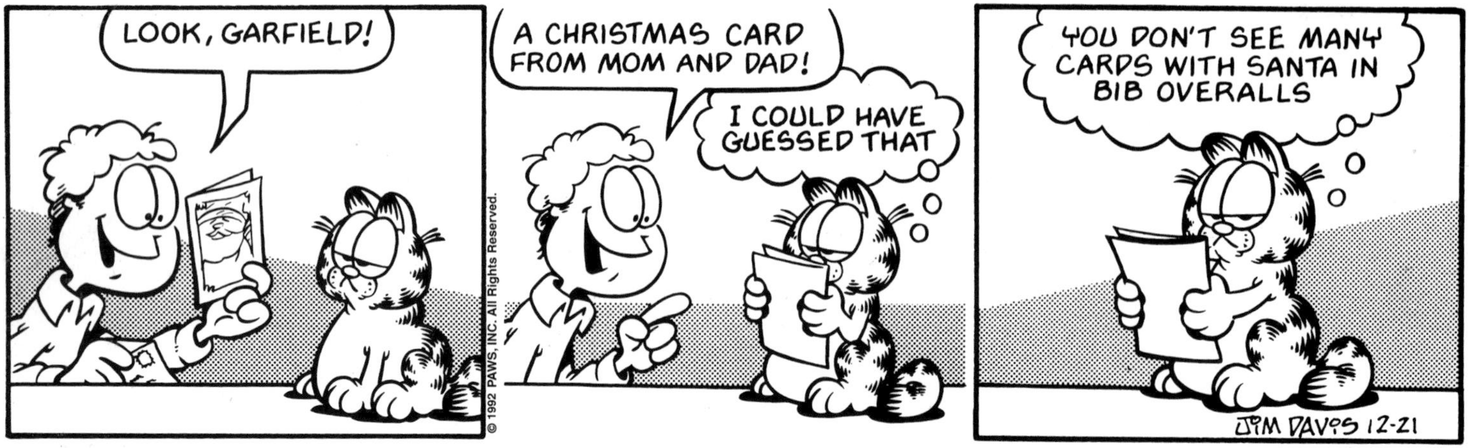
LOOK, GARFIELD!
A CHRISTMAS CARD FROM MOM AND DAD!
I COULD HAVE GUESSED THAT
YOU DON'T SEE MANY CARDS WITH SANTA IN BIB OVERALLS
JIM DAVIS 12-21
© 1992 PAWS, INC. All Rights Reserved.

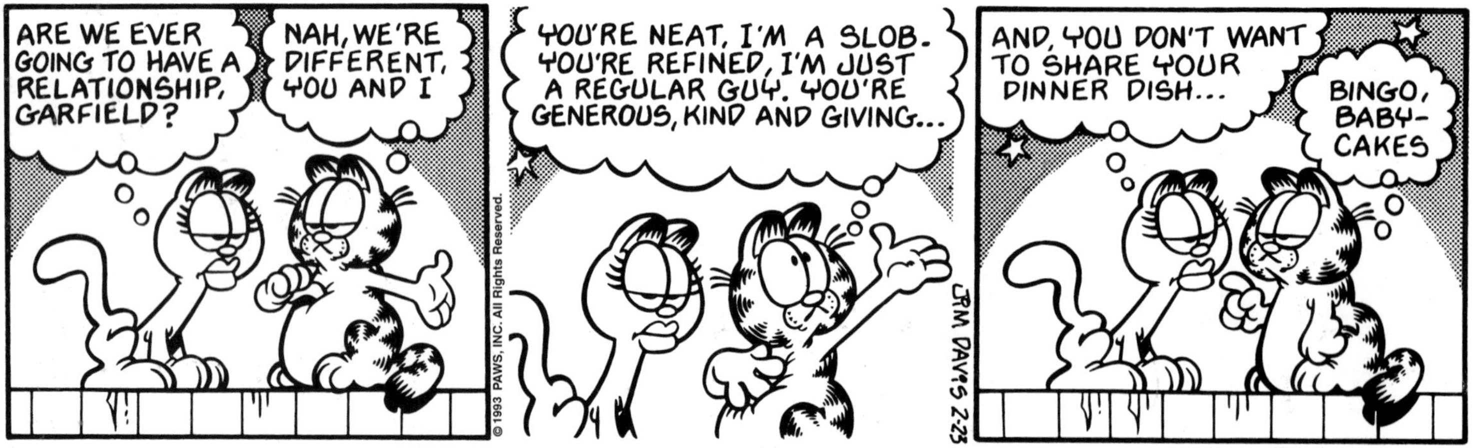
ARE WE EVER GOING TO HAVE A RELATIONSHIP, GARFIELD?
NAH, WE'RE DIFFERENT, YOU AND I
YOU'RE NEAT, I'M A SLOB. YOU'RE REFINED, I'M JUST A REGULAR GUY. YOU'RE GENEROUS, KIND AND GIVING...
AND, YOU DON'T WANT TO SHARE YOUR DINNER DISH...
BINGO, BABY-CAKES
JIM DAVIS 2-23
© 1993 PAWS, INC. All Rights Reserved.

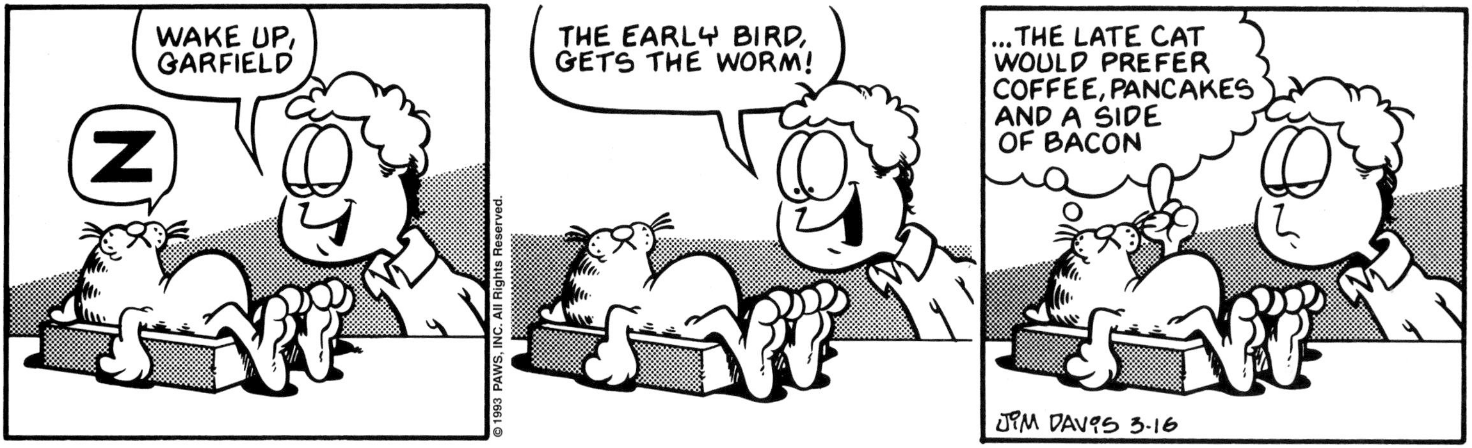
WAKE UP, GARFIELD
Z
THE EARLY BIRD, GETS THE WORM!
...THE LATE CAT WOULD PREFER COFFEE, PANCAKES AND A SIDE OF BACON
JIM DAVIS 3-16
© 1993 PAWS, INC. All Rights Reserved.

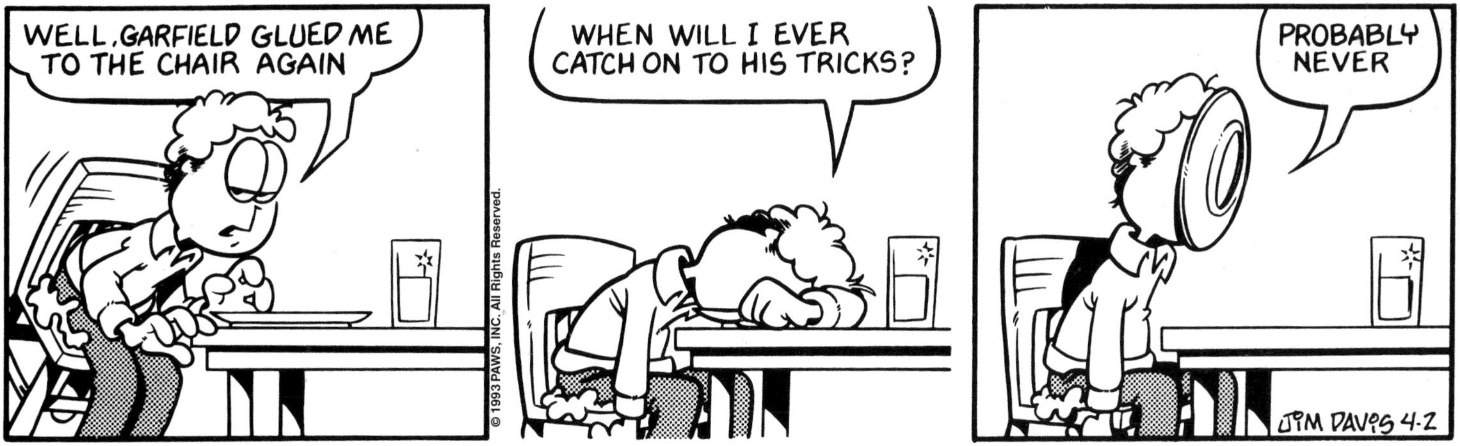
WELL, GARFIELD GLUED ME TO THE CHAIR AGAIN
WHEN WILL I EVER CATCH ON TO HIS TRICKS?
PROBABLY NEVER
JIM DAVIS 4-2
© 1993 PAWS, INC. All Rights Reserved.

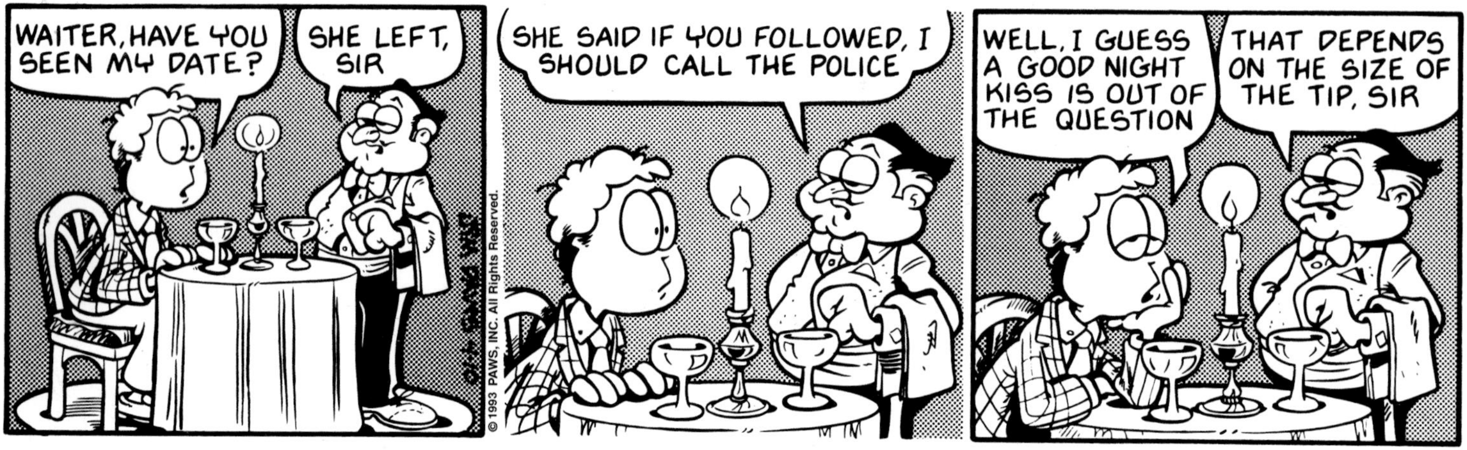
WAITER, HAVE YOU SEEN MY DATE?
SHE LEFT, SIR
JPM DAVIS 4-10
© 1993 PAWS, INC. All Rights Reserved.
SHE SAID IF YOU FOLLOWED, I SHOULD CALL THE POLICE
WELL, I GUESS A GOOD NIGHT KISS IS OUT OF THE QUESTION
THAT DEPENDS ON THE SIZE OF THE TIP, SIR

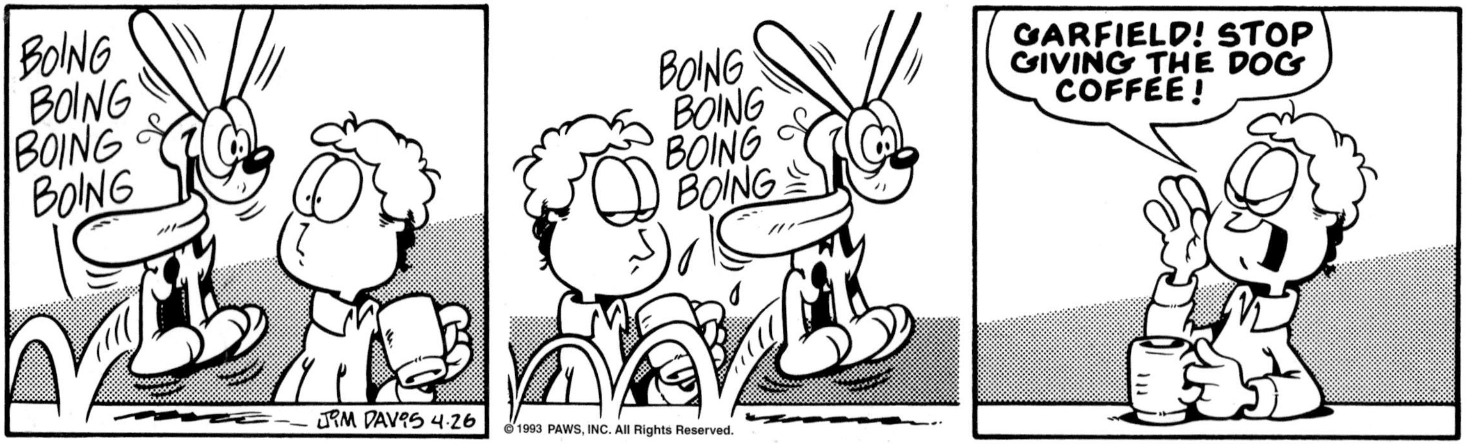
BOING BOING BOING BOING
JIM DAVIS 4-26
© 1993 PAWS, INC. All Rights Reserved.
BOING BOING BOING BOING
GARFIELD! STOP GIVING THE DOG COFFEE!

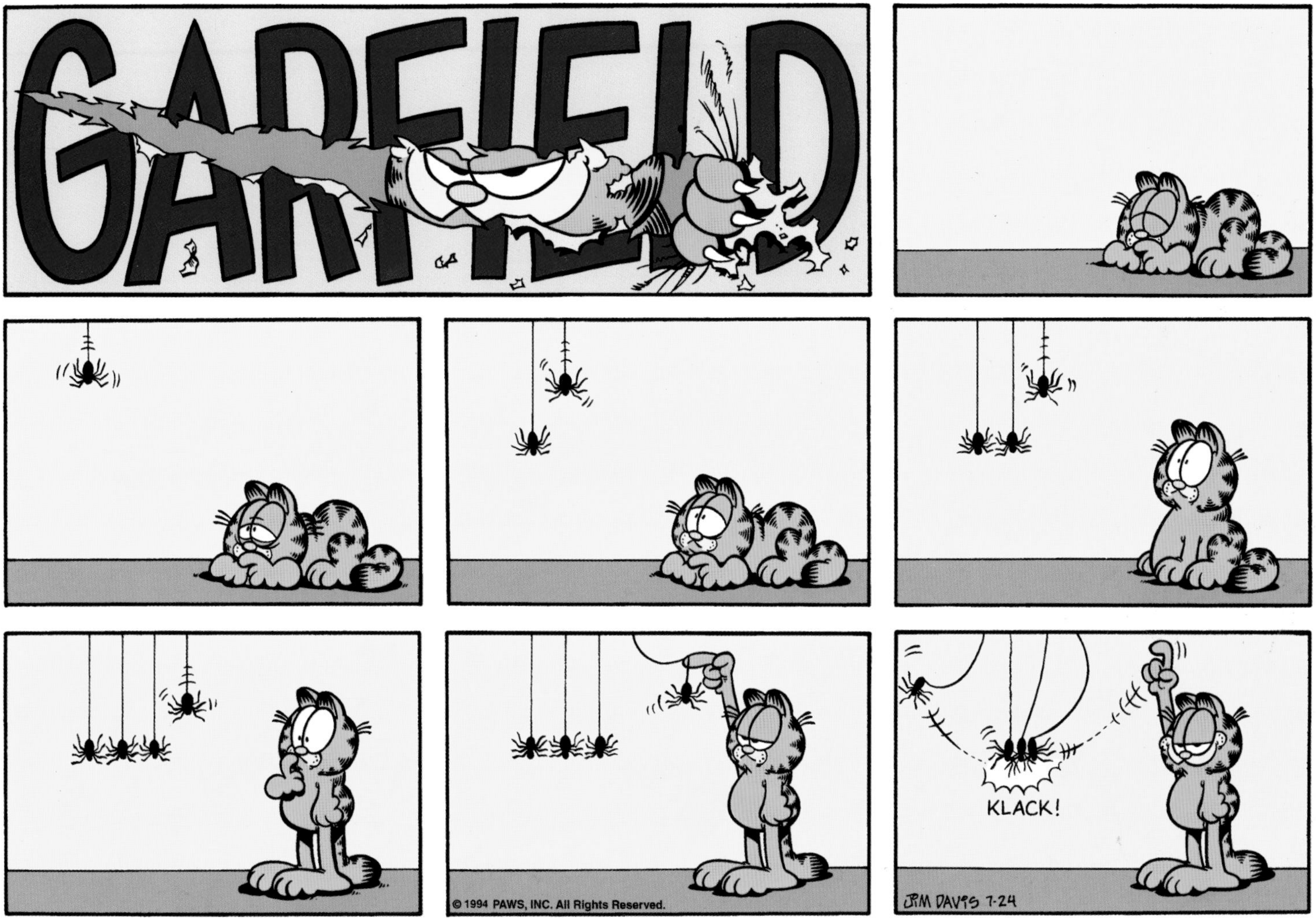
GARFIELD
KLACK!
© 1994 PAWS, INC. All Rights Reserved.
JIM DAVIS 7-24

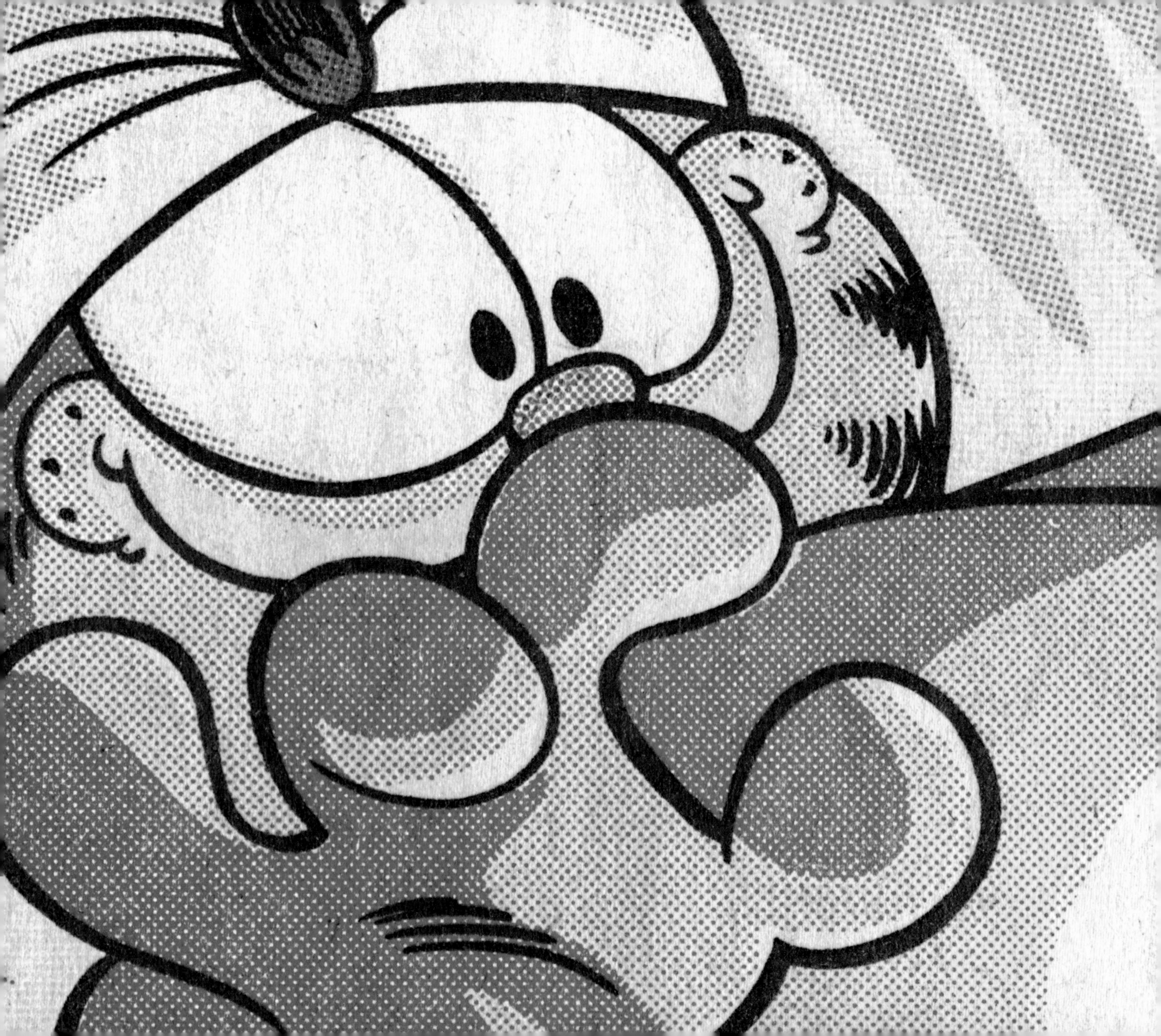

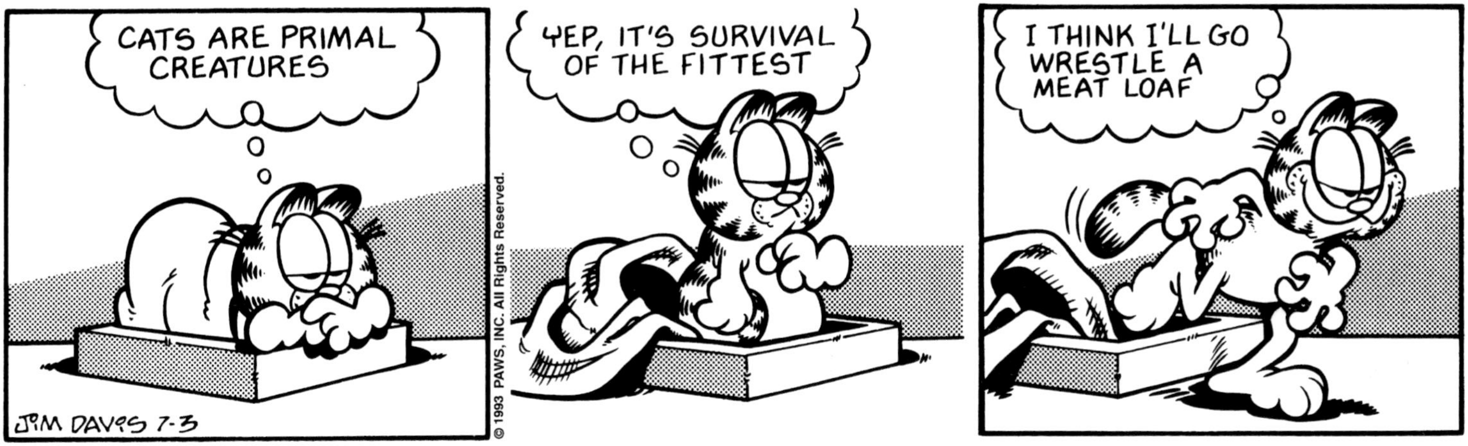
CATS ARE PRIMAL CREATURES
JIM DAVIS 7-3
© 1993 PAWS, INC. All Rights Reserved.
YEP, IT'S SURVIVAL OF THE FITTEST
I THINK I'LL GO WRESTLE A MEAT LOAF

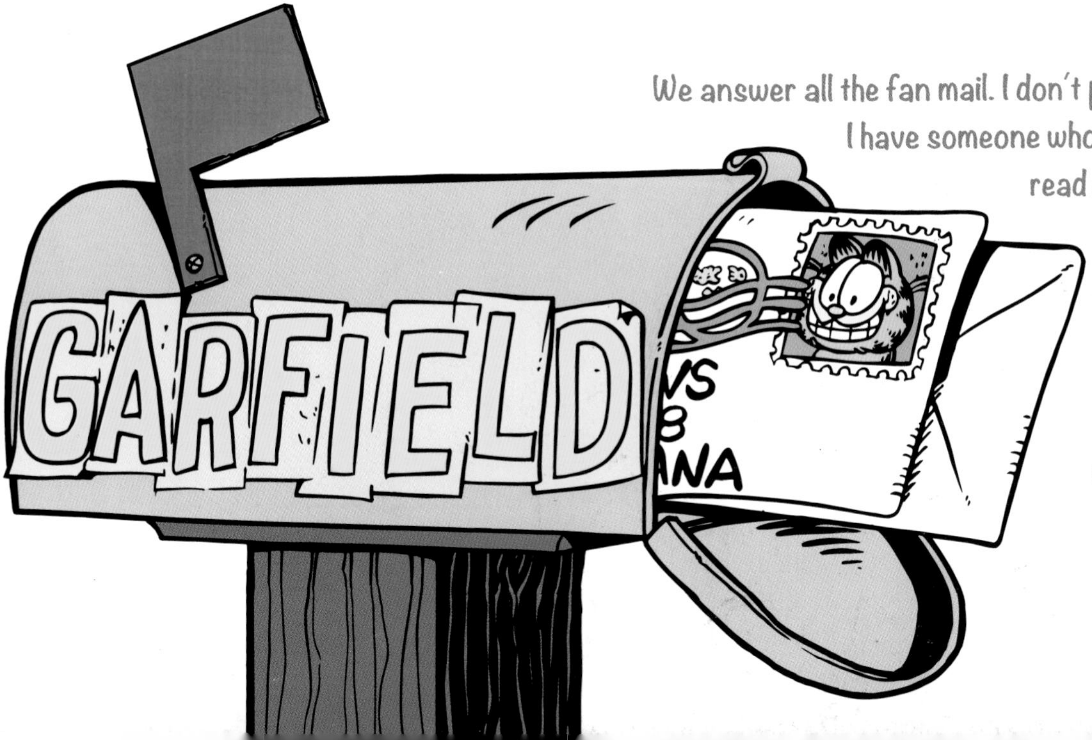
GARFIELD

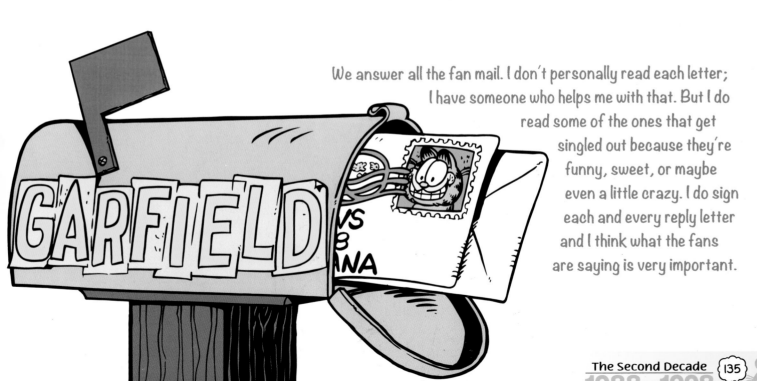

We answer all the fan mail. I don't personally read each letter; I have someone who helps me with that. But I do read some of the ones that get singled out because they're funny, sweet, or maybe even a little crazy. I do sign each and every reply letter and I think what the fans are saying is very important.

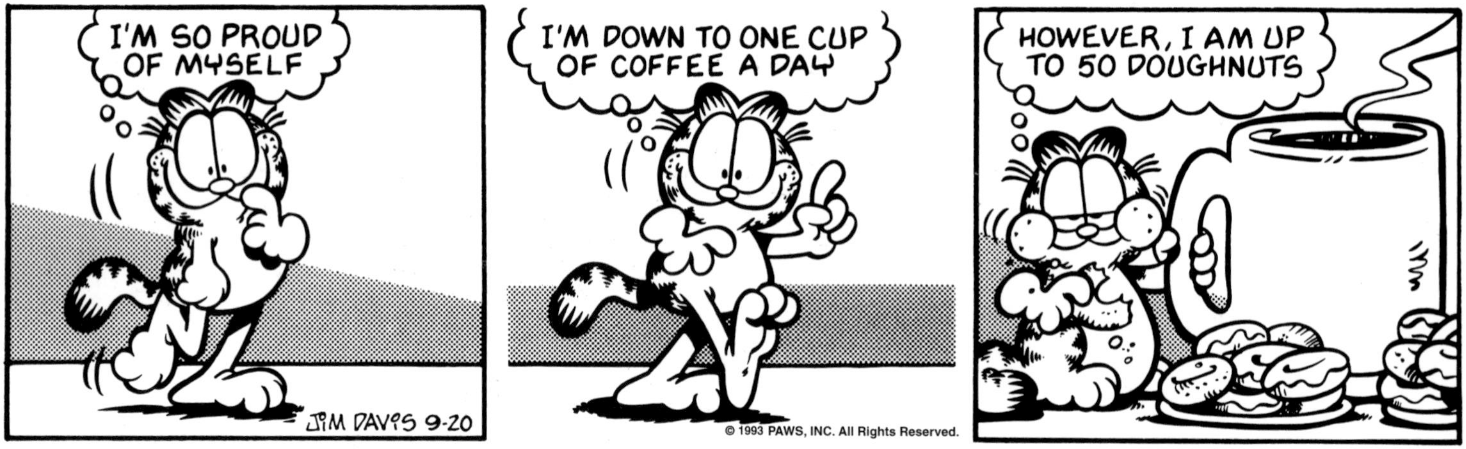
I'M SO PROUD OF MYSELF
JIM DAVIS 9-20
I'M DOWN TO ONE CUP OF COFFEE A DAY
© 1993 PAWS, INC. All Rights Reserved.
HOWEVER, I AM UP TO 50 DOUGHNUTS

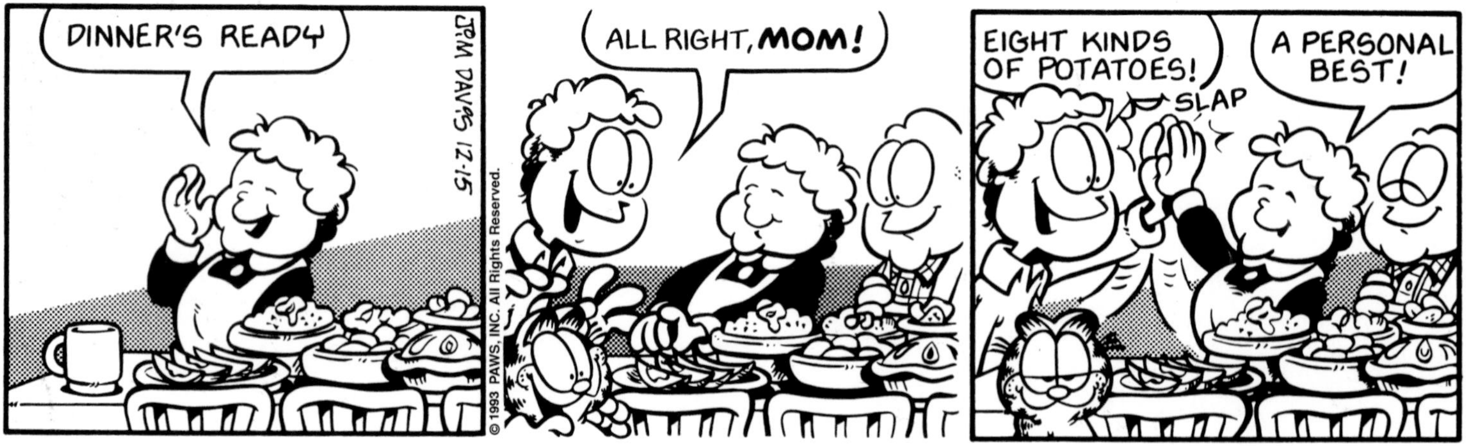
DINNER'S READY
JIM DAVIS 12-15
© 1993 PAWS, INC. All Rights Reserved.
ALL RIGHT, **MOM!**
EIGHT KINDS OF POTATOES!
SLAP
A PERSONAL BEST!

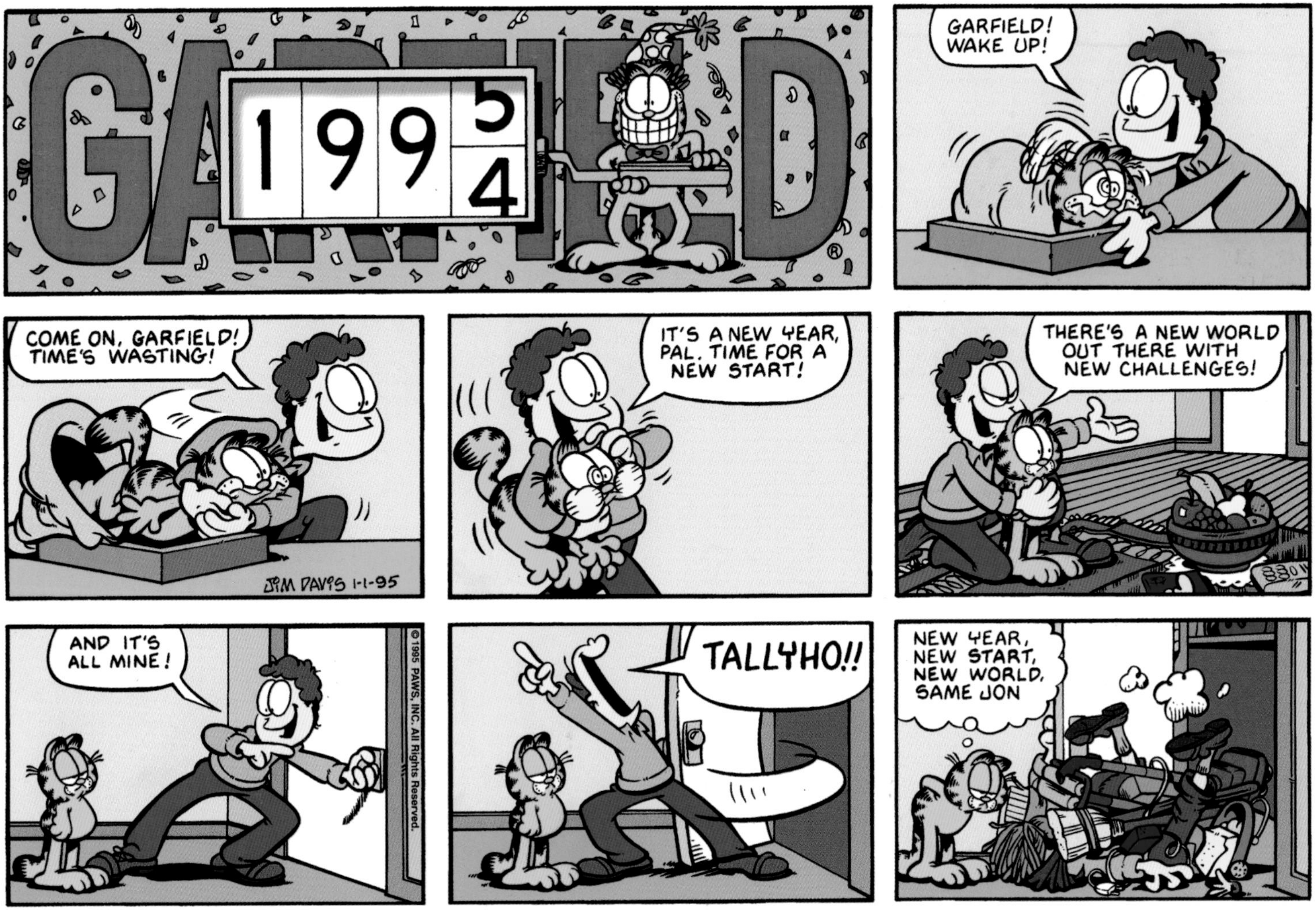
GARFIELD
1995
1994
GARFIELD! WAKE UP!
COME ON, GARFIELD! TIME'S WASTING!
JIM DAVIS 1-1-95
IT'S A NEW YEAR, PAL. TIME FOR A NEW START!
THERE'S A NEW WORLD OUT THERE WITH NEW CHALLENGES!
AND IT'S ALL MINE!
© 1995 PAWS, INC. All Rights Reserved.
TALLYHO!!
NEW YEAR, NEW START, NEW WORLD, SAME JON

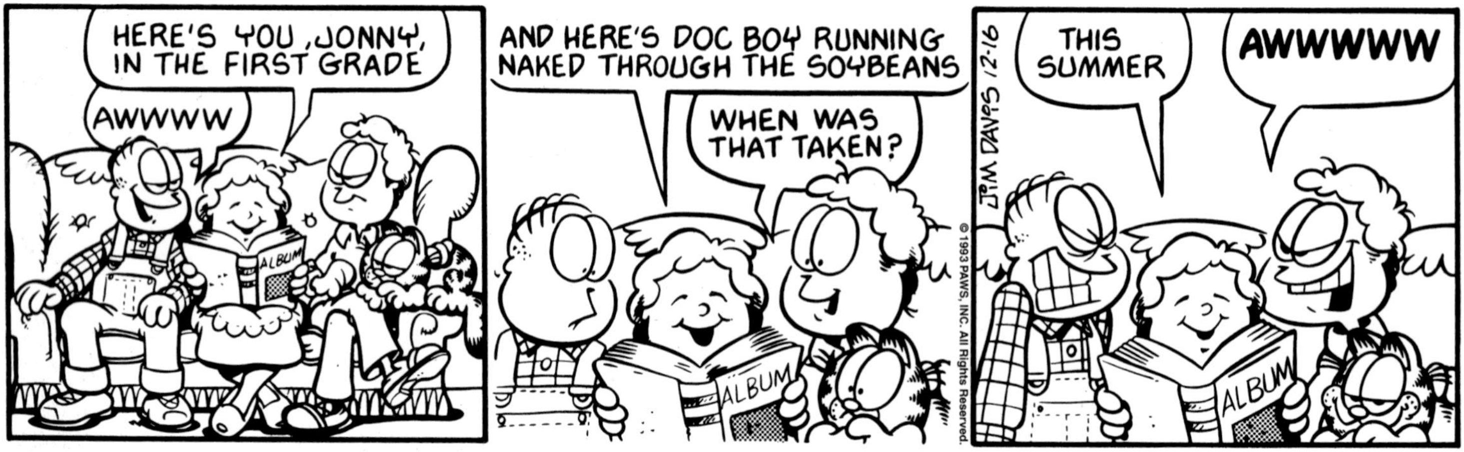
HERE'S YOU, JONNY, IN THE FIRST GRADE
AWWWW
ALBUM
AND HERE'S DOC BOY RUNNING NAKED THROUGH THE SOYBEANS
WHEN WAS THAT TAKEN?
ALBUM
JIM DAVIS 12-16
© 1993 PAWS, INC. All Rights Reserved.
THIS SUMMER
AWWWWW
ALBUM

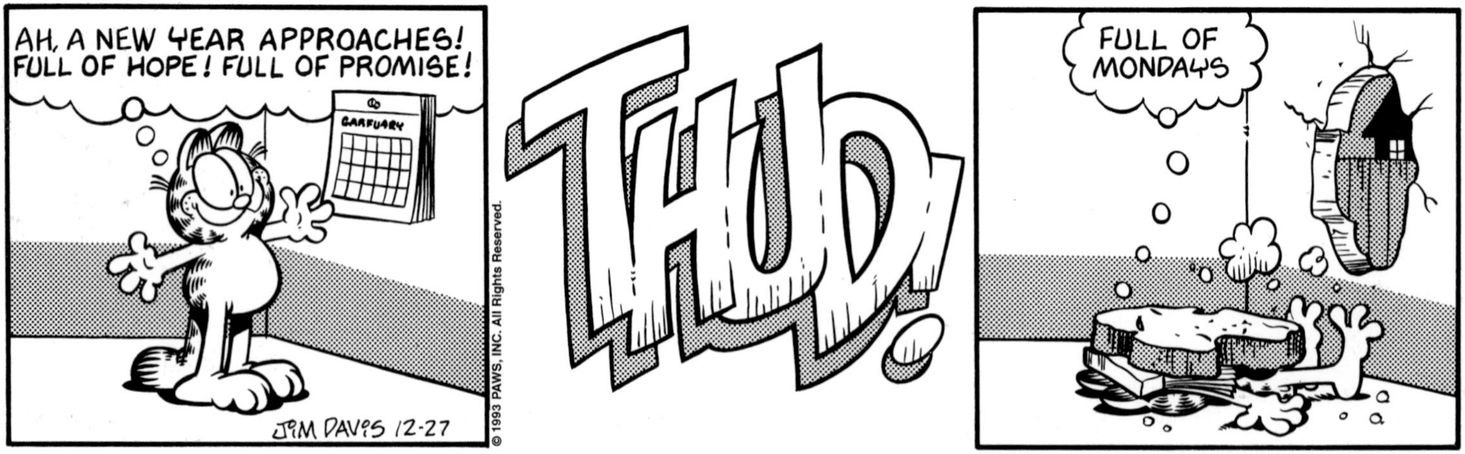
AH, A NEW YEAR APPROACHES! FULL OF HOPE! FULL OF PROMISE!
GARFUARY
JIM DAVIS 12-27
© 1993 PAWS, INC. All Rights Reserved.
THUD!
FULL OF MONDAYS

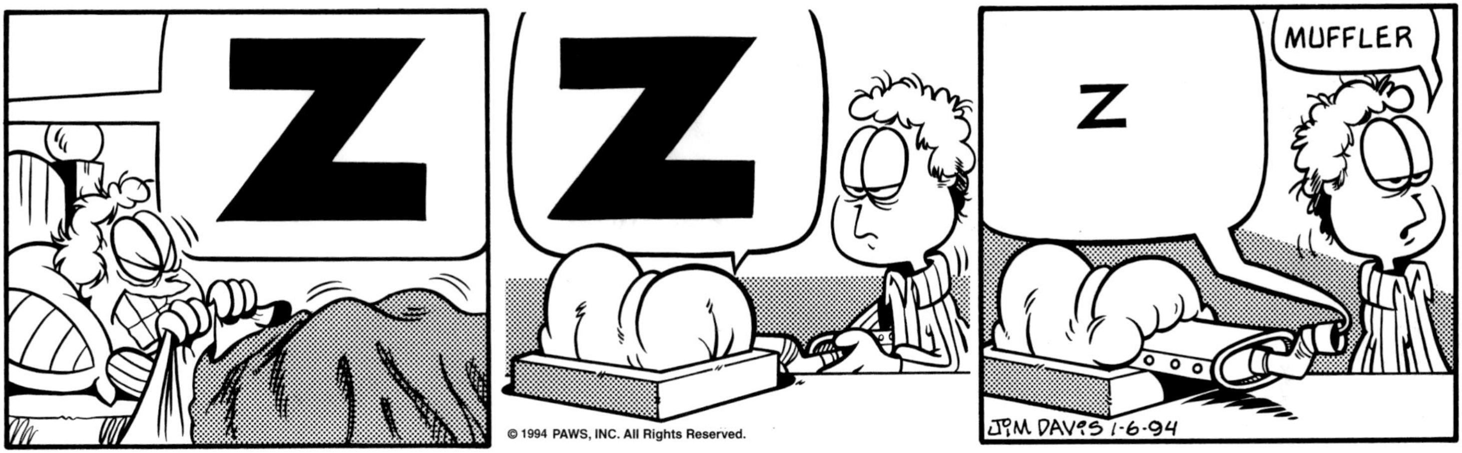
Z
Z
Z
MUFFLER
© 1994 PAWS, INC. All Rights Reserved.
JIM DAVIS 1-6-94

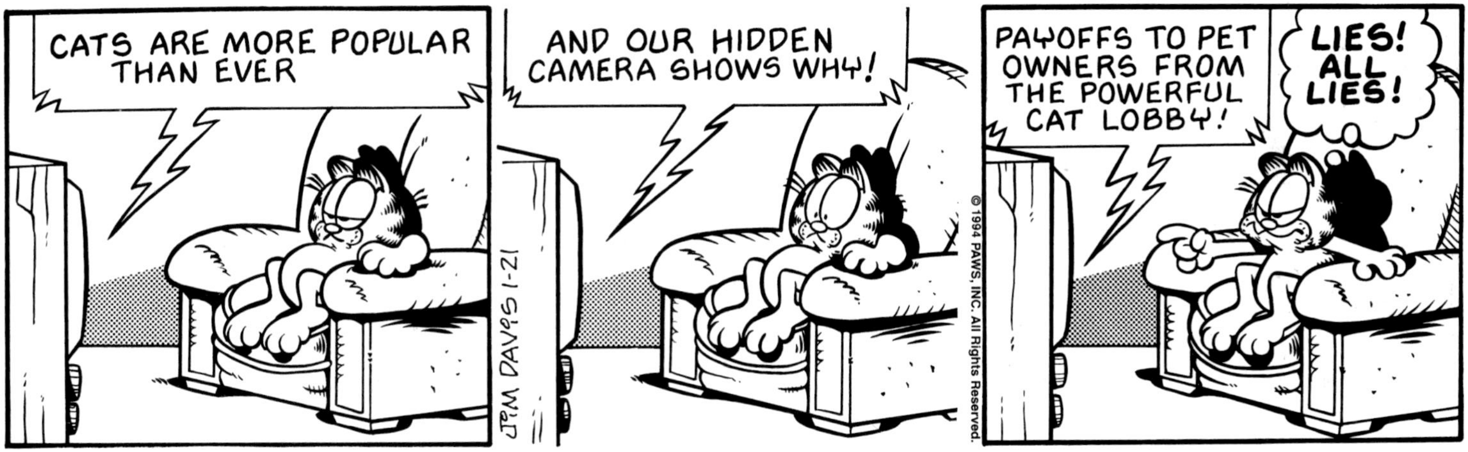
CATS ARE MORE POPULAR THAN EVER
AND OUR HIDDEN CAMERA SHOWS WHY!
PAYOFFS TO PET OWNERS FROM THE POWERFUL CAT LOBBY!
LIES! ALL LIES!
JIM DAVIS 1-21
© 1994 PAWS, INC. All Rights Reserved.

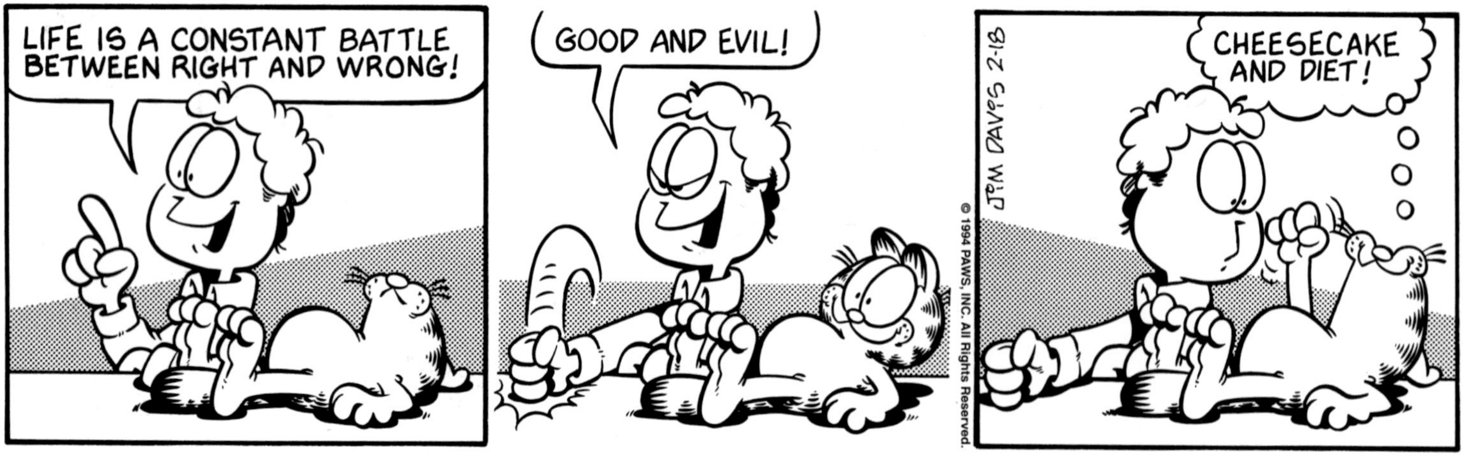
LIFE IS A CONSTANT BATTLE BETWEEN RIGHT AND WRONG!
GOOD AND EVIL!
CHEESECAKE AND DIET!
JIM DAVIS 2-18
© 1994 PAWS, INC. All Rights Reserved.

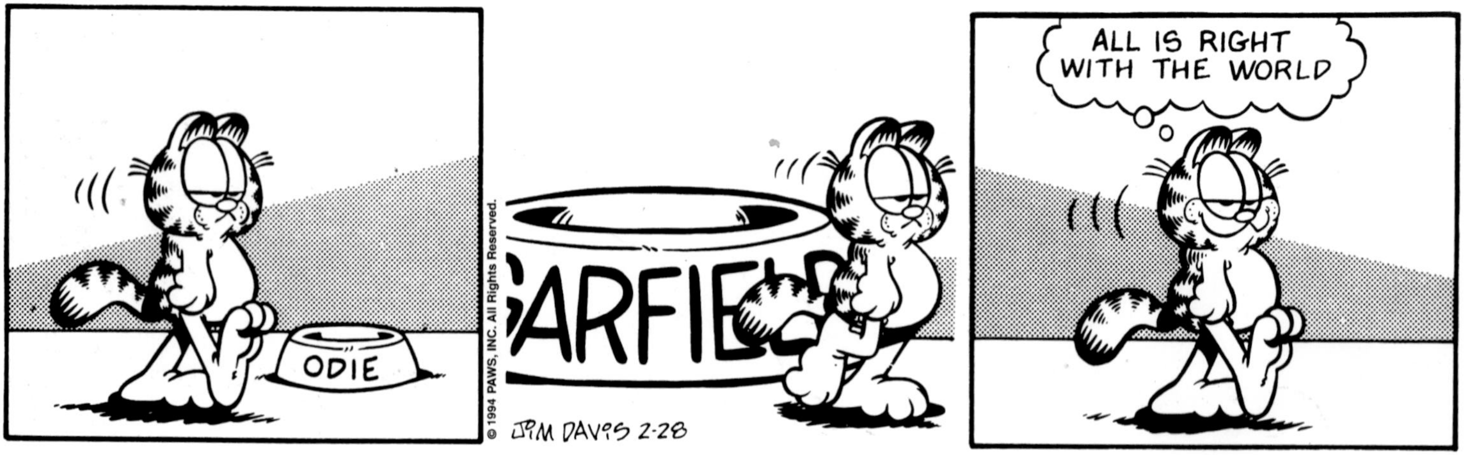
ODIE
GARFIE
© 1994 PAWS, INC. All Rights Reserved.
JIM DAVIS 2-28
ALL IS RIGHT WITH THE WORLD

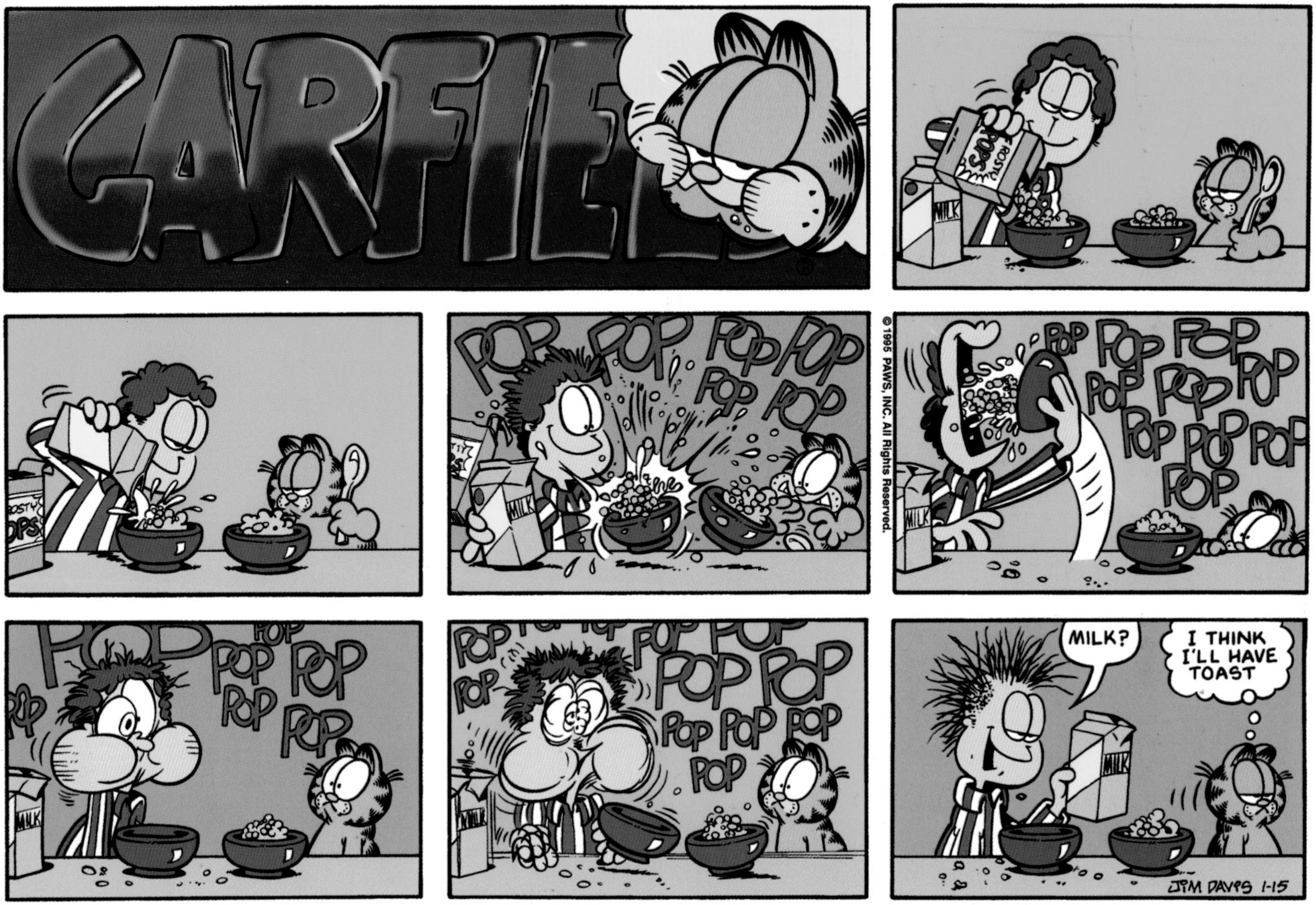
GARFIELD
MILK
POP POP POP POP POP POP
© 1995 PAWS, INC. All Rights Reserved.
POP POP POP POP POP POP POP POP POP POP POP
POP POP POP POP POP POP
POP POP POP POP POP POP POP POP POP
MILK?
I THINK I'LL HAVE TOAST
JIM DAVIS 1-15

I'm glad people want to have Garfield on their coffee cups, T-shirts, or on a poster. He's really a character with many expressions and attitudes, and I think it's neat if someone can relate to the character enough to want to demonstrate that by owning something "Garfield." It's flattering. Garfield's success has opened up many doors for me, allowed me to live a comfortable life, allowed me to travel and see things I might never have seen.

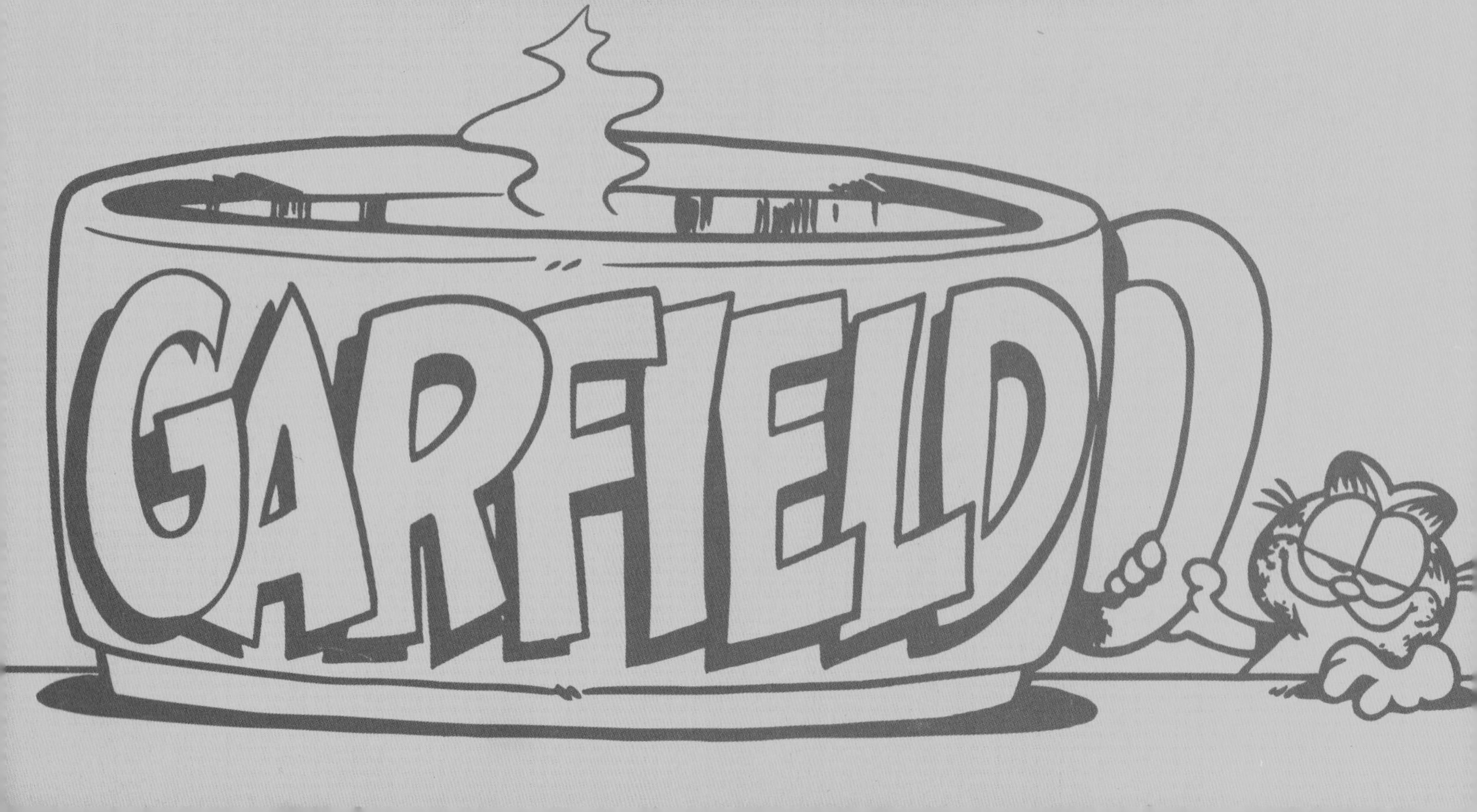
GARFIELD

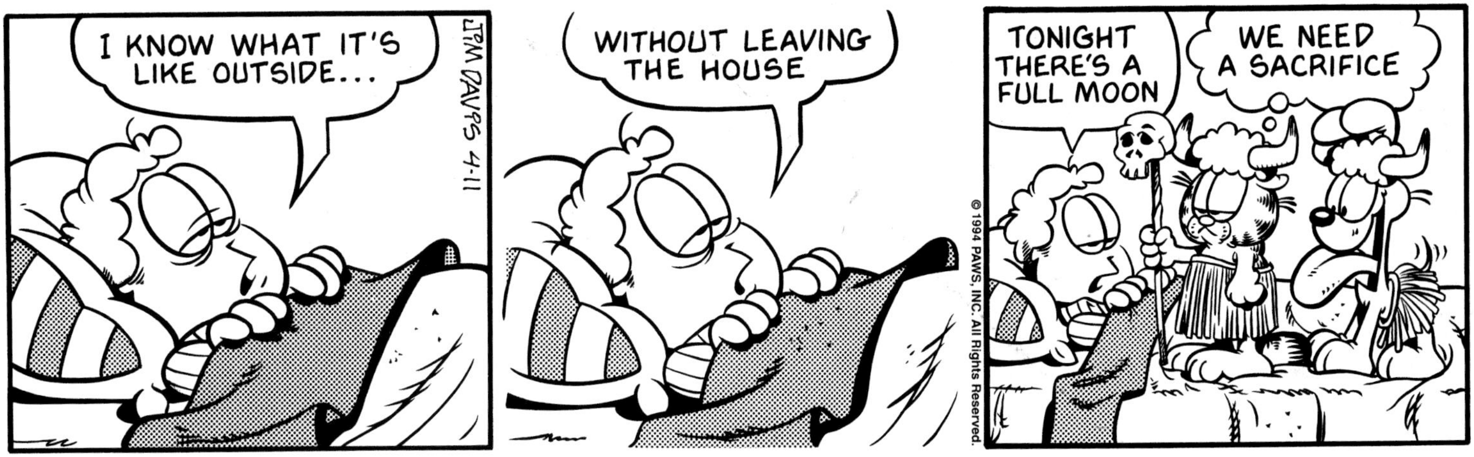

I KNOW WHAT IT'S LIKE OUTSIDE...
JIM DAVIS 4-11
WITHOUT LEAVING THE HOUSE
TONIGHT THERE'S A FULL MOON
WE NEED A SACRIFICE
© 1994 PAWS, INC. All Rights Reserved.

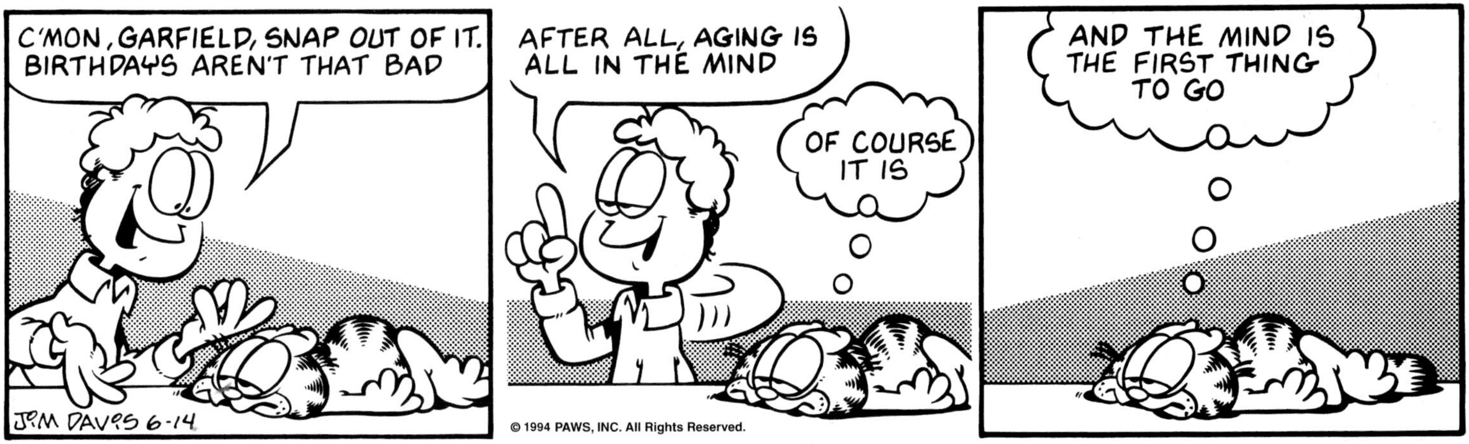

C'MON, GARFIELD, SNAP OUT OF IT. BIRTHDAYS AREN'T THAT BAD
JIM DAVIS 6-14
AFTER ALL, AGING IS ALL IN THE MIND
OF COURSE IT IS
© 1994 PAWS, INC. All Rights Reserved.
AND THE MIND IS THE FIRST THING TO GO

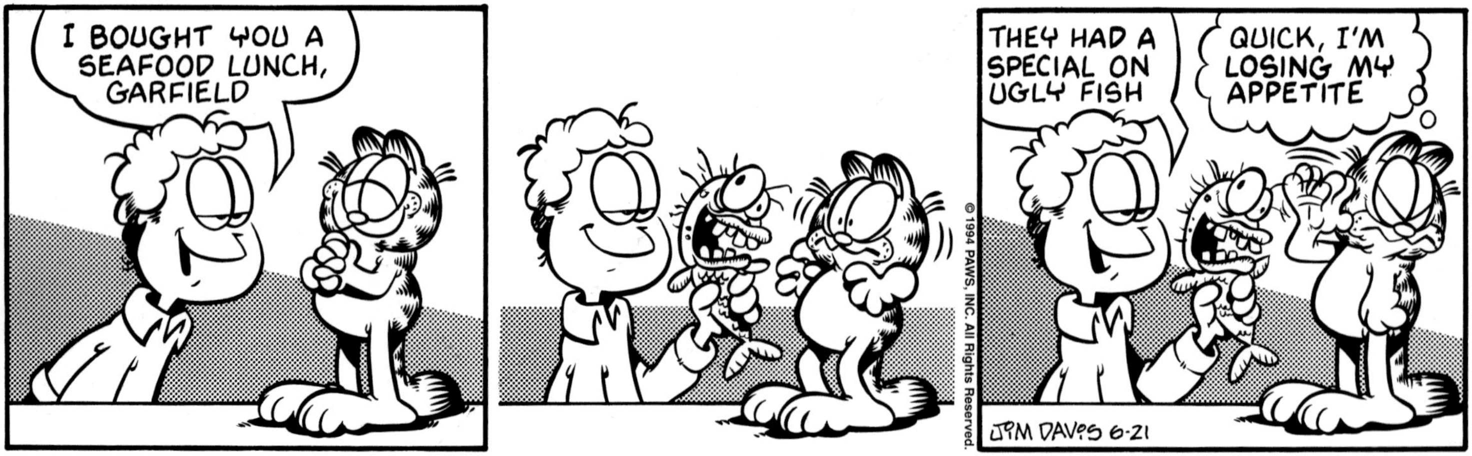
I BOUGHT YOU A SEAFOOD LUNCH, GARFIELD
THEY HAD A SPECIAL ON UGLY FISH
QUICK, I'M LOSING MY APPETITE
JIM DAVIS 6-21

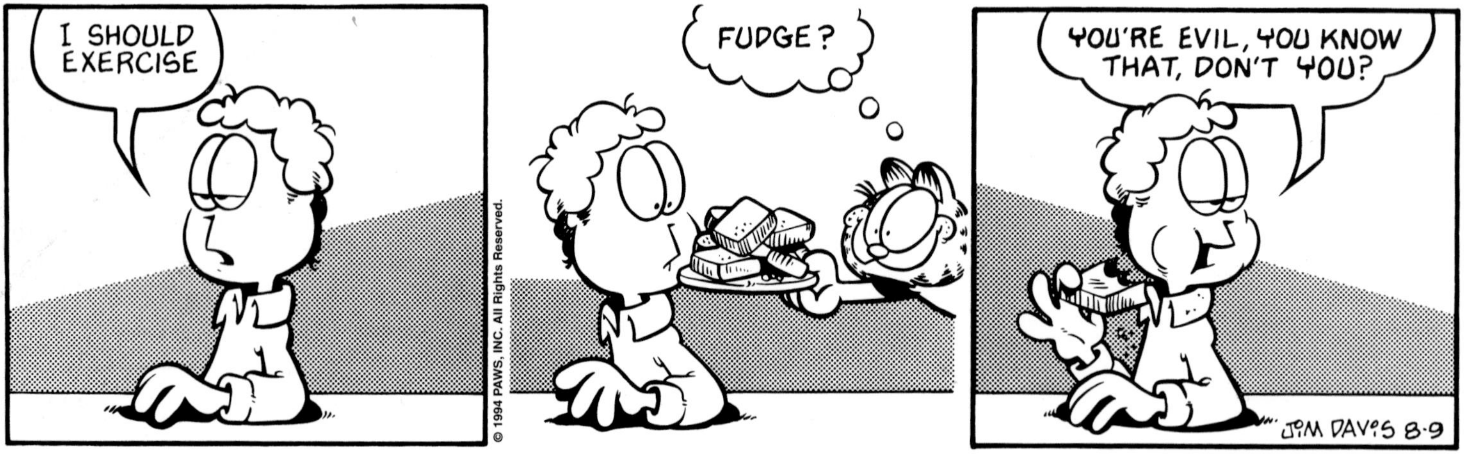
I SHOULD EXERCISE
FUDGE?
YOU'RE EVIL, YOU KNOW THAT, DON'T YOU?
JIM DAVIS 8-9

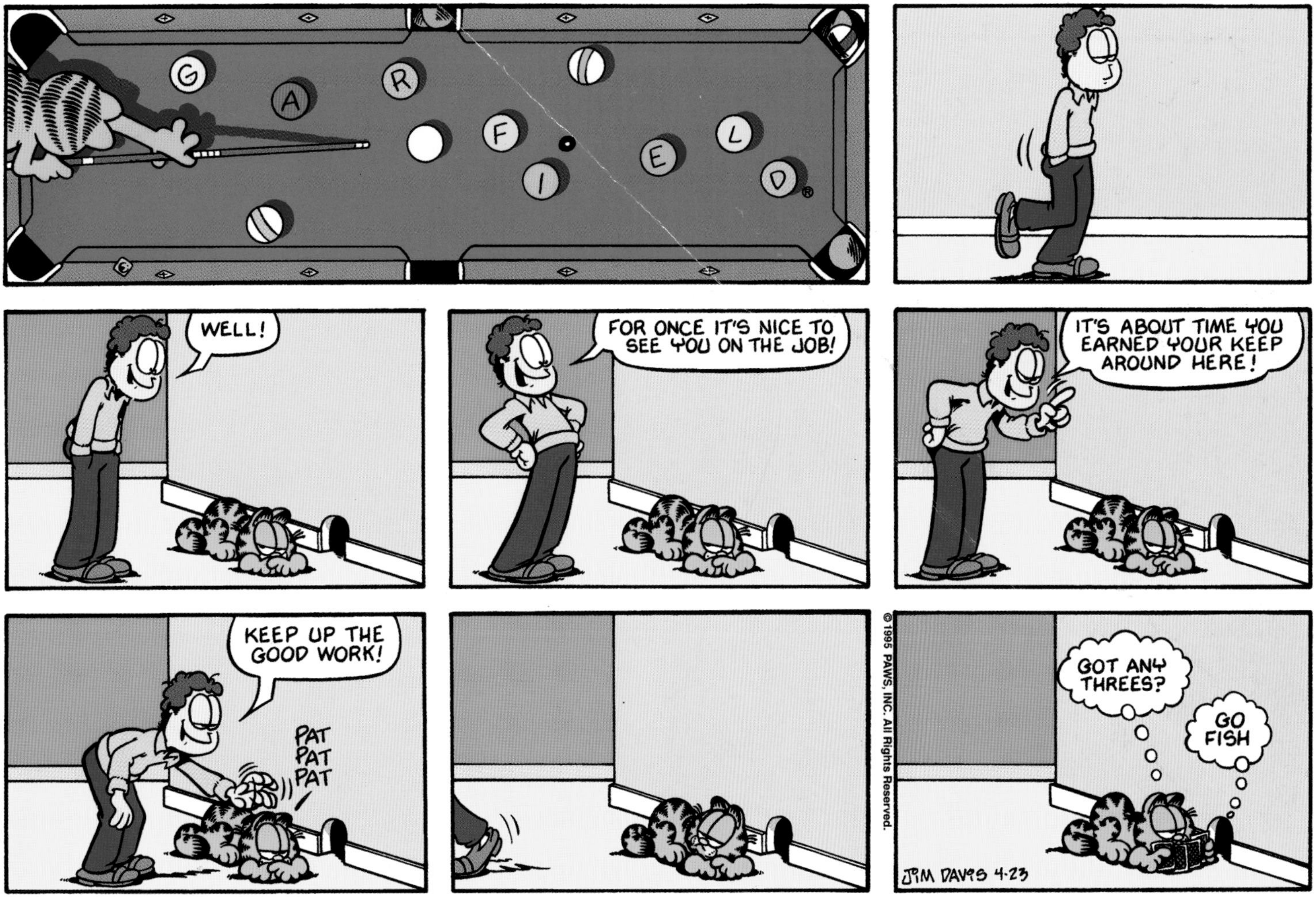
G
A
R
F
I
E
L
D
WELL!
FOR ONCE IT'S NICE TO SEE YOU ON THE JOB!
IT'S ABOUT TIME YOU EARNED YOUR KEEP AROUND HERE!
KEEP UP THE GOOD WORK!
PAT PAT PAT
GOT ANY THREES?
GO FISH
JIM DAVIS 4-23

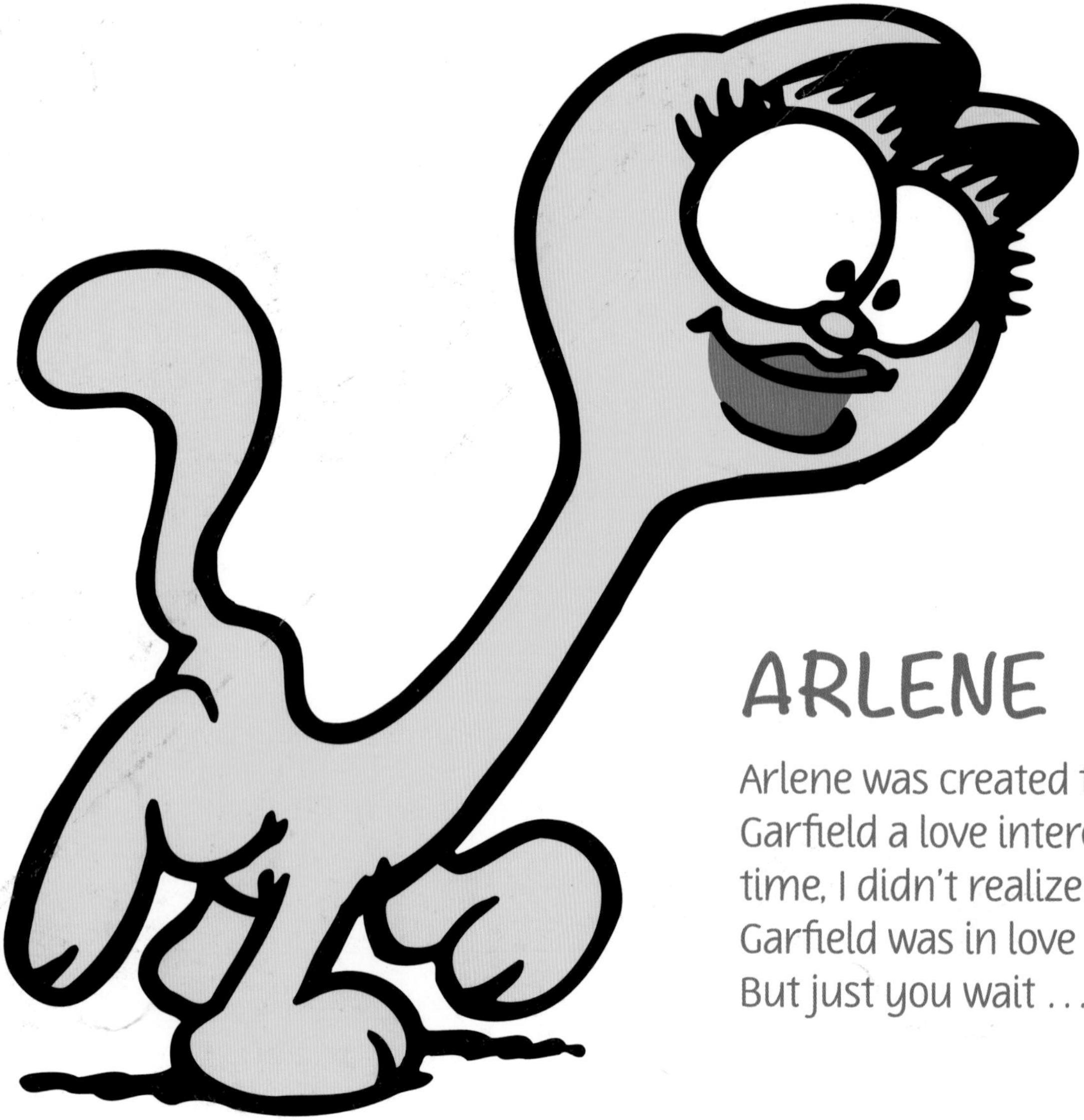

ARLENE

Arlene was created to give Garfield a love interest. At the time, I didn't realize how much Garfield was in love with himself! But just you wait . . .

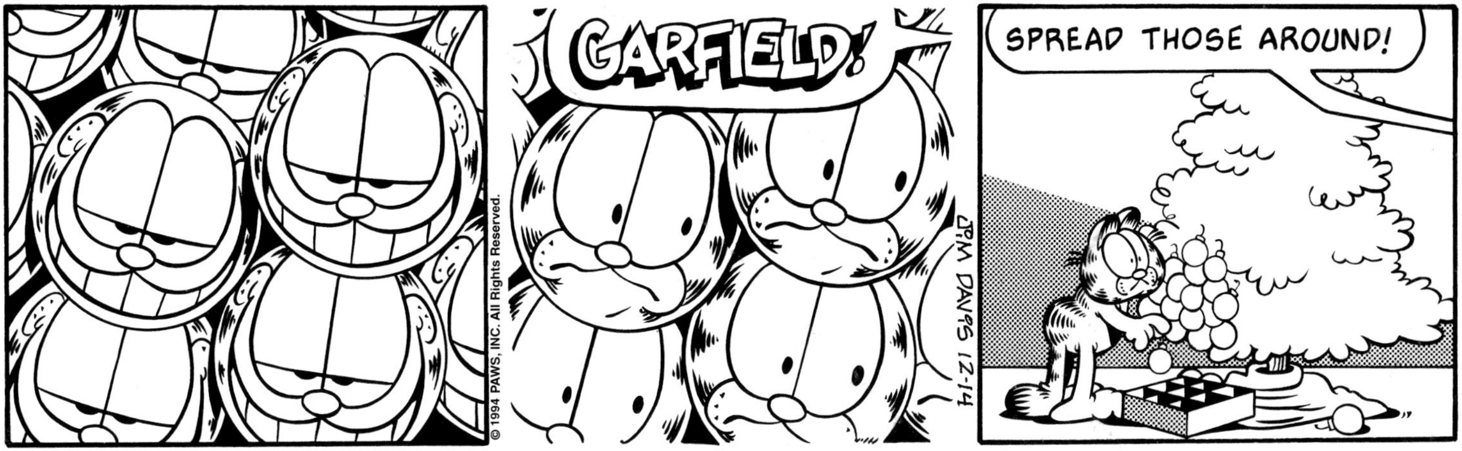
© 1994 PAWS, INC. All Rights Reserved.
GARFIELD!
JIM DAVIS 12-14
SPREAD THOSE AROUND!

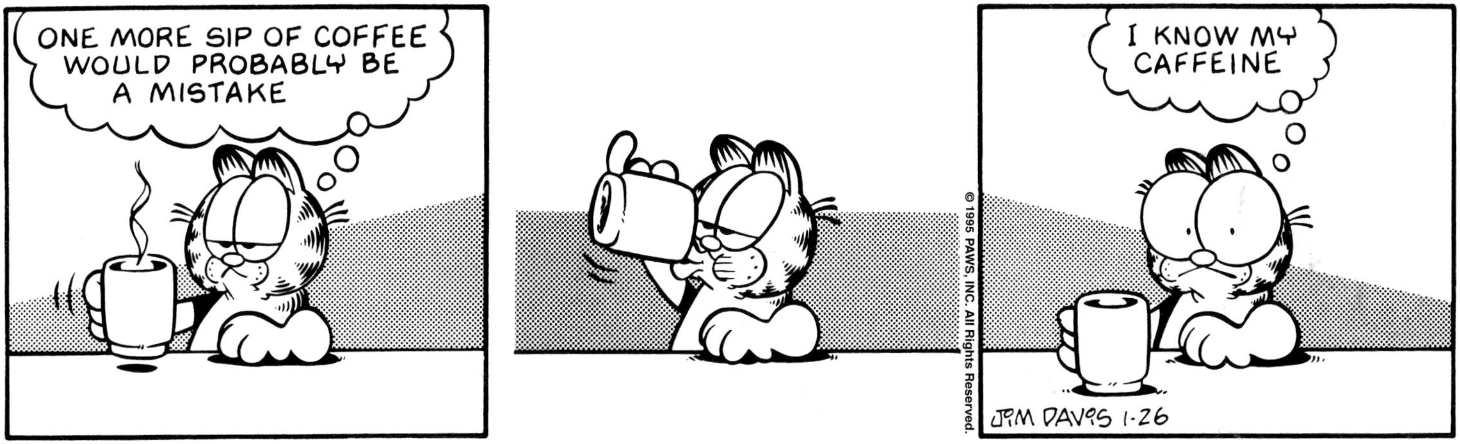
ONE MORE SIP OF COFFEE WOULD PROBABLY BE A MISTAKE
© 1995 PAWS, INC. All Rights Reserved.
I KNOW MY CAFFEINE
JIM DAVIS 1-26

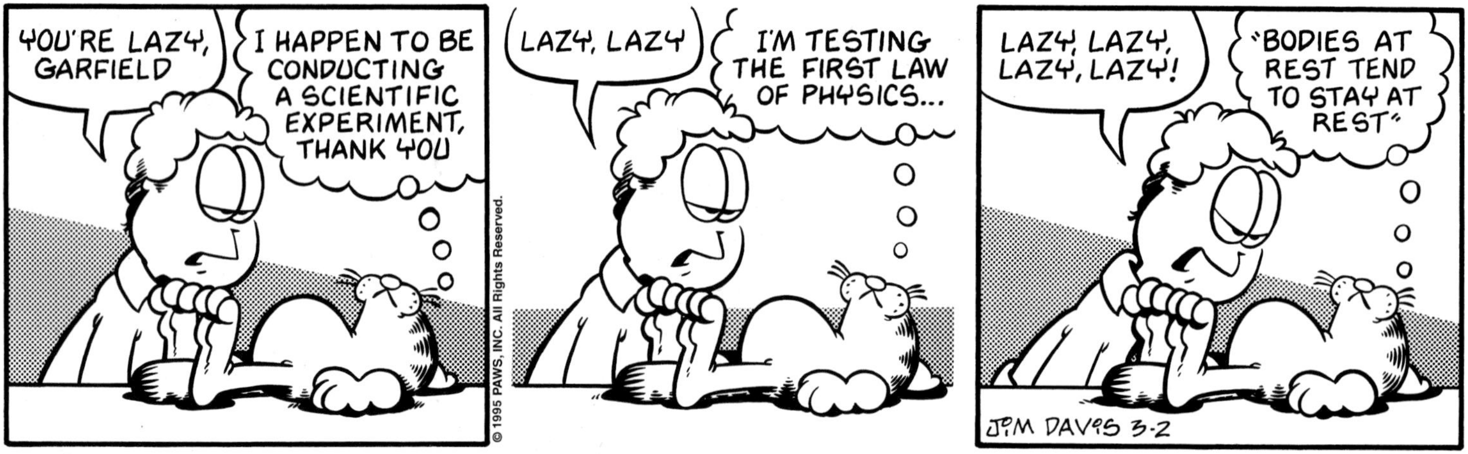
YOU'RE LAZY, GARFIELD
I HAPPEN TO BE CONDUCTING A SCIENTIFIC EXPERIMENT, THANK YOU
LAZY, LAZY
I'M TESTING THE FIRST LAW OF PHYSICS...
LAZY, LAZY, LAZY, LAZY!
"BODIES AT REST TEND TO STAY AT REST"
© 1995 PAWS, INC. All Rights Reserved.
JIM DAVIS 3-2

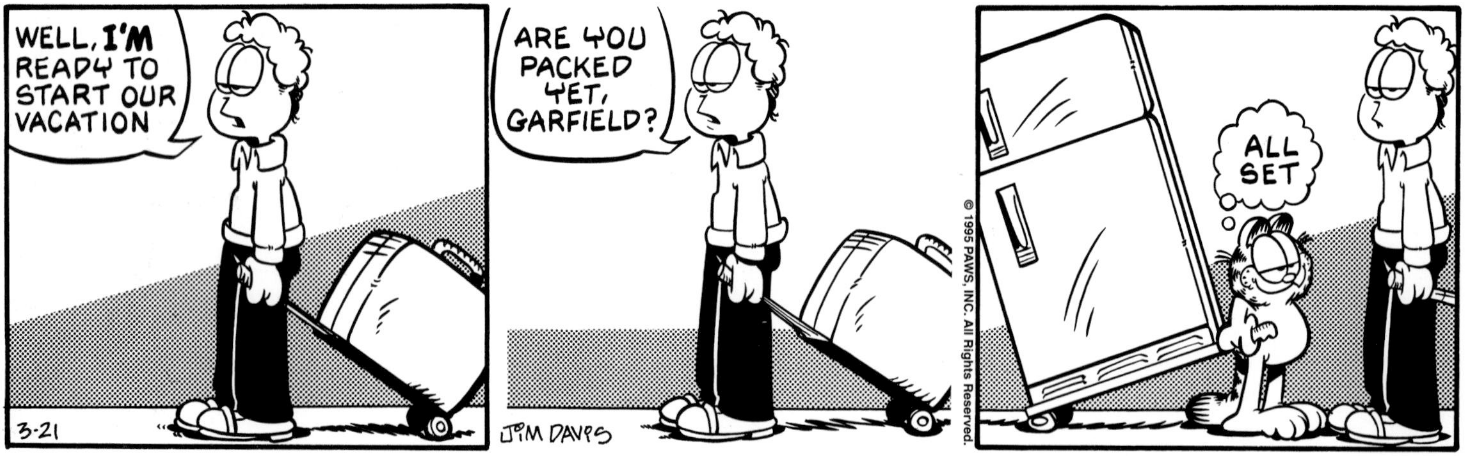
WELL, I'M READY TO START OUR VACATION
3-21
ARE YOU PACKED YET, GARFIELD?
JIM DAVIS
ALL SET
© 1995 PAWS, INC. All Rights Reserved.

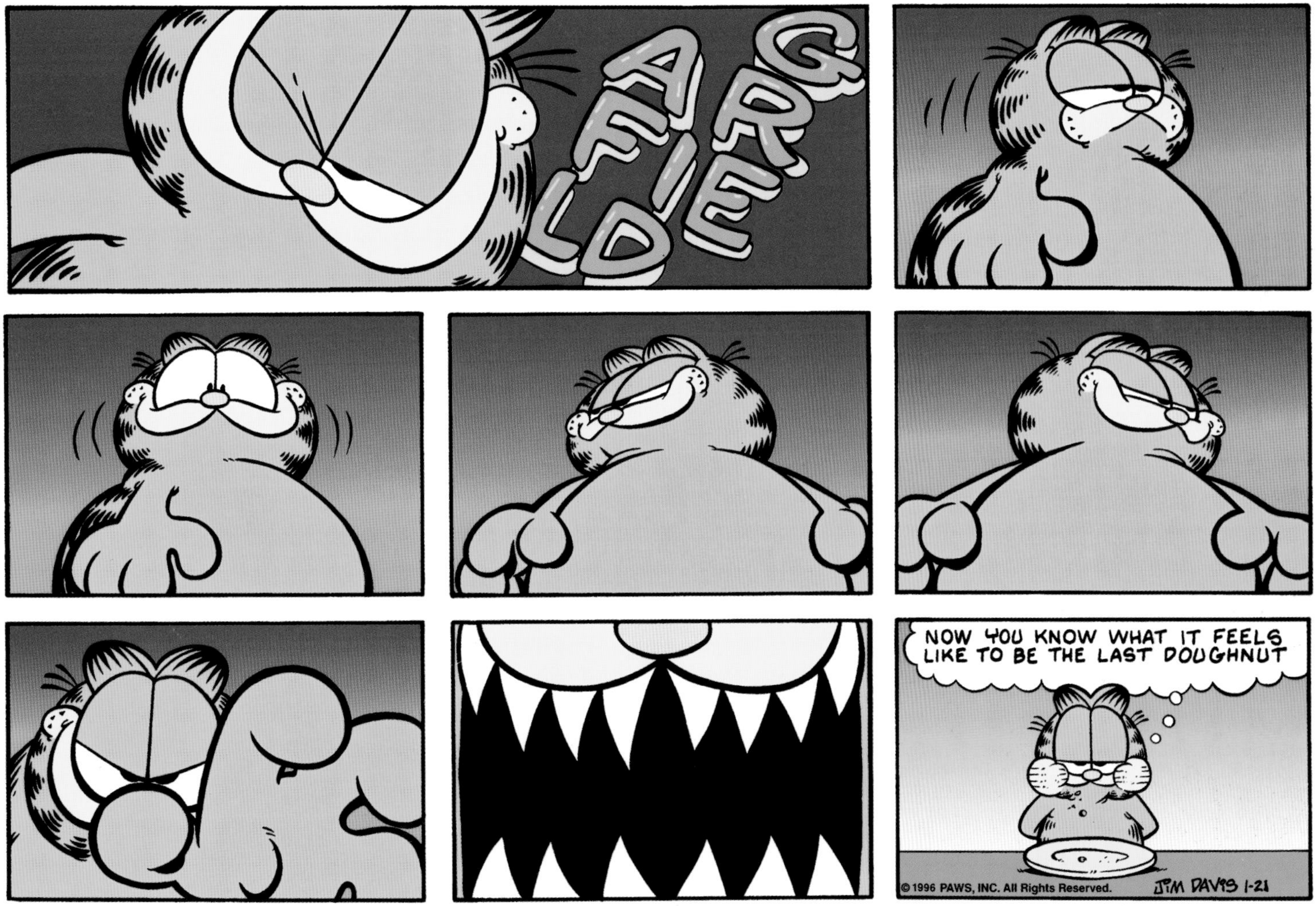
GARFIELD
NOW YOU KNOW WHAT IT FEELS LIKE TO BE THE LAST DOUGHNUT
© 1996 PAWS, INC. All Rights Reserved.
JIM DAVIS 1-21

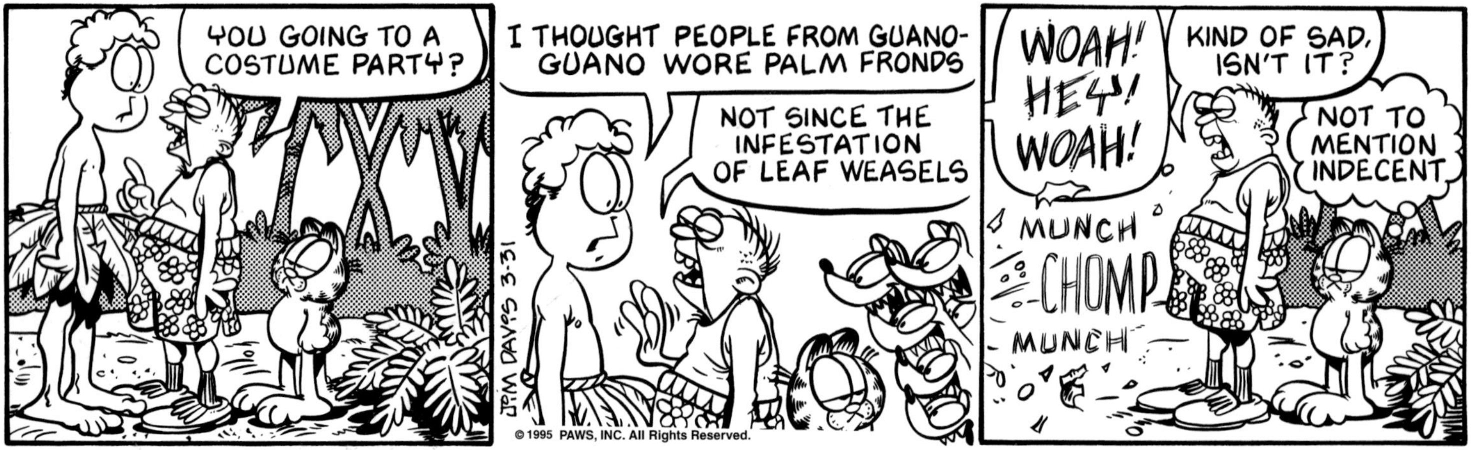
YOU GOING TO A COSTUME PARTY?
I THOUGHT PEOPLE FROM GUANO-GUANO WORE PALM FRONDS
NOT SINCE THE INFESTATION OF LEAF WEASELS
WOAH! HEY! WOAH!
MUNCH
CHOMP
MUNCH
KIND OF SAD, ISN'T IT?
NOT TO MENTION INDECENT
JIM DAVIS 3-31
© 1995 PAWS, INC. All Rights Reserved.

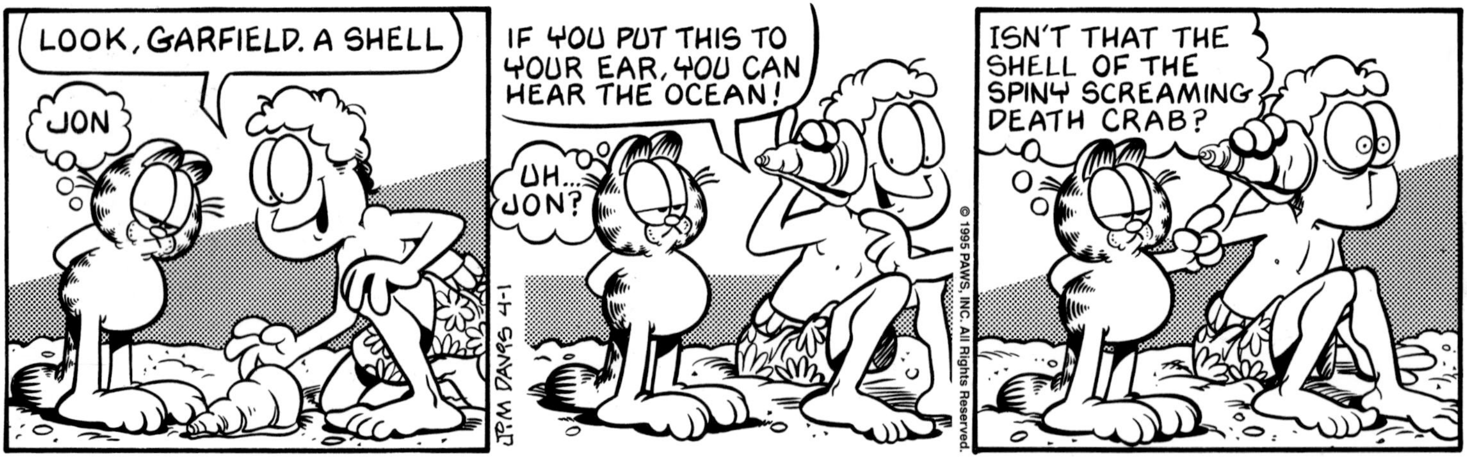
LOOK, GARFIELD. A SHELL
JON
IF YOU PUT THIS TO YOUR EAR, YOU CAN HEAR THE OCEAN!
UH... JON?
ISN'T THAT THE SHELL OF THE SPINY SCREAMING DEATH CRAB?
JIM DAVIS 4-1
© 1995 PAWS, INC. All Rights Reserved.

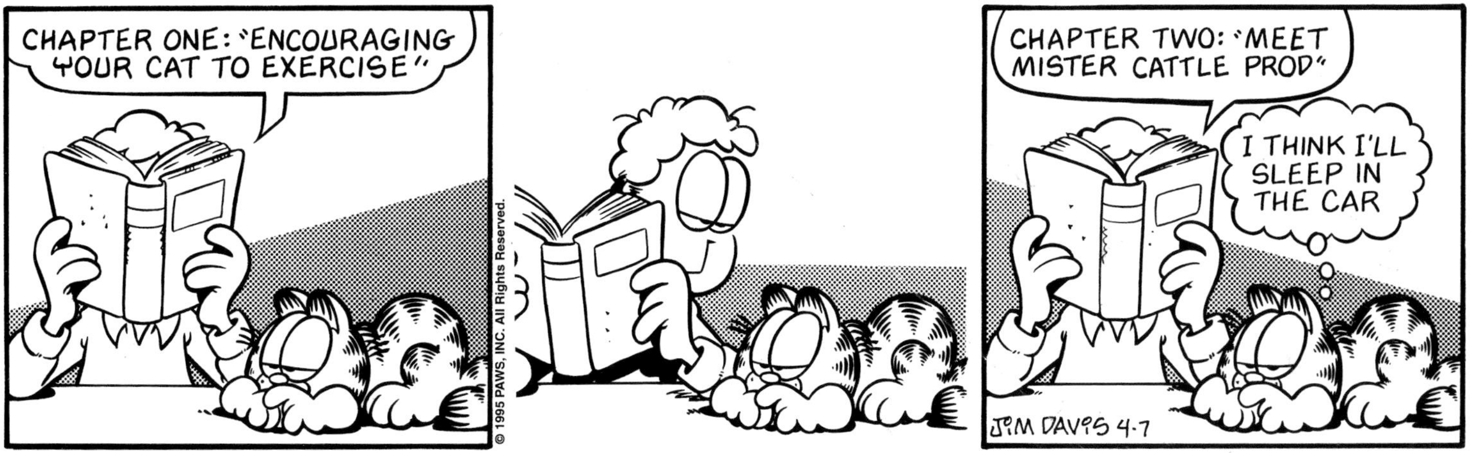
CHAPTER ONE: "ENCOURAGING YOUR CAT TO EXERCISE"
© 1995 PAWS, INC. All Rights Reserved.
CHAPTER TWO: "MEET MISTER CATTLE PROD"
I THINK I'LL SLEEP IN THE CAR
JIM DAVIS 4-7

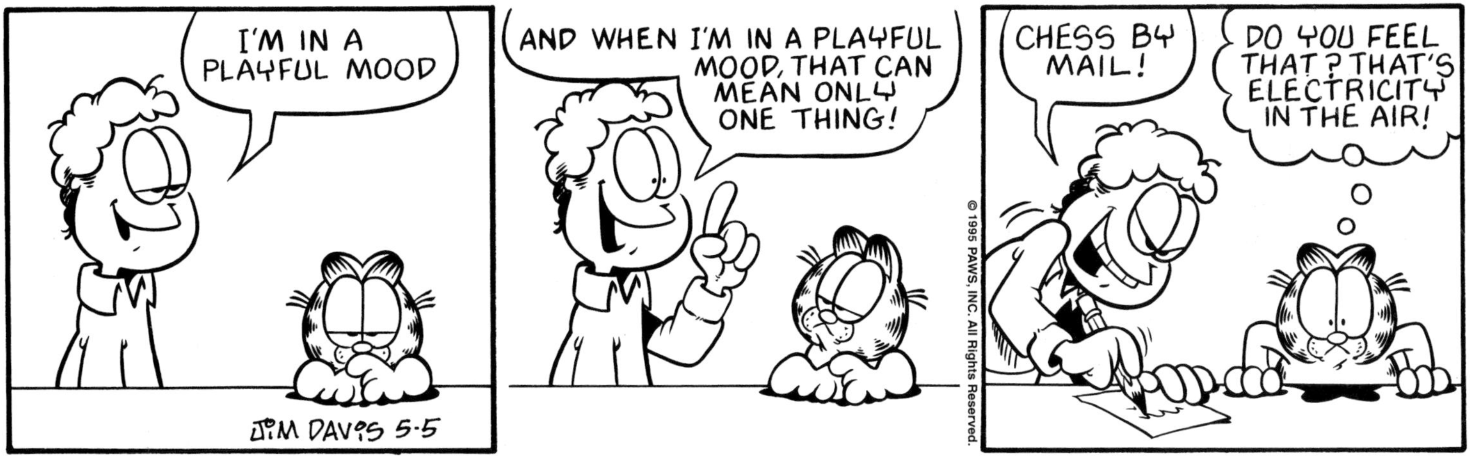
I'M IN A PLAYFUL MOOD
JIM DAVIS 5-5
AND WHEN I'M IN A PLAYFUL MOOD, THAT CAN MEAN ONLY ONE THING!
© 1995 PAWS, INC. All Rights Reserved.
CHESS BY MAIL!
DO YOU FEEL THAT? THAT'S ELECTRICITY IN THE AIR!

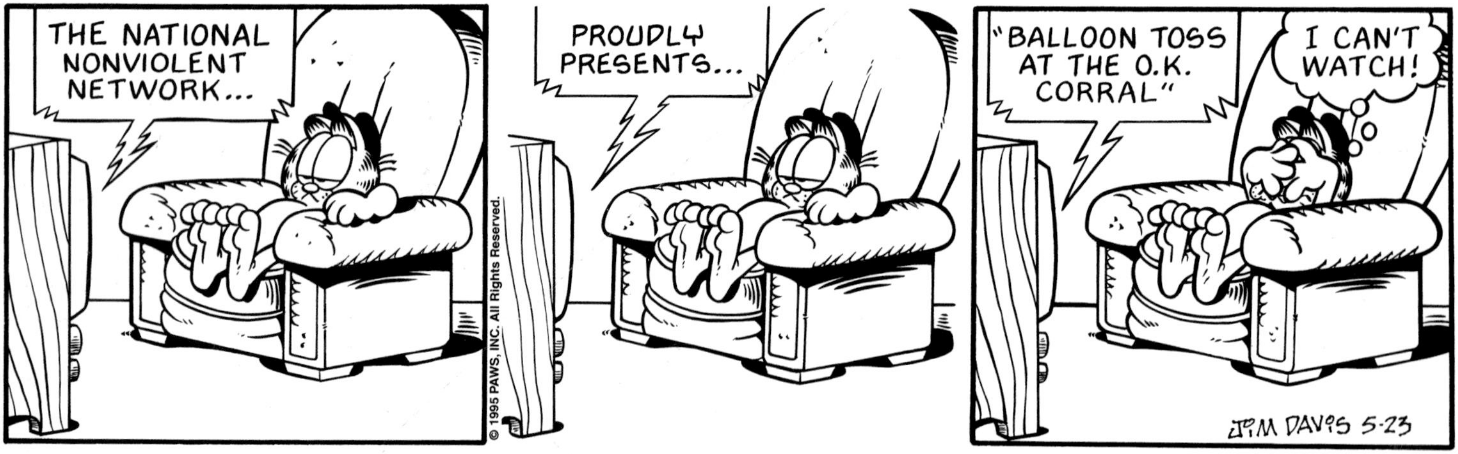
THE NATIONAL NONVIOLENT NETWORK...
PROUDLY PRESENTS...
"BALLOON TOSS AT THE O.K. CORRAL"
I CAN'T WATCH!
JIM DAVIS 5-23

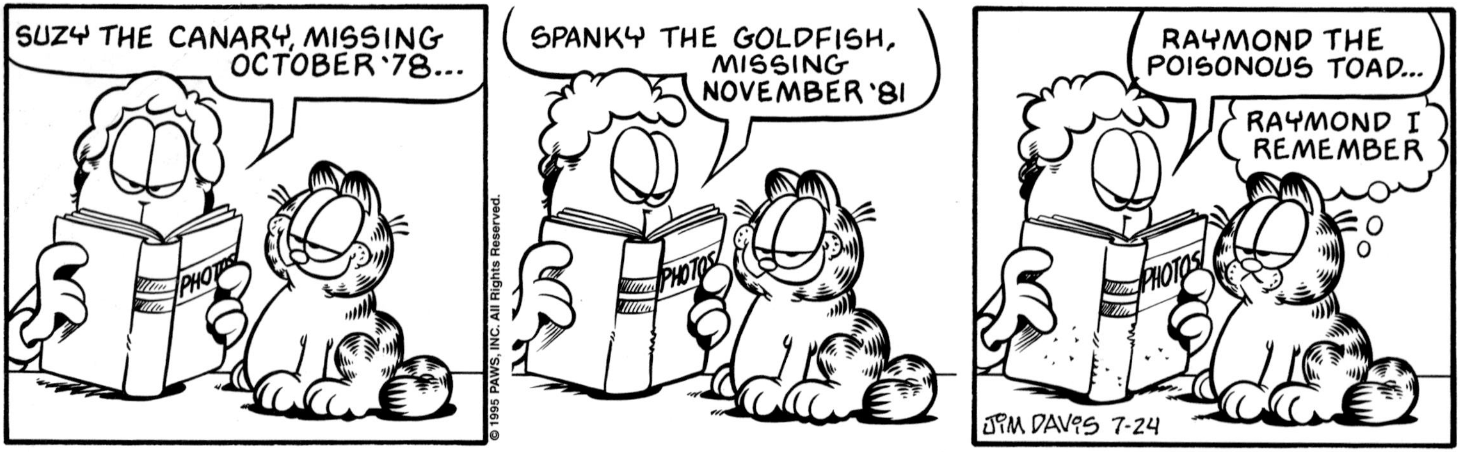
SUZY THE CANARY, MISSING OCTOBER '78...
SPANKY THE GOLDFISH, MISSING NOVEMBER '81
RAYMOND THE POISONOUS TOAD...
RAYMOND I REMEMBER
PHOTOS
JIM DAVIS 7-24

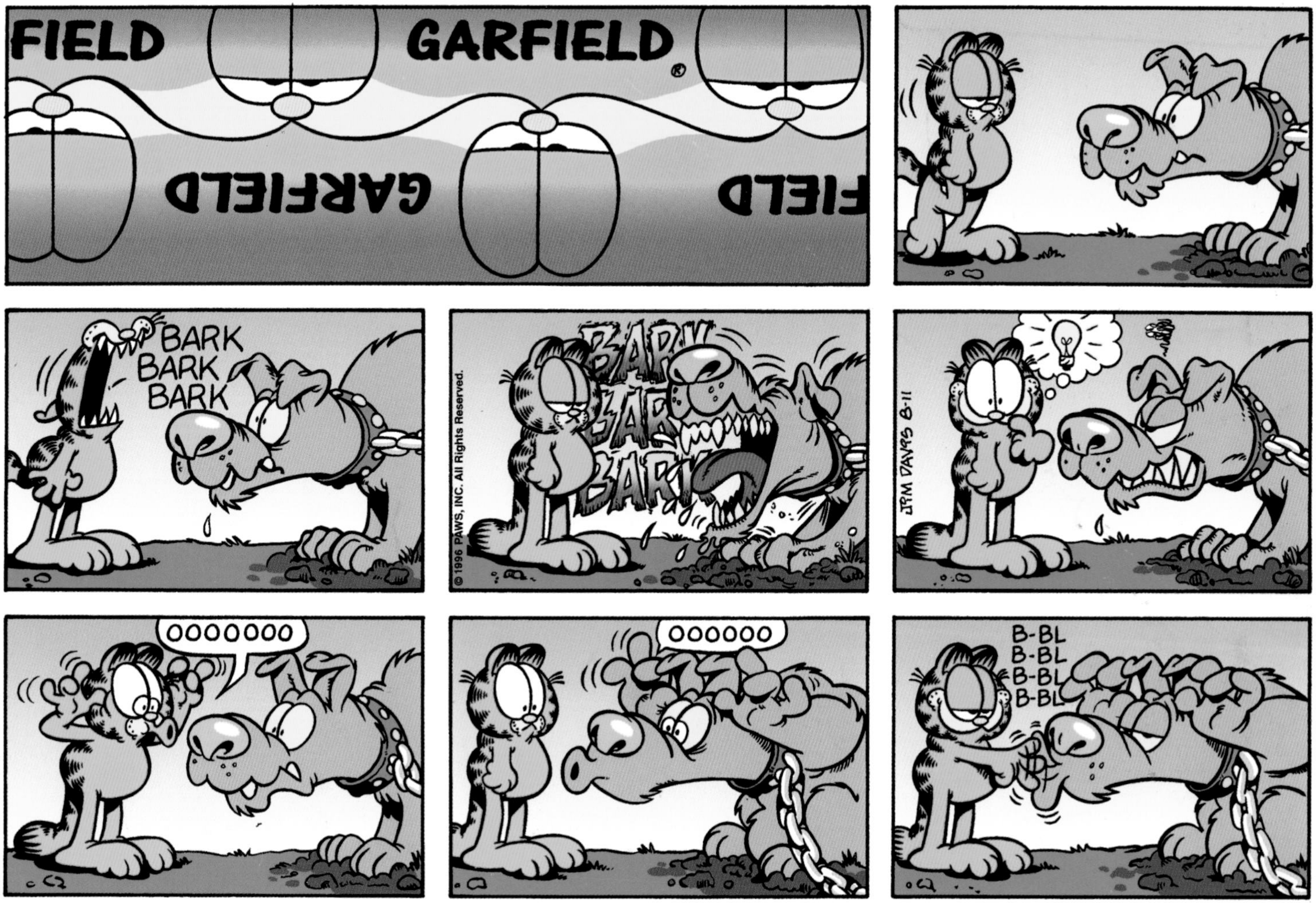
GARFIELD
BARK
BARK
BARK
BARK
BARK
BARK
© 1996 PAWS, INC. All Rights Reserved.
JPM DAVIS 8-11
OOOOOOO
OOOOOO
B-BL
B-BL
B-BL
B-BL

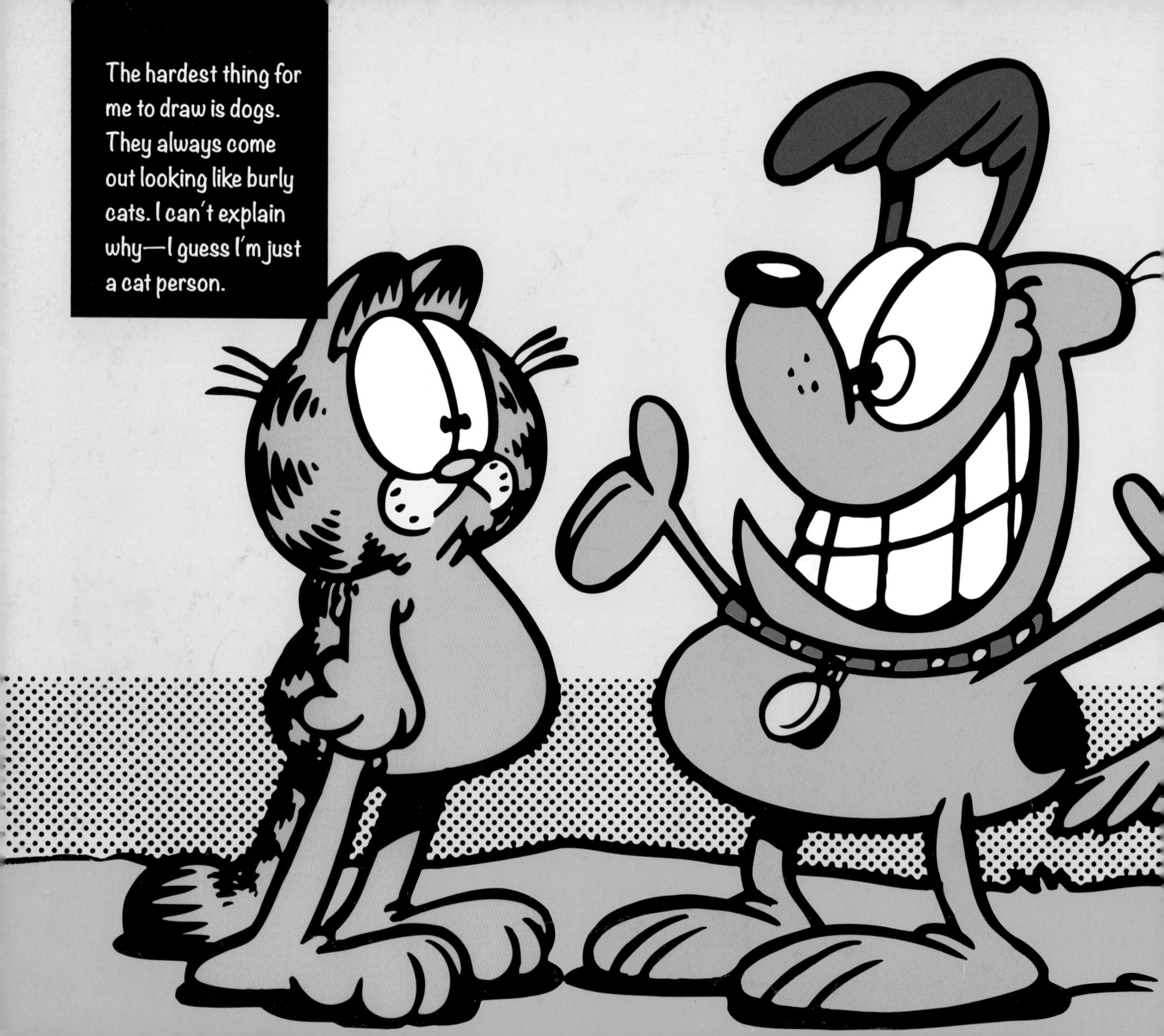

The hardest thing for me to draw is dogs. They always come out looking like burly cats. I can't explain why—I guess I'm just a cat person.

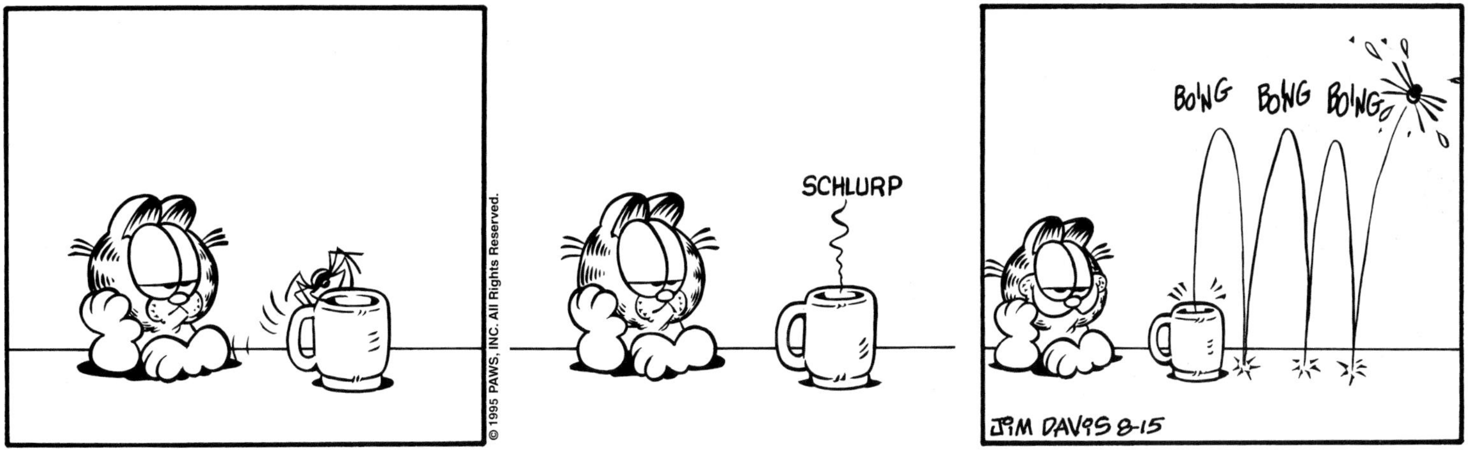
© 1995 PAWS, INC. All Rights Reserved.
SCHLURP
BOING
BOING
BOING
JIM DAVIS 8-15

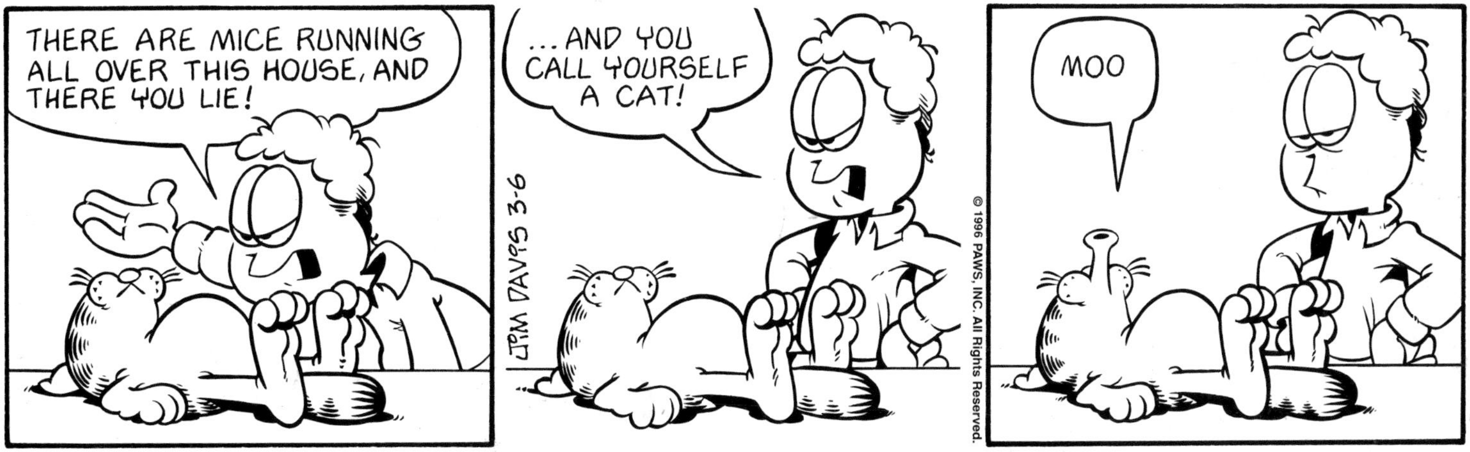
THERE ARE MICE RUNNING ALL OVER THIS HOUSE, AND THERE YOU LIE!
JIM DAVIS 3-6
...AND YOU CALL YOURSELF A CAT!
© 1996 PAWS, INC. All Rights Reserved.
MOO

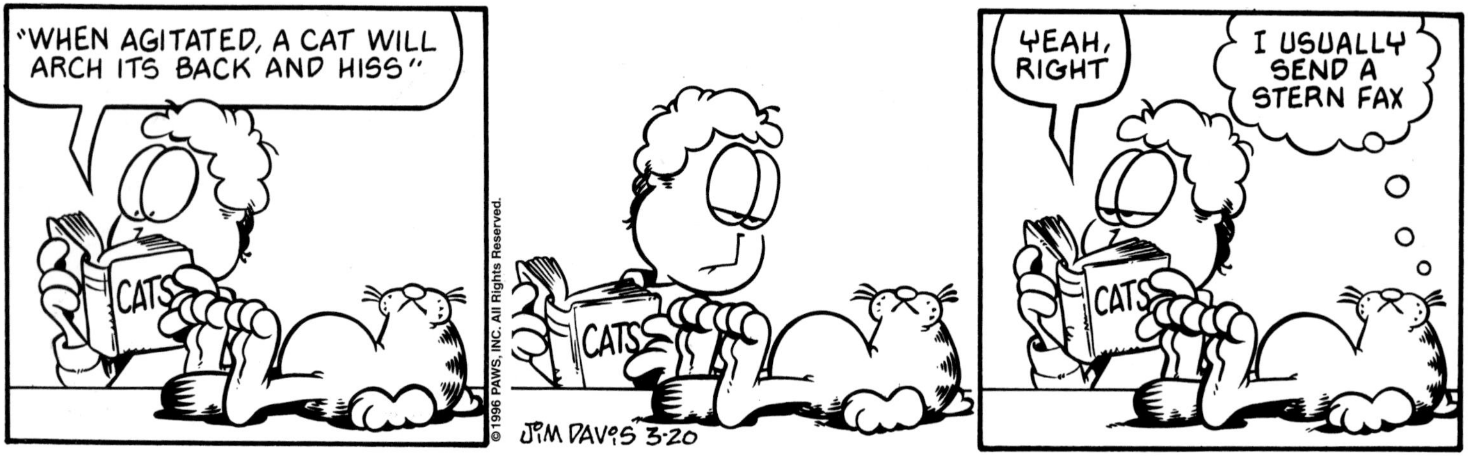
"WHEN AGITATED, A CAT WILL ARCH ITS BACK AND HISS"
CATS
© 1996 PAWS, INC. All Rights Reserved.
JIM DAVIS 3-20
YEAH, RIGHT
I USUALLY SEND A STERN FAX

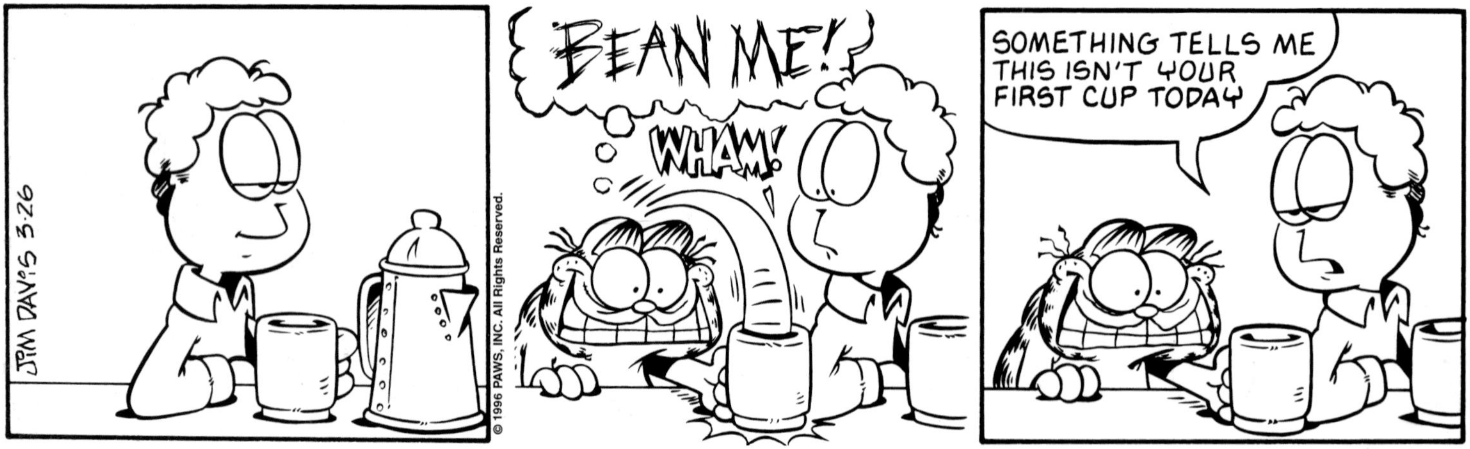
JIM DAVIS 3-26
© 1996 PAWS, INC. All Rights Reserved.
BEAN ME!
WHAM!
SOMETHING TELLS ME THIS ISN'T YOUR FIRST CUP TODAY

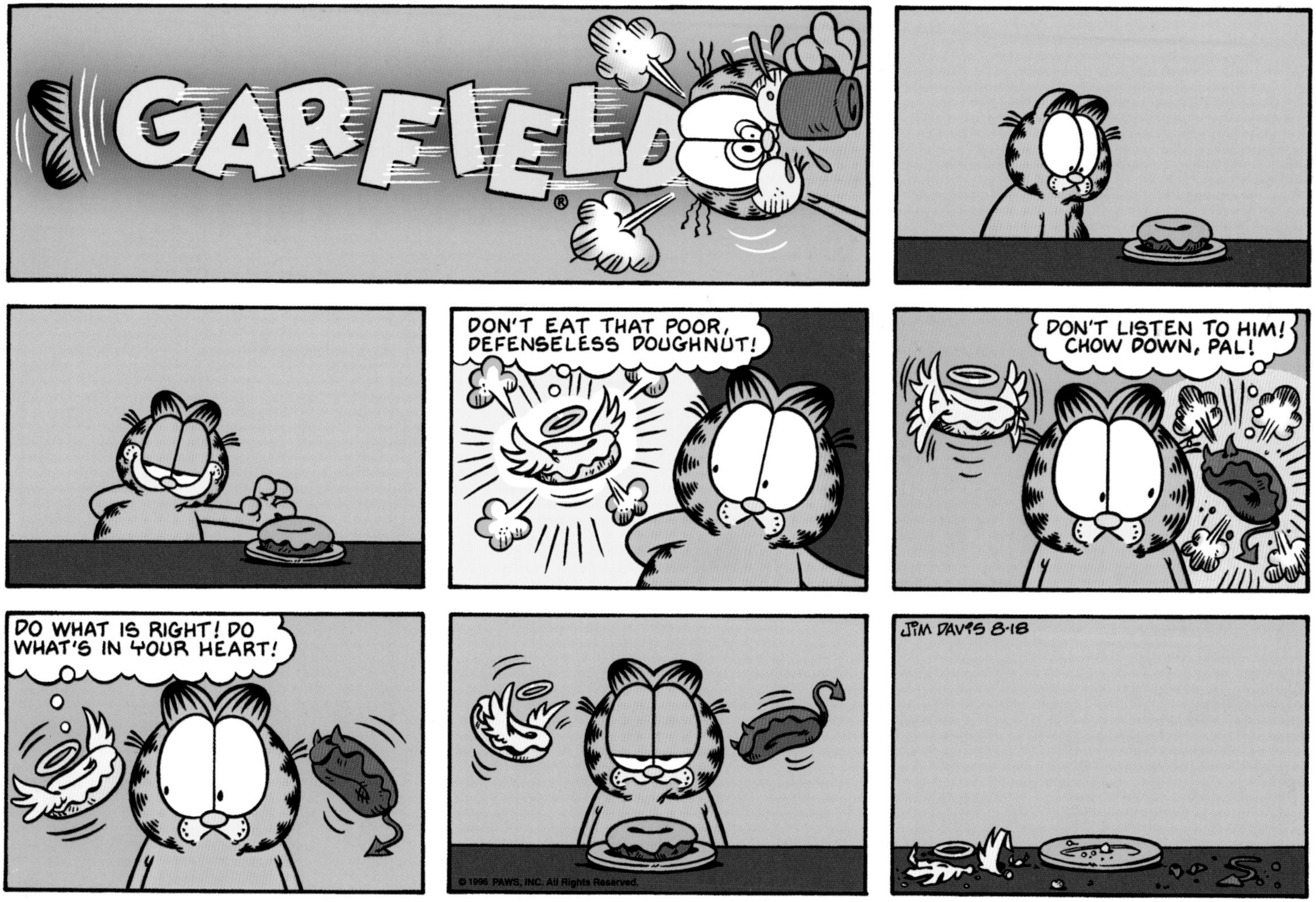
GARFIELD®
DON'T EAT THAT POOR, DEFENSELESS DOUGHNUT!
DON'T LISTEN TO HIM! CHOW DOWN, PAL!
DO WHAT IS RIGHT! DO WHAT'S IN YOUR HEART!
© 1996 PAWS, INC. All Rights Reserved.
JIM DAVIS 8-18

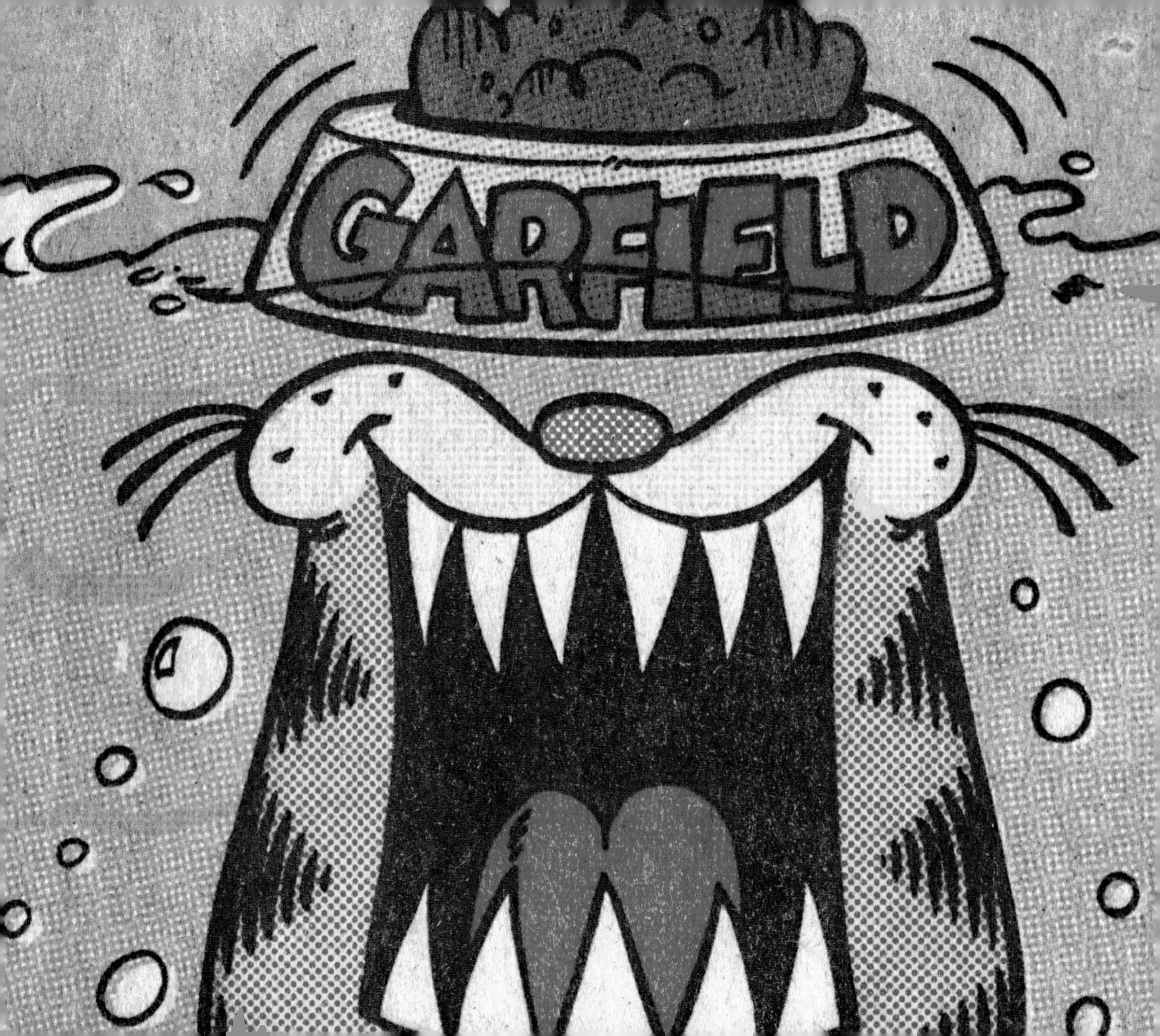
GARFIELD

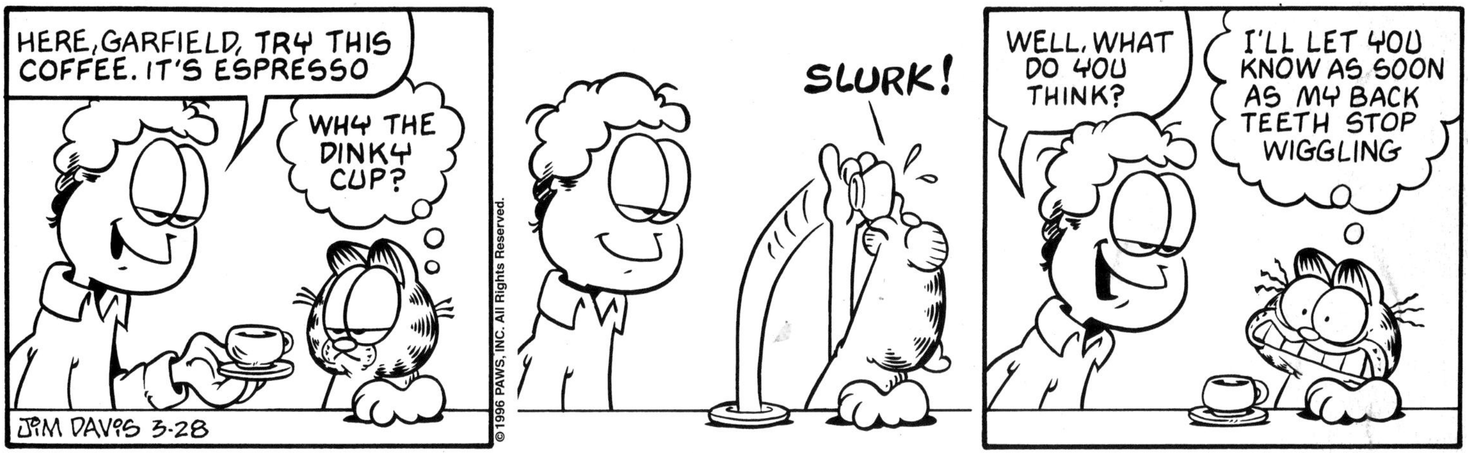
HERE, GARFIELD, TRY THIS COFFEE. IT'S ESPRESSO
WHY THE DINKY CUP?
JIM DAVIS 3-28
© 1996 PAWS, INC. All Rights Reserved.
SLURK!
WELL, WHAT DO YOU THINK?
I'LL LET YOU KNOW AS SOON AS MY BACK TEETH STOP WIGGLING

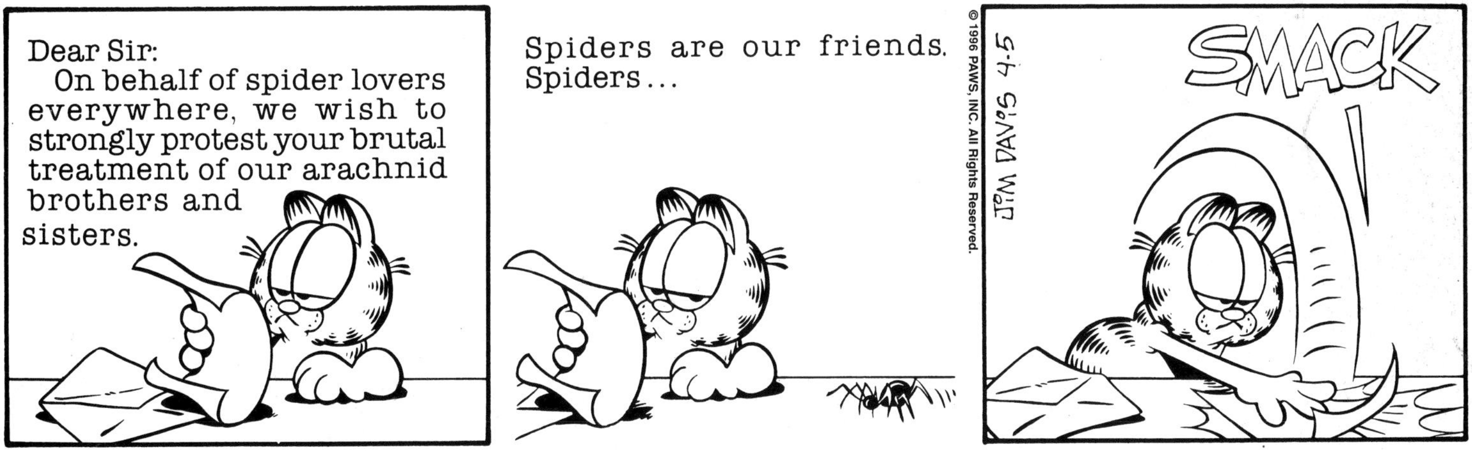
Dear Sir:
On behalf of spider lovers everywhere, we wish to strongly protest your brutal treatment of our arachnid brothers and sisters.
Spiders are our friends. Spiders...
© 1996 PAWS, INC. All Rights Reserved.
JIM DAVIS 4-5
SMACK

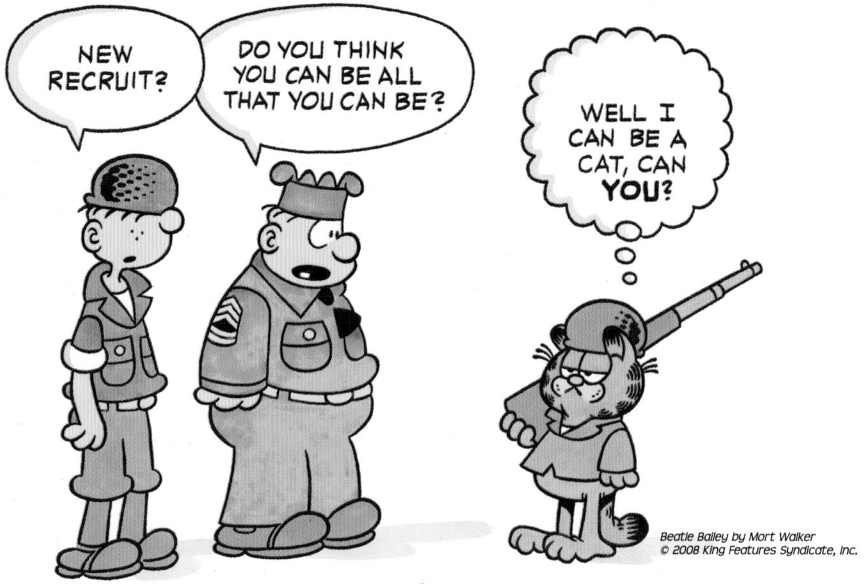
NEW RECRUIT?
DO YOU THINK YOU CAN BE ALL THAT YOU CAN BE?
WELL I CAN BE A CAT, CAN **YOU**?
Beetle Bailey by Mort Walker
© 2008 King Features Syndicate, Inc.

My dad's favorite strip is *Beetle Bailey*. How's that for awkward?

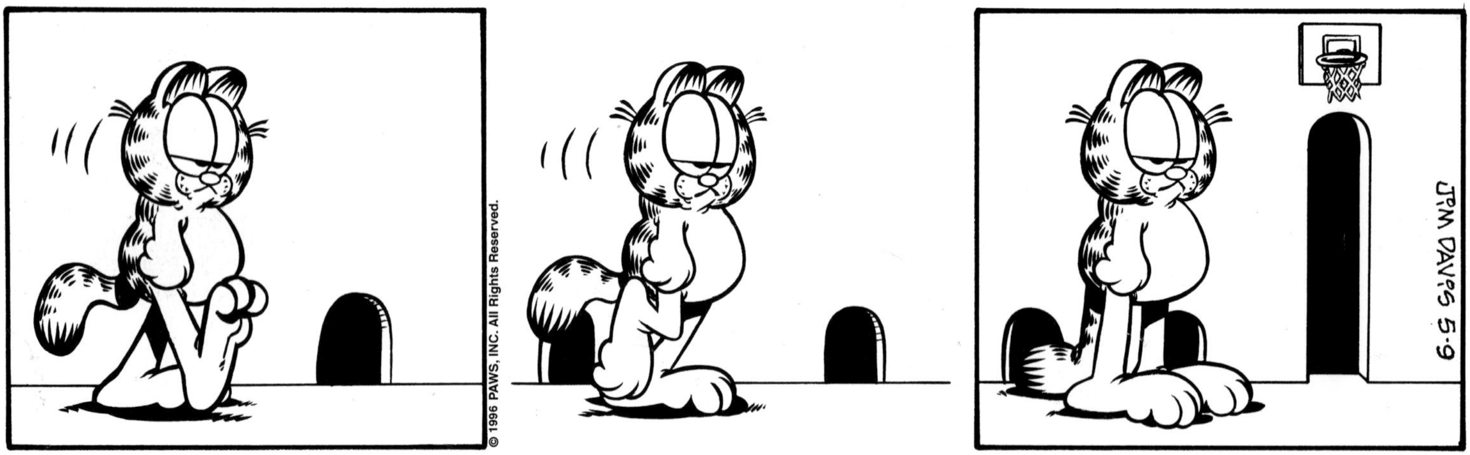
© 1996 PAWS, INC. All Rights Reserved.
JIM DAVIS 5-9

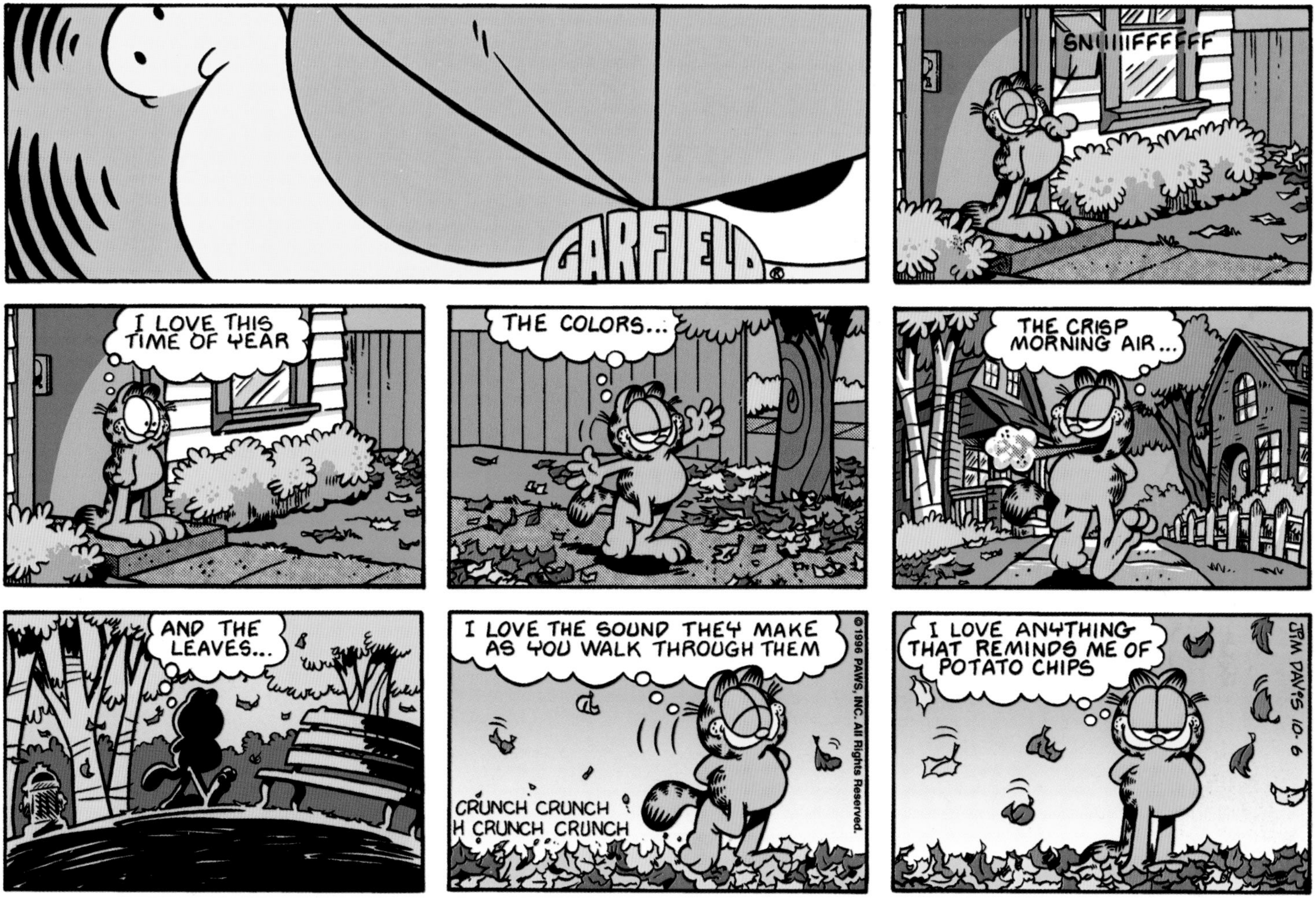
GARFIELD®
SNIIIIIFFFFFF
I LOVE THIS TIME OF YEAR
THE COLORS...
THE CRISP MORNING AIR...
AND THE LEAVES...
I LOVE THE SOUND THEY MAKE AS YOU WALK THROUGH THEM
CRUNCH CRUNCH
H CRUNCH CRUNCH
© 1996 PAWS, INC. All Rights Reserved.
I LOVE ANYTHING THAT REMINDS ME OF POTATO CHIPS
JIM DAVIS 10-6

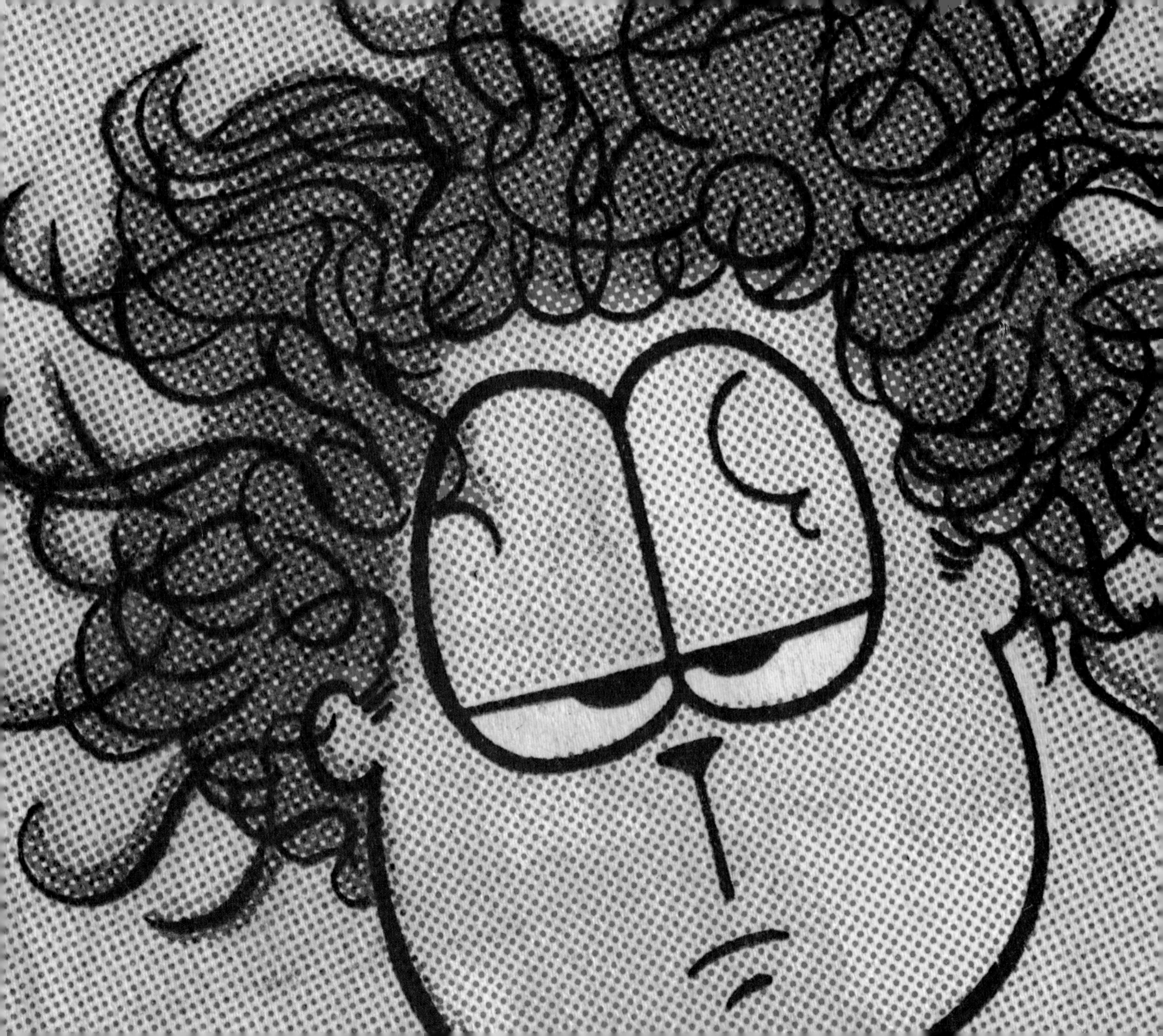

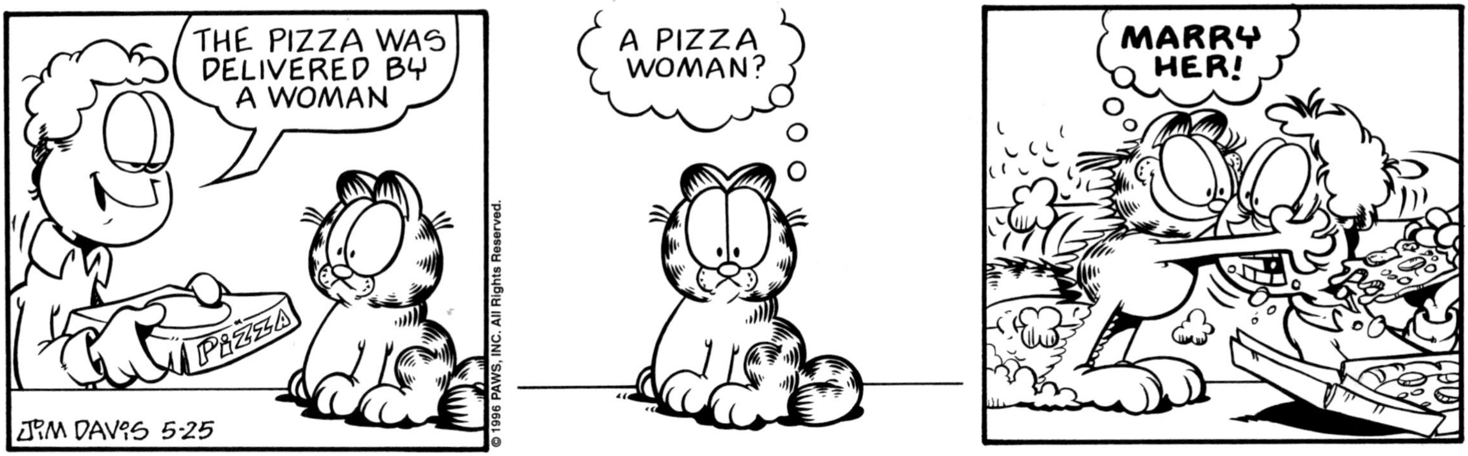
THE PIZZA WAS DELIVERED BY A WOMAN
JIM DAVIS 5-25
© 1996 PAWS, INC. All Rights Reserved.
A PIZZA WOMAN?
MARRY HER!

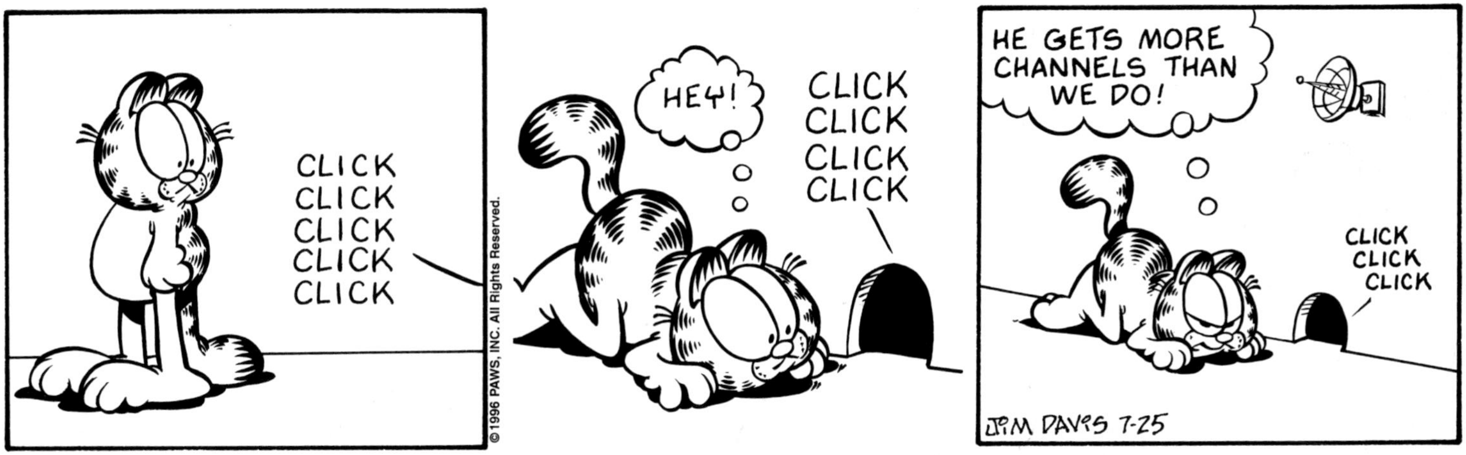
CLICK CLICK CLICK CLICK CLICK
© 1996 PAWS, INC. All Rights Reserved.
HEY!
CLICK CLICK CLICK CLICK
HE GETS MORE CHANNELS THAN WE DO!
CLICK CLICK CLICK
JIM DAVIS 7-25

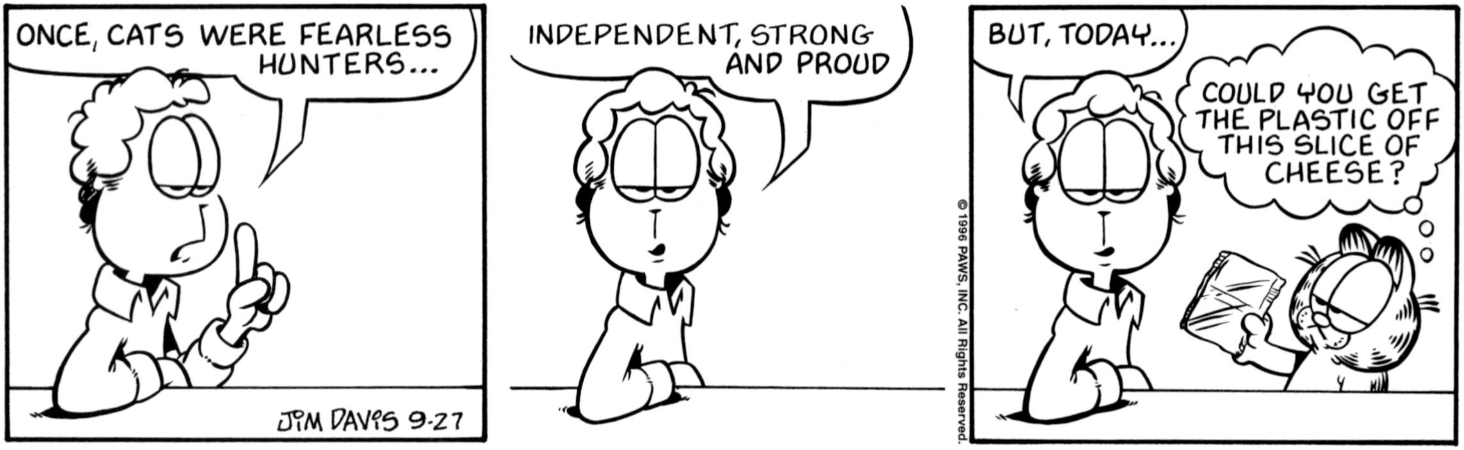
ONCE, CATS WERE FEARLESS HUNTERS...
JIM DAVIS 9-27
INDEPENDENT, STRONG AND PROUD
BUT, TODAY...
COULD YOU GET THE PLASTIC OFF THIS SLICE OF CHEESE?
© 1996 PAWS, INC. All Rights Reserved.

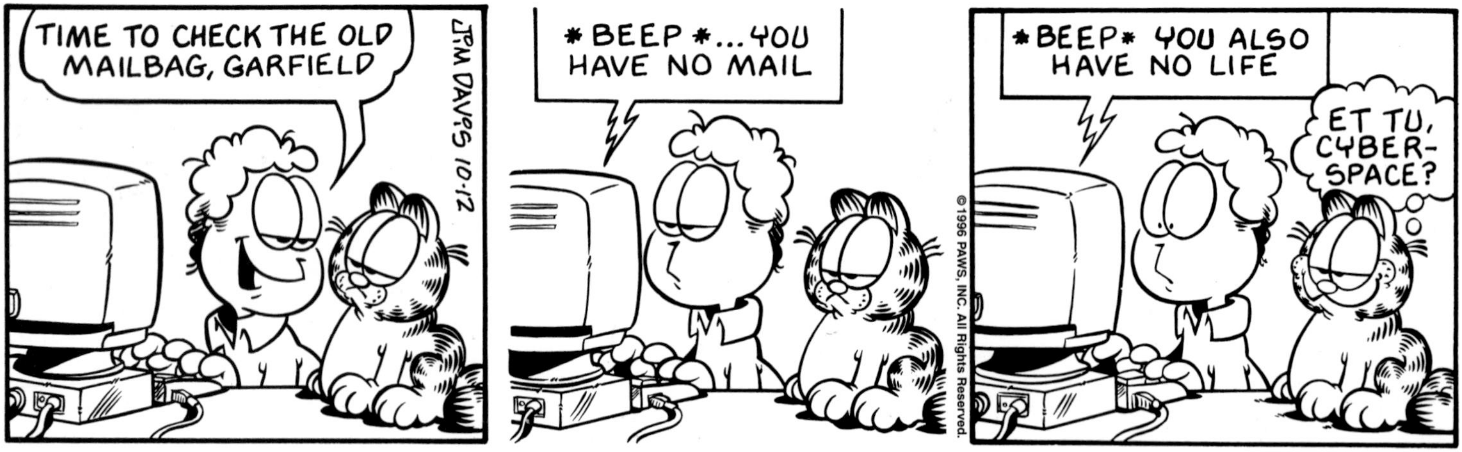
TIME TO CHECK THE OLD MAILBAG, GARFIELD
JIM DAVIS 10-12
BEEP... YOU HAVE NO MAIL
BEEP YOU ALSO HAVE NO LIFE
ET TU, CYBER-SPACE?
© 1996 PAWS, INC. All Rights Reserved.

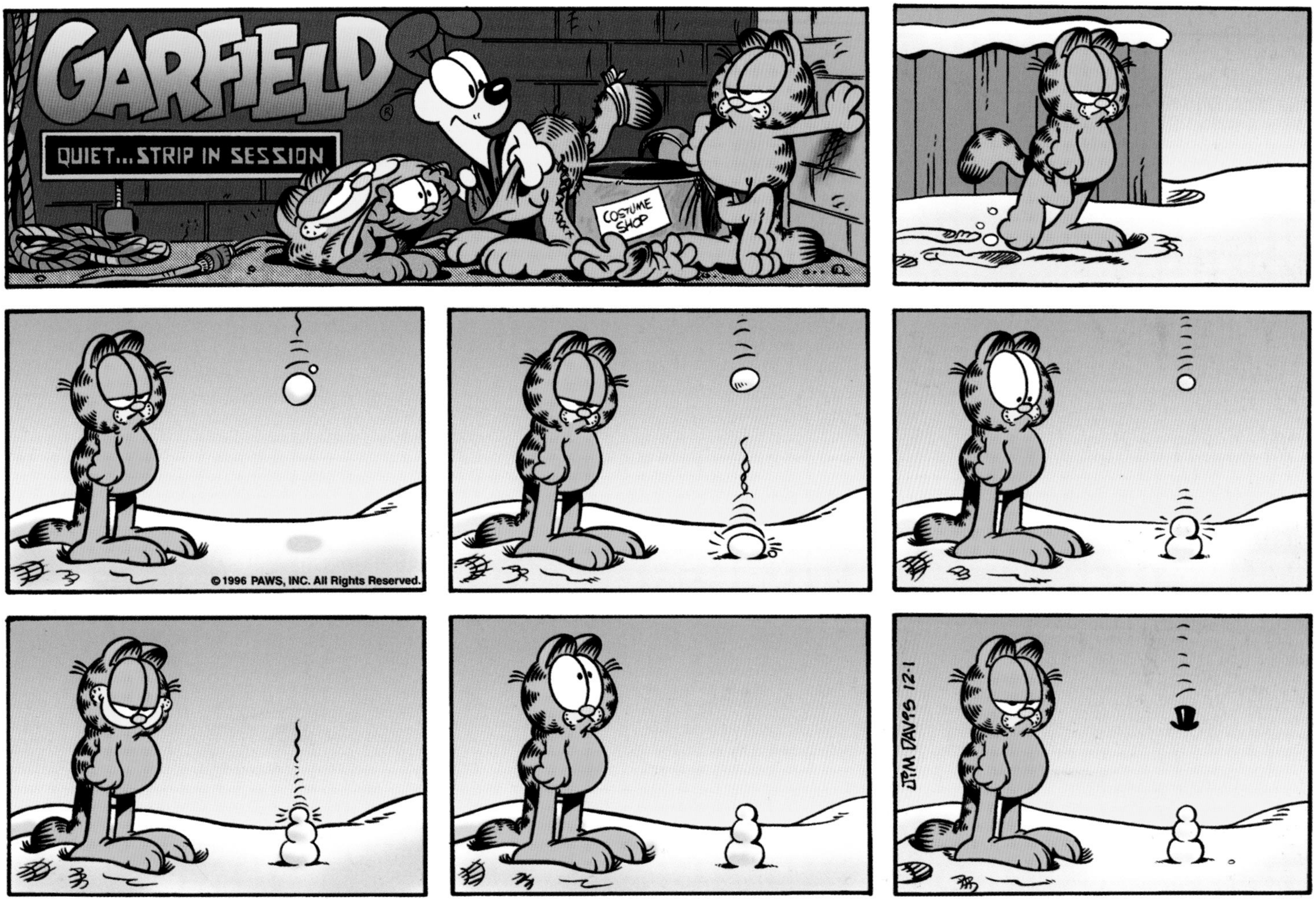
GARFIELD
QUIET...STRIP IN SESSION
COSTUME SHOP
© 1996 PAWS, INC. All Rights Reserved.
JIM DAVIS 12-1

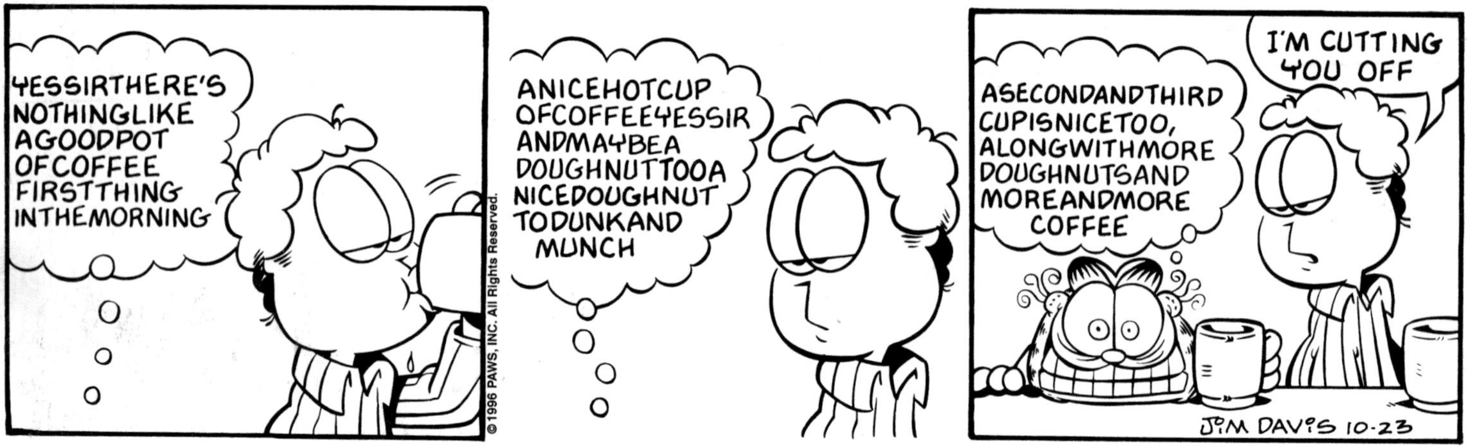

YESSIRTHERE'S NOTHINGLIKE AGOODPOT OFCOFFEE FIRSTTHING INTHEMORNING
©1996 PAWS, INC. All Rights Reserved.
ANICEHOTCUP OFCOFFEEYESSIR ANDMAYBEA DOUGHNUTTOOA NICEDOUGHNUT TODUNKAND MUNCH
ASECONDANDTHIRD CUPISNICETOO, ALONGWITHMORE DOUGHNUTSAND MOREANDMORE COFFEE
I'M CUTTING YOU OFF
JIM DAVIS 10-23

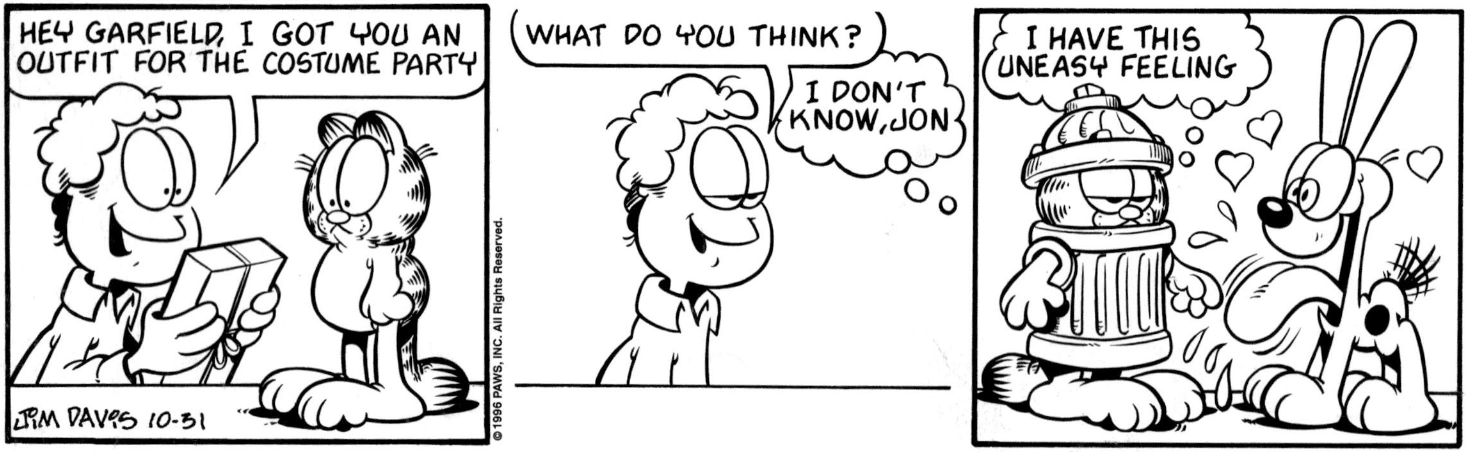

HEY GARFIELD, I GOT YOU AN OUTFIT FOR THE COSTUME PARTY
JIM DAVIS 10-31
©1996 PAWS, INC. All Rights Reserved.
WHAT DO YOU THINK?
I DON'T KNOW, JON
I HAVE THIS UNEASY FEELING

MY DATE IS IN SHOW BUSINESS, GARFIELD

WE MET AT THE CARNIVAL

TONIGHT I DINE WITH "ZELDA, THE TOAD WOMAN"

DON'T FORGET TO TAKE A JAR OF FLIES

JIM DAVIS 3-28

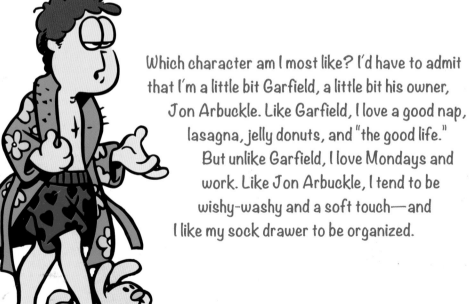

Which character am I most like? I'd have to admit that I'm a little bit Garfield, a little bit his owner, Jon Arbuckle. Like Garfield, I love a good nap, lasagna, jelly donuts, and "the good life." But unlike Garfield, I love Mondays and work. Like Jon Arbuckle, I tend to be wishy-washy and a soft touch—and I like my sock drawer to be organized.

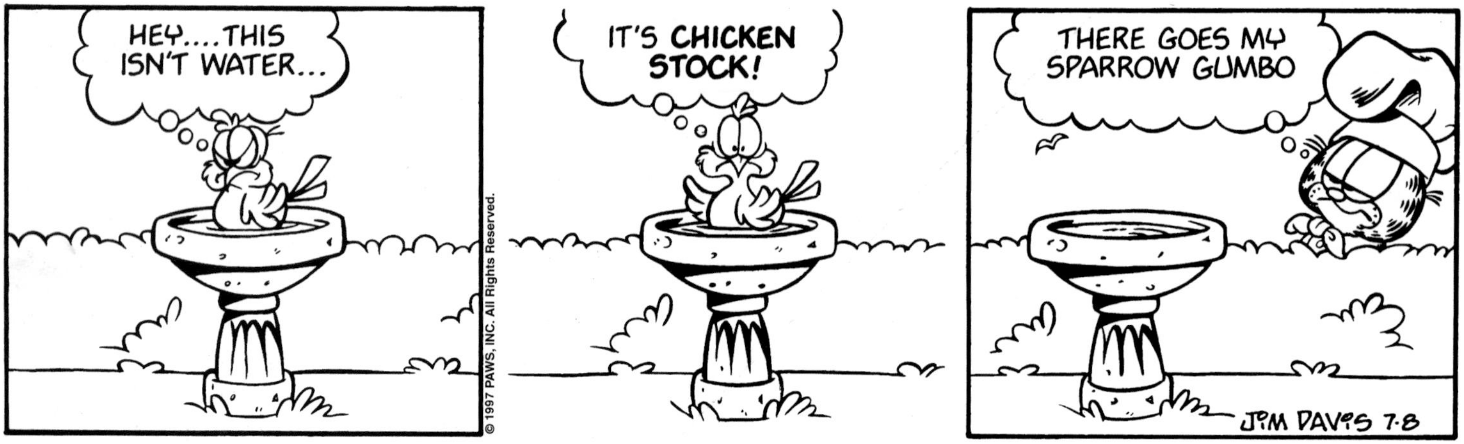
HEY....THIS ISN'T WATER...
IT'S CHICKEN STOCK!
THERE GOES MY SPARROW GUMBO
JIM DAVIS 7-8
© 1997 PAWS, INC. All Rights Reserved.

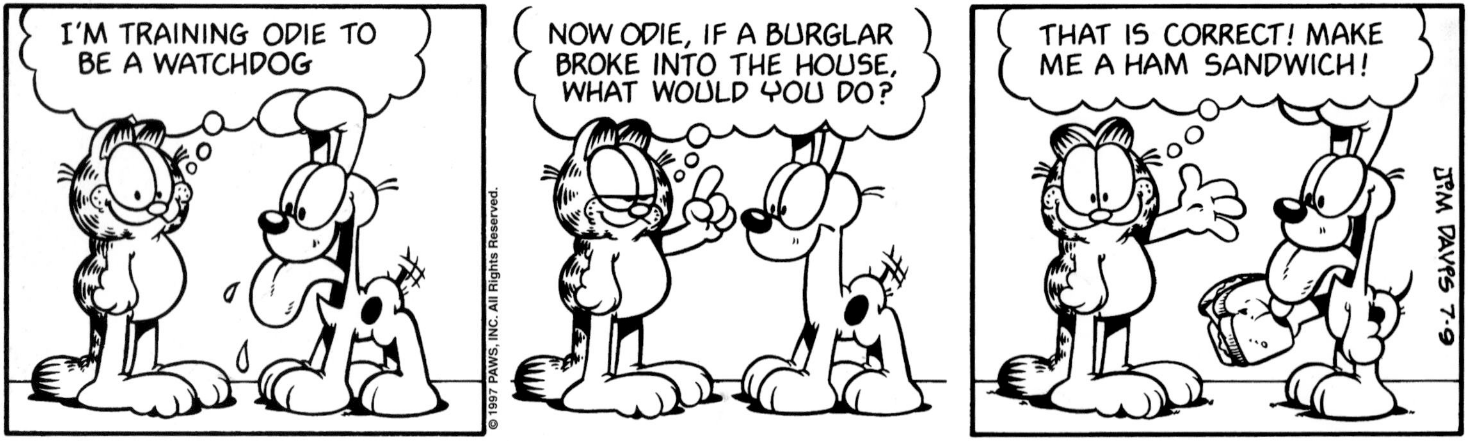
I'M TRAINING ODIE TO BE A WATCHDOG
NOW ODIE, IF A BURGLAR BROKE INTO THE HOUSE, WHAT WOULD YOU DO?
THAT IS CORRECT! MAKE ME A HAM SANDWICH!
JIM DAVIS 7-9
© 1997 PAWS, INC. All Rights Reserved.

garfield®
SIGH...
BOY, AM I DEPRESSED
© 1997 PAWS, INC. All Rights Reserved.
BZZZZ BZZZZ BZZZZ
JIM DAVIS 11-9
TEASE TEASE TEASE TEASE
TEASE TEASE TEASE TEASE
REE REE REE
PAINT PAINT PAINT
FUNNY... I FEEL BETTER
I DO WHAT I CAN

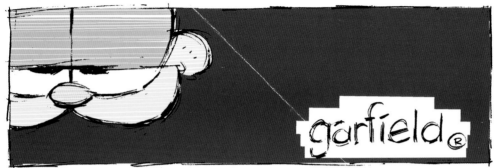

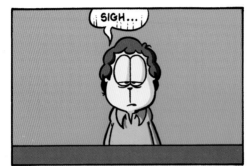

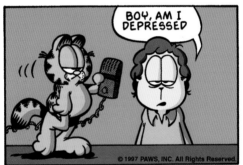

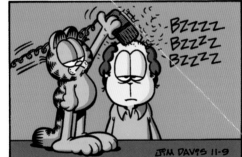

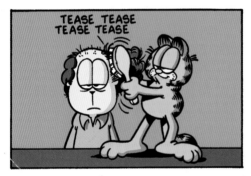

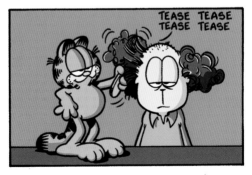

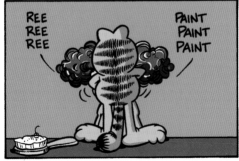

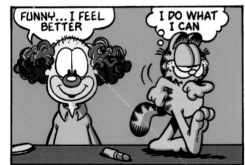

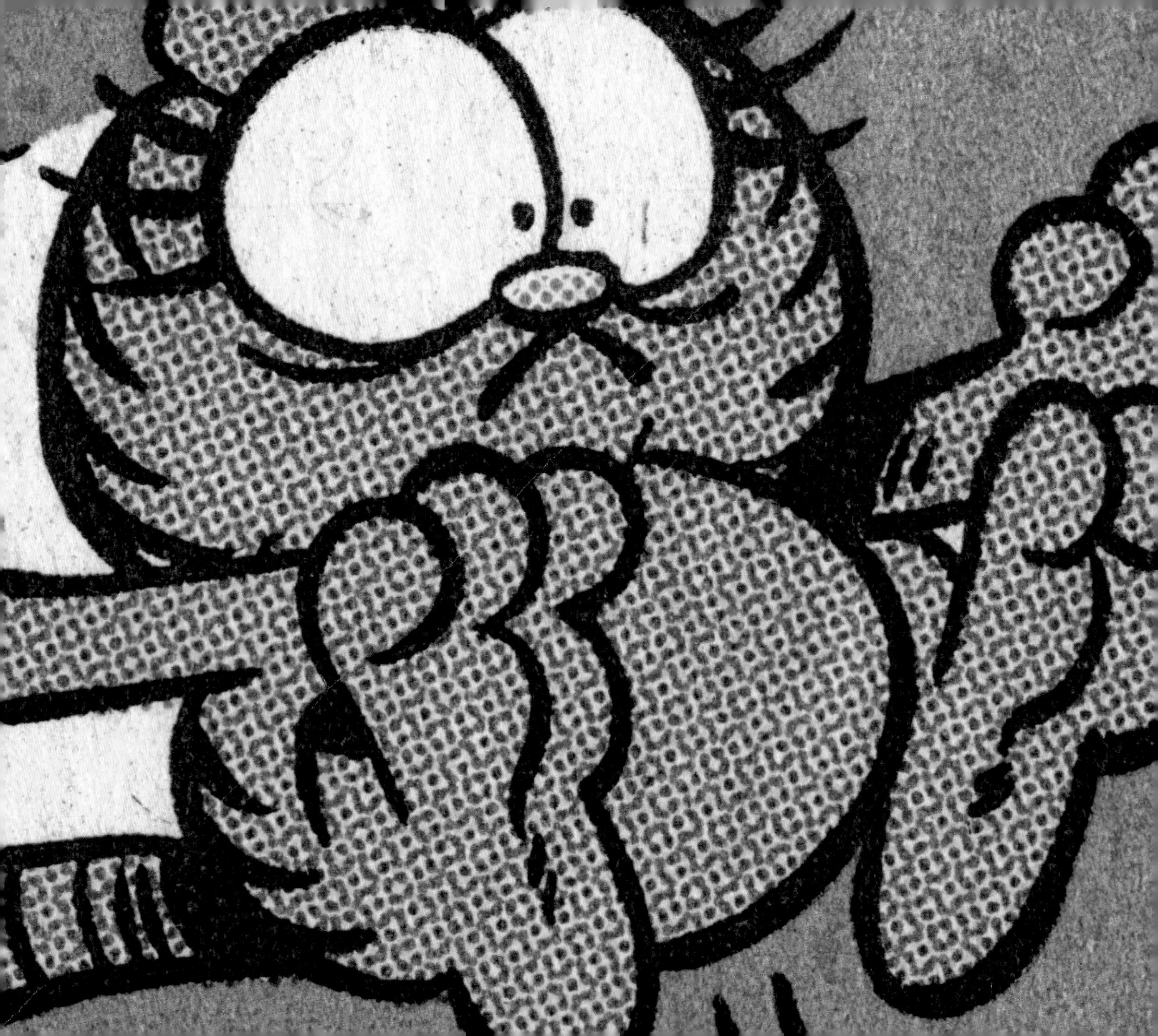

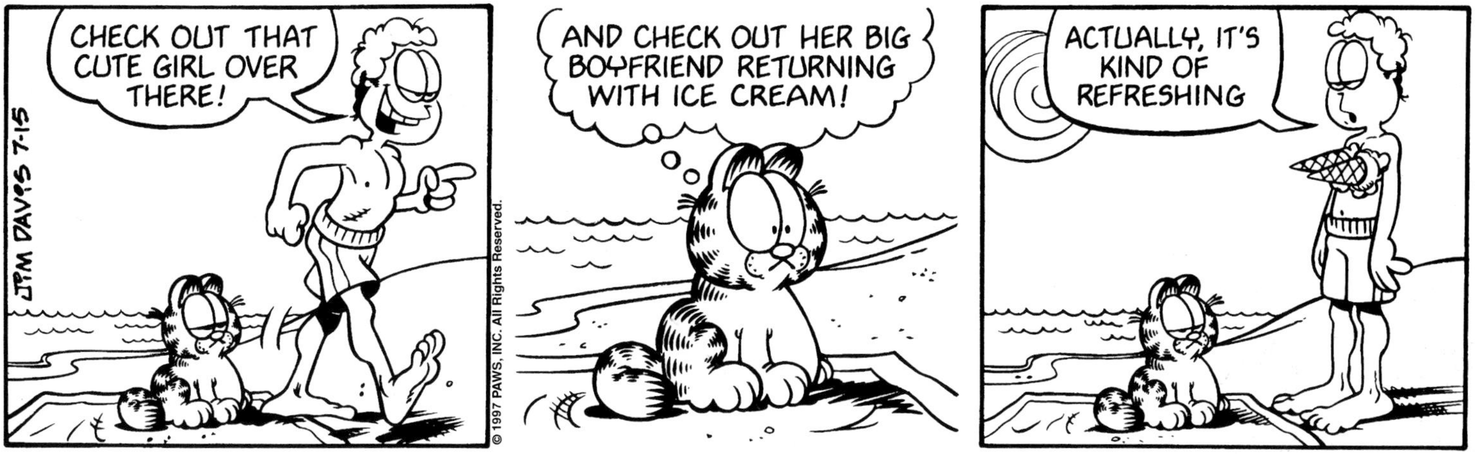
CHECK OUT THAT CUTE GIRL OVER THERE!
JIM DAVIS 7-15
© 1997 PAWS, INC. All Rights Reserved.
AND CHECK OUT HER BIG BOYFRIEND RETURNING WITH ICE CREAM!
ACTUALLY, IT'S KIND OF REFRESHING

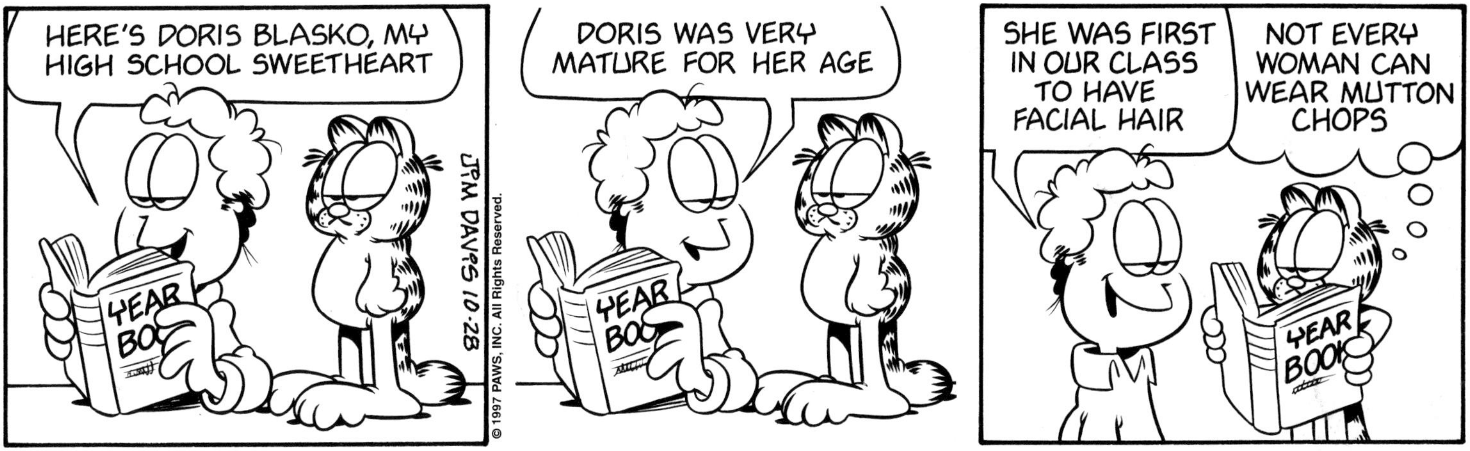
HERE'S DORIS BLASKO, MY HIGH SCHOOL SWEETHEART
YEAR BOO
JIM DAVIS 10-28
© 1997 PAWS, INC. All Rights Reserved.
DORIS WAS VERY MATURE FOR HER AGE
YEAR BOO
SHE WAS FIRST IN OUR CLASS TO HAVE FACIAL HAIR
NOT EVERY WOMAN CAN WEAR MUTTON CHOPS
YEAR BOOK

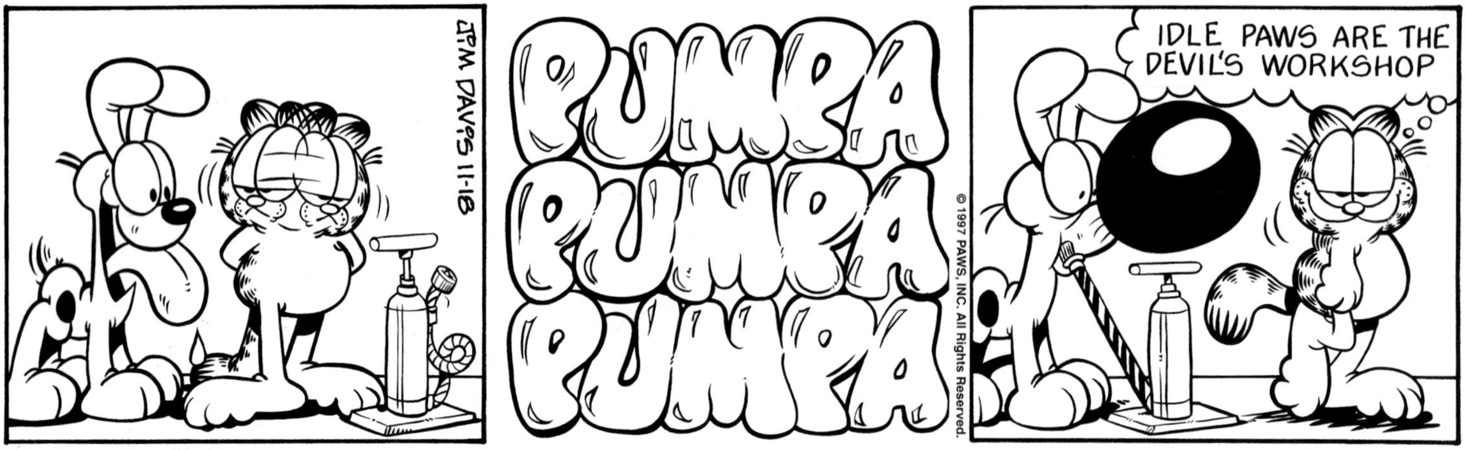
JIM DAVIS 11-18
PUMPA PUMPA PUMPA
© 1997 PAWS, INC. All Rights Reserved.
IDLE PAWS ARE THE DEVIL'S WORKSHOP

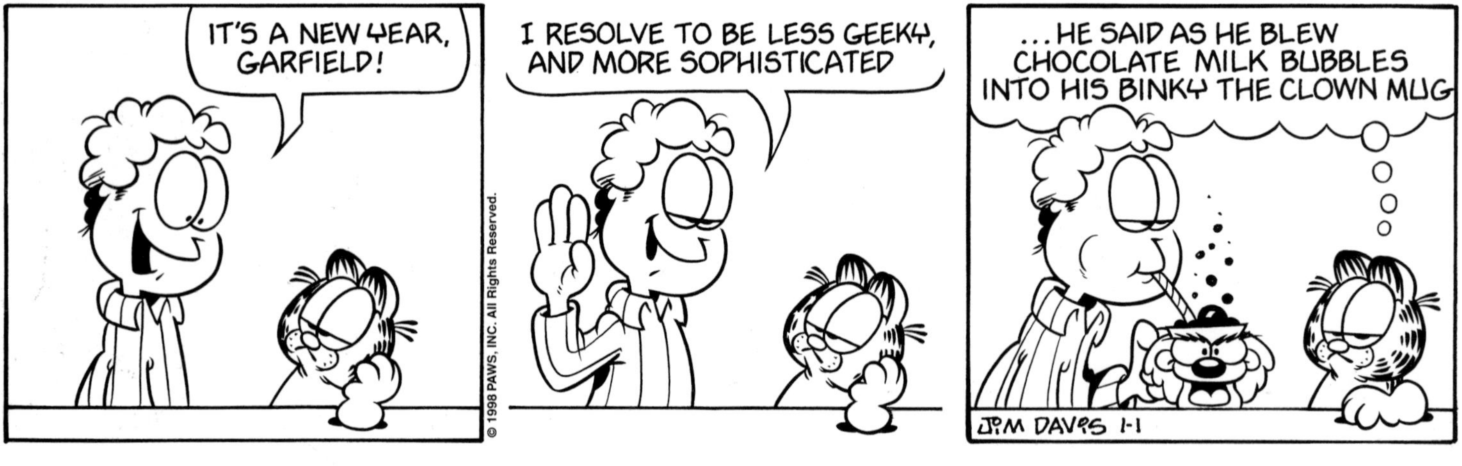
IT'S A NEW YEAR, GARFIELD!
© 1998 PAWS, INC. All Rights Reserved.
I RESOLVE TO BE LESS GEEKY, AND MORE SOPHISTICATED
...HE SAID AS HE BLEW CHOCOLATE MILK BUBBLES INTO HIS BINKY THE CLOWN MUG
JIM DAVIS 1-1

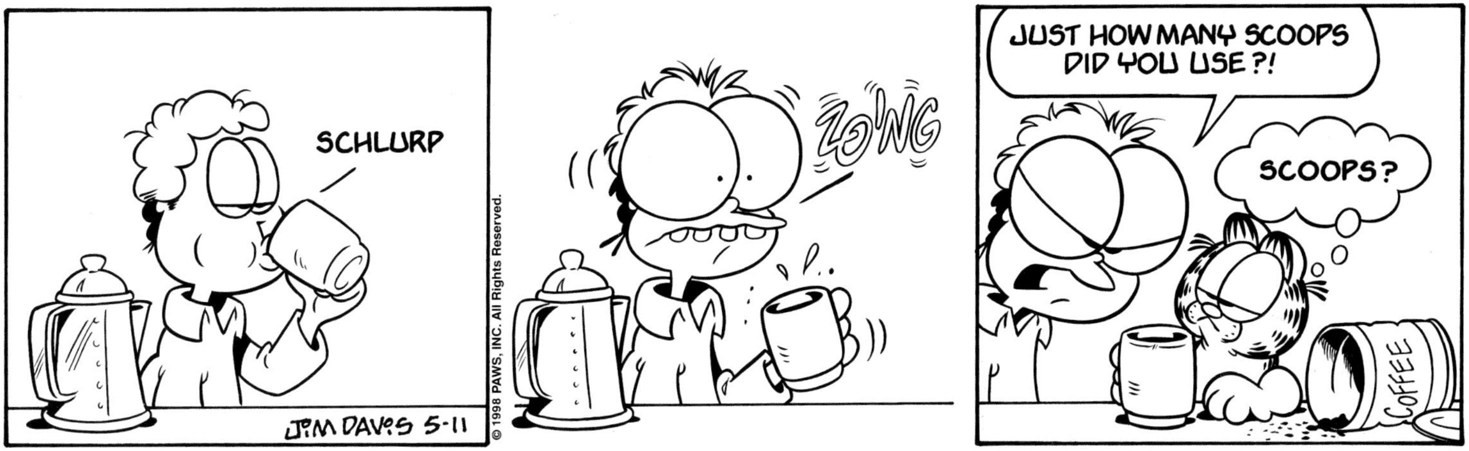
SCHLURP
ZO'NG
JUST HOW MANY SCOOPS DID YOU USE?!
SCOOPS?
COFFEE
JIM DAVIS 5-11
© 1998 PAWS, INC. All Rights Reserved.

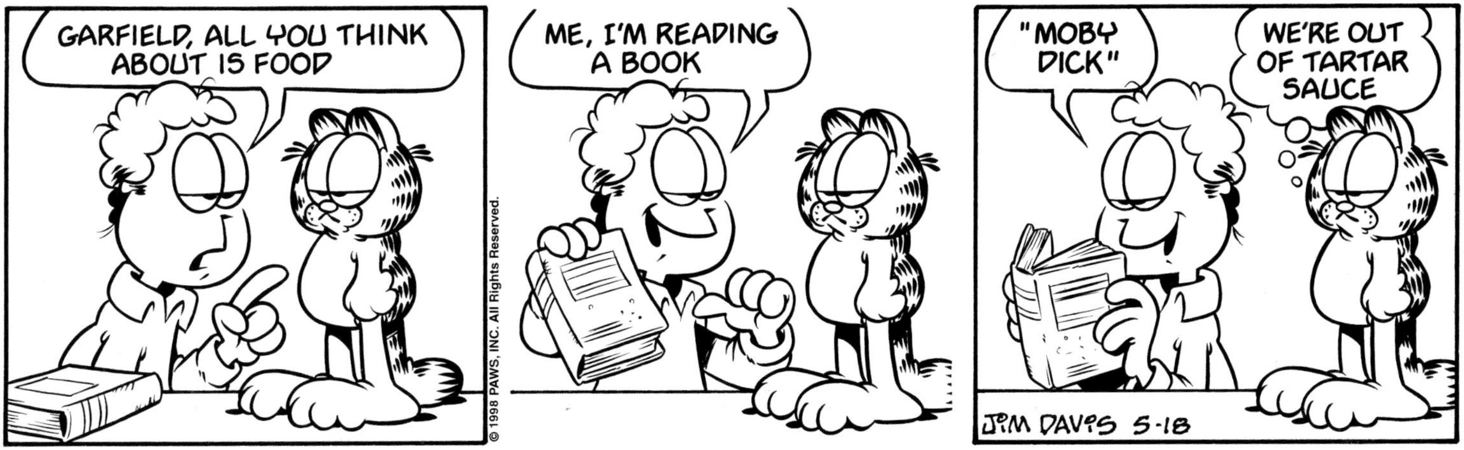
GARFIELD, ALL YOU THINK ABOUT IS FOOD
ME, I'M READING A BOOK
"MOBY DICK"
WE'RE OUT OF TARTAR SAUCE
JIM DAVIS 5-18
© 1998 PAWS, INC. All Rights Reserved.

The Third Decade
1998–2008

Life has been good to Garfield. He's now the most widely syndicated comic strip in the world with more than 2,500 newspapers in more than a hundred countries!

In this decade, we finally started doing something about something we'd known for twenty years. Garfield was helping people learn to read. Pictures make it easier for some people to understand what the words mean.

Now that academia is starting to embrace this concept, we formed the Professor Garfield Foundation to provide free online content to support the advancement of literacy. It's nice to give back.

And what about Garfield? He's still maturing. I'm still trying to write that one perfect gag that makes the whole world laugh. But, you know, a part of me hopes I never find it . . .

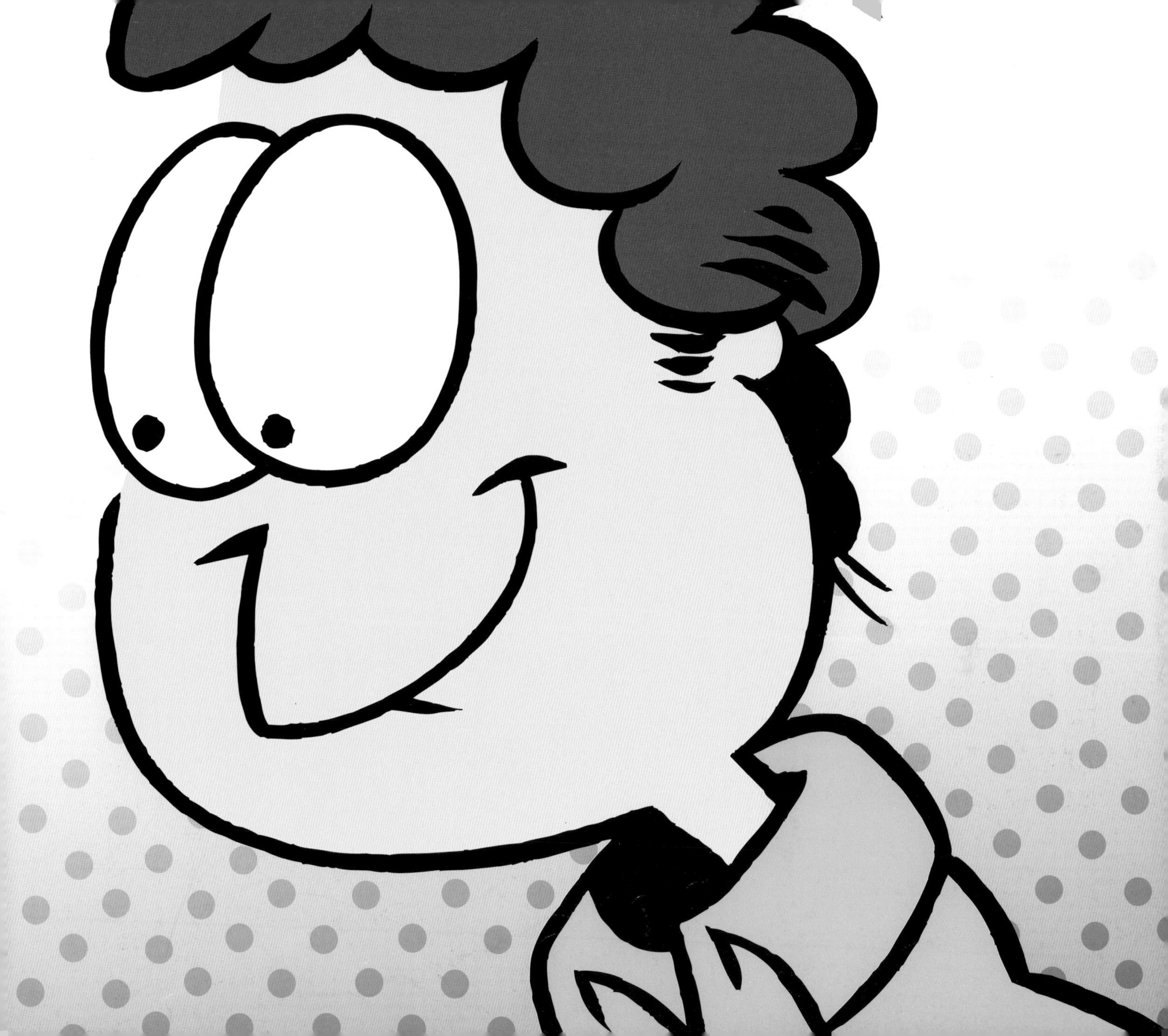

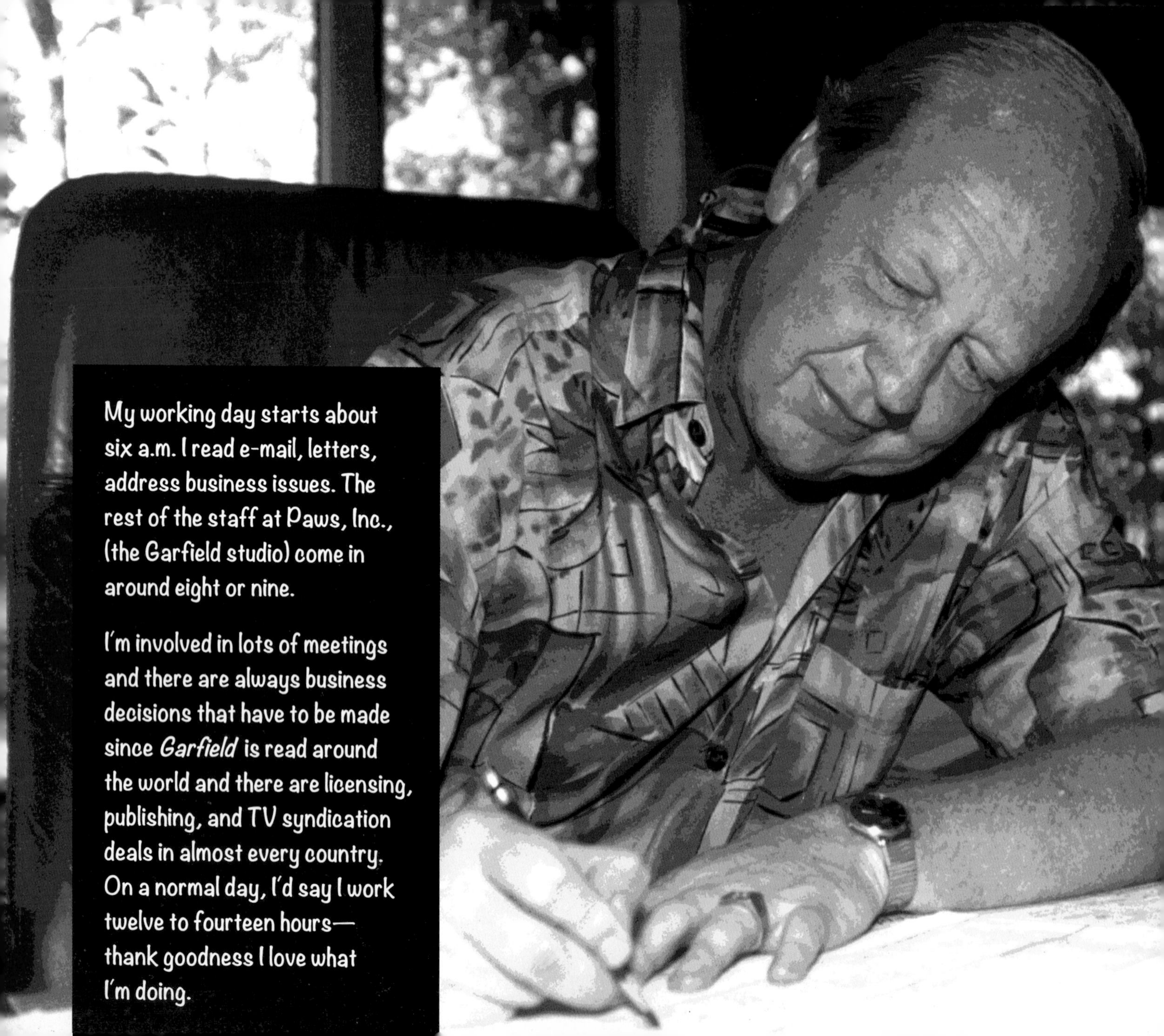

My working day starts about six a.m. I read e-mail, letters, address business issues. The rest of the staff at Paws, Inc., (the Garfield studio) come in around eight or nine.

I'm involved in lots of meetings and there are always business decisions that have to be made since *Garfield* is read around the world and there are licensing, publishing, and TV syndication deals in almost every country. On a normal day, I'd say I work twelve to fourteen hours—thank goodness I love what I'm doing.

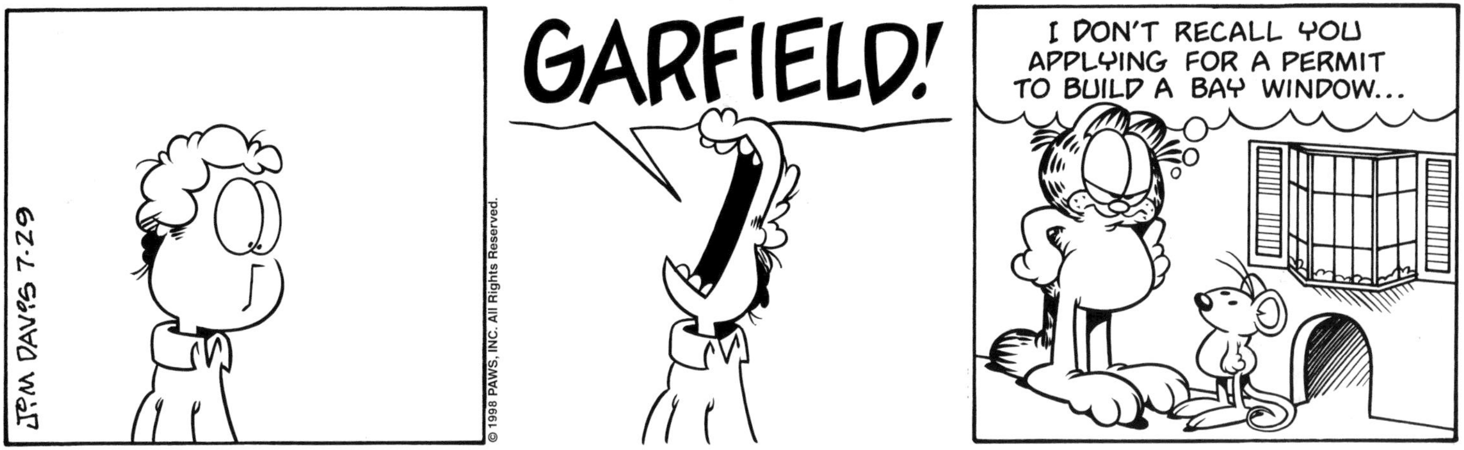
JIM DAVIS 7-29
GARFIELD!
© 1998 PAWS, INC. All Rights Reserved.
I DON'T RECALL YOU APPLYING FOR A PERMIT TO BUILD A BAY WINDOW...

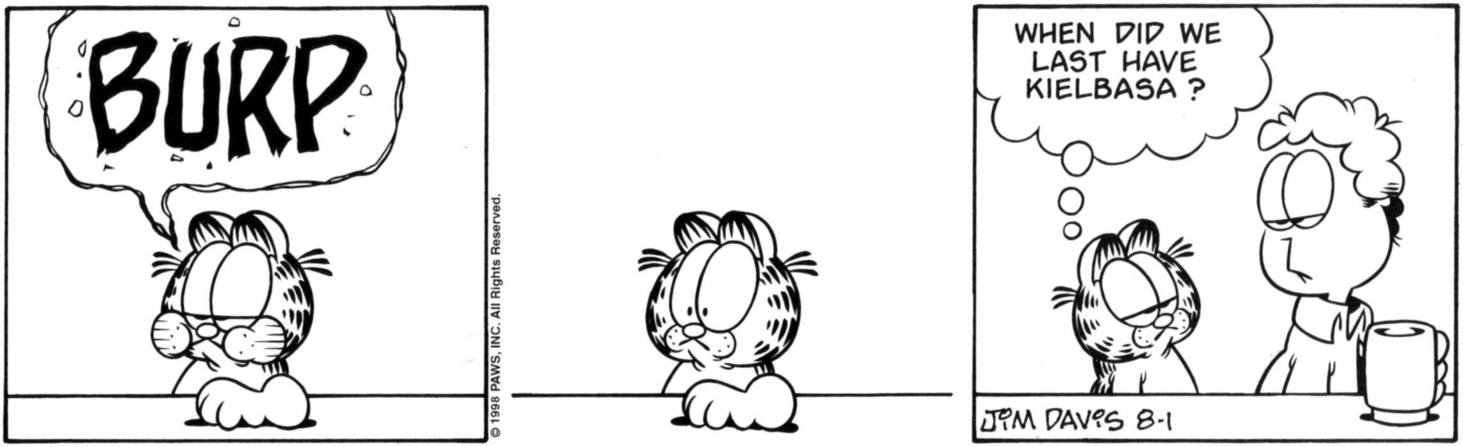
BURP
© 1998 PAWS, INC. All Rights Reserved.
WHEN DID WE LAST HAVE KIELBASA ?
JIM DAVIS 8-1

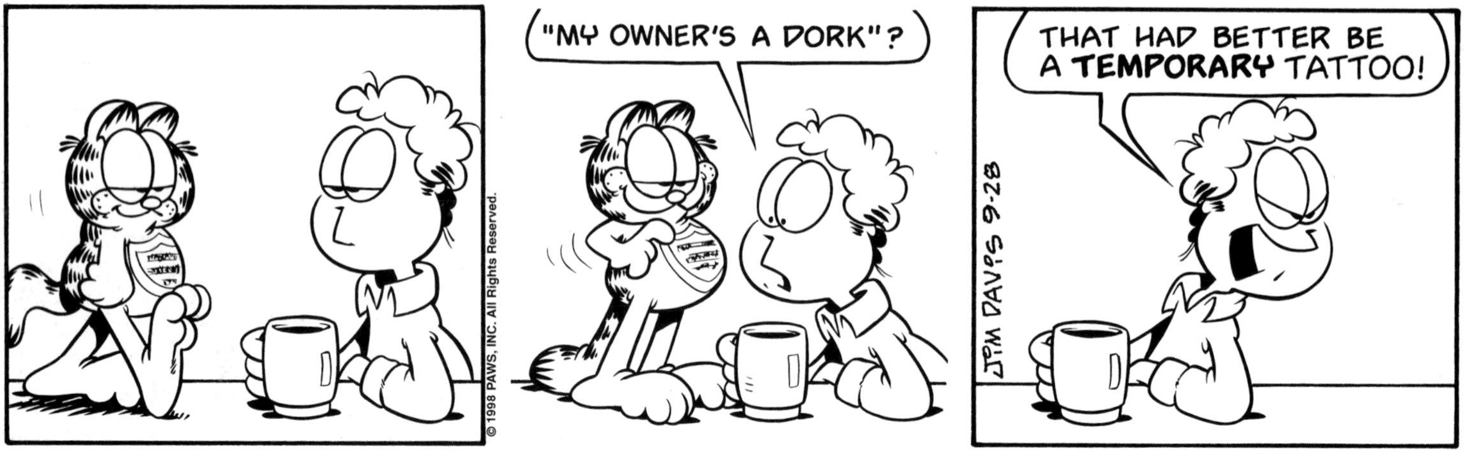
© 1998 PAWS, INC. All Rights Reserved.
"MY OWNER'S A DORK"?
THAT HAD BETTER BE A **TEMPORARY** TATTOO!
JIM DAVIS 9-28

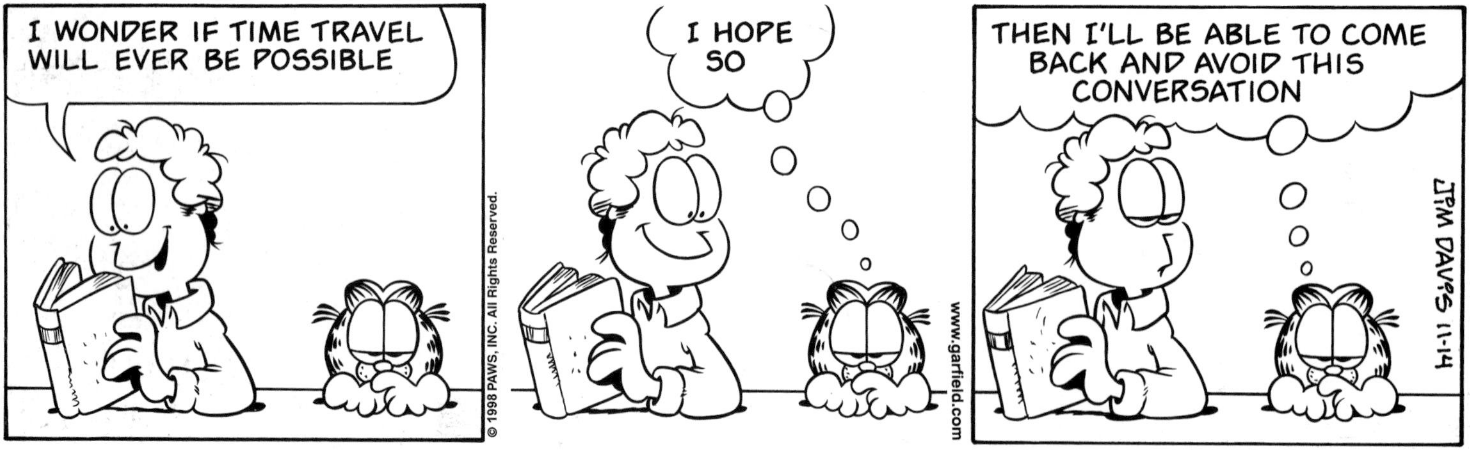
I WONDER IF TIME TRAVEL WILL EVER BE POSSIBLE
© 1998 PAWS, INC. All Rights Reserved.
I HOPE SO
www.garfield.com
THEN I'LL BE ABLE TO COME BACK AND AVOID THIS CONVERSATION
JIM DAVIS 11-14

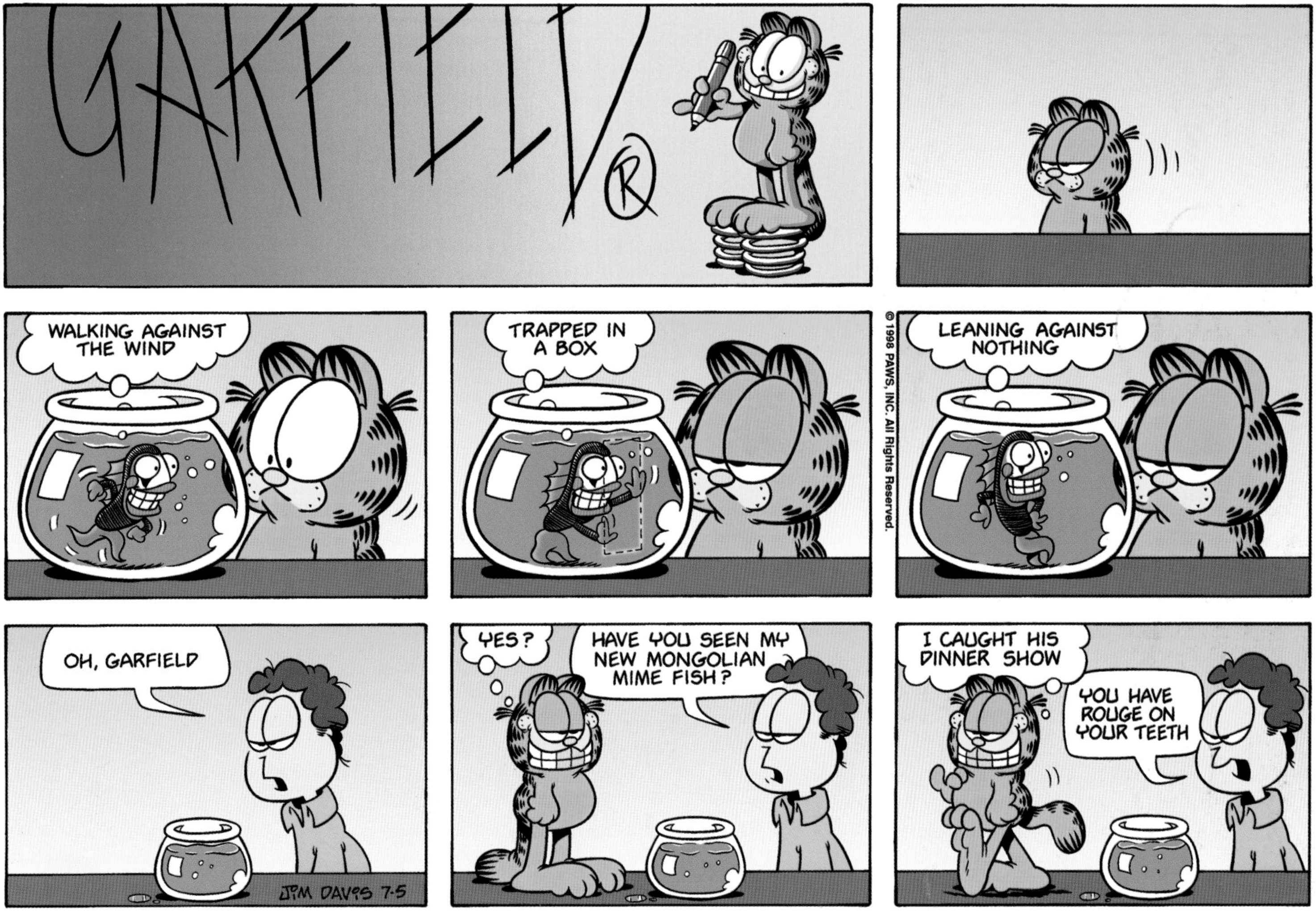
GARFIELD®
WALKING AGAINST THE WIND
TRAPPED IN A BOX
© 1998 PAWS, INC. All Rights Reserved.
LEANING AGAINST NOTHING
OH, GARFIELD
JIM DAVIS 7-5
YES?
HAVE YOU SEEN MY NEW MONGOLIAN MIME FISH?
I CAUGHT HIS DINNER SHOW
YOU HAVE ROUGE ON YOUR TEETH

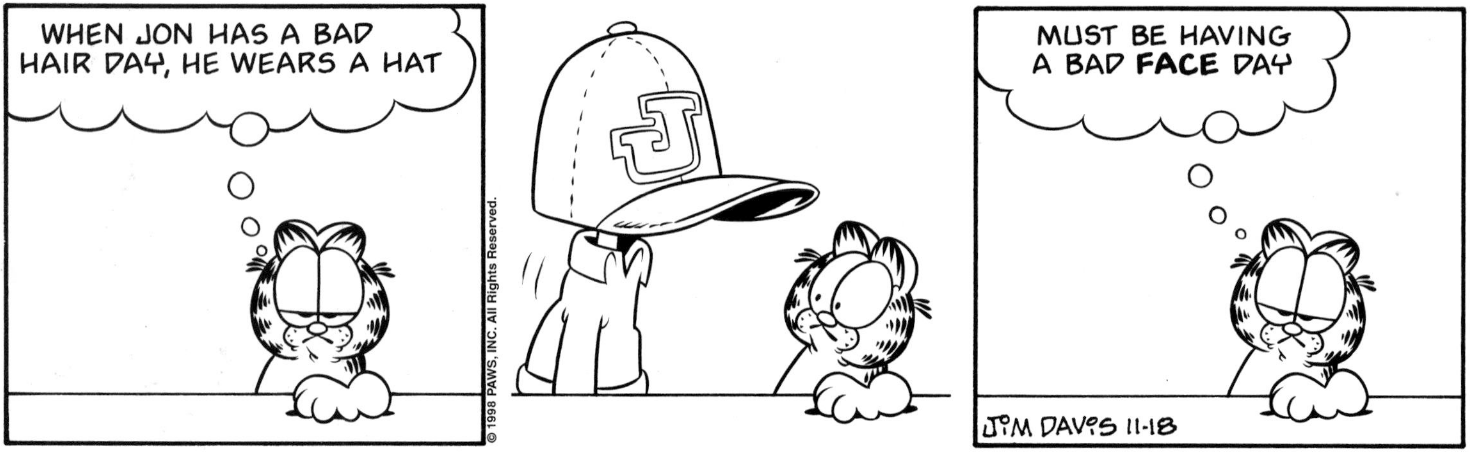
WHEN JON HAS A BAD HAIR DAY, HE WEARS A HAT
© 1998 PAWS, INC. All Rights Reserved.
MUST BE HAVING A BAD **FACE** DAY
JIM DAVIS 11-18

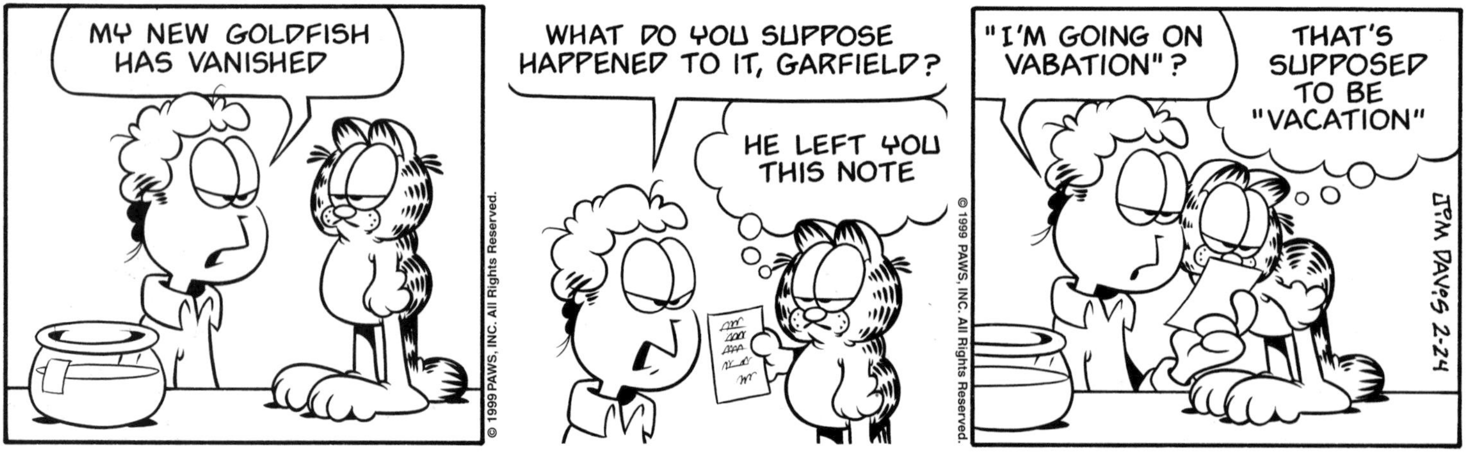
MY NEW GOLDFISH HAS VANISHED
© 1999 PAWS, INC. All Rights Reserved.
WHAT DO YOU SUPPOSE HAPPENED TO IT, GARFIELD?
HE LEFT YOU THIS NOTE
© 1999 PAWS, INC. All Rights Reserved.
"I'M GOING ON VABATION"?
THAT'S SUPPOSED TO BE "VACATION"
JIM DAVIS 2-24

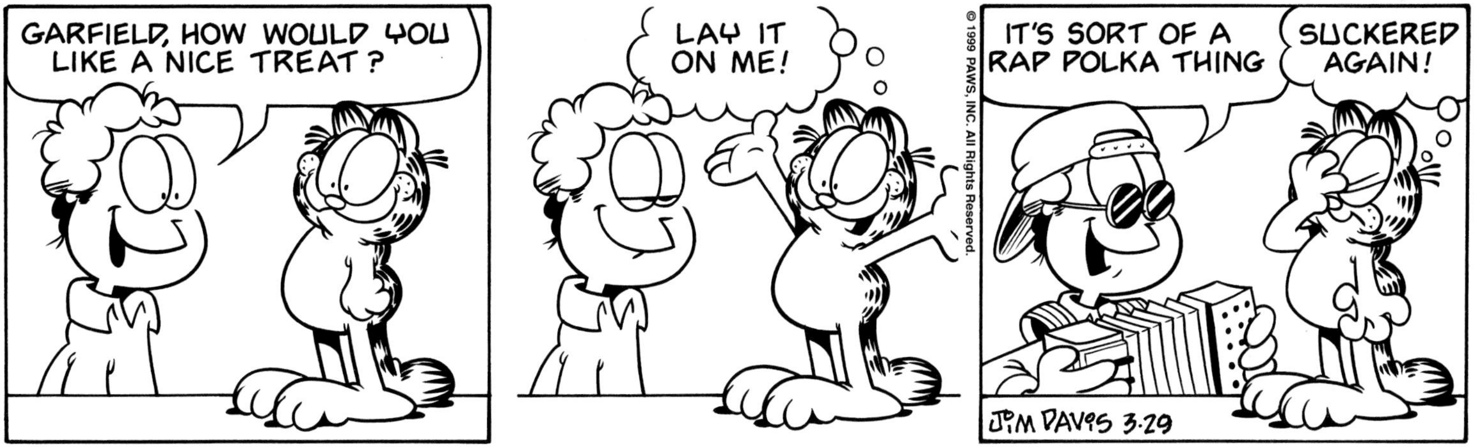
GARFIELD, HOW WOULD YOU LIKE A NICE TREAT?
LAY IT ON ME!
IT'S SORT OF A RAP POLKA THING
SUCKERED AGAIN!
JIM DAVIS 3·29

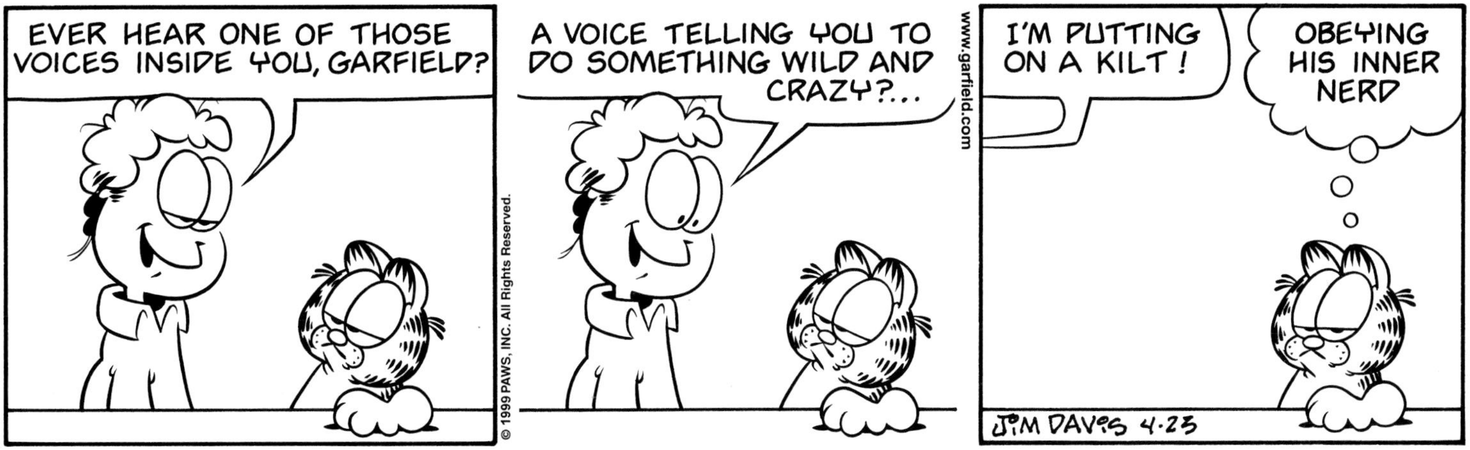
EVER HEAR ONE OF THOSE VOICES INSIDE YOU, GARFIELD?
A VOICE TELLING YOU TO DO SOMETHING WILD AND CRAZY?...
I'M PUTTING ON A KILT!
OBEYING HIS INNER NERD
JIM DAVIS 4·23

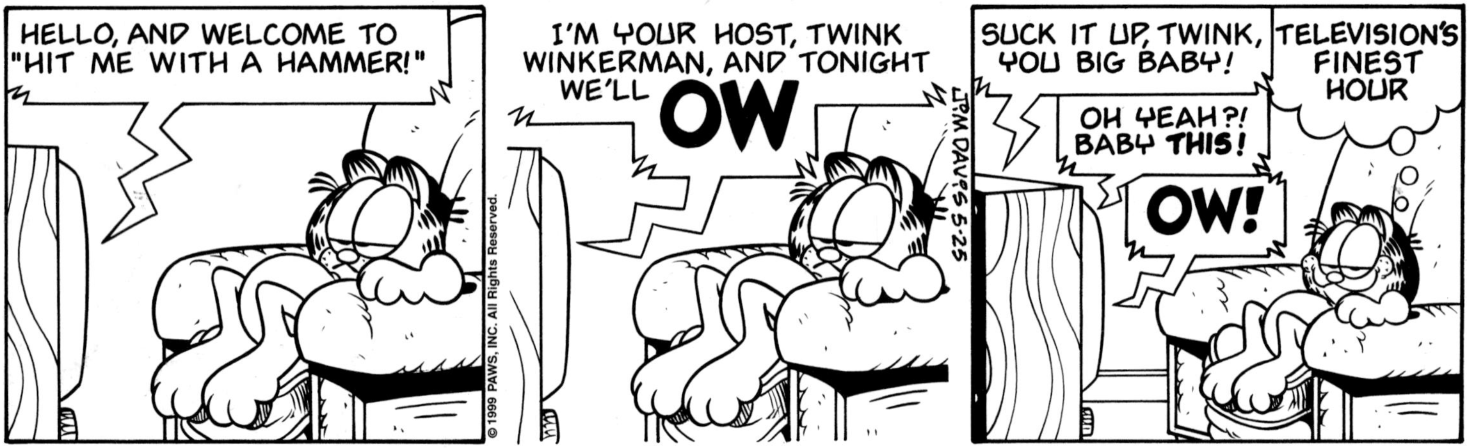
HELLO, AND WELCOME TO "HIT ME WITH A HAMMER!"
I'M YOUR HOST, TWINK WINKERMAN, AND TONIGHT WE'LL
OW
SUCK IT UP, TWINK, YOU BIG BABY!
OH YEAH?! BABY THIS!
OW!
TELEVISION'S FINEST HOUR
JIM DAVIS 5-25
© 1999 PAWS, INC. All Rights Reserved.

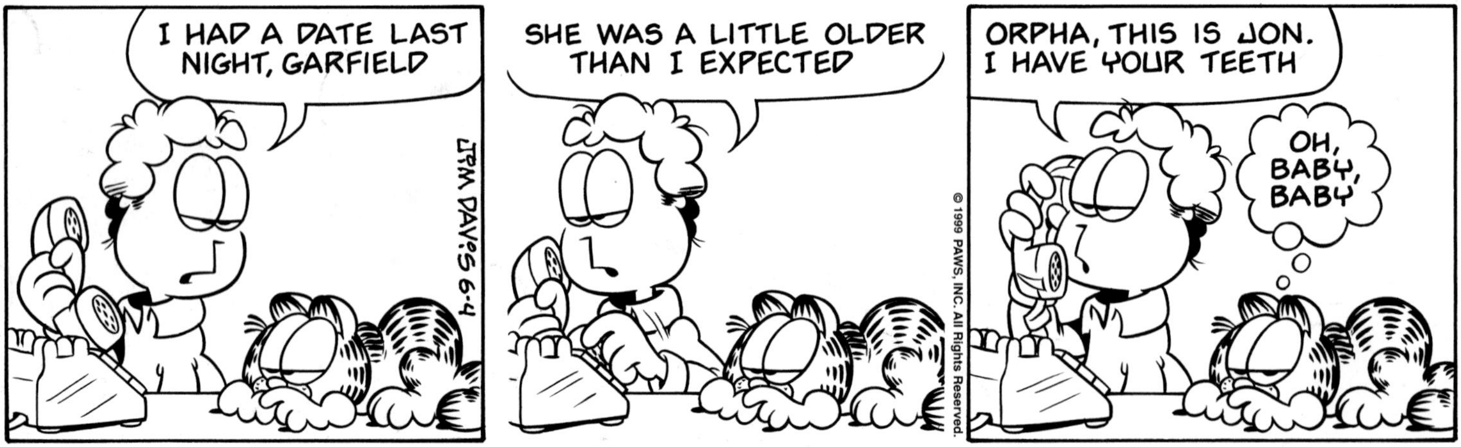
I HAD A DATE LAST NIGHT, GARFIELD
SHE WAS A LITTLE OLDER THAN I EXPECTED
ORPHA, THIS IS JON. I HAVE YOUR TEETH
OH, BABY, BABY
JIM DAVIS 6-4
© 1999 PAWS, INC. All Rights Reserved.

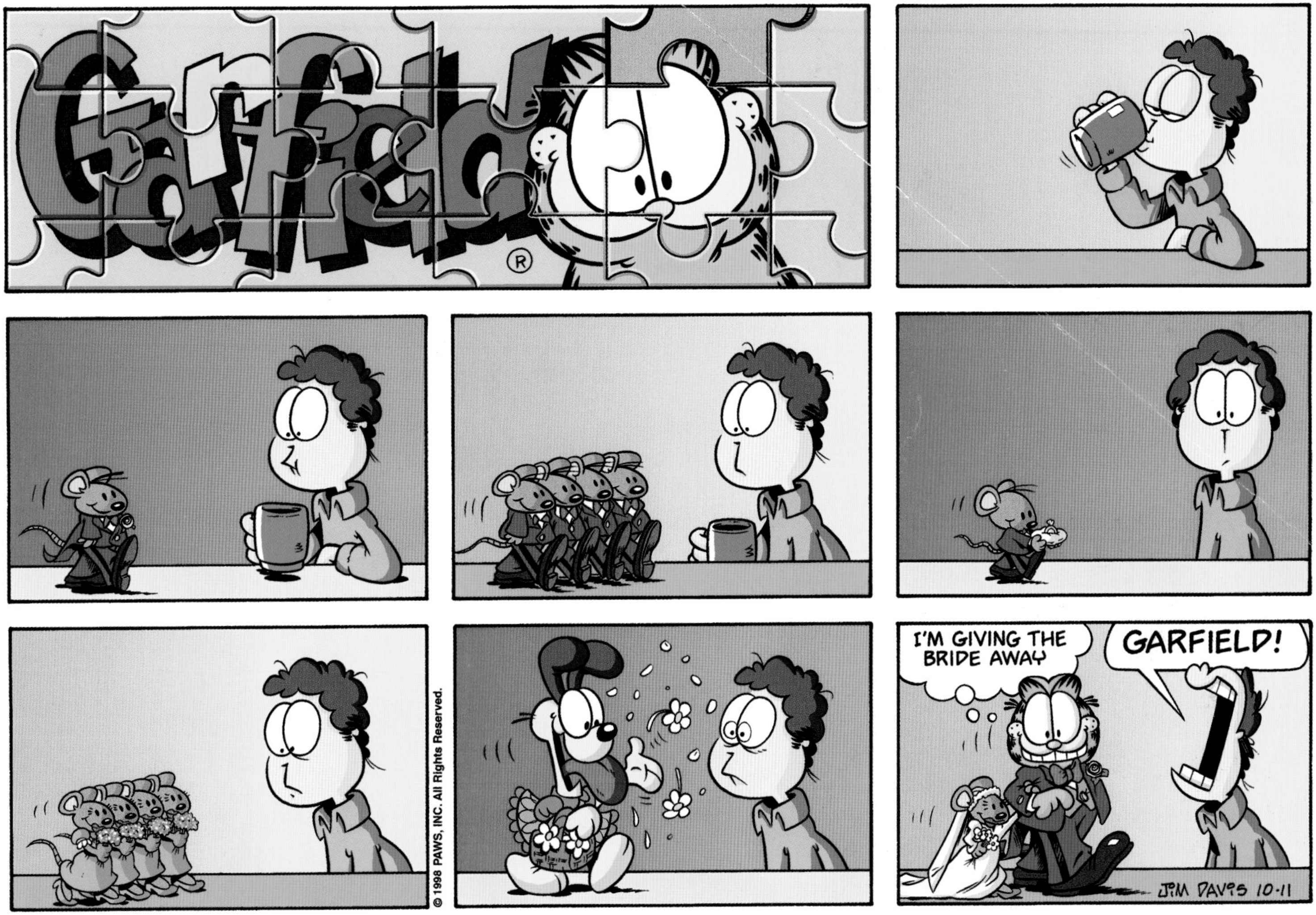
Garfield
I'M GIVING THE BRIDE AWAY
GARFIELD!
JIM DAVIS 10-11

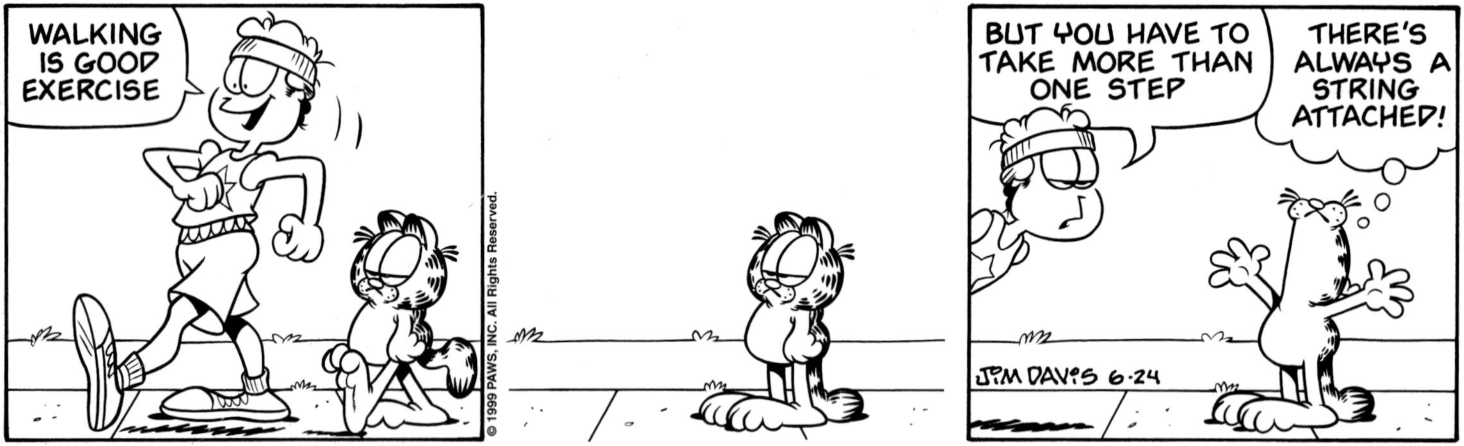
WALKING IS GOOD EXERCISE
© 1999 PAWS, INC. All Rights Reserved.
BUT YOU HAVE TO TAKE MORE THAN ONE STEP
THERE'S ALWAYS A STRING ATTACHED!
JIM DAVIS 6-24

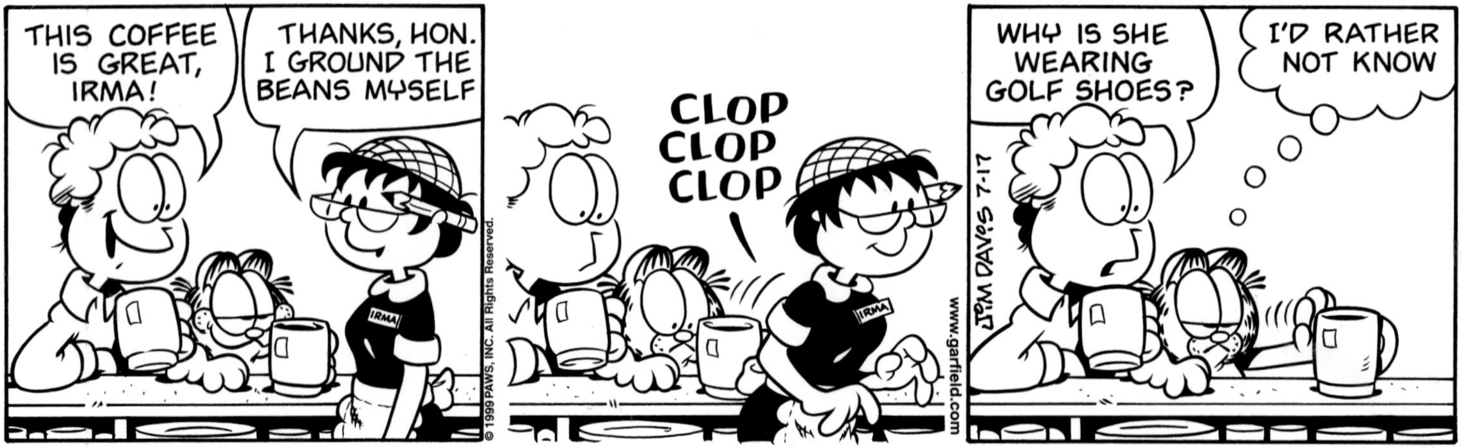
THIS COFFEE IS GREAT, IRMA!
THANKS, HON. I GROUND THE BEANS MYSELF
IRMA
© 1999 PAWS, INC. All Rights Reserved.
CLOP CLOP CLOP
www.garfield.com
JIM DAVIS 7-17
WHY IS SHE WEARING GOLF SHOES?
I'D RATHER NOT KNOW

RESPECT IS AN IMPORTANT PART OF A PET-OWNER RELATIONSHIP, GARFIELD
WOULDN'T YOU AGREE?
PERHAPS YOU WOULDN'T
JIM DAVIS 8-2
© 1999 PAWS, INC. All Rights Reserved.

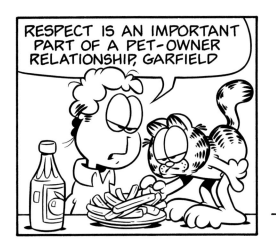

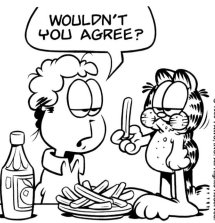

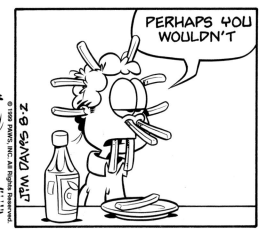

The comic strip and the licensing programs are two independent entities. To be honest, I've learned a lot about Garfield from working on plush and in animation. I get to see more sides of his personality working with him in other mediums. So for me, it's helped the feature.

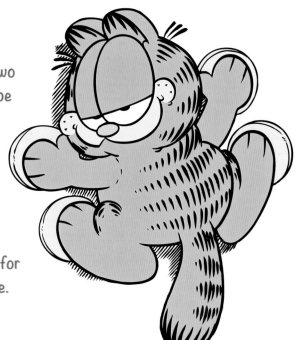

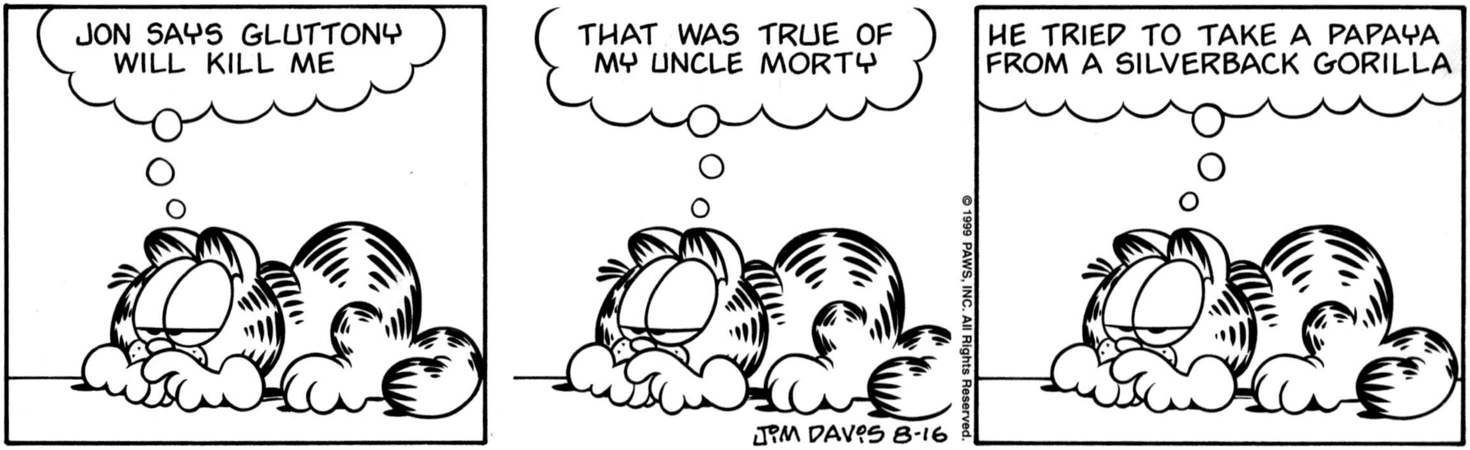
JON SAYS GLUTTONY WILL KILL ME
THAT WAS TRUE OF MY UNCLE MORTY
HE TRIED TO TAKE A PAPAYA FROM A SILVERBACK GORILLA
JIM DAVIS 8-16
© 1999 PAWS, INC. All Rights Reserved.

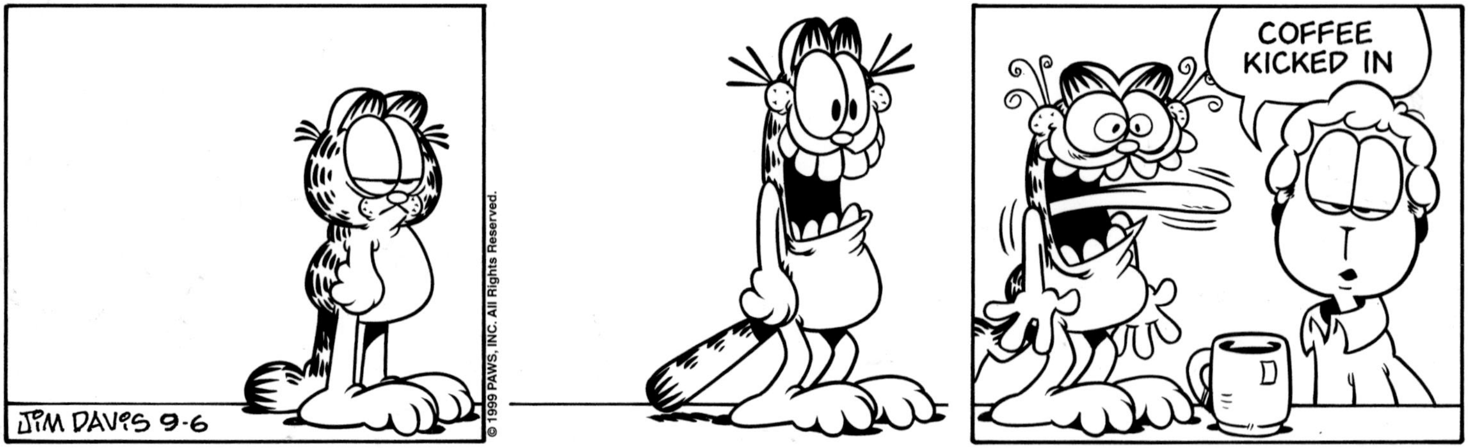
JIM DAVIS 9-6
© 1999 PAWS, INC. All Rights Reserved.
COFFEE KICKED IN

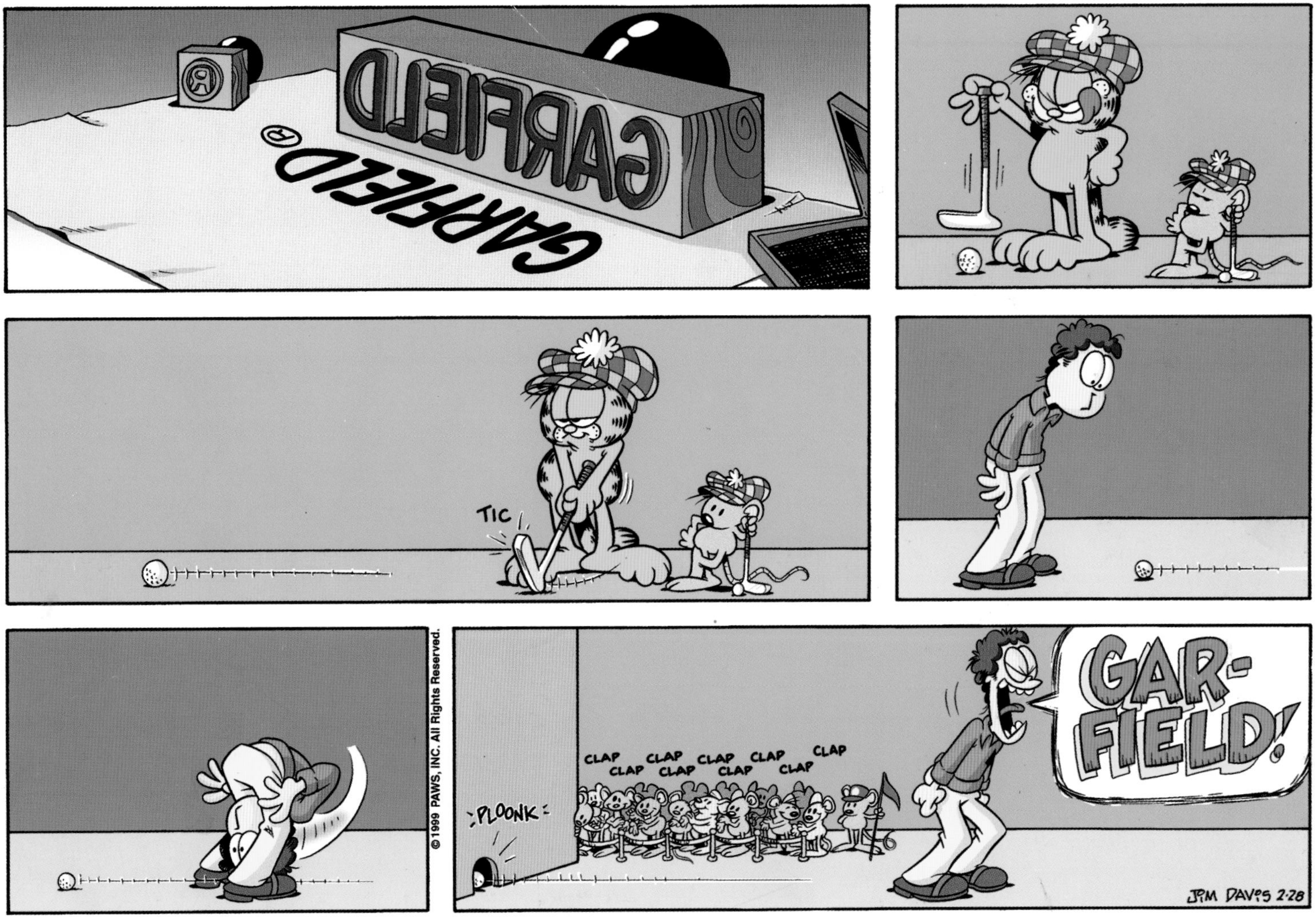
GARFIELD®
TIC
PLOONK
CLAP CLAP CLAP CLAP CLAP CLAP CLAP CLAP CLAP
GAR-FIELD!
JIM DAVIS 2-28

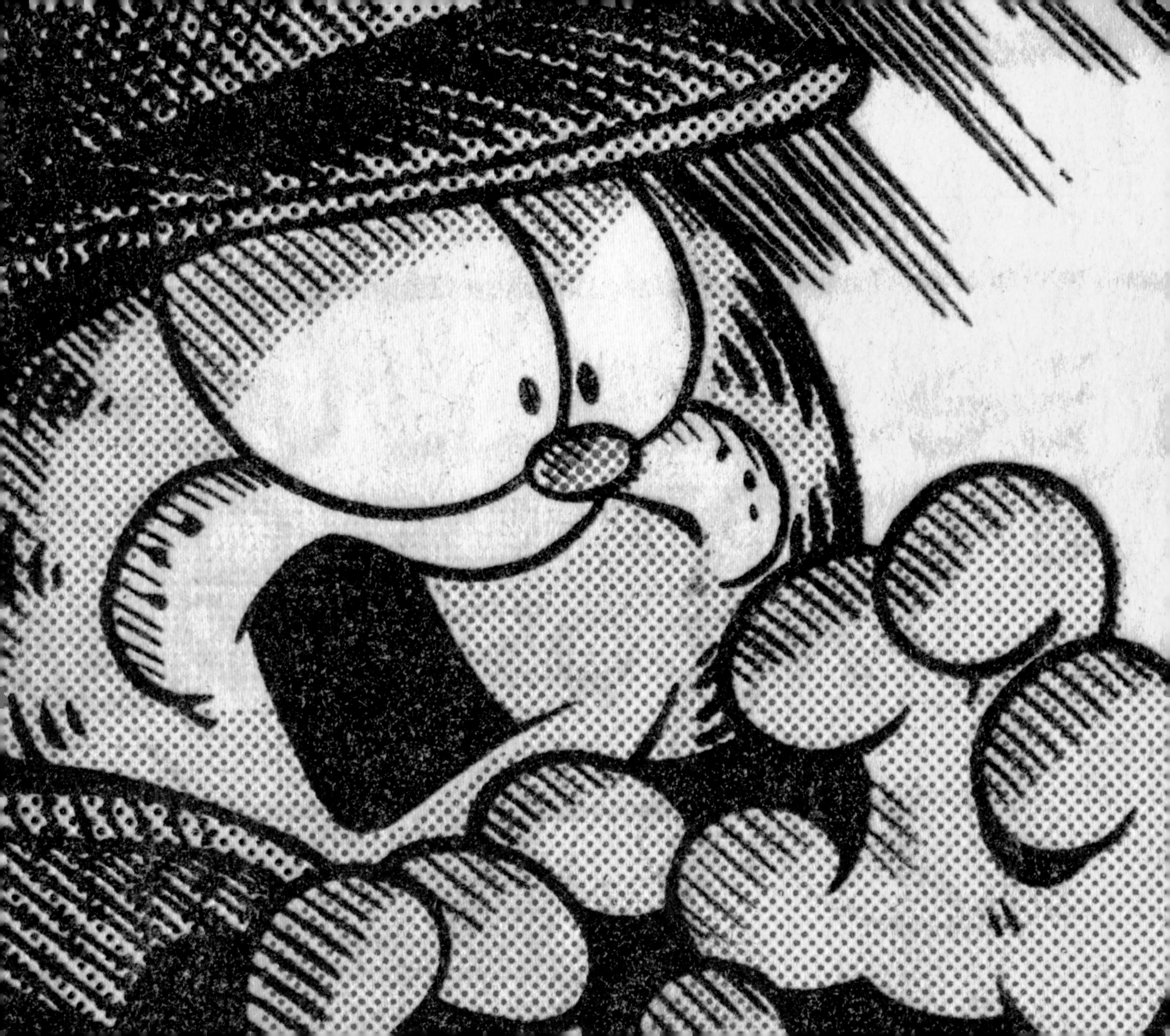

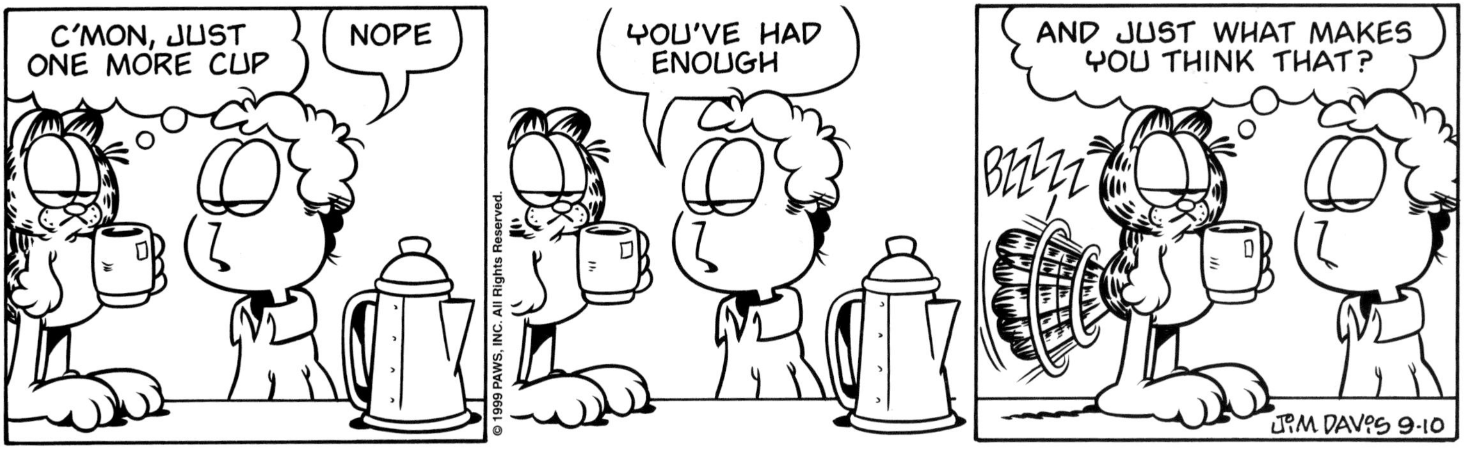
C'MON, JUST ONE MORE CUP
NOPE
© 1999 PAWS, INC. All Rights Reserved.
YOU'VE HAD ENOUGH
AND JUST WHAT MAKES YOU THINK THAT?
BZZZZZ
JIM DAVIS 9-10

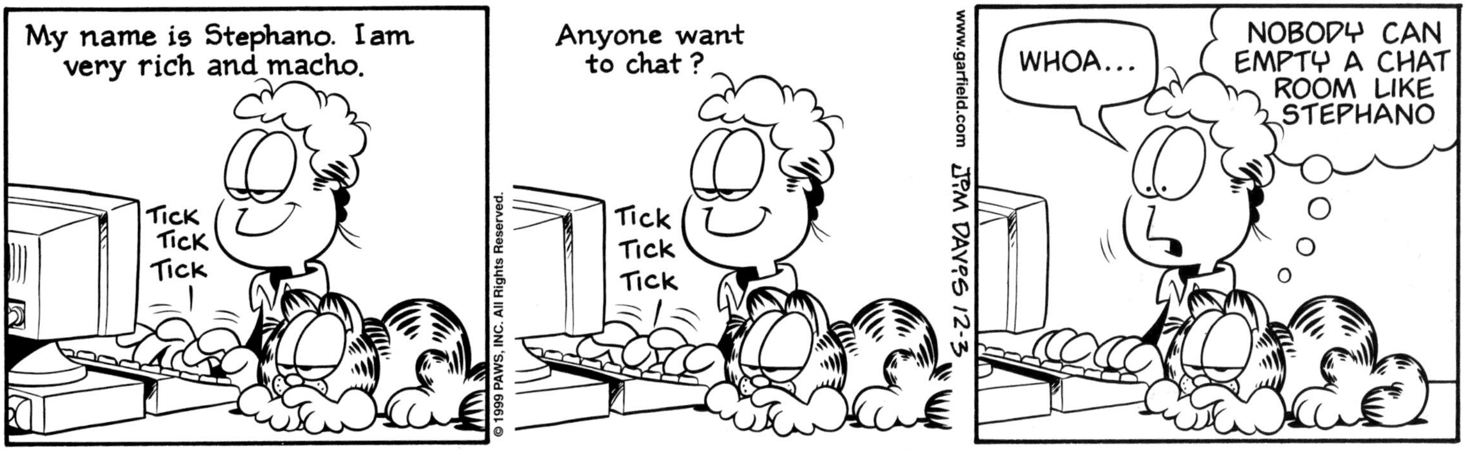
My name is Stephano. I am very rich and macho.
Tick Tick Tick
© 1999 PAWS, INC. All Rights Reserved.
Anyone want to chat?
Tick Tick Tick
www.garfield.com
JIM DAVIS 12-3
WHOA...
NOBODY CAN EMPTY A CHAT ROOM LIKE STEPHANO

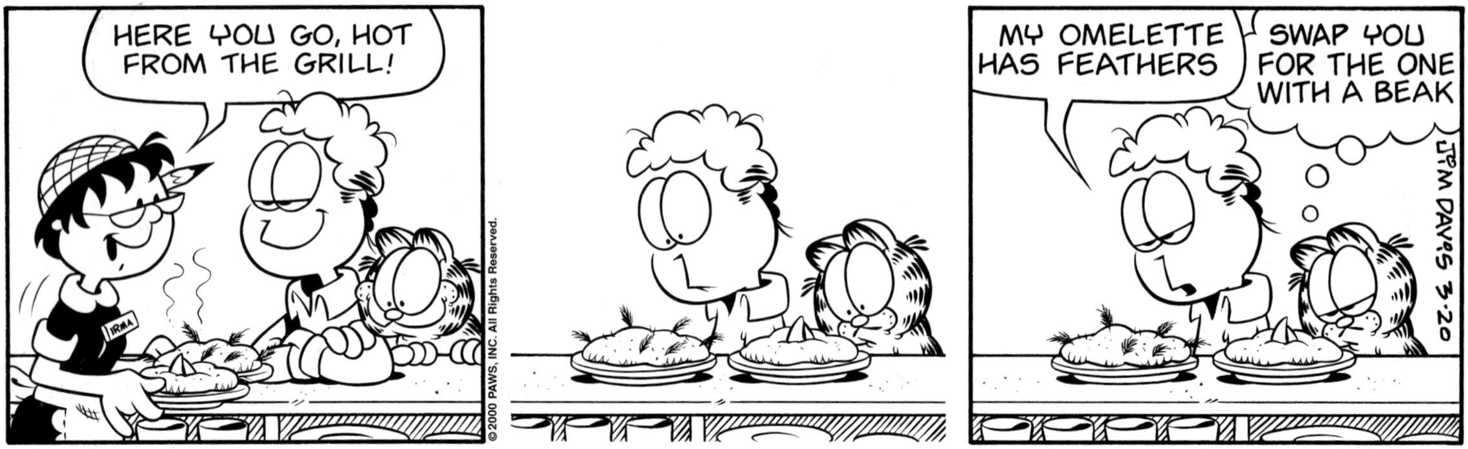
HERE YOU GO, HOT FROM THE GRILL!
IRMA
MY OMELETTE HAS FEATHERS
SWAP YOU FOR THE ONE WITH A BEAK
JPM DAVPS 3-20

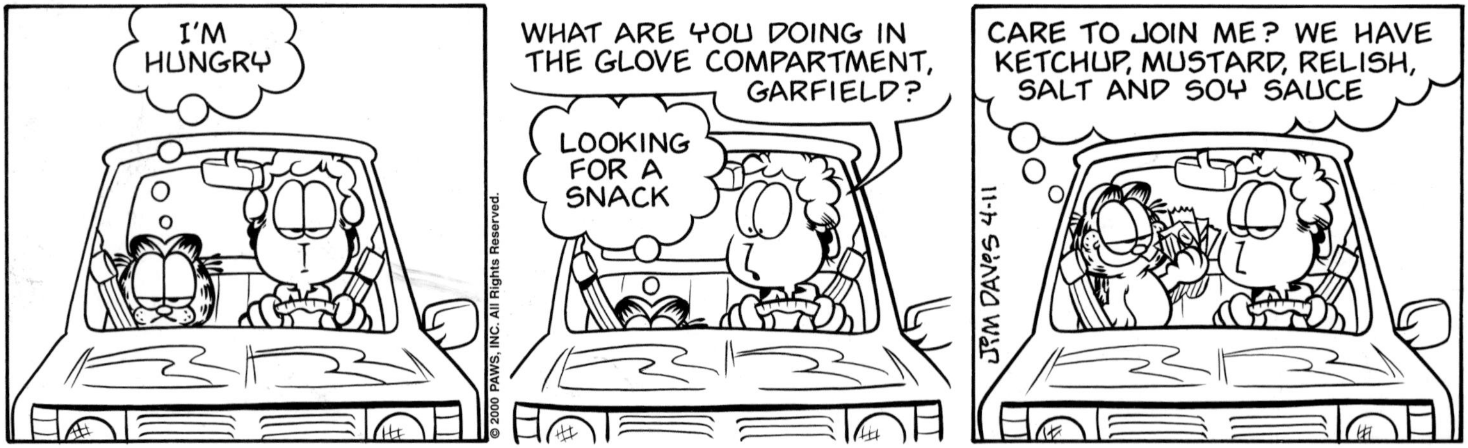
I'M HUNGRY
WHAT ARE YOU DOING IN THE GLOVE COMPARTMENT, GARFIELD?
LOOKING FOR A SNACK
CARE TO JOIN ME? WE HAVE KETCHUP, MUSTARD, RELISH, SALT AND SOY SAUCE
JPM DAVPS 4-11

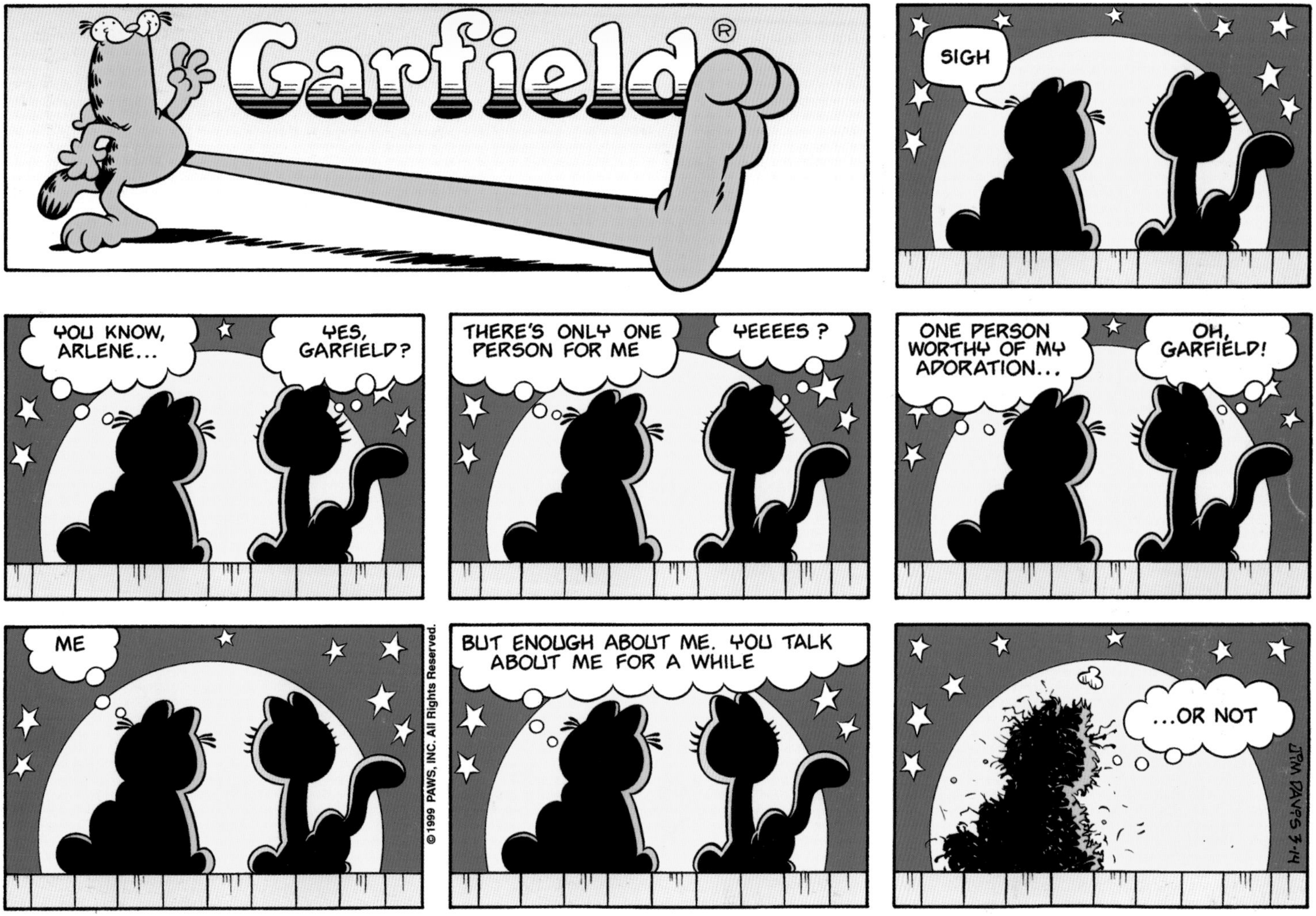
Garfield®
SIGH
YOU KNOW, ARLENE...
YES, GARFIELD?
THERE'S ONLY ONE PERSON FOR ME
YEEEES ?
ONE PERSON WORTHY OF MY ADORATION...
OH, GARFIELD!
ME
© 1999 PAWS, INC. All Rights Reserved.
BUT ENOUGH ABOUT ME. YOU TALK ABOUT ME FOR A WHILE
...OR NOT
JPM DAVPS 3-14

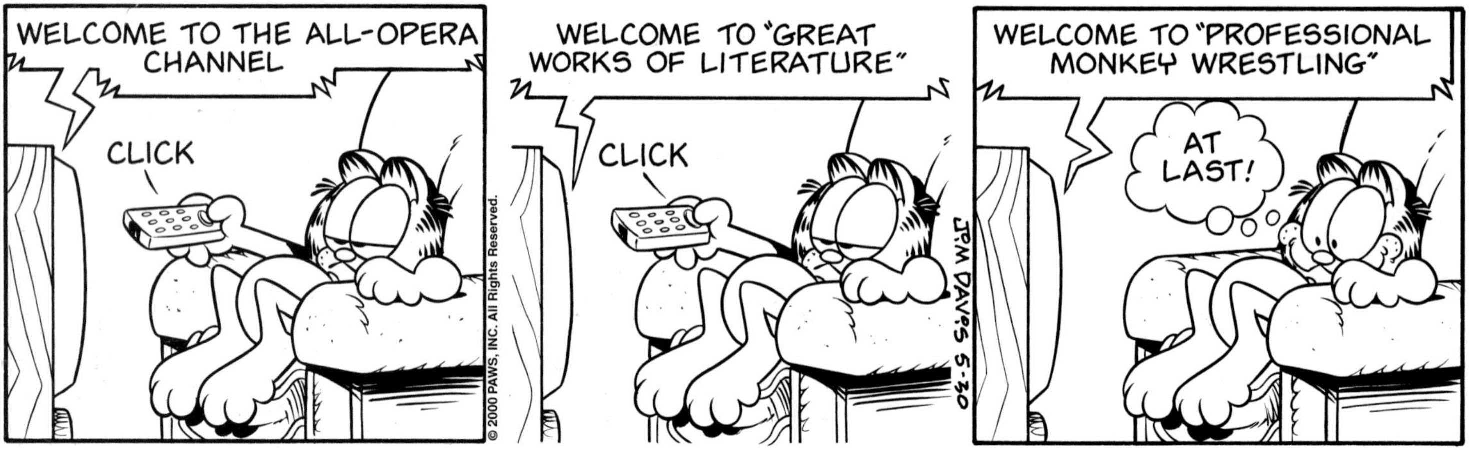
WELCOME TO THE ALL-OPERA CHANNEL
CLICK
WELCOME TO "GREAT WORKS OF LITERATURE"
CLICK
WELCOME TO "PROFESSIONAL MONKEY WRESTLING"
AT LAST!
JIM DAVIS 5-30

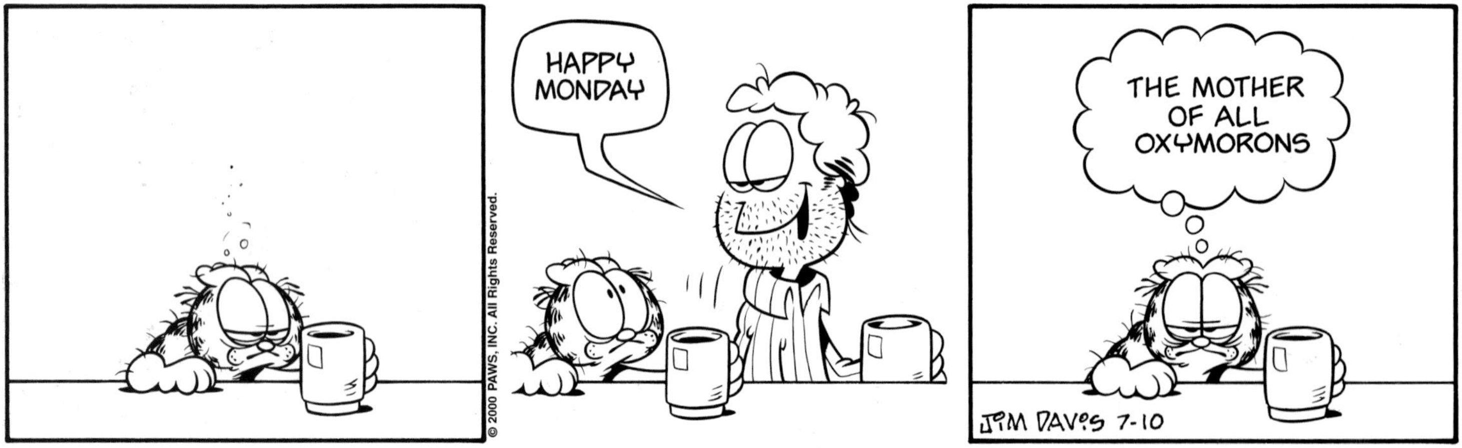
HAPPY MONDAY
THE MOTHER OF ALL OXYMORONS
JIM DAVIS 7-10

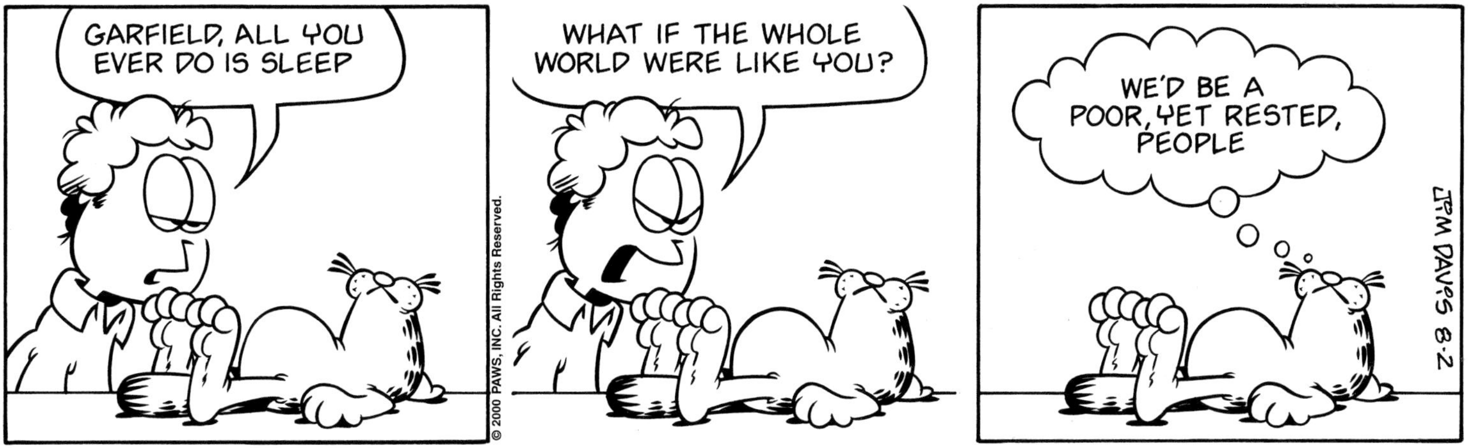
GARFIELD, ALL YOU EVER DO IS SLEEP
WHAT IF THE WHOLE WORLD WERE LIKE YOU?
WE'D BE A POOR, YET RESTED, PEOPLE
JPM DAVPS 8-2
© 2000 PAWS, INC. All Rights Reserved.

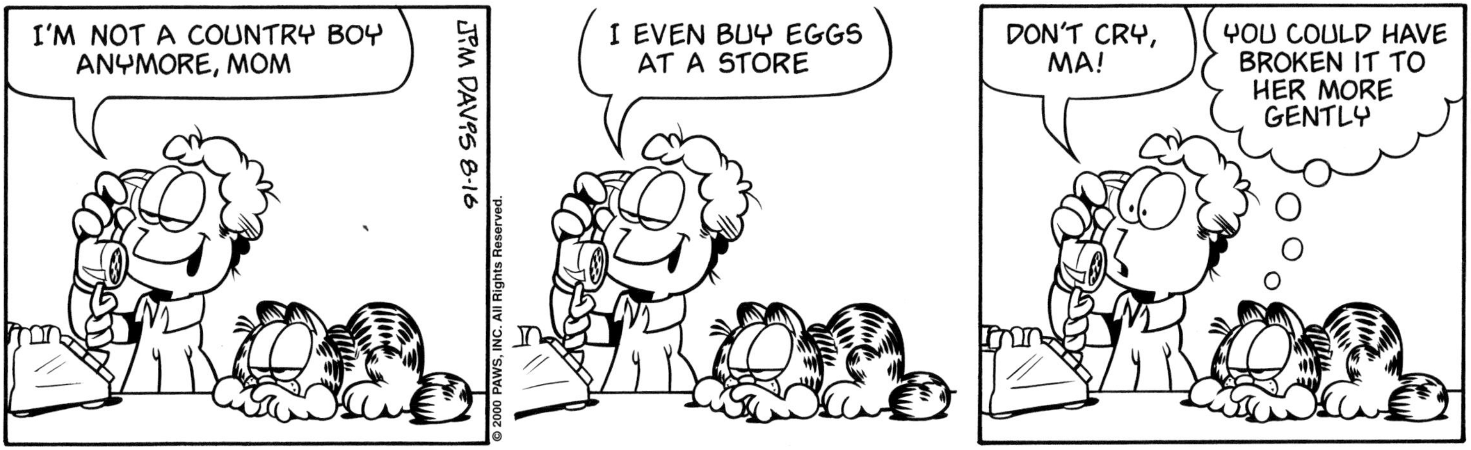
I'M NOT A COUNTRY BOY ANYMORE, MOM
JPM DAVPS 8-16
I EVEN BUY EGGS AT A STORE
DON'T CRY, MA!
YOU COULD HAVE BROKEN IT TO HER MORE GENTLY
© 2000 PAWS, INC. All Rights Reserved.

Does Garfield get smarter as he gets older? I don't think he's changed too much, personality-wise, over the years. He's pretty much the same self-centered, lazy, egotistical, lasagna-loving, coffee-drinking, dog-hating cat he's always been. He does seem to be catching on to new technologies: DVD players, computers, cell phones—so in that way, he's smarter.

www.coffeequick.com
TIC TIC TIC
www.garfield.com
CLICK
DING-DONG
© 2000 PAWS, INC. All Rights Reserved.
I NOW OFFICIALLY LOVE THE INTERNET
JIM DAVIS 9-7

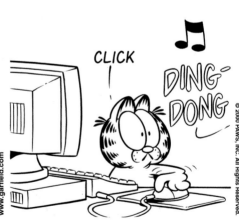

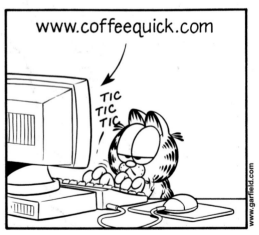

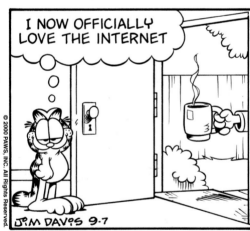

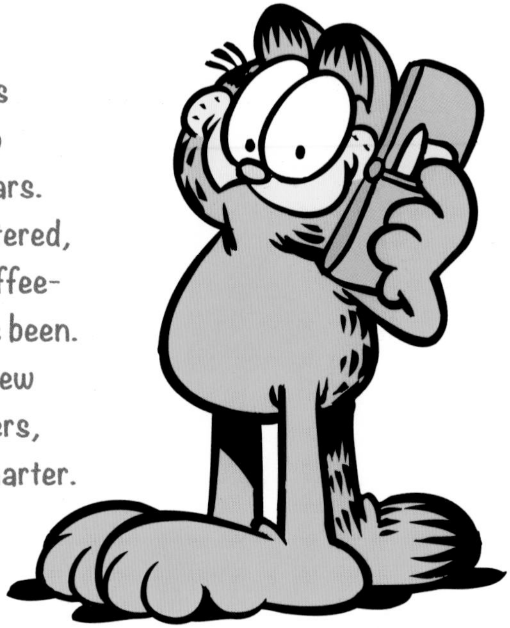

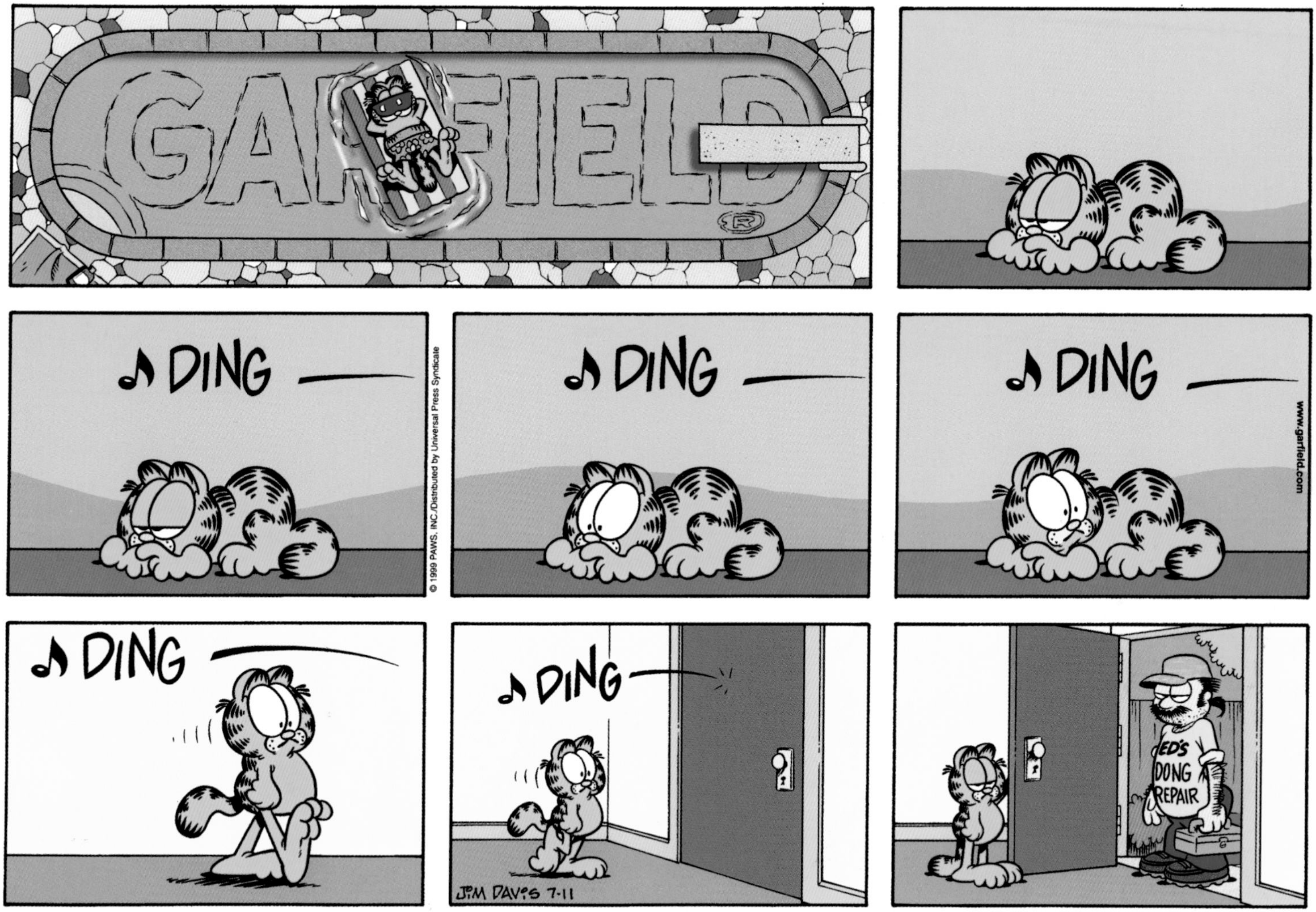
GARFIELD ®
DING
DING
DING
DING
DING
ED'S DONG REPAIR
JIM DAVIS 7-11
© 1999 PAWS, INC./Distributed by Universal Press Syndicate
www.garfield.com

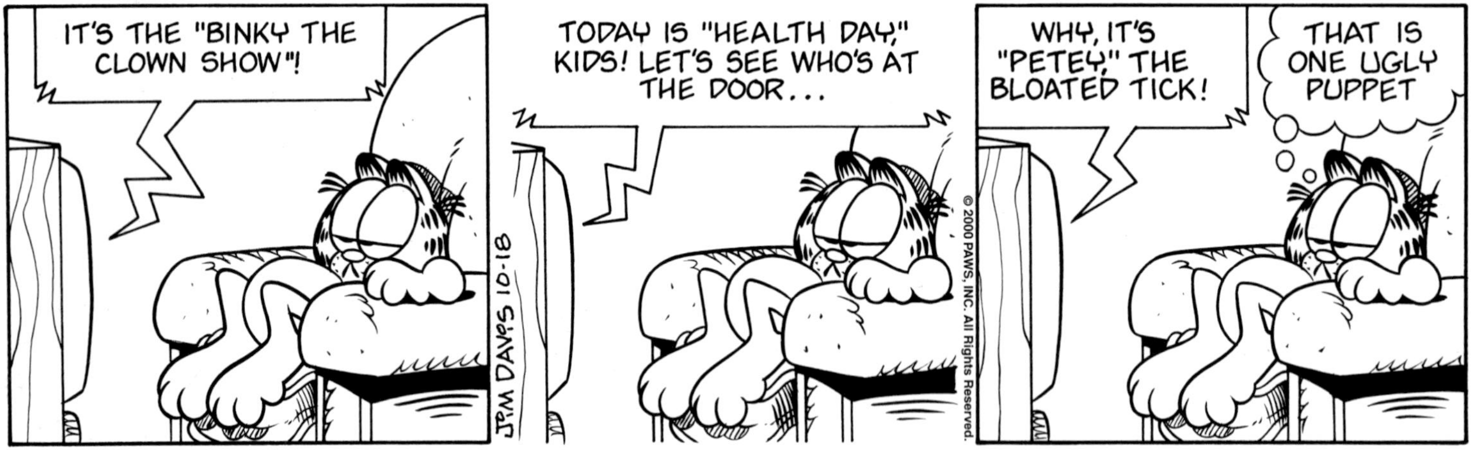

IT'S THE "BINKY THE CLOWN SHOW"!
JIM DAVIS 10-18
TODAY IS "HEALTH DAY," KIDS! LET'S SEE WHO'S AT THE DOOR...
© 2000 PAWS, INC. All Rights Reserved.
WHY, IT'S "PETEY," THE BLOATED TICK!
THAT IS ONE UGLY PUPPET

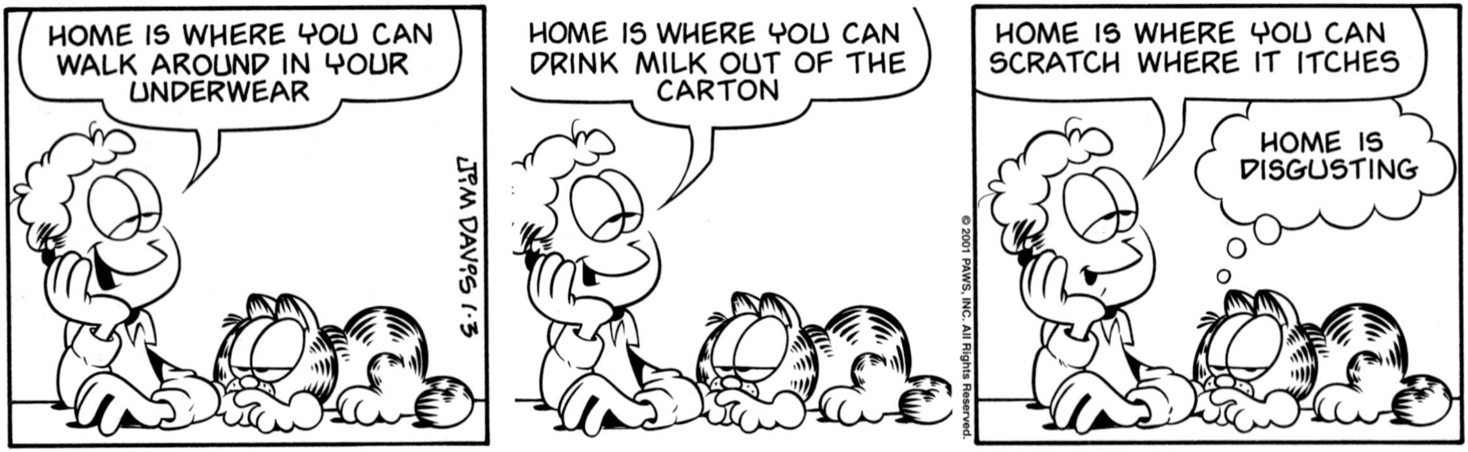

HOME IS WHERE YOU CAN WALK AROUND IN YOUR UNDERWEAR
JIM DAVIS 1-3
HOME IS WHERE YOU CAN DRINK MILK OUT OF THE CARTON
© 2001 PAWS, INC. All Rights Reserved.
HOME IS WHERE YOU CAN SCRATCH WHERE IT ITCHES
HOME IS DISGUSTING

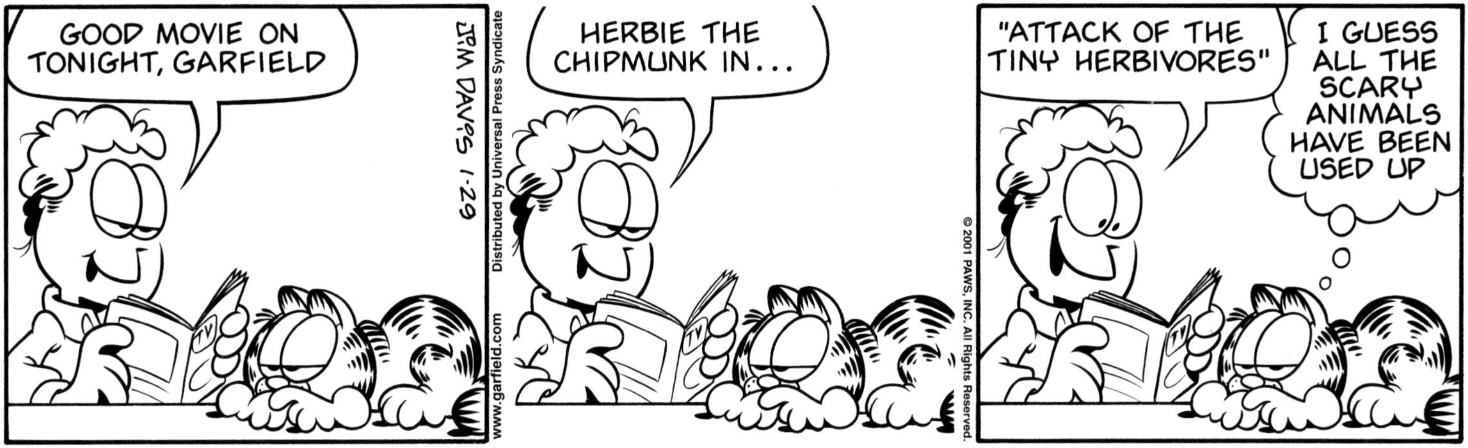
GOOD MOVIE ON TONIGHT, GARFIELD
HERBIE THE CHIPMUNK IN...
"ATTACK OF THE TINY HERBIVORES"
I GUESS ALL THE SCARY ANIMALS HAVE BEEN USED UP
JPM DAVPS 1-29
Distributed by Universal Press Syndicate
www.garfield.com
© 2001 PAWS, INC. All Rights Reserved.

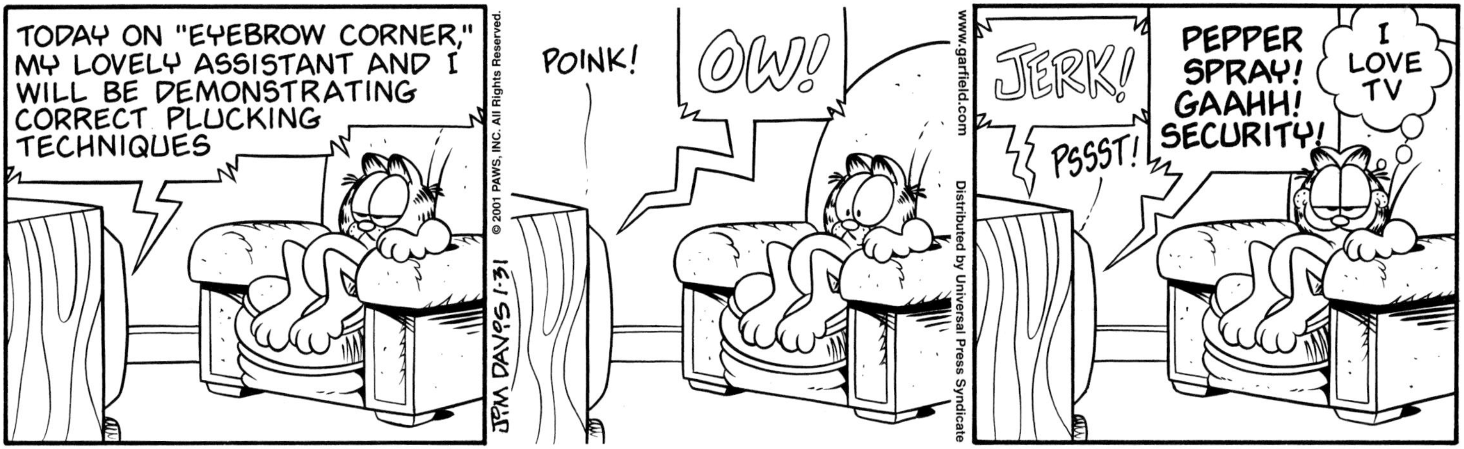
TODAY ON "EYEBROW CORNER," MY LOVELY ASSISTANT AND I WILL BE DEMONSTRATING CORRECT PLUCKING TECHNIQUES
POINK!
OW!
JERK!
PSSST!
PEPPER SPRAY! GAAHH! SECURITY!
I LOVE TV
JPM DAVPS 1-31
© 2001 PAWS, INC. All Rights Reserved.
www.garfield.com
Distributed by Universal Press Syndicate

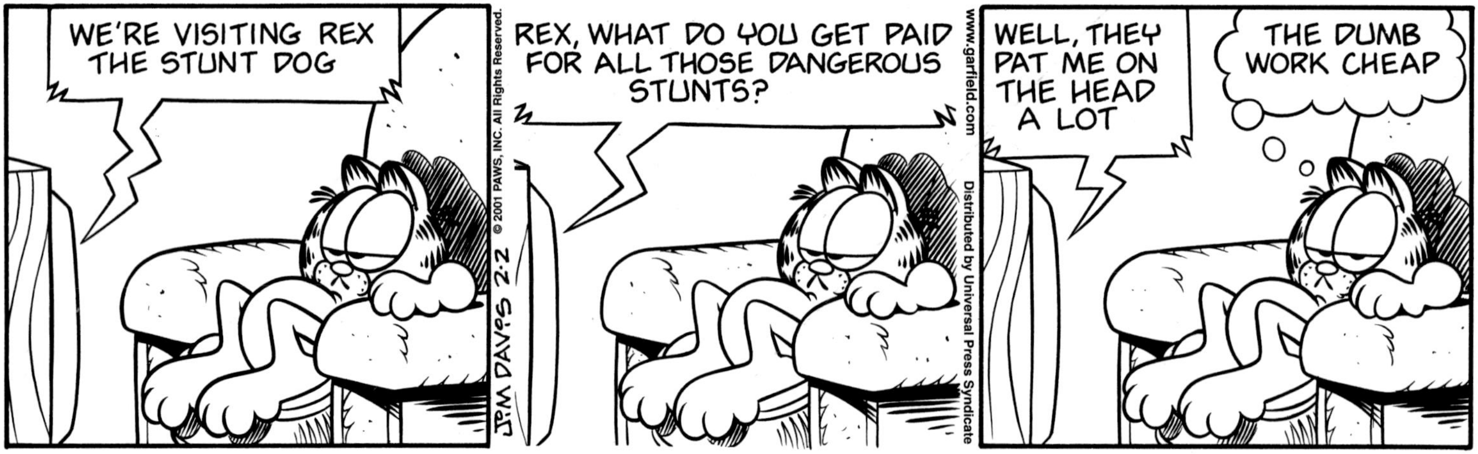
WE'RE VISITING REX THE STUNT DOG
REX, WHAT DO YOU GET PAID FOR ALL THOSE DANGEROUS STUNTS?
WELL, THEY PAT ME ON THE HEAD A LOT
THE DUMB WORK CHEAP
JPM DAVPS 2·2
© 2001 PAWS, INC. All Rights Reserved.
www.garfield.com
Distributed by Universal Press Syndicate

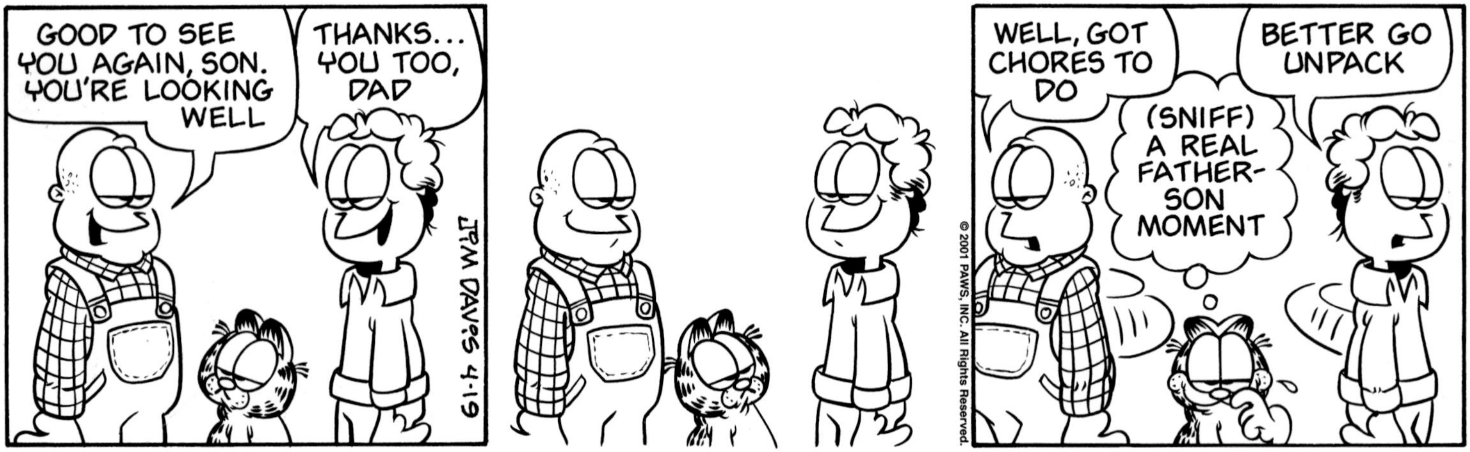
GOOD TO SEE YOU AGAIN, SON. YOU'RE LOOKING WELL
THANKS... YOU TOO, DAD
JPM DAVPS 4·19
WELL, GOT CHORES TO DO
(SNIFF) A REAL FATHER-SON MOMENT
BETTER GO UNPACK
© 2001 PAWS, INC. All Rights Reserved.

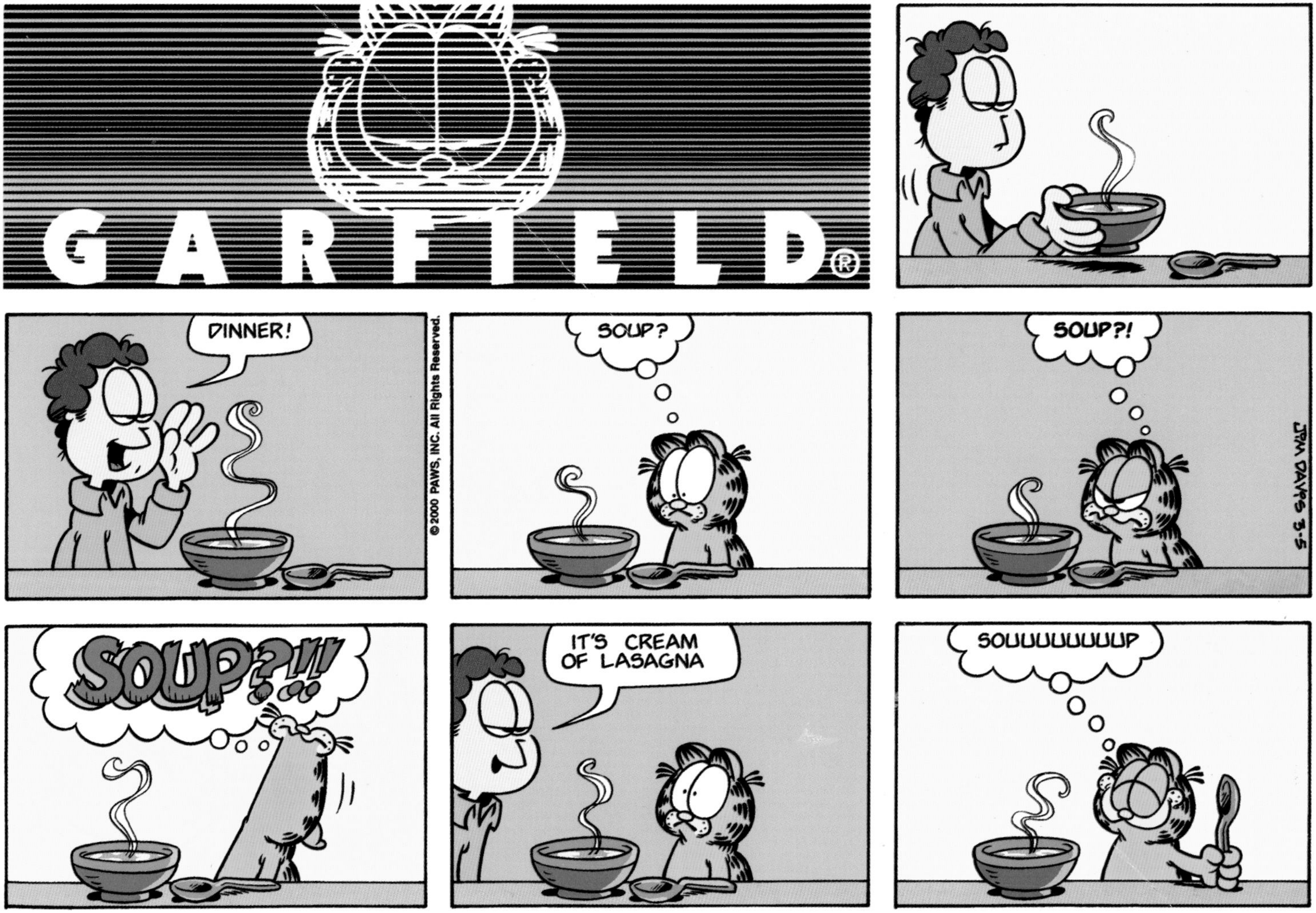
GARFIELD®
DINNER!
© 2000 PAWS, INC. All Rights Reserved.
SOUP?
SOUP?!
JPM DAVIS 3-5
SOUP?!!
IT'S CREAM OF LASAGNA
SOUUUUUUUUP

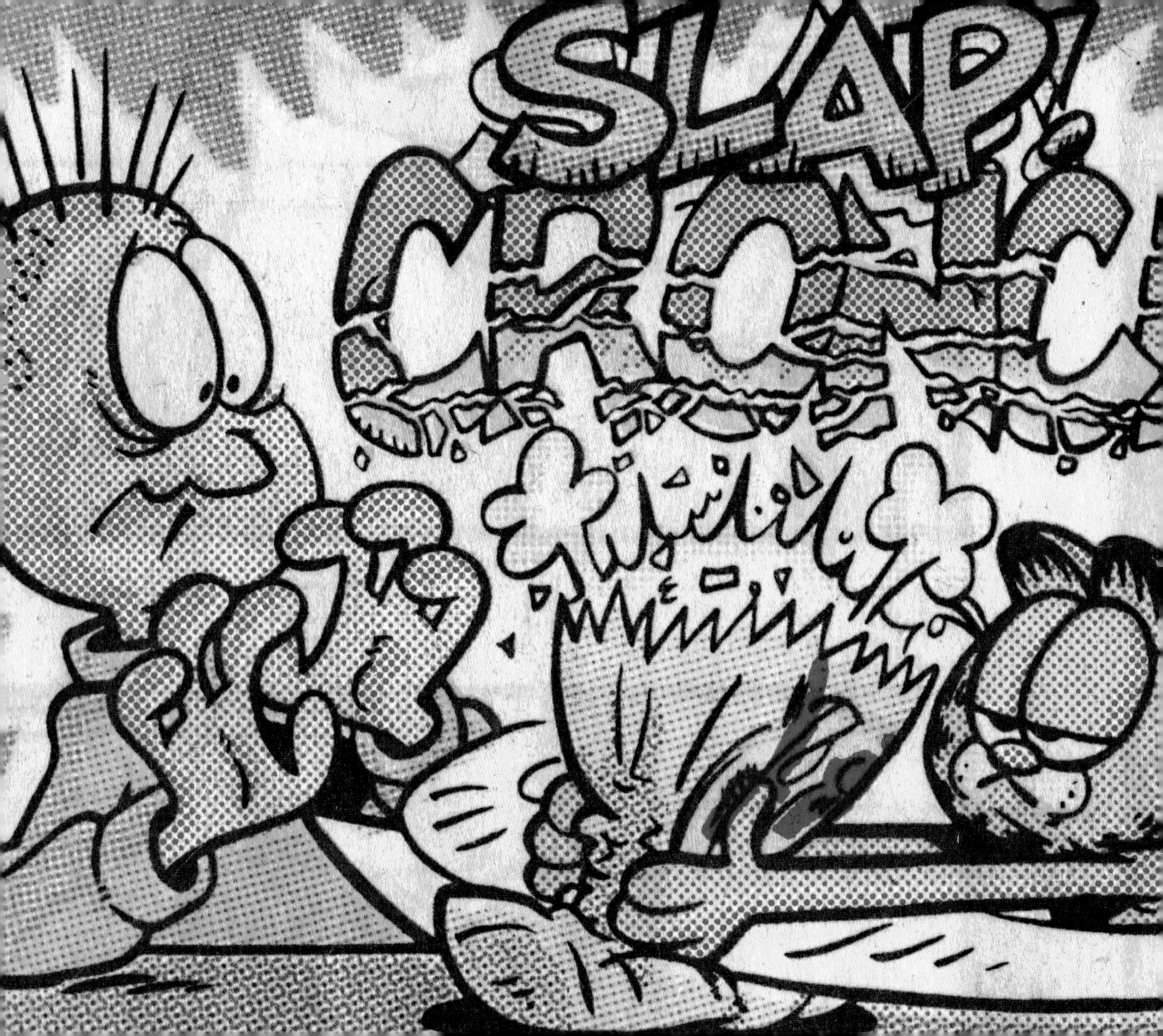
SLAP!
CRACK

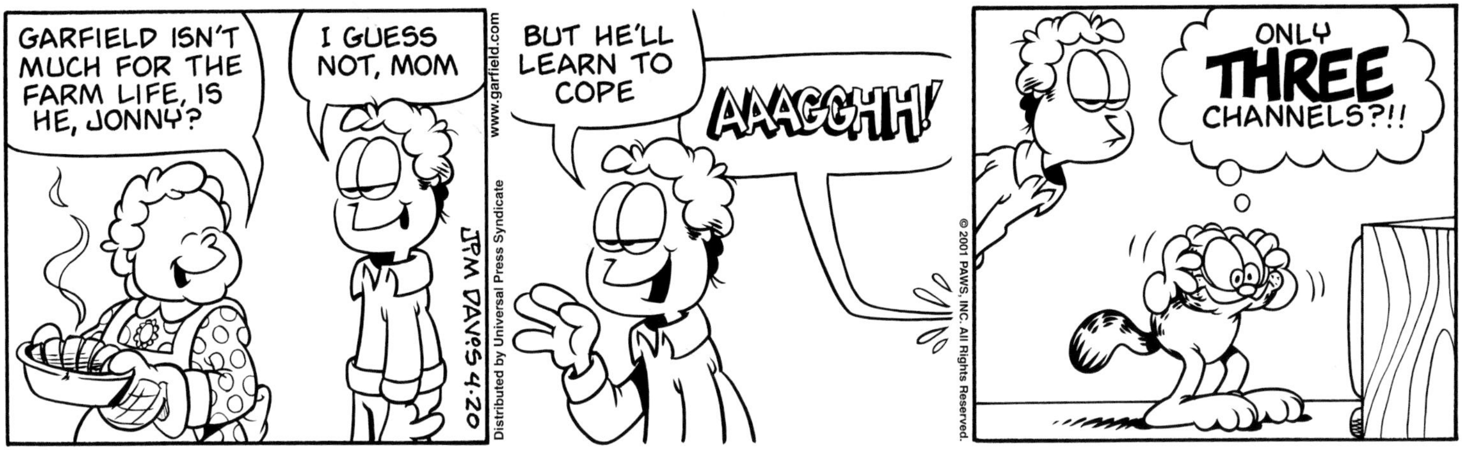
GARFIELD ISN'T MUCH FOR THE FARM LIFE, IS HE, JONNY?
I GUESS NOT, MOM
JIM DAVIS 4·20
www.garfield.com
Distributed by Universal Press Syndicate
BUT HE'LL LEARN TO COPE
AAAGGHH!
© 2001 PAWS, INC. All Rights Reserved.
ONLY THREE CHANNELS?!!

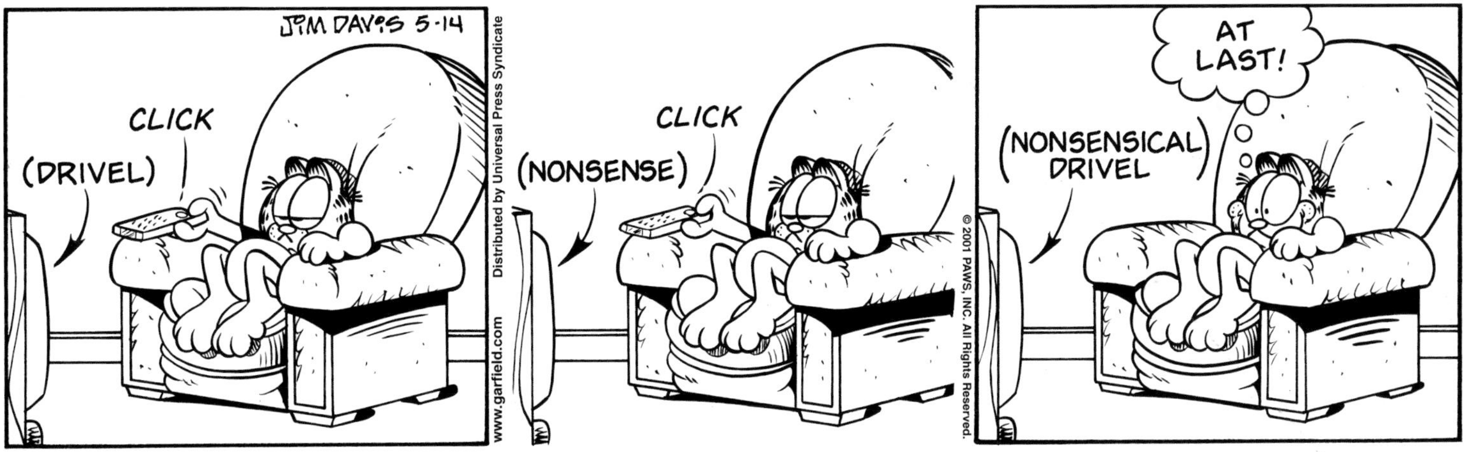
JIM DAVIS 5·14
CLICK
(DRIVEL)
www.garfield.com
Distributed by Universal Press Syndicate
CLICK
(NONSENSE)
© 2001 PAWS, INC. All Rights Reserved.
AT LAST!
(NONSENSICAL DRIVEL)

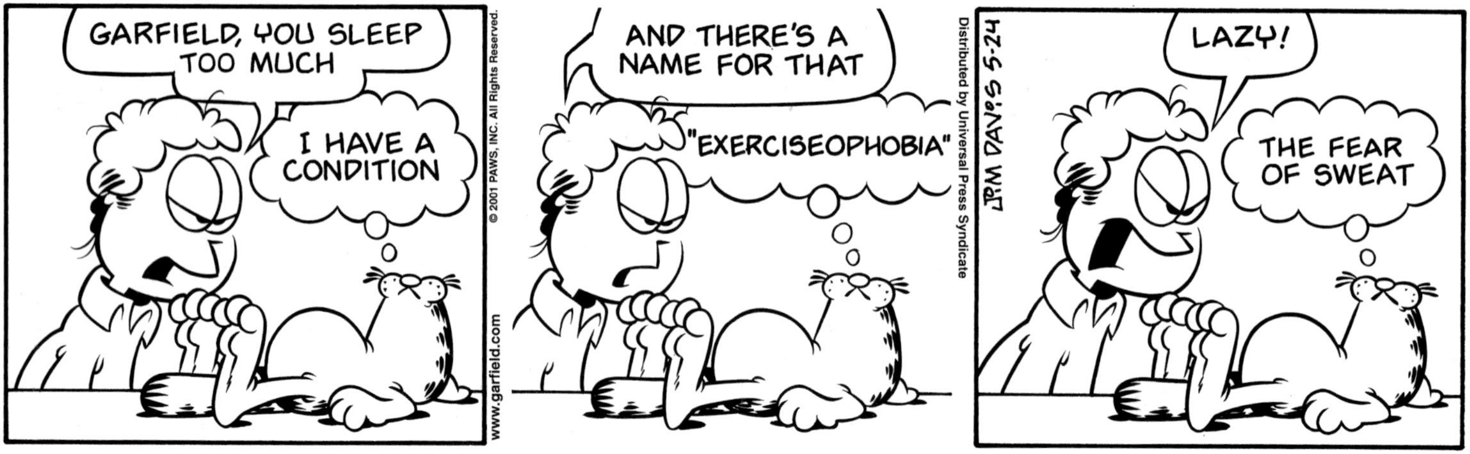
GARFIELD, YOU SLEEP TOO MUCH
I HAVE A CONDITION
© 2001 PAWS, INC. All Rights Reserved.
www.garfield.com
AND THERE'S A NAME FOR THAT
"EXERCISEOPHOBIA"
Distributed by Universal Press Syndicate
JIM DAVIS 5-24
LAZY!
THE FEAR OF SWEAT

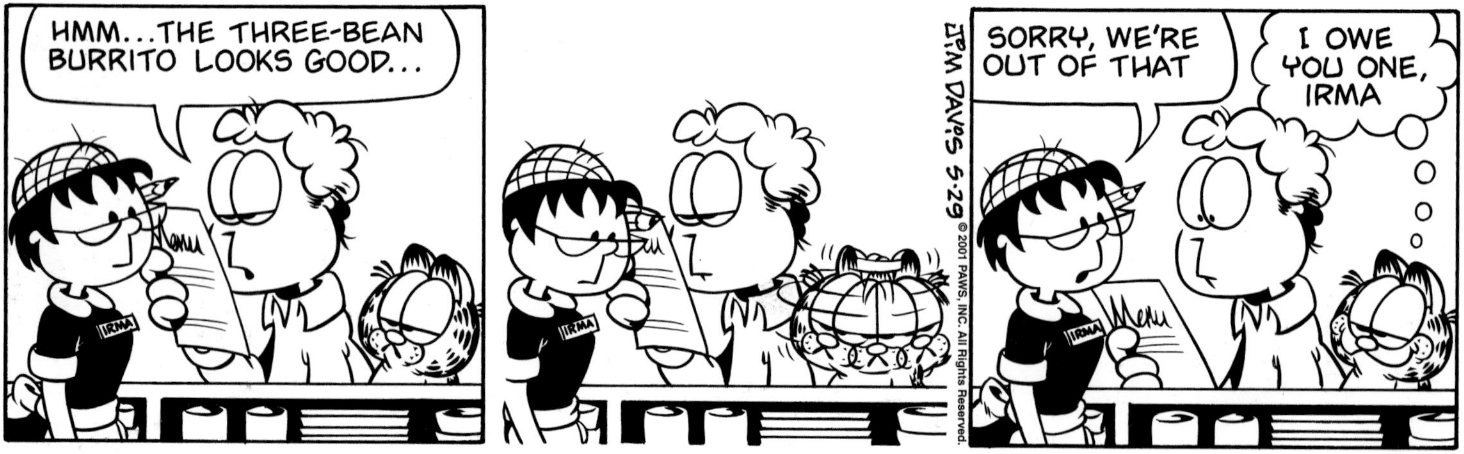
HMM...THE THREE-BEAN BURRITO LOOKS GOOD...
JIM DAVIS 5-29
© 2001 PAWS, INC. All Rights Reserved.
SORRY, WE'RE OUT OF THAT
I OWE YOU ONE, IRMA

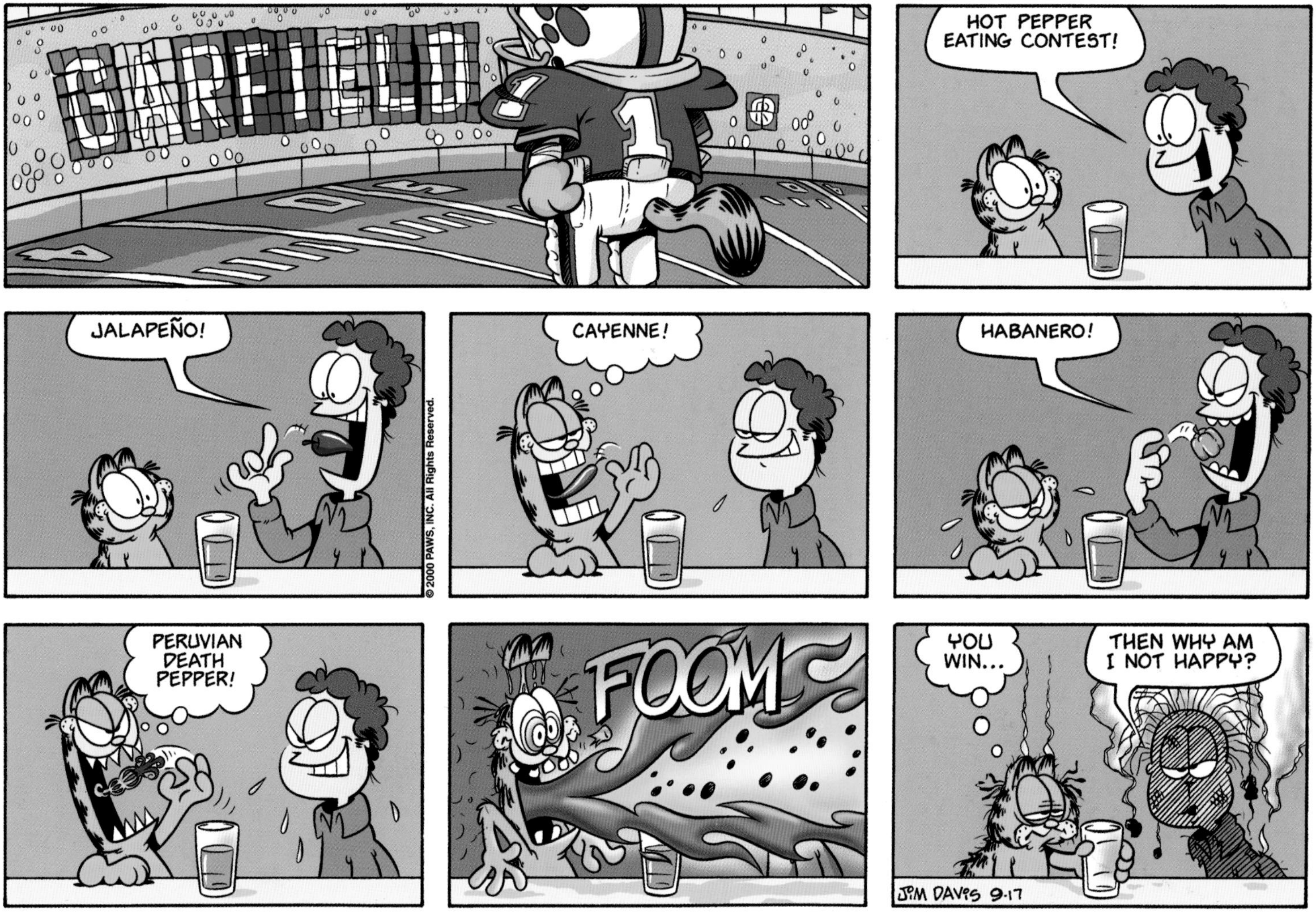
GARFIELD
1
HOT PEPPER EATING CONTEST!
JALAPEÑO!
© 2000 PAWS, INC. All Rights Reserved.
CAYENNE!
HABANERO!
PERUVIAN DEATH PEPPER!
FOOM
YOU WIN...
THEN WHY AM I NOT HAPPY?
JIM DAVIS 9-17

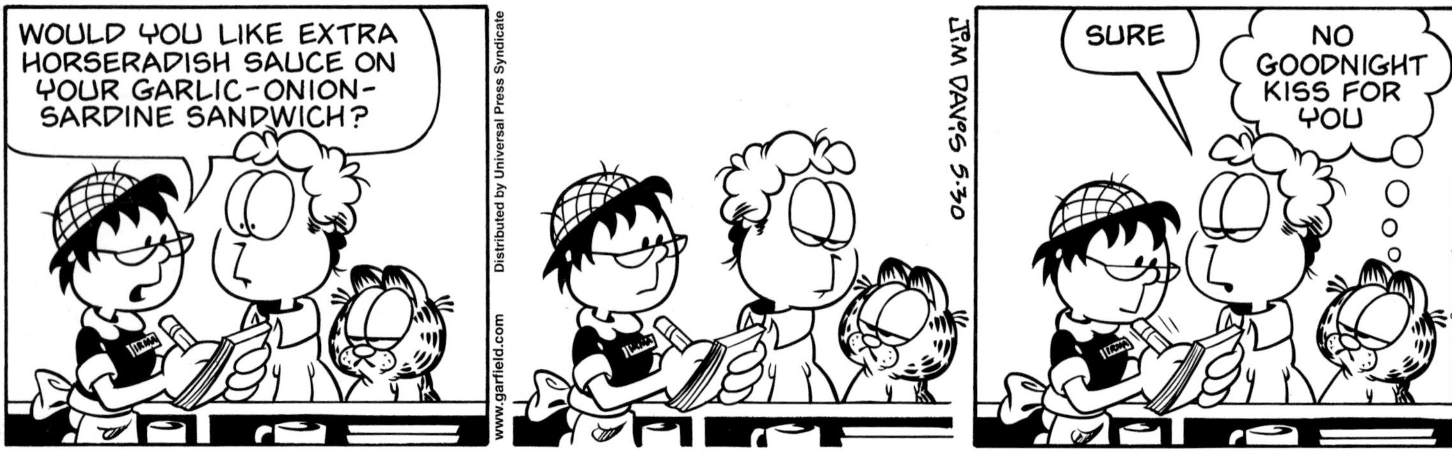
WOULD YOU LIKE EXTRA HORSERADISH SAUCE ON YOUR GARLIC-ONION-SARDINE SANDWICH?
SURE
NO GOODNIGHT KISS FOR YOU
JIM DAVIS 5-30
Distributed by Universal Press Syndicate
www.garfield.com
© 2001 PAWS, INC. All Rights Reserved.

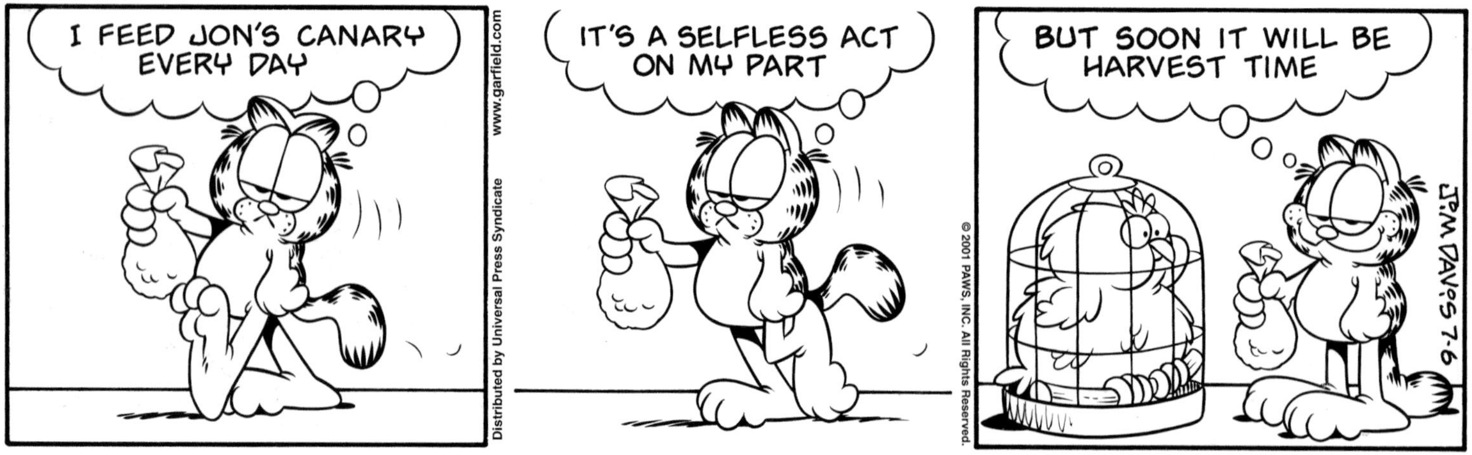
I FEED JON'S CANARY EVERY DAY
IT'S A SELFLESS ACT ON MY PART
BUT SOON IT WILL BE HARVEST TIME
JIM DAVIS 7-6
www.garfield.com
Distributed by Universal Press Syndicate
© 2001 PAWS, INC. All Rights Reserved.

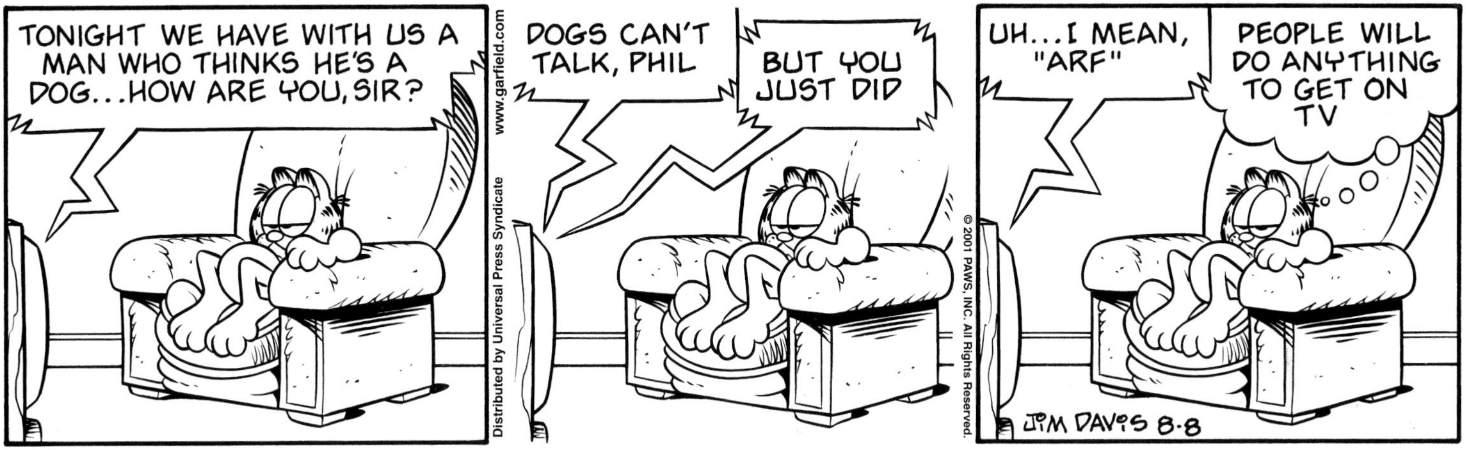
TONIGHT WE HAVE WITH US A MAN WHO THINKS HE'S A DOG...HOW ARE YOU, SIR?
www.garfield.com
Distributed by Universal Press Syndicate
DOGS CAN'T TALK, PHIL
BUT YOU JUST DID
© 2001 PAWS, INC. All Rights Reserved.
UH...I MEAN, "ARF"
PEOPLE WILL DO ANYTHING TO GET ON TV
JIM DAVIS 8-8

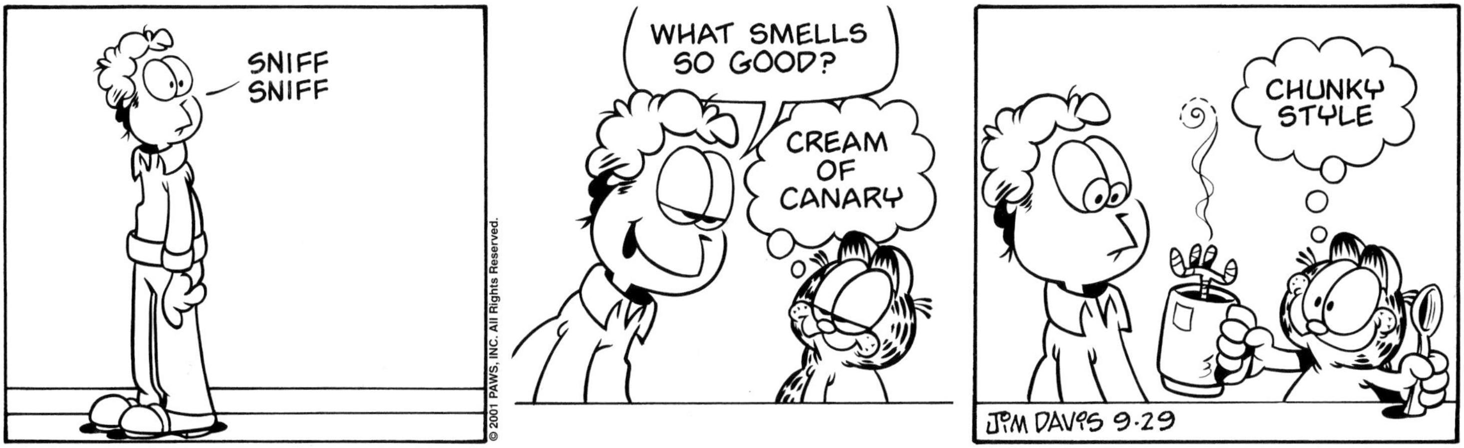
SNIFF SNIFF
© 2001 PAWS, INC. All Rights Reserved.
WHAT SMELLS SO GOOD?
CREAM OF CANARY
CHUNKY STYLE
JIM DAVIS 9-29

I was raised with farm cats, none quite like Garfield. I now have a fat tiger cat who lives at the studio named Spunky, and recently adopted a brown tiger kitten from Action for Animals, via PetSmart. We renamed the kitten Nermal; it was originally named Charlie Brown.

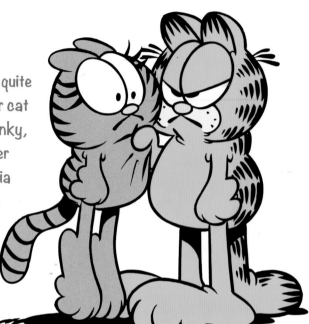

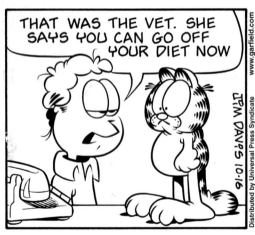

THAT WAS THE VET. SHE SAYS YOU CAN GO OFF YOUR DIET NOW
JIM DAVIS 10-16
www.garfield.com
Distributed by Universal Press Syndicate
THUD
© 2001 PAWS, INC. All Rights Reserved.
ARE YOU ALL RIGHT?!
QUICK! MOUTH-TO-MEAT LOAF RESUSCITATION!

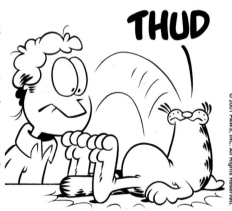

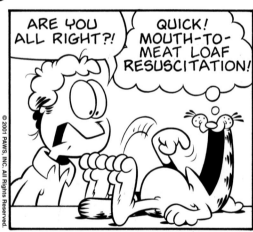

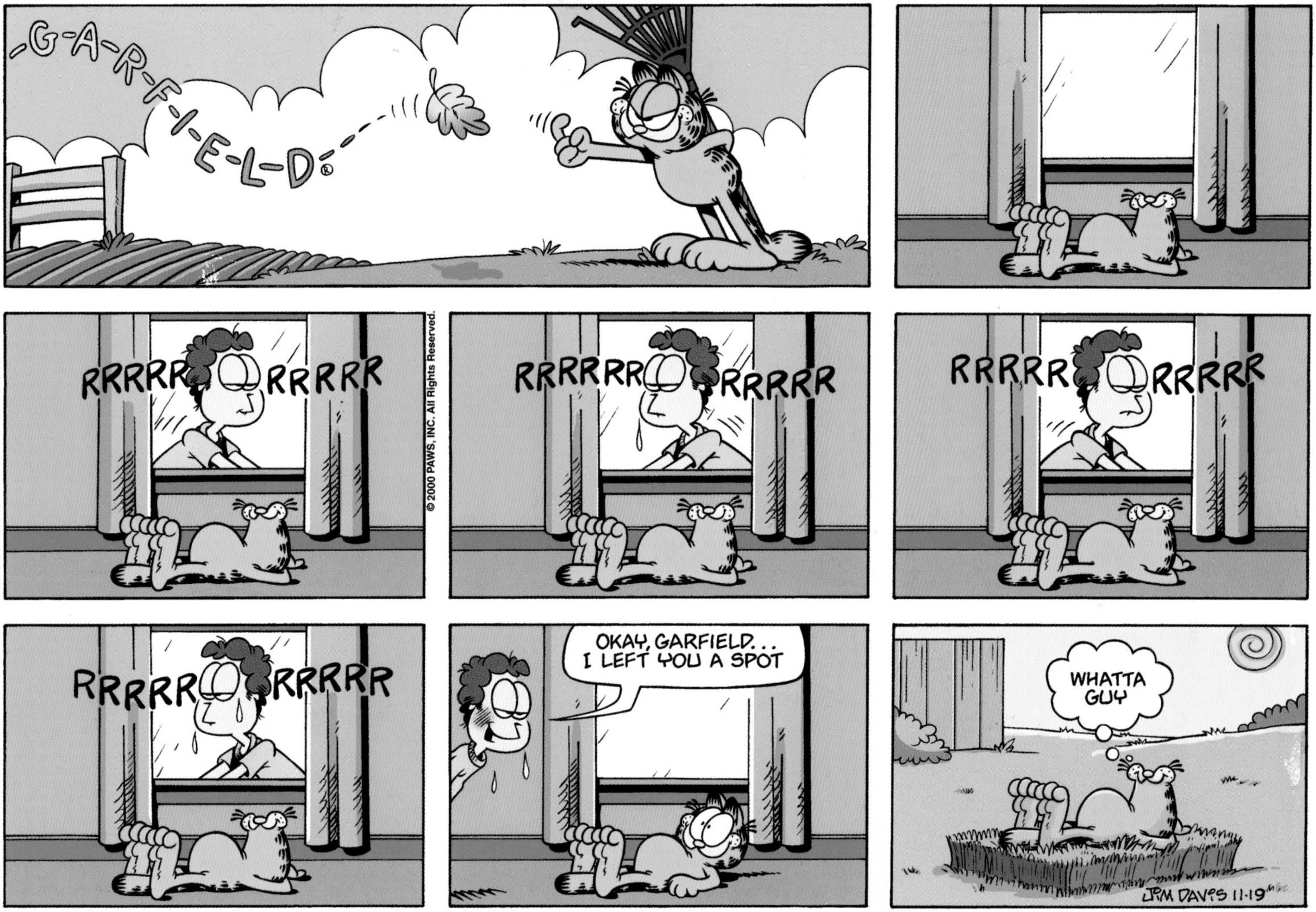
G-A-R-F-I-E-L-D®
RRRRR RRRRR
RRRRRR RRRRR
RRRRR RRRRR
RRRRR RRRRR
OKAY, GARFIELD... I LEFT YOU A SPOT
WHATTA GUY
JIM DAVIS 11-19

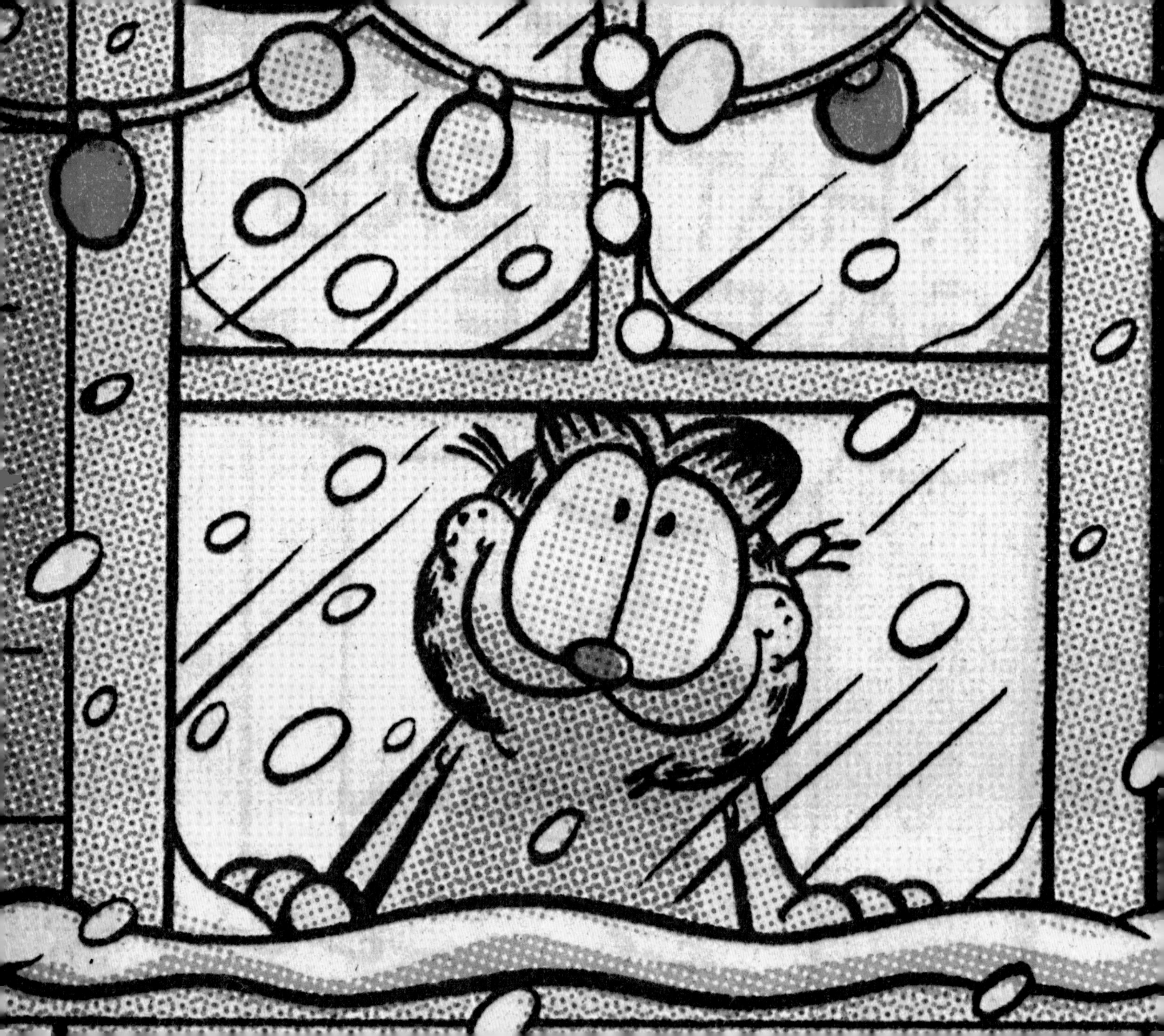

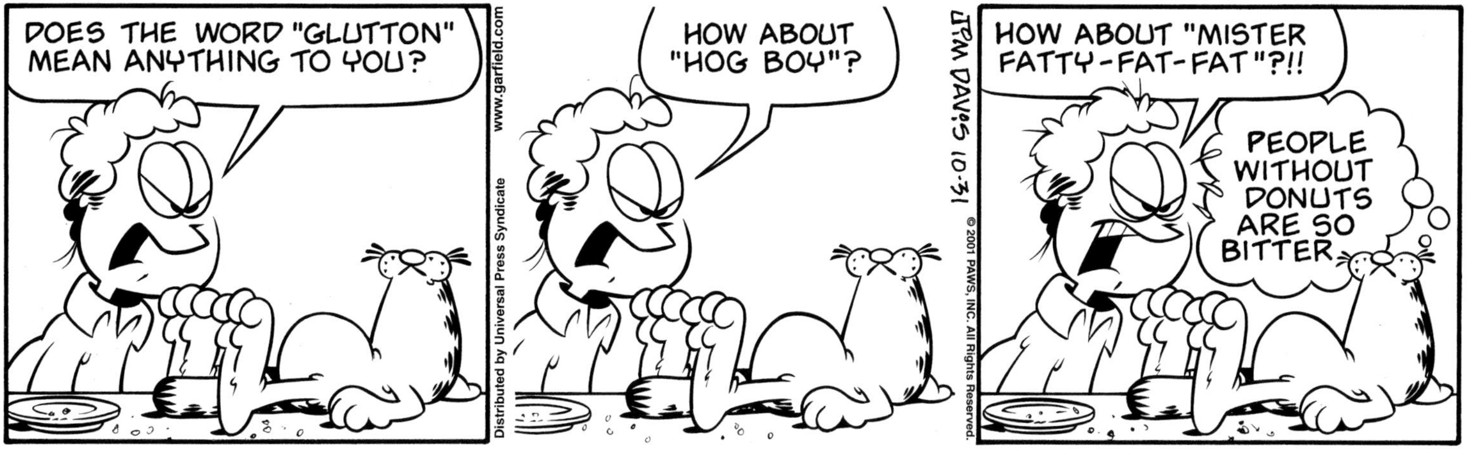
DOES THE WORD "GLUTTON" MEAN ANYTHING TO YOU?
HOW ABOUT "HOG BOY"?
HOW ABOUT "MISTER FATTY-FAT-FAT"?!!
PEOPLE WITHOUT DONUTS ARE SO BITTER
JIM DAVIS 10-31
www.garfield.com
Distributed by Universal Press Syndicate
© 2001 PAWS, INC. All Rights Reserved.

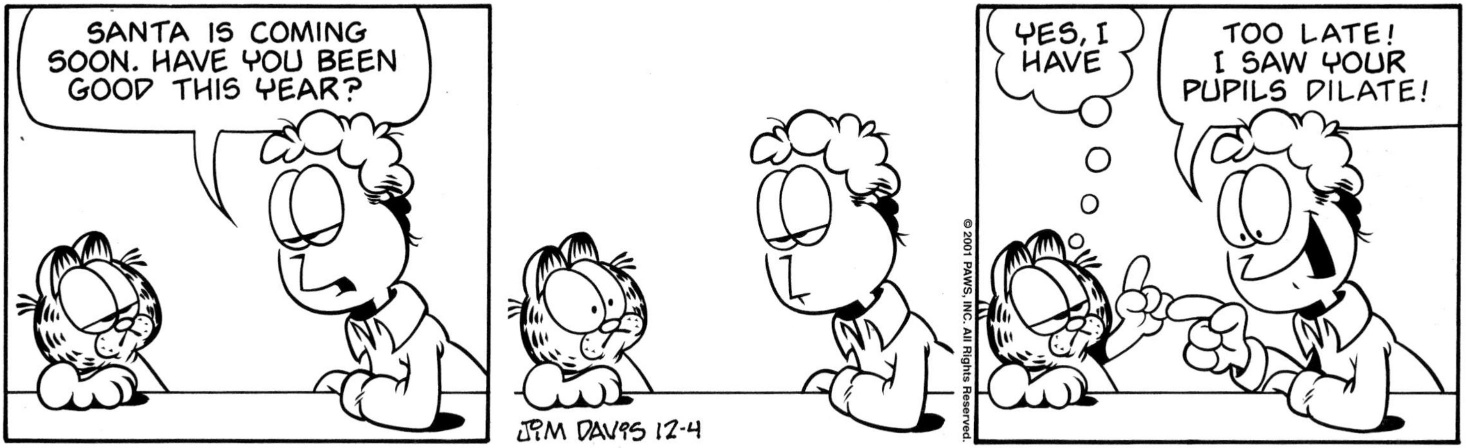
SANTA IS COMING SOON. HAVE YOU BEEN GOOD THIS YEAR?
YES, I HAVE
TOO LATE! I SAW YOUR PUPILS DILATE!
JIM DAVIS 12-4
© 2001 PAWS, INC. All Rights Reserved.

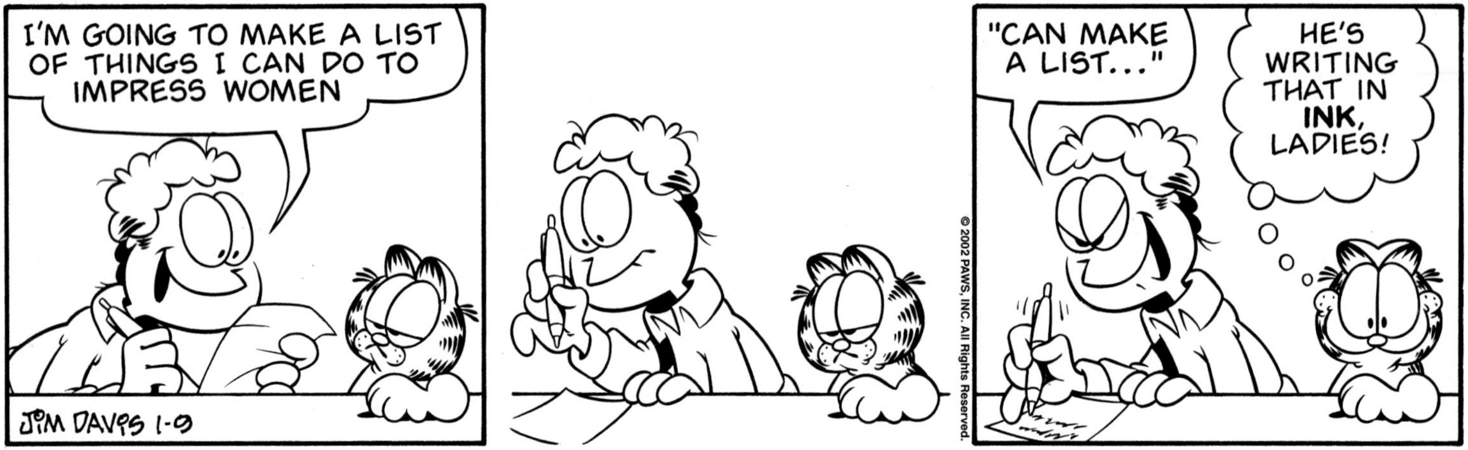
I'M GOING TO MAKE A LIST OF THINGS I CAN DO TO IMPRESS WOMEN
JIM DAVIS 1-9
"CAN MAKE A LIST..."
HE'S WRITING THAT IN **INK**, LADIES!
© 2002 PAWS, INC. All Rights Reserved.

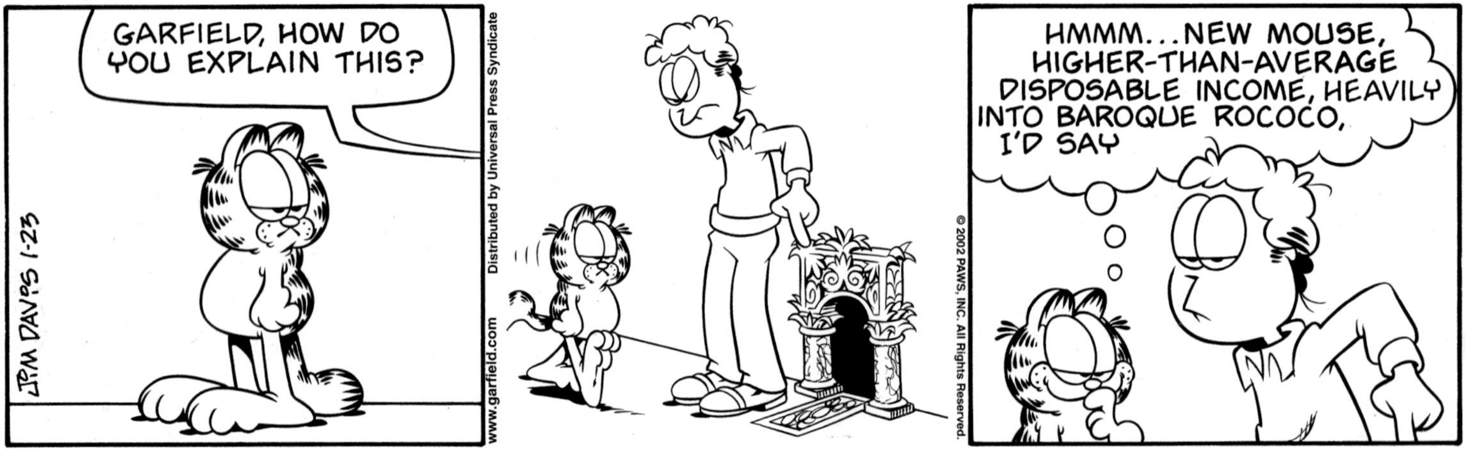
GARFIELD, HOW DO YOU EXPLAIN THIS?
JIM DAVIS 1-23
Distributed by Universal Press Syndicate
www.garfield.com
HMMM...NEW MOUSE, HIGHER-THAN-AVERAGE DISPOSABLE INCOME, HEAVILY INTO BAROQUE ROCOCO, I'D SAY
© 2002 PAWS, INC. All Rights Reserved.

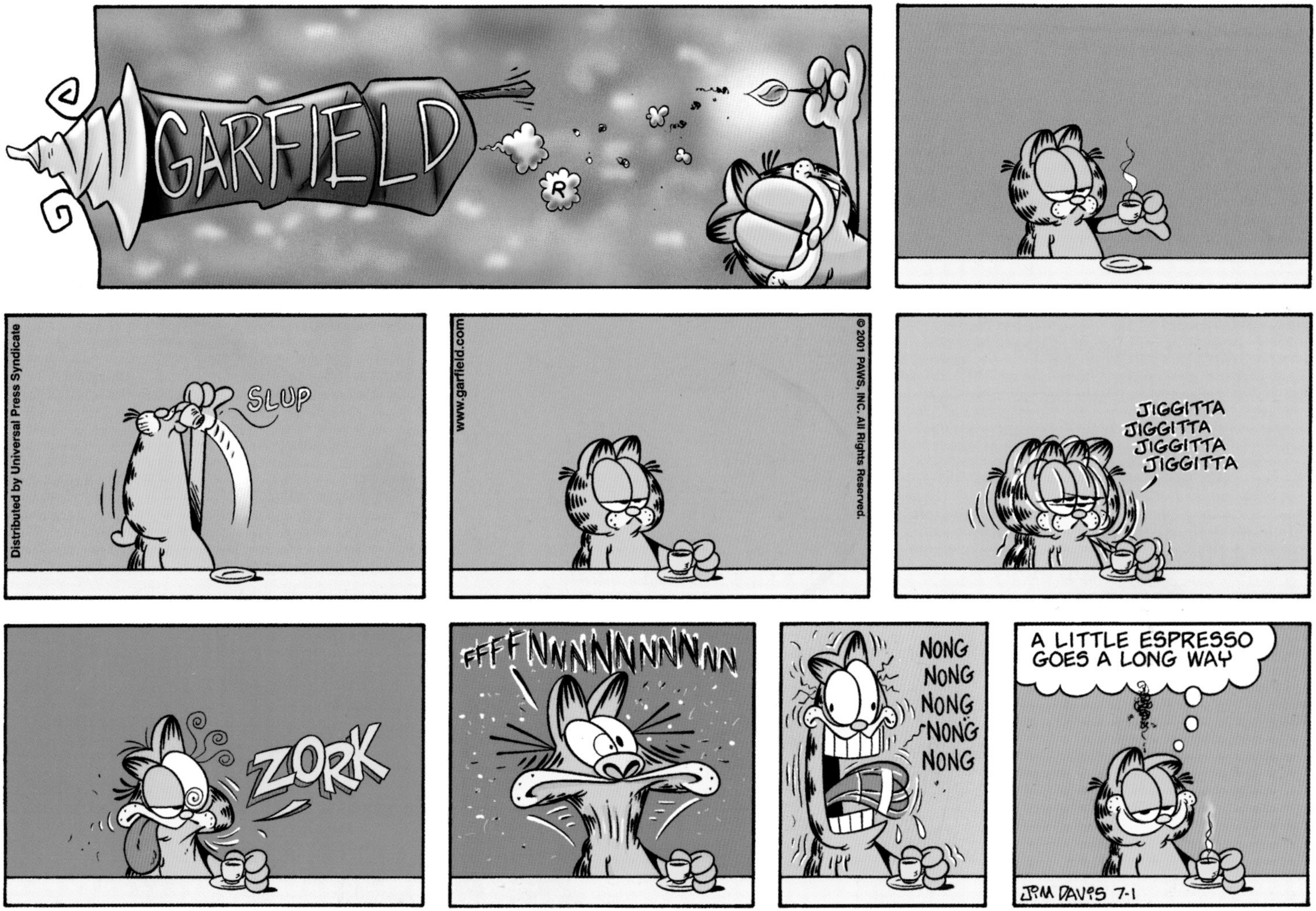
GARFIELD
Distributed by Universal Press Syndicate
SLUP
www.garfield.com
© 2001 PAWS, INC. All Rights Reserved.
JIGGITTA
JIGGITTA
JIGGITTA
JIGGITTA
ZORK
FFFFNNNNNNNNNNNN
NONG
NONG
NONG
NONG
NONG
A LITTLE ESPRESSO GOES A LONG WAY
JIM DAVIS 7-1

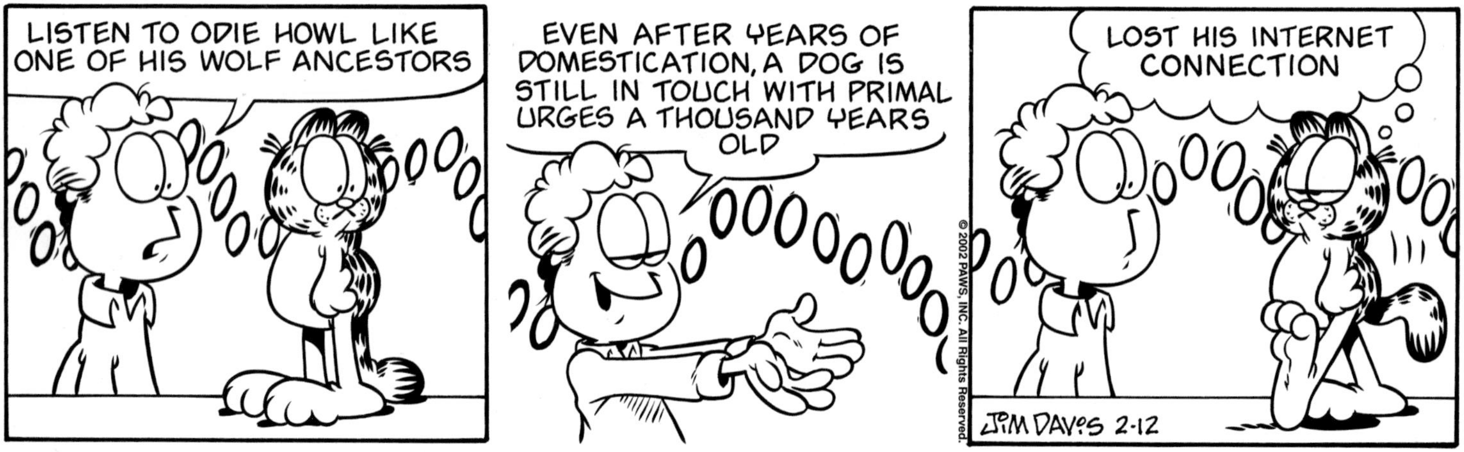
LISTEN TO ODIE HOWL LIKE ONE OF HIS WOLF ANCESTORS
EVEN AFTER YEARS OF DOMESTICATION, A DOG IS STILL IN TOUCH WITH PRIMAL URGES A THOUSAND YEARS OLD
LOST HIS INTERNET CONNECTION
JIM DAVIS 2-12
© 2002 PAWS, INC. All Rights Reserved.

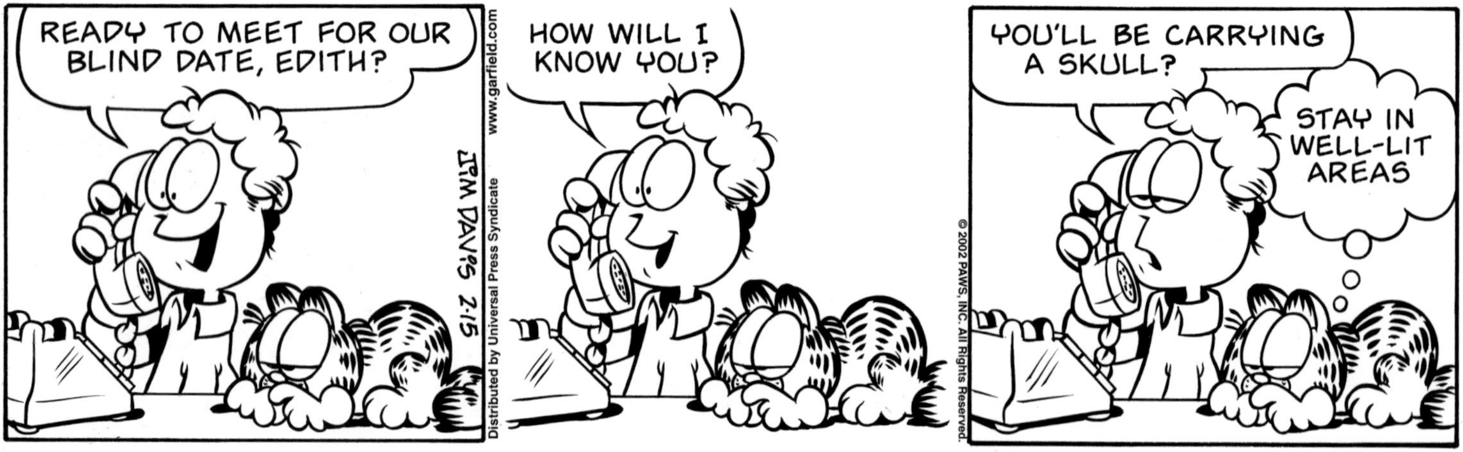
READY TO MEET FOR OUR BLIND DATE, EDITH?
JIM DAVIS 2-15
www.garfield.com
Distributed by Universal Press Syndicate
HOW WILL I KNOW YOU?
YOU'LL BE CARRYING A SKULL?
STAY IN WELL-LIT AREAS
© 2002 PAWS, INC. All Rights Reserved.

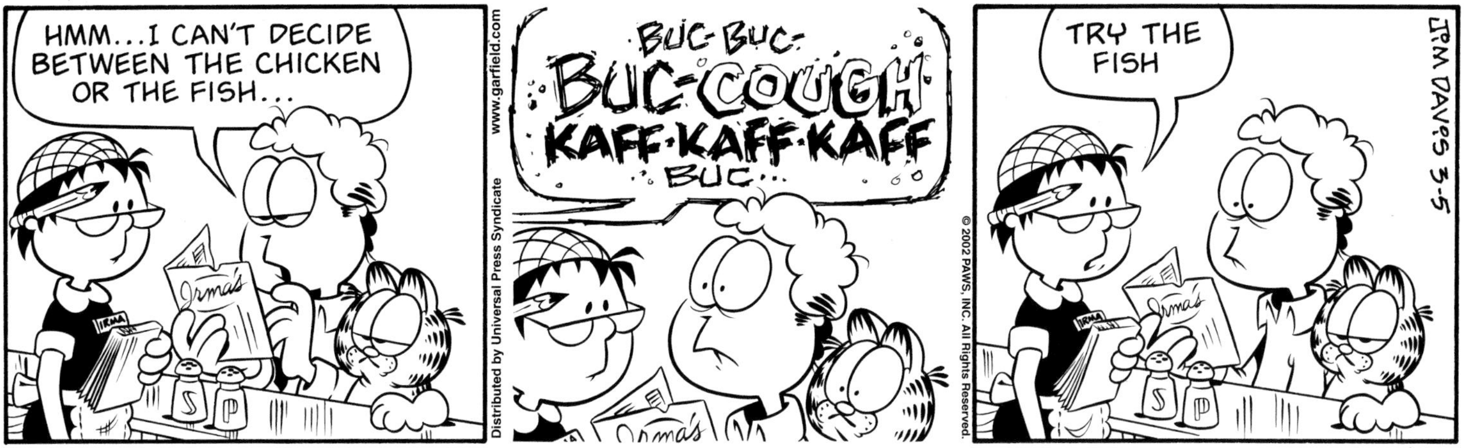
HMM...I CAN'T DECIDE BETWEEN THE CHICKEN OR THE FISH...
www.garfield.com
Distributed by Universal Press Syndicate
BUC-BUC-
BUC-COUGH
KAFF-KAFF-KAFF
BUC
TRY THE FISH
JIM DAVIS 3-5
© 2002 PAWS, INC. All Rights Reserved.

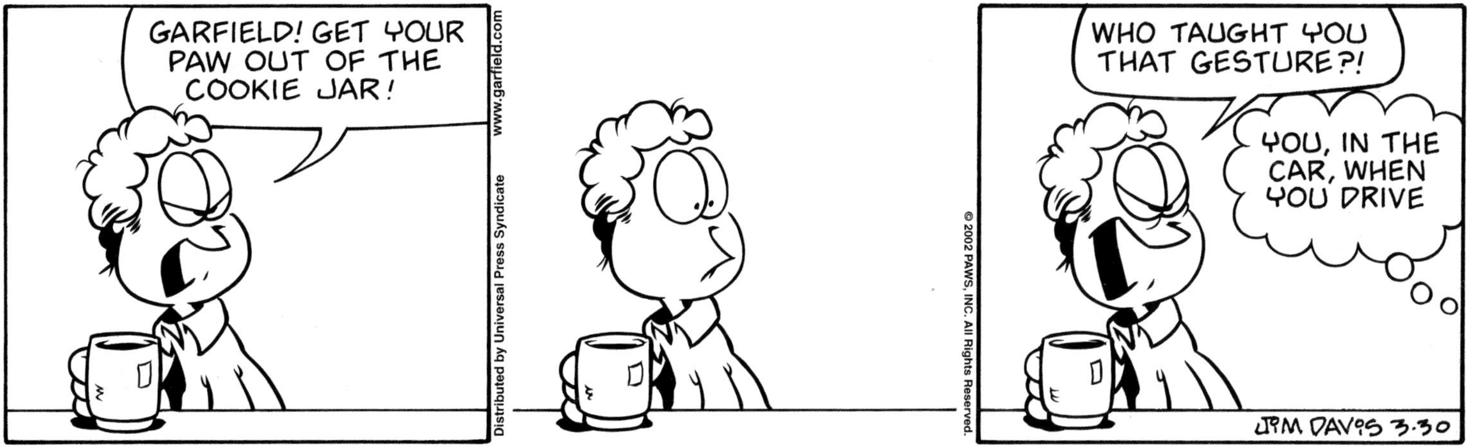
GARFIELD! GET YOUR PAW OUT OF THE COOKIE JAR!
www.garfield.com
Distributed by Universal Press Syndicate
© 2002 PAWS, INC. All Rights Reserved.
WHO TAUGHT YOU THAT GESTURE?!
YOU, IN THE CAR, WHEN YOU DRIVE
JIM DAVIS 3-30

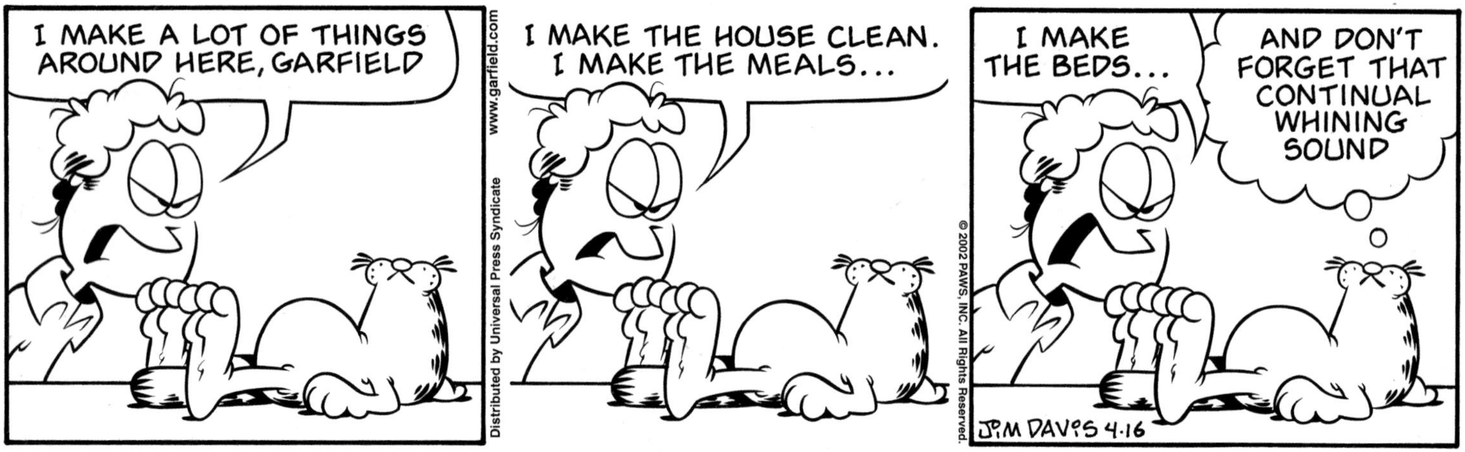
I MAKE A LOT OF THINGS AROUND HERE, GARFIELD
www.garfield.com
Distributed by Universal Press Syndicate
I MAKE THE HOUSE CLEAN. I MAKE THE MEALS...
© 2002 PAWS, INC. All Rights Reserved.
I MAKE THE BEDS...
AND DON'T FORGET THAT CONTINUAL WHINING SOUND
JIM DAVIS 4.16

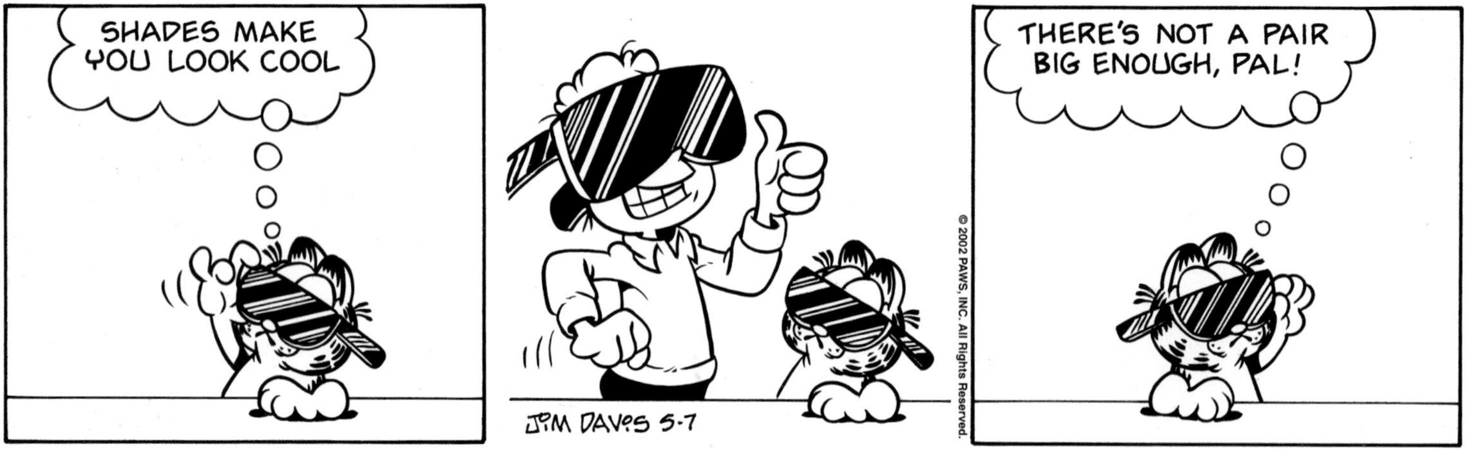
SHADES MAKE YOU LOOK COOL
JIM DAVIS 5.7
© 2002 PAWS, INC. All Rights Reserved.
THERE'S NOT A PAIR BIG ENOUGH, PAL!

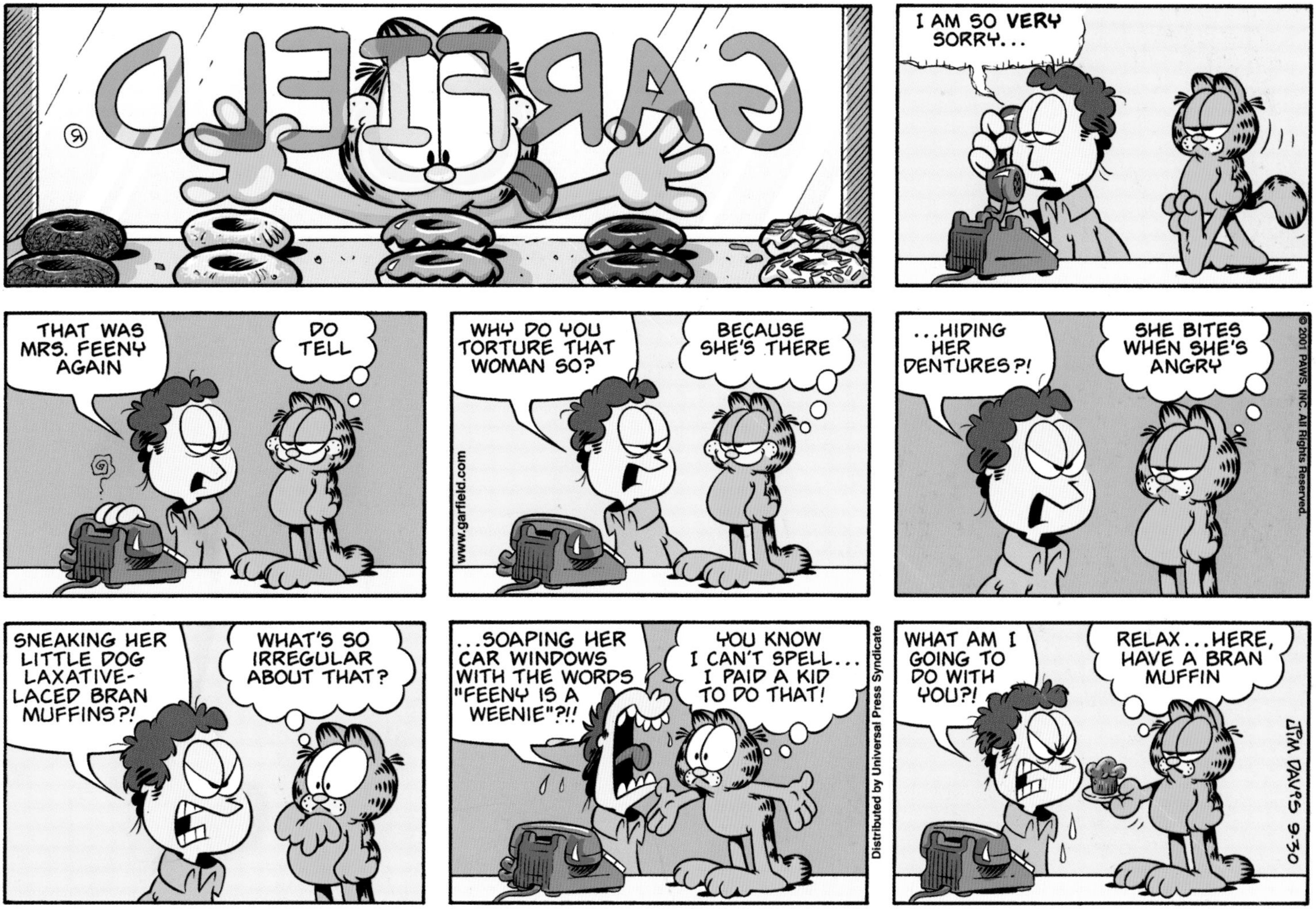
GARFIELD
I AM SO VERY SORRY...
THAT WAS MRS. FEENY AGAIN
DO TELL
WHY DO YOU TORTURE THAT WOMAN SO?
BECAUSE SHE'S THERE
...HIDING HER DENTURES?!
SHE BITES WHEN SHE'S ANGRY
SNEAKING HER LITTLE DOG LAXATIVE-LACED BRAN MUFFINS?!
WHAT'S SO IRREGULAR ABOUT THAT?
...SOAPING HER CAR WINDOWS WITH THE WORDS "FEENY IS A WEENIE"?!!
YOU KNOW I CAN'T SPELL... I PAID A KID TO DO THAT!
WHAT AM I GOING TO DO WITH YOU?!
RELAX...HERE, HAVE A BRAN MUFFIN
www.garfield.com
© 2001 PAWS, INC. All Rights Reserved.
Distributed by Universal Press Syndicate
JIM DAVIS 9-30

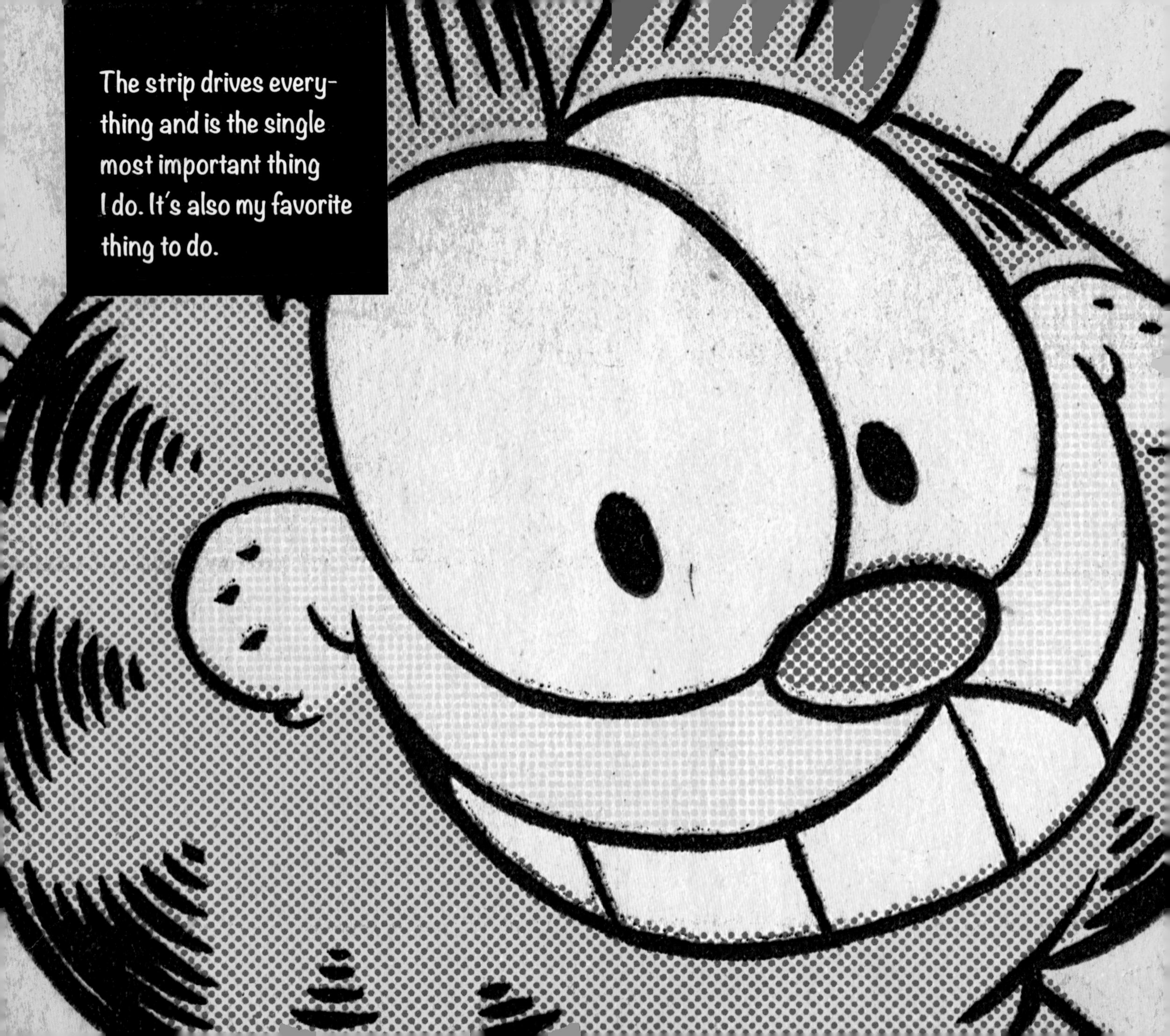

The strip drives everything and is the single most important thing I do. It's also my favorite thing to do.

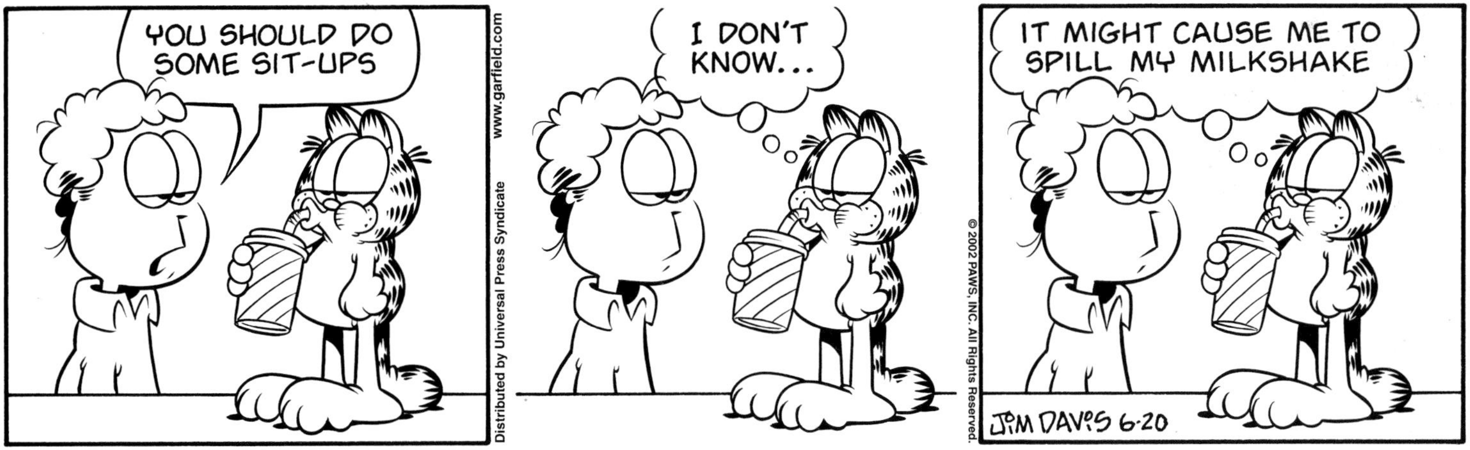
YOU SHOULD DO SOME SIT-UPS
I DON'T KNOW...
IT MIGHT CAUSE ME TO SPILL MY MILKSHAKE
www.garfield.com
Distributed by Universal Press Syndicate
© 2002 PAWS, INC. All Rights Reserved.
JIM DAVIS 6-20

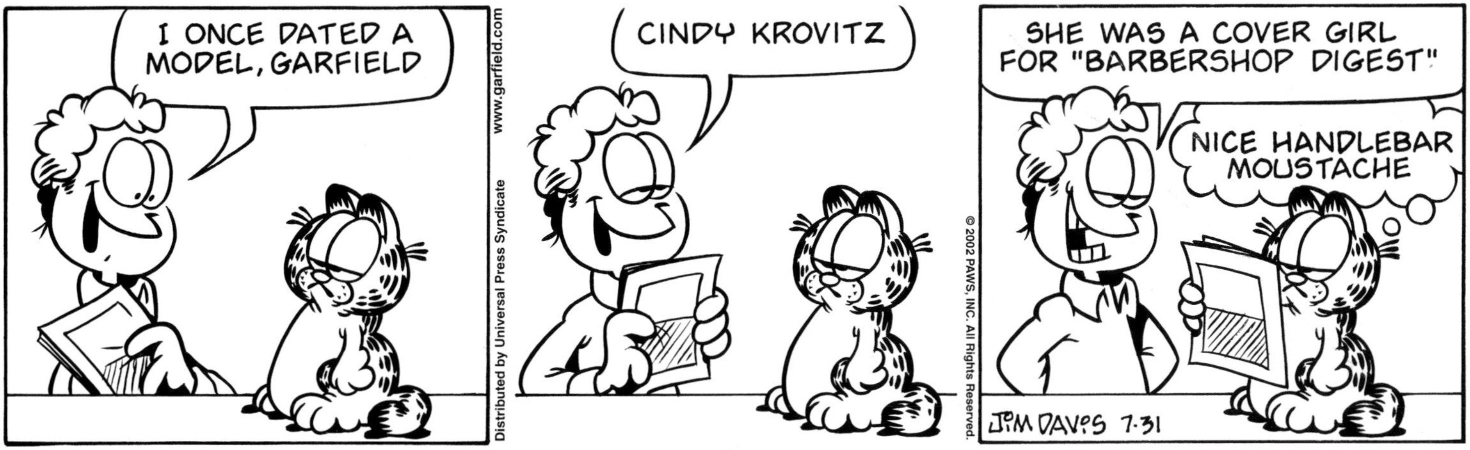
I ONCE DATED A MODEL, GARFIELD
CINDY KROVITZ
SHE WAS A COVER GIRL FOR "BARBERSHOP DIGEST"
NICE HANDLEBAR MOUSTACHE
www.garfield.com
Distributed by Universal Press Syndicate
© 2002 PAWS, INC. All Rights Reserved.
JIM DAVIS 7-31

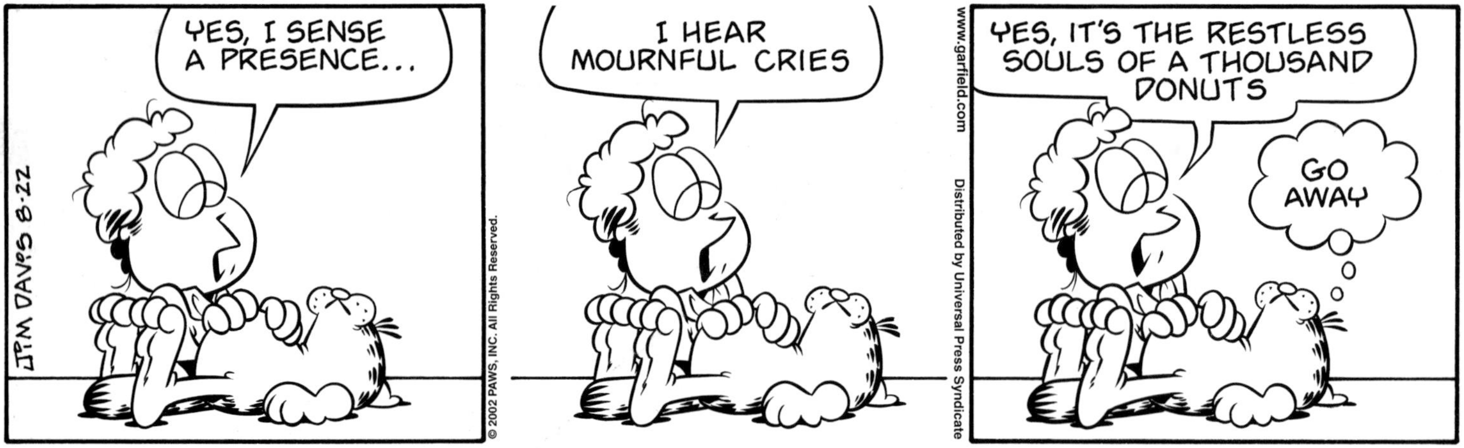
JIM DAVIS 8·22
YES, I SENSE A PRESENCE...
© 2002 PAWS, INC. All Rights Reserved.
I HEAR MOURNFUL CRIES
www.garfield.com
Distributed by Universal Press Syndicate
YES, IT'S THE RESTLESS SOULS OF A THOUSAND DONUTS
GO AWAY

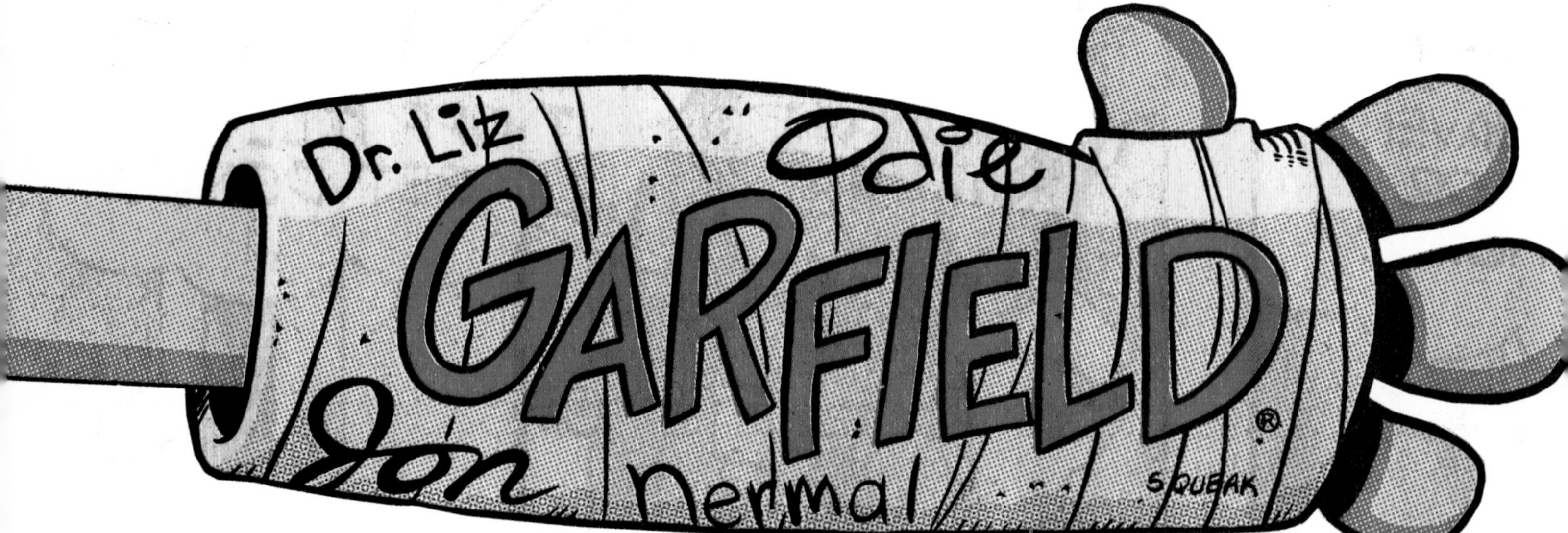
Dr. Liz
Odie
GARFIELD®
Jon
nermal

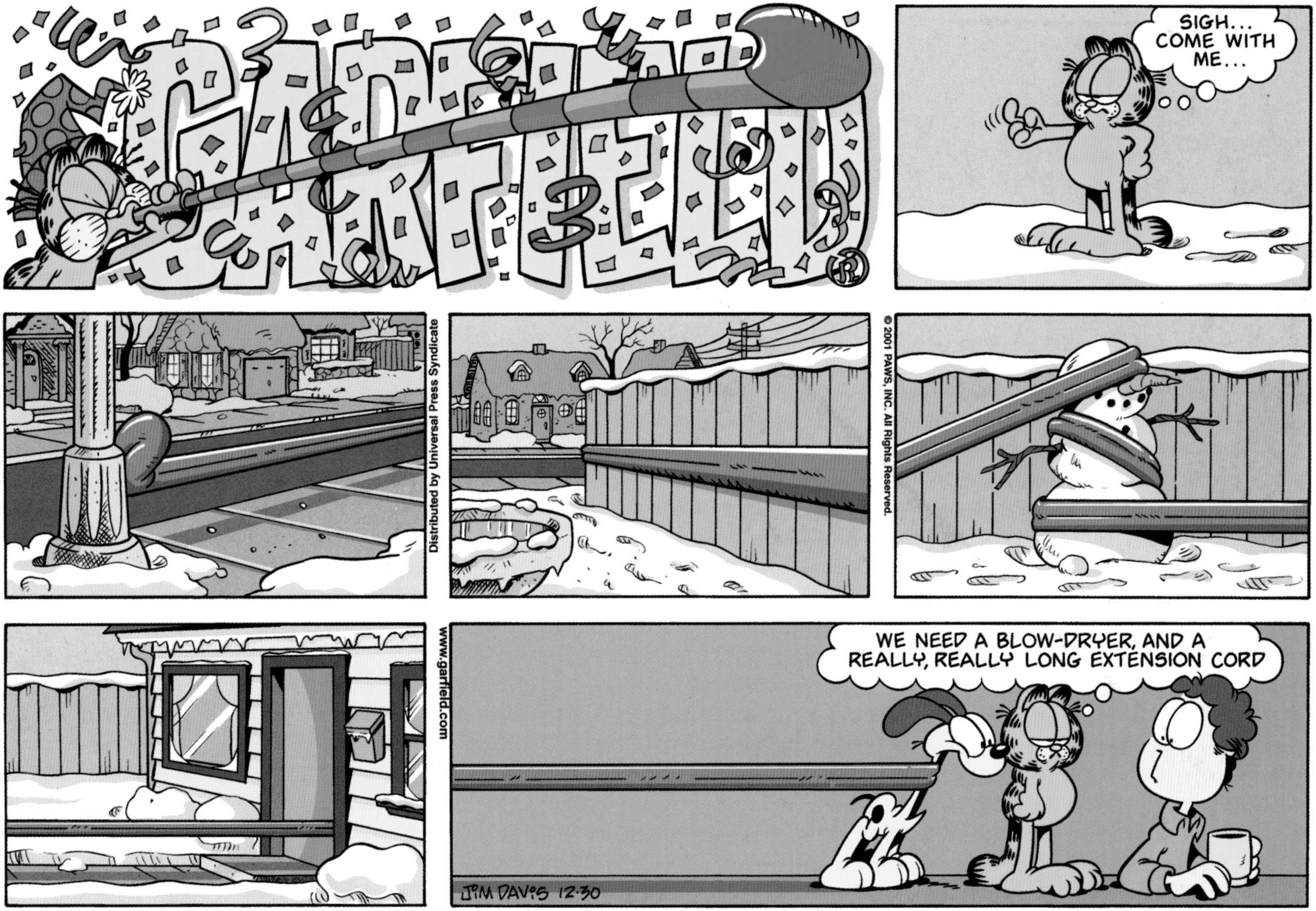
GARFIELD
SIGH... COME WITH ME...
Distributed by Universal Press Syndicate
© 2001 PAWS, INC. All Rights Reserved.
www.garfield.com
WE NEED A BLOW-DRYER, AND A REALLY, REALLY LONG EXTENSION CORD
JIM DAVIS 12-30

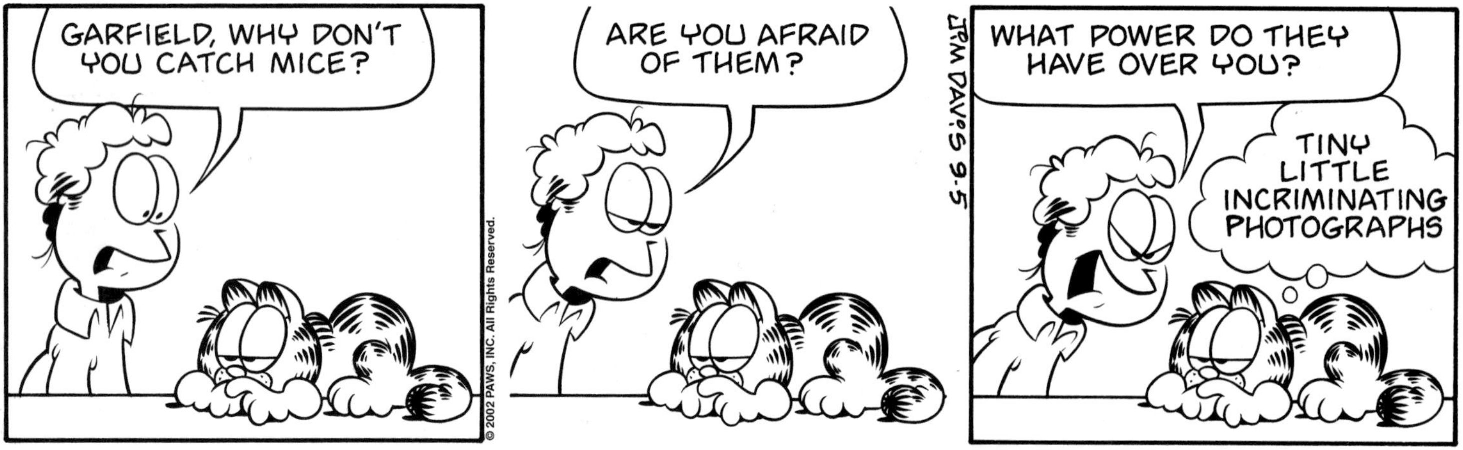
GARFIELD, WHY DON'T YOU CATCH MICE?
ARE YOU AFRAID OF THEM?
WHAT POWER DO THEY HAVE OVER YOU?
TINY LITTLE INCRIMINATING PHOTOGRAPHS
JIM DAVIS 9-5
© 2002 PAWS, INC. All Rights Reserved.

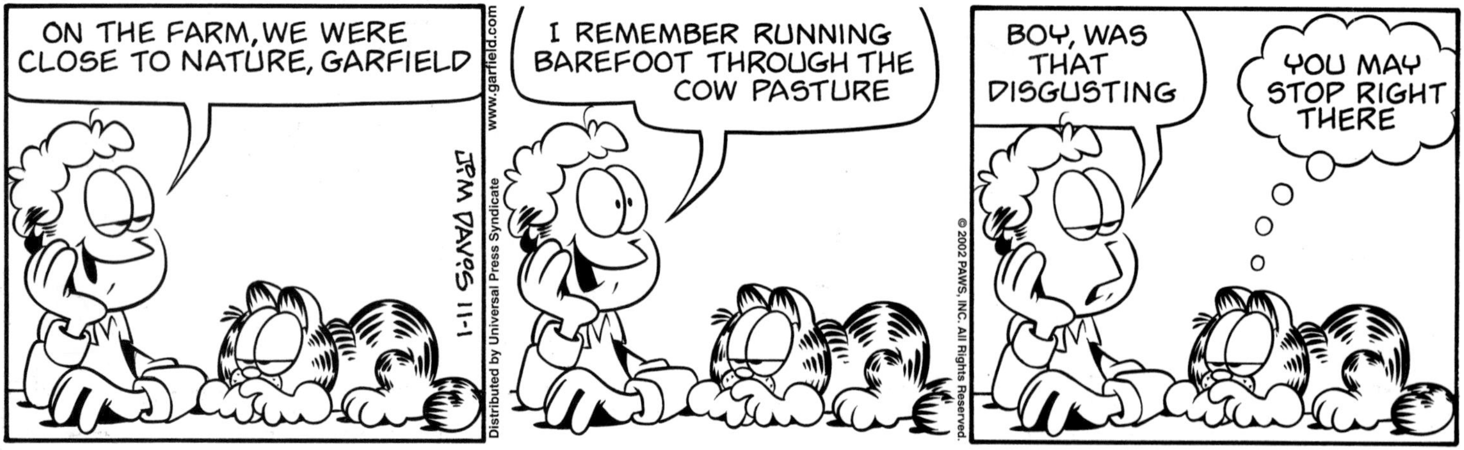
ON THE FARM, WE WERE CLOSE TO NATURE, GARFIELD
I REMEMBER RUNNING BAREFOOT THROUGH THE COW PASTURE
BOY, WAS THAT DISGUSTING
YOU MAY STOP RIGHT THERE
JIM DAVIS 11-1
www.garfield.com
Distributed by Universal Press Syndicate
© 2002 PAWS, INC. All Rights Reserved.

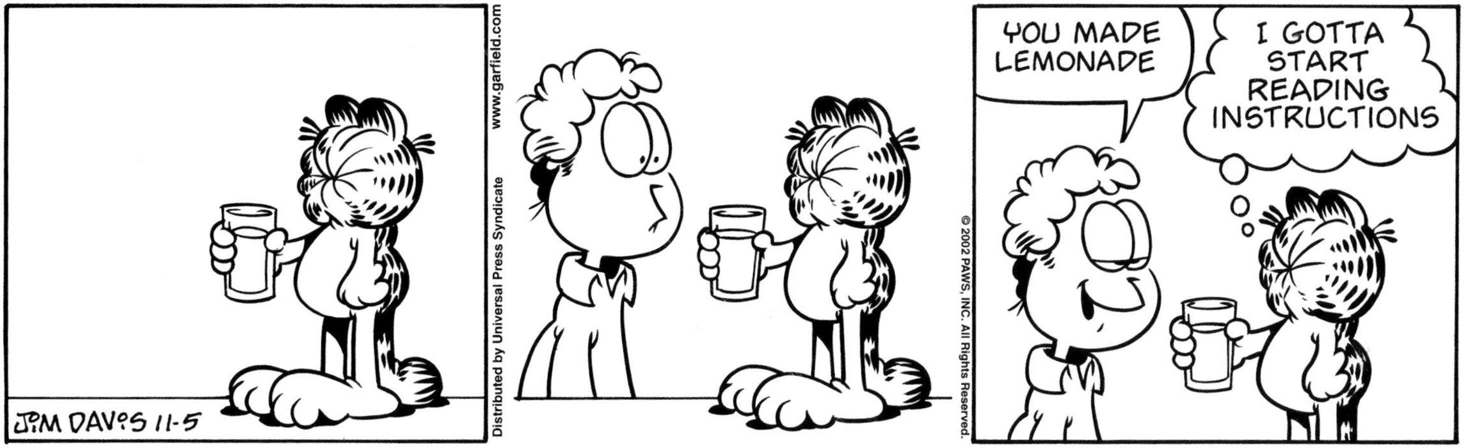
JIM DAVIS 11-5
www.garfield.com
Distributed by Universal Press Syndicate
YOU MADE LEMONADE
I GOTTA START READING INSTRUCTIONS
© 2002 PAWS, INC. All Rights Reserved.

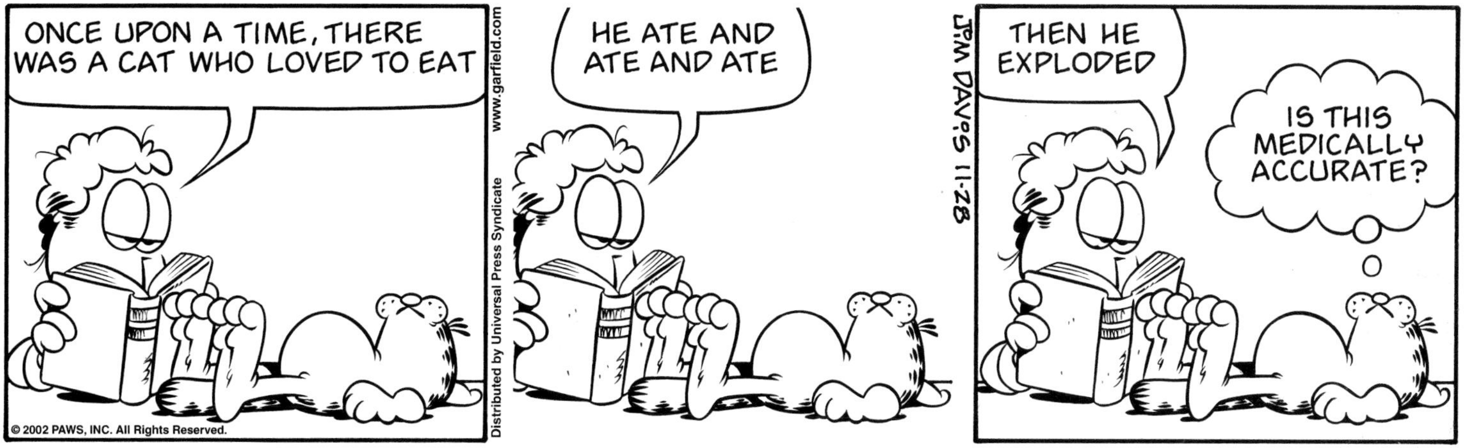
ONCE UPON A TIME, THERE WAS A CAT WHO LOVED TO EAT
© 2002 PAWS, INC. All Rights Reserved.
www.garfield.com
Distributed by Universal Press Syndicate
HE ATE AND ATE AND ATE
JIM DAVIS 11-28
THEN HE EXPLODED
IS THIS MEDICALLY ACCURATE?

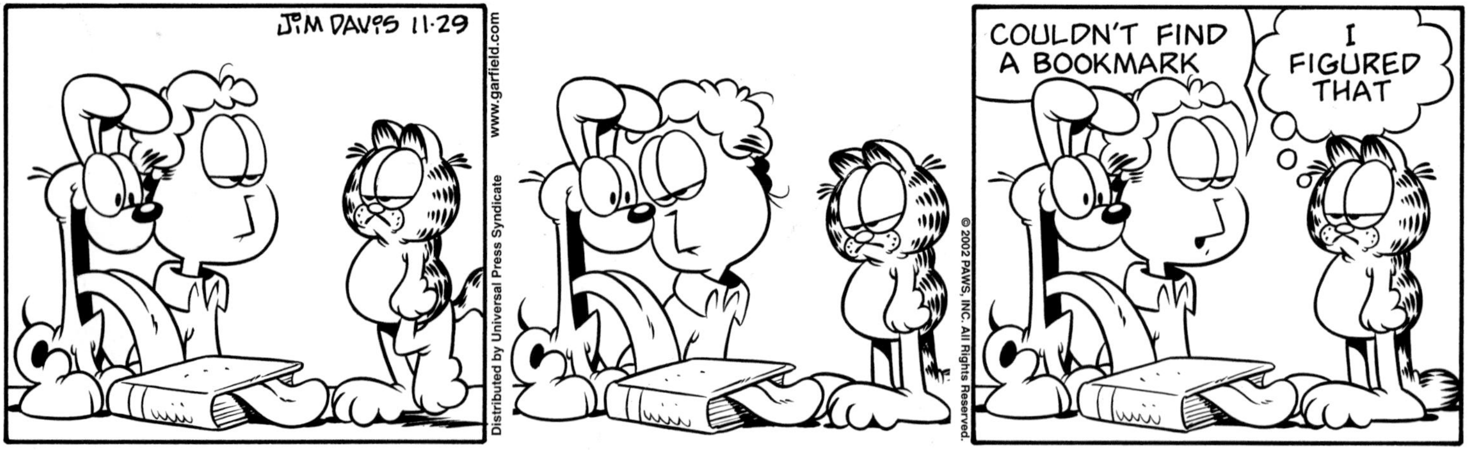
JIM DAVIS 11-29
www.garfield.com
Distributed by Universal Press Syndicate
COULDN'T FIND A BOOKMARK
I FIGURED THAT
© 2002 PAWS, INC. All Rights Reserved.

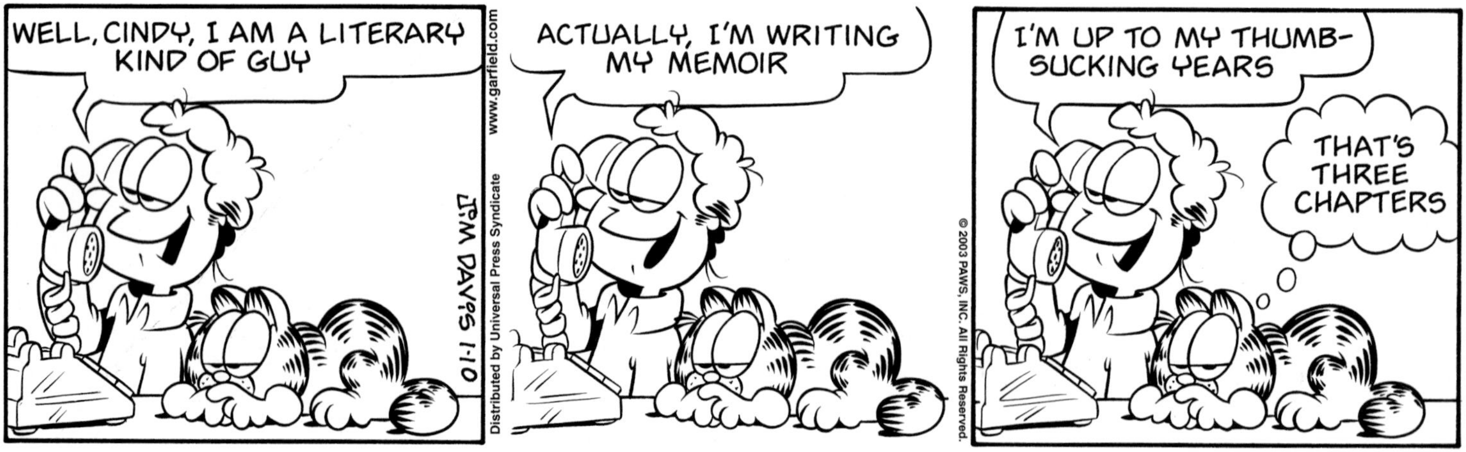
WELL, CINDY, I AM A LITERARY KIND OF GUY
JIM DAVIS 1-10
www.garfield.com
Distributed by Universal Press Syndicate
ACTUALLY, I'M WRITING MY MEMOIR
I'M UP TO MY THUMB-SUCKING YEARS
THAT'S THREE CHAPTERS
© 2003 PAWS, INC. All Rights Reserved.

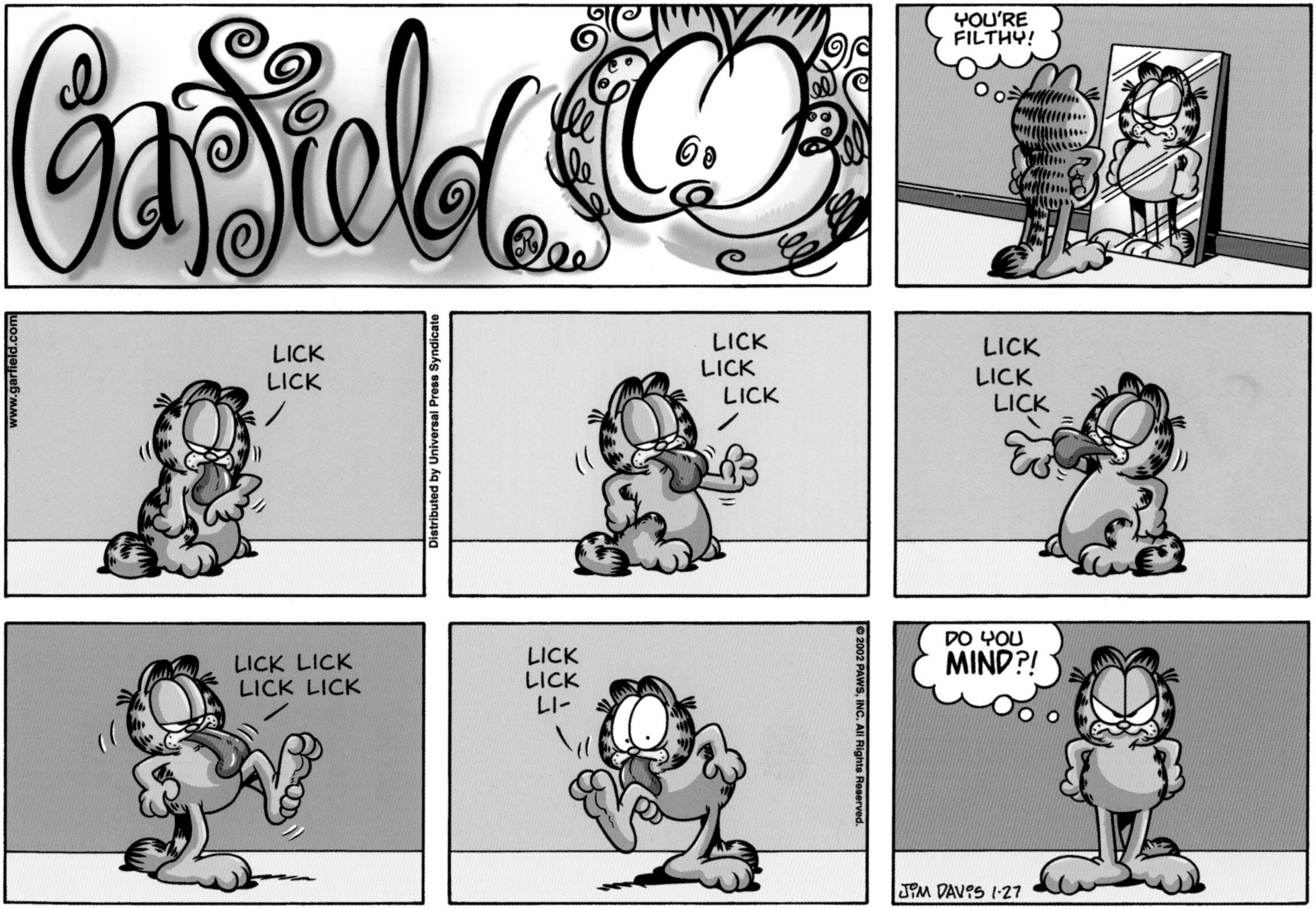
Garfield
YOU'RE FILTHY!
www.garfield.com
LICK LICK
Distributed by Universal Press Syndicate
LICK LICK LICK
LICK LICK LICK
LICK LICK LICK LICK
LICK LICK LI-
© 2002 PAWS, INC. All Rights Reserved.
DO YOU MIND?!
JIM DAVIS 1-27

DAD

Jon's dad is my dad, Jim. Yep, I'm from a long line of Jim Davises. Dad always said, "If you do something, do it right." He grows one heck of a tomato plant.

MOM

Jon's mom is modeled after my mom, Betty. When I wasn't doing chores, Mom was always putting paper and a pencil in my hand. She claims that my being a cartoonist is all her fault.

DOC BOY

David "Doc" Davis is my real-life brother. He lives about 150 yards from my house. We hit golf balls across the yard at each other. I usually use an 8-iron. No injuries yet. And yes, we both grew up on the family farm.

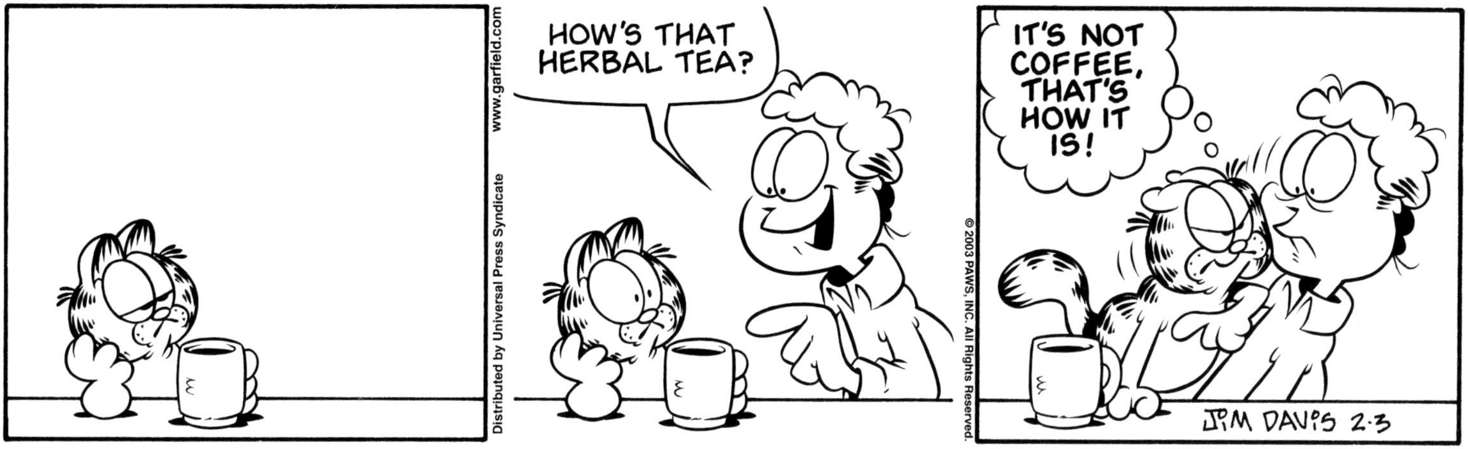
HOW'S THAT HERBAL TEA?
IT'S NOT COFFEE, THAT'S HOW IT IS!
JIM DAVIS 2-3
www.garfield.com
Distributed by Universal Press Syndicate
© 2003 PAWS, INC. All Rights Reserved.

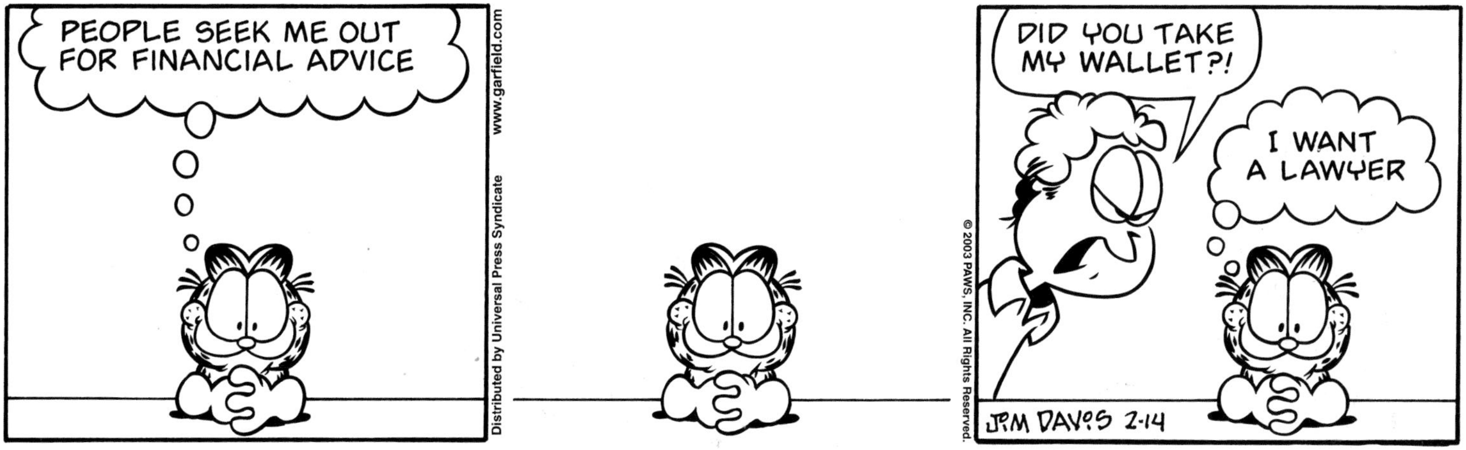
PEOPLE SEEK ME OUT FOR FINANCIAL ADVICE
DID YOU TAKE MY WALLET?!
I WANT A LAWYER
JIM DAVIS 2-14
www.garfield.com
Distributed by Universal Press Syndicate
© 2003 PAWS, INC. All Rights Reserved.

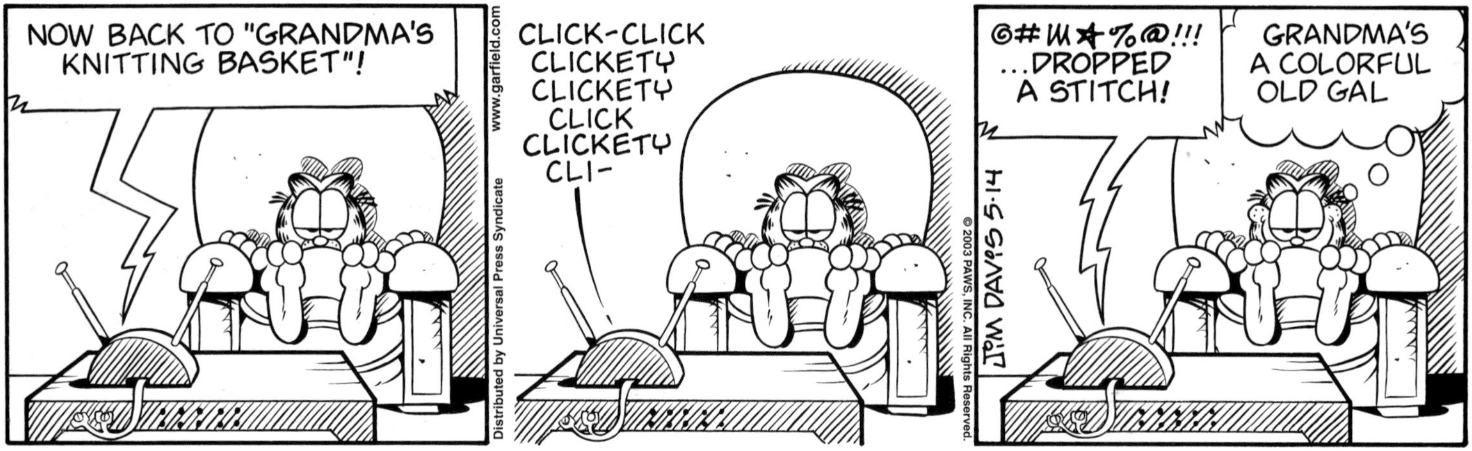
NOW BACK TO "GRANDMA'S KNITTING BASKET"!
www.garfield.com
Distributed by Universal Press Syndicate
CLICK-CLICK CLICKETY CLICKETY CLICK CLICKETY CLI-
© 2003 PAWS, INC. All Rights Reserved.
JIM DAVIS 5-14
©#Ш✯%@!!! ...DROPPED A STITCH!
GRANDMA'S A COLORFUL OLD GAL

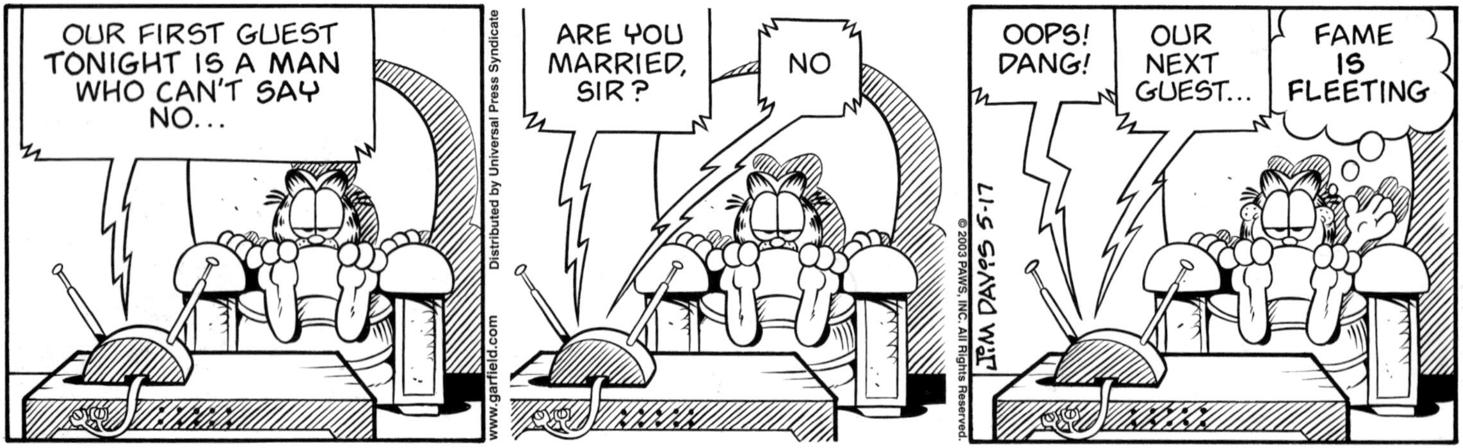
OUR FIRST GUEST TONIGHT IS A MAN WHO CAN'T SAY NO...
Distributed by Universal Press Syndicate
www.garfield.com
ARE YOU MARRIED, SIR?
NO
© 2003 PAWS, INC. All Rights Reserved.
JIM DAVIS 5-17
OOPS! DANG!
OUR NEXT GUEST...
FAME IS FLEETING

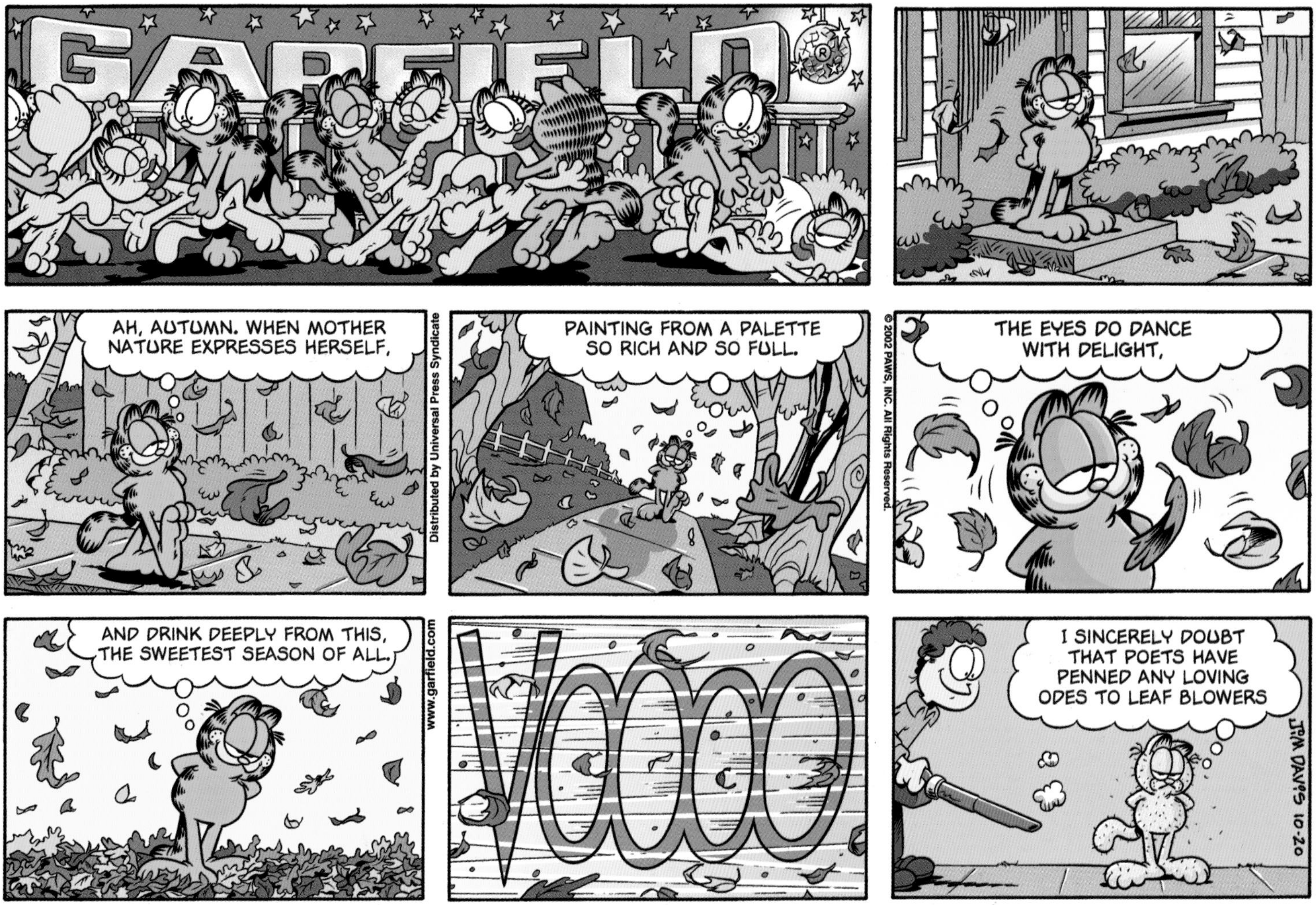
GARFIELD
AH, AUTUMN. WHEN MOTHER NATURE EXPRESSES HERSELF,
Distributed by Universal Press Syndicate
PAINTING FROM A PALETTE SO RICH AND SO FULL.
© 2002 PAWS, INC. All Rights Reserved.
THE EYES DO DANCE WITH DELIGHT,
AND DRINK DEEPLY FROM THIS, THE SWEETEST SEASON OF ALL.
www.garfield.com
VOOOOO
I SINCERELY DOUBT THAT POETS HAVE PENNED ANY LOVING ODES TO LEAF BLOWERS
JIM DAVIS 10-20

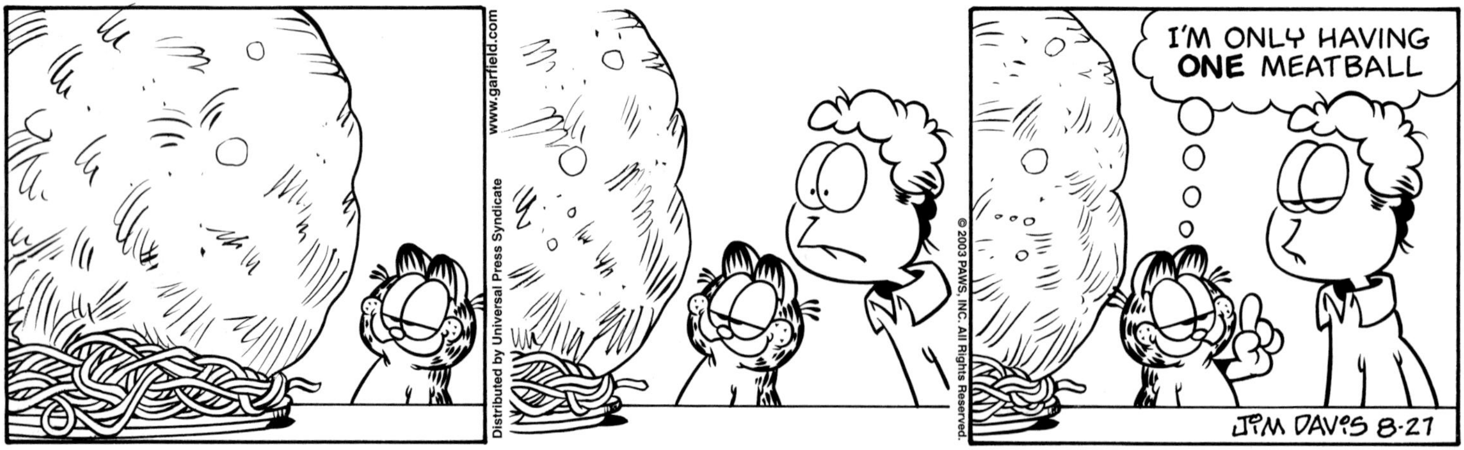
www.garfield.com
Distributed by Universal Press Syndicate
© 2003 PAWS, INC. All Rights Reserved.
I'M ONLY HAVING ONE MEATBALL
JIM DAVIS 8-27

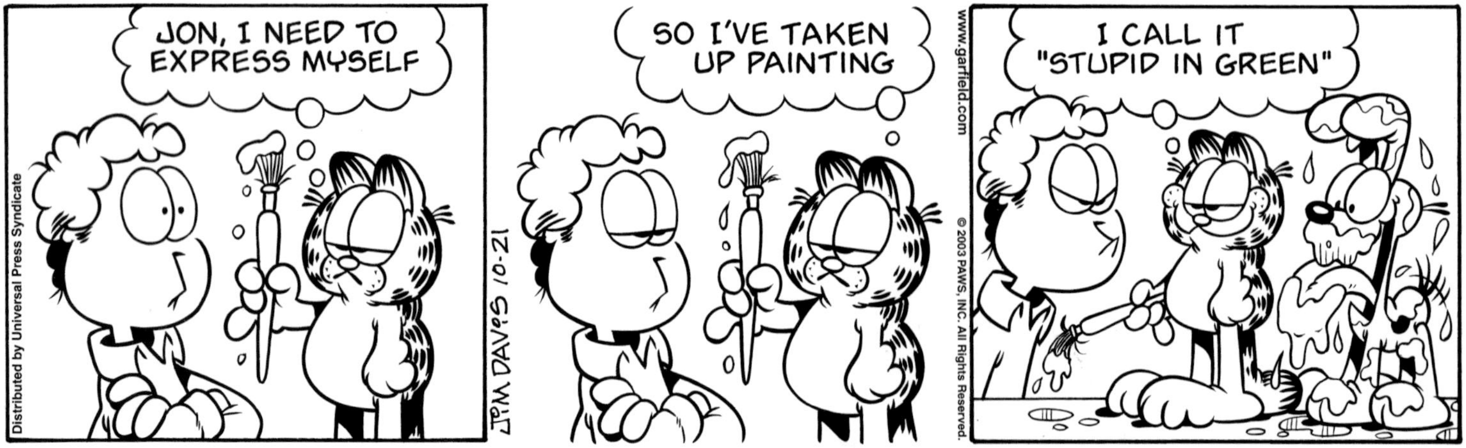
JON, I NEED TO EXPRESS MYSELF
Distributed by Universal Press Syndicate
JIM DAVIS 10-21
SO I'VE TAKEN UP PAINTING
www.garfield.com
© 2003 PAWS, INC. All Rights Reserved.
I CALL IT "STUPID IN GREEN"

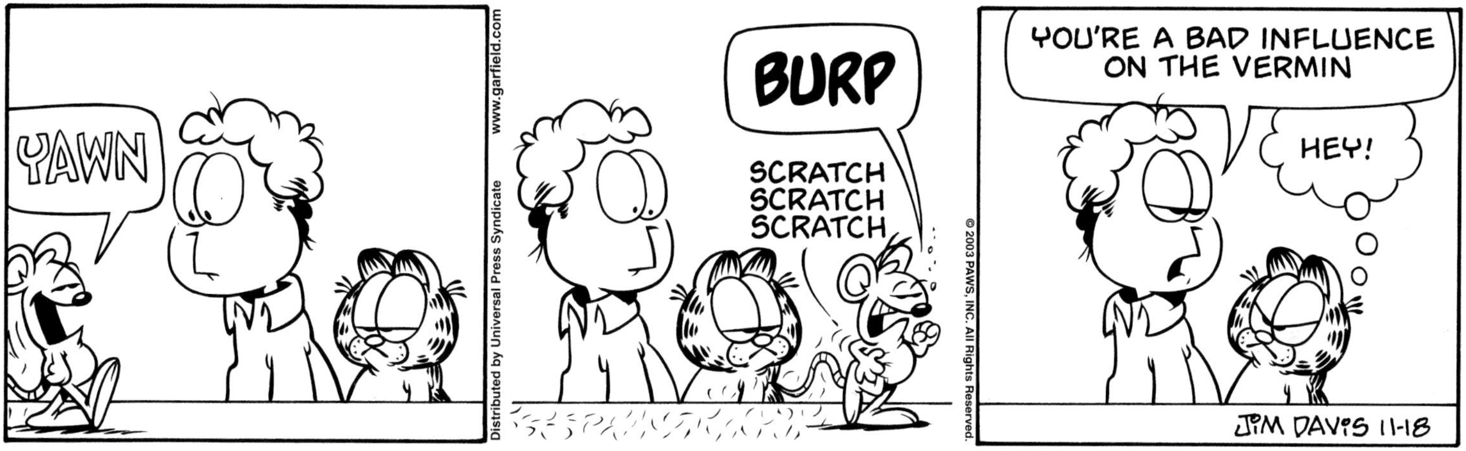
YAWN
www.garfield.com
Distributed by Universal Press Syndicate
BURP
SCRATCH
SCRATCH
SCRATCH
© 2003 PAWS, INC. All Rights Reserved.
YOU'RE A BAD INFLUENCE ON THE VERMIN
HEY!
JIM DAVIS 11-18

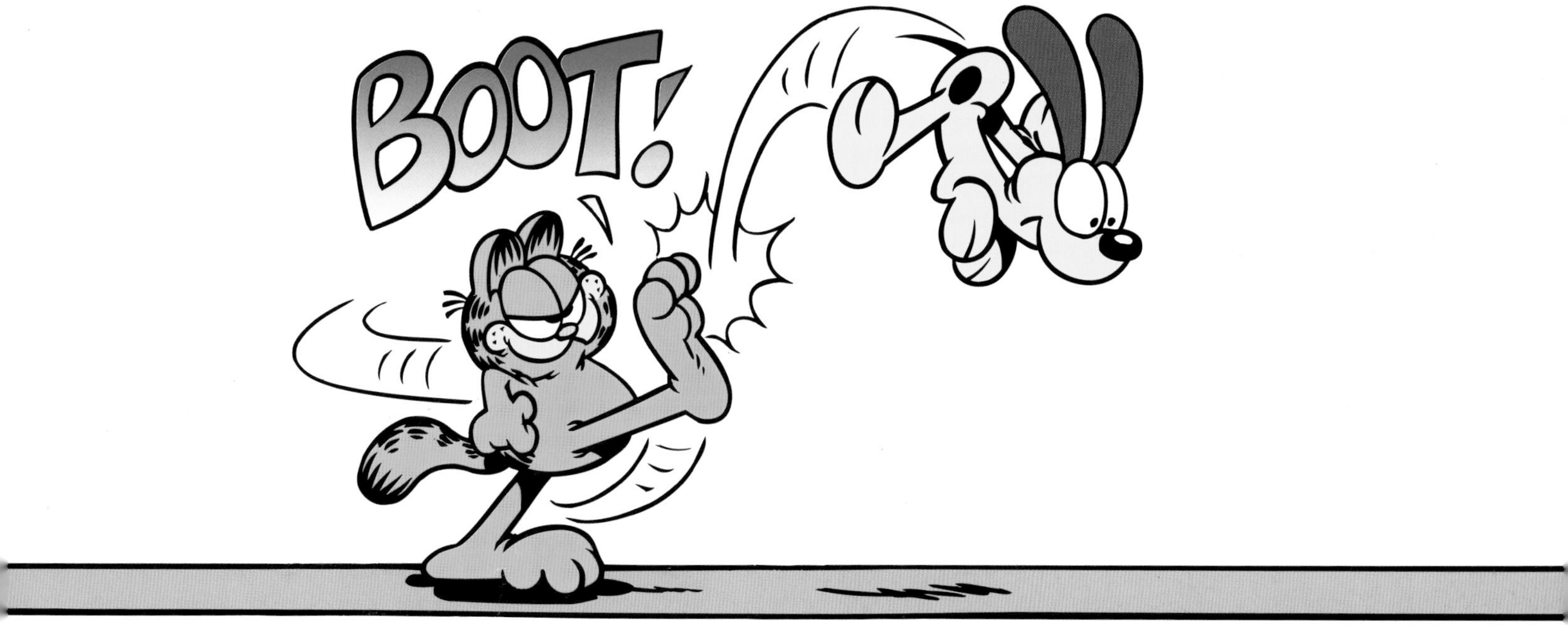
BOOT!

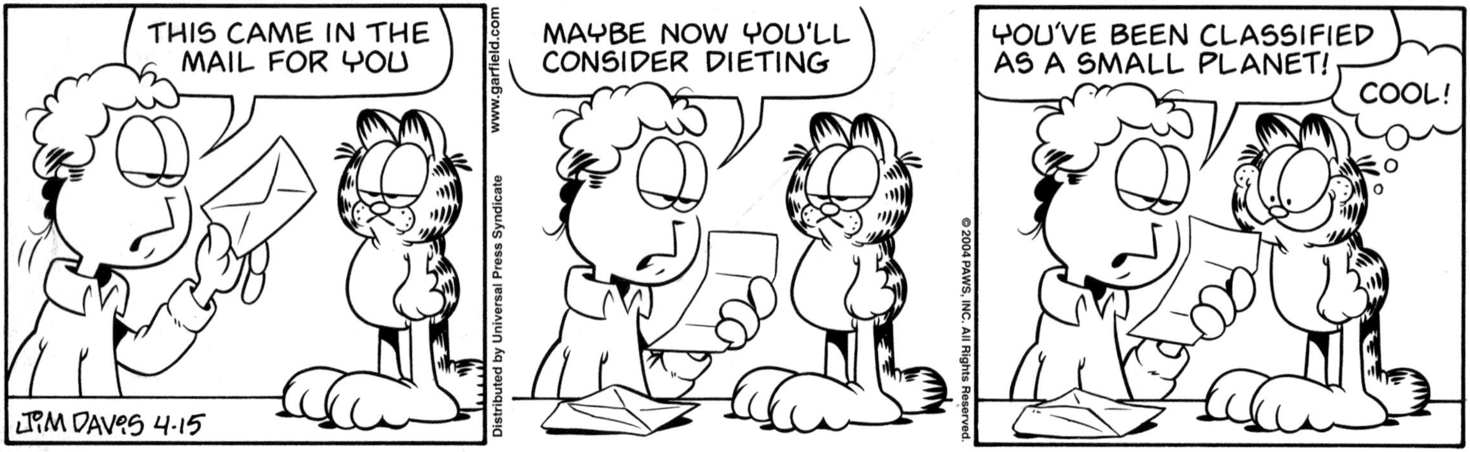
THIS CAME IN THE MAIL FOR YOU
JIM DAVIS 4-15
www.garfield.com
Distributed by Universal Press Syndicate
MAYBE NOW YOU'LL CONSIDER DIETING
© 2004 PAWS, INC. All Rights Reserved.
YOU'VE BEEN CLASSIFIED AS A SMALL PLANET!
COOL!

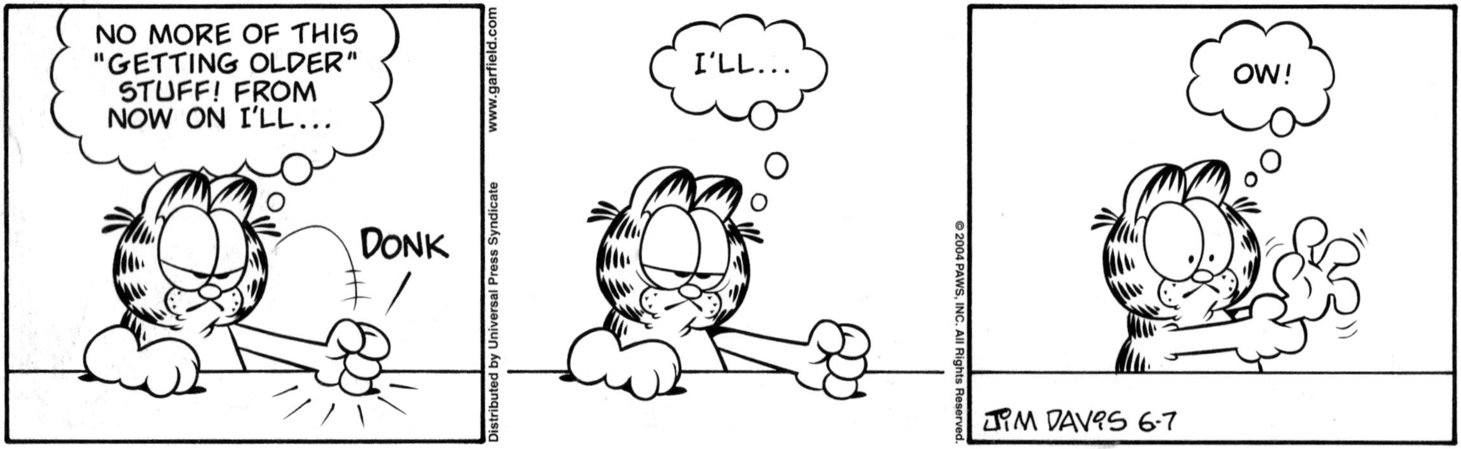
NO MORE OF THIS "GETTING OLDER" STUFF! FROM NOW ON I'LL...
DONK
www.garfield.com
Distributed by Universal Press Syndicate
I'LL...
© 2004 PAWS, INC. All Rights Reserved.
OW!
JIM DAVIS 6-7

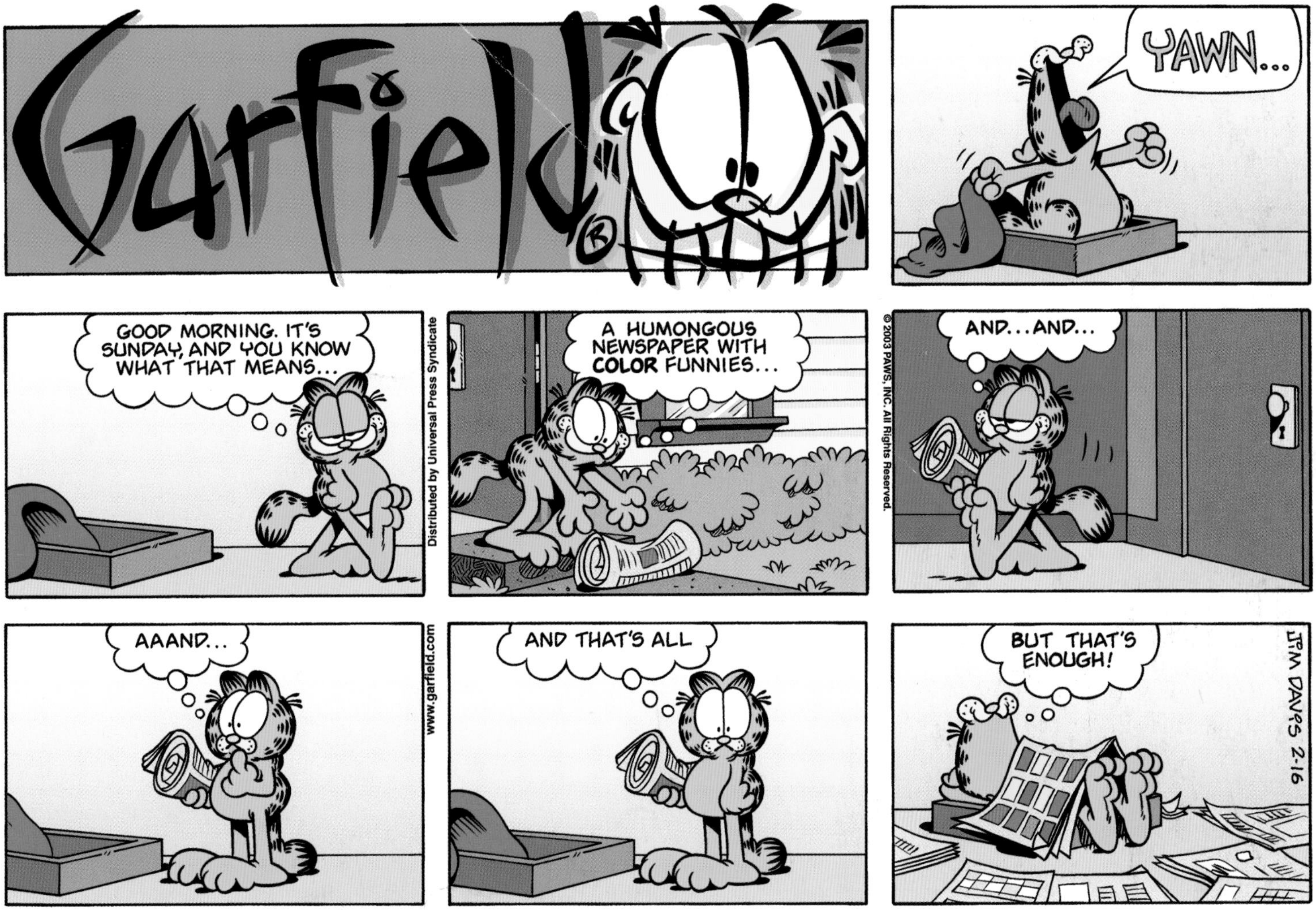
Garfield®
YAWN...
GOOD MORNING. IT'S SUNDAY, AND YOU KNOW WHAT THAT MEANS...
Distributed by Universal Press Syndicate
A HUMONGOUS NEWSPAPER WITH COLOR FUNNIES...
© 2003 PAWS, INC. All Rights Reserved.
AND...AND...
AAAND...
www.garfield.com
AND THAT'S ALL
BUT THAT'S ENOUGH!
JIM DAVIS 2-16

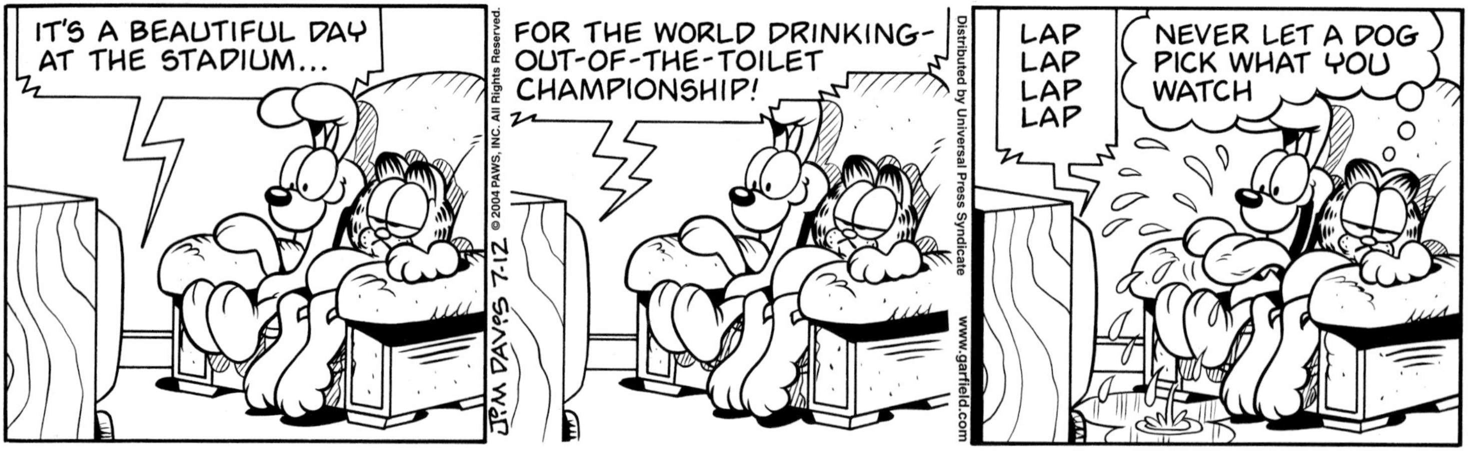
IT'S A BEAUTIFUL DAY AT THE STADIUM...
© 2004 PAWS, INC. All Rights Reserved.
JPM DAVPS 7-12
FOR THE WORLD DRINKING-OUT-OF-THE-TOILET CHAMPIONSHIP!
Distributed by Universal Press Syndicate
www.garfield.com
LAP LAP LAP LAP
NEVER LET A DOG PICK WHAT YOU WATCH

Neil Simon said, "No one character should always have the upper hand." I try to let Odie get Garfield back every few months, but he could probably stand to do it more.

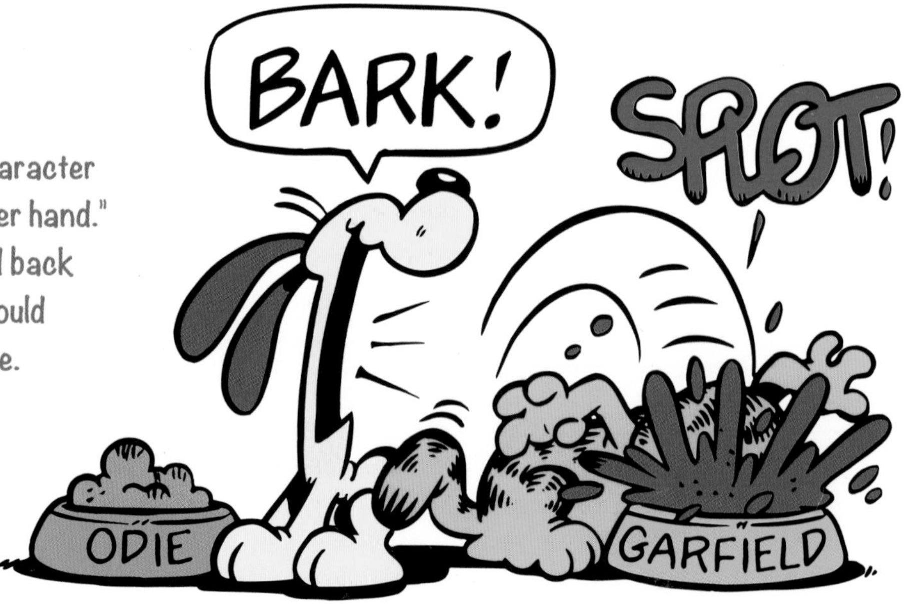
BARK!
SPLOT!
ODIE
GARFIELD

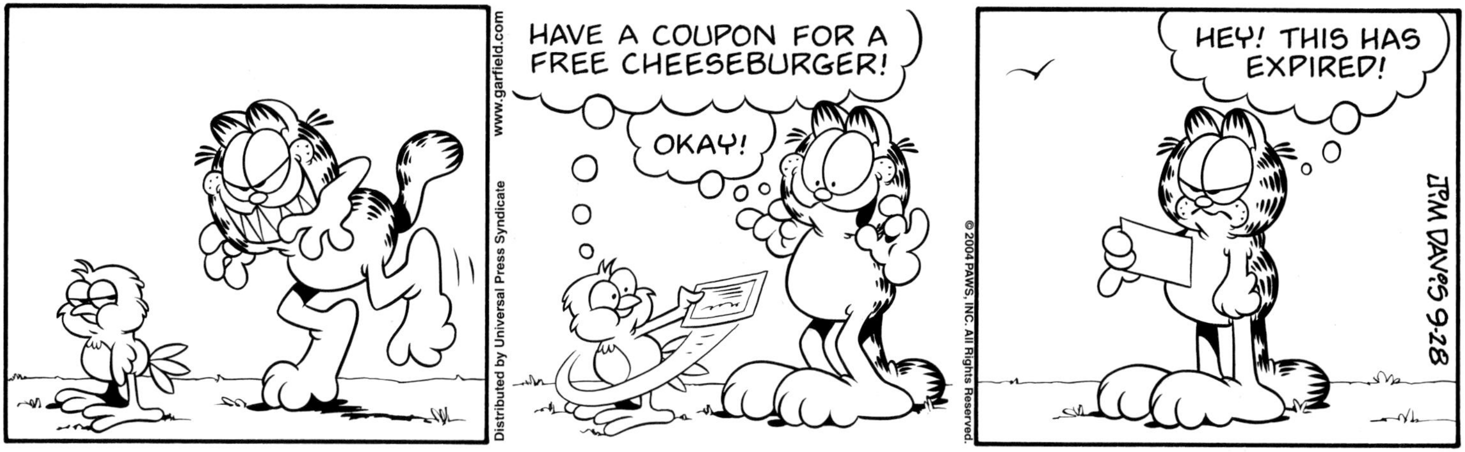
HAVE A COUPON FOR A FREE CHEESEBURGER!
OKAY!
HEY! THIS HAS EXPIRED!
JPM DAVIS 9-28
www.garfield.com
Distributed by Universal Press Syndicate
© 2004 PAWS, INC. All Rights Reserved.

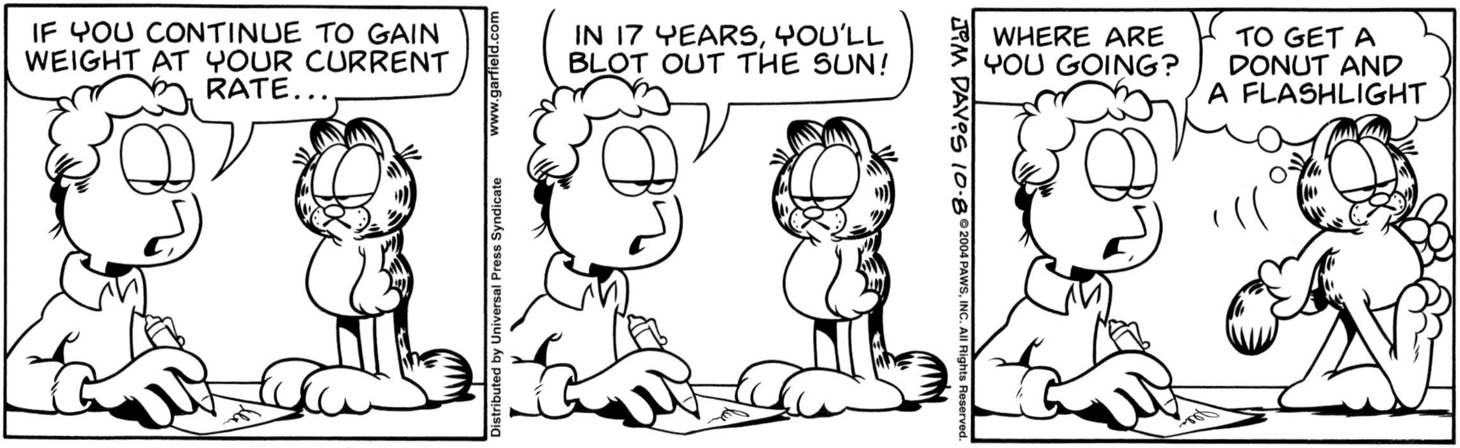
IF YOU CONTINUE TO GAIN WEIGHT AT YOUR CURRENT RATE...
IN 17 YEARS, YOU'LL BLOT OUT THE SUN!
WHERE ARE YOU GOING?
TO GET A DONUT AND A FLASHLIGHT
JPM DAVIS 10-8
www.garfield.com
Distributed by Universal Press Syndicate
© 2004 PAWS, INC. All Rights Reserved.

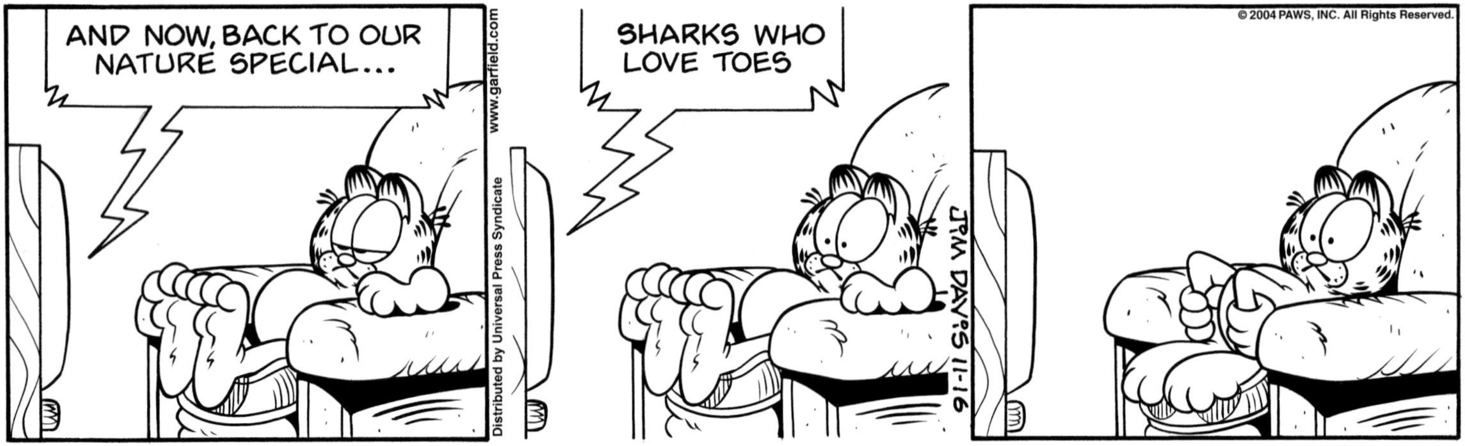
AND NOW, BACK TO OUR NATURE SPECIAL...
SHARKS WHO LOVE TOES
www.garfield.com
Distributed by Universal Press Syndicate
JPM DAVIS 11-16
© 2004 PAWS, INC. All Rights Reserved.

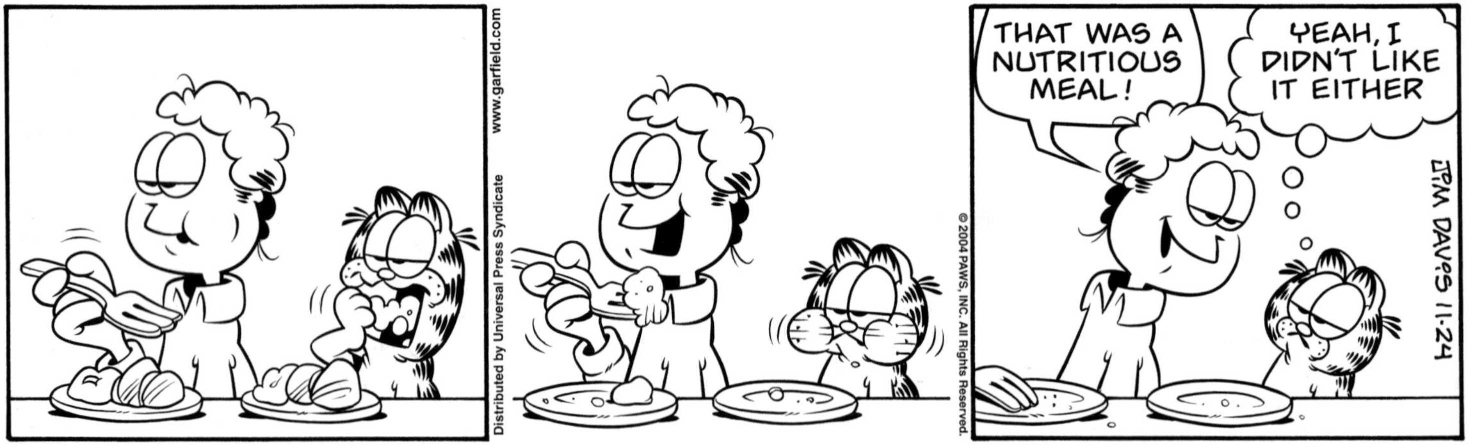
www.garfield.com
Distributed by Universal Press Syndicate
© 2004 PAWS, INC. All Rights Reserved.
THAT WAS A NUTRITIOUS MEAL!
YEAH, I DIDN'T LIKE IT EITHER
JPM DAVIS 11-24

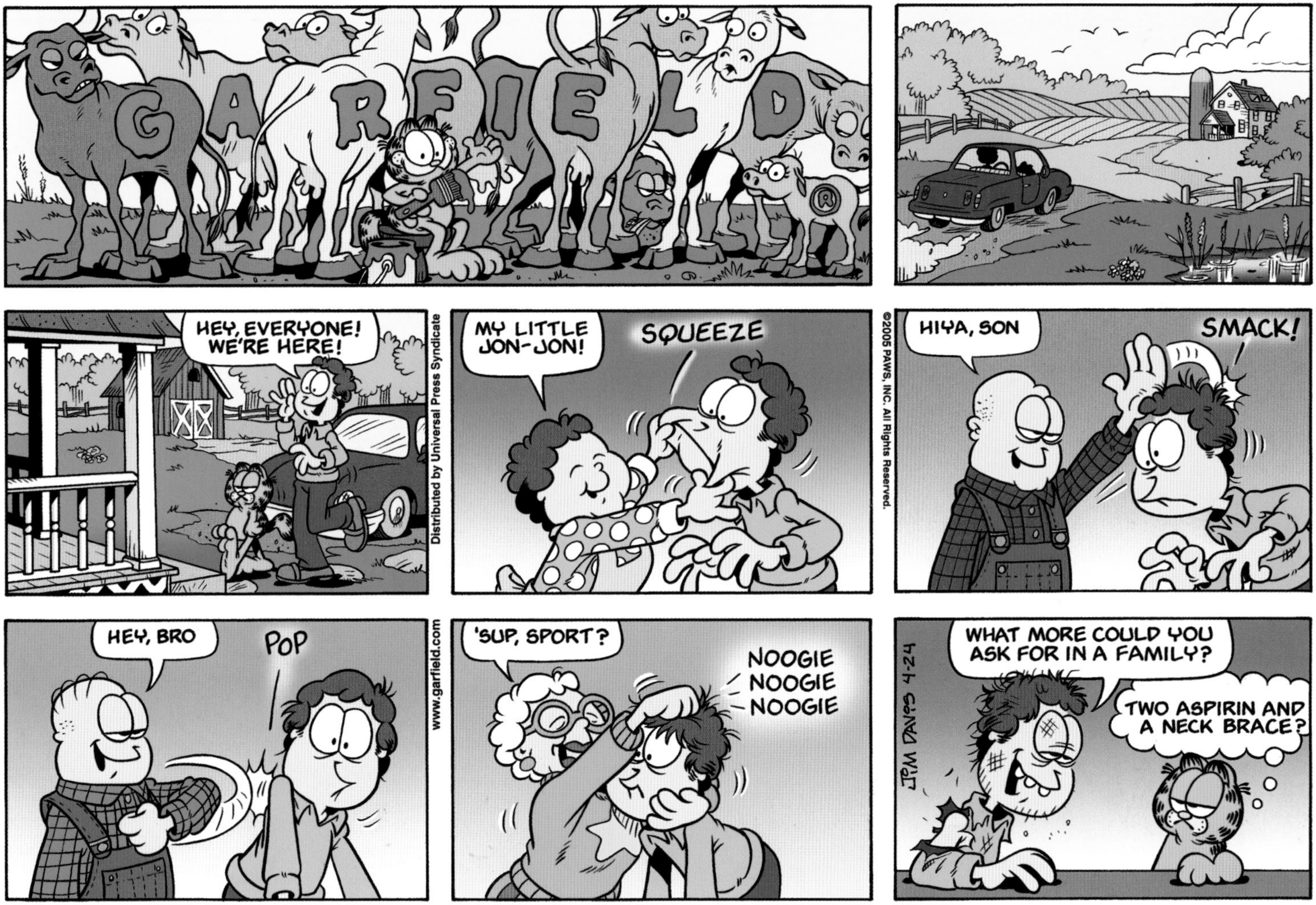
GARFIELD
HEY, EVERYONE! WE'RE HERE!
Distributed by Universal Press Syndicate
MY LITTLE JON-JON!
SQUEEZE
©2005 PAWS, INC. All Rights Reserved.
HIYA, SON
SMACK!
HEY, BRO
POP
www.garfield.com
'SUP, SPORT?
NOOGIE
NOOGIE
NOOGIE
JIM DAVIS 4-24
WHAT MORE COULD YOU ASK FOR IN A FAMILY?
TWO ASPIRIN AND A NECK BRACE?

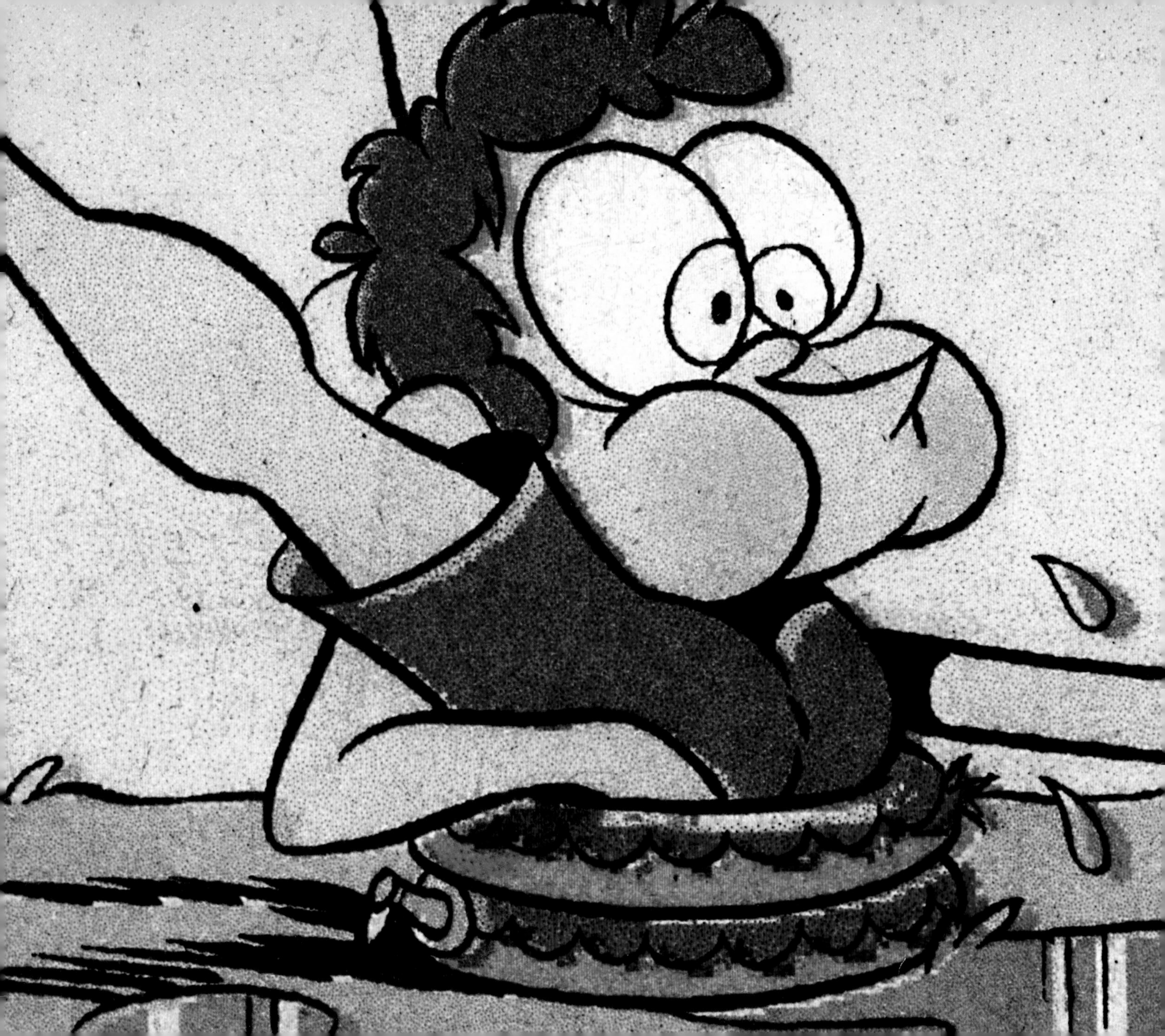

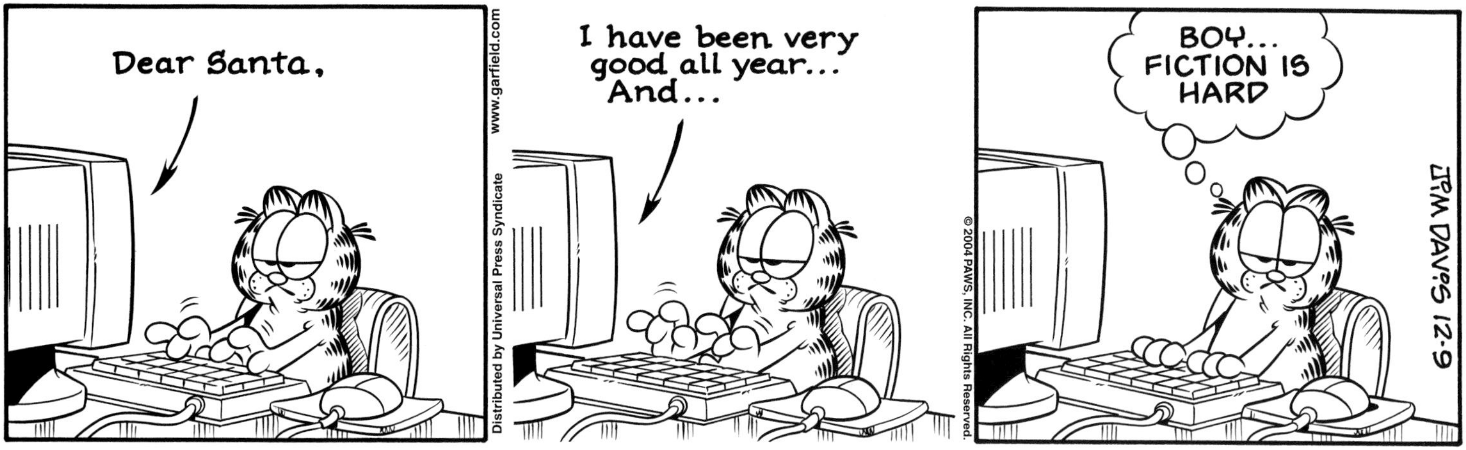
Dear Santa,
I have been very good all year... And...
BOY... FICTION IS HARD
JIM DAVIS 12-9
www.garfield.com
Distributed by Universal Press Syndicate
© 2004 PAWS, INC. All Rights Reserved.

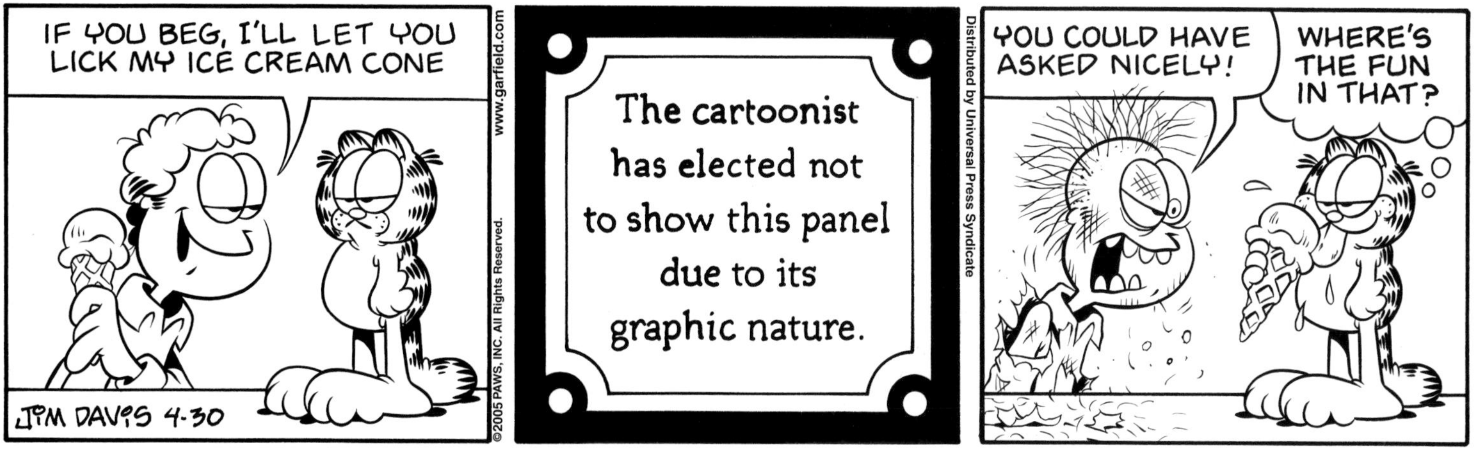
IF YOU BEG, I'LL LET YOU LICK MY ICE CREAM CONE
JIM DAVIS 4-30
www.garfield.com
©2005 PAWS, INC. All Rights Reserved.
The cartoonist has elected not to show this panel due to its graphic nature.
Distributed by Universal Press Syndicate
YOU COULD HAVE ASKED NICELY!
WHERE'S THE FUN IN THAT?

When I was growing up, Christmas was definitely the event of the year for us. It was the time Davie (my younger brother) and I would get the "big stuff" we'd been asking for all year.

Of course, actually getting the "big stuff" depended entirely on the success of Mom and Dad's crop that year. During a bad year, we'd probably get essential items like slippers, pajamas, and clothing. But during a good year, we received the essentials, plus some great toys. I remember the year I received a red pedal-driven jeep and Dave got a rocking horse.

Mom spent weeks before Christmas making cookies and candies, which we traded with neighbors, family, and friends. Dad spent the week before Christmas trying not to act excited.

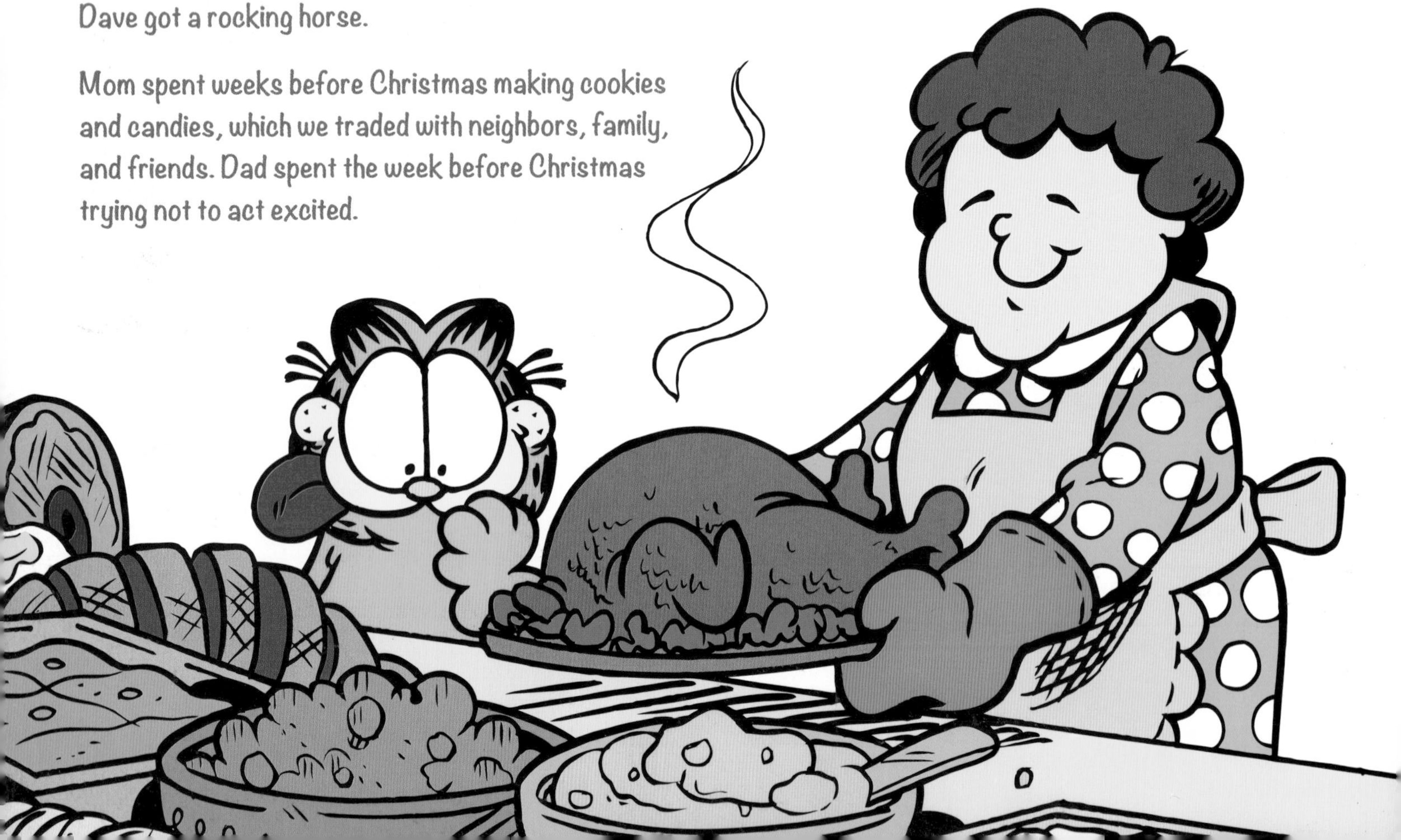

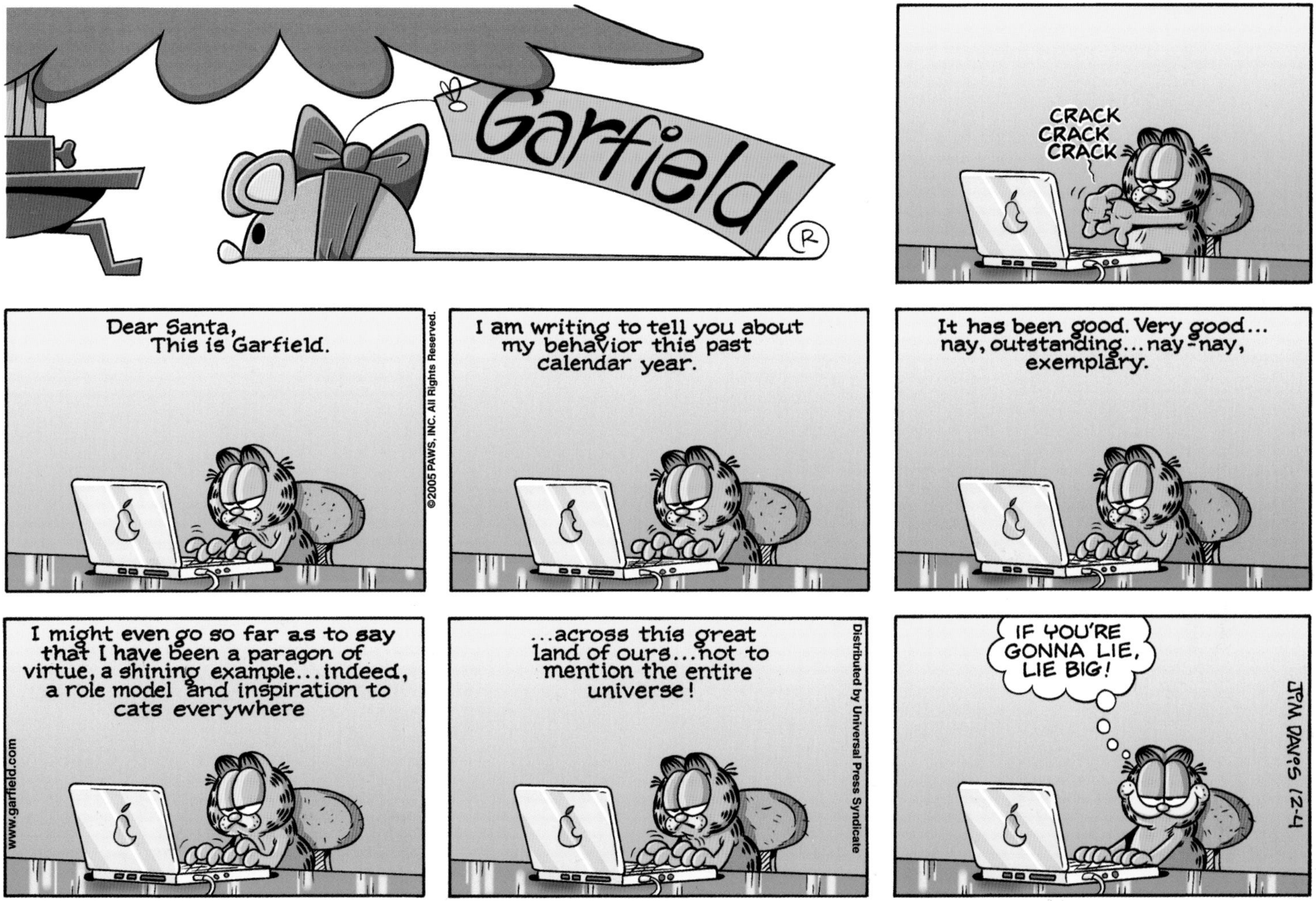
Garfield
CRACK CRACK CRACK
Dear Santa, This is Garfield.
©2005 PAWS, INC. All Rights Reserved.
I am writing to tell you about my behavior this past calendar year.
It has been good. Very good... nay, outstanding... nay-nay, exemplary.
I might even go so far as to say that I have been a paragon of virtue, a shining example... indeed, a role model and inspiration to cats everywhere
www.garfield.com
...across this great land of ours... not to mention the entire universe!
Distributed by Universal Press Syndicate
IF YOU'RE GONNA LIE, LIE BIG!
JPM DAVPS 12-4

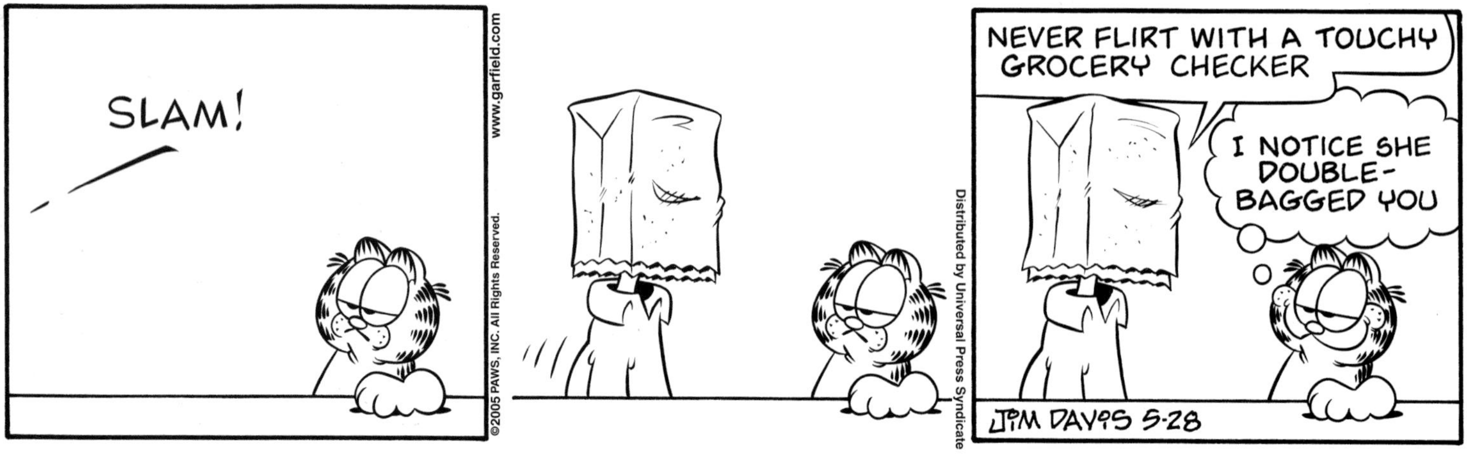
SLAM!
www.garfield.com
©2005 PAWS, INC. All Rights Reserved.
Distributed by Universal Press Syndicate
NEVER FLIRT WITH A TOUCHY GROCERY CHECKER
I NOTICE SHE DOUBLE-BAGGED YOU
JIM DAVIS 5-28

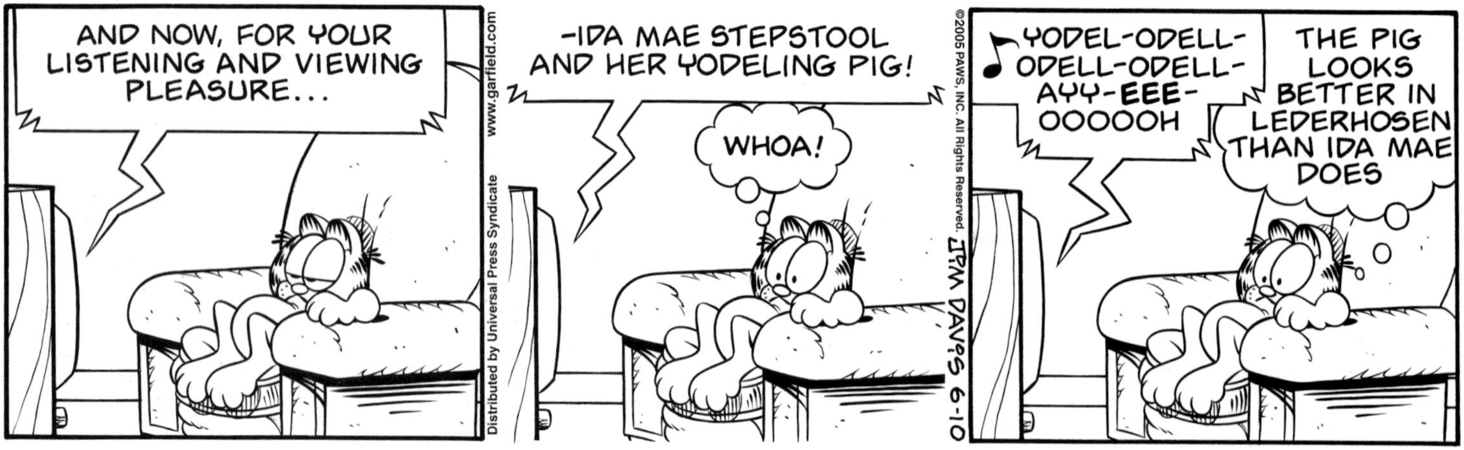
AND NOW, FOR YOUR LISTENING AND VIEWING PLEASURE...
www.garfield.com
Distributed by Universal Press Syndicate
-IDA MAE STEPSTOOL AND HER YODELING PIG!
WHOA!
©2005 PAWS, INC. All Rights Reserved.
JIM DAVIS 6-10
YODEL-ODELL-ODELL-ODELL-AYY-EEE-OOOOOH
THE PIG LOOKS BETTER IN LEDERHOSEN THAN IDA MAE DOES

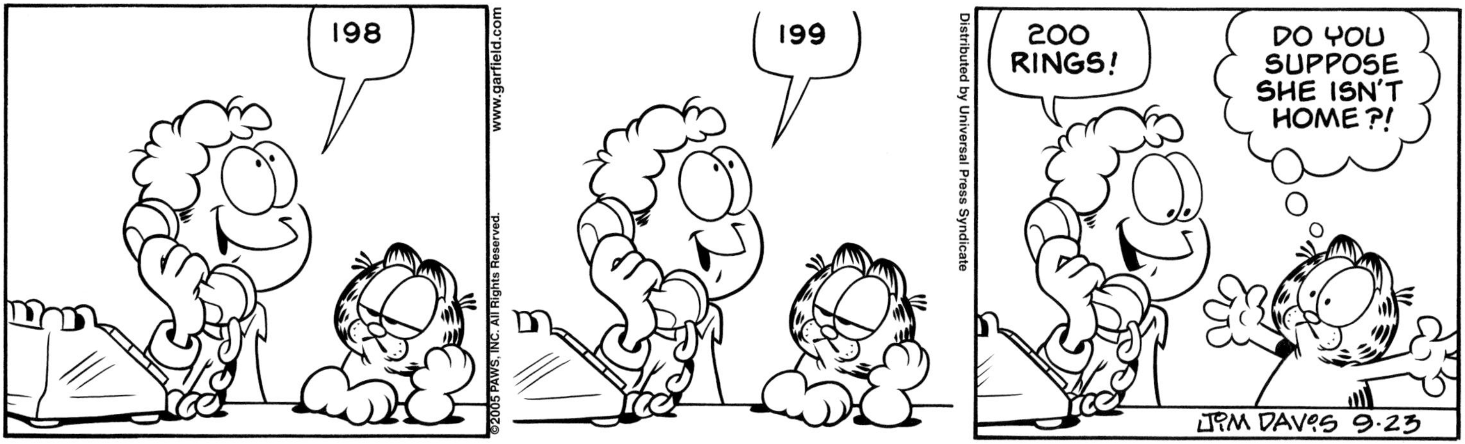
198
199
200 RINGS!
DO YOU SUPPOSE SHE ISN'T HOME?!
JIM DAVIS 9-23
www.garfield.com
©2005 PAWS, INC. All Rights Reserved.
Distributed by Universal Press Syndicate

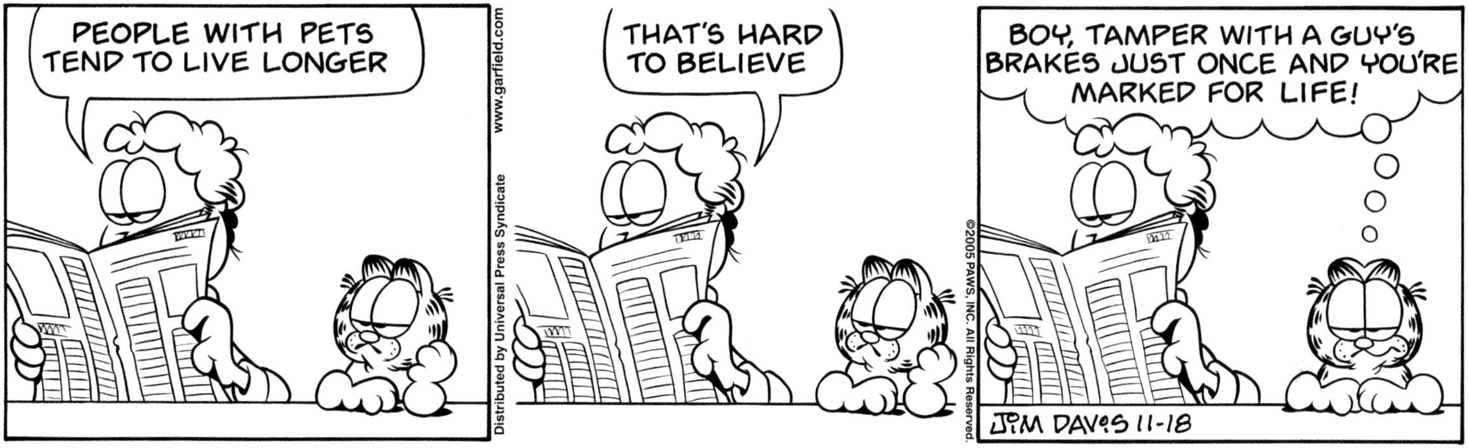
PEOPLE WITH PETS TEND TO LIVE LONGER
THAT'S HARD TO BELIEVE
BOY, TAMPER WITH A GUY'S BRAKES JUST ONCE AND YOU'RE MARKED FOR LIFE!
JIM DAVIS 11-18
www.garfield.com
Distributed by Universal Press Syndicate
©2005 PAWS, INC. All Rights Reserved.

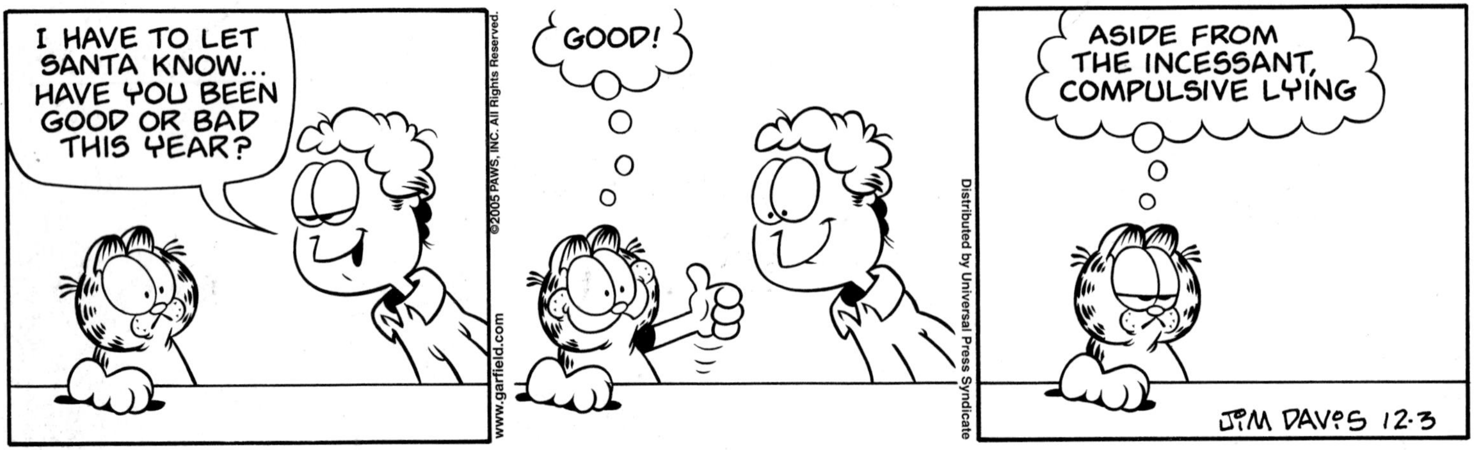
I HAVE TO LET SANTA KNOW... HAVE YOU BEEN GOOD OR BAD THIS YEAR?
©2005 PAWS, INC. All Rights Reserved.
www.garfield.com
GOOD!
Distributed by Universal Press Syndicate
ASIDE FROM THE INCESSANT, COMPULSIVE LYING
JIM DAVIS 12-3

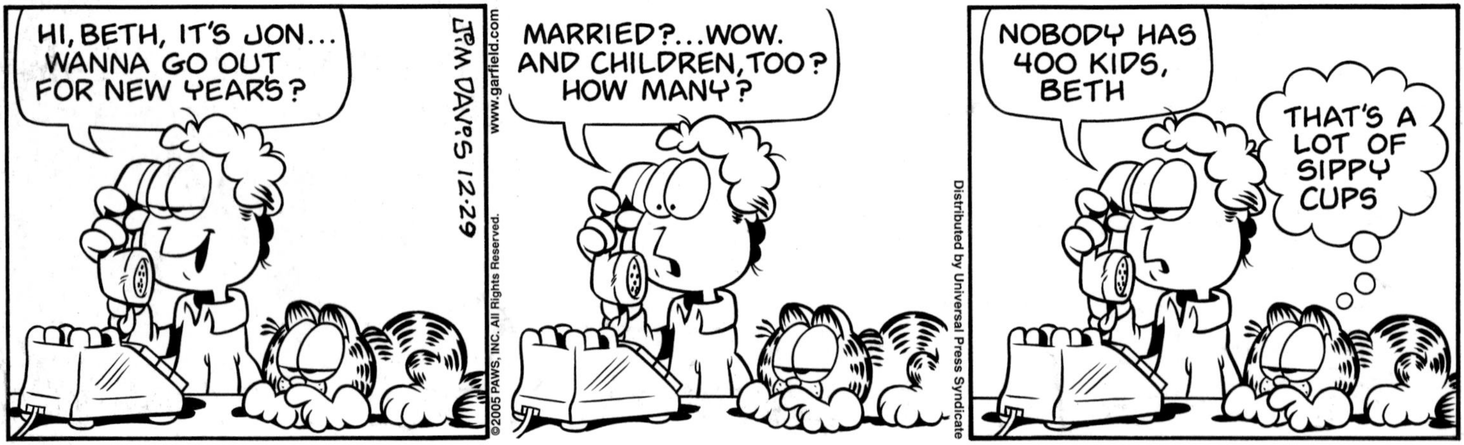
HI, BETH, IT'S JON... WANNA GO OUT FOR NEW YEAR'S?
JIM DAVIS 12-29
www.garfield.com
©2005 PAWS, INC. All Rights Reserved.
MARRIED?...WOW. AND CHILDREN, TOO? HOW MANY?
Distributed by Universal Press Syndicate
NOBODY HAS 400 KIDS, BETH
THAT'S A LOT OF SIPPY CUPS

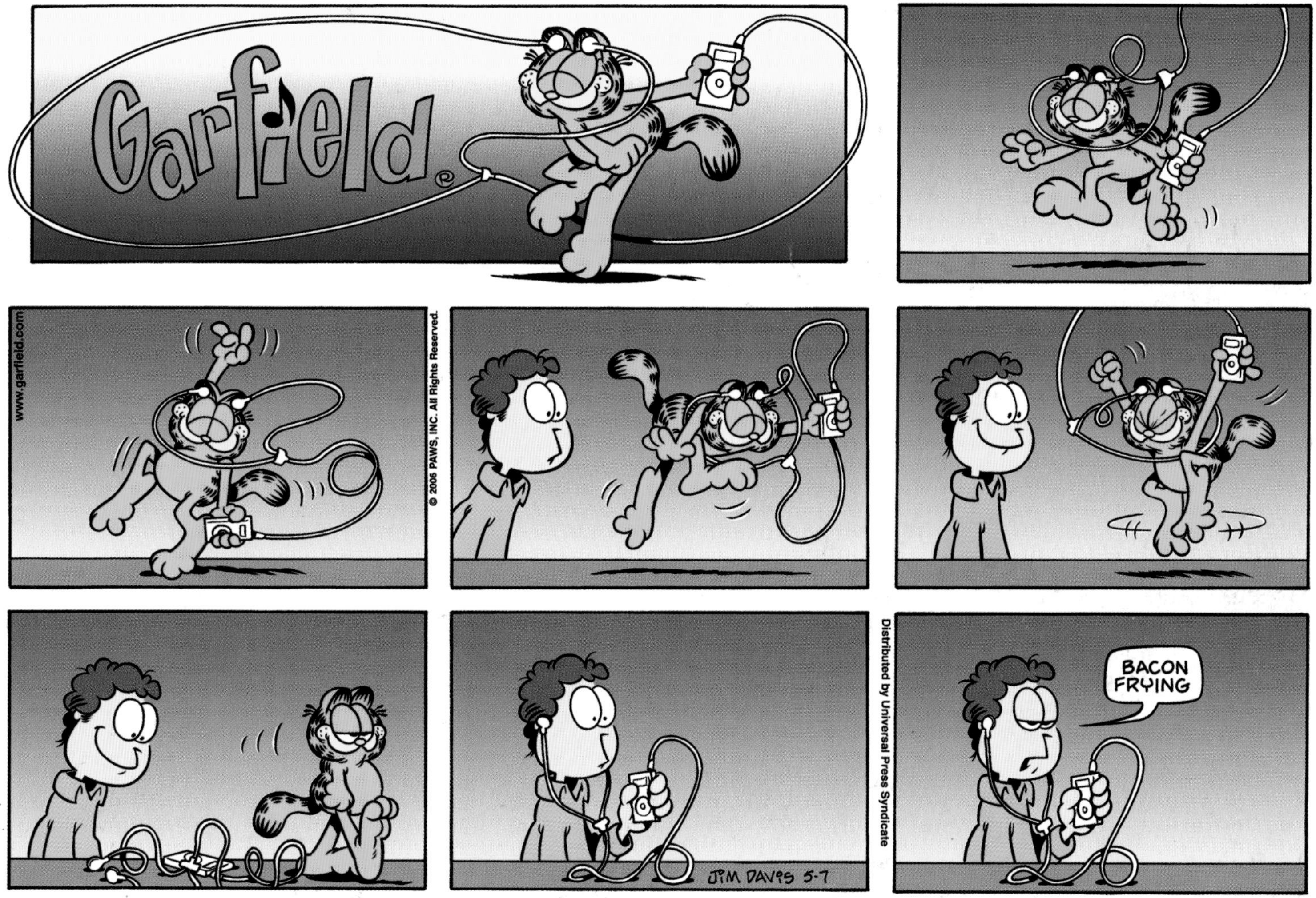
Garfield
www.garfield.com
© 2006 PAWS, INC. All Rights Reserved.
Distributed by Universal Press Syndicate
JIM DAVIS 5-7
BACON FRYING

IRMA

If you've ever found yourself on a diner barstool, drinking a cup of coffee and eating a piece of pie, you've met Irma. Her name may have been Marge, but she called you "honey" and could easily "take you out" if you forgot the tip.

LIZ

Every nerd has a dream. Liz has been Jon's dream for years. Finally, in 2006, Jon got his date and seems to have won Liz's heart. How is Garfield going to process having to share Jon ... and with a *vet* no less? It may take another thirty years to find out.

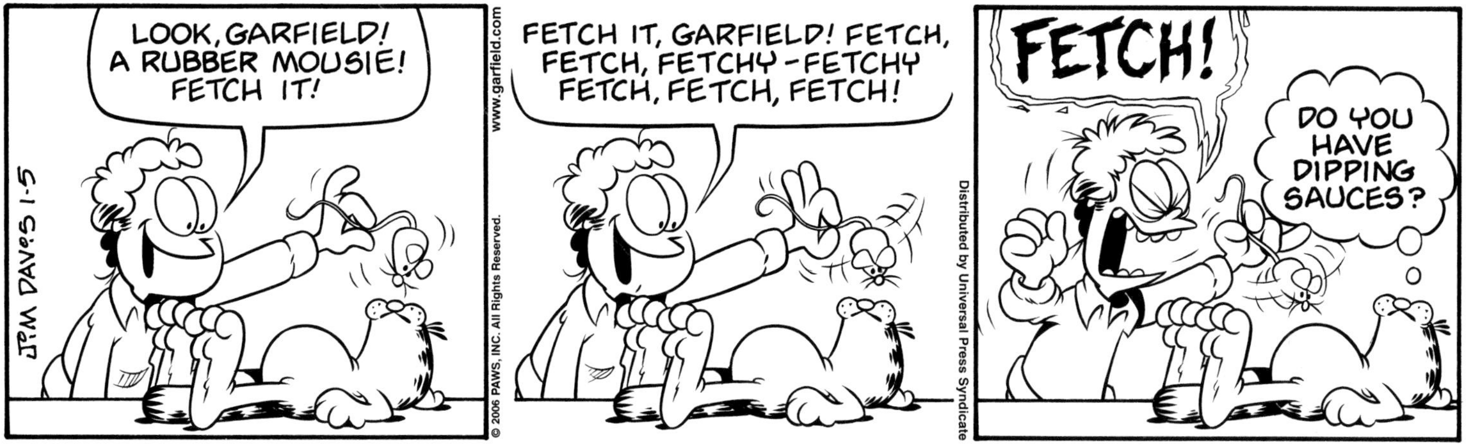
LOOK, GARFIELD! A RUBBER MOUSIE! FETCH IT!
JIM DAVIS 1-5
© 2006 PAWS, INC. All Rights Reserved.
www.garfield.com
FETCH IT, GARFIELD! FETCH, FETCH, FETCHY-FETCHY FETCH, FETCH, FETCH!
Distributed by Universal Press Syndicate
FETCH!
DO YOU HAVE DIPPING SAUCES?

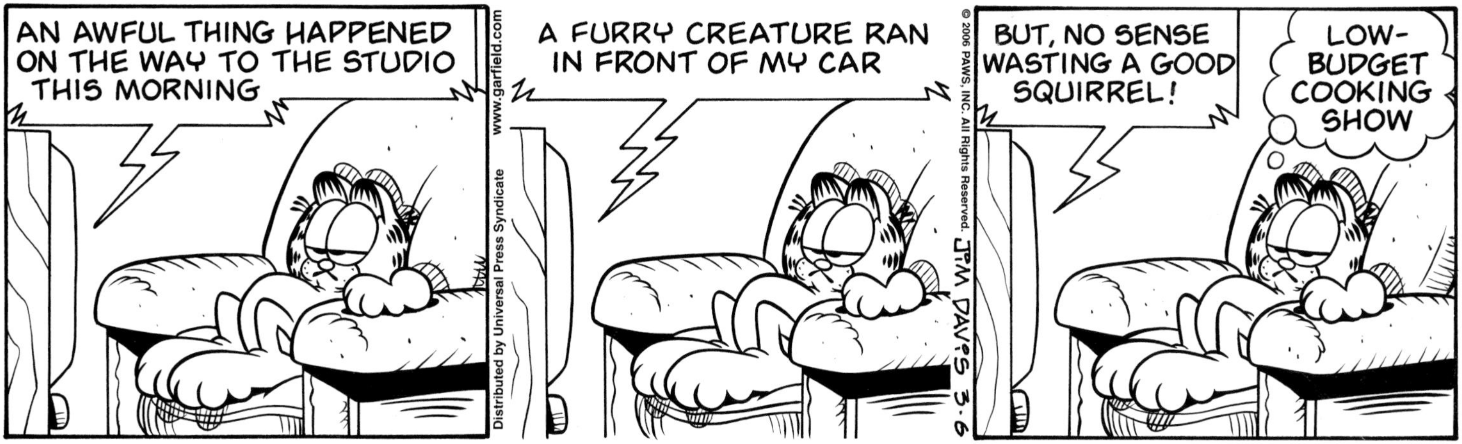
AN AWFUL THING HAPPENED ON THE WAY TO THE STUDIO THIS MORNING
www.garfield.com
Distributed by Universal Press Syndicate
A FURRY CREATURE RAN IN FRONT OF MY CAR
© 2006 PAWS, INC. All Rights Reserved.
JIM DAVIS 3-6
BUT, NO SENSE WASTING A GOOD SQUIRREL!
LOW-BUDGET COOKING SHOW

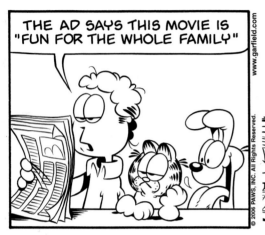

THE AD SAYS THIS MOVIE IS "FUN FOR THE WHOLE FAMILY"
www.garfield.com
© 2006 PAWS, INC. All Rights Reserved.
JPM DAVIS 4-26
Distributed by Universal Press Syndicate
HEY, WE'RE FAMILY, RIGHT?
IN A DYSFUNCTIONAL SORTA WAY

I think Garfield is pithier and more profound now than he ever was before. I don't think it's that Garfield has changed dramatically since his beginning; it's more that society has, and humor in general is much sharper and more cutting than before.

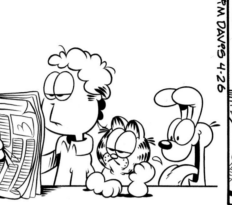

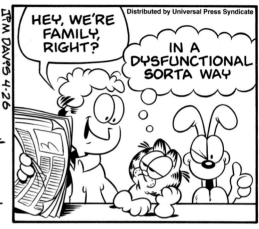

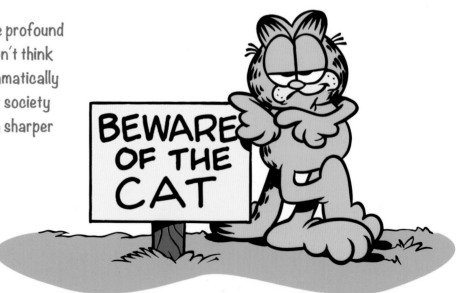

BEWARE OF THE CAT

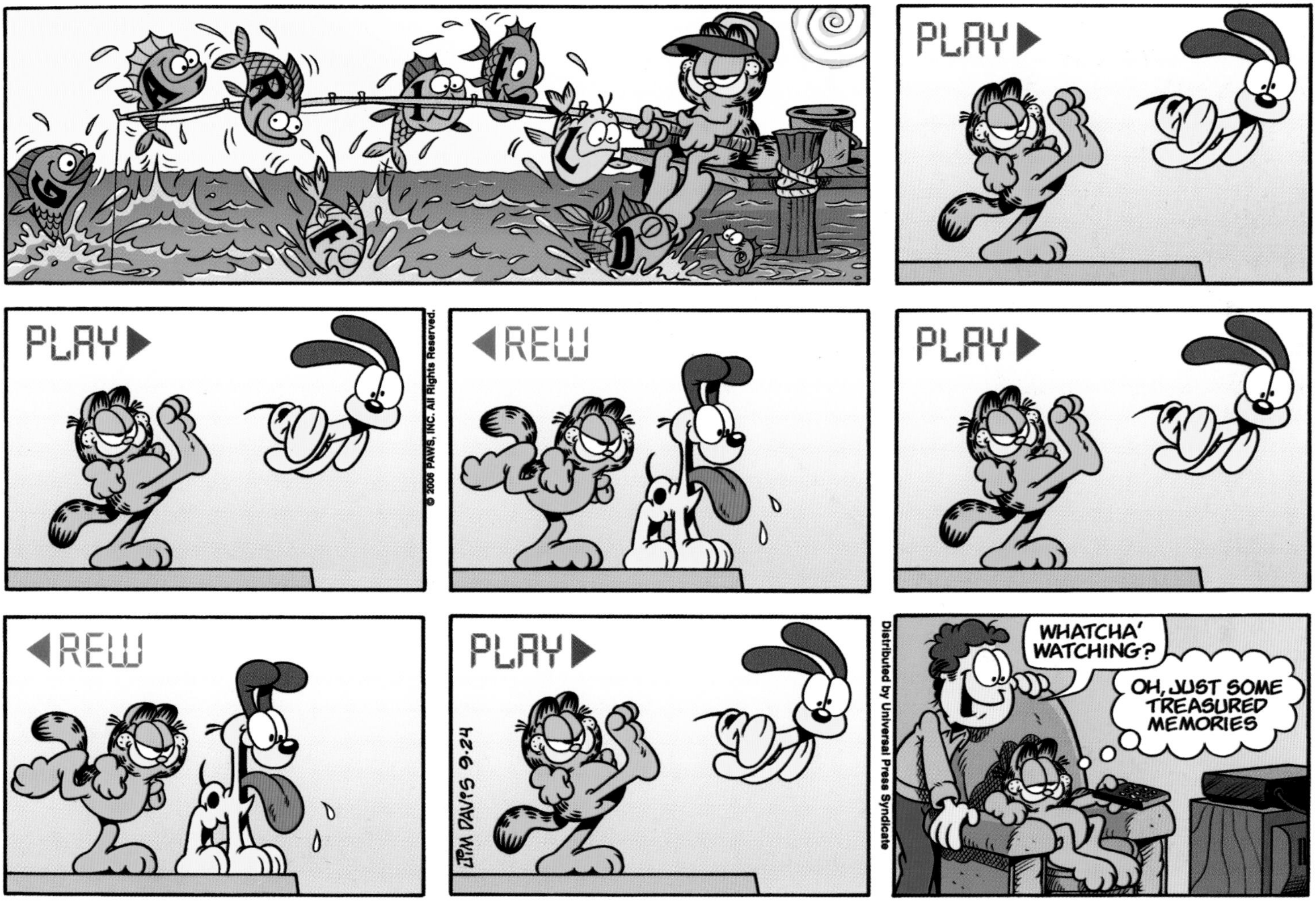
PLAY
PLAY
REW
PLAY
REW
PLAY
WHATCHA' WATCHING?
OH, JUST SOME TREASURED MEMORIES
JPM DAVIS 9-24

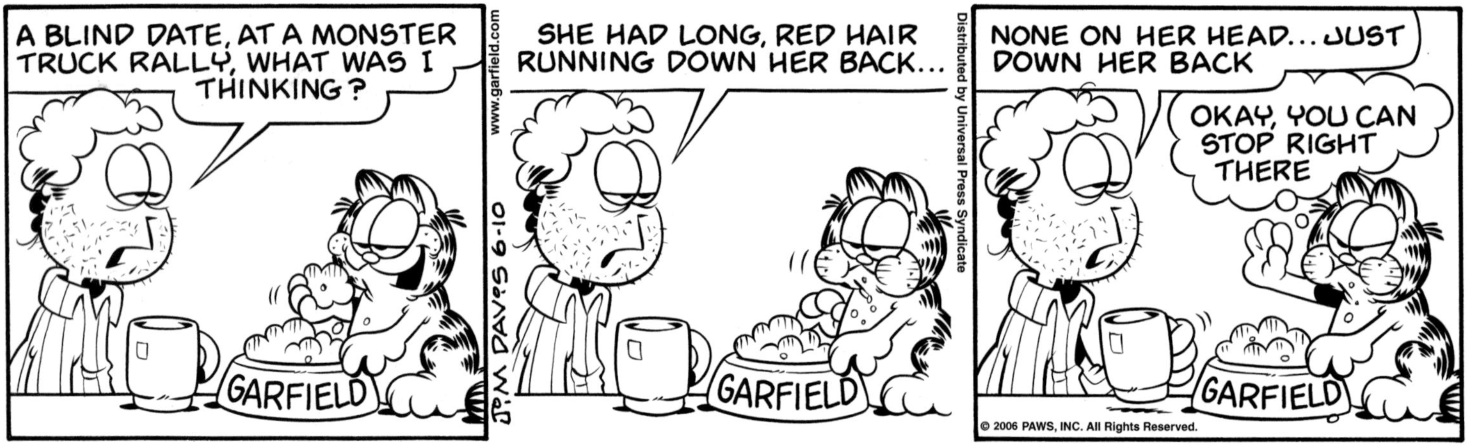
A BLIND DATE, AT A MONSTER TRUCK RALLY, WHAT WAS I THINKING?
GARFIELD
www.garfield.com
JPM DAVIS 6-10
SHE HAD LONG, RED HAIR RUNNING DOWN HER BACK...
GARFIELD
Distributed by Universal Press Syndicate
NONE ON HER HEAD... JUST DOWN HER BACK
OKAY, YOU CAN STOP RIGHT THERE
GARFIELD
© 2006 PAWS, INC. All Rights Reserved.

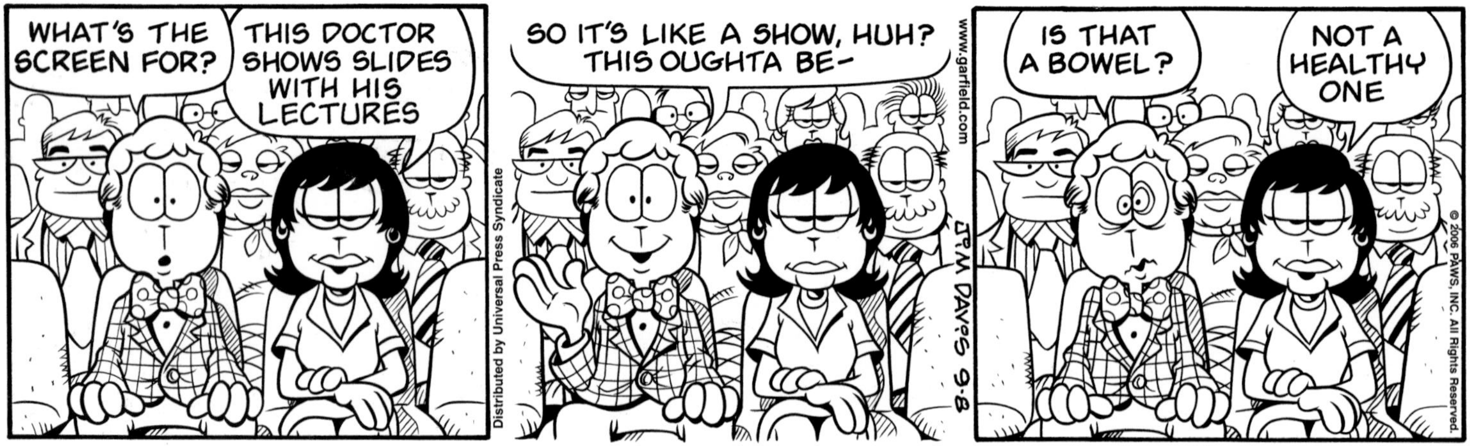
WHAT'S THE SCREEN FOR?
THIS DOCTOR SHOWS SLIDES WITH HIS LECTURES
Distributed by Universal Press Syndicate
SO IT'S LIKE A SHOW, HUH? THIS OUGHTA BE-
JPM DAVIS 9-8
www.garfield.com
IS THAT A BOWEL?
NOT A HEALTHY ONE
© 2006 PAWS, INC. All Rights Reserved.

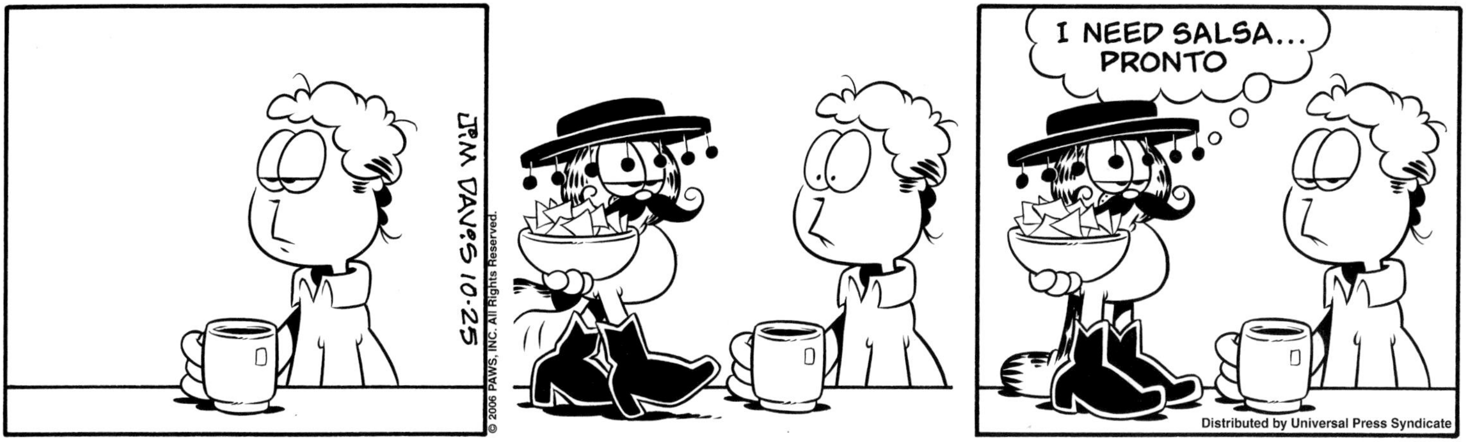
JIM DAVIS 10-25
I NEED SALSA... PRONTO
Distributed by Universal Press Syndicate

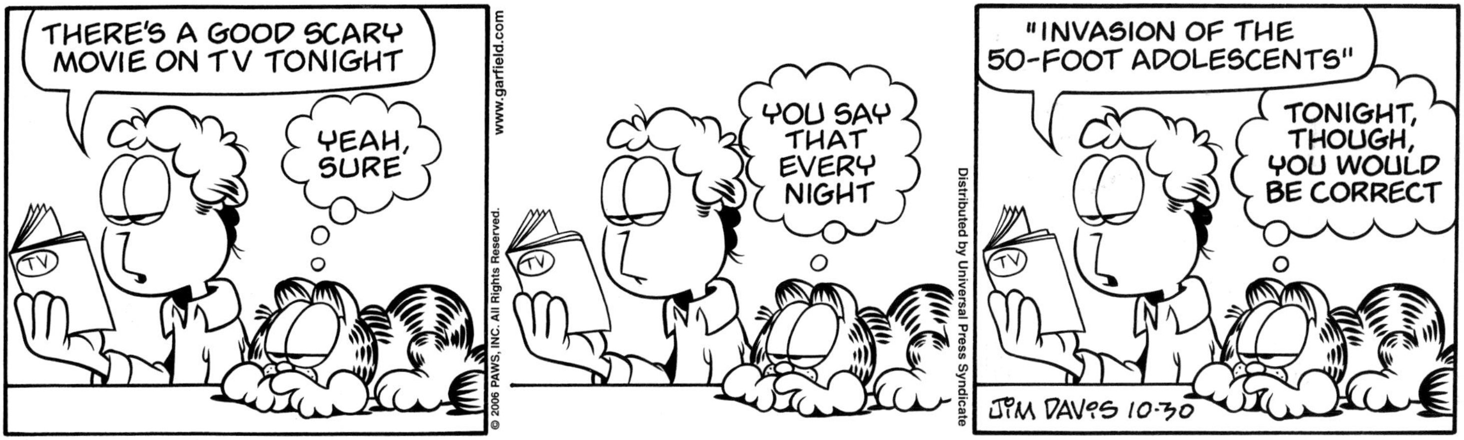
THERE'S A GOOD SCARY MOVIE ON TV TONIGHT
YEAH, SURE
YOU SAY THAT EVERY NIGHT
"INVASION OF THE 50-FOOT ADOLESCENTS"
TONIGHT, THOUGH, YOU WOULD BE CORRECT
JIM DAVIS 10-30

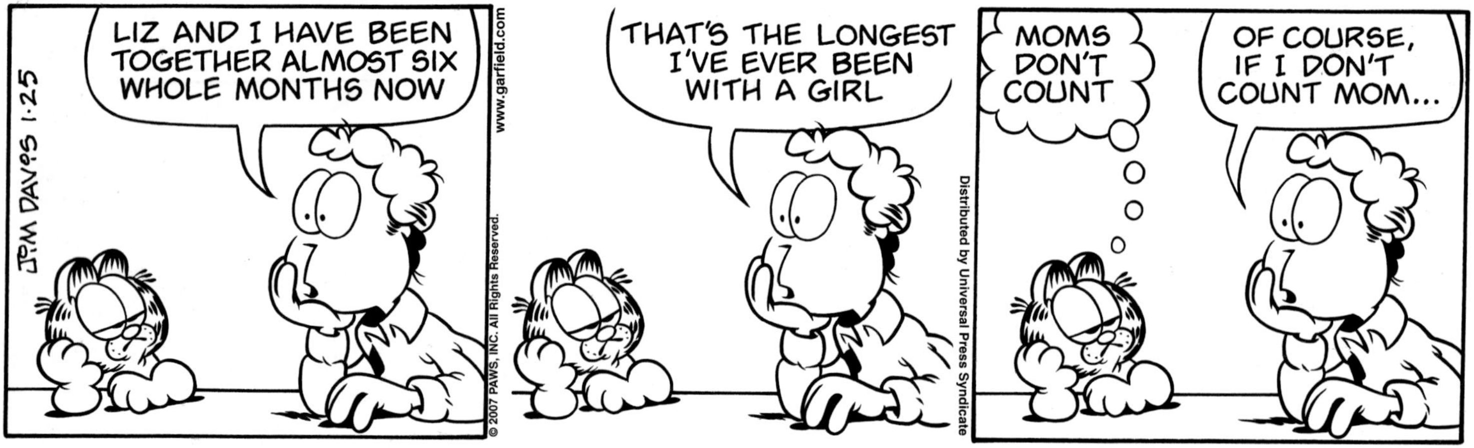
LIZ AND I HAVE BEEN TOGETHER ALMOST SIX WHOLE MONTHS NOW
THAT'S THE LONGEST I'VE EVER BEEN WITH A GIRL
MOMS DON'T COUNT
OF COURSE, IF I DON'T COUNT MOM...
JIM DAVIS 1·25
www.garfield.com
© 2007 PAWS, INC. All Rights Reserved.
Distributed by Universal Press Syndicate

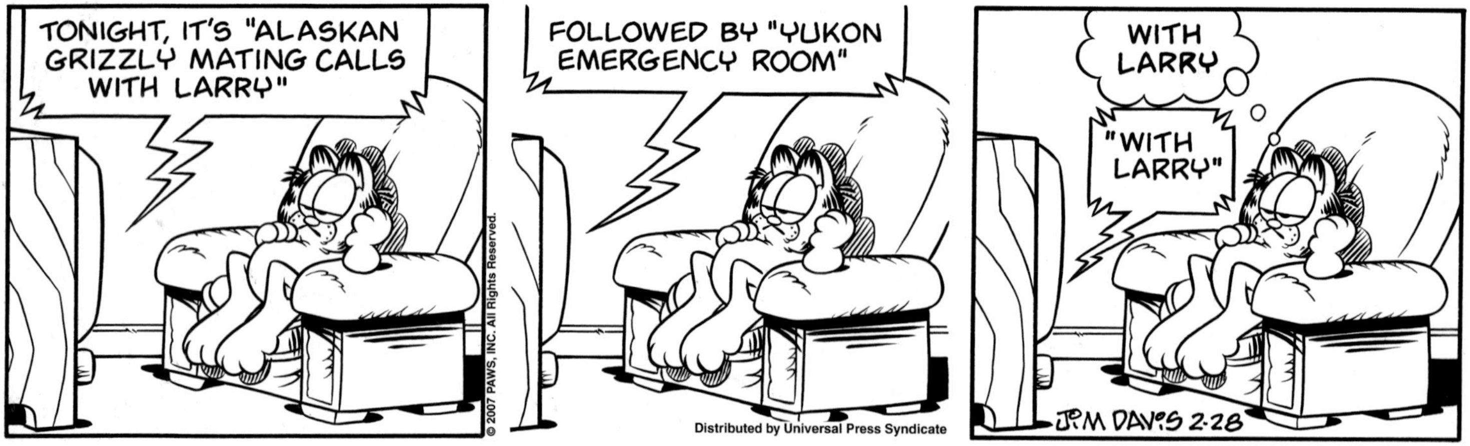
TONIGHT, IT'S "ALASKAN GRIZZLY MATING CALLS WITH LARRY"
FOLLOWED BY "YUKON EMERGENCY ROOM"
"WITH LARRY"
WITH LARRY
© 2007 PAWS, INC. All Rights Reserved.
Distributed by Universal Press Syndicate
JIM DAVIS 2·28

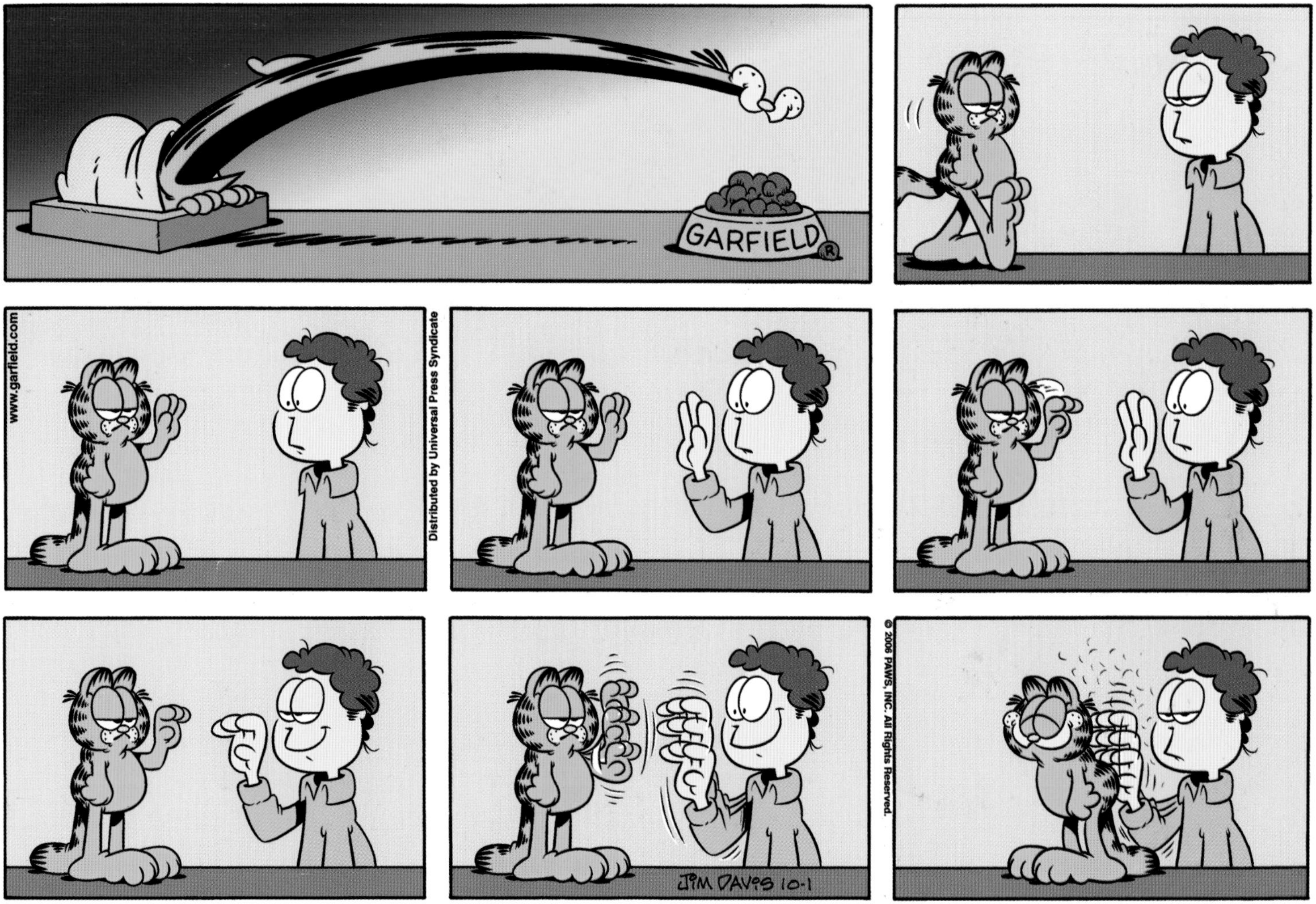
GARFIELD®
www.garfield.com
Distributed by Universal Press Syndicate
© 2006 PAWS, INC. All Rights Reserved.
JIM DAVIS 10-1

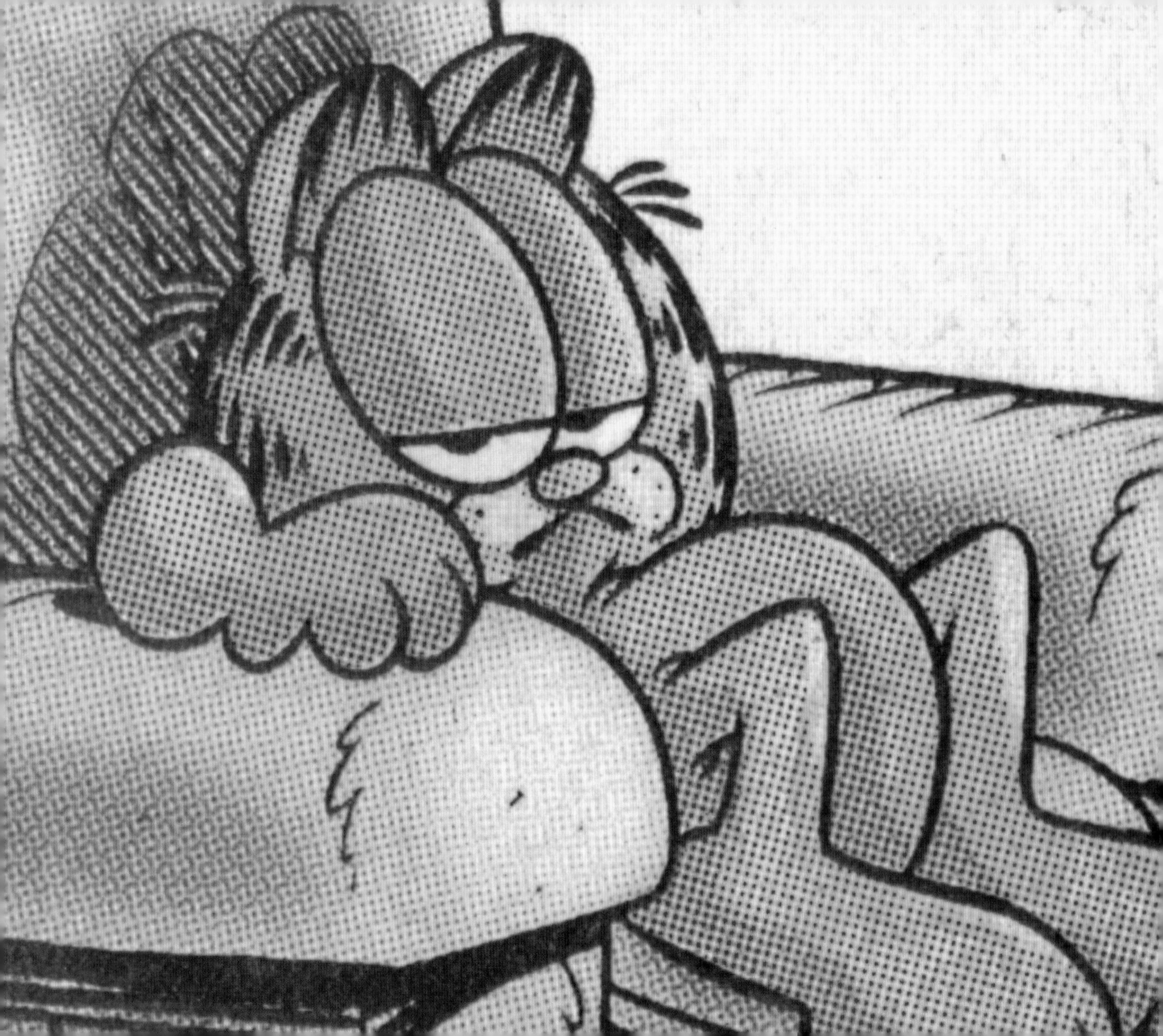

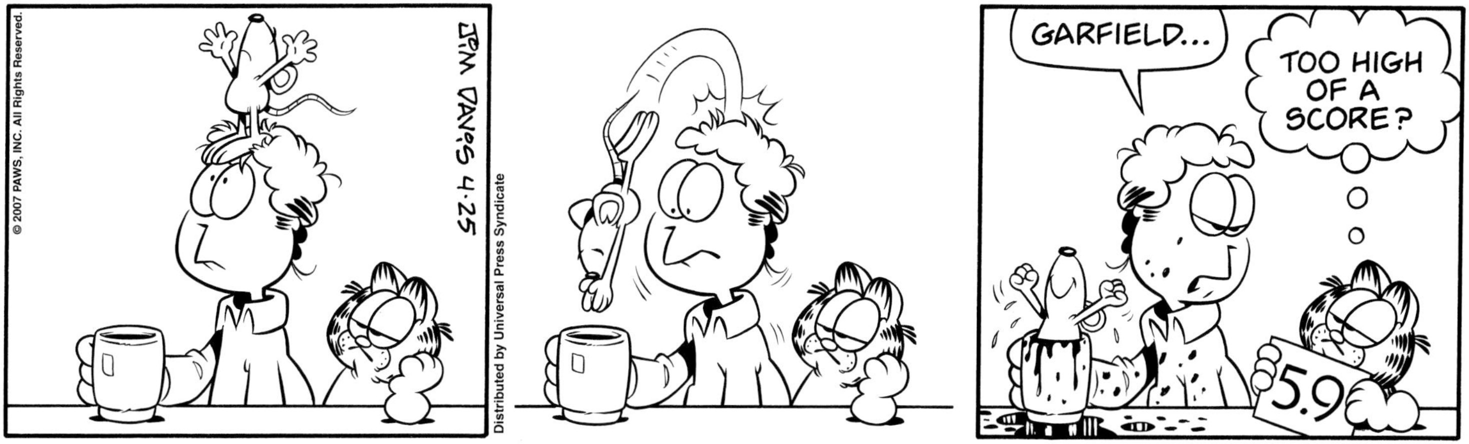
© 2007 PAWS, INC. All Rights Reserved.
JIM DAVIS 4·25
Distributed by Universal Press Syndicate
GARFIELD...
TOO HIGH OF A SCORE?
5.9

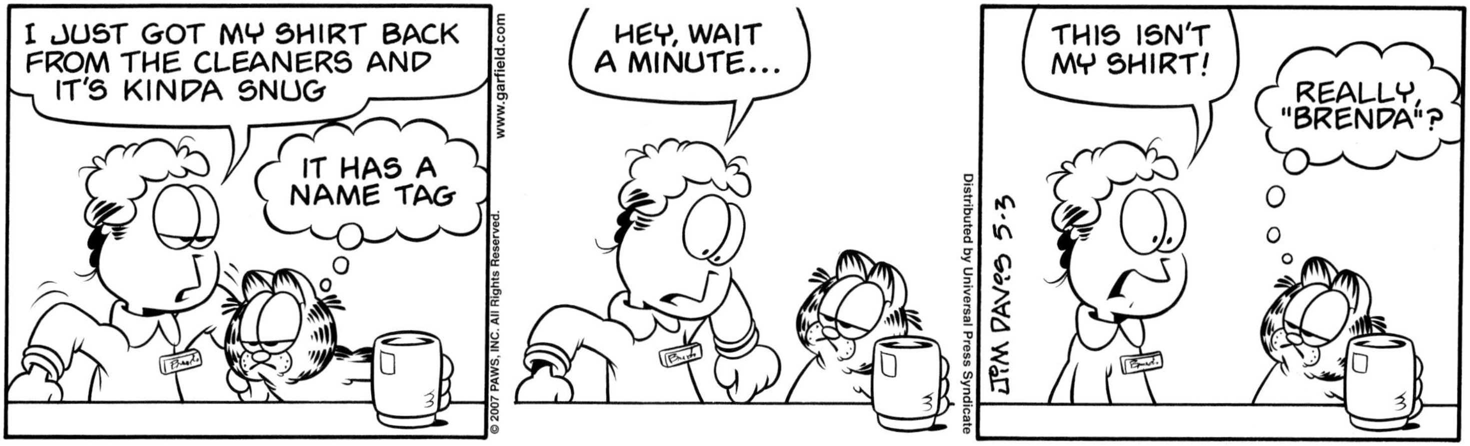
I JUST GOT MY SHIRT BACK FROM THE CLEANERS AND IT'S KINDA SNUG
IT HAS A NAME TAG
www.garfield.com
© 2007 PAWS, INC. All Rights Reserved.
HEY, WAIT A MINUTE...
Distributed by Universal Press Syndicate
JIM DAVIS 5·3
THIS ISN'T MY SHIRT!
REALLY, "BRENDA"?

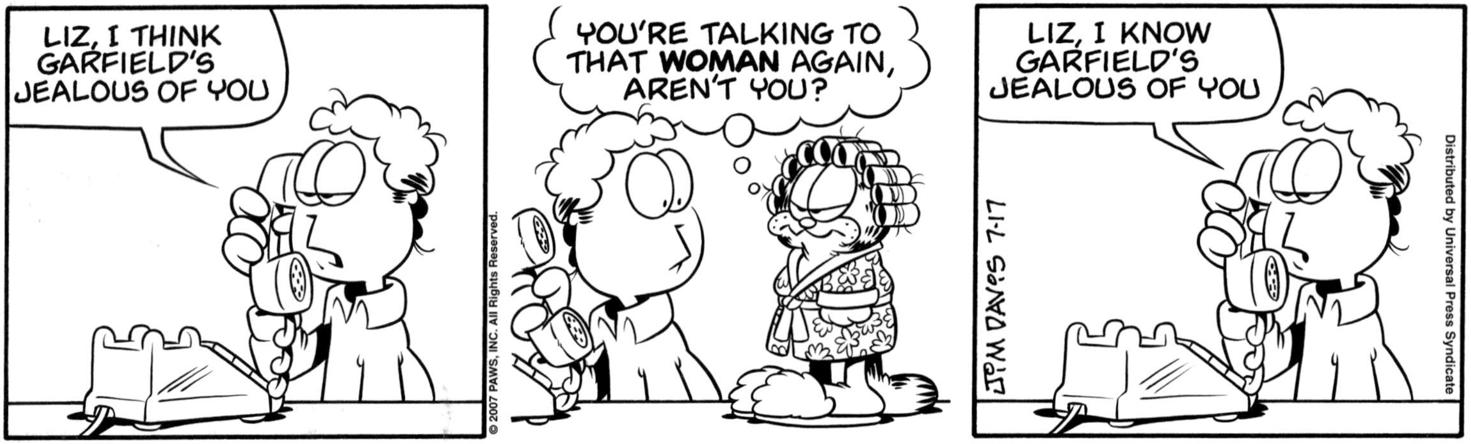
LIZ, I THINK GARFIELD'S JEALOUS OF YOU
YOU'RE TALKING TO THAT **WOMAN** AGAIN, AREN'T YOU?
LIZ, I KNOW GARFIELD'S JEALOUS OF YOU
JPM DAVIS 7-17
© 2007 PAWS, INC. All Rights Reserved.
Distributed by Universal Press Syndicate

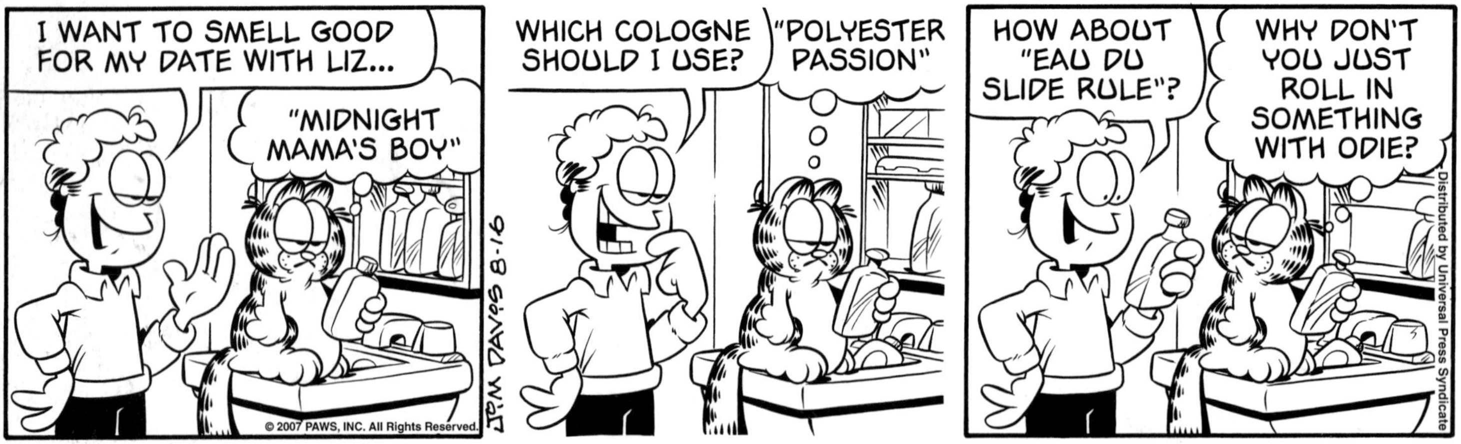
I WANT TO SMELL GOOD FOR MY DATE WITH LIZ...
"MIDNIGHT MAMA'S BOY"
WHICH COLOGNE SHOULD I USE?
"POLYESTER PASSION"
HOW ABOUT "EAU DU SLIDE RULE"?
WHY DON'T YOU JUST ROLL IN SOMETHING WITH ODIE?
JPM DAVIS 8-16
© 2007 PAWS, INC. All Rights Reserved.
Distributed by Universal Press Syndicate

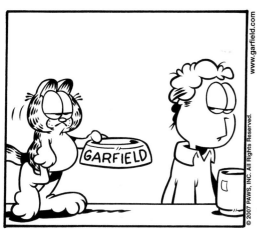

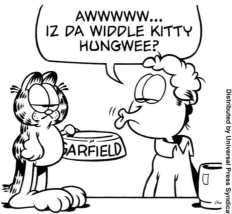

GARFIELD
www.garfield.com
© 2007 PAWS, INC. All Rights Reserved.
AWWWWW... IZ DA WIDDLE KITTY HUNGWEE?
GARFIELD
Distributed by Universal Press Syndicate
GARFIELD
RECKON SO
JIM DAVIS 9-4

As far as future plans for *Garfield,* who knows? When I sit down and write it each time, I have no idea what he's going to do, what direction he's going to go, or what new character will pop into the strip. It's always a big surprise for me as well as the readers.

GARFIELD

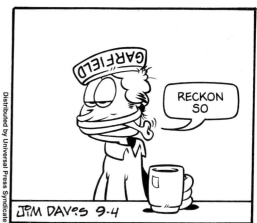

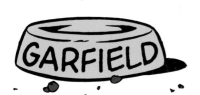

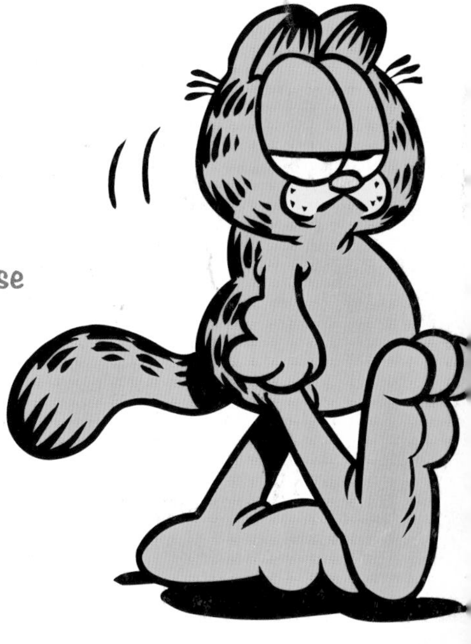

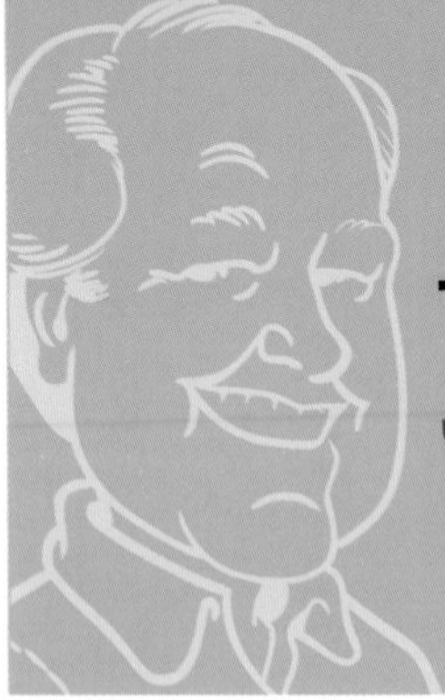

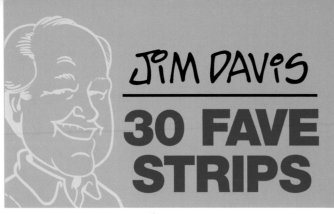

JIM DAVIS

30 FAVE STRIPS

I have a simple philosophy for writing gags: If I'm giggling, chances are the joke I'm working on is going to make other people laugh. For one reason or another, these really cracked me up. Enjoy!

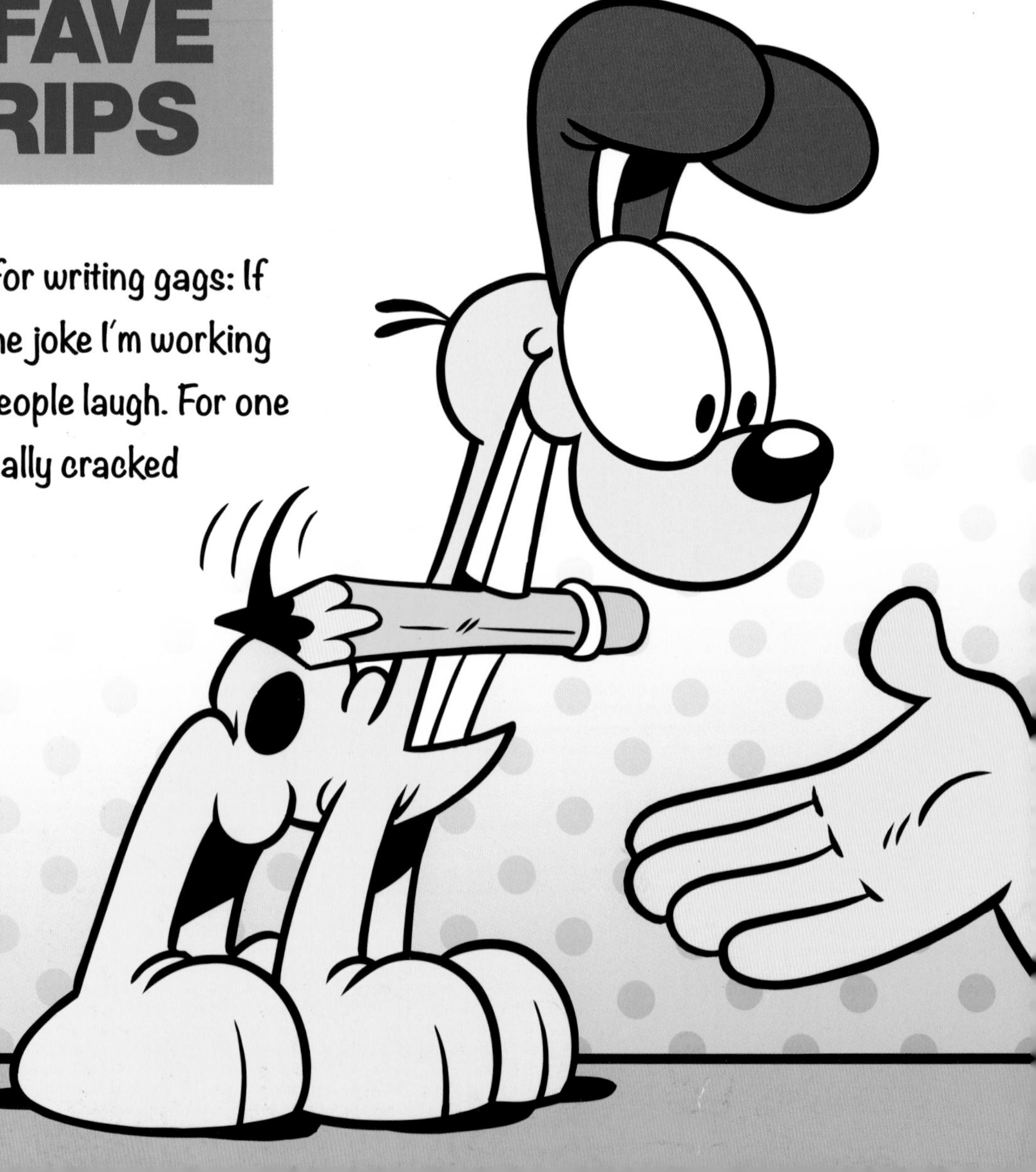

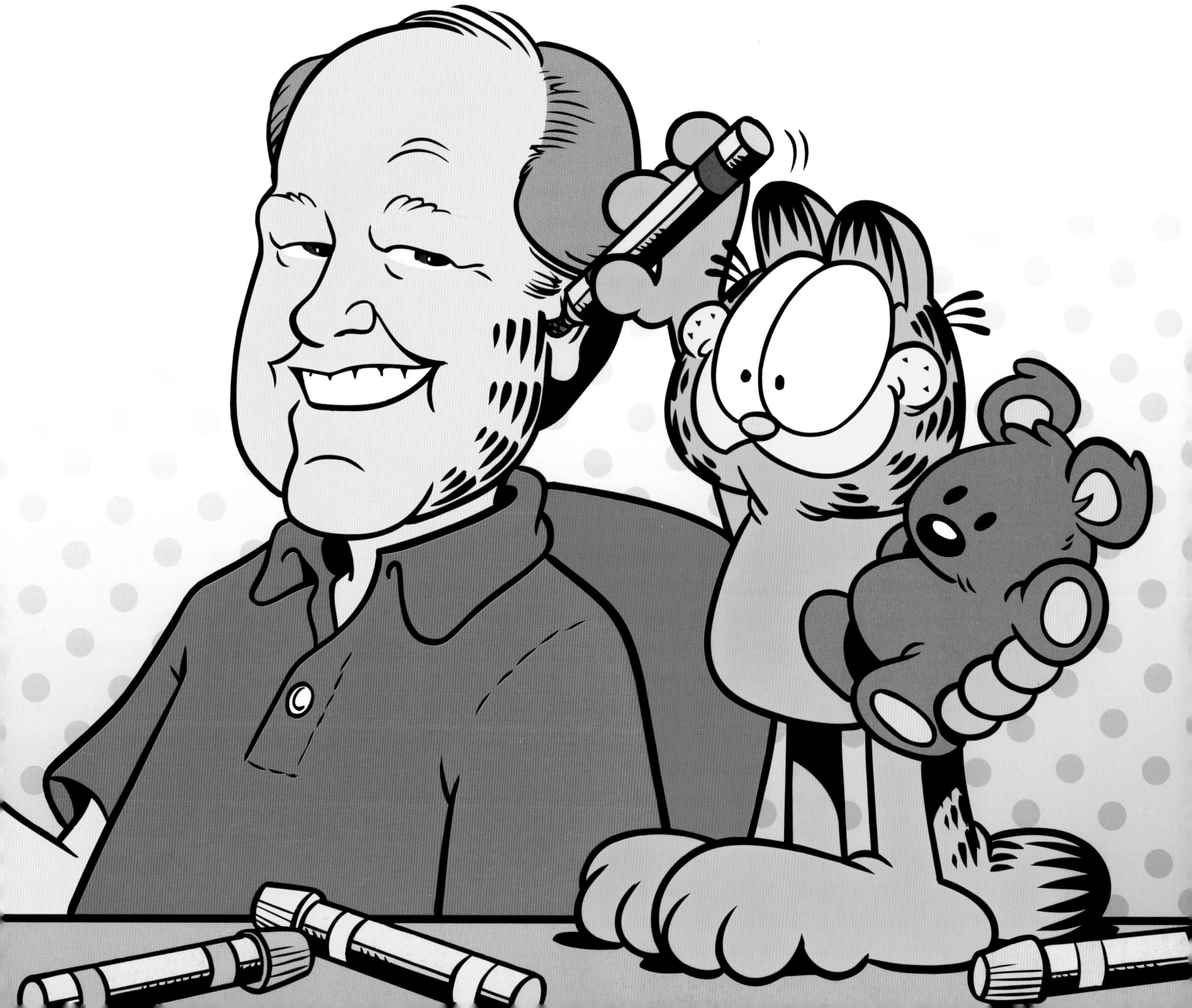

HI, THERE...I'M JON ARBUCKLE. I'M A CARTOONIST, AND THIS IS MY CAT, GARFIELD.
JIM DAVIS 6-19
© 1978 PAWS, INC. All Rights Reserved.
HI, THERE. I'M GARFIELD. I'M A CAT, AND THIS IS MY CARTOONIST, JON.
OUR ONLY THOUGHT IS TO ENTERTAIN YOU.
FEED ME.

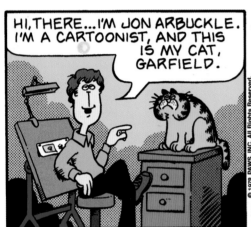

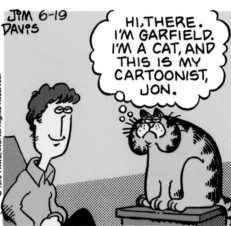

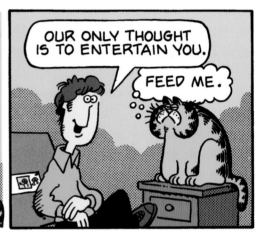

This is my first and my favorite strip. It's one of the very few times that Jon talked about what he does. The strip is a bit prophetic. I still consider myself to be in the entertainment biz.

A MOUSE! GET IT!
GARFIELD! YOU DIDN'T EVEN TRY!
© 1978 PAWS, INC. All Rights Reserved.
SHOW ME A GOOD MOUSER, AND I'LL SHOW YOU A CAT WITH BAD BREATH.
6-21
JIM DAVIS

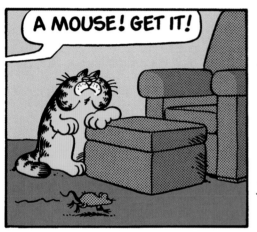

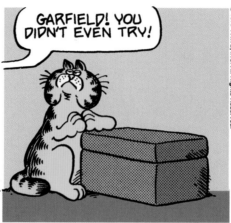

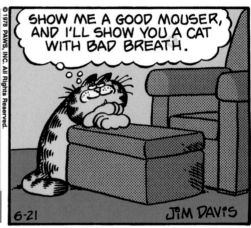

This was a defining strip for Garfield. He not only set himself apart from stereotypical cats, but he established himself as a human in a cat suit.

CLICK!
JIM DAVIS
2-12
SHOOP!
© 1982 PAWS, INC. All Rights Reserved.
FASTER THAN THE SPEED OF DARK

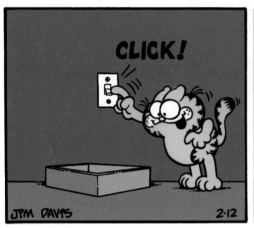

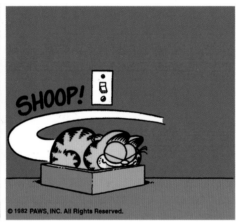

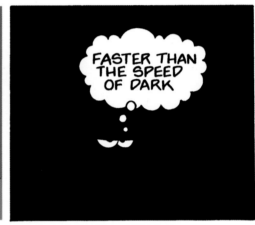

On very rare occasions, I will use a gag supplied by a trusted source. This trusted source was my dad. That was more than twenty-five years ago, and I haven't been able to get him to write another one!

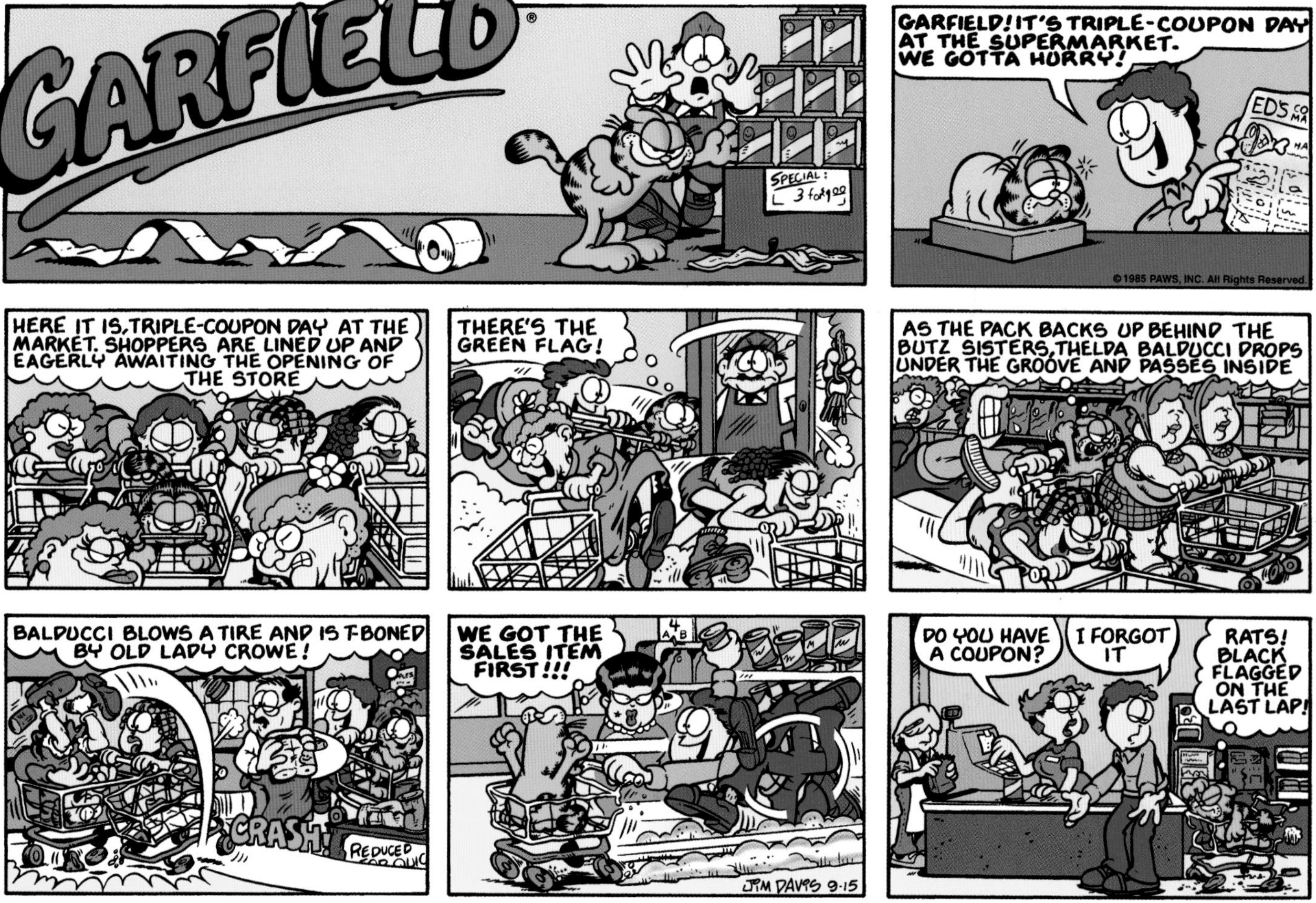
GARFIELD®
SPECIAL: 3 for $1.00
GARFIELD! IT'S TRIPLE-COUPON DAY AT THE SUPERMARKET. WE GOTTA HURRY!
ED'S
© 1985 PAWS, INC. All Rights Reserved.
HERE IT IS, TRIPLE-COUPON DAY AT THE MARKET. SHOPPERS ARE LINED UP AND EAGERLY AWAITING THE OPENING OF THE STORE
THERE'S THE GREEN FLAG!
AS THE PACK BACKS UP BEHIND THE BUTZ SISTERS, THELDA BALDUCCI DROPS UNDER THE GROOVE AND PASSES INSIDE
BALDUCCI BLOWS A TIRE AND IS T-BONED BY OLD LADY CROWE!
CRASH!
WE GOT THE SALES ITEM FIRST!!!
JIM DAVIS 9-15
DO YOU HAVE A COUPON?
I FORGOT IT
RATS! BLACK FLAGGED ON THE LAST LAP!

This strip was a deliberate effort to stuff as much art and action into a Sunday page as humanly possible. It was hard work, but great fun! Even Mr. Whipple (remember him?) makes a cameo appearance.

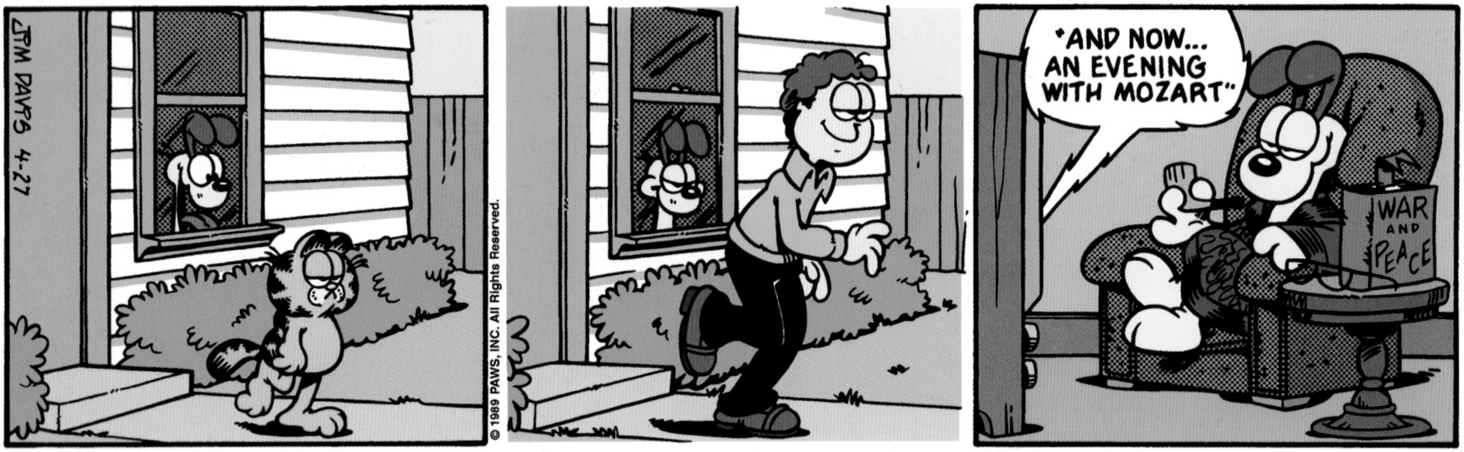
JIM DAVIS 4-27
© 1989 PAWS, INC. All Rights Reserved.
"AND NOW... AN EVENING WITH MOZART"
WAR AND PEACE

This is the only time I've shown what
Odie is really like off-camera.

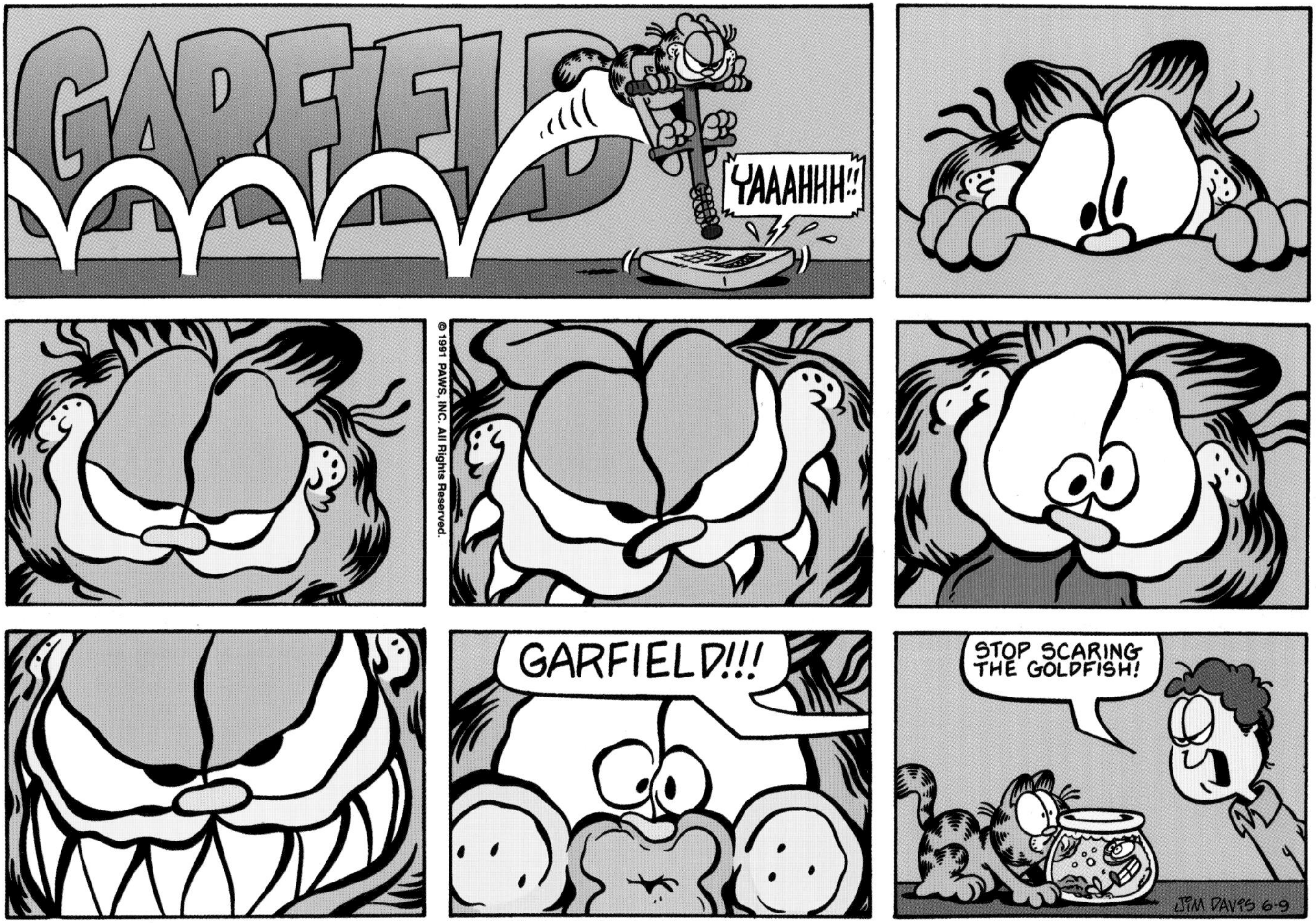
GARFIELD
YAAAHHH!!
© 1991 PAWS, INC. All Rights Reserved.
GARFIELD!!!
STOP SCARING THE GOLDFISH!
JIM DAVIS 6-9

In the trade, we call this a wallpaper gag with a reveal. I love teasing the reader with seemingly nonsensical action for most of the strip, and then revealing its logic in the last frame. It's also a great excuse to do silly drawings.

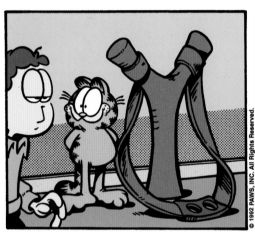

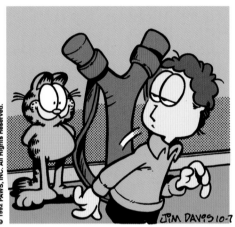

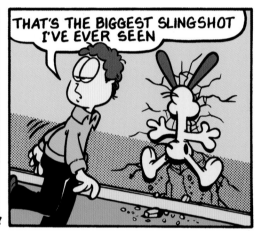

© 1992 PAWS, INC. All Rights Reserved.
JIM DAVIS 10-7
THAT'S THE BIGGEST SLINGSHOT I'VE EVER SEEN

One ingredient of comedy is exaggeration . . .
. . . and it doesn't get much bigger than this.

GARFIELD, I HAVE TO ADMIRE YOUR TENACITY
JIM DAVIS 3-25
© 1993 PAWS, INC. All Rights Reserved.
YOU'VE PULLED SOME DUMB STUNTS
BUT THIS IS THE WORST
FEED THE TEETH!

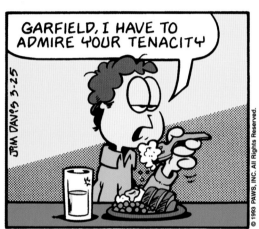

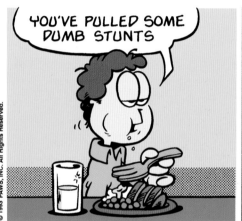

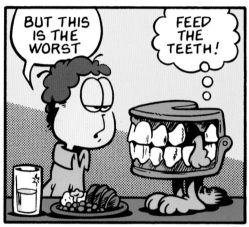

Some gags don't make a lot of sense . . . and they don't have to if they're silly enough. This one's very silly.

WE'RE VISITING JON'S FAMILY FOR CHRISTMAS
JIM DAVIS 12-18
IT'S PEACEFUL HERE ON THE FARM
© 1993 PAWS, INC. All Rights Reserved.
C'MON, GARFIELD! WE'RE GOING TO PLAY "TOUCH THE UDDER"
AND WEIRD

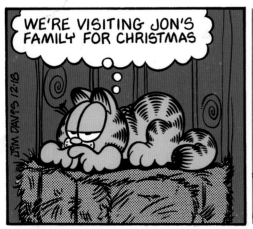

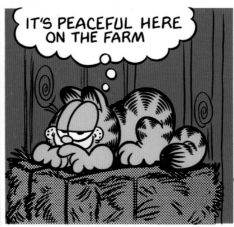

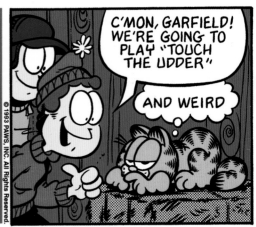

Now and then I can't resist a nostalgic trip back to my childhood on the farm. Oh, the fun Doc Boy and I had . . . ha, ha, ha . . . .

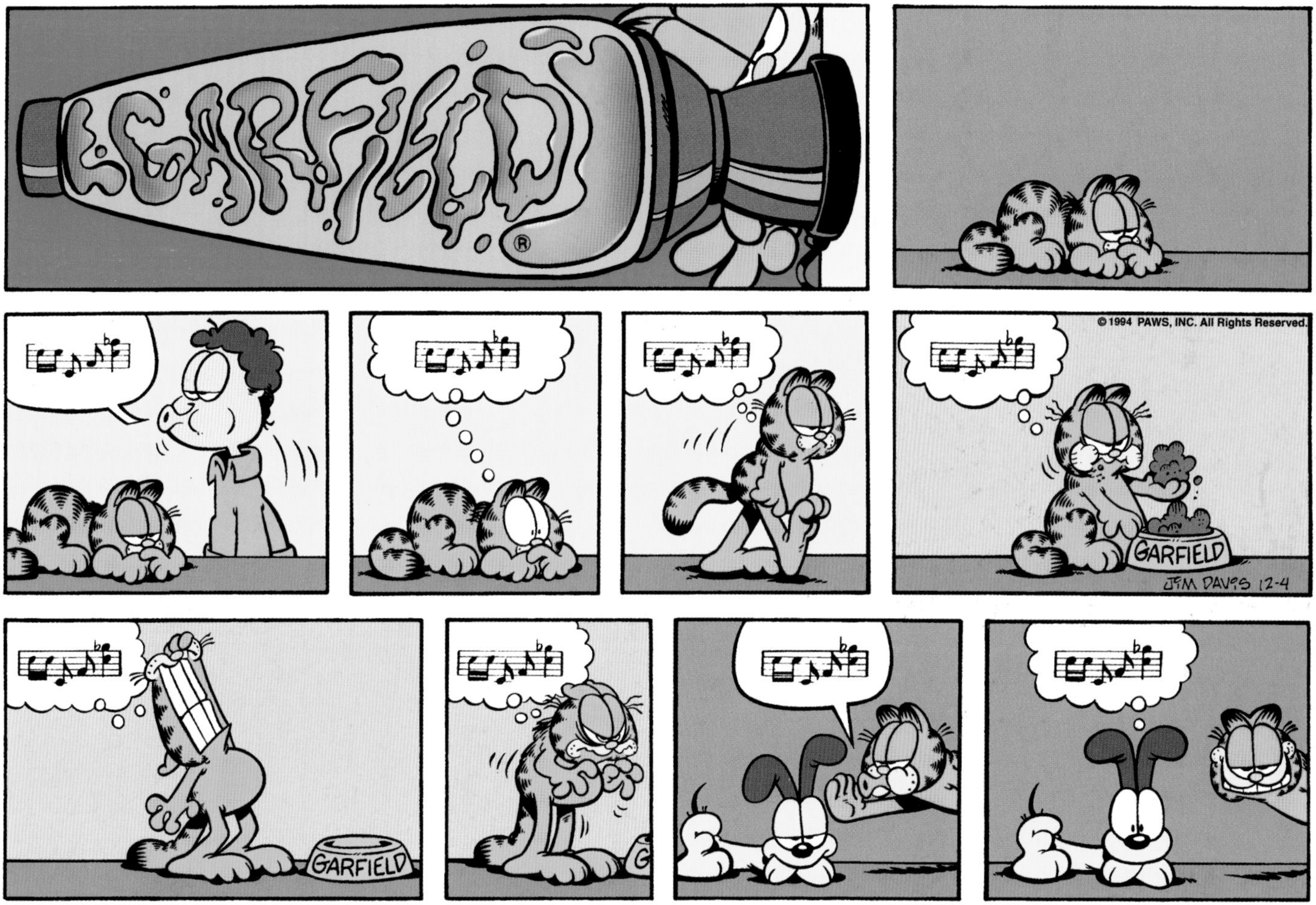
GARFIELD®
© 1994 PAWS, INC. All Rights Reserved.
GARFIELD
JIM DAVIS 12-4
GARFIELD

I read somewhere that the best way to get a pesky tune out of your head was to sing it out loud. Of course, that means that someone else is going to hear it, and pick it up . . . like a head cold. It's a small world after all.

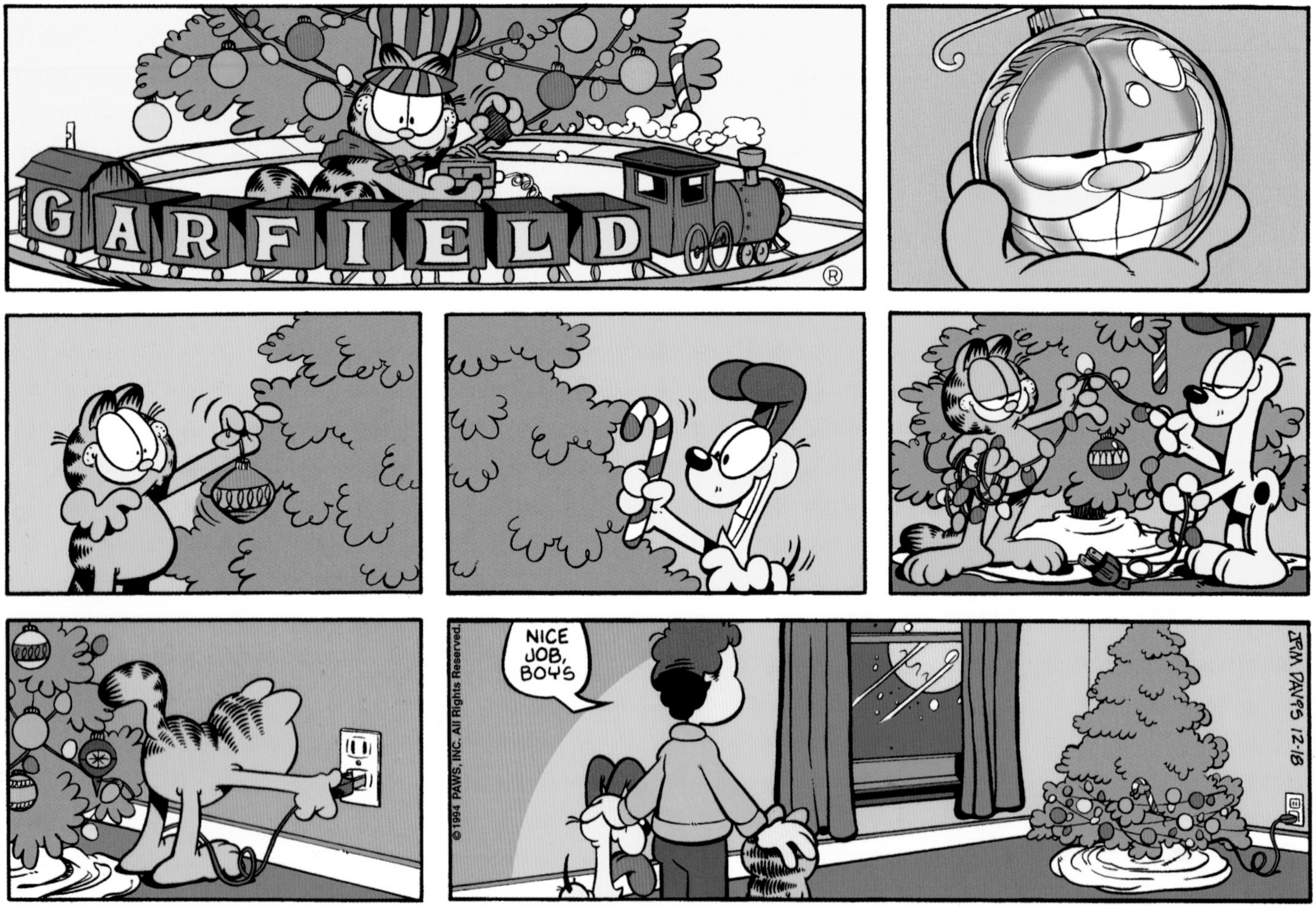
GARFIELD
NICE JOB, BOYS
JIM DAVIS 12-18
© 1994 PAWS, INC. All Rights Reserved.

When our oldest son was eighteen months old, he wanted to decorate the Christmas tree. He couldn't reach very high, and all the ornaments were hung together in one spot. It's the most beautiful Christmas tree I've ever seen.

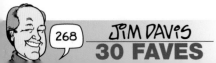

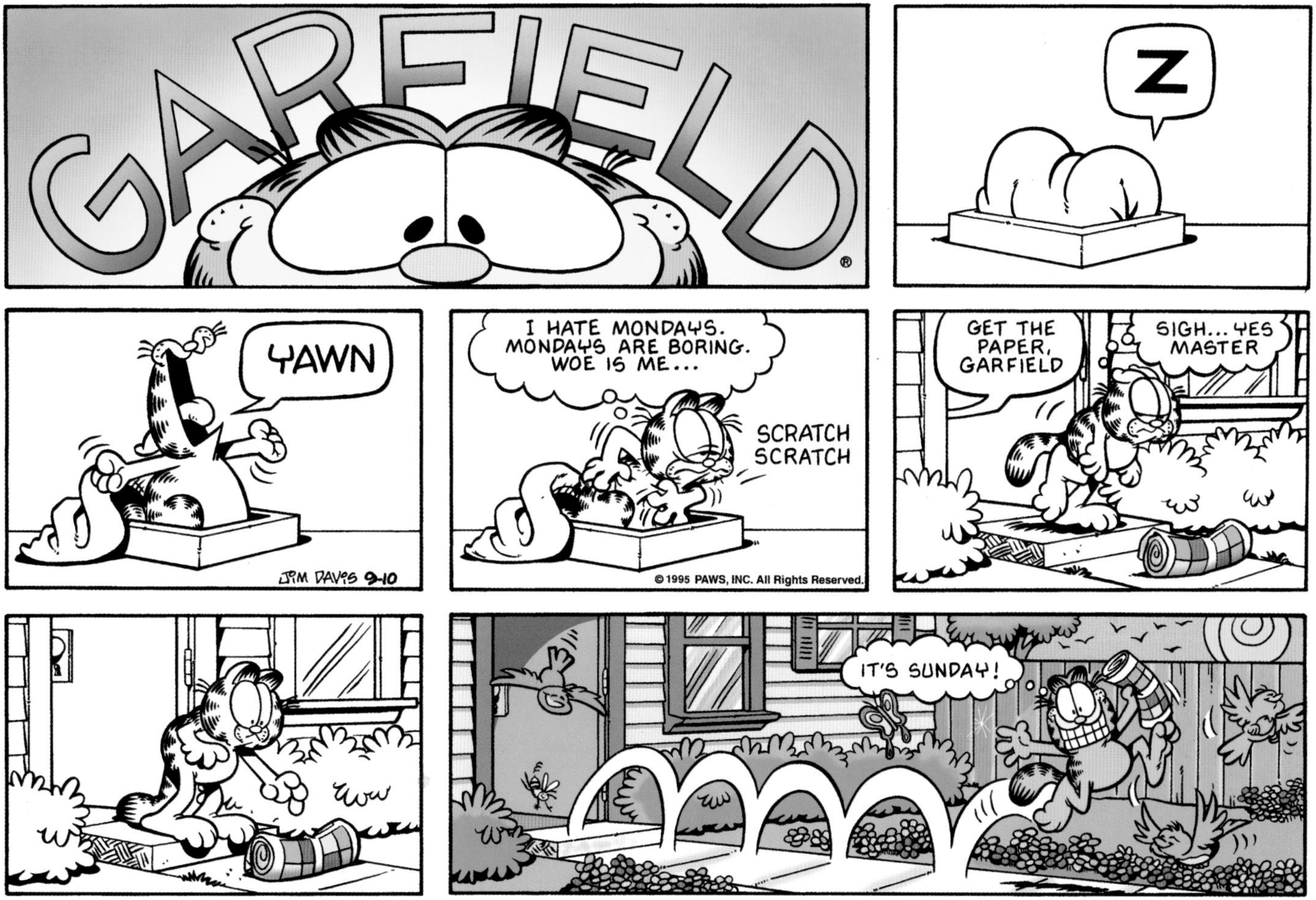
GARFIELD®
Z
YAWN
JIM DAVIS 9-10
I HATE MONDAYS. MONDAYS ARE BORING. WOE IS ME...
SCRATCH SCRATCH
© 1995 PAWS, INC. All Rights Reserved.
GET THE PAPER, GARFIELD
SIGH... YES MASTER
IT'S SUNDAY!

Ever wake up on what you thought was a work/school day and discover that it was a weekend? Remember that feeling of euphoria as you realize it's going to be a good—nay, great—day? Life is good!

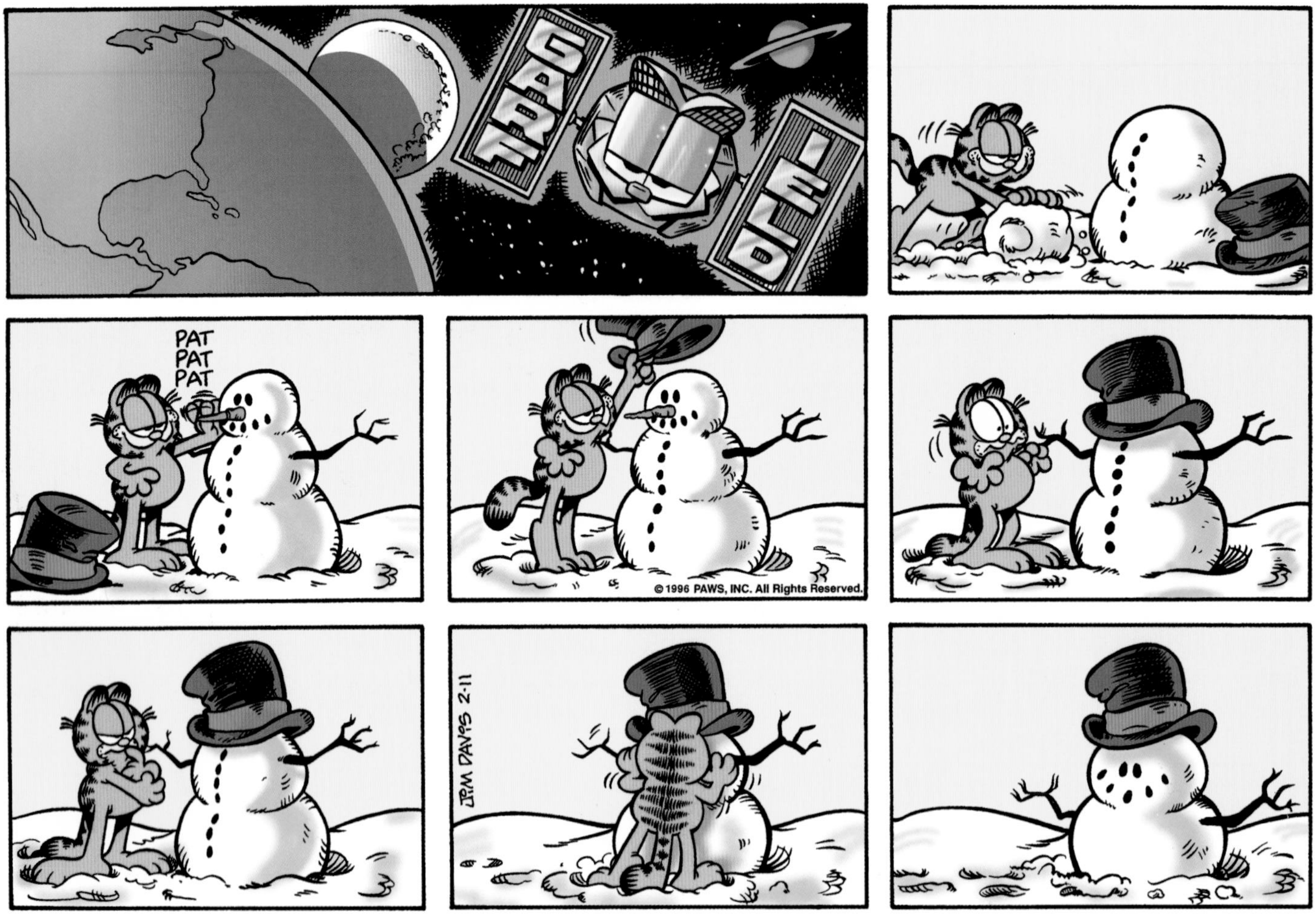
GARFIELD
PAT
PAT
PAT
© 1996 PAWS, INC. All Rights Reserved.
JIM DAVIS 2-11

The creative process is simply problem solving. How do you get your heroine off the railroad track? How do you get your cartoon cat out of a tree? What do you do if your snowman's hat is too big? This is my nod to the process.

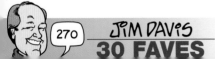

CEREAL IS NOT HEALTHY
OH, IT'S NUTRITIOUS ENOUGH....
BUT, EVER TRY TO PASS A DECODER RING?
JIM DAVIS 11·19

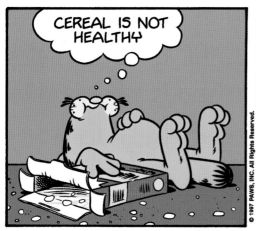

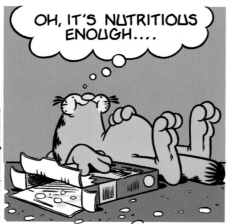

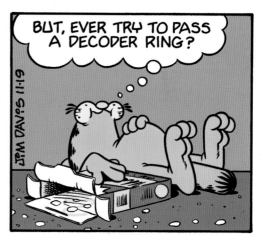

I know, I know. The "decoder ring" reference really dates me. However, many comics readers are in their forties and up . . . I hope.

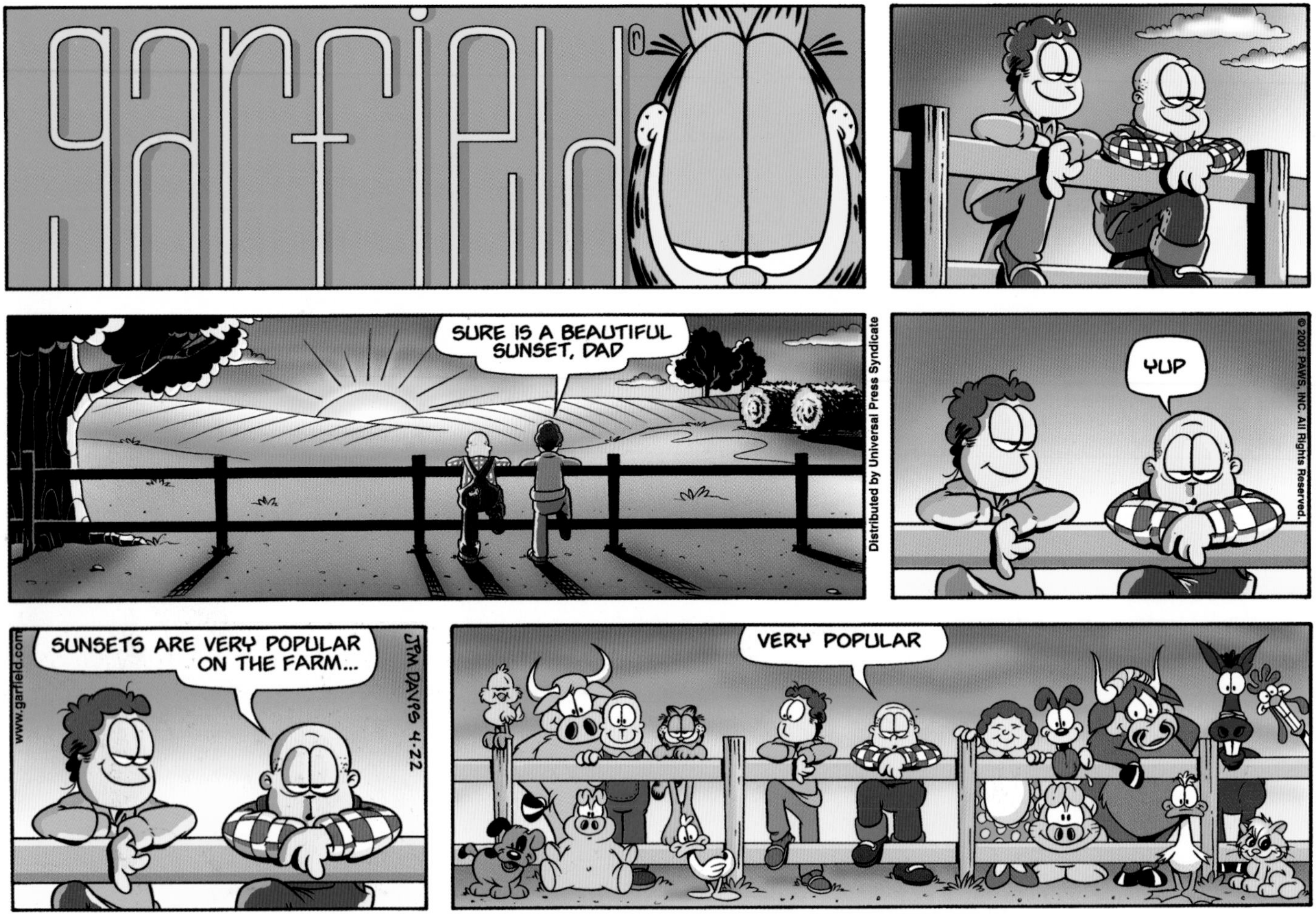
garfield®
SURE IS A BEAUTIFUL SUNSET, DAD
Distributed by Universal Press Syndicate
YUP
© 2001 PAWS, INC. All Rights Reserved.
www.garfield.com
SUNSETS ARE VERY POPULAR ON THE FARM...
JIM DAVIS 4-22
VERY POPULAR

Growing up on the farm, Dad, Mom, Doc, and I watched a lot of sunsets while leaning on the fence. We didn't talk much, but it was quality time. Orson, Booker, and Roy from the *U.S.Acres* strip slipped into the last frame.

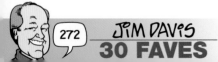

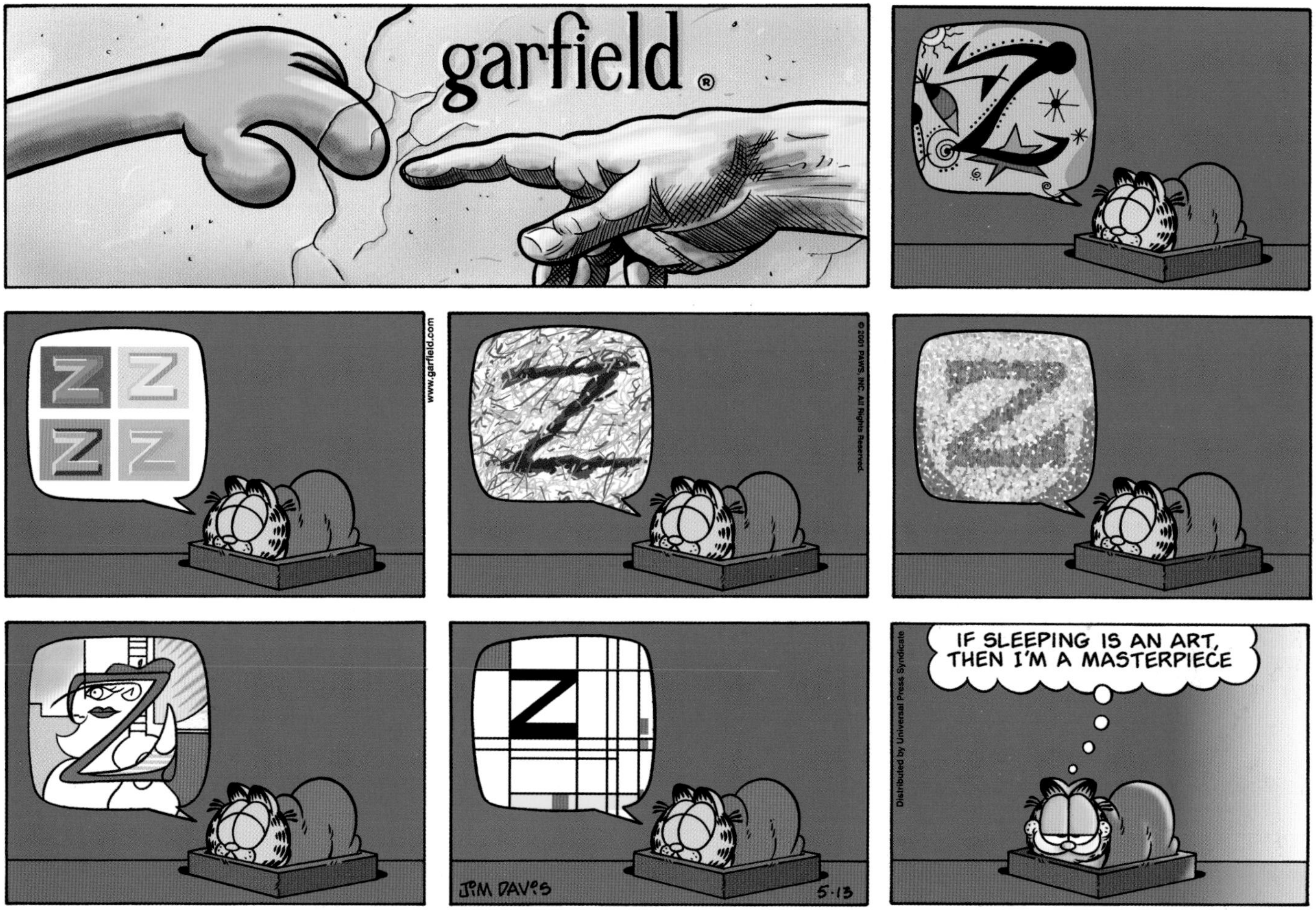
garfield®
www.garfield.com
© 2001 PAWS, INC. All Rights Reserved.
Distributed by Universal Press Syndicate
JIM DAVIS
5-13
IF SLEEPING IS AN ART, THEN I'M A MASTERPIECE

Technology has finally allowed us to have more fun with the art. Art imitates art in this, my homage to Michelangelo, Miró, Warhol, Pollock, Seurat, Picasso, and Mondrian.

SQUEEK
SQUEEK
SQUEEK
Distributed by Universal Press Syndicate
SQUEE
www.garfield.com
© 2002 PAWS, INC. All Rights Reserved.
JIM DAVIS 8-16
I'M ON, AREN'T I ?

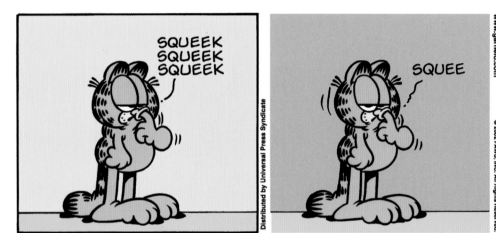

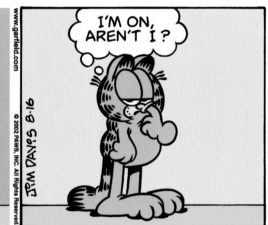

You can count on one hand the number of times that
I've allowed Garfield to step outside of the strip.
But I couldn't resist this one.

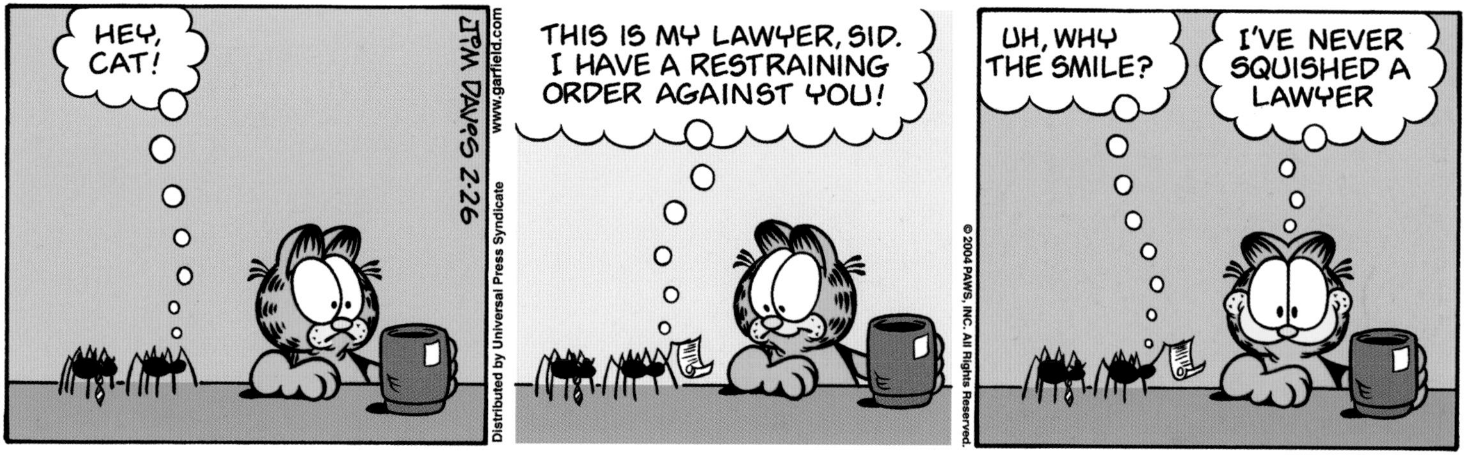
HEY, CAT!
JIM DAVIS 2-26
www.garfield.com
Distributed by Universal Press Syndicate
THIS IS MY LAWYER, SID. I HAVE A RESTRAINING ORDER AGAINST YOU!
© 2004 PAWS, INC. All Rights Reserved.
UH, WHY THE SMILE?
I'VE NEVER SQUISHED A LAWYER

Luckily, I received no adverse mail from lawyers over this strip. Maybe they don't read the comics . . . .

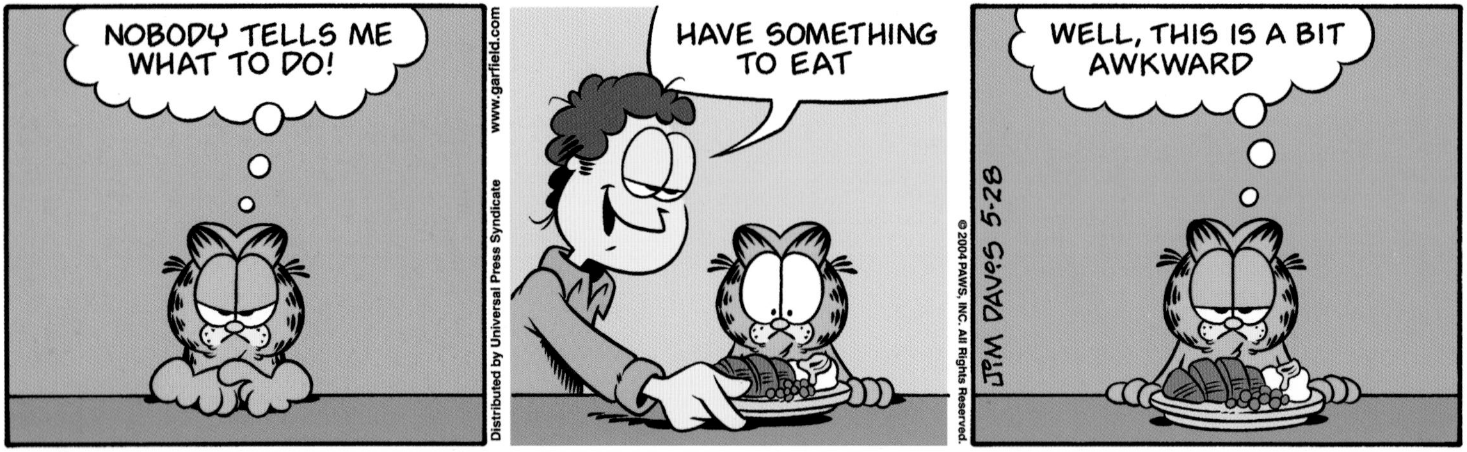
NOBODY TELLS ME WHAT TO DO!
Distributed by Universal Press Syndicate www.garfield.com
HAVE SOMETHING TO EAT
© 2004 PAWS, INC. All Rights Reserved.
JIM DAVIS 5-28
WELL, THIS IS A BIT AWKWARD

This is one of the few times that Garfield is at a loss for words. Of course, he's never claimed to be perfect.

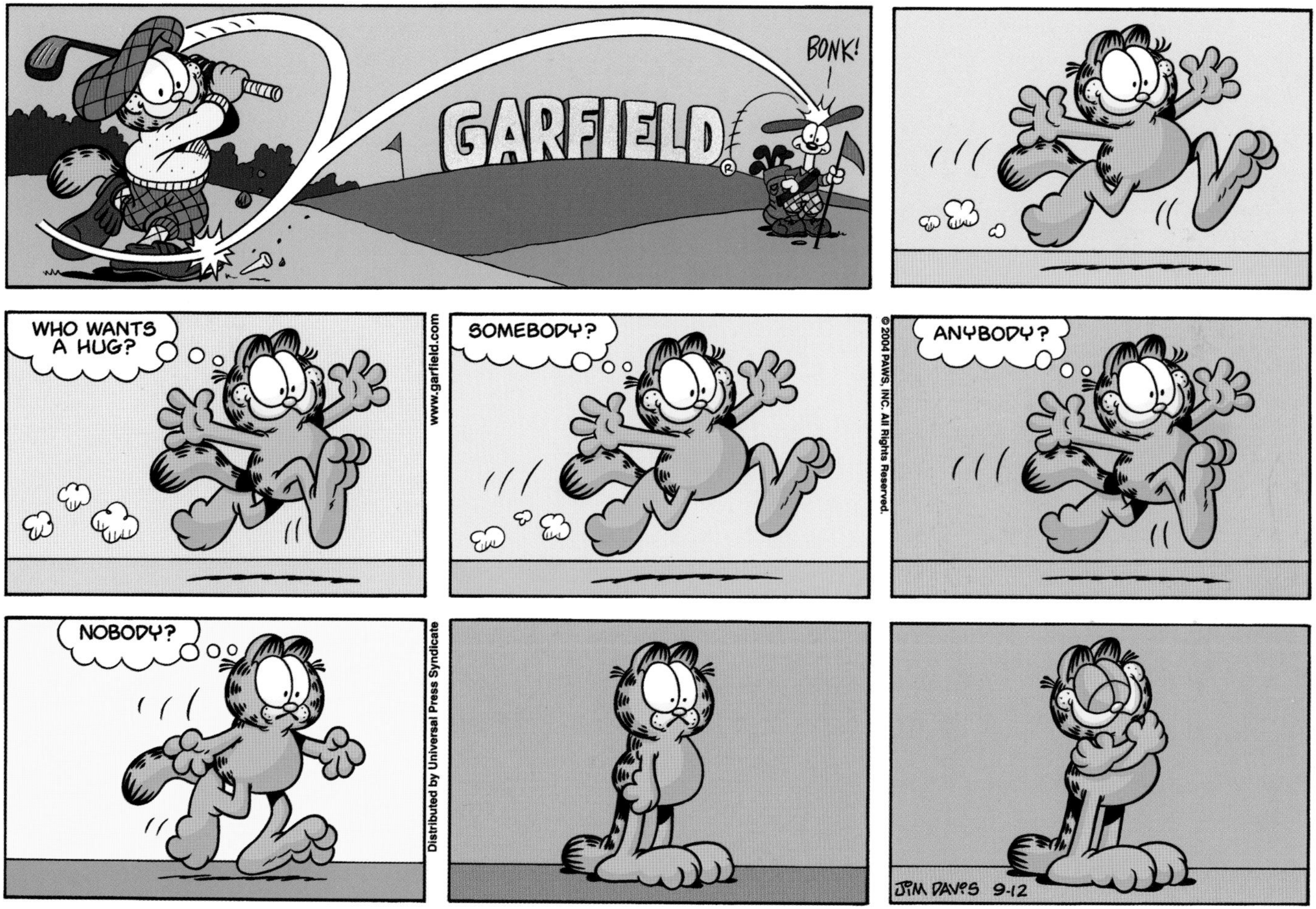
BONK!
GARFIELD®
WHO WANTS A HUG?
www.garfield.com
SOMEBODY?
© 2004 PAWS, INC. All Rights Reserved.
ANYBODY?
NOBODY?
Distributed by Universal Press Syndicate
JIM DAVIS 9-12

I don't do political or social commentary in the strip, but sometimes I can't help but share a philosophy. I feel you have to love yourself before you can love others, or, as Garfield says, "If you don't indulge yourself, nobody will."

IN ANSWER TO YOUR MANY LETTERS...
BOOT
www.garfield.com
©2005 PAWS, INC. All Rights Reserved.
YES...
CRASH!
JIM DAVIS 7-1
Distributed by Universal Press Syndicate
ODIE DOES DO ALL HIS OWN STUNTS!

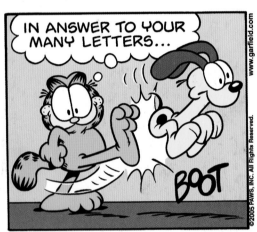

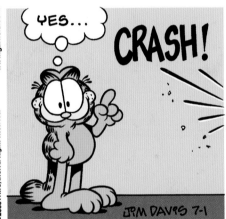

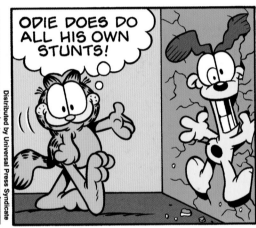

Fortunately, what may be violence on television is called a sight gag in a comic strip. No dogs were harmed in the performance of this strip.

www.garfield.com
©2005 PAWS, INC. All Rights Reserved.
Distributed by Universal Press Syndicate
SO THAT'S WHY THE CEILING FAN STOPPED
JIM DAVIS 8-23

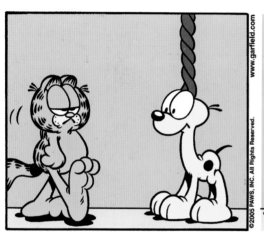

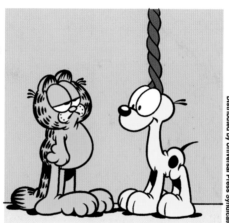

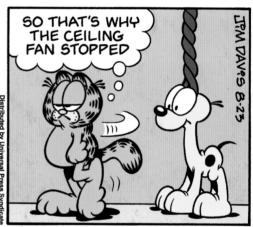

Sometimes it's what you don't show that makes a gag work. All I do in the last frame is give the reader a hint. Some jokes are funnier if you have to work for them!

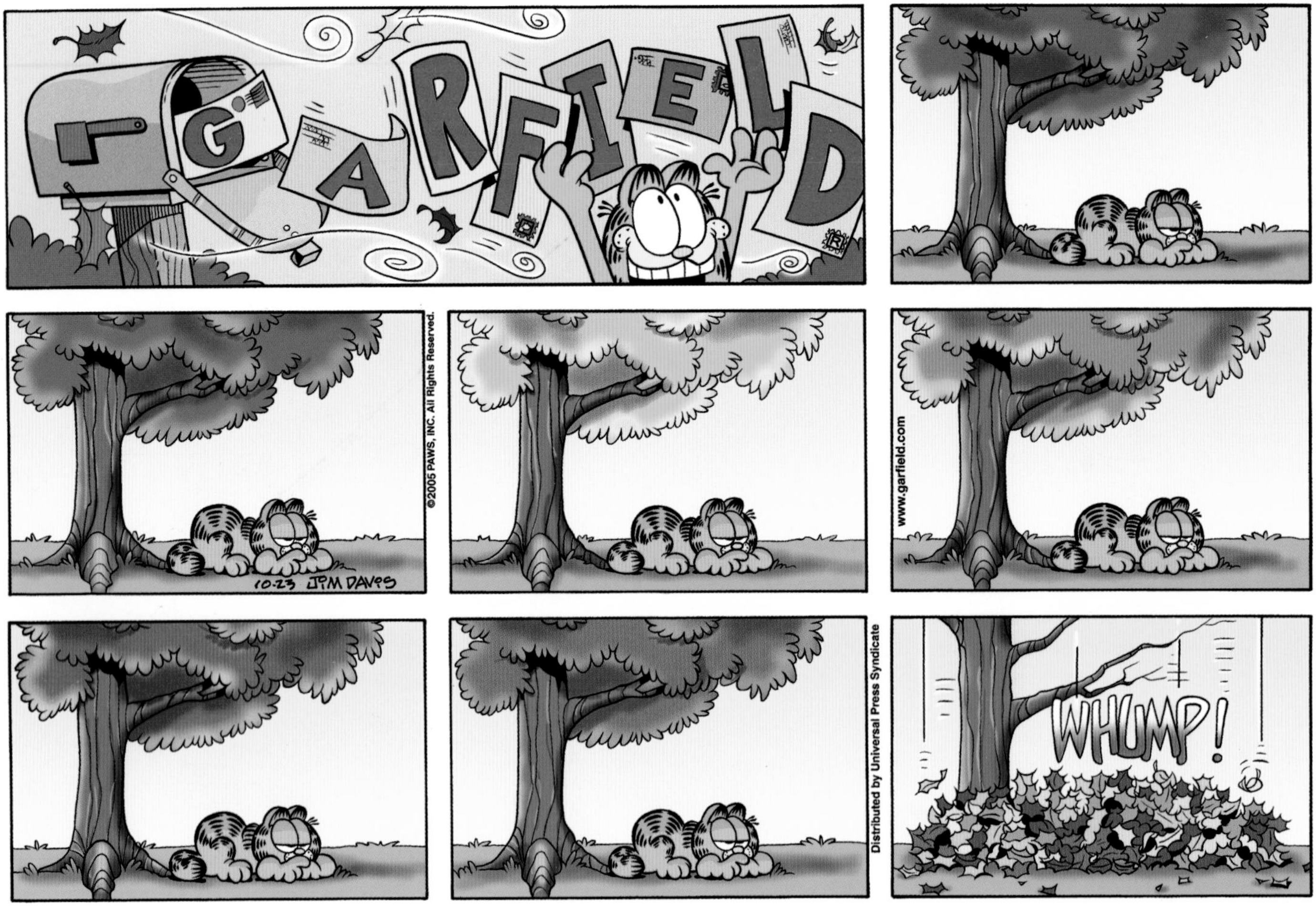
GARFIELD
©2005 PAWS, INC. All Rights Reserved.
10-23 JIM DAVIS
www.garfield.com
Distributed by Universal Press Syndicate
WHUMP!

Autumn is a wonderful season to feature in a comic strip. It's a colorful and magical time of year. Garfield loves autumn, as do I. There's only one drawback: Autumn is entirely too short.

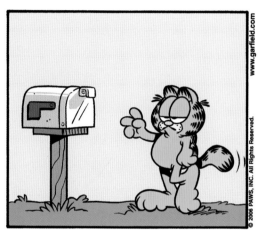

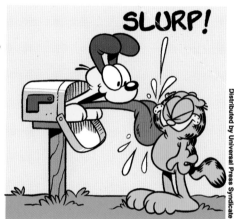

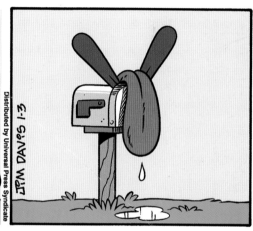

www.garfield.com
© 2006 PAWS, INC. All Rights Reserved.
SLURP!
Distributed by Universal Press Syndicate
JIM DAVIS 1-3

Now and then I get a funny image in my head that just begs to get into a strip. In this case, I worked from the last panel to the first.

WHAT'S IT ALL MEAN, GARFIELD? WHAT'S LIFE ALL ABOUT?
I'LL SAY TUNA
JIM DAVIS 1-19
© 2007 PAWS, INC. All Rights Reserved.
Text GARFIELD to 26642 US ONLY
Distributed by Universal Press Syndicate

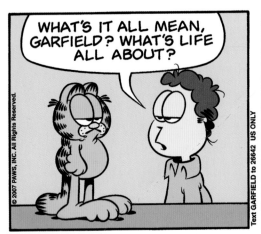

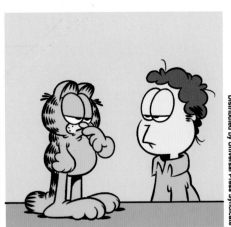

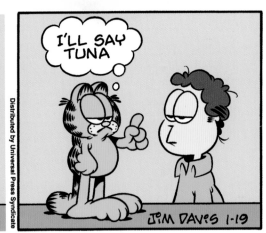

This is about as deep as Garfield gets. You know what?
This may be what life really is about.

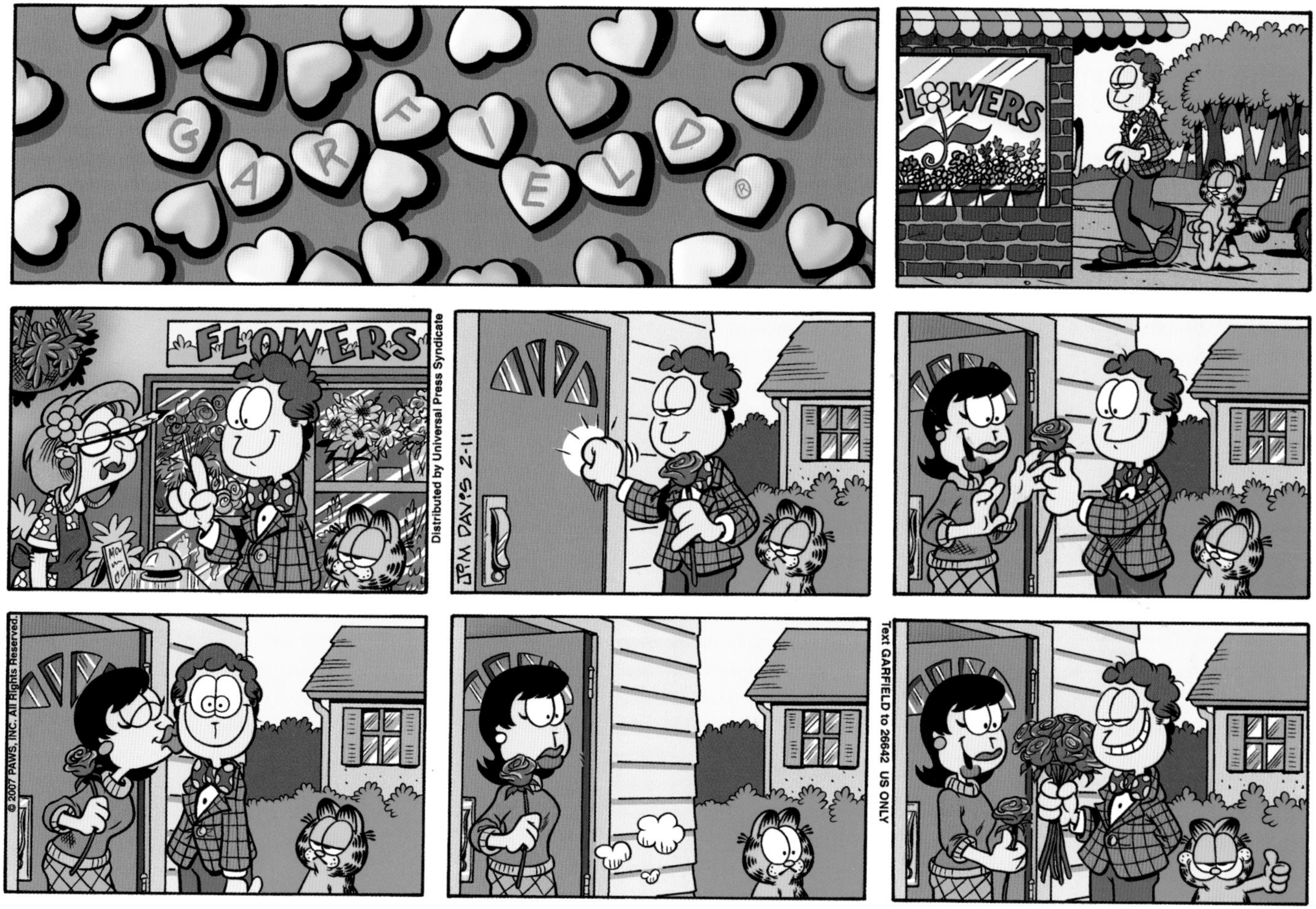
GARFIELD®
FLOWERS
FLOWERS
Distributed by Universal Press Syndicate
JIM DAVIS 2-11
© 2007 PAWS, INC. All Rights Reserved.
Text GARFIELD to 26642 US ONLY

After Garfield turned twenty-five, we asked our biggest fans if they'd change anything about the strip. The majority said, "Give Jon a life!" After pursuing Liz for over a quarter of a century, Jon's persistence should count for something . . . .

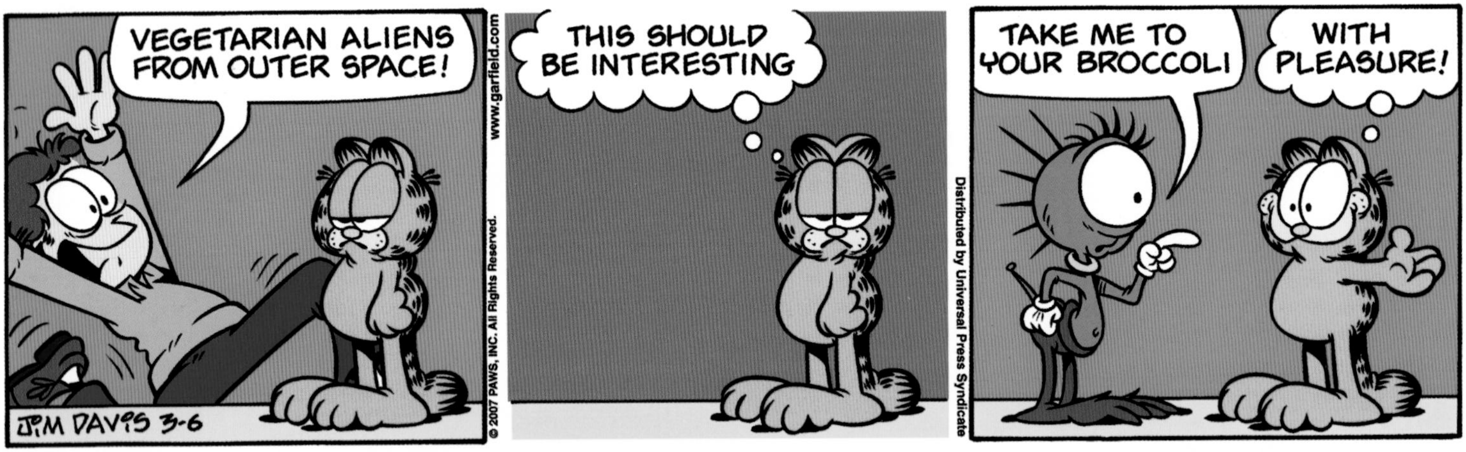
VEGETARIAN ALIENS FROM OUTER SPACE!
JIM DAVIS 3-6
© 2007 PAWS, INC. All Rights Reserved.
www.garfield.com
THIS SHOULD BE INTERESTING
Distributed by Universal Press Syndicate
TAKE ME TO YOUR BROCCOLI
WITH PLEASURE!

For some gags to work, the reader has to make a leap of faith.
This is about as far as I go.

DOG NEWS
www.garfield.com
© 2007 PAWS, INC. All Rights Reserved.
DOG NEWS
WHOA...
Distributed by Universal Press Syndicate
DOG NEWS
YOU GUYS WILL SNIFF PRETTY MUCH ANYTHING, WON'T YOU?
JIM DAVIS 8-7

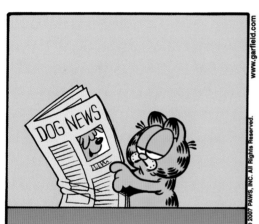

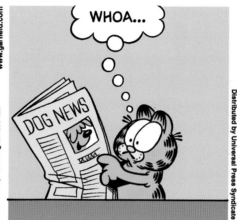

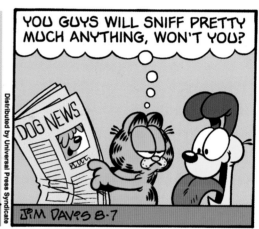

Part of dog humor is how direct and, well, earthy they are.
You notice that I didn't show a dog actually sniffing anything.
I'm too classy for that.

JIM DAVIS 8-25
© 2007 PAWS, INC. All Rights Reserved.
HAAAACK
www.garfield.com
Distributed by Universal Press Syndicate
YOU'RE GONNA NEED SOME TRAFFIC CONES FOR THAT ONE

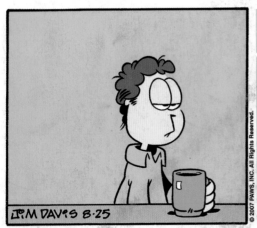

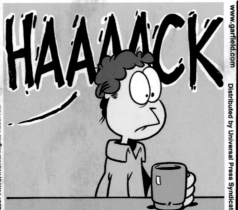

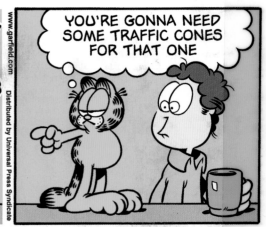

This gag is for cat owners. Yes, this graphically exposes the seamy side of owning a cat.

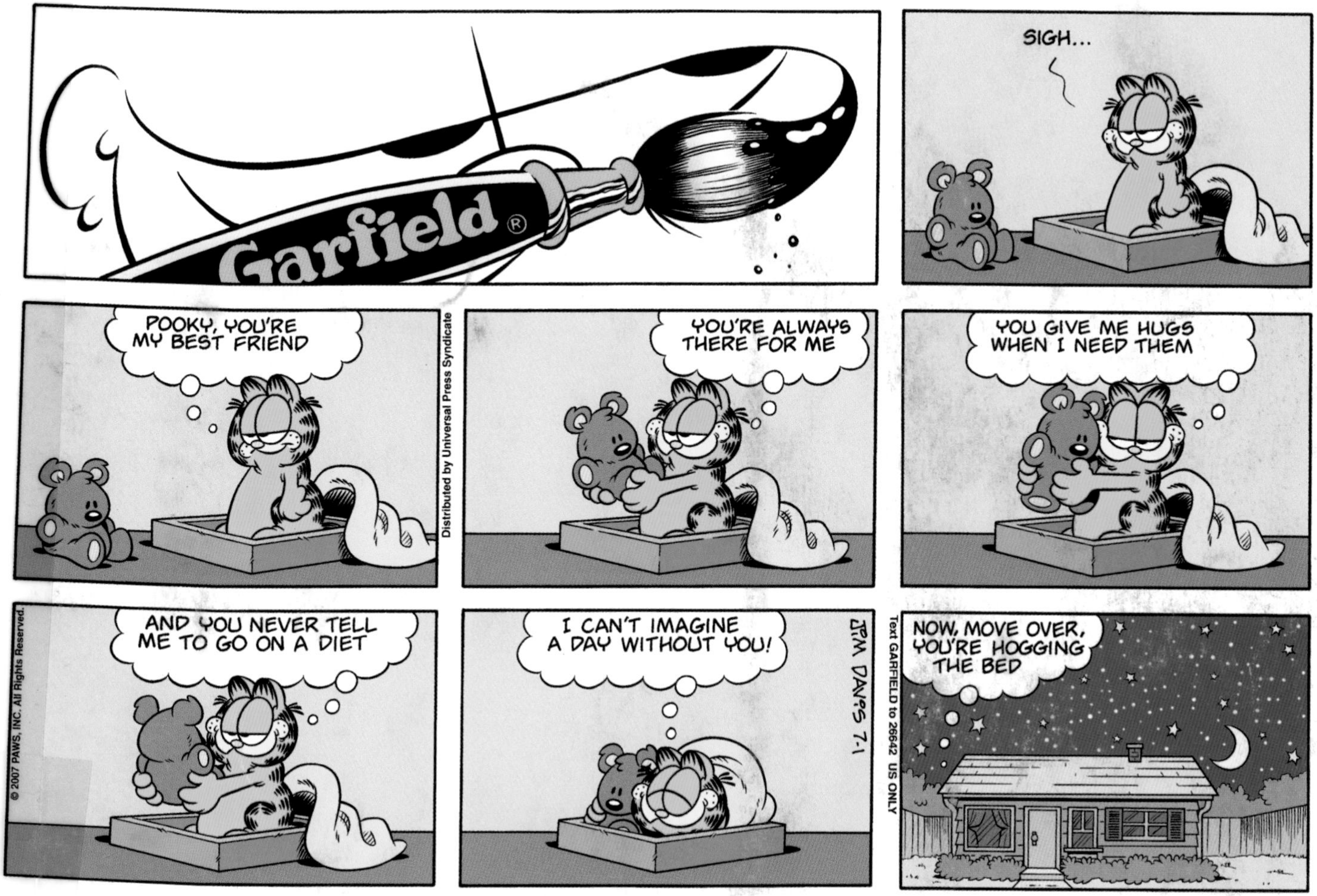
Garfield®
SIGH...
POOKY, YOU'RE MY BEST FRIEND
YOU'RE ALWAYS THERE FOR ME
YOU GIVE ME HUGS WHEN I NEED THEM
AND YOU NEVER TELL ME TO GO ON A DIET
I CAN'T IMAGINE A DAY WITHOUT YOU!
NOW, MOVE OVER, YOU'RE HOGGING THE BED
Distributed by Universal Press Syndicate
© 2007 PAWS, INC. All Rights Reserved.
JIM DAVIS 7-1
Text GARFIELD to 26642 US ONLY

Valette Greene was my first assistant. She was a dear, sweet lady who loved people and pets. She passed away a while back. This strip was written for her. In the last panel, her name is in the stars. I can hear her laughing now.